MW01042626

The CSI Project Delivery Practice Guide

The CSI Project Delivery Practice Guide

Construction Specifications Institute

WILEY

John Wiley & Sons, Inc.

Copyright © 2011 by Construction Specifications Institute. All rights reserved

Published by John Wiley & Sons, Inc., Hoboken, New Jersey

Published simultaneously in Canada

For general information about our other products and services, please contact our Customer Care Department within the United States at (800) 762-2974, outside the United States at (317) 572-3993 or fax (317) 572-4002.

Wiley also publishes its books in a variety of electronic formats. Some content that appears in print may not be available in electronic books. For more information about Wiley products, visit our web site at www.wiley.com.

Library of Congress Cataloging-in-Publication Data:

ISBN 978-0-470-63519-3 (pbk); ISBN 978-0-470-94018-1 (ebk); ISBN 978-0-470-94019-8 (ebk); ISBN 978-0-470-95126-2 (ebk); ISBN 978-0-470-95145-3 (ebk); ISBN 978-1-118-00688-7 (ebk)

Printed in the United States of America

10 9 8 7 6 5

Contents

Preface

Beginning with the publication of the first *Manual of Practice* (MOP) in 1967 continuing through the publication of its successor document, the *Project Resource Manual* (PRM), it has been the intent of the Construction Specifications Institute (CSI) that these publications embody accepted standards for the preparation of construction specifications and project manuals, and a detailed source of information on quality documentation for the life cycle of a facility.

Through these publications, CSI has sought to aid owners, designers, specifiers, contract administrators, contractors, construction product representatives, and facility managers in the performance of their jobs.

In 2008, CSI began an effort to update the knowledge formerly contained in the MOP and PRM to present it anew and ensure its continued relevance. As with the earlier collections of this knowledge, the intent is to provide an authoritative resource on the organization, preparation, use, and interpretation of construction documents, encompassing the entire life cycle of a facility from conception through facility management.

To accomplish this update CSI established the Practice Guides Task Team. One of the task team charges was to organize the presentation of this information into modules to support areas of practice where CSI currently offers certificates and certifications, such as Project Delivery addressed by the Construction Documents Technology (CDT) certificate, Specifications, addressed by the Certified Construction Specifier (CCS) certification, Contract Administration addressed by the Certified Construction Contract Administrator (CCCA) certification, and Product Representation addressed by the Certified Construction Product Representative (CCPR) certification, as well as other areas of practice for which education and certification may be developed.

To keep current with changes in the industry, the Task Team also reviewed other CSI documents and standards, and updated references to them that appear in the Practice Guides. A similar effort was made to incorporate changes in contract documents produced by The American Institute of Architects (AIA) and the Engineers Joint Construction Documents Committee (EJCDC), and to introduce the new standard contract documents developed by the ConsensusDOCS Coalition.

The Task Team also recognized the growing impact of "green" or sustainable practices on the subject matter contained in the Practice Guides. Each Practice Guide now addresses the topic of sustainable practice to some degree while a more detailed examination of the topic is planned for a future Sustainable Practice Guide.

Two other topics that have had an impact on the Practice Guides are: Building Information Modeling (BIM) and Integrated Project Delivery (IPD). The growing impact of BIM on the practice of specification writing and its potential impact on quality documentation made a discussion of this topic imperative. Likewise IPD has grown in importance over the past several years and has had an impact on the way practitioners relate to the process of creating and interpreting construction documents.

The Practice Guide Series is not intended to be composed of static documents but to be a living set of guides with the capacity to change and be updated as the construction industry changes around them. The input of users of this Series will be critical to the future updating of the Series and the authors and reviewers welcome feedback from users.

Description of the *CSI Project Delivery Practice Guide*

The CSI Project Delivery Practice Guide is the introductory volume in the Practice Guide Series. This Guide presents an overview of the process needed to conceive, design, construct, and maintain the built environment. This Guide describes the many parts of that process and the inter-related role of the various participants in the process. It is intended to be a guide to the steps in the life cycle of a project that begins with an owner's conception of the project, continues through the design and construction phases, and results in the successful operation and maintenance of the project after construction is complete. As the introductory volume in the Series, *The CSI Project Delivery Practice Guide* creates a foundation for the other, more specialized Practice Guides that follow. To those individuals seeking a more specialized knowledge of a particular topic such as construction specification writing or construction contract administration, this Practice Guide provides a starting point, one that is a key to understanding those more specialized topics. *The CSI Project Delivery Practice Guide* gives participants in the design and construction industry the tools that they need to effectively deliver a project.

Additional CSI publications that complement the Practice Guides are available for download to purchasers of the Practice Guides. The following documents can be obtained at www.wiley.com/go/csipracticeguides:

- MasterFormat® numbers and titles
- UniFormat™
- SectionFormat™/PageFormat™
- Sample CSI Forms
- GreenFormat™ questionnaire
- Practice Guide Glossary

To access the content on this site, you will need the unique Access Code printed on the card included with this book. If you have purchased an ebook version of this title, please contact Customer Care at 877-762-2974 or at http://support.wiley.com for a unique Access Code in order to take advantage of the web site.

Acknowledgments

No project of this magnitude can be accomplished single-handedly. In the best CSI tradition many people volunteered to write, review, and contribute to the production of the CSI Practice Guides. CSI wishes to recognize the following people who contributed in many ways to this project. If we omitted anyone's name it was inadvertent not intentional.

Ross G. Spiegel, FCSI, CCS, CCCA, FAIA, LEED AP BD+C
Chairman, Practice Guides Task Team

Author of *The CSI Project Delivery Practice Guide:*
Walter R. Scarborough, CSI, CCS, CCCA, AIA, SCIP

Practice Guide Task Team Members:
George Wade Bevier, CSI, CCS, SCIP, LEED AP
Ellen Kay Crews, FCSI, CCS, FMP
Kathryn A. D'Andrea, CSI, CCS
Dennis J. Hall, FCSI, CCS, CCCA, FAIA, SCIP
Gregory J. Marking, FCSI, CCS, CCCA, AIA, NCARB, LEED AP
Wiley N. McMillan, Jr., FCSI, CCPR
Chris Pechacek, CSI, LEED AP
Jim Rains, CSI, AIA
James M. Robertson, FCSI, CCS, FAIA, NCARB
Walter R. Scarborough, CSI, CCS, CCCA, AIA, SCIP
Paul W. Simonsen, RA, FCSI, CCS, CCCA, LEED AP, NCARB, SCIP
Paul M. Sternberg, CSI, CCS, CCCA, AIA, LEED AP, NCARB

CSI Certification Committee Members 2008–2010
Ann G. Baker, RA, CSI, CCS, CCCA, LEED AP, SCIP
Peter A. Baker, CSI, CCPR, RCI
Joseph Berchenko, CSI, CCS, AIA
Bill Coady, CSI, CCPR
Sheryl L. Dodd-Hansen, FCSI, CCS, CCCA
George A. Everding, CSI, CCS, CCCA, AIA, LEED AP
Raymond E. Gaines, FCSI, CCS, AIA
Richard G. Howard, CSI, CCS, AIA, NCARB, SCIP
Gregory J. Markling, FCSI, CCS, CCCA, AIA, LEED AP, NCARB
Wiley N. McMillan, Jr., FCSI, CCPR
Kay M. Melcher, CSI, CCS, LEED AP
Jonathan M. Miller, FCSI, CCS, CCCA, AIA, SCIP
Stephen E. Nash, CSI, CCS, CCCA, AIA, LEED AP
George Rosamond, FCSI, CCS, AIA, LEED AP
Marilyn G. Smith, CSI, CCS, AIA, SCIP
Robert B. Swan, CSI, CCS, CCCA, AIA
Robert W. Teller, FCSI, CCS, CCCA, LEED AP
J. Peter Tolson, CSI, CCS, CCCA

Lisa Turner, CSI, CCPR, LEED AP
Sandra M. Velleca, FCSI, CCS, CCCA
M. Keith West, CSI, CCPR
Laurence E. Wightman, III, CSI, CCPR, AHC

CSI Education Committee Members 2008–2010
Mary-Alice Avila, RA, CSI, CCS, LEED AP, MS
Loren R. Berry, FCSI, CDT, AIA, NCARB
Marc C. Chavez, CSI, CCS, CCCA, AIA, SCIP
Gregory J. Markling, FCSI, CCS, CCCA, AIA, LEED AP, NCARB
Robert T. Matschulat, CSI, CCS, AIA, AIA
Jack P. Morgan, RA, CSI, CCS, CCCA, AIA, NCARB
Stephen E. Nash, CSI, CCS, CCCA, AIA, AIA, LEED AP
David S. Proudfit, FCSI, CCS, AIA
Casey F. Robb, FCSI, CCPR, LEED AP
Paulette K. Salisbury, FCSI, CDT
Walter R. Scarborough, CSI, CCS, CCCA, AIA, SCIP
Gregory W. Sprinkel, FCSI, CDT
Grady W. Whitaker, Jr., FCSI
Jim F. Whitfield, FCSI, CCPR, CTC, LEED AP

CSI Technical Committee Members 2008–2010
Gary L. Beimers, FCSI, CDT
Lane J. Beougher, FCSI, CCS, CCCA, AIA, LEED AP
George Wade Bevier, CSI, CCS, SCIP, LEED AP
Tom R. Deines, FCSI, CCCA
Nina M. Giglio, CSI, CCS, SCIP
Mark J. Kalin, FCSI, CCS, FAIA
Michael MacVittie, CSI, AIA
Richard C. Master, CSI, AIA
Larry Nordin, CSI, CCS, AIA, ALA
James M. Robertson, FCSI, CCS, FAIA, NCARB
Paul M. Sternberg, CSI, CCS, CCCA, AIA, LEED AP, NCARB
David A. Stutzman, CSI, CCS, AIA, SCIP
Robert S. Weygant, CSI, CDT, SCIP

CSI Staff
Greg Ceton, CSI, CDT, Director of Technical Services

Chapter 1
Introduction to *The CSI Project Delivery Practice Guide*

1.1   Introduction

Designing and constructing buildings, civil structures, industrial facilities, interior design projects, and other structures and facilities is one of humankind's most difficult endeavors in spite of the fact that it is a common activity. All facilities start as a project that takes a journey through a sophisticated and complex process in order to come into being. Talented individuals with advanced education, specialized knowledge, well-developed decision-making abilities, and in some cases professional licenses are required to manage, direct, and monitor the process. All that talent and skill has to be marshaled and brought together to converge on a common goal of producing a project. Then a considerable amount of both time and money are required to accomplish the goal. Yet out of the need for shelter, protection, and comfort, we design and construct facilities to house the activities of our private and public lives, both individually and socially. We aspire to create facilities that are useful, functional, visually pleasing, and enjoyable to occupy.

This journey is called the project delivery process, and this practice guide presents the many pieces and parts that compose that process. While this practice guide is not about creating and designing facilities, it is about the logistics of project delivery from conception to occupancy. It provides insight into the vast array of activities that are either required or necessary in the delivery process. Not every concept presented in this practice guide will be necessary for every project. The information contained in the practice guide is useful to anyone, at any level, who owns, designs, engineers, constructs, installs, supplies, or manages a facility.

1.2   Understanding Project Delivery as Foundational Knowledge

The purpose of this practice guide is to educate individuals about project delivery from the global, or big picture, perspective. Project delivery is not specialized, like designing or constructing; it is generalized. Understanding the concepts of project delivery allows

1

stakeholders and participants to be able to provide more effective services no matter what delivery path the project takes. While there are six project delivery methods identified in this practice guide, the reality is that there are as many variations of these project delivery methods as there are individuals that make project decisions.

This practice guide is the foundation for all of the other practice guides developed and published by CSI. The ideas, concepts, and information presented in the other practice guides builds on this practice guide to present more specialized information about other topics. For example, developing a working understanding of *The CSI Construction Specifications Practice Guide* and *The CSI Construction Contract Administration Practice Guide* depends on first understanding the information of *The CSI Project Delivery Practice Guide.*

Every individual that is a stakeholder or participant in the design and construction of anything in the built environment should have a foundational understanding of how projects are delivered. An understanding of the information in this practice guide as an introduction to project delivery is important. Much of what design and construction professionals do is founded on the information presented in these chapters.

As will be seen, successful project delivery depends on the melding of the following aspects into a process with a specific purpose:

- An owner that has a defined plan for a facility
- Individuals, firms, and companies to produce the design and make the appropriate decisions
- Contracts that comprehensively and effectively establish and define the roles and responsibilities of the stakeholders and participants
- Well-developed and sufficient construction documentation
- Organized construction project management and scheduling
- Individuals and companies to provide and install the required materials

1.3 Magnitude of Design and Construction Information Available

Information that is available about the design and construction of projects and facilities has advanced light-years over the last several decades. For example, in the 1970s, when information was needed about a product, material, or construction technique—if it existed at all and could be found by telephone calls to possible sources—it was only as immediately available as waiting on the mail to be delivered. There were few books, few periodicals, and few resources, and the information that was available was not easily found.

Today, there is an enormous amount of design and construction information available instantly, and it is growing at an astonishing rate. Individuals are being flooded every day with an ocean of information from many sources. For those random instances when information is not immediately available, it can usually be generated in a short time and immediately made available to the one requesting the information. Essentially, there are numerous sources for everything anyone would want to know at any time.

There is a relatively small and exclusive class of inventions that has fundamentally changed society's ability to communicate, which has revolutionized the nature of information, knowledge, and understanding. The printing press, electricity and the countless devices it powers, capturing and creating images (photography, television, recordings, etc.), and wired and wireless communication capabilities are a few of the most significant inventions. A case could be made that information overload began with Gutenberg's invention of the printing press. Now, the amount of information that is available through the Internet is staggering—it has forever changed the nature of knowledge. One of the reasons the Internet is significant is that information is now available to anyone, anywhere, anytime. The Internet has become the preferred method for accessing information about the design and construction of the built environment.

1.3.1 Books

Throughout human history, there have always been those that want to make their knowledge available to others. However, the opportunity to do so has been limited by the means of producing it for consumption by others. We know that the printing press fundamentally changed that. Today, the technology to publish books is widely available, and there is now a huge volume of books available on a limitless number of topics from many different sources. While the breadth of knowledge may not be as extensive as the Internet, there is nevertheless a massive amount of information available.

While books capture knowledge, one of their major limitations is that books only capture knowledge through a specific point in time (usually six months or so prior to publication because of prepublication production). It is not until a new edition is published that the knowledge contained in a book can be advanced, improved, updated, or expanded. Other limitations include the distribution and availability of books. Unless a book is purchased via the Internet, the availability of books still depends on shipping, stocking, and shelf display to be available to purchasers. Books face an uncertain future and will in all likelihood give way to Internet-based information.

1.3.2 Periodicals

There are a number of periodicals available for a vast range of specialized design and construction topics. In fact, a periodical can probably be found for just about any subject. Increasingly, they are available on the Internet as well as in printed editions. Unlike books, periodicals are published frequently and have the capability to be more current. An asset of periodicals is that they can be archived and thus accumulate a sizeable body of specialized knowledge. Many professional and trade associations publish periodicals for their members, and their periodicals are usually available to anyone who is interested.

1.3.3 Professional Associations, Societies, and Institutes

A profession is a vocation or occupation in which individuals obtain specialized, extensive, and advanced education or training for the purpose of supplying unbiased counsel or service to others for compensation. A license is frequently required, based on a competency examination that is administered by a governmental jurisdiction (usually a state), before an individual can be legally identified as a professional of a particular discipline. The same jurisdiction establishes and enforces licensing laws that regulate professional practice and conduct. Once licensed, a professional is legally obligated to practice in such a manner as to protect the public and to perform services within the scope of the licensing laws. Professionals should exercise reasonable care and competence by applying the same technical knowledge and skill ordinarily applied by reasonably prudent professionals practicing under similar conditions and circumstances.

An association is a group of professionals, and those aspiring to be professionals, who voluntarily agree to be a part of an organization for the purpose of pursuing common interests and to promote the status of the membership. Also known as societies and institutes, a professional association is composed of professionals who are practitioners of a particular occupation, skill, or discipline who promote the advancement of knowledge of their profession. Since professionals are licensed by a jurisdiction, a professional association complements the jurisdiction by providing oversight of their members and monitoring professional activities.

The advancement of specialized knowledge is important to a professional association. Significant effort is expended to develop, collect, evaluate, and disseminate intrinsic knowledge for the benefit of professionals and the public. Because professionals are usually involved with disciplines in which knowledge evolves based on research, experience, and technical developments, most professional associations, as well as licensing jurisdictions, require a commitment from professionals to continuing their education to remain aware of new developments as well as issues and challenges facing the profession.

1.3.4 Standards

Standards establish uniform guidelines, criteria, methods, processes, and practices for a particular building product, assembly, or technology and are covered in more detail in Chapter 4.

1.3.5 Trade Associations

Trade associations are organizations of companies that compete with each other in a particular business or industry and are primarily interested in advancing their products and services. Activities of trade associations include the development of management practices, enforcement of ethics, promotion of their members, and public relations. Trade associations often establish and maintain skill certifications for technicians and they provide a valuable service to society by policing their respective businesses and industries.

Trade associations make an important contribution to the design and construction of facilities because they frequently originate, maintain, and distribute technical standards that, while voluntary, govern the manufacture, fabrication, and installation of products, materials, and equipment. Also, technical publications, newsletters, and customer service departments may be available for the purpose of education and advancing an understanding of practices that may be unique to an industry. Because they have the most knowledge and understanding of their products and work, trade associations are considered to be the authority of that industry. Their standards are frequently the basis of construction specifications.

1.3.6 Manufacturer Associations

In some industries, manufacturer associations are similar to professional and trade associations except they are a consortium of manufacturers that promote the interests of their industry through member distributors, wholesalers, retailers, other associations, and installers. Through consensus among members, they work to improve the quality of their products.

1.3.7 Research Agencies

While not as extensive as trade and manufacturer associations, there are independent agencies that research building products, materials, and equipment. Effort is expended for the purpose of understanding and improving the nature of the design and construction of facilities.

1.3.8 Manufacturers

Manufacturers that supply materials, products, and equipment for the construction of facilities are a vastly diversified group and are essentially spread over the entire planet. In addition to being in the business of selling their products, manufacturers are motivated to advance a better understanding of the products they manufacture and they make a significant contribution to the advancement of knowledge of the design and construction of facilities. Manufacturers have a vested interest in purchasers and users understanding the qualities, characteristics, and potentials of their products. Manufacturer representatives are a crucial part of communicating technical information, and they provide a valuable service to other stakeholders and participants.

One of the most noticeable manifestations of the explosion of information in the design and construction professions and industries directly involves manufacturers. In years past, the most effective method of making information available was the distribution of hundreds of product information ring binders that have become synonymous with designers. Today, the number of ring binders in offices is decreasing as manufacturers make their information available over the Internet.

There are several other important contributions made by manufacturers. It is common for manufacturers to make their research-and-development departments available for inquiries, and they strive to provide high-quality customer service not only for owners, but for designers and constructors as well. Some manufacturers demonstrate a commitment to the quality of their products by certifying, licensing, or approving those individuals and companies that install them.

1.3.9 Continuing Education Opportunities

Common to all of the organizations described above are the continuing education opportunities available for individual or in-office presentations; local, regional, state, and national conferences; Internet webinars, and design or trade publications. Most professionals are required by professional associations and licensing jurisdictions to take a specified number of continuing education sessions. The number of opportunities available is extensive and easily accessible.

One of the longest-running programs, offering continuing education since 1949, is the Department of Engineering Professional Development program at the University of Wisconsin at Madison. There are many classes offered covering building codes; commissioning; construction; heating, ventilating, and air conditioning (HVAC); electrical; plumbing; fire protection; structural; high-performance buildings; and green buildings.

1.4 Managing Information

It is well known that information is one of our most valuable commodities, and it is expanding at what seems to be a logarithmic pace. Information about the design and construction of facilities is no exception. We live in a time when the amount of knowledge we need to possess about what we do increases every day. Like never before, it is of utmost importance to understand how to manage the information that is required of stakeholders and participants in the design and construction of facilities. This process is information intensive from project conception to occupancy, and continues for the life of the facility. The need for information management is especially important for product representatives and specifiers.

A computer and a connection to the Internet empowers individuals in profound ways and permits an ability to seek knowledge without limitation. Therefore, managing information has become a common part of the life of a professional. Managing information requires skill in finding, filtering, evaluating, and storing the information necessary to accomplish the design and construction of a facility. Important considerations for managing information and converting it to knowledge include the following:

- Is the information relevant sufficient, and accurate?
- Is the information timely?
- Is the information from a trustable source?
- Is the information a fact (verifiable), opinion (requires interpretation), or propaganda (not verifiable)?
- Is the information supported by other information or evidence?
- Is the information related to authoritative sources, such as a standard?

Knowledge empowers individuals, and acquiring knowledge is an individual responsibility. The knowledge necessary to succeed in any endeavor can be found in four realms:

1. *What We Know.* Personal education and training; lessons learned from personal experiences; resources we absorb and understand
2. *Resources within Reach.* Books, periodicals, articles, and research in our personal libraries
3. *Accessible Information.* Information accessible over the Internet or from others
4. *Whom We Know.* Colleagues, manufacturers, manufacturer's representatives, and research agencies

1.5 The Nature of the Project and Facility

The terms *project* and *facility* are used throughout this practice guide, and while they appear to have the same meaning, they are actually distinctively different.

- *Project* describes the process of planning, designing, documenting for procurement and construction, procuring, contracting, and constructing a facility for delivery to its owner. The goal of a project is the facility, and this practice guide is largely about the process of that delivery. The term *project* can refer to the object of the delivery process or the delivery process itself. The design and construction (delivery process) of a project is a unique combination of a scope of work (extent), its budget (cost), and its schedule (time).

- *Facility* is the completed project as a constructed entity intended for a specific purpose and function.

Philosophically, the process to deliver a facility is the confluence of an owner that wants a new facility with those that provide the aesthetic and technical design and those that construct that design. An owner wants something, it is designed, and then it is constructed. Around this simple conceptual idea is a large number of individuals, professionals, firms, companies, and agencies that work toward that goal.

Chapter 2
Stakeholders and Participants

2.1 | Introduction

The design and construction of a project that, upon completion, becomes a facility, requires the merging of the collective needs, ideas, talents, knowledge, and services of a widely diverse group of individuals and businesses that provide specialized services. Positive interaction among the teams begins with understanding the basic responsibilities of each team throughout the process and taking into consideration what each can do to contribute to another's success.

The Owner Team wants or needs a new or renovated facility.

The Architect/Engineer (A/E) Team provides design services addressing project requirements and designing the facility wanted or needed.

The Contractor Team provides construction services and is responsible for the many forces that are necessary to build the designed facility.

The Supplier Team provides technical and knowledgeable information to the other three teams and furnishes the materials and products required to build the designed facility.

In addition to being part of one of these teams, every individual is either a stakeholder or a participant based on the interests they have in the course of the project.

- *Stakeholders* are those individuals or organizations that are actively involved in a major portion of the project delivery process and have some type of interest in the project, such as investment, operational, or reputation, which may be positively or negatively affected by the constructed facility.
- *Participants* are those individuals or organizations that are active in only a portion of the project delivery process and have indirect interests that are not affected by the constructed facility.

The design and construction of every project has a unique personality because it is performed by a distinct group of individuals organized in the four teams described earlier that have never existed before and will most likely never exist again in the same arrangement.

2.2 The Owner Team

The term *owner* is the universal designation given to the entity that starts a sophisticated process of design and construction that will satisfy their need for a new or renovated building or facility. The owner initiates the project, assumes the risk, provides funding, controls and manages the design and construction process, approves of design and construction activities, and is the principal stakeholder. Unless the owner is an individual, typically one or more people will be charged with the responsibility to represent the interests of the owner and to orchestrate the activities of all four teams simultaneously.

The owner may or may not ultimately occupy the facility. The owner is usually the occupant of a residential project; however, for some projects, the owner is not always the occupant, as can be seen from the following:

- Administrators of the facilities department of a school district might have schools designed and constructed for the children of the families that live in the district.
- A developer builds multifamily apartments to rent, condominiums to sell, or other types of facilities for an owner to lease.
- The principals of a business might have a new building designed and constructed as the regional branch of the business.
- A state department of transportation might have new streets and infrastructure designed and constructed for a new or existing neighborhood.

In some instances, a project may be so large and complex that there might be two or more entities that are the owners. An example would be a sports stadium in which a facility management company, ownership representatives of a basketball team, and ownership representatives of a hockey team each have an interest in the project, contribute to its funding, and are the principal stakeholders. Sometimes a municipality, county, or state may also be a stakeholder. For projects of this complexity, the stakeholders might retain another company to manage the process, represent their interests, and direct the design and construction process.

2.2.1 Private Owners

The first of the two owner classifications involves facilities that will be owned by entities in the private sector. The distinguishing factor of the private sector is that the funding does not include money derived from taxation, and the user is not a public entity, unless a facility is constructed to be leased or purchased by a governing agency.

An individual is the most basic type of owner. Depending on their financial resources, individuals can own any one of many different types of facilities that are built to produce income or to house their business.

There are many private institutions that might build a facility for a particular function. An example would be facilities constructed by the board of directors of a private school or university. In many instances, individuals do not own the facility; instead the owner may be a company, a corporation, or a board of trustees.

Real estate development companies initiate and complete projects that are eventually either income-producing investments or will be sold to other individuals, companies, or investors. Development companies might focus on multifamily residential projects, hotels, health care facilities, office buildings, or complete neighborhood developments.

A company or a corporation might also be the owner of a building or facility. In addition, a group of companies or corporations might join forces to own a facility, as in the example of the large sports venue discussed above.

2.2.2   Public Owner

The second of the two owner classifications involves facilities that will be owned by entities in the public sector. The distinguishing factor of the public sector is that the funding is derived from some type of taxation. Public entities can be in many forms (i.e., federal, state, county, city, or town). They can also be a governing agency, a department of a public entity, or a centralized agency that initiates and manages the design and construction, such as the General Services Administration of the federal government.

It is not uncommon for a governing agency to dictate the design and construction process of any of the project delivery methods by their own rules or regulations. Examples of aspects of the process that may be different from the same process in the private sector include the following:

- How design work is awarded
- Use of drawings, conventions, and specifications required by the agency
- How the architect's construction administration and the contractor's project management will be conducted
- How applications for payment are processed
- Warranties and guarantees

2.2.3   Advisers

Owners frequently require the services of other individuals and businesses to assist with their role and responsibilities in controlling and managing the design and construction process. Advisers to the owner may include the following:

- Financial institutions, which arrange project financing
- Attorneys, who coordinate legal and contractual issues
- Insurance companies, which provide risk coverage
- Real estate agents, who assist with property acquisition
- Appraisers, who advise about specific sites, costs, and market types
- Marketing companies, which assist with advertising

2.2.4   Design Team Consultants Retained by Owner

Since the land on which the facility will be designed and constructed is owned by the project owner, there are several consultants the owner may engage to provide important information to the A/E and contractor teams.

2.2.4.1 Surveyors

Surveyors examine and survey the site and document the existing condition of the land. They also determine and document the ground surface topography and existing natural and constructed improvements that are either above ground or below ground.

2.2.4.2 Environmental Engineers

If the land on which the project will rest includes unique geographical assets, environmental engineers might be required to assist the owner in being environmentally sensitive to the assets.

2.2.4.3 Geotechnical Engineers

Geotechnical engineers examine the soil strata beneath the surface and the subsurface geological formation, and make recommendations for the design of the building foundations.

2.2.4.4 Hazardous Materials and Abatement Consultant

The hazardous materials and abatement consultant examines existing buildings for the presence of hazardous materials, such as asbestos, and prepares remediation recommendations and/or documents.

2.2.4.5 Traffic Engineers

Traffic engineers examine traffic usage and patterns over existing freeways, streets, and roads in anticipation of their expansion. They recommend facilities that would accommodate existing and future traffic.

2.2.4.6 Sustainability Consultants

Sustainability consultants recommend opportunities for being environmentally sensitive and advise about the sustainability properties of materials and products. If the project is seeking a specific Green Building rating, sustainability consultants assist with evaluations and decision making to achieve the rating. They may participate in construction administration.

2.2.4.7 Wetlands Biologists

Wetlands biologists examine existing wetlands in the path of development, identify and evaluate environmentally sensitive areas, and make recommendations for minimizing damage to the wetlands by construction.

2.2.4.8 Wildlife Biologists

Wildlife biologists examine existing wildlife that would be affected by development and makes recommendations for minimizing its impact.

There are some instances when the owner retains other consultants to provide services to the A/E and contractor teams for various reasons. Such consultants may include the following:

2.2.4.9   Design Engineers

Some owners may retain some or all of the engineers and consultants that are traditionally retained as part of the A/E team.

2.2.4.10   Testing and Inspection Agencies

For the purpose of ensuring that certain portions of the facility are being constructed according to project requirements, these agencies provide the owner with quality assurance (QA) and quality control (QC) by verifying that specific project elements and components comply with the contract documents and code requirements.

2.2.4.11   Commissioning Authority

Evaluates, tests, and analyzes newly constructed building mechanical and electrical systems, and operational equipment, to determine if they will function according to the project design criteria.   See discussion later in this chapter.

2.2.5   Occupants

After construction of a facility is completed, there are a variety of occupants that include the following:

2.2.5.1   Facility Manager

Commercial facilities typically have an individual, either a staff member or a service company, that implements maintenance and operations programs to ensure that the facility continues to function according to its intended purposes during occupancy and use. The facility manager may participate in the planning and design of the project or subsequent alteration, renovation, or addition projects.

2.2.5.2   Facility Users

Facility users are the people for which the facility was designed and constructed to conduct activities in accordance with its intended purpose. In some complex facilities, such as hospitals, the users may provide valuable input to the A/E team and assist with designing a facility that will meet spatial and functional requirements.

2.2.5.3   Visitors

In addition to the needs and requirements of the facility users, consideration must be given to those that visit the facility.

2.2.6   Utility Service Providers

Utility service providers are not part of the owner team in the same sense as those described above; however, this category is included here because the relationship between the providers and the owner continues for the life of the facility.

The owner arranges and contracts for the various public and regulated private utility providers that will furnish electrical power, natural gas, domestic water, sewerage removal, stormwater control, and communications services to the completed facility. After the owner has entered into the appropriate agreements, the design and contractor teams assist with the coordination of these utility services.

2.2.7 Authorities Having Jurisdiction

Like the utility service providers, authorities having jurisdiction are also not part of the owner team but the relationship continues after construction.

Authorities having jurisdiction (AHJs) include building code officials, zoning officials, inspectors, and regulatory agencies. They protect the public's health, safety, and welfare by administering laws, codes, and other regulations governing the project.

2.3 The Design Team

The design team works with the owner to deliver a facility meeting the owner's vision and requirements. The process of transforming the owner's vision and requirements, as expressed in the decisions and conclusions composing the project conception, from original concepts, visions, and ideas to the documentation required for construction, requires various disciplines of aesthetic and technical design services. Normally, A/E services are obtained by the owner separately or may be included as a part of a delivery method, such as the design-build (D-B) project delivery method. Design services may involve only one discipline or be very complex and require an A/E and various consultants with specific expertise. Using specialized design skills, the design team is usually responsible for the following services:

- Addressing the planning issues, including those involving the AHJs
- Assisting the owner in determining the design program and requirements
- Designing a project that reflects the owner's visions and meets the design program and requirements
- Identifying codes and regulations applicable to the design
- Researching, evaluating, and selecting products
- Producing the procurement and construction documents
- Administering the construction contract
- Providing QA procedures and QC reviews

Selection of A/E design services is usually based on qualifications, experience, and/or unique design skills or abilities, and not simply lowest price. It is prudent to select A/E design services that are appropriate for the project requirements and are consistent with the owner's vision of the facility desired. For example, small firms will not have the experience, staff, or capabilities to provide design services for a very large project, such as a sports venue, hotel, office complex, or high-rise building. Also, a large firm may provide far too many services for a small project or produce a creative and technical design that is more suited for a large project rather than a small project.

A very large number of projects have been produced in the past, and continue to be produced, utilizing traditional design services, which typically include the following broadly defined design services that can be used with any of the project delivery methods:

- Originating the design concept
- Creating the design schematically
- Developing the design in more detail
- Preparing the contract and/or construction documentation

While not always the case, this diversified collection of design professionals is directed, managed, and coordinated by a single professional or firm. This professional or firm is primarily responsible for the major portion of the design and subcontracts with other design professionals with specialized talents required to complete the design. Leadership of the design team could be provided by any of the following:

- *Buildings:*
  - Architect for the design-bid-build (D-B-B) and design-negotiate-build (D-N-B) delivery methods
  - Developer, contractor, or A/E for the D-B delivery method
  - Owner's program manager for complex projects, using any of the delivery methods
  - The facilities department for a business that requires buildings in multiple geographic locations that might be built by any of the delivery methods
  - The construction manager for the construction management delivery method
  - Owner for the owner-build (O-B) delivery method
  - Curtain wall consultant for the renovations of the exterior wall of an existing building for the D-B-B and D-N-B delivery methods
- *Tenant Improvements.* Interior designer for the D-B-B and D-N-B delivery methods
- *Municipal Infrastructure.* Civil engineer for the D-B-B delivery method
- *Industrial Facilities.* Mechanical engineer for any of the delivery methods
- *Transportation Improvements.* Governmental agency's public works department

The design team is universally referred to as the A/E (architect/engineer). The A/E team may be composed of any of the design professionals named below. Each of these terms can be used to refer to any individual professional, or to the business firm, that provides those particular design services. In order to use the title of architect or engineer, an individual must have a college degree, pass a licensing examination, and be duly and currently licensed in the state in which the project is located. With the exception of individual residences and possibly some very small commercial projects, the work of architects and engineers must include a seal attached to their work products, which are also known as *instruments of service.* Consultants are individuals or firms that have specialized knowledge and a significant amount of experience in a design discipline and provide specialized design services. These individuals may or may not be required to be licensed.

The terms *architect, engineer,* and *consultant* reflect the education and specialized training, governmental licensure, and sphere of design in which they practice. These individuals may also have other titles that reflect their role within their respective businesses and the responsibility they have as one of the design professionals contributing to the design of a project. The roles and responsibilities discussed below for architects, engineers, and consultants are generally the same for any of the project delivery methods.

2.3.1 Architect

The architect is responsible for the aesthetic and technical design of a project and for managing the design services provided by engineers and consultants for utility systems and other systems and equipment in the building not traditionally part of the services of an architect. Roles and responsibilities vary within firms of varying sizes, but generally include the following positions:

2.3.1.1 Principal-in-Charge

The principal-in-charge (PIC):

- Is typically an owner, principal, or officer of the firm that bears ultimate responsibility for the project and is final decision maker for the firm
- Is authorized to sign and commit the firm to binding contracts
- May or may not seal the documents
- Provides global "high-altitude" management and is not involved with day-to-day activities
- Represents the firm to others
- Usually is not involved in the details of design, documents, or construction
- Usually does not meet with product manufacturer representatives or suppliers

2.3.1.2 Project Manager

The project manager (PM):

- May or may not be an owner or principal of the firm, but is usually an officer
- May or may not be authorized to sign and commit the firm to binding contracts
- May or may not seal the documents
- Provides general "middle-altitude" management of the architect's staff, engineers, and consultants and is involved with day-to-day activities
- Guides the project through the design portion of the project delivery method
- Has controlling responsibility for the various phases and activities of the design process
- May or may not meet with product manufacturer representatives or suppliers

2.3.1.3 Programmer

Services may be provided by a programming consultant outside the firm. The programmer:

- Is generally reserved for large, complex projects such as hospitals
- Meets with the owner and user groups to interpret the design requirements and develop a program that will be used to arrange the spatial relationships between functions and areas of the project
- Usually is not involved with the construction documents or construction administration
- Does not meet with product representatives or suppliers

2.3.1.4 Project Designer

The project designer:

- Creates the aesthetic design for the project which may be limited to the exterior if an interior designer is part of the design team
- Meets with product representatives or suppliers
- Selects materials and products and, subject to owner approval, has decision-making power for the exterior design
- Usually is not involved with the construction documents or construction administration

2.3.1.5 Interior Designer

Services may be provided by an interior design consultant outside the firm. The interior designer:

- Creates the aesthetic design for the interiors of the project
- Makes recommendations for interior finishes, including color coordination
- Designs interior spaces and furniture layouts
- Meets with product representatives or suppliers
- Selects materials and products and, subject to owner approval, has decision-making power for the interior design
- May or may not be involved with the construction documents or construction administration

2.3.1.6 Project Architect

The project architect (PA):

- Provides some "low-altitude" management of the architect's staff
- Directs, manages, and coordinates the day-to-day activities of the production of the construction documents
- Coordinates the construction documents with the engineers and consultants
- Meets with product representatives or suppliers
- Generally determines the assembly of materials and products
- Has some amount of decision-making power, which is usually limited to the documents

2.3.1.7 Job Captain

The job captain:

- Probably does not have client contact
- Works primarily for the project architect to produce the construction drawings; may direct the work of the drafters, but has no other management responsibilities
- Has no decision-making power or influence over the aesthetic design, construction documents, or construction administration

2.3.1.8 Drafter

The drafter:

- Does not have client contact
- Works for the job captain on the construction drawings and has no management responsibilities
- Has no decision-making power or influence over the aesthetic design, construction documents, or construction administration

2.3.1.9 Specifier

Services may be provided by an independent specifications consultant. The specifier:

- Provides material and product research
- Prepares clear, concise, correct, and complete written specifications based on the design and tailored to the construction drawings
- Does not select, but may recommend or influence, the selection of the exterior and interior materials and products that are exposed to view; may select or influence the selection of materials and products that are not exposed to view
- Assists PM, PA, and others with decisions about the technical aspects of the aesthetic design and construction drawings

2.3.1.10 Construction Administrator

The construction administrator (CA):

- Administers the construction contract
- Works with the owner and contractors during construction
- Generates and/or processes change orders, supplemental instructions, and change requests
- Reviews submittals, observes the work, responds to questions, and interprets the construction documents
- Reviews contractor's applications for payment and requests for substitutions
- May have limited decision-making power about the project design

Even though the preceding role and responsibility descriptions are for architectural firms, other design firms will have many of the same, or similar, roles and responsibilities. Also, not all of these roles will be found on every project. The size of the project will determine which are necessary. For example, the project manager may also be project designer and project architect for small projects, whereas large projects may need several project managers and a larger number of project architects.

2.3.2 Civil Engineer

The civil engineer:

- Is responsible for the technical and engineering design of the site for the following:
  - Improvements, such as streets, roads, paving, plazas, and retaining walls
  - Service utilities, such as water, sewer, energy, communications, and storm drainage

- Shaping the topography of the land, such as earthwork, cut and fill grading
- Provides construction drawings and specifications
- Participates in construction administration

2.3.3 Structural Engineer

The structural engineer:

- Is responsible for the technical and engineering design of the building structural support frame, including footings and foundations
- Provides construction drawings and specifications
- Participates in construction administration

2.3.4 Mechanical Engineer

The mechanical engineer:

- Is responsible for the technical and engineering design of the movement and distribution of heated and cooled air, ventilation, and removal of odors, including the necessary equipment
- Provides construction drawings and specifications
- Participates in construction administration

2.3.5 Electrical Engineer

The electrical engineer:

- Is responsible for the technical and engineering design of the supply and distribution of lighting, power, and communication systems, including the necessary equipment
- Provides construction drawings and specifications
- Participates in construction administration

2.3.6 Plumbing Engineer

The plumbing engineer:

- Is responsible for the technical and engineering design of the supply and distribution of domestic water, removal of sewerage, directing rainwater off the roof, and medical gas systems for hospitals, including the necessary equipment
- Provides construction drawings and specifications
- Participates in construction administration

2.3.7 Landscape Architect

The landscape architect:

- Is responsible for the aesthetic and technical design of the trees, shrubs, lawns, plants, furnishings, plazas, courtyards, and visual improvements to exterior areas of the site
- Provides construction drawings and specifications
- Participates in construction administration

2.3.8 Fire Protection Engineer

The fire protection engineer:

- Is responsible for the technical and engineering design of the supply and distribution of active fire suppression systems, including the necessary equipment
- Advises, assists, and makes recommendations for the following:
  - Determining the need for passive fire protection materials and assemblies
  - Functional design to protect life and property
- May provide construction drawings and specifications
- May participate in construction administration

2.3.9 Exterior Enclosure Consultant

The exterior enclosure consultant:

- Advises, assists, and makes recommendations for the aesthetic and technical design of the building envelope enclosure; may be responsible for, or influence, the selection of materials and products
- May provide construction drawings and specifications
- May participate in construction administration

2.3.10 Roofing and Waterproofing Consultant

The roofing and waterproofing consultant:

- Advises, assists, and makes recommendations for the roofing and waterproofing systems; may be responsible for, or influence, the selection of materials and products
- May provide construction drawings and specifications
- May participate in construction administration

2.3.11 Cost Estimator

The cost estimator:

- Prepares detailed estimates of probable construction cost of a project
- May be a professional in independent practice or on the staff of the contractor

2.3.12 Code Consultant

The code consultant:

- Advises, assists, makes recommendations, and evaluates the design for compliance with the applicable building codes
- Assists with obtaining permits from AHJs

2.3.13 Sustainability Consultant

The sustainability consultant:

- Advises, assists, and makes recommendations for being environmentally sensitive and for sustainable properties of materials and products
- Assists with evaluations and decision making if the project is seeking a specific Green Building rating
- May participate in construction administration

2.3.14 Commissioning Consultant

See discussion later in this chapter.

2.3.15 Food Service Consultant

The food service consultant:

- Is responsible for planning and the technical design of commercial kitchens and the necessary equipment
- May prepare construction drawings and specifications
- May participate in construction administration

2.3.16 Building Transportation Consultant

The building transportation consultant:

- Is responsible for performing traffic studies and selecting the equipment for elevators, escalators, moving walks, and dumbwaiters
- May prepare construction drawings and specifications
- May participate in construction administration

2.3.17 Parking Consultant

The parking consultant:

- Is responsible for the technical design and layout of parking areas and parking garages
- May prepare construction drawings and specifications
- May participate in construction administration

2.3.18 Swimming Pool, Fountain, and Water Feature Consultant

The swimming pool, fountain, and water feature consultant:

- Is responsible for the aesthetic and technical design of the materials, products, finishes, and equipment to control water in a design feature
- May prepare construction drawings and specifications
- May participate in construction administration

2.3.19 Building Maintenance Equipment Consultant

The building maintenance equipment consultant:

- Is responsible for determining how the exterior wall will be accessed for maintenance, such as window washing and selecting the equipment
- May prepare construction drawings and specifications
- May participate in construction administration

2.3.20 Acoustical Consultant

The acoustical consultant advises, assists, and makes recommendations for the control, improvement, and containment of sounds and noise within the facility.

2.3.21 Lighting Design Consultant

The lighting design consultant advises, assists, and makes recommendations for lighting portions of the facilities, frequently to emphasize the facility design or to focus on an accent.

2.4 The Contractor Team

Constructing a project involves significant time, money, and personnel to convert a project design into a physical facility. Construction services typically include the following:

- Cost estimating
- Time scheduling
- Contracting
- Procurement (bidding, negotiating, purchasing)
- Management of construction

Unlike the selection of design services, selecting construction services could be exclusively based on being the lowest bidder of several contractors competitively bidding the project. Contractor selection may also be based on reputation, previous relationship with the owner or A/E, or special qualifications or experience constructing the specific type of project involved. The owner may select the contractor by a competitive bidding process or negotiation in which the basis of selection is more than construction cost alone. In such a process, the owner seeks proposals (negotiations) in which contractors state desired aspects of a proposed agreement rather than respond to the requirements of procurement documents as is normal in the D-B-B project delivery method.

As will be discussed in more detail in the chapters about the various project delivery methods, there are six primary project delivery methods, and several of variations are possible. One of the primary differences between the methods is in how the contractors, subcontractors, and suppliers are contracted for materials, products, and installation services.

Construction services may be combined with design services or may be obtained during or after the design process. Each type of project delivery will necessitate different sequencing of the construction process. When multiple contracts are involved, some contracts may be procured under a bidding process, while other services on the same project may be obtained through negotiated contracts or unit price contracts. Project delivery methods will be discussed, including the roles and responsibilities of the participants and whether construction services are obtained with complete construction documents or partial design documents. Regardless of how services are provided, it is prudent to obtain references and qualifications for the firm performing the actual construction. One of the most significant aspects of these qualifications is the financial capacity and bond capacity.

Project management services may be utilized early in the project delivery process to complement design services. These management services may simply involve establishing construction costs of the design or may be more formally established as project management or construction management. Construction expertise is extensive and diverse, and this expertise is offered similar to other professional services. Depending on the nature of these services, some jurisdictions may or may not require licensure of construction management services. Services such as estimating or management may not require licensing, whereas actual construction may require licensing to protect the public. Construction contractors with extensive experience can add tremendous value to any team.

Constructing a project requires knowledge of its numerous components as well as management skills to ensure that participants work together in harmony to complete a facility. Much construction is performed by specialists in many different trades. These specialists are usually employed by a contractor as subcontractors. A project may have numerous contractors and/or subcontractors, each performing a particular portion of the work. Each of these construction services may be provided under different types of agreements.

2.4.1 Contractor

The contractor enters into an agreement with the owner to build the facility described in the documents produced by the design team. The term *contractor* is used universally in this practice guide and is used to refer to the entity that constructs a facility. The contractor uses their management abilities to gather the various labor forces, subcontractors, and material, product, and equipment suppliers required to construct the facility.

Management expertise that contractors bring to the project delivery process includes the following:

- Experience in the construction of facilities
- Knowledge of factors that influence cost, time, and quality

- Ability to manage multiple subcontractors and suppliers
- Ability to manage complex construction operations and dynamic site activities
- Ability to manage cash flow and project accounting
- Skill in bidding and awarding contracts and subcontracts
- Experience with managing a construction budget in a risk-based setting

2.4.1.1 Principal-in-Charge

The PIC is typically an owner, principal, or officer of the firm that bears ultimate responsibility for the project and is final decision maker for the firm. The PIC:

- Is authorized to sign and commit the firm to binding contracts
- Provides global "high-altitude" management and is not involved with day-to-day activities
- Represents the firm to others
- Usually is not involved in the details of construction

2.4.1.2 Project Manager

The PM:

- May or may not be an owner or principal of the firm, but is usually an officer
- May or may not be authorized to sign and commit the firm to binding contracts
- Provides general "middle-altitude" management of the contractor's staff, suppliers, and subcontractors, and is involved with day-to-day activities
- Guides the project through the construction portion of the project delivery method

2.4.1.3 Estimator

The estimator determines the cost of the work, which will be basis of the agreement between the owner and contractor, from among a variety of suppliers and subcontractors.

2.4.1.4 Supervisor

The supervisor:

- May or may not be authorized to sign and commit the firm to binding contracts
- Directs, manages, and coordinates the day-to-day activities of the contractor's staff, suppliers, and subcontractors, and is involved with day-to-day activities

2.4.1.5 Accountant

The accountant processes incoming invoices, monitors the disbursement of funds to suppliers and subcontractors, and assists with preparation of applications for payment.

2.4.1.6 Layout Technician

The layout technician establishes, monitors, and maintains dimensional and benchmark control over the work.

2.4.1.7 Safety Director

The safety director establishes, monitors, and maintains safety on the construction site in general and among subcontractors.

2.4.1.8 Sustainability Consultants

Sustainability consultants:

- Recommend opportunities for being environmentally sensitive and advises about the sustainability properties of materials and products
- Assist with evaluations and decision making if the project is seeking a specific Green Building rating

2.4.2 Subcontractor *✳ PART OF CONTRACTOR TEAM*

A subcontractor is an individual or business that provides the labor, materials, and services required for the construction of a specific portion of the work as defined by the contractual relationship with the prime contractor. A critical aspect of this relationship is that a subcontractor is obligated to the prime contractor in the same manner as the prime contractor is obligated to the owner. This is known as "flow-through" provisions so that there is consistency in the various contractual arrangements for a project.

2.5 The Supplier Team

The supplier team is composed of a wide variety of companies that are part of the delivery method simply because they will furnish the materials and products for the facility to be constructed. The supplier team consists of individuals, organizations, and companies involved in the manufacture, promotion, and sale of construction materials, products, equipment, and systems.

Before proceeding with the discussion of this team, it is helpful to establish a few definitions for those that are on the supplier team:

- *Manufacturer.* Manufactures or produces materials, products, and equipment to be incorporated in a project
- *Distributor.* Buys, inventories, and resells materials, products, components, assemblies, and equipment to others that can be either fabricated or directly incorporated into the project
- *Supplier.* Furnishes or supplies products or services for the project, but does not perform labor at the site

- *Fabricator.* Assembles in a location other than the project site, of various materials, products, and equipment into a form that can be more efficiently installed or constructed on the project site using fewer installing personnel and taking less time than would be necessary if the original materials and products not fabricated

In addition to making printed and web site information available to the other teams, manufacturers, distributors, suppliers, and fabricators utilize representatives to provide sales and consulting services to the other teams.

2.5.1   Forms of Representation

Manufacturers use several forms of product representation to market their products. The responsibilities vary greatly, depending on the form of representation. Some product representatives represent multiple manufacturers, while others represent only one.

2.5.1.1   Manufacturers' Employees

Many manufacturers employ a staff to market and sell their products. Depending on the company's size, a single employee may perform several functions. Manufacturers' employees may have different titles, depending on the manufacturer. Regardless of the title, they are responsible for some aspect of representing the manufacturers' products to the project team.

Manufacturers' employees are agents, sell a product or perform a service, and are excluded from representing other manufacturers' products. These employees speak for the manufacturers, which assume liability for the representatives' actions.

Manufacturers' employees usually receive a salary, and, depending on the manufacturer, some may make a commission on sales. The company normally reimburses expenses.

Three of the more common types of manufacturers' employees include sales, marketing, and technical staff:

- *Sales Employees.* Sales employees are responsible for making sales appointments, quoting pricing information, taking purchase orders, and arranging for product shipment if the manufacturer does not have a separate order-processing department. Often, these individuals have held other positions in the company and are thoroughly familiar with the manufacturing process. They can usually advise on nonstandard items and unique technical installation problems. Sales employees typically work toward a sales quota or goal.
- *Marketing Employees.* Marketing employees research the market to determine what is important to buyers and decision makers. Their research evaluates and targets buyers and decision makers, assists in establishing criteria for the product that satisfies their clientele, and provides information to price the product competitively. Another responsibility is to develop advertising strategies and determine the suitable methods, media, and quantity of advertising. These employees are often responsible for forecasting future sales so manufacturers can effectively plan future production.

- *Technical Employees*. Technical employees answer inquiries from the design and construction teams, present seminars, and perform other educational activities such as technical training. Though technical employees do not often sell, they provide a vital service to the project team on evaluation, selection, specification, and proper product use. Technical employees work with engineering departments in the development of specific details or product modification. Sometimes they are asked to provide warranty information, observe product installation, or trouble-shoot an installation problem.

2.5.1.2 Independent Sales Representatives

Manufacturers may promote their products through contracts with independent sales representatives to provide this service. Independent sales representatives typically have established contacts with A/Es, contractors, subcontractors, and perhaps owners within a defined geographic area. The agreements between manufacturers and independent sales representatives usually stipulate a specific geographic area of activity. A manufacturer wishing to penetrate a new territory can do so quickly by using established independent sales representatives to market through their contacts. It is often more economical for a small- or medium-sized manufacturer to contract for these services with an experienced local representative than to have a direct employee sales force.

Independent sales representatives, through a contractual agreement with a manufacturer, derive their income through commissions on sales and are responsible for their own business costs. They may be paid a fee to distribute manufacturers' literature or write specifications that include a manufacturer's product or system. It is also common for manufacturers to pay independent sales representatives a fee for service when marketing a new product. National and global marketing requires the interaction of independent sales representatives in different geographic areas to work on the same project. When project design occurs in one region and construction in another, the commission on sales is often split between the representatives. If the product is specified but not used, no commission is paid. Some representative agreements with manufacturers may include commission based on a percentage of sales from the geographic area or registered projects.

Even though they may have agreements with several manufacturers, independent sales representatives usually do not represent competing products or those that present a conflict of interest. However, occasionally an overlap in product lines may occur. Such an overlap might exist if a representative carries a generic product from one manufacturer and a high-performance product of another. Although similar, the products are not competing for the same market.

Another form of agreement for independent sales representatives is a subrepresentative agreement. This form of agreement is typically made between two product representatives; one has a contract to represent a particular product for a large territory, but needs assistance covering another part of that territory.

Independent sales representatives are responsible for servicing other members of the project team in the same manner as manufacturers' sales employees. The product manufacturer may also rely on information from the independent sales representative to forecast sales.

Independent sales representatives may combine different forms of representation. For example, an independent sales representative may have an agreement to be a representative of one manufacturer and a distributor for another. A manufacturer may have a sales force to represent some territories, but independent sales representatives or distributors represent and sell in others. The decision to combine forms of representation is usually the result of an evaluation of the geographic area. A territory may have a high concentration of construction in a single location, such as a large city, while other areas that need representation are widely spread, such as a rural state.

2.5.2 The Dual Nature of Representation

Product representatives are ambassadors, in a sense, for manufacturers and suppliers, and they play an important role throughout the design and construction process in each of the project delivery methods.

The primary reason product representatives are valuable assets to the design and construction process is the dual nature of their function and role.

- *Consultant.* The most active aspect of the role of a product representative is that they function as the provider of technical information necessary to allow the materials and products to be incorporated into the project. Product representatives can do the following:
  - Provide skills necessary to promote a product for its intended purpose and then provide advice on its proper installation.
  - Advise owners, A/Es, contractors, and subcontractors on product options, limitations, cost, and maintenance. These services carry with them a burden of responsibility because A/Es, owners, contractors, and subcontractors rely on the product representative's advice.
  - Provide technical assistance and information during design; provide estimates during the bidding, negotiation, and purchasing; and make recommendations and observations during product installation.
  - Provide maintenance and warranty requirements at contract closeout.
- *Sales.* The other aspect of the role of product representatives is that they provide consultation for the purpose of selling their materials and products to the builders of the project. Some product representatives also act as subcontractors and may install their products as well. A supplier team involved with the design team, construction team, and owner team early in a project helps to ensure that a specified product or system is used and specified properly. This early involvement may also provide the supplier team with a competitive advantage, when products are being selected and purchased.

Product representatives should be aware of project requirements, including specified functional and performance criteria, prebid submittal conditions, necessary delivery dates, and procedures for proposing substitutions. Most effective assistance occurs when product representatives interact with members of the project team and review the construction documents to understand the requirements.

Effective product representatives usually possess the following broad areas of knowledge and skills:

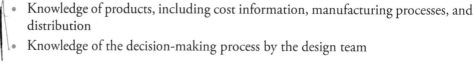

- Knowledge of products, including cost information, manufacturing processes, and distribution
- Knowledge of the decision-making process by the design team

- Knowledge of the construction process, documents, procedures, and participants
- Sales skills

To be integral participants in the design and construction process, product representatives should understand the principles of effective technical assistance, and understand the constraints of project scheduling. Effective product representatives understand the value of time—theirs and that of other team members. Time well spent early in the initial design phases can save time for the design team and for all project team members during construction.

Effective interaction by the supplier team requires expert knowledge to educate the other project team members about available products, systems, and installation methods; provide technical assistance during project design and construction; and ensure proper installation and use of products and systems. The supplier team works with the owner and design teams to identify products that are suitable for particular project conditions and requirements.

The supplier team works with the contractor team by providing information necessary for proper delivery, storage, and installation of products and systems.

2.5.3 Distribution of Materials

The movement of materials, products, components, assemblies, and equipment to either intermediators or directly to the project site is a complex logistical operation for suppliers. The delivery of materials to the project site has to occur according to the construction schedule in order for the construction to proceed smoothly. For example, the traditional and logistical supply chain for consumer products has three levels: the producer, the wholesaler, and the retailer.

Distributors have agreements (written or oral) with manufacturers to buy, inventory, and resell products to buyers. Distributors derive a profit on the sale of a product or system and usually do not work on a commission basis as independent sales representatives do. Distributors may be stocking distributors who maintain an inventory, or nonstocking distributors, sometimes referred to as *dealers*. A distributor's agreement with the manufacturer may be for a specific geographic area and time period. The agreement sometimes contains a sales objective that may be used to evaluate performance. Geographic areas can be broken into two types of territories: exclusive and nonexclusive. An exclusive territory is one in which the manufacturer has an agreement with a distributor or a specific period during which that particular distributor is the sole distributor that can sell the manufacturer's product in the specific geographic area. For example, ABC Manufacturer signs an agreement with XYZ Distributor for the exclusive rights to all sales in Your Town, USA, for one year. Though the distributor may be legally bound to the geographic area, once a material is purchased, the manufacturer no longer has control of the product and it can then be resold anywhere.

The nonexclusive territory is a more common arrangement for distributors in highly populated areas. In a nonexclusive territory, a manufacturer may decide to have more than one distributor because of sales potential, or the territory may be too large to be sufficiently covered by one company. Several arrangements for these distributors may exist. Each distributor has a pricing structure based on volume, credit rating, level of participation in the sale, and rating with the manufacturer. Subdistributors may buy from the master distributor or from the manufacturer at a different pricing structure. Some manufacturers give distributors a significant discount because of the volume of material they purchase.

2.6 Team Selection Process

Each project delivery method requires a wide variety of participants from many design and construction disciplines. These participants are brought together by agreements that should be compatible, depending on the relationships established by the project delivery method selected. For example, in the D-B-B delivery method, the A/E and contractor are under separate contracts with the owner, whereas under D-B method, the A/E and contractor are under one contract with the owner. Each contract under a delivery method most likely will have a subset of contracts for consultants, subcontractors, and suppliers.

It is important that the project delivery method be determined early in the process because in some instances the design and construction of the project may be concurrent. Most project owners utilize the advice of experienced consultants such as an A/E or contractor to select the best project delivery method. Together they consider many factors, including project cost, complexity, time for completion, and market conditions. The contractor lends expertise and experience to help the owner determine the best project delivery method.

2.6.1 Selecting the Team

Selection of team participants takes knowledge and skill and may be outside of the owner's expertise. There are firms, such as development consultants specializing in certain project types, that can assist in getting a project under way. The selection process will be somewhat different, depending on whether the selection is for an A/E, a contractor, or a design-builder. Any of these processes may begin with a request for proposal (RFP) from an owner or an offer from a firm wishing to be considered.

A prerequisite of a good project is ensuring that each team participant has the education, practical experience, and skills to carry out their respective responsibilities effectively and in concert with other team participants. An effective project team works together harmoniously and focuses on the same goal. The team often includes the owner's personnel, A/E, cost consultants, a contractor, and possibly a construction manager. Suppliers and product representatives may not have contractual relations until products are purchased but may provide vital advice prior to actual construction. Coordination and communication among team participants is vitally important for a successful project. Building good working relationships enhances the entire process.

The owner should keep in mind the project concept and mission when assembling the team. The owner should consider the work that needs to be done and skills and expertise required to perform the work. If specialized design is crucial, it is worthwhile to ensure that the team includes special consultants.

Part of what enhances successful and harmonious relations among team participants is allowing all of them adequate time to do their job properly. This emphasizes the importance of a clear and concise project schedule.

With qualified personnel working together on a regular basis, the project manager can develop effective in-house team building to suit the requirements of a variety of clients and projects.

2.6.2 Selecting an A/E

The A/E is generally selected by the owner based on the A/E firm's expertise in a particular type of project. The A/E may have experience in a wide range of project types but may be known for having innovative techniques and solutions. The A/E may be selected by the owner independent of the construction team or may be combined with construction, as in the D-B delivery method. There are three primary methods for selecting an A/E.

2.6.2.1 Direct Selection/Negotiation of Services

Obtaining design services can be a daunting task for an owner, especially an inexperienced owner that will build only one facility in their lifetime. Some of the simplest ways of retaining an A/E may be one of the following:

* A recommendation from a friend or associate
* Retaining an A/E that provided services on a previous project
* Based on seeing an existing facility in the area or in a periodical

Those owners with previous experience in design and construction may use direct selection as their primary means of obtaining design services. To the A/E this is known as a *returning client*. The direct selection process saves time and money for the participants involved. The client saves the efforts of research, interviews, and specific documentation of requirements. For the A/E, the process saves expenses of identifying markets, making presentations, and assessing capabilities and consultants required for the project. Direct selection may be the result of the A/E's reputation in certain design types. Some A/Es have demonstrated creative solutions and unique use of materials in their designs. These solutions to problems have received recognition through awards and publication. Most A/E firms specialize in certain project types and have developed significant expertise in those markets.

Some owners have established facilities and operations and are familiar with the design and construction process. These owners may have prior relationships with A/Es and other participants. Under these circumstances, the owner will contact specific firms with whom they have had successful past projects. At this point, the direct selection is a matter of discussions and meetings relative to the extent of the project, the owner's design criteria, and the project budget. With a mutual understanding of everyone's schedules, these discussions and communications turn to negotiations of a fee for these design services.

2.6.2.2 Request for Proposal for Services

The more sophisticated way of obtaining design services is to respond to a detailed RFP that requests information about experience, qualifications, and recommendations from previous owners. For example, a recent RFP for the renovation of an existing federal building included the following categories of information:

* Description and parameters of the project
* Responsibilities of the design professionals
* Project schedule
* Necessary team participants
* Terms and conditions of the design contract
* Scope of services required
* Green Building Rating System scorecard
* Compensation

- Proposal preparation requirements
- Request for basic information and history of the firm
- Request for biographical information for principals and personnel
- Request for organizational chart of the team structure
- Request for commitment to various disclosure statements such as the following:
  - Previous litigation activity
  - Possible conflicts of interest
  - Authorizations to conduct business
  - Anticollusion statements
  - Tax certification affidavit
  - Nondiscrimination statements
  - Payment to subcontractors and suppliers
  - Release of claims
- Proposal executed on offer form
- Fee proposal
- Evaluation factors and criteria

Federal, state, and local governmental agencies, real estate developers, large organizations such as hospitals, and school districts are among those entities that have developed forms that are used for the design and construction of projects. A federal form that is commonly known among A/Es is SF 330—Architect-Engineer Qualifications—which is used by federal agencies to obtain information from potential A/Es about their professional qualifications.

The federal government and most state and local agencies obtain design services according to a common process known as *qualifications-based selections*. For federal projects, the Brooks A-E Act (40 USC 1101–1104) requires the federal government to announce publicly the requirements for A/E services for upcoming projects. After submission of qualified proposals, not less than three highly qualified firms are to be selected that have demonstrated competence and professional qualifications according to the specific criteria published in the public announcement. Beginning with the most highly qualified firm, the act then requires the agency to negotiate a contract at a fair and reasonable price based on the information contained within the proposal.

2.6.2.3 Design Competitions for Services

Design competitions are sometimes utilized when a high-profile project or a unique solution is being sought for a facility. The intent for a design competition is to select an aesthetic and technical design from among a group of potential design solutions according to the quality of the solutions to the established design criteria, such as a program and an intended site. In an open design competition, design proposals from any design professional (not always limited to A/Es) may be submitted for consideration. In a closed competition, only a preselected group of design professionals may submit a design proposal.

Design competitions require significant work by the design professional and can be very costly. The owner who proposes a design competition should be willing to provide some form of compensation to the design professional of the design that is selected. Design competitions may also be combined with, or in conjunction with, construction services such as in a D-B project delivery.

As with any competition, rules need to be established, and an independent jury of peers is prudent to retain objectivity in the selection process. This jury of peers usually consists of other A/Es who can objectively evaluate different solutions based on the initial criteria. These other A/Es can best understand how the designs can meet the criteria and benefit the owner. Frequently, the jury may include stakeholders that have an interest in the decision-making process. Notwithstanding the controversy surrounding the proposals and selection, the redevelopment of the World Trade Center site in New York City after the tragic 9-11 event is a prominent example of a design competition. For private projects, an owner is entitled to select any design solution believed to be the best solution according to whatever reasons the owner deems important.

Competition for design services in conjunction with construction services, such as the D-B project delivery method, offers unique opportunities and a holistic approach to the project. This type of design competition usually involves teams that are self-assembled through previous affiliations on other projects. These teams involve A/Es and construction firms working together to solve the owner's needs though an efficient design within the owner's established budget. These competitions usually involve exploration of alternative construction systems, scheduling, and other evaluations to achieve a solution that goes beyond design to include a projected final cost and schedule.

2.6.3 Selecting a Contractor

Depending on the project delivery method to be used for a project, a contractor may be brought into a project early in its life cycle. A contractor may provide preliminary pricing for design or may be part of a D-B entity seeking a negotiated contract. Some public agencies may be required to obtain preconstruction services through a competitive bidding process. In any case, the contractor's qualification should be considered relative to the type of project involved.

2.6.3.1 Bidding versus Negotiating

Obtaining pricing and selecting a contractor is usually the procurement stage of a project. Whether an owner is a private entity or a public agency will determine if there are restrictions on this process. In either case, the owner's project requirements and basis of design will require documentation. Obtaining pricing from several contractors is known as *competitive bidding* (design-bid-build project delivery method), whereas a dialog (with or without a proposed design) with a single-prime contractor is known as *negotiating* (design-negotiate-build project delivery method). These two delivery methods are discussed in more detail in Chapter 7, "Project Delivery."

2.6.3.2 Qualifications

Some owners may require contractors to provide information regarding their capability to do the work from both a physical and a financial standpoint. In a D-B-B project delivery, this information may be required from all bidders at the time the bids are received or at a predetermined time after receipt of bids, or it may be required only from the apparent low bidder prior to award of contract. Associations such as the American Institute of Architects (AIA; Document A305, Contractor's Qualification Statement) and Associated General Contractors (AGC; ConsensusDOCS Form 220, Contractor Statement of Qualifications for Engineered Construction and ConsensusDOCS Form 221, Contractor Statement of Qualifications, Specific Project) have standard forms for recording essential information in a format that permits comparison and evaluation.

The aspects of workmanship and excellence are not easily documented, so contacting references and actually visiting projects might provide good insight into the contractor's qualifications.

2.6.3.3 Subcontractors

Almost all construction contracts can be subdivided into units of work, and subcontractors may accomplish the work of each unit. Within each unit of work, a separate system of competitive bidding occurs, with a number of subcontractors competing on a price basis within their own field. The bid submitted by the prime bidder will be made up of a number of these subbids. AGC also has standard forms for recording essential information (ConsensusDOCS Form 721, Subcontractor Statement of Qualifications, Specific Project).

2.6.4 Selecting a Construction Manager

Once an owner decides that one of the two types of construction management project delivery methods is appropriate for a project, the construction manager may be selected through negotiations. Construction managers may be selected directly based on an established relationship or may submit their qualifications in response to an RFP. Depending on the method selected, qualifications will vary based on whether the construction manager is an adviser or a contractor. The construction management project delivery method is discussed in more detail in Chapter 7, "Project Delivery."

2.6.5 Selecting a Design-Builder

Once an owner determines that the D-B project delivery method is the most appropriate delivery method for a project, there are several ways to obtain services.

2.6.5.1 Direct Selection

For direct selection, the owner should have a performance program and project description. When selecting a design-builder, the owner should be able to convey the program to those being considered to provide D-B services. By comparison, traditional A/E services might include helping the owner define the program. In talking to design-builders, the owner must be very clear on the goals and purpose of the project. These requirements need to be documented and may be in the form of performance requirements. In some instances, the owner may engage a separate A/E to prepare a program and preliminary design documents under a variation referred to as bridging. The selected design-builders are then invited to submit preliminary proposals based on the owner's performance program and project description. The design-builders' proposal normally includes information on their experience, design, construction capability, and financial condition. The owner evaluates the proposals, selects the design-builder, and negotiates the contract.

2.6.5.2 Competitive Bidding

Competitive bidding may be used for the selection of a design-builder, especially when public funds are involved or when the owner's financing method requires a single stipulated sum. Because precise information is not available to the design-builders, competitive bidding may be more difficult. The owner's performance program and project description and criteria for evaluating information in the proposals should be clear and accurate to ensure a fair and competitive evaluation. A formal programming effort by the owner is necessary to produce a detailed performance program for use by the bidders. Competitive bidding for D-B services requires a greater investment by the owner in the production of a well-developed project description and a greater investment on the design-builder's part to arrive at a competitive and accurate bid.

2.6.5.3 Request for Proposal and Qualifications

Prior to issuing an RFP, the owner may issue a request for qualifications to solicit information about potential design-builders. The information received in response to the request for qualifications helps the owner discern the qualifications of those who may be considered for the project. The owner may want to have this information before the RFP is sent. This may help to narrow the field, as the RFP is sent only to those who have been approved or prequalified.

The request for qualifications may request the following information:

- Licensing of architects, engineers, and contractors in the jurisdiction where the project is located.
- Experience with similar projects.
- Experience in the selected project delivery method (for example, negotiated agreements, D-B, or D-B-B).
- Bonding capacity. Even if the owner is not requiring it, the fact that the entity can be bonded is important and provides insight into both the financial stability and performance record of the entity.
- Specific experience for specific types of projects. If the project under consideration has special requirements, the A/E may be required to have that type of experience. Some types of experience are more important than others. For example, if the project is a six-lane highway with several large intersections and raised roadways, the experience of a highway paving/construction company may not be adequate if it has worked only on ground level. Or a firm with experience in speculative office buildings may not have the expertise to complete a hospital.
- A certain level of project excellence. What types of projects has the A/E completed and to what level of requirements? For example, different requirements would apply to an apartment complex, a housing development, and a four-star luxury hotel.
- Financial statements, as an indication of a company's financial strength and stability. The owner may want to know how long the firm has been in business and what its record is for timely payments to consultants, subcontractors, and suppliers.
- A description of the project team participants. Is this an established team with experience with numerous projects, one previous project, or none? What is the experience of the team in working together?
- Adequate team participants, management, and support staff. They should have experience as well, and they should have worked with the other participants.
- The experience of the individuals proposed for key positions.
- Professional organizations and civic organizations that the firm or team participants are active in. Can this participation positively influence the project?

- In some cases, participation by team participants who are disadvantaged business enterprises, minority business enterprises, or women-owned business enterprises may be required.
- A description of the entity's record on timely completion of projects—whether on time, ahead of schedule, or late. If late, what were the reasons?
- Adequate resources, in the form of equipment to support the work, office space, and secretarial or administrative support, must be available for the project. The firm must have enough capital to cover its expenses during the project.
- A description of experience in maintaining projects within established budgets and value analysis.
- A record of requests for information, substitutions, and change orders from recent projects. Reasons for the changes should also be included.

The D-B project delivery method is discussed in more detail in Chapter 7.

2.7 Partnering and Collaboration

A project team that functions together and works toward mutual goals can be greatly improved by the concepts of partnering and collaboration. The success of any project is reflective of how well the participants worked together to achieve the end results. The ultimate goal is a project constructed on time, on budget, and meeting the owner's requirements.

Partnering is a concept of teamwork or team building. This concept may be required to help ensure cooperative efforts and proactive solutions. This concept is usually implemented by having a managerial consultant bring the participants together for an interactive session. Team participants set priorities and goals to achieve. This concept may also involve a pledge by those involved to make every attempt to resolve issues without conflict. Partnering as a concept attempts to make all team participants partners in the process of executing the work and completing the facility. A weakness of this technique develops when participants do not follow the priorities and goals established in the partnering session.

Collaboration is another term reflecting the need to cooperatively work together. Collaboration may simply be people working together as a team. Unfortunately, in today's world, participants are scattered in numerous locations and not in the same office or even the same town. Current computer systems, networks, the Internet, and extranets permit quick transfer of data. This can permit online, live, interactive documents and data. Software and services have been developed that permit multiple participants to access files to input, modify, and comment on the data available. This instantaneous processing of data can save precious time, which can result in cost savings. As these data are made available in the public computer domain, there are new issues of privacy and authority. Most of the software and services can establish rights of access and rights to modify or alter this information. This live information can become extremely valuable to the owner and facility manager of a completed project and the resulting facility.

Ideally, partnering and collaboration will aid in the project delivery process, will assist in the production of documents of a higher quality and with a higher standard of care, and will serve the practical needs of the participants in the design and construction process.

2.8 Commissioning

A type of design and construction specialist that is increasingly becoming a part of project delivery methods is a commissioning authority. Commissioning is being discussed separately from the four teams above because it can be a part of the owner team, the A/E team, or the contractor team. It will be discussed here as a consultant for the owner.

Originally developed for mechanical and electrical system construction, the commissioning process has expanded to include the validation of the project delivery process entirely from the concept stage, including programming, through design, contract document preparation, procurement, and construction, and into the operations and maintenance activities in facilities management. The purpose of commissioning has been established by the Building Commissioning Association as providing "... documented confirmation that building systems function according to criteria set forth in the project documents to satisfy the owner's operational need" (www.bcxa.org, accessed on April 3, 2010).

Total project commissioning engages the use of a specialist known as a *commissioning authority,* or sometimes *agent,* who is usually an independent entity not affiliated with the other participants of the project team. The commissioning authority is engaged to verify the quality of the project in relation to the owner's project requirements. This is different from normal construction administration, which verifies the quality by checking its compliance with the contract documents.

The process of total project commissioning begins by documenting the owner's project requirements, the basis of the design proposed to solve those requirements, and how the variety of systems and assemblies will work together to provide those solutions. At each stage in the project's life cycle, procedures can be implemented to monitor how the criteria are being incorporated and whether the criteria will achieve results. This commissioning continues through the design and construction process to obtain assurances and minimize errors and omissions.

Most of today's projects are complex in their very nature and require numerous components, elements, systems, and assemblies to work together to provide solutions. As an example, the environment of a space is controlled by the enclosure of that space, as well as the equipment that provides the light, temperature, and humidity control. The owner's project requirement may simply be 72 degrees Fahrenheit with 30 percent relative humidity as a performance criterion. Numerous systems and assemblies need to work together to achieve this desired result. The type and extent of glazing, insulation, materials resisting infiltration of water, air, and moisture vapor, and other materials are equally as important and must be consistent with the mechanical equipment and its design. Equipment alone is not the answer to the owner's need for environmental control. If energy efficiency and sustainability are a concern, these add other aspects to the design solution. Each aspect can add complexity to the project and requires numerous integrated systems and assemblies for the final solution.

As a project moves from design through construction documentation and actual construction, every aspect can impact the final outcome. A mere substitution may jeopardize the original intent and cause a failure of the design. The commissioning authority acts on the owner's behalf to ensure that the process provides the results intended. Total commissioning can help an owner who is not familiar with the design, the construction, and the many high-tech systems that exist. This commissioning may also help owners who do not have the required in-house staff or facility managers.

Complex systems can include security, fire suppression, automation, environmental controls, telecommunications, networks, data, and systems specific to process equipment. The integration of these systems and assemblies requires greater involvement of all concerned and requires extensive cooperation. Today's complex issues may require an owner to add a commissioning authority to ensure that the completed facility operates as intended. The commissioning authority should view the project as a whole, determine the interdependence of systems, and develop means to verify compliance with original intent.

Much as design takes an owner's project requirements and converts it into a physical solution, commissioning is used to monitor these processes to ensure it meets the original requirements. Commissioning should be more than monitoring the process and should be proactive in its attempts to ensure rather than control the quality. Commissioning can be as simple as a series of checklists or as complex as computer software. As with any other process involving more participants and monitoring, this can add paperwork, time, and additional cost to each participant's effort.

Chapter 3
Facility Life Cycle

3.1 Introduction

Facilities of every form, type, extent, or use have a beginning, a service life, and an ending.

The origin of every facility starts as an original thought in the mind of someone. The thought is nurtured and developed and then, if found to be viable, becomes the catalyst for determining if the facility is feasible. At this point, the idea for a facility becomes a project and the project delivery process starts. When it is decided that a new, renovated, or expanded facility is feasible, decisions have to be made and the details of what is needed have to be programmed. At some point, those with the capabilities for design enter the process and assist with shaping the ideas and programming into physical forms, the purpose of which is to satisfy the needs for the facility. Also, at some point, those with the capabilities for construction join the process and assist with the details of constructability. When the process matures to the point that sufficient construction documents have been prepared, construction begins. When the completion of the construction draws near, certain activities take place to move the project from construction to occupancy and the establishment of facility management. When all the activities of design and construction are fully completed, the project delivery process ends and the facility starts living its useful life. Some facilities will exist for a few decades, while other facilities might last centuries, all the while having to be managed. This sequence of activities is known as the facility life cycle.

3.2 The Nature of the Facility Life Cycle

The generalized facility life cycle description in the previous paragraph can be organized in a variety of ways. This practice guide is built around a facility life cycle developed by CSI that is detailed in Section 3.4. However, before it is discussed, it would be helpful to review others that have been proposed by other professional associations.

3.2.1 American Institute of Architects (AIA)

THE AMERICAN INSTITUTE OF ARCHITECTS

AIA Document B101—Standard Form of Agreement Between Owner and Architect has been the project delivery method used by the architectural profession for many years and thousands of projects. *The Architect's Handbook of Professional Practice*,

14th edition, published by John Wiley & Sons in 2008, identifies the following phases:

- *Schematic Design Phase* (p. 525). Schematic design establishes the general scope, conceptual design, and scale and relationships among the components of a project. The primary objective is to arrive at a clearly defined, feasible concept and to present it in a form that achieves client understanding and acceptance. The secondary objectives are to clarify the project program, explore the most promising alternative design solutions, and provide a reasonable basis for analyzing the cost of the project.
- *Design Development Phase* (p. 526). During design development, the design team works out a clear, coordinated description of all aspects of the design. This typically includes fully developed floor plans, sections, exterior elevations, and, for important areas or aspects of the building, interior elevations, reflected ceiling plans, wall sections, and key details. Often these become the basis for the construction documents.
- *Construction Documentation Phase* (pp. 531–532). The development of the construction documentation is an extension of the design process. Decisions on details, materials, products, and finishes all serve to reinforce the design concept—and begin the process of translating the concept into reality. The project documents typically consist of the project manual and the project drawings.
  - The drawings include architectural, structural, mechanical, electrical, civil, landscape, interior design, and other specialty drawings.
  - The project manual typically includes the following:
    - Bidding requirements
    - Contract forms and supplements
    - Contract conditions
    - Specifications
- *Bidding or Negotiation Phase* (p. 562). In the bidding/negotiation phase, the architect assists the client in obtaining competent construction bids or negotiating the construction contract.
- *Construction Contract Administration Phase* (p. 574). … The architect has authority to act on the owner's behalf … Throughout the construction phase, the architect serves as the representative of, as well as an adviser and consultant to, the owner. During the architect's visits to the job site, CA duties include the following:
  - Becoming generally familiar with the work through site visits
  - Keeping the owner informed about the progress and quality of the portions of the complete work
  - Reporting observed defects and deficiencies in the work, and deviations from the construction schedule
  - Determining in general if the work, when fully completed, will be in accordance with the contract documents
  - Other more specific responsibilities include the following:
    - Reviewing submittals
    - Payment certifications
    - Project closeout

3.2.2 The Associated General Contractors of America (AGC)

AGC outlines the project delivery process of a project in five phases that is also closely related to project management. The following is taken from *Project Delivery Systems for*

Construction, published by the Associated General Contractors of America in 2004, page 20:

- *Real Estate.* The "real estate" phase consists of locating and purchasing real property; identifying its appropriate use; arranging for zoning, permitting, and environmental compliance; and handling other front-end development issues.
- *Financing.* "Financing" is the process of obtaining funds to pay for and develop real property.
- *Design.* The "design" phase includes all architecture and engineering work associated with building improvements on real property. Includes programming and predesign activities.
- *Construction.* In the "construction" phase, improvements are made to real property.
- *Occupancy.* In the "occupancy" phase, the finished construction product is leased or sold, and basic property management services such as operations and maintenance are set up. This phase also includes decommissioning at the end of the project's useful life.

3.2.3 Engineers Joint Contract Documents Committee (EJCDC)

EJCDC Document E-500—Standard Form of Agreement Between Owner and Engineer for Professional Services, and Its Exhibits, has been used by the engineering profession, especially for civil, infrastructure, and utilities work. The facility life cycle phases are organized as follows:

- *Study and Report Phase.* The owner's requirements are defined and clarified, and governmental authority requirements are analyzed; alternate solutions are identified and evaluated; and a report is prepared to advise the owner of the conceptual design criteria and the opinion of probable construction costs.
- *Preliminary Design Phase.* Along with surveys and existing property information, the final design criteria, drawings, specifications, and descriptions of the project are prepared; the opinion of probable construction costs is revised.
- *Final Design Phase.* Drawings and specifications indicating the scope, extent, and character of the work to be performed are prepared; adjustments to the opinion of construction costs are made; and bidding documents are finalized.
- *Bidding or Negotiating Phase.* The owner is assisted with advertising for bids, obtaining the bids, and managing the process.
- *Construction Phase.* Along with other services, the following are provided:
  - General administration of the construction contract
  - Selecting the independent testing laboratory
  - Visits the site, observes the construction, and identifies defective work
  - Clarifies and interprets the documents and issues modifications
  - Reviews and takes action on submittals
  - Determines the amount the contractor should be paid
  - Decides disagreements between the owner and contactor
  - Determines the substantial completion of the work
- *Postconstruction Phase.* Assists with adjusting equipment and systems and assists with training the owner's staff.

3.3 Integrated Project Delivery

Integrated Project Delivery (IPD) is a newly emerging delivery method that promises to be more inclusive than the other delivery methods. IPD is included in this chapter because, unlike the other project delivery methods, IPD can also be seen as a comprehensive facility life cycle. The AIA California Council has issued *Integrated Project Delivery—A Working Definition*, published by McGraw-Hill Construction, updated May 15, 2007, which defines IPD as the following:

> Integrated Project Delivery (IPD) is a project delivery approach that integrates people, systems, business structures and practices into a process that collaboratively harnesses the talents and insights of all participants to reduce waste and optimize efficiency through all phases of design, fabrication and construction.

AIA California Council has also issued *Integrated Project Delivery: A Guide*, published by McGraw-Hill Construction in 2007, that establishes the flow of a project from conceptualization through implementation and closeout that can seen in the following stages:

- *Conceptualization [Expanded Programming]* (p. 24). ... begins to determine WHAT is to be built, WHO will build it, and HOW it will be built.
- *Criteria Design [Expanded Schematic Design]* (p. 25). ... the project begins to take shape. Major options are evaluated, tested and selected.
- *Detailed Design [Expanded Design Development]* (p. 26). ... concludes the WHAT phase of the project. ... all key decisions are finalized ... comprises much of what is left to the Construction Documents phase under traditional practice. ...
- *Implementation Documents [Construction Documents]* (p. 27). ... efforts shifts from WHAT is being created to documenting HOW it will implemented ... complete the determination and documentation of how the design intent will be implemented, not to change or develop it. The traditional shop drawing process is merged into this phase as constructors, trade contractors, and suppliers document how systems and structure will be created ... generates the documents that third parties will use for permitting, financing, and regulatory purposes.
- *Agency Coordination* (p. 28). Use of BIM (Building Information Modeling) and early involvement and validation by agencies shortens the final permitting process. Agency review commences in Criteria Design and increases in intensity during the final review period. This early involvement minimizes agency comments and required changes to the design as submitted for permit.
- *Buyout* (p. 29). ... early involvement of key trade contractors and vendors, so buyout of work packages they provide occurs through development of prices throughout the design phases, culminating at the conclusion of Implementation Documents.
- *Construction [Construction/Construction Contract Administration]* (p. 30). ... construction contract administration is primarily a quality control and cost monitoring function. Because of the greater effort put into the design phases, construction under IPD will be much more efficient.
- *Closeout* (p. 31). An intelligent 3D model can be delivered to the owner ... greatly depends upon the business terms by the parties ... compensation incentives or penalties ... warranty obligations, occupancy, and completion notifications, remain unchanged ...

3.4 Construction Specifications Institute

The life cycle of a facility, from concept through construction, to use and eventual deconstruction (demolition), follows a number of stages, as illustrated in Figure 3.1.

- *Project Conception.* An owner identifies a need and completes planning activities to verify feasibility, secure financial resources, develop a facility program, and identify a site.
- *Project Delivery.* The owner determines the project delivery method to be used and assembles a project team.
- *Design.* The project team evaluates preliminary studies, collected data, program requirements, and the budget and schedule to seek issues and form design solutions. Typically the design process occurs in a series of phases (schematic design, design development).
- *Construction Documents.* The A/E team prepares the graphic and written documents needed to define the project for pricing, regulatory approvals, and construction purposes.
- *Procurement (Bidding/Negotiating/Purchasing).* The project price is determined. Project price may be determined prior to, in conjunction with, or following development of construction documents, depending on the project delivery method selected.
- *Construction.* The project is constructed in accordance with the contract documents and regulatory requirements.
- *Facility Management.* The completed facility is placed in service. This includes operations and maintenance procedures.

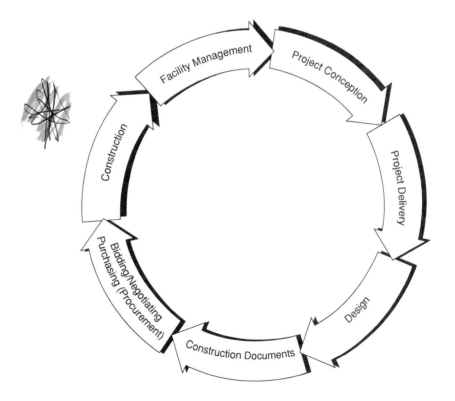

Figure 3.1
Facility Life Cycle

- *Project Conception.* The facility evaluation may identify needs that lead to expansion, remodeling, renovation, or restoration of an existing facility to accommodate growth or changes in function, or may result in abandonment, deconstruction, sale, or adaptive reuse of an existing facility.

A project, regardless of type, will nearly always undergo similar stages in its evolution from idea to tangible result as illustrated in Table 3.1. An owner may envision a new regional shopping center; a school district may require new campuses to meet population growth; a city may need to rehabilitate its sewage treatment facilities; a state or federal agency may launch new highway construction projects; or a family may simply decide to build a new home. The duration of each stage depends on the extent of the project, the number of participants involved, and the efficiency the participants apply to their respective contractual responsibilities.

The precise beginning and end of a project may be blurred, depending on the point of view from which it is defined. The life cycle runs from conception of an idea to the eventual deconstruction/demolition of the facility and subsequent reuse of the site. Some facilities may be slated for preservation or rehabilitation and never see the wrecking ball. The stages include project conception, project delivery, design, construction documents, procurement (bidding/negotiating/purchasing), construction, facility management including evaluation/modification, and decommissioning/deconstruction.

3.4.1 Project Conception

Project conception consists of activities that transform the needs or aspirations of the owner into a clear concept on which the project can be designed and built.

3.4.1.1 Feasibility Studies

Preliminary studies establish project feasibility and impact on the owner, prospective sites, and community. Feasibility studies and market analyses help owners identify existing conditions and future trends and define specific needs. For example, a major hotel corporation, before committing substantial funds toward a specific project, may assess the economic condition of a community, its population growth, travel and tourism industry, the existing supply of competing hotels and their occupancy rates, local construction costs, and land prices. Such information helps determine whether or not the idea is economically sound and whether projected construction costs, operating expenses, and revenue have the potential for a satisfactory return on investment.

3.4.1.2 Programming

Programming establishes and prioritizes the owner's goals and requirements for the project.

3.4.1.3 Site Selection

Identify potential project sites. Site selection and analysis may include specific studies of environmental impact, zoning restrictions, governmental regulations, pedestrian or vehicular accessibility, available utilities, and soil conditions. If the project involves renovation or rehabilitation, the owner may also need a detailed survey and report of existing conditions.

Table 3.1 **Typical Project Stages**

Stages	Activities	Documents Produced		
		Owner	A/E	Contractor
Project Conception	Feasibility Study Programming Site Analysis Site Selection	Program Budget Schedule	Reports Analysis Recommendations	
Design	Schematic Design	Surveys Geotechnical Data	Schematic Drawings 　Sketches 　Renderings 　Diagrams Conceptual 　Plans 　Elevations 　Sections Preliminary Project 　Description Cost Projections	
	Design Development		Drawings 　Plans 　Elevations 　Sections 　Typical Details Engineering 　Design Criteria 　Equipment Layouts Outline Specifications Revised Cost Projections	
Construction Documentation	Construction Documents (or Final Design)	Solicitation Instructions for Procurement Bid/Proposal Form General Conditions Supplementary Conditions	Detailed Drawings 　Plans 　Elevations 　Sections 　Details 　Schedules Specifications Bidding Requirements Revised Cost Projections	
Bidding/Negotiating/Purchasing	Competitive Bidding or Contract Negotiations Direct Purchasing of Goods and Supplies	Request for Proposal Purchase Orders	Addenda	Bid Bid Security
Construction	Mobilization Construction Contract Administration Project Closeout	Payment Certificates	Modifications	Permits Schedules Shop Drawings Certificates Record Documents Warranties Operation and Maintenance Data
Facility Management	Occupancy Operation/Maintenance Evaluation Repairs	Maintenance Records	Postoccupancy 　Reports or Analysis	Warranty Service 　Records

3.4.1.4 Budgeting

Developing a preliminary project description and budget should provide the owner with enough information to clearly communicate the fundamental project requirements to the design team and construction team in subsequent stages.

The primary participants are the owner, the owner's advisers, and individual consultants, who assist the owner in these critical preliminary processes. Depending on the extent of the owner's vision, the participants may include:

- Insurance, financial, real estate, and legal advisers to assist the owner in assessing financial resources, risk factors, and potential sites for the project
- Programming consultants to prioritize the owner's goals and requirements
- Authorities having jurisdiction (AHJs), including zoning officials, health officials, transportation officials, and building officials involved with identifying and clarifying applicable regulations and requirements
- Testing agencies to evaluate attributes of prospective sites
- Estimators and construction budgeting consultants to convert information from preliminary and programming studies into construction cost information
- Contractors and construction managers to advise the owner about procedures, coordination, and other factors affecting project scheduling
- Product representatives who can provide specific information about construction procedures, project components, systems, and subsystems
- Architect/engineers (A/Es) to provide professional advice regarding project types and other design-related information
- Facility managers hired by the owner

The advisers provide information that the owner and other participants may use to complete activities in this and subsequent project stages. The primary documentation in the project conception includes:

- Reports and recommendations of studies and tests
- Written facility program
- Preliminary cost estimates
- Preliminary schedules

3.4.2 Project Delivery

At some point in the process, the owner needs to determine the project delivery method to be used: design-bid-build (D-B-B), design-negotiate-build (D-N-B), design-build (D-B), construction management, owner-build (O-B), or Integrated Project Delivery. Factors affecting the decision include the owner's qualifications, experience, and capacity; the project extent; and the time requirements. The chosen method will ultimately affect the nature and extent of work for the design team and contractor team.

3.4.3 Design

The AIA defines design as occurring in three distinct phases: schematic design, design development, and construction documents. The Engineers Joint Contract Documents

Committee (EJCDC) defines design in two phases: preliminary design and final design phase, which includes construction documents. The Design-Build Institute of America (DBIA) defines design in two phases: schematic design and design development, which includes construction documents. For the purpose of this practice guide, design is defined as having two phases: schematic and design development.

The primary participants in the design process include the owner, the facility manager, the A/E and subconsultants, product representatives, design builders, construction managers, building officials, and cost estimators. Commissioning agents may also become involved at this stage of a project. Deliverables are contractually required information. Deliverables in each phase include graphic and written design documents and estimates of project cost. A successful project requires the cooperation of all project team participants to facilitate communication and fulfillment of responsibilities.

3.4.3.1 Schematic Design

To execute schematic design, the owner must identify and secure a suitable site and assemble a design team. The participants will review and evaluate the owner's budget and program and present alternative approaches to design, based on the project delivery. During schematic design, site plan and area relationships may be defined; the general size, shape, and massing of elements determined; elevations and exterior finishes established; and conceptual design criteria for structural, mechanical, and electrical systems identified. Written documents usually consist of preliminary project descriptions and preliminary estimates of probable construction cost projections. Preliminary project descriptions describe systems, materials, products, and performance criteria. The owner reviews and approves the recommendations of the project team so that design can progress.

Deliverables include:

- Schematic drawings and preliminary project descriptions to illustrate the general form, scale, and relationship of the major project components, and the type of construction proposed
- Preliminary estimates of probable cost for the owner's approval
- Preliminary project schedules

3.4.3.2 Design Development

The design development phase follows the owner's approval of the schematic design and any necessary program or budget adjustments. The emphasis shifts from overall relationships and functions to more technical issues of constructability and integration of systems and components. Aesthetic concerns move from massing and arrangement to materials, surfaces, and details.

Design development phase documents fix and describe the size and character of the entire project, including architectural, structural, mechanical, and electrical systems. Drawings at this phase include plans, elevations, and sections that provide more detail of the various systems and components. The structural, mechanical, and electrical systems are usually developed by selecting the type of system and then determining preliminary sizes of equipment and routing of services. Plans are developed, exterior elevations refined, typical construction details worked out, and many product and material selections are made. Outline specifications are used to record such decisions and to describe to the owner the materials, products, and systems selected, as well as any special construction conditions or special contract requirements. The graphic and written documents serve as the basis for revised cost projections, and the outline specifications also serve as a checklist for the subsequent development of detailed documents.

Participants, including AHJs, product representatives, manufacturers of systems and subsystems, special consultants, and entities, may take part in these activities.

Deliverables include:

- Technical information about special systems and subsystems to be incorporated into the project
- Outline specifications and drawings to establish the size and character of the entire project, including architectural, structural, mechanical, and electrical systems
- Updated schedules
- Updated cost estimates

3.4.4 Construction Documents

The construction documents stage is based on the owner-approved design development documents and any further adjustments in the extent of the project or the project budget. During this stage the A/E prepares documents that will be used to file for permits and approvals from AHJs and to obtain prices upon which a bid or a negotiated contract can be based. The procurement documents include procurement requirements, contracting forms, conditions of the contract, specifications, contract drawings, and resource drawings. Of these documents, the contracting forms, conditions of the contract, specifications, and contract drawings become part of the legal contract for construction when the agreement between the owner and the contractor is executed, as they describe the work and the rights, duties, and responsibilities of the parties. The contracting forms and the general conditions may be standard documents that the owner has selected or approved for use on the project, or may be custom documents produced by legal counsel and supplied to the A/E for incorporation into the construction documents.

3.4.5 Procurement (Bidding/Negotiating/ Purchasing)

In a D-B-B project, the link between design and execution of a project is an agreement between the owner and the contractor. This is most often achieved through competitive bidding evaluation or through the process of negotiation with a prequalified contractor. The procurement stage allows the prospective contractor to examine procurement documents, visit the site, request clarifications and interpretations, propose substitutions, and, finally, prepare a bid or price for executing the work. The A/E's responsibilities include responding to requests for information or clarifications, evaluating proposed substitutions, and issuing addenda to document changes made during the procurement period. Acceptance of the contractor's bid or negotiated sum and other conditions will result in award of a contract and commencement of work.

In D-B, the agreement between the owner and D-B participants is different from the traditional D-B-B project delivery method. Under D-B project delivery, a design-builder contracts directly with the owner to both design and construct the facility.

3.4.6 Construction

Construction traditionally begins with the <u>execution of an owner-contractor agreement</u> and is often the most demanding stage of any project. It tests the constructability of the design and accuracy of the project budget; it requires the coordinated efforts of more participants than any previous or subsequent stages; it demands the highest levels of administrative skills; and it exposes the participants to the greatest levels of financial risk. During construction, the contractor's responsibilities include performing the work of the project in accordance with the contract documents, including project coordination, complying with project quality provisions, submittal procedures, execution of the work, contract closeout procedures, and compliance with warranty provisions. The A/E is normally responsible for construction administration, including monitoring the contractor's compliance with the contract by reviewing submittals, providing construction evaluation services, evaluating proposals for contract modifications, certifying applications for payment, and making final inspections of work for contract closeout. The owner's responsibilities include providing information necessary for preserving the contractor's lien rights, furnishing surveys and legal information regarding the site, processing payments, approving contract modifications, providing owner-furnished products or services in a timely manner, and accepting the project upon completion. Commissioning agents are involved to ensure that the constructed project conforms to the owner's requirements as identified in the facility program and defined by the construction documents. The deliverables include the completed facility, record documents, operations and maintenance manuals, maintenance materials, and warranties.

3.4.7 Facility Management

The longest stage in the life cycle commences when the facility is put into use and maintained by the facility manager. Participants are generally limited to the owner, facility users, and facility manager; however, members of the original project team may be called upon by the owner for periodic evaluation of how components, systems, and subsystems are performing.

Commencing with substantial completion, the contractor is under a defined period of obligation to correct defects in the project. Manufacturers of certain project components may also be obligated to fulfill the terms of special product warranties and maintenance procedures. Participants in these activities include the owner, A/E, contractor, construction manager, product representatives, and facility manager.

During occupancy, owners and facility managers maintain and evaluate the performance of project components, subsystems, and systems to assess their life cycle cost and determine their suitability for continuing use. Participants may include A/Es, facility managers, facility users, commissioning agents, testing agencies, or manufacturer's representatives. An A/E may be engaged to make a formal assessment of a facility's condition. Maintenance professionals, contractors, and testing agencies may also be involved in making evaluations. Deliverables include formal evaluations or reports on the findings of the participants. Evaluations should result in recommendations on the project's disposition options: to modify the facility to accommodate changes in capacity or use, to sell the facility and purchase or plan a new one, or to demolish and plan a new facility on the existing site.

3.4.7.1 Evaluation/Modification

When portions of a facility deteriorate or become obsolete through technological demands, changes in laws and regulations, or changes in use, modification (alteration, renovation, or restoration) becomes necessary. Participants and deliverables will be similar to those in the design and construction stages previously described.

3.4.7.2 Decommissioning/Deconstruction/Demolition

This marks the end of the facility's useful life and gives way to the beginning of an entirely new project and facility life cycle.

Chapter 4
Codes, Regulations, and Standards

4.1 Introduction

Human beings naturally gather in groups and pursue a vast diversity of activities. To maintain civilized order, laws become necessary to control those activities socially and personally. Laws also continue the always necessary effort of establishing unity, harmony, and shared values.

One of the hallmarks of the unity, harmony, and shared values of the United States is the need for and existence of mandatory codes and regulations and voluntary standards, which provide for the health, safety, and welfare of those that occupy and use buildings and other structures. Today, there are not many parts of the built environment that are not covered by a code, regulation, or standard. Outcomes that might not otherwise occur and the prevention of undesirable or hazardous outcomes from occurring are important purposes of influencing and controlling the creation, construction, maintenance, and ultimately the disposal of buildings.

Codes, regulations, and standards establish minimum requirements for the design and construction of the buildings and other structures that compose the built environment. Unfortunately, far too many of the requirements in codes, regulations, and standards came into being because of the tragic and sometimes considerable loss of life and property. The notion of having minimum requirements for buildings and other structures has taken a permanent place in the collective goal of preventing tragedies, some from happening a first time and others from happening again, for protecting property, and for setting a socially acceptable minimum level of quality of habitation.

For certain projects, jurisdictions overlap, and coordination of requirements by the A/E is necessary. The most stringent authority having jurisdiction (AHJ) requirement normally takes precedence if requirements of two different jurisdictions are in conflict. However, some AHJs may enforce requirements that are different from those of the higher AHJ, and the design may have to demonstrate compliance with both requirements. Normally, however, each level of requirement is developed in concert with those of a higher AHJ to prevent conflict and duplication.

Laws and regulations governing construction are enforced at federal, state, and local levels of government to protect the health, safety, and welfare of the public and ensure the integrity of completed projects. The AHJ over the project is normally determined by project location, except for federal government projects, which are constructed in widely varying locations and subject to federal regulations, which also differ according to the agency building and/or occupying the facility.

As design, manufacturing, and construction expertise moves outside the borders of the United States, the issue of interchangeability of codes, regulations, and standards presents a unique challenge. Generally, codes, regulations, and standards developed in the United States are not usually accepted in other nations, and those of other nations are not accepted in the United States. Because of this, the International Organization for Standardization (ISO; www.iso.org) is developing codes, regulations, and standards that are universally acceptable throughout the world.

4.2 Authorities Having Jurisdiction

The governmental structure of the federal government grants individual states the responsibility and authority to administer activities within their respective state jurisdictions. States then grants counties and cities the responsibility and authority to administer activities within their respective jurisdictions through legislative enabling acts. Thus, it is up to the citizens of a county or city jurisdiction to determine which codes and regulations they want as the standards by which they will govern themselves.

Thus, one of the controlling factors in the design and construction of buildings are the codes that are adopted and the regulations that are written for the respective jurisdiction. Once adopted or written, a jurisdictional department or agency becomes the authority for the citizens of that jurisdiction for the following:

- Applications for and issuing of permits
- Interpretations of provisions
- Enforcement of requirements through approvals or by withholding approvals
- Inspection of newly constructed buildings or structures
- Condemnation of buildings and structures or portions thereof not in compliance with the code or regulation

4.3 Codes

Codes specify minimum requirements for the design and construction of new and renovated buildings for the safety of persons and the protection of property. The A/E must have a thorough knowledge of the codes governing the project and must consider their impact on the design from the earliest stages through the completion of construction documents.

Building codes are developed and maintained by model code-writing organizations. By working with building design and construction professionals, product manufacturers, building officials, AHJs, concerned citizens, and other interested groups, these organizations endeavor to be on the leading edge of available research, design concepts, and building products providing safety. A variety of code products is available for adoption by any AHJ, usually towns, cities, counties, and states. Before a model building code can become the building code for a jurisdiction, it has to be adopted by that AHJ. Once adopted, they then are responsible for enforcing that building code within their jurisdiction. The AHJ does not have to adopt the model code in its entirety; the AHJ can adopt any portions desired and then modify it for their own purposes. The most commonly known building codes are the various codes developed by the International Code Council (www.iccsafe.org) and include the following:

- International Building Code
- International Electrical Code
- International Energy Code
- International Existing Building Code
- International Fire Code
- International Fuel Code
- International Mechanical Code
- International Performance Code
- International Plumbing Code
- International Private Sewage Code
- International Property Maintenance Code
- International Residential Code

The model codes are updated on a periodic basis, which is usually three years or so. There are multiple internal committees in the code-writing organization—each with responsibility for maintaining a specific part of a code—that continuously work to maintain viable and useful codes. Members of these committees are experienced professionals from both government and business who volunteer their time and talent to continually update the content of a code.

4.3.1   Design and Construction Requirements

Building codes provide requirements governing the following:

- Use and occupancy classifications
- Building heights and areas
- Types of construction
- Fire-resistance-rated construction
- Interior finishes
- Life safety requirements, including fire protection systems
- Means of egress
- Accessibility
- Interior environment
- Energy efficiency
- Exterior wall construction
- Roof assemblies and rooftop structures
- Structural design, tests, and special inspection requirements
- Soils and foundations
- Materials used in structures, including concrete masonry, metals, wood, glass, gypsum board, and plastics
- Elevators and conveying systems

- Special construction, including awnings, canopies, signs, towers, swimming pools, manufactured dwellings and structures, tents, membrane structures, temporary structures, pedestrian walkways, and tunnels
- Plumbing systems
- Heating, ventilating, and air conditioning (HVAC) systems
- Electrical systems
- Maintenance of public thoroughfares and rights-of-way
- Safety measures related to construction
- Requirements for existing structures
- Maintenance requirements for existing structures
- Tanks and underground structures
- Seismic design
- Weather-related design (e.g., hurricane, tornado)
- Alternative materials and methods of construction

4.3.2 Fire and Life Safety Requirements

Building codes address the life safety of occupants and fire protection of property and include the following:

- Structural stability
- Occupancy load hazards
- Fire performance characteristics of building materials, including flame spread and smoke development
- Means of egress
- Areas of refuge for disabled occupants
- Access to the site and building by police, fire, and rescue services
- Fire-resistant construction
- Explosion resistance
- Fire protection systems, including detection systems, and fire suppression systems
- Smoke evacuation systems
- Alarms and emergency communication systems
- Emergency power generation
- Lightning protection/surge protection/electrical system stabilization
- Prevention of panic by moving occupants toward visible, unobstructed exits within a reasonable distance

Protection of occupants is achieved by the combination of:

- Prevention of ignition
- Detection of fire
- Control of fire development
- Confinement of the effects of fire
- Extinguishment of fire

* Refuge or evacuation facilities
* Staff reaction
* Providing fire safety information

4.3.3 AHJ Plan Reviews and Permits for Construction

The project construction documents must demonstrate compliance with the building code because the AHJ will conduct a plan review process, and the construction documents and comments made by the AHJ will be the basis of issuing a building permit for construction. Essentially, the AHJ has to be satisfied that the design is in compliance with the building code. The AHJ will continue to monitor the project by periodic inspections throughout the construction stage to ensure compliance.

As construction and the governing laws have become more complex, so has the permitting process. Published guides are available to facilitate the plan approval process. For some projects, it may be appropriate to conduct a predevelopment conference with the AHJ to identify issues that will affect the project. Early meetings are followed up by additional meetings later in the design process to discuss possible areas of conflict with the building code or to document corrections issued by the AHJ. At these meetings, agreements may be reached regarding code compliance issues.

If the project will be subject to competitive bidding, the plan review process should be complete prior to issuing the construction documents for bidding. It allows for incorporation of required code-related changes to the documents. However, not completing the plan review prior to bidding may cost the A/E additional time during the construction stage to account for revisions and additional work.

4.3.4 Evaluation Reports

An important service offered by model code-writing organizations is their evaluation of building materials and products. A manufacturer can submit product information, test reports, and other information for their products to the organization for evaluation. If the material or product is determined to be in compliance with the model code, an evaluation report will be issued indicating the acceptance. Primarily for local building officials, the evaluation reports are available to anyone wanting to research building materials and products.

4.4   Regulations

Regulations, sometimes known as ordinances, tend to be developed and written by respective AHJs for a specific purpose or intent for use within their jurisdiction. Unlike codes, regulations sometimes impose sanctions, or fines, for failing to comply with the requirements. A commonly known regulation is a zoning ordinance, created to regulate how land within city limits will be used.

4.4.1 Zoning, Deed Covenants, and Regulations

Codes, covenants and restrictions may restrict the type of facility, its use, and its functions. Sites may be classified by such terms as commercial, residential, industrial, institutional, recreational, or agricultural. Local regulations control land use and limit the size, type, and density of improvements. In one area, a high-density housing project is encouraged, while nearby there may be minimum lot sizes of an acre or more. In some parts of the country, zoning restrictions are very rigid, while other areas are more flexible—perhaps because they are hoping to encourage economic development.

There are other types of zoning restrictions that challenge the nature and type of project located there. In some zoning categories, limitations are placed on the amount of land that may be developed, covered with paving, or otherwise utilized. This may be called the allowable site coverage, expressed in terms of the occupant density or footprint of the facility. Setback restrictions and floor area restrictions may be included with zoning and may dictate the distance that the facility must be from the property lines and other structures.

Parking requirements and restrictions may have a significant impact on the design and location of the facility. The same is true of the location and size of loading zones. Both issues are particularly relevant in urban areas and for infill projects.

Height restrictions take their cue from the landscape of the neighborhood. They prevent a single facility from towering above its neighbors, blocking sight lines, casting shadows on neighboring facilities, and altering the look of a neighborhood. Tall facilities may also be a hazard in areas near airports or where extremely high winds pose a significant threat.

A facility's style, aesthetics, and form may also be dictated by deed covenants and zoning (particularly if the project is in a historic district), including the following:

- The type and quantity of exterior materials permitted
- Limitations on the colors utilized
- Quantity of neighborhood fabric, both interior and exterior, which must be maintained in renovation or addition

Landscaping requirements may also be defined by zoning. Some jurisdictions may require buildings to have gardens or public plazas or even public art. If a project is located near wetlands, certain types of indigenous plantings may be required to fit with the local flora or to regulate and filter runoff. Trees and other vegetation, removed from one area of a site for facility functional reasons, may have to be relocated or replaced in another part of the site, to meet master zoning planning criteria.

The owner must also consider zoning implications from its own perspective, such as the surrounding land use and adjacent facilities' impact on the proposed facility.

If there is a zoning problem, it is possible to request a variance (change). Sometimes variances are almost impossible to get, while in other cases they will pass the local AHJ with few objections. Owners should research what the probability for approval might be, and whether similar variances passed. Also it will be beneficial to determine whether the process will be long and expensive.

In addition to zoning and other property use restrictions, regulatory agencies may require precautions to keep soil, chemicals used during construction, storm water runoff, and other pollutants from running off the site.

4.4.2 Site Use and Environmental Requirements

Although local zoning laws determine the suitability of a site for a specific use, the local department of health and the Environmental Protection Agency (EPA) will influence project design by enforcing regulations to protect adjacent properties, existing facilities, waterways, the atmosphere, and other natural resources surrounding the site. Issues include:

- Management of wastewater
- Management of stormwater
- Erosion and sedimentation control
- Airborne emissions caused by proposed facility construction and operations

These regulations may affect design in the following ways:

- Size and number of structures permitted
- Occupancy levels
- Position of facilities and related structures on the site
- Ratio of open/green space required
- Amount of pavement, parking, and outdoor lighting allowed
- Environmental protection features, such as filters, acoustical isolation of equipment, and pollutant emission control
- Other isolation and protection features, such as retention ponds, embankments, site drainage provisions, and wastewater treatment equipment

The Clean Water Act is a federal policy that affects design and construction by controlling the amount and type of pollutants that may be discharged into public waterways. Design of reservoirs, detention structures, and waste disposal projects such as landfills and wastewater treatment facilities may be affected by the provisions of that law. Processing and manufacturing facilities must also be designed to ensure compliance with AHJ environmental requirements in effect during the facility management stages of the project life cycle.

The amount of volatile organic compounds emitted by paints, special coatings, and other construction products is regulated by state laws, which affects design, manufacturing, and product selection. Local AHJs may have additional environmental requirements that may affect design.

4.4.3 Occupational Safety and Health Requirements

Through legislation and oversight, the Occupational Safety and Health Administration (OSHA) protects worker health and safety in the workplace. OSHA regulations affect the design of commercial and industrial projects. While the A/E is not responsible for safety on construction sites, the contractor is required to comply with OSHA regulations that cover the following categories related to the workplace safety practices:

- Electrical wiring, fixtures, and controls
- Exits and access
- Fire protection

- Housekeeping and general work environment
- Illumination
- Sanitation and health
- Signs, labels, markings, and tags
- Ventilation
- Walking and work surfaces

Machines and equipment standards include the following:

- Appliances and electrical utilization
- Compressed gas and compressed air equipment
- Conveyors
- Crawler, locomotive, and truck cranes
- Overhead and gantry cranes
- Derricks
- Hand and portable powered tools
- Machinery and machine guarding
- Miscellaneous equipment used in general industry (lifts, scaffolds, ladders, and platforms)
- Miscellaneous equipment used in special industries (bakeries, laundries, pulp and paper mills, logging, sawmills, textiles)
- Trucks

Materials standards include the following:

- Hazardous materials (air contaminants, anhydrous ammonia, compressed gases, explosives, inflammable and combustible liquids, ionizing radiation, liquefied petroleum gases)
- Hazardous locations due to materials
- Materials handling and storage
- Materials-handling machines and equipment

Employee standards include the following:

- Ionizing radiation protection
- Medical and first aid
- Personnel protection in tanks and confined spaces
- Personal protective equipment
- Skills and knowledge

Power source standards include the following:

- Electrical power
- Explosive-actuated power
- Pneumatic power
- Steam power
- Miscellaneous power sources used in special industries

Process standards include the following:

- Abrasive blasting
- Dry grinding, polishing and buffing, exhaust systems
- Process, dip, and open surface tanks
- Processing plants and operations
- Special industries and related processes
- Spray finishing
- Welding, cutting, and brazing

Owners should have detailed knowledge of their facility operations related to worker safety and emergency procedures.

4.4.4 Accessibility Requirements

Federal law prohibits discrimination on any basis, including, but not limited to, physical disabilities. Thus, owners and operators of places of public accommodation must provide accessibility to facility users.

National accessibility standards have been adopted in response to this need. The Architectural Barriers Act of 1968 was passed by Congress to provide access to facilities designed, built, altered, or leased with federal funds. The Americans with Disabilities Act (ADA) of 1990 extended the responsibility for uniform accessibility to state, local, and private entities, including businesses, restaurants, and other facilities used by the public.

The basis for accessibility standards in the United States is the International Code Council/American National Standards Institute (ICC/ANSI) A117.1 Standard on Accessible and Useable Buildings and Facilities. This standard is incorporated into the Uniform Federal Accessibility Standards and the Americans with Disabilities Act Accessibility Guidelines (ADAAG).

AHJs will determine the accessibility requirements for the project. They may be more stringent than the referenced ANSI accessibility standard. Categories of accessibility related to sites and structures include:

- Space allowance and reach ranges
- Accessible routes
- Protruding objects
- Ground and floor surfaces
- Parking and passenger loading zones
- Curb ramps
- Ramps
- Stairs
- Elevators
- Platform lifts (wheelchair lifts)
- Windows
- Doors
- Entrances
- Drinking fountains and water coolers
- Water closets

- Toilet stalls
- Urinals
- Lavatories and mirrors
- Bathtubs
- Shower stalls
- Toilet rooms
- Bathrooms, bathing facilities, and shower rooms
- Sinks
- Storage
- Handrails, grab bars, and tub and shower seats
- Controls and operating mechanisms
- Alarms
- Detectable warnings
- Signage
- Telephones
- Fixed or built-in seating and tables
- Assembly areas
- Automated teller and vending machines
- Dressing and fitting rooms
- Saunas and steam rooms
- Benches

AHJ's typically enforce special requirements for the following types of facilities:

- Restaurants and cafeterias
- Medical care facilities
- Business, mercantile, and civic facilities
- Libraries
- Transient lodging
- Transportation facilities
- Judicial, legislative, and regulatory facilities
- Detention and correctional facilities
- Residential housing
- Public rights-of-way
- Recreation facilities

The A/E must understand and incorporate the accessibility guidelines applicable to the design of the project.

4.4.5 Health and Sanitary Requirements

Health and sanitary requirements include regulations for plumbing systems, septic systems, nursing and health care facilities, child care facilities, public swimming pools, and food preparation, processing, and serving areas.

Indoor air quality is also an important design consideration. The local department of environment control usually enforces these requirements. Areas of primary concern include:

- Outdoor replacement air
- Airborne particulates and chemicals emitted by building materials
- The presence of mold and bacteria
- The presence of hazardous materials

4.5 Standards

Standards establish uniform guidelines, criteria, methods, processes, and practices for a particular building product, assembly, or technology. Standards are usually developed and maintained by a consensus of members of an association, society, council, or institute directly involved with the service, product, or installation, which is the subject of the standard. Standards reflect conditions within an industry in which the majority of manufacturers and/or installers agree are the standard of care for their industry; hence they are referred to as industry standards. Unlike codes and regulations, which are mandatory, standards are usually voluntary unless included as a provision of a code or regulation.

Standards become minimum requirements for providing services, or for the manufacture, fabrication, and installation of materials, products, and equipment. Standards are the common language for an industry and, if compliance is specified, they can predict the results of an activity.

Standards include the following types with corresponding examples:

- *Materials Standards.* ASTM B 211, Standard Specifications for Aluminum and Aluminum-Alloy Extruded Bars, Rods, Wires, Shapes, and Tubes
- *Product Standards.* Engineered Wood Association (APA) APAPS-1, Construction and Industrial Plywood
- *Design Standards.* American Concrete Institute International (ACI) ACI 318, Building Code Requirements for Structural Concrete
- *Installation Standards.* National Fire Protection Association International (NFPA) 13, Standard for the Installation of Sprinkler Systems
- *Test Method Standards.* ASTM E 119, Standard Test Methods for Fire Tests of Building Construction and Materials
- *Performance Standards.* ASTM F 1487, Standard Consumer Safety Performance Specification for Playground Equipment for Public Use

Some standards are so comprehensive and well developed that a code-writing organization references them in a building code as the basis of a required provision. For example, the International Code Council (ICC) lists the standards included in the International Building Code as one of the last chapters of the code. Examples include the following:

- American Society for Civil Engineers (ASCE) 7, Minimum Design Loads for Buildings and Other Structures
- American Society for Testing of Materials (ASTM) E 119, Test Method for Fire Tests of Building Construction and Materials

- The Masonry Society (TMS) 602, Specification for Masonry Structures
- American National Standards Institute/American Society of Mechanical Engineers (ANSI/ASME) A17.1, Safety Code for Elevators and Escalators

Any portion of a standard, or the entire standard, can be incorporated in the specifications for a project by referring to its developing association name, number, title, or other designation. The standard then becomes a reference standard, and it becomes a part of the specifications just as though included. Incorporation of a standard into specifications by reference takes advantage of an established body of knowledge developed by an industry and saves the A/E the work of writing elaborate and lengthy specifications. When using a standard as a reference standard, caution should be exercised according to the following:

- Standards can create duplication and contradiction within the contract documents.
- Standards can contain embedded options.
- Standards generally refer to minimum requirements.
- Standards might contain undesired requirements.
- AHJs may enforce different editions of the same standard, which might have conflicting requirements.

4.5.1 Standards Development Process

ASTM International's publication *Standards: The Corporate Edge—A Handbook for the Busy Executive* has proposed three rules that are important considerations for the development process of a standard:

- Rule 1: The process should be open.
- Rule 2: Every participant is equal and the process should not be dominated by one interest.
- Rule 3: Decisions should be made by consensus.

4.5.2 Standards Development Organizations

One classification of the groups that develop standards is independent, for-profit, standards development organizations. There are several organizations that are very prominent in the design and construction industry.

ASTM International (ASTM; www.astm.org) is one of the best-known organizations that develop standards for test methods, specifications, guides, practices, classifications, and terminology, which now total more than 12,000. ASTM's stated mission statement is:

To be recognized globally as the premier developer and provider of voluntary consensus standards, related technical information, and services that

Promote public health and safety, support the protection and sustainability of the environment, and the overall quality of life;
Contribute to the reliability of materials, products, systems and services; and
Facilitate international, regional, and national commerce.

American National Standards Institute (ANSI; www.ansi.org) considers itself the voice of the U.S. voluntary consensus standards and conformity assessment systems, and safeguarding their integrity. ANSI also oversees the creation, promulgation, and use of thousands of norms and guidelines that directly impact many business fields.

The mission of the National Fire Protection Association (NFPA; www.nfpa.org) is to reduce the worldwide burden of fire and other hazards on the quality of life by providing and advocating consensus codes and standards intended to minimize the possibility and effects of fire and other risks through research, training, and education.

Underwriters Laboratories (UL; www.ul.com) is another group that has a global reach and is an independent product safety certification organization that evaluates thousands of products and has written over 1,000 standards for safety.

FM Global (FMG; www.fmglobal.com) believes the majority of all property loss is preventable and provides comprehensive global commercial and industrial property insurance; engineering-driven underwriting and risk management solutions; groundbreaking property loss prevention research; and prompt, professional claims handling. Also, FMG writes standards, tests materials, products, and assemblies, and provides certification services.

4.5.3 Governmental Standards Development Agencies

Another classification of the groups that develop standards is governmental agencies.

The Occupational Safety and Health Administration (OSHA; www.osha.gov) endeavors to assure safe and healthful conditions for workers. OSHA is authorized to enforce the standards developed under the Occupational Safety and Health Act of 1970, and assists and encourages states to ensure safe and healthful working conditions by providing for research, information, education, and training in occupational safety and health.

The National Institute of Standards and Technology (NIST; www.nist.gov) promotes U.S. innovation and industrial competitiveness by advancing measurement science, standards, and technology in ways that enhance economic security and improve our quality of life.

The Consumer Product Safety Commission (CPSC; www.cpsc.gov) is charged with protecting the public from unreasonable risks of serious injury or death from thousands of types of consumer products under their jurisdiction.

4.6 Associations, Societies, Councils, and Institutes

Associations, which may also be called societies, councils, or institutes, also develop standards for their respective interests. Associations have a vested interest in the existence of a common language, understanding, beliefs, and standards of care within their respective industries. Typical authors are architects, engineers, scientists, technologists, manufacturers, and product users. The standards are based on research conducted by, or the empirical experiences of, its membership and those who are knowledgeable about the particular standard subject.

An association is initially founded by a small group of interested individuals that eventually grows into a stand-alone, nonprofit or for-profit business, and is administered by volunteers from its membership or by a paid staff. Funding for associations is derived from membership dues, sales of standards and other publications, or services provided to others. There are many advantages for the membership of associations as well as those that seek information about the respective industry. Distinguishing characteristics of associations include the following:

- Provides a forum for collaboration concerning the common issues important to a respective industry
- Gathers empirical information, experiences, and lessons learned from its membership
- Develops a body of knowledge unique to a respective industry
- Facilitates networking within the association as well as outside the membership
- Promotes and advocates its membership and their respective contributions
- Hosts national or regional conventions or shows that provide product displays, networking, and educational opportunities that sometimes results in published proceedings
- Develops, writes, publishes, and offers voluntary standards
- Researches certain aspects of an industry
- Publishes periodicals
- Offers continuing education opportunities to its membership and other interested groups
- Participates in public relations activities such as advertising and lobbying
- Fosters opportunities for charitable events
- Sets the ethical standards for its membership

There are many associations that are focused on the design and construction of buildings and other structures and can generally be divided into the following categories:

- Trade
- Manufacturing
- Professional
- Industry

4.6.1 Reference Standards

One of the most effective ways of utilizing the vast body of knowledge found in standards is to incorporate them strategically in the specifications as needed. When this is done, the standards are identified as reference standards and they become a part of the specifications just as if they were included in their entirety.

There are many advantages of reference standards, including the following:

- *Quality Assurance.* The organizations that develop standards are experts in their respective fields of interest, and their standards are the product of extensive research, experience, and lessons learned.
- *Uniformity.* Standards represent the consensus of a national network of manufacturers within a field of interest.

- *Reduced Conflict and Duplication.* To reduce duplication and conflict between standards, ANSI coordinates standards development and adopts and promotes the standards developed by its accredited members.
- *Reduced Work.* Incorporation of standards into the specifications by reference saves the time required for writing an elaborate and lengthy text. A reference standard should be reviewed and its content and purpose understood before including it in the specifications.

Users of reference standards should be familiar with the following issues:

- *Applicability.* The standards most appropriate for the product and application should be specified.
- *Quality.* Reference standards often define quality in terms of minimum requirements. The minimum requirements may be so restrictive that they exclude most commercially available materials, or they may be so liberal that nearly anything produced can meet them.
- *Availability.* Participants should maintain a current library of reference standards specified and understand the specified standards and how they apply to the product.
- *Duplication and Conflict.* Requirements of one standard may conflict with another when two or more are used for a given product, which may increase the possibility of using an inferior product.
- *Optional Provisions.* Some standards contain optional provisions including categories, classes, or groups from which applicable properties must be selected.
- *Multiple Standards.* Standards usually contain references to other related standards. Users must understand the effect of the additional references; otherwise, conflicts of information and optional provisions may affect the project in undesirable ways.

4.6.2   Manufacturer Standards and Certifications

There are several ways an individual manufacturer or an alliance of manufacturers can demonstrate a commitment to the quality of the products they manufacture or fabricate:

- *Company Standards.* A manufacturer or fabricator has the option of developing and imposing a standard for their production that is more restrictive than a traditional or commonly used standard developed by one of the organizations described earlier.
- *Consensus Standards.* A variation of a company standard is a group of manufacturers of the same or similar product voluntarily agreeing to be bound to a standard developed by a consensus of the manufacturers.
- *Manufacturer Certifications.* Manufacturers may require fabricators or installers of their products to be certified by the manufacturer as a condition of the sale or a condition before a warranty can be issued.

Chapter 5
Contracts and Legal Issues

5.1 Introduction

The design and construction process of a facility is accomplished by a series of complex and interrelated activities that, depending on the size of the facility, can involve a large number of people, services, building products, and enormous sums of money. Agreements are the foundation for establishing, organizing, and managing these activities. It should be noted that the terms *contract* and *agreement* are interchangeable terms, and for purposes of this practice guide have the same meaning. While having an agreement between two parties is not always mandatory, it is good and prudent business practice to have agreements for services and products, even if the project is small.

Contracts accomplish a number of things, including the following:

- The expectations of each party are protected because a duty is imposed on each party to perform according to the agreed-upon terms.
- They signify that there is a "meeting of the minds" that the two parties are freely and mutually agreeing to the stipulated terms.
- They bind the two parties until the terms of the agreement are fulfilled.
- To protect each party, contracts are enforceable by the courts should disputes and conflicts arise.

5.2 Owner, Architect/Engineer, and Contractor Tripartite Relationships

The simplest manner of explaining the essence of a project is that it is a collection of relationships among three diverse groups, as illustrated in Figure 5.1, that come together for the common purpose of focusing a wide range of talents and abilities on the planning, design, documentation, construction, and management of a building or other facility. While each project is unique and has its own distinct personality that is influenced by the project delivery method and the type of project, it is still characterized by this tripartite relationship among ownership, design, and construction.

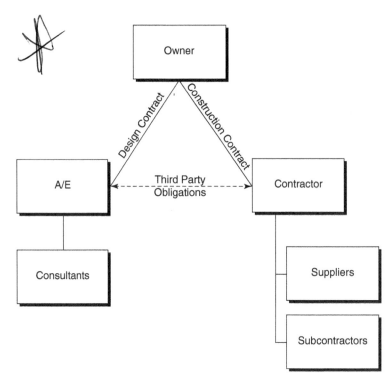

Figure 5.1
The tripartite relationship for ownership, design, and construction of a project. While this is based on the traditional Design-Bid-Build (D-B-B) and the Design-Negotiate-Build (D-N-B) project delivery methods, this relationship still applies to the other project delivery methods, except the contractual arrangements, which may be different.

5.3 Elements of a Contract

A contract is established when two parties agree to be bound in a relationship defined by obligations or promises. Usually, one party agrees to pay money to another party that will provide a service or product—in a sense, design and construction services are provided to accomplish a product, which is the building.

Before design and construction agreements are discussed, it is helpful to understand the general elements that are required before a contract is said to legally exist. Once a contract exists, in the event of a dispute or claim, courts will interpret the contract terms unless the contract does not adequately address the issue in question, at which time the law will be the basis of an interpretation. Contracts generally include the following basic elements:

- *Offer and Acceptance.* Contracts should include an offer by one party that, when accepted by the other party, imposes a duty to specifically perform the scope of work described in the contract.
- *Mutual Consent.* Contracts should reflect the meeting of the minds of the parties, which is objectively provable by the offer and acceptance.
- *Capacity.* Contracts should signify that both parties are competent and have the ability to fulfill their respective promises or obligations.
- *Scope of Work.* Contracts should include a description of the work that is required for an exchange of consideration.
- *Consideration.* Contracts should include an exchange of something of value, usually money, which should be adequate for performing the work.
- *Good Faith.* Contracts should be based on the parties' acting in good faith.

- *Legality.* Contracts should not violate public policy within a jurisdiction in order to be enforceable. In other words, the terms are not enforceable if they violate laws at any level.
- *Remedy for Breach of Contract.* Contracts should include a way of seeking remedy if a promise is breached.
- *Written.* Contracts should be rendered as a formally written document. Existence of an oral, or verbal, contract is difficult to prove. There is a long-time observation that explains the essence of oral agreements well: an oral contract isn't worth the paper it is written on. Since meeting of the minds is the foundation of a contract, in an oral contract the understandings of the terms of the agreement are only as good as what each party remembers or believes the terms were at the time of agreement. If both parties agree to the terms, an oral contract is enforceable; however, if there is disagreement, the terms are difficult to enforce.
- *Signatures.* Contracts come into existence at the time both parties accept the terms by signifying such by the signatures of responsible individuals that have the authority to bind the party to a contract.

5.4 Standard Agreement Forms

Several professional associations and government agencies have developed various standard agreement forms. This standardization of forms is desirable because it may save preparation time and offer reasonable assurance of a complete and accurate document. Through repeated use, forms with standardized clauses have become well understood by owners, architects/engineers (A/Es), suppliers, and contractors and are less subject to misinterpretation. The agreement form should be reviewed carefully by the owner's legal counsel before modification to satisfy specific project requirements.

The standard agreement forms contain wording that has a history of being interpreted and adjudicated by the legal profession and the courts, and modifications should be made with caution and not without review by an attorney. Modifications to one document may require coordination with and modification to another. For example, modifications without proper coordination with the associated conditions of the contract may create conflicts and problems within the contract documents.

Private projects tend to rely on standard agreement forms that have been developed, monitored, and maintained by professional associations; however, some corporations and government agencies have developed specific forms that must be used in their contracts. In today's world, the use of standard agreement forms, modified for the specific project, instead of using custom-drafted agreements is considered by many to be good professional practice.

- *American Institute of Architects* (AIA; www.aiadocuments.org). AIA has developed and continues to maintain standardized agreement forms for all of the project delivery methods. AIA probably has the most extensive collection of forms available, as can be seen in the following categories and families:
  - Document Series:
    - A: Owner-contractor documents
    - B: Owner-architect documents
    - C: Architect-consultant documents

- D: Architect-industry documents
- E: Exhibits
- G: Contract administration and project management forms
- Document Families:
  - Conventional
  - Small project
  - Construction manager-adviser
  - Construction manager-constructor
  - Interiors
  - Design-build
  - Integrated Project Delivery
  - Digital practice
  - International
  - Contract administration and project management forms
- *Engineers Joint Contract Documents Committee* (EJCDC; http://content.asce.org/ ejcdc/). A coalition between the American Council of Engineering Companies (ACEC), the American Society of Civil Engineers (ASCE), The Associated General Contractors of America (AGC), and the National Society of Professional Engineers (NSPE) for the purpose of developing and encouraging contract documents. They reflect the knowledge of the many engineers, owners, contractors, and other construction-related professionals that are represented on a central committee. The forms are in the following series groupings:
  - Design-bid-build documents
  - Construction-related documents
  - Owner-engineer documents
  - Engineer-subconsultant documents
  - Environmental remediation documents
  - Procurement documents
  - Funding agency documents
  - Design-build documents
  - Joint venture between engineers documents
  - Peer review documents
  - Guides, commentaries, and references
- *Design-Build Industry of America* (DBIA; www.dbia.org). The standardized agreement forms of DBIA are exclusively focused for the design-build project delivery method and include owner and design-builder agreements and general conditions.
- *Associated General Contractors of America* (AGC; www.agc.org): Jointly drafted by 23 industry associations including owners, contractors, subcontractors, designers, and surety professionals, AGC's ConsensusDOCS address all project delivery methods, and are in the following series groupings:
  - Construction and program management documents
  - General contracting documents
  - Collaborative agreement documents
  - Design-build documents
  - Construction management documents
  - Subcontracting documents
- *Construction Specifications Institute* (CSI; www.csinet.org): The standard forms developed by CSI are for the various activities of construction contract administration.

While an owner has the right to use custom-drafted agreements for its projects, caution is advised because the project delivery of design and construction is a very complex process. Without impugning the skill and abilities of the legal profession, it would be difficult to replace documents that have evolved over a number of years based on case law and the number of projects for which they have been used. Standardized agreement forms provide many advantages for projects, including the following:

- Language consistency and enforcement predictability enhances industry stability across the nation.
- Legal preparation time, and therefore expense, is less than for custom-drafted documents.
- They reflect both industry practices and customs, or may be based on a consensus of those that use the forms.
- Risks and responsibilities are assigned to the party that is best able to control them or protect from unexpected costs.
- They were developed with the understanding that they would be tailored by attorneys to fit the unique requirements of a specific project.

5.5 Example—Contract between Owner and Contractor

A typical construction agreement between an owner and a contractor would include many of the following provisions:

- *Preamble.* Records the date of the agreement and the legal identification of the project.
- *Identification of Parties.* Indentifies the legal names of the parties entering into the agreement, specifically the owner and contractor. Addresses and phone numbers would also be included to provide a location where proper notice (as required by various terms and actions) can be delivered.
- *Identification of Other Participants.* Identifies other participants who affect the agreement and may include the A/E for the project or a construction manager as adviser (CMa), and refers to their contract documents for the rights and authority assigned to them.
- *Contract Documents.* Enumerates the graphic and written documents (drawings and specifications) that constitute the work required by the contract, and incorporates them by reference in the contract, thus establishing them as contract documents. The list may also make reference to documents (revisions, clarifications, and modifications) that might be issued after the effective date of the agreement to modify the original contract documents.
- *Scope of Work.* Brief description of the scope of the work required to be performed in accordance with the contract documents, including labor, materials, equipment, and services to fulfill the obligations of one of the parties. The work may be the complete project when a single-prime contract is required by the project delivery method, or a specific portion of the project when multiple-prime contracts are required.
- *Date of Commencement of the Work.* A date, determined and issued by the owner in writing, as a notice to the contractor of when the work can proceed. The date

should be carefully considered to allow for review of all required preconstruction submittals. If a notice to proceed is designated in the agreement form, it should be issued after all matters relating to the contract and the start of construction operations have been determined and the required preconstruction submittals have been submitted and reviewed.

- *Date of Substantial Completion of the Work.* Establishes a number of days (preferably calendar days rather than work days) for the duration of the work, or a specific date when the work is to be completed and the owner can occupy the project or a designated portion thereof for its intended use. The time requirements will have been met when the work is substantially complete, even if a few minor items may remain to be completed or corrected. There are occasions when delay, beyond the time limit stated in the contract documents, will cause damage to the owner.

- *Liquidated Damages.* Establishes a fixed monetary amount per day, as a result of failure by the contractor to complete the work by the date of substantial completion, a stipulated time, or by a stated calendar date. The amount per day should be stated in the agreement and referenced in the procurement instructions and in the conditions of the contract. The owner, under advice from legal counsel, should determine both the type of damages to be covered or excluded and the amount per day that is stipulated due from the contractor. The inclusion of a liquidated damages clause in a contract is generally considered to be in lieu of actual damages for delay. If there is no liquidated damages clause, however, the contractor may still be liable for actual damages.

- *Incentives, Bonuses, and Penalties.* Establishes an incentive or a bonus if the project is completed early, or a penalty amount if the project is completed late. Although this is not a required or a necessary condition when imposing liquidated damages, it is highly recommended if the owner will benefit from early completion.

- *Contract Sum.* Establishes the amount (from an accepted bid or negotiated amount) that is to be paid for the performance of the contract, which includes accepted alternates, and, when permitted, adjustments resulting from minor changes negotiated after receiving bids or prices.

- *Adjustment of Contract Sum.* Provides that the owner has the right to make changes to the work without invalidating the terms of the contract. Without such a provision, changes might not be permitted. Such changes might require appropriate adjustments in the contract sum.

- *Unit Prices.* The additive and deductive costs for the work of certain designated items that are based on estimated quantities of work included from the bid form, or may include unit price items that are negotiated at the time of executing the agreement. Unit prices may be used to determine the value of changes in the work.

- *Payment Procedures.* Establishes the requirements for preparing and processing applications for payment, and the time periods for submitting applications and receiving payment. This article might also establish an interest rate for monies not paid when due.

- *Due Dates for Payments.* Establishes the dates mutually acceptable to the parties, considering the time required to prepare an application for payment, for the A/E to review and certify the application for payment, and for the owner to make the payment within the time limits identified in the contract documents.

- *Work Completed.* Establishes the provision that the contractor may be paid for work completed and in place, as well as for materials or equipment not incorporated in the work but delivered and suitably stored and protected on-site.

- *Materials and Equipment Stored Off-Site.* Establishes the provision that certification and payment will be permitted for materials and equipment stored off-site if it is stored at a mutually agreed location, properly protected and insured, with clear title to owner.
- *Cutoff Date.* Establishes the date on which the work is evaluated for payment; it should normally be not fewer than 10 days prior to the payment date to allow for the A/E to assess the evaluation and issue a certificate for payment, and the owner to make payment within the time provided in the contract documents. The contractor may prefer an additional few days to allow time to prepare the application.
- *Payment at Substantial Completion.* Establishes the percentage of the contract sum that will be due upon substantial completion. The amount to be stipulated for the percentage retained at substantial completion should be decided by the owner and the owner's legal counsel with advice from the A/E.
- *Due Date for Final Payment.* Establishes the time, frequently 30 to 60 days after substantial completion, at which point the owner will make final payment to the contractor if the work is finally completed. However, it may be stipulated that this time period is subject to specific requirements of the project and, further, that this date is binding only if the work is in fact fully completed.
- *Progress Payments and Retainage.* Establishes a monthly date, mutually acceptable to the parties, for progress payments to be made. Additional paragraphs might be added to cover Retainage percentages prior to and upon substantial completion. Traditionally, owners pay 90 to 95 percent of earned sums, retaining the remainder to ensure full performance of the contract. The amount retained is often governed by local custom and, for public work, by state or federal regulations or statutory requirements. This procedure provides the owner with some degree of assurance that the contractor will perform the work expeditiously, but it also may increase project costs because a contractor will compensate for the amount of Retainage in its price. A fair and effective practice is for the owner to place retained funds into interest-bearing escrow accounts. The funds remain under control of the owner until project completion, at which time the Retainage, plus the interest accrued, is paid to the contractor. Other customary procedures are to reduce the amount of Retainage from 10 percent to 5 percent after the project is 50 percent complete, or retain 10 percent of payments due until the project is 50 percent complete and not retain on payments due thereafter.
- *Miscellaneous Provisions.* States that where reference is made in the agreement to a provision of the general conditions or another contract document, the reference refers to that provision as amended or supplemented by other provisions of the contract documents. Miscellaneous provisions might also state that interest can be applied to payments under the contract documents that are due and unpaid, at a predetermined rate.
- *Termination or Suspension.* Establishes that the contract may be terminated or suspended by the owner or contractor, and includes the causes that are permitted as the reason for the termination of suspension.
- *Signatures.* Authorized representatives of the parties to the agreement bind the parties to each other by placing signatures at the end of the contract. The agreement form should be executed in ample quantities so that each party—and, where necessary, other stakeholders—will have access to the original agreement documents. Also included may be signatures of witnesses and corporate seals.

5.6 Contract Types

The structure and contract types for the contractual relationships among the stakeholders and participants are influenced by the project delivery method. As the project delivery method is determined, the fundamental decision to be made is whether to use a single-prime contract or multiple-prime contracts.

A prime contract designates an original contract between two original parties for an original purpose. When either of these parties enters into a contract with another party for work that is associated with, or will be part of, the original purpose, it is called a *subcontract.* An original party can have any number of subcontracts with other parties, however, the original agreement is not modified in any way by a subcontract. For example, an architect enters into a contract, which is a subcontract, with a structural engineer to provide the structural design and engineering services for the project of which the architect has a prime contract with an owner to provide design services. Likewise, a contractor enters into a contract, which is a subcontract, with a specialty, or trade, contractor to provide products and installation for the project of which the contractor has a prime contract with an owner to provide construction services. It is common for subcontracts to include similar duties, rights, and responsibilities as in the original contract.

5.6.1 Single-Prime Contract

A common form of construction contracting involves a single contract. The selected contractor and the owner enter into an agreement formalizing their relationship and their obligations. The contractor then constructs the project in accordance with the contract documents. Typically, the contractor will have a portion or perhaps a majority of the work performed by subcontractors.

Figure 5.2 is a diagram of a single-prime contract construction project. This diagram represents the basic design-bid-build or design-negotiate-build type of project delivery. Note that the owner has a contractual relationship with both the A/E and the contractor. The A/E has agreements with consultants and the contractor has agreements with subcontractors, but the A/E and the contractor have no agreement with each other. The A/E, depending on the terms of the owner-A/E contract, may provide construction contract administration services. Consultants to the A/E must communicate with the owner and the contractor through the A/E, and specifications prepared by consultants must reflect this relationship. For example, consultants should not designate themselves to process submittals directly to and from the contractor.

Neither the owner nor the A/E has a contractual relationship with suppliers, subcontractors, or sub-subcontractors. Communication with these entities must always be through the contractor. The project specifications should not be directed or addressed to subcontractors or suppliers.

The single-prime contract is usually the simplest type of construction contract to administer. Centralization of responsibility—one owner, one contractor, and one construction contract—can result in simpler project scheduling and coordination. Even though the contractor may divide the work into subcontracts, the contractor remains solely responsible for all of the work needed to fulfill the contract. The lines of responsibility to the owner are clearly defined.

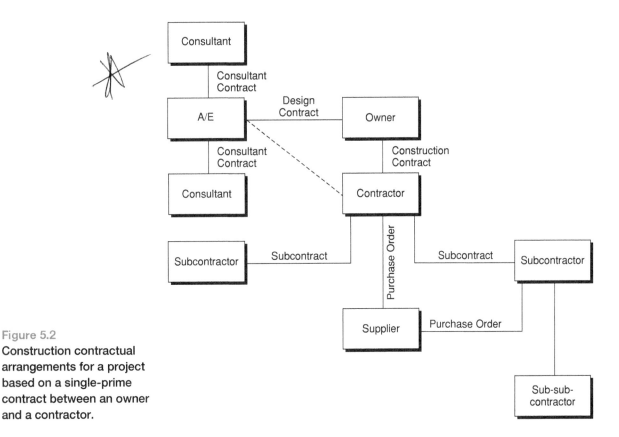

Figure 5.2
Construction contractual arrangements for a project based on a single-prime contract between an owner and a contractor.

5.6.2 Multiple-Prime Contracts

In a multiple-prime construction project, the work is divided among several contractors, and each enters into a separate prime contract with the owner. For example, a building project might be divided into six scopes of work for site construction, general construction, masonry work, mechanical work, plumbing work, and electrical work, and the owner enters into a prime contract with each contractor for each scope of work. These multiple-prime contracts are applicable to both architectural and engineering type projects. Figure 5.3 illustrates the contractual relationships of a multiple-prime contract arrangement. Multiple-prime contracts may be a result of the fast-track scheduling (described later) or may be used to control procurement.

For the multiple-prime projects, the A/E might prepare a separate set of documents for each contract. With several prime contractors on a single project, the A/E, construction manager, or owner-builder must define how the work will be divided into each contract and coordinated. The documents must include a clear summary outlining the extent of each contract. Thorough coordination is critical because separate contractors will be involved with certain parts of the project. Unless someone (a contractual entity) is assigned responsibility and authority for coordination, the owner may assume the responsibility to coordinate between the multiple-prime contracts. Claims between contracts are an evitable circumstance, and the required detailed coordination of documents and contracts can add expense to a project. Multiple-prime contracts often require construction management for effective coordination, particularly on projects of large scope or significant complexity. This is in contrast to a single-prime contract project where it is the contractor who divides the work among subcontractors and is responsible for coordination.

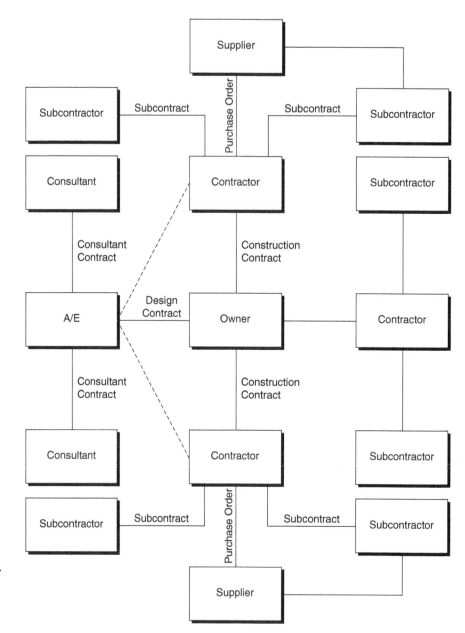

Figure 5.3
Construction contractual arrangements for a project based on multiple-prime contracts between an owner and several contractors.

Several organizations have standard agreement forms that are compatible with their respective contract conditions and are tailored to specific types of project delivery and basis of payment. The owner, in consultation with their legal counsel, should determine the appropriate contractual conditions and forms of agreements that should be used for a project. These conditions and agreements should be coordinated and compatible with other project agreements and contracts to ensure that duties, rights, and responsibilities are consistent among stakeholders and participants. These contract conditions and agreements must be compatible for the A/E and the contractor to ensure that liabilities and responsibilities are properly assigned. An example is design liability versus construction liability and the proper types of insurance for these issues. In some types of project delivery methods, these responsibilities may be combined; however, the licensing requirements and liability issues need to be clearly delineated in the contract conditions and agreements. The proper contract conditions and agreements are significant issues to ensure proper execution of the work.

Standard agreements have a long history of legal precedence, are under constant review, and are reissued on a periodic basis. These agreements include compatible agreements for the most construction participants even though these participants may not be members of the organization. The primary purpose of these agreements is to ensure proper documentation of the duties and responsibilities, while ensuring compatibility with other participants.

Numerous other agreements are utilized during the design and construction of the project. These other agreements are required to delegate work to consultants, subcontractors, and suppliers. The significance of these subagreements is to ensure that the terms and responsibilities are similar to the primary agreements between the owner and the A/E or the owner and contractor. Use of agreements from the same association ensures coordinated wording of terms and legal issues. The separation of work and the respective scope of work are the primary areas of claims and disputes.

5.8 Compatibility of Agreements

Regardless of the number of participants in a specific project, each agreement (design services and construction services) should be consistent and compatible with the other. The participants in a design and construction project work together to create the facility. When duties affect other parties, it is important that each respective participant's role should be consistently stated in each other's agreement. The design agreement should indicate who will perform construction administration. Conversely, the agreements with those who will provide other services such as construction administration should adequately include services required to ensure that the design is properly executed in accordance with the documents prepared. Other provisions might be required if construction management services are involved in the project delivery. Standard forms of agreements for all participants should be obtained from the same organization to ensure compatible contract conditions.

Each duty that affects another party under a separate agreement should be clearly delineated in its respective agreements. Contractual agreements have important legal consequences and, as such, should be reviewed by each party's legal counsel. Duties and responsibilities are liabilities that can be forced through legal actions. Many agreements have several forms of alternative dispute resolution to avoid costly legal processes. Hopefully, the utilization of compatible agreements, mutual understanding, and a cooperative effort can be a good aid toward a successful project.

5.9 Design Team Coordination

The key to effective design team coordination is good communication, attention to detail, reviewing the interface between design disciplines, and a sufficient number of decisions that are proportionate for the stage of work. Sufficient time must be dedicated to performing coordination tasks. A well-planned, executed, and enforced coordination program can result in fewer addenda items, fewer requests for interpretation, fewer change orders, fewer disputes, and reduced project costs. Ideally, the documents for construction, prepared by the architect and the other design team members, will be as consistent as if they were prepared and produced by one source.

Coordination may be just as difficult when project design team members are on the A/E staff as when they are multiple outside consultants. There are three components of project design team coordination:

- *Organization.* Selecting team members and establishing management procedures
- *Execution.* Project design and production of construction documents
- *Quality Assurance:* Meetings, checklists, communication, and checking and cross-checking construction documents

Incomplete coordination among design team members is an important issue within the construction industry. Following are some of the problems that can result from incomplete coordination:

- *Duplications.* Duplications occur when part of, or the entire same element of, work is specified in more than one section of the specifications, or indicated in more than one drawing. Duplications violate the Construction Specifications Institute (CSI) principle of "say it once and in the right place." Duplication is an opportunity for discrepancies that alter the uniform basis for procurement and cause confusion. In turn, this can result in higher construction costs, faulty construction, disputes, decreased document credibility, and increased exposure to liability.
- *Omissions.* Omissions occur when information concerning an element of work is inadvertently excluded from the construction documents. Omissions are often caused by a lack of understanding of the responsibilities of the various design disciplines and the absence of a joint checklist.
- *Discrepancies.* Discrepancies develop when conflicting information is shown in two or more locations of the drawings and specifications. Lack of knowledge by the team leader or team members of the procurement requirements, contract document requirements, agreements, insurance, bonds, or the conditions of the contract increases the possibility of discrepancies and conflicts.
- *Division 01 Responsibility.* Although Division 01—General Requirements is usually the responsibility of the design team leader, it affects all divisions and requires input from all disciplines.
- *Terminology Differences.* Terminology often differs between drawings and specifications because the two sets of documents are not usually prepared by the same individual.

Among the design team members, there are many areas of the construction documents that require coordinating attention; however, the following are the more critically important areas to spend sufficient time to coordinate:

- The relationship between the construction documents as a multidisciplined representation with the design concept
- The two-way relationship between the architectural drawings and each of the other design disciplines
- The relationship between the drawings and the specification

5.10 Important Legal Issues

It is not the intent of this practice guide to dispense legal advice; however, there are several issues design professionals and the construction industry should understand are important to the project delivery process.

5.10.1 Need for a Written Historical Record

The importance of the need for a written historical record during the performance of a contract should never be underestimated or taken lightly. In the event of a lawsuit, the purpose of the discovery phase is for the attorneys to discover facts that are pertinent and relevant. One of the ways this is accomplished is by examining the written history: contracts, drawings, specifications, submittals, formal modification documentation, meeting reports, correspondence, e-mails, and even handwritten notes kept by individuals. Stakeholders and participants should understand the following about the importance of keeping good records:

- Every document becomes part of the historical record and is discoverable.
- Each document should be clearly written, professional in demeanor, accurate in detail, and contain sufficient information to describe or document the issue at hand.
- Documentation will usually be examined years after being written, so the information should be written in such a way that the information can be accurately understood by both the writer and others at a future time.
- Others who access the documents will make interpretations and draw conclusions on what the words say and the meanings conveyed.
- The records and documents will be assembled to form a chronological sequence of events of the design and construction, including actions, decisions and lack of decisions, problems, errors, omissions, delays, disputes, deficiencies, resolutions, and the presence or absence of individuals or information at critical times.
- In addition to discovering information, there is an irresistible attraction to finding the "smoking gun" that will be used to implicate a party or shift the blame or focus in another direction.

The story told by the reconstruction of the design and construction processes may very well provide the necessary information to determine liability and recourse for the party damaged.

5.10.2 Professional Standard of Care

Most professionals are required by law to possess advanced, specialized education or training and to be licensed by the state in which they practice. Consequently, because professionals have unique knowledge and capabilities, society expects them to practice in such a manner as to achieve a professional standard of care. Since rules and standards cannot be comprehensively developed in advance of every situation a professional will encounter, they are expected to use their unique knowledge, exercise judgment, and special skill in the pursuit of their respective practice. Also, outcomes cannot be guaranteed, and professionals are not expected to be perfect or infallible. Therefore, to what standard can professionals be held?

Professionals have a duty to clients and society at large to practice according to the general principle of a standard of reasonable care. The standard of reasonable care is defined as taking the same course of action as another reasonable and prudent professional in the same area would have taken under the same circumstances. Professionals are held to a higher standard than the average person.

5.10.3 Professional Negligence

If professionals do not exercise the standard of reasonable care, they may be negligent in the performance of their actions or lack of actions. Negligence occurs when the professional does not use the unique knowledge and special skill in making decisions and judgments. While a professional is not negligent if a wrong decision is made in good faith under the standard of care, failing to take an appropriate action can be held to be negligent. For an action or lack of action to be negligent the following elements are necessary:

- The professional has a duty to conform to a certain standard of conduct to protect another party against unreasonable risk. It should be noted that, in addition to the other party to an agreement, professionals have a duty to protect the public.
- The professional did not conform to the required standard.
- There is a causal connection between the professional and the injury done to the other party.
- A legally protected interest of the other party has been injured.

5.10.4 Compliance with Building Codes, Laws, and Regulations

The individual or entity that designs a facility, or a portion of a facility, is also responsible for complying with the design requirements required by the authority having jurisdiction (AHJ; laws, statutes, ordinances, codes, rules and regulations, and lawful orders of public authorities). Traditionally, the design professional has been responsible for this duty; however as design-build and Integrated Project Delivery become more commonly used, design decisions are not always made by the design professionals. The contractor is entitled to a reasonable expectation that the construction documents provided by the owner are sufficient for the purpose intended, including compliance with the AHJ design requirements.

The individual or entity that constructs a facility or a portion of a facility, as indicated on the contract documents, is not required to ascertain if the facility complies with the AHJ design requirements. If the constructor discovers the facility design is not in conformity with the AHJ design requirements, or is made aware of the nonconformity, the constructor is obligated to seek direction from the owner and designer. If the constructor fails to perform this obligation, the constructor may be responsible for the cost of the damages to the owner. If the constructor does perform this obligation, the constructor is not liable to the owner or architect for damages due to errors, inconsistencies, or omissions in the contract documents.

5.10.5 *Spearin* Doctrine

A U.S. Supreme Court decision in 1918, *United States v. Spearin,* 248 U.S. 132, 39Ss. Ct., 63 L.Ed.2d 166 (1918), is a key case that has far-reaching implications for the design professions and the construction industries. Basically, *Spearin* holds that a contractor is entitled to rely on the construction documents provided by the owner to be sufficient for their intended purpose and is not responsible for the consequences of defects (errors, inconsistencies, or omissions) in the contract documents.

5.10.6 Actions Can Change the Terms of a Contract

Each participant in the design and construction process should understand the importance of performing his or her respective duties according to the terms of their contracts. If an action or activity is performed that is not part of the contract, it can be held that that particular action or activity is now part of the contract. Also, if an action or activity that is in the contract is not performed, a party can be held in breach of contract.

5.10.7 Interpretation by the Courts

One of the ways the understanding of legal issues can be advanced is to examine the manner in which courts interpret specifications in the event of litigation resulting from a claim during construction. By knowing how courts interpret contract documents, specifications can be produced that are more likely to hold up to the scrutiny of litigation. Courts will interpret specifications in the same manner as they interpret contracts according to the following rules:

- *Autonomy to Contract.* The foundation of contract law is that two parties are mutually free to determine the terms of an agreement, within the bounds of lawful activities, for a specific purpose. Those that do so are seen as having the capacity to contract for products or services.
- *Entire Agreement.* When questions are being considered, the court will search for the meanings of the words used and the purposes of the contract provisions. The documents will be interpreted in the effort to establish the intention of the parties. If ambiguities or conflicts are found, then other contract documents will be examined in the effort to find definitions and meanings. If an issue under consideration is of a technical nature, the specifications will be examined.
- *Specific Takes Precedence over General.* When specific information is written, the courts interpret it as intentional for the work and will be given more importance than general information or printed provisions.
- *Trade Customs.* If the contract documents do not adequately establish the intentions of the contract provisions, then the court may rely on the customs and practices of an industry or a trade. If the specifications include references to trade association standards, then that may be examined before bringing in trade customs.

- *Practical Interpretation.* Ambiguous provisions will be interpreted by the court according to the practical meanings placed on it by the parties to the contract.
- *Construction Against the Drafter.* Ambiguous provisions will be interpreted against the party drafting the provision on the basis that the drafter had superior knowledge of the subject matter and should have been more specific or accurate in the preparation of the provision.

Chapter 6
Project Planning

6.1 Introduction

Ranging from the simplest building to the largest development that includes multiple buildings, underground infrastructure, roadways, and streets, that might cost several billion dollars, every facility requires a knowledgeable and experienced project team of individuals, firms, and companies that are responsible for the process of bringing it into existence. However, before anything can be designed or constructed, a considerable amount of planning is necessary to deliver whatever the project is to be as a facility. The project delivery process can be described in the simplest way as planning and then execution of the plan.

Regardless of the project work (extent), its budget (cost), and its schedule (time), or the project delivery method selected, the appropriate amount of planning must be completed to enable the project delivery process to be successful. The more complete the planning, the more smoothly the project will proceed. For example, if the owner's needs, financing, and budgets are developed before consideration is given to the applicable zoning restrictions affecting the allowable height of a facility, the owner's budget may require adjustment to accommodate a different project form.

6.2 Project Conception

Project conception is the stage in the facility life cycle in which the project is planned and is characterized by the following activities:

- Due diligence investigations
- Site selection
- Facility programming
- Facility performance criteria
- Anticipating the cost of the work
- Setting the project schedule

Some of the activities associated with this stage are known as *programming, planning,* or *predesign.* The decision-making process during this stage provides the foundation for successful progression through subsequent project stages. Project conception is often a creative stage for the owner; it requires a clear understanding of project values and goals, which become the basis of many decisions. A facility program documents these decisions, resulting in a framework for future design decisions, operational procedures, and determining project feasibility.

This process requires specialists in concept development who can prioritize the values and goals, integrate them with the facts provided by preliminary studies, and make recommendations. Project conception requires various participants and coordination of tasks, some of which can be carried out concurrently. Depending on the extent and complexity of the owner's requirements, participants may include:

- Facility programmers
- Architects/engineers (A/Es)
- Facility managers
- Facility users
- Developers or development consultants
- Product representatives
- Construction managers
- Project managers
- Design-builders
- Contractors

Additional participants may include the following, who can assist in providing information and services to refine and support the project concept:

- Financial advisers
- Realtors
- Urban planners
- Authorities having jurisdiction (AHJs)
- Community representatives
- Legal advisers

6.3 Due Diligence Investigations

While envisioning the future facility as the beginning of a project, the owner may conduct a series of due diligence investigations to determine its viability. These investigations are carried out by the owner, independently or in consultation with a development consultant and other specialists, to identify the conditions and influences that will shape the project concept and clarify the owner's values and goals. Whether purchasing or leasing real estate, the owner must take care to perform proper due diligence investigations of the property to ensure that it meets the owner's needs. Due diligence investigations should begin as soon as the property is identified and before the owner is contractually bound to purchase or lease the property.

Preliminary studies may include:

- Feasibility studies to evaluate the owner's available and prospective financial resources
- Impact studies to determine the effect of the facility on the surrounding community
- Physical facilities evaluations, identifying potential for reuse, adaptation, salability, or leaseability

- Site studies to determine the availability, viability, and cost of suitable sites
- Studies to determine other factors that might influence the owner's decision to relocate or stay in an existing facility

Some investigations are brief and involve few participants other than the owner, internal personnel, and users. Other investigations, especially those involving complex financial projections, social impact, and site evaluations, require more time and involve specialists who can provide information upon which sound decisions can be based. The owner's experience with project conception and organizational resources will also determine the effectiveness and duration of due diligence investigations. On public projects, the same task may take longer because of legal processes, funding, and the scrutiny of the public as the project progresses.

If the owner's vision is broad or complex, involving a large site and multiple stages of growth, master planning should be considered. Master plans define long-term development strategies. In this process, the owner's resources, operations, and vision are evaluated for their adaptability to successive, complementary improvements with minimal disruption to existing operations, culminating in an integrated long-term strategy. Master planning benefits projects such as manufacturing plants, resource industries, governmental buildings, universities, schools, retail complexes, hospitals, and planned residential communities by sustaining their overall vision for growth. To be effective, the owner should engage A/Es, planners, financial experts, and development consultants with successful master planning experience.

Due diligence investigations are essentially preparatory steps for the subsequent involvement of specialists who evaluate and summarize the owner's requirements through programming. Programming may not be completed until the due diligence investigations are complete. Ultimately, the investigations provide information to aid the owner in evaluating values, goals, and needs in order to facilitate clearer communication with subsequent project participants. Every stage of the project life cycle presents the owner with options. The choices made during each stage affect subsequent stages.

6.3.1 Financial Studies

Financial studies evaluate the various economic aspects of an owner's vision. If the vision is not financially viable, the project will probably not be feasible. If there is a substantial difference between the vision and viability, the project may need to be abandoned. Experienced owners have a sense of financial feasibility based on their knowledge of the design and construction process, as well as financial parameters.

If project success depends on generating revenue, then demographics and market evaluations must support the owner's expectations. If the owner has a record of successful projects, financial studies for similar projects may not be extensive and may involve few participants outside the owner's staff. In the absence of project experience and resources, the owner should engage outside consultants to conduct financial studies. Financial studies should provide the owner with a clear understanding of the financial restrictions affecting the project's size and material requirements by evaluating the following:

- *Owner's Financial Condition.* An evaluation by a financial analyst will reveal the extent of the owner's present monetary resources. Business owners usually maintain current financial statements about their companies or organizations and use them as templates through which they visualize and act.

- *Life Cycle Cost.* Life cycle cost involving both operational and maintenance cost and expenses should be analyzed.
- *Value of Existing Facilities.* The financial analysis describes options for constructing a new facility or determining the extent of modification to an existing facility. It provides factual information with respect to an existing facility's adaptability and resale options. A/Es and real estate appraisers are often engaged by owners to help make sound evaluations of physical facilities.
- *Available Funding.* Sufficient funds are required to plan, construct, and, when complete, operate and maintain a facility. The extent of funding the owner is able to secure affects the size and characteristics of the project. Project conception cannot be effective until this type of study is complete. Funding may be separated into construction funds (capital cost) and operations and maintenance funds. Together, these represent the life cycle cost. Some owners place greater emphasis on the construction cost and may not realize the long-term effect on the eventual total life cycle cost.
  - A private-sector owner often seeks a construction loan for projects, in which credit history and project type will be important factors. However, the owner may need to consider alternative sources of funds, including liquidation of assets, private investment, philanthropic donations, venture capital, government grants, or tax and bond revenue.
  - A public sector owner will attain its project funding through public sources such as capital projects budget, bonds, or matching grants, and these may require the approval of the federal, state, and local government or the voters in a governmental jurisdiction. Public funding and approvals may take months or years.
- *Timing.* This is especially important in securing funds. Bank loans should be secured when interest rates are relatively low. Philanthropic donations or government grants must be applied for well in advance of when the funds are needed. Private investment and venture capital require experienced marketing strategies to make their solicitations successful. The success of tax and bond issue proposals depends on several factors, including the state of the economy, how receptive the public will be to the proposed improvements, and other competing issues on the public agenda at the time they are proposed.

6.3.2 Community Impact Studies

The feasibility of a project is also directly related to the impact it will have on the project site and surrounding community. A proposed development or project may affect public facilities and utilities, which may need to be modified to accommodate the impact of the project. Also a new, large complex may impact other concurrent community projects already in advanced planning stages, some negatively and some positively, which may, in turn, affect the overall success of this new project.

Community impact studies address:

- *Operations.* A project involving renovations or additions can have a measurable impact on the owner's existing operations and may affect the project scheduling and project cost. A retail owner may consider scheduling remodeling work during periods of off-peak business hours to avoid inconvenience to customers. Also, schools typically schedule renovations during the summer months when children are not in and around the school. However, in a case where there are no long off-peak periods, the project must be completed in as short a period as possible so operations can resume.

- *Relocation.* A relocation project may have an even greater impact, depending on the nature of the operations. The owner of a facility must consider the effects of relocation on its users, employees, suppliers, and customers and the effect of downtime on the facility use or the owner's operations during the relocation. The mobility of key employees, the cost of relocation, and the availability of a trained workforce may be a factor in determining whether the owner relocates or remodels the existing facility. If the relocation is significant in terms of its distance from the existing facility, the project will significantly affect the lives of employees. The owner should consider the availability of suitably trained personnel for the new location when key employees who are bound by other commitments cannot relocate. The costs for relocation may include transporting equipment and furnishings, as well as the costs of relocating key employees to a new facility.
- *Environmental Impact.* A project site may be in a sensitive area and require an environmental impact study to evaluate the effects the project will have on local wetlands, wildlife, surface runoff, drainage, and certain buffer zones or green-space requirements. If a percentage of wetlands is usurped by the project, the owner might be required to add wetlands elsewhere. An owner might have to mandate porous pavement in a parking area to permit the unimpeded flow of groundwater. Environmental requirements for reforestation, stream protection, erosion control, and surface water runoff containment may have to be addressed.
- *Public Facilities and Utilities Impact.* The impact of a project on the community's infrastructure, including transportation systems, utilities, and other services, may involve an impact study, if required by the local community.
- *Economic Impact.* A major facility may play a significant role in the local economy, for both taxes and employment. Whether a facility stays in an existing location or is considering a new location, this impact could be a factor that needs a study or other form of documentation.

6.3.3 Site Studies

Site studies are a key activity of the project conception stage. Site studies are a series of coordinated investigations by specialists to determine a site's suitability for its intended purposes throughout its life cycle. A/Es and Realtors can provide valuable assistance to the owner in locating potential sites and evaluating them for cost and ability to accommodate the project. Sites can range from existing facilities, with the potential for owner-specific adaptation to existing buildings that may be demolished for a new facility, to an entirely different site in another part of the community.

The site will need to be surveyed to obtain information on the topography, easements, site utilities, as well as to establish the property lines. After the survey, the owner might be surprised to learn that a certain percentage of the property is unusable or subject to certain restrictions.

6.3.3.1 Environmental Issues

An environmental study that evaluates the site should reveal whether a potential site is contaminated or environmentally sensitive, which will greatly affect its usefulness for a project and future value. Sites that have been contaminated with chemicals by previous owners may be referred to as *brownfields.* These sites are not necessarily the same type of sites that may contain hazardous materials within existing structures. Hazardous materials surveys are discussed later. Environmentally problematic sites will affect project cost, project schedule, and the latitude the owner has in adapting it for the project. Public records and special testing are necessary for making these determinations.

Financial institutions are extremely reluctant to finance projects located on contaminated sites, so alternative financing may be necessary if such conditions are encountered. Federal programs and grants for restoring contaminated sites are available; however, application processes usually have long waiting periods. In addition, sites deemed "environmentally or politically sensitive" may be subject to lawsuits or other legal actions to restrict development on the site.

Federal, state, and local environmental regulations affect sites. Protection of the public and the physical environment may require controlling water usage, vehicular traffic, precipitation runoff, waste disposal, or the preservation of beaches, forested areas, and wetlands. An environmental impact statement (EIS) quantifies and describes the effect the project will have on the environment. Perhaps a prime example of this is construction on wetlands. Often, a site looks nothing like a wetland, and it isn't until surveys or geotechnical evidence shows up that the owner is aware of the property's wetland status, the implications of which are complex. There may be parts of the site that may be required to be excluded from potential development and construction. Or the owner may be required to pay for wetlands restoration, mitigation, or creation in other locations.

Use of environmentally sensitive sites, such as wildlife habitats, wetlands, and riparian areas, are increasingly scrutinized by the public and restricted through legislation. Any project, even a public park, may have problematic aspects when it involves environmentally sensitive sites. Special approvals by federal, state, and local AHJs may be required, prolonging the project conception stage. Procedural guides recognized and accepted by AHJs are available from governmental and nongovernmental agencies such as the following from ASTM International:

- *ASTM E 1527 Standard Practice for Environmental Site Assessments.* Phase I Environmental Site Assessment defines the practice in conducting an environmental site assessment of real estate with respect to the range of contaminants within the scope of Comprehensive Environmental Response, Compensation, and Liability Act (CERCLA) and petroleum products.
- *ASTM E 1903 Standard Guide for Environmental Site Assessments.* Phase II Environmental Site Assessment Process ASTM E 1903 defines a process intended to gather information about the previous ownership and property uses to determine whether hazardous substances or products have been disposed of or released there, in order to satisfy one element of the innocent purchaser defense to CERCLA liability.

One of the most significant aspects of sustainability is how the design and construction of facilities should be conducted in the physical environment. Areas of environmental concern that may require study include the following:

- Soil erosion, waterway sedimentation, and airborne dust during construction activities
- Environmental impact of facilities on a site
- Density of development, including reuse of existing facilities

- Sites contaminated with dangerous chemicals and hazardous materials
- Reduction of the use of automobiles by using other forms of transportation, vehicles fueled by alternative energy types, and higher parking densities
- Preservation of natural assets and promotion of biodiversity
- Pollution from and management of stormwater runoff containing contaminates

Owners, practicing their due diligence, are advised to retain recognized accredited consultants to perform this type of review.

6.3.3.2 Hazardous Material Surveys

Like subsurface investigations, these surveys are conducted by specialists to determine the extent of hazardous conditions on the site. Structures built before 1970 may contain materials that are presently considered health hazards with emerging environmental acts and regulations, including petroleum wastes, underground fuel tanks, toxic chemicals such as polychlorinated biphenyls (PCBs), and refrigerants in abandoned equipment. Hazardous material surveys reveal the type and extent of these materials.

Hazardous materials require special handling and disposal procedures and will affect project cost. Even vacant sites may have contaminated soils and hazardous fill that may have to be removed before any construction may begin. Most standard contracts, include provisions indicating the concealed and unknown conditions, will require clarification and may require costly additional work. Hazardous material surveys will reduce the owner's exposure to costly unscheduled delays during the construction stage of the project.

6.3.3.3 Geotechnical Investigations

Geotechnical investigations provide information on the hidden, subsurface conditions. This work describes the soil type and its stability, helping the owner to decide what type of design and construction method is suitable. These are conducted by geotechnical engineers who take representative samples of soil from the site and prepare reports of site conditions based on laboratory analysis. These surveys may also detect underground streams and potential moisture or water-level problems. Once again, this information determines where the facility will sit on the site, its design, and what type of construction is most suitable.

6.3.3.4 Archeological Surveys

Public entities often require archeological surveys or at least literature reviews before construction can start. For example, almost any coastal site or river floodplain and many urban sites may have historic or prehistoric artifacts that require the input of an archeologist; other parts of the country may have artifacts from Native Americans or early settler occupation. Another example is the discovery of unmarked graves.

6.3.3.5 Other Governments

An unusual but nevertheless important type of site study addresses the implications of planning projects on sites governed by other governments. This may involve Native American tribes or foreign embassies within our country.

6.3.4 Existing Facility Evaluations

If an existing facility will be part of the project concept, an investigation will help determine its suitability for adaptation to the owner's needs and goals. Such an evaluation may include the following:

- Functional Evaluation:
  - Ability to meet the basic functional requirements
  - Ability to be renovated and expanded
- Facility Systems Evaluation:
  - Condition of major operating systems and subsystems, including controls, environmental equipment, fire suppression, electrical system, security, and fire alarms
  - Condition of service utilities such as water, sewerage, electrical, and communications
- Structural Evaluation: Structural integrity of gravity and lateral/seismic components, including the condition of foundations, floors, and superstructure
- Environmental Evaluation:
  - Presence of hazardous materials, such as lead piping or lead-based paints, asbestos, mold, formaldehyde, or refrigerants in abandoned equipment

Table 6.1 **Facility Assessment**

Project Type	Potential Effects/Considerations	Action
Minor re-engineering or rehabilitation	Lowest expense Minor schedule considerations Few disruptions Most constraining Need for future changes most likely	Adjust facility or operations to suit existing and planned conditions
Modifications/ Expansion	Lower expense Brief schedule duration Moderately disruptive Moderately constraining Need for future changes very likely	Adapt existing facility or major systems/subsystems/components to accommodate current and future facility operations
Relocation/Adaptive re-use	Moderate expense Moderate schedule duration Moderately disruptive Moderately constraining Need for future changes likely	Within the existing facility this may fall into an O&M activity, depending upon its magnitude Lease or buy available facilities and relocate
New construction	High expense Long schedule duration Few disruptions Few constraints Need for future changes less likely	Design and build new facility to suit planned operations
New construction, multiple projects or phases of development	Highest expense Longest schedule duration Fewest disruptions Fewest constraints Master planning helps avoid problems related to growth	Perform comprehensive master planning Design and build a new facility to suit operations while retaining other options for growth

- Indoor air quality
- Noise introduced into the neighborhood during construction and during facility operations
- Studies of light and shadow that affect adjacent properties such as public parks
- Water and air infiltration that can affect the structural and thermal integrity of components, including corrosion and movement
- Energy consumption
- Accessibility Evaluation: Evaluation for conformance with accessibility requirements

This list covers only the primary physical aspects that should be performed in evaluating an existing facility. Other types of construction projects, such as the expansion of a highway, modification of a waste treatment facility, or the restoration of a historic site, will require additional types of investigative studies.

Table 6.1 is an example that shows the types of general conclusions an owner may draw from a facilities assessment and the potential effects.

6.4 Site Selection

If an owner does not already have a site for the anticipated facility, then a site should to be obtained before the programming is completed. Choosing a site is an important consideration for a facility because for as long as the facility exists, it will be on one site and in one neighborhood or community. The site should be located in a setting that is conducive, suitable, and fitting to the purpose for the facility. Retail businesses need to be within populated areas that are of sufficient size to support the business, schools need to be centrally located within the community they serve, and golf courses are usually located within areas that have naturally attractive assets.

A/Es often assist an owner with the search, evaluation, selection, and acquisition of a site. Before a site is acquired, the owner should be convinced the property will be suitable for the facility, and the only way to make this determination is by performing studies of various kinds. While the full range of site studies, as detailed in here and later, are not all required, the necessary studies should be performed to justify the acquisition. More extensive site studies can be performed after the site is acquired but before programming has been completed.

If a project involves an existing facility, a detailed survey and report of existing conditions should be made so that, when it is time for the design, there is information available for use. Also, the information will be important for the development of the design and construction documents for the project.

The actual purchase price of the site may be the primary component; however, other services involving fees are required to complete this process, such as the following:

- Real estate fees, which are typically included in the purchase price of sites "for sale" or may be paid by the seller in attempts to acquire a site. Government of public agencies may require other techniques for site acquisition. Fair market values by certified appraisers or means of valuation may be required by local law. Difficult sites required for public use may eventually lead to condemnation or even rights of eminent domain.
- An environmental impact statement or report should be completed. If a site is purchased before determining the project's requirements, all of the owner's objectives may not be achievable.

6.4.1 Location

Location is a universal attribute of successful projects of all types. The real estate cliché is "location, location, location" and is an accurate characterization for locating facilities. But often a combination of factors contributes to this success. Key attributes related to site location include:

- Natural features, such as geography (topography) and climate
- Public utilities and services, including availability and capacity necessary to operate the facility
- Economic resources, including proximity to complementary business interests, natural and other material resources, and even competing business interests that may stimulate business activity
- Access to transportation infrastructure(s) including highways, airports, waterways, and railroads, which may be critical to the viable operation of the facility
- Human resources, such as proximity to skilled labor, customer bases, volunteers, and other potential project participants
- Proximity to schools and universities, churches, libraries, museums, and other cultural magnets that anchor populations, which can contribute to further economic development

6.4.2 Land Development Regulations

State legislatures are empowered to enable cities, villages, counties, or townships with the authority to establish, manage, and enforce land development control regulations. One of the most common regulations is zoning, which defines the permitted and conditional uses of land by regulating the type and size of a facility, its use, its function, and the density of improvements. Sites may be classified for commercial, residential, industrial, institutional, recreational, or agricultural uses. In one area, a high-density housing project is encouraged, while nearby there may be minimum lot sizes of an acre or more. In some parts of the country, zoning restrictions are very rigid, while other areas are more flexible—perhaps because they are hoping to encourage economic development.

There are other types of zoning restrictions that challenge the nature and type of project located there. In some zoning categories, limitations are placed on the amount of land that may be developed, covered with paving, or otherwise utilized. This may be called the allowable site coverage, expressed in terms of the occupant density or footprint of the facility. Setback restrictions and floor area restrictions may be included with zoning and may dictate the distance that the facility must be from the property lines and other structures.

Parking requirements and restrictions may have a significant impact on the design and location of the facility. The same is true of the location and size of loading zones. Both issues are particularly relevant in urban areas and for infill projects.

Height restrictions take their cue from the landscape of the neighborhood. They prevent a single facility from towering above its neighbors, blocking sight lines, casting shadows on neighboring facilities, and altering the look of a neighborhood. Tall facilities may also be a hazard in areas near airports or where extremely high winds pose a significant threat.

A facility's style, aesthetics, and form may also be dictated by deed covenants and zoning (particularly if the project is in a historic district), including the following:

- The type and quantity of exterior materials permitted
- Limitations on the colors utilized
- Quantity of neighborhood fabric, both interior and exterior, which must be maintained in renovation or addition

Landscaping requirements may also be defined by zoning. Some jurisdictions may require buildings to have gardens or public plazas or even public art. If a project is located near wetlands, certain types of indigenous plantings may be required to fit with the local flora or to regulate and filter runoff. Trees and other vegetation, removed from one area of a site for facility functional reasons, may have to be relocated or replaced in another part of the site, to meet master zoning planning criteria.

The owner must also consider zoning implications from its own perspective, such as the surrounding land use and adjacent facilities' impact on the proposed facility.

If there is a zoning problem, it is possible to request a change. If the project concept does not conform to the site's permitted uses, an organized appeal to the zoning authority for a zoning variance will be necessary. This process can be lengthy and may require the participation of experts, increasing both cost and time before they are resolved. Owners should research what the probability for approval might be, and whether similar variances passed. Also it will be beneficial to determine whether the process was long and expensive.

In addition to zoning and other property use restrictions, regulatory agencies may require precautions to keep soil, chemicals used during construction, stormwater runoff, and other pollutants from running off the site.

6.4.3 Surrounding Conditions

Local economic and social conditions should be considered while selecting potential sites, as they will have significant effects on the owner's operations, both immediately and in the long run. A site located near a large airport may be ideally suited for a package-handling facility requiring access to air transportation routes. However, it may not be acceptable for other projects, such as schools, laboratories, housing projects, and other facility types where high noise levels will affect the owner's operations.

6.4.4 Other Site Concerns

Marketability is a key factor in the decision to remodel or relocate existing facilities. Owners of highly specialized facilities may be financially unable to relocate for this reason. In some locales, the cost of the site alone may well offset the cost of relocation, as facilities built "out of town" 50 years ago are now "in town" and the land is much more valuable. Conversely, the "in town" location may not be close to preferred methods of transportation, such as major highways and rail systems for distributing goods or obtaining raw materials.

Time and money are also factors in the site selection and acquisition. If a site does not immediately meet the requirements of the project, addressing the problems and limitations may be costly and time consuming. Site limitations may require legal help, additional feasibility and impact studies, permitting applications and fees, and other steps that will, invariably, slow the process.

6.4.5 Acquisition and Purchase

If a site under consideration does not meet all of the owner's requirements, or if there are problems with the site, the owner may have several options. If the site can be purchased at a lower cost, it might still be worthwhile. If there are ways to handle the site limitations, perhaps there would be enough difference in cost to resolve these issues. Alternately, a site that meets all the project criteria may be prohibitively expensive and affect other project assemblies, components, and elements.

If the site is a former landfill, there may be significant cost for bringing in new clean fill. If the soil on the site is not the correct type for supporting a structure, there may be significant cost for soil stabilization techniques or removal and replacement. If environmental cleanup is required, determining the extent of the contamination and cleaning up the site could be extremely costly. If the site has existing structures above or below grade, costs for demolition and removal need to be considered. Drainage problems or underground streams can also be costly problems, if they can be solved. Remote sites may require upgraded or new transportation, utility, and communication infrastructures, especially if the purchase price for the site or an existing facility is very low. Most purchase agreements related to site or facility acquisition involve two steps:

1. The buyer submits an offer. The conditions of the offer are based on receiving information from an evaluation of the site or facility that satisfies the buyer's requirements.
2. On the basis of receiving a favorable evaluation that favors the buyer's requirements, the purchase is completed.

Due diligence involves a careful analysis of all of the issues related to the site or facility within the timeline established in the purchase agreement. The evaluation may require several studies to examine all potential problems with the property. Examples include identification of existing environmental hazards, identification of development restrictions, and identification of any unique soil conditions that might impact the cost of development. This is information the buyer needs to know before completing the purchase.

Most purchase agreements allow for a specific time period to complete the due diligence evaluations, such as 60 days or more, so completion of the necessary studies needs to be timely and allow sufficient time for the buyer to evaluate them.

6.5 Facility Programming

Originally directed to his clients, William M. Pena, an architect with CRS in Houston, published a little book in 1969, *Problem Seeking: An Architectural Programming Primer*, which has become the timeless classic book on programming. Now in its fourth edition and with a co-author, Steven A. Parshall, *Problem Seeking* (4th edition, Wiley, 2001) defines programming as a process that starts with defining a problem and concludes with the requirements for developing a solution to the problem. While not limited to architecture, *Problem Seeking* can be used by anyone who is involved with methodically analyzing problems and proposing objectives for a course of action.

Problem Seeking proposes that facility programming is a two-phase process that proceeds from general to particulars and is associated with the schematic design and design development phases of design:

- Schematic programming identifying the broad visionary owner goals, user preferences, image, functional requirements, movement, activity adjacencies, and facility demographics. As schematic programming ends, schematic design begins.
- Program development includes the organization of the vast amount of detailed information collected in impact studies and site analysis during the initial stages of information collection. As program development ends, design development begins. The critical activity is transforming the owner's broad visionary goals into a physical form: "If programming is problem seeking, then design is problem solving" (p. 15).

Problem Seeking indicates there are four considerations that should be identified in the following terms:

- Function (What will happen in the facility?)
- Form (What will the facility look like and feel like?)
- Economy (What is the budget and quality?)
- Time (What will the time be to achieve the facility?)

The logic continues by indicating that there are five consecutive steps to the programming process:

1. Establish goals (What does the owner want to achieve?)
2. Collect and analyze facts (What is known?)
3. Uncover and test concepts (How are the goals achieved?)
4. Determine needs (What is needed and how much will it cost?)
5. State the problem (What is the direction the design should take?)

Together, these four considerations and five steps forms a matrix identified by *Problem Seeking* as a Programming Information Index (see Table 6.2). The terms contained in the matrix are key words that search for the appropriate information.

6.5.1 Step 1: Establish Goals

A/Es need to know and understand the owner's goals and values, in addition to the basic project needs. Goal statements included in the facility program must be useful and relevant for the A/E. The goals need to be quantifiable and measurable, such as an owner's goal to "provide a good environment" or to "get the most for the money." Green Building rating system programs, such as the U.S. Green Building Council (USGBC) and Leadership in Energy and Environmental Design ™ (LEED ™) provide a set of standards with measurable, recognized categories that owners can set as an industry-recognized goal for the project. Every project is a combination of various needs and influences, including functional considerations, existing conditions, aesthetics, economics, regulations, social considerations, environmental concerns, and time.

Table 6.2 An adaptation of a chart originally included in the *Architectural Registration Handbook: A Test Guide for Professional Exam Candidates,* published jointly in 1973 by the National Council of Architectural Registration Boards (NCARB) and Architectural Record (pp. 36–37)

	Goals	Facts	Concepts	Needs	Problem

Function
 	
1. People
2. Activities
3. Relationships
	Mission
	Maximum number
	Individual identity
	Interaction/privacy
	Hierarchy of values
	Prime activities
	Security
	Progression
	
	Segregation
	Encounters
	Transportation/
	  parking
	Efficiency
	Priority of
	  relationships
		Statistical data
		Area parameters
		Personnel forecast
		User characteristics
		Community
		  characteristics
		Organizational
		  structure
		
		Value of potential
		  loss
		Time-motion study
		Traffic analysis
		Behavior patterns
		Space adequacy
		Type/intensity
		ADA
			Service grouping
			People grouping
			Activity grouping
			Priority
			Hierarchy
			Security controls
			Sequential flow
			Separated flow
			Mixed flow
			
			Functional
			  relationships
			Communications
				Area requirements
				• By organization
				• By space type
				• By time
				• By location
				Parking
				  requirements
				Outdoor spaces
				
				Alternatives
					Unique and
					important
					performance
					requirements
					that will shape a
					facility's design

Form
 	
1. Site
2. Environment
3. Performance
  Level
	Bias on site
	  elements
	Environmental
	  response
	Efficient land use
	Community relations
	Community
	  relations
	Community
	  improvements
	Physical comfort
	Life safety
	Social/psychologi-
	  cal environment
	Individuality
	Wayfinding
	Projected image
	Owner expectations
		Site analysis
		Soil analysis
		Zoning
		Climate
		Code surveys
		Surroundings
		Psychological
		  implications
		Point of reference/
		  entry
		Cost/ft²
		Layout efficiency
		Equipment costs
		Area per unit
			Enhancements
			Special foundations
			Density
			Environmental
			  controls
			Safety
			Neighbors
			Home-based offices
			On premise: fixed
			  free, group address
			Off premise:
			  satelite, telecom-
			  muting, virtual
			  office, hoteling
			Orientation
			Accessibility
			Character
			Quality control
				Site development
				  costs
				Environmental
				  influences on
				  costs
				Facility cost/ft²
				Overall facility
				  efficiency factor
					Major form consid-
					erations affecting
					the design of the
					facility

Economy
 	
1. Initial
  Budget
2. Operating
  Costs
3. Life Cycle
  Costs
	Extent of funds
	Cost effectiveness
	Maximum return
	Return on investment
	Minimizing operational
	  costs
	Maintenance on
	  operational costs
	Reduction of life
	  cycle costs
	Sustainability
		Cost parameters
		Maximum budget
		Time-use factors
		Market analysis
		Energy source costs
		Activities and
		  climate factors
		Economic factors
		Economic data
		Green Building
		  rating systems
			Cost control
			Efficient allocation
			Multifunctional/
			  versatility
			Merchandising
			Energy
			  conservation
			Cost reduction
			Recycling
			Value analysis
				Budget estimate
				  analysis
				Balance budget
				Cash flow analysis
				Energy budget
				Operating costs
				Green building
				  rating
				Life cycle costs
					The initial budget
					and its influence
					on the fabric and
					geometry of the
					facility

Time
 	
1. Past
2. Present
3. Future
	Historic
	  preservation
	Static/dynamic
	  activities
	Change
	Growth
	Occupancy date
	Availability of funds
		Significance
		Space parameters
		Activities
		Projections
		Durations
		Escalation factors
			Adaptability
			Tolerance
			Convertibility
			Expansibility
			Linear/concurrent
			  scheduling
			Phasing
				Escalation
				Time schedule
				Time/cost
				  schedule
					Implications
					of change and
					growth on life cycle
					performance

- *Functional Considerations.* Responding to "What is going to happen in a facility?" The functionality of the facility has to be determined during planning so that the design can be tailored to the reasons the facility is needed.
  - In a building, this deals with individuals and groups of people, the relationships between them, and their activities.
  - In a manufacturing plant, this deals with a process that involves elements, the activities involved in each step of the process, and the relationship of each activity to produce something in a cost-efficient manner.
  - When underground utility infrastructures are extended into future growth areas of a community, this deals with the capacity of the services for the anticipated growth. Growth beyond the extension is an important consideration for the success of the utilities to handle the loads.
  - In a major freeway interchange, this deals with how the interchange will impact the existing as well as future traffic patterns and efficiency in moving vehicles through the interchange.
- *Existing Conditions.* Inadequacy, obsolescence, or failure of existing facilities to meet present and future owner requirements should be discovered and addressed by the programming.
- *Aesthetics.* Form, space, color, and texture affecting the physical, physiological, and psychological well-being of the facility user primarily, and secondarily its setting within the built environment are significant requirements for acceptance of the facility.
- *Economics.* Because a project requires expending significant financial resources, projects are generally conceived when new economic opportunities make execution possible. A strong upsurge in a sector of the economy, the offer of a subsidy or grant, the dissolution of a major competitor, or a tax incentive may stimulate visions of expansions or improvements. Conversely, corporate executives and managers often use the decision to plan and renovate or construct as a catalyst for organizational or administrative change.
- *Regulations.* Changes to laws, codes, and regulations affect design, construction, and use of facilities. Such laws may include the Americans with Disabilities Act (ADA), which has mandated major changes in existing public facilities as well as requirements affecting the ways new projects should be designed. The Clean Water Act resulted in thousands of wastewater treatment facility projects across the United States.
- *Social Considerations.* Public agencies may have needs for facilities such as utilities, streets and highways, bridges, dams, libraries, firehouses, parks, recreation facilities, and schools. Social problems require social solutions. A defined social solution can be incorporated into a design through the programming process.
- *Environmental Concerns.* The awareness of all living creatures and components of the natural and human-made environment and the evolution of sustainable balanced relationships is important for reducing the impact the facility will have on the natural environment.
- *Time.* The owner's time requirements are important considerations that are expressed in a project schedule.
- *Other.* The desire to create a unique environmental or sustainable statement, preserve a historic site, commemorate an event or person, or provide an opportunity for innovation may motivate a project.

Motivated by one or a combination of these factors, the owner initially identifies the values and goals for the project. Most owners' initial values and goals require a validation process. This process involves three steps: collecting and analyzing the facts, identifying and testing concepts, and determining the real needs.

6.5.2 Step 2: Collect and Analyze Facts

The facts need to be presented clearly and objectively. It is important to collect impartial information. Preconceptions must be avoided. Opinions must be evaluated and tested. Retain only information that might have direct bearing on the defined goals, organizing them into categories, such as aesthetics, economics, regulations, social considerations, environmental concerns, and time. Examples of facts involving numbers might include: 400-seat lecture hall, six classrooms with a maximum of 24 students each, a 500-vehicle parking lot, an interchange required for an urban shopping facility, or a complex in a community of 200,000.

Preliminary studies are important to facility programming only if they are relevant. Preliminary studies, discussed elsewhere in this chapter, are used to describe existing conditions of the site, including the physical, legal, climatic, and aesthetic aspects. Preliminary studies and their conclusions are required to complete the facility program. The detailed information that supports the conclusions, while not required in the schematic design, is often required in design development. The sources of the preliminary studies are from many diverse disciplines, such as geotechnical, finance, real estate, sociological, and urban planning.

Organizations such as governments and private-sector owners often complete this task with in-house facility programmers and production personnel, to prevent technology espionage. The facility programmer must have the organizational skills to filter out what is really important to the owner and the wisdom to guide the owner through the process objectively. The information acquired during preliminary studies and issues relative to the specific project are important to the programming process. These studies and issues will affect the detailed functional decisions and should be carried out in the early stages of information collection, to avoid revisiting a detailed functional analysis. The experienced facility programmer can reduce the time frame and avoid missing major elements required in the complete conceptual process.

6.5.3 Step 3: Uncover and Test Concepts

The term *concept,* as used here, relates to the programming process. *Programming concepts* refer to abstract ideas that are intended as functional solutions to an owner's performance problems without regard to the physical response. It is important to clearly understand that programming concepts are concerned with performance problems, and design concepts address design problems. For example, convertibility is a programmatic concept; a demountable partition is a corresponding design concept.

To illustrate the programmer's task, an owner provides a scrapbook full of diverse styles and features desired in a house, such as a Scandinavian kitchen, Louis XIV dining suite, Japanese living room, and Shangri-la porch. The programmer must seek solutions to the problems inherent in this eclectic information.

Regardless of the facility type, some concepts are common to every project, whether it be housing, institutions, shopping centers, or manufacturing. These recurring concepts include character/image, density, service grouping, activity grouping, people grouping, relationships, communication, orientation, flexibility, safety, security controls, energy conservation, environmental controls, phasing, and cost control. All of these concepts must be prioritized at some time during the facility programming process.

Prioritizing is an important part of facility programming. This is especially true when the project budget cannot accommodate all of an owner's needs or there are specific site or project constraints or restrictions. For example, a corporation may wish to ensure that its economic goals receive a higher position in the hierarchy, perhaps followed by aesthetic, environmental, and social considerations. A highway commissioner may place a higher value on the social and environmental impact of a new expressway interchange than on economic or aesthetic values. A citizens' group involved in planning a community project, such as a hiking trail, may base most of their decisions on environmental and social issues as well, although their project may be quite different in character from the expressway interchange.

An experienced owner—one who has previously worked through the project life cycle or substantial portions of it firsthand—might have a clearer sense of the key goals that should be manifested in the project and can reconcile them with the project budget without a great deal of assistance from other participants. The owner with little or no experience in programming might be less efficient, experience greater difficulty in setting priorities, and require more professional guidance to achieve the desired goals within budget. A facility programmer may be hired by the owner to assist in this process. Facility programmers utilize research techniques, including objective listening skills in interviews, recording of meaningful data during a walk-through study of an existing facility, comprehensive space inventories, system observations, and knowing when and how to develop and administer questionnaires.

Failure to complete a prioritizing process at the conceptual project stage can lead to poor design decisions, which will plague subsequent project stages and the completed facility throughout its life cycle. Prioritizing the collected facts is the initial filtering activity, which is repeated through every phase and stage of the project.

6.5.4 Step 4: Determine Needs

Determining the needs is the initial economic feasibility test for the proposed space requirements and the expected performance level against a proposed budget. The conceptual budgeting process provides a second filter, prioritizing the essential or real needs from the wants or commonly termed *wish list* that plagues projects from conception to completion and throughout their life cycle. It is human nature to push the budget to the limit. Wants must be distinguished from real needs. A wants/needs confrontation occurs whenever the owner defines the problem in terms of architectural solutions rather than functional requirements. The programmer must determine the assumptions on which the owner based the solutions and evaluate these. An owner may have a clear understanding of functional requirements but fail to relate them to financial position.

An objective needs assessment requires a framework to insert the owner's goals, the activities, and facts or conditions impacting the activities required to achieve goals. This assessment will include criteria to establish the project's performance level. To realistically validate goals, test the proposed space requirements and the expected level of performance against a budget. A balance must be achieved between functional economic, social, environmental, and aesthetic considerations. An imbalance will require recycling to reevaluate goals, facts, and concepts. In some facilities, the considerations may not have an equal weight; nevertheless, they should be considered in each step.

6.5.5 Step 5: State the Problem

The facility program document must be a clear, simple statement of the problem and include organized and edited information, free from irrelevance. The owner's values and goals statements should be expressed in quantitative and qualitative terms that describe the essence and uniqueness of the facility. There should be statement categories dealing with function, aesthetics/form, economics, regulations, social considerations, environmental concerns, and time. The key issue statements listed under each category should be limited to those dealing with unique, not universal, aspects of the problem. The statements should ideally be expressed in performance terms so as not to rule out different expressions of form. The expression of form is the A/E's role.

A facility program should include:

- An introduction explaining the programming process utilized
- An executive summary describing the project and its background
- The owner's program (value and goal) statements
- A summary of relevant facts, including preliminary studies, site studies, relevant information, and statistical projections
- Concepts including organizational structure, functional relationships, priorities, and operational models
- Space requirements expressed in terms of facility functions and their related activities, physical and environmental requirements of each programmed space, and space adjacencies analysis utilizing flow diagrams

Formats have been developed to assist in the process. Some of these are tabular bar charts, diagrammatic matrices, narrative space descriptions describing activities within the space, bubble diagrams, and zoning sketches.

The complete, often voluminous, preliminary studies, site studies, survey information, and budgeting information are generally contracted separately by an owner. They should be included as appendices to the main programming document. The facility programmer should review the preliminary studies and advise the owner what preliminary information is essential to be incorporated into the program statements (values and goals). Some of these studies, such as geological and topography surveys, will be utilized in the procurement (bidding/negotiating/purchasing) and construction stages, in addition to the design phases. An A/E can advise an owner on the scope of these preliminary studies and surveys to avoid repeating the process later in the project.

6.6 Facility Performance Criteria

Requirements documented in a facility program may be expressed in unit measure and quantities and as performance criteria. Performance criteria may be developed using various methods or software. The more the project requirements are expressed in performance criteria, the more flexibility the A/E or design-builder has in creating a facility design.

Performance factor checklists, as shown in Figure 6.1, organized into groups by the way they influence design, can identify important requirements for each element of the design.

Factors Affecting Built Element Performance

Amenity, Comfort – Factors that affect the comfort, convenience, or pleasure of the occupants. Most are stated in positive terms, because they are the reason for the building, existence.

- heat/cold
- wind, drafts
- water intrusion, leakage
- humidity, condensation
- light, glare
- sound, noise
- convenience, accessibility
- cleanliness
- odor
- appearance
- texture, feel
- privacy

Health, Safety – Factors that relate to occupants' well-being, not usually optional. Most are referred to as "hazards"; many are hazards generated by the building itself and are usually expressed using verbs like "prevent," "minimize," or "avoid."

- emergency (egress/alarm)
- falling, tripping, slipping
- cutting, breakable materials
- fire source
- ignitibility, combustibility
- fire spread
- smoke
- accidental explosion
- electrical shock
- radiation
- chemicals

- disease, infection
- vermin, animals
- intrusion, security, terrorism
- pollution
- flood
- hurricane, tornado
- vehicular collision

Structure – Important only because a building must be self-supporting. Most are expressed as a necessity to sustain a certain load with not more than a certain deflection, movement, or other consequence.

- static, dead loads
- live, vertical loads
- horizontal, wind loads
- seismic loads
- impact loads
- concentrated loads

Durability – Relevant because the building consists of physical materials that will inevitably wear out. Most are framed as resistance to a negative or degrading influence, in terms of commonly specified properties of building materials.

- life span
- exposure to touch
- moisture, condensation
- corrosion, chemical action
- rot, fungus, insects
- dirt, grease, stains
- cleaning, scrubbing
- abrasion, scratching

- impact, bending, loading
- temperature changes
- atmosphere, pollution
- light, ultraviolet light
- vandalism
- animals
- hurricane, tornado
- flood
- vehicular collision

Operational, Maintenance – Relevant because buildings have to be operated and maintained whether we like it or not and the types of materials used influence the cost and ease of operation or maintenance. Most are expressed with regard to the ease of doing something, as opposed to what happens to the material when that action is taken (which is usually a durability factor). Most are very difficult to prove because, though they come down to cost of operation, those costs are often difficult to pin down.

- reduction of power, water, fuel use
- ease of use
- minimization of misuse
- reduction of by-products, waste
- ease of cleaning
- minimization of cleaning required
- ease of service (equipment)
- minimization of service required
- ease of repair
- ease of replacement
- minimization of theft
- ease of location
- ease of adding on, adaptability

Figure 6.1   Factors Affecting Built Element Performance

6.7 Anticipating the Cost of the Work

One of the most important considerations during the planning for a project is anticipating what the new facility will cost to design and construct. It is incumbent upon the owner to understand the many factors that will be associated with the project and to estimate their costs. It is important that an initial budget be determined before the owner proceeds too far into the project delivery process. The initial budget will evolve somewhat as the project proceeds and the design is developed. Throughout the design portion of the project delivery process, the anticipated cost of the work should be continuously monitored and the design should be aligned to the cost, or the cost aligned to the design.

6.7.1 Project Funding

The sources of project funding will influence the delivery method and the pricing method that will be used. Privately funded projects may be competitively bid or negotiated, according to the owner's preference for the project delivery method selected. Traditionally, law required contractors for publicly funded projects to be selected by the competitively bid process because the funds are from publicly generated revenue, such as tax revenue or publicly issued bonds. However, many AHJs have determined that it is in the public's interests to procure projects according to the design-build delivery method.

In order to reduce time constraints and administrative burdens on public owners, small public projects may be contracted without competitive bidding according to administrative rules and monetary limits established within individual public jurisdictions. This enables the public owner to complete projects of limited scope and respond to emergencies without going through the standard bidding procedures required for larger, complex projects. The estimated probable construction cost of the project determines whether a project is contracted without formal bidding procedures. To allow for the effects of economic inflation, public owners may periodically increase the limits under which they may contract without competitive bidding.

The public owner may select contractors for small projects from a qualified contractor listing. Contractors are added to or removed from the listing according to established administrative guidelines. To apply, contractors must submit their qualifications for evaluation. They may also be required to submit labor rates and standard percentages for overhead and profit for time- and material-based contracts.

6.7.2 Project Budget

Once the functional needs (the program) have been established by the owner and the preliminary studies have been collected and analyzed, a project budget can be formulated. Figure 6.2 illustrates the affect of conceptual budget decisions on the subsequent project stages. As the project develops through each stage, more players become involved and major changes are not as possible without additional funding. The project budget should include projections of all of the costs associated with the entire project. A project budget may consider initial construction cost only or may include projected costs of operation. Including the operations and maintenance costs in a project budget will provide a better understanding of the total life cycle costs. If a project is of a speculative nature and will be sold in a short period of time, less emphasis is usually placed on the long-term operation and maintenance cost, which will, in turn, eventually impact the life cycle cost.

The project budget should not be confused with the construction budget. Costs are generally divided into two categories: hard costs and soft costs. Hard costs include tangible components of the completed project, and soft costs are all other items. Project budget soft costs include the following:

- *Due Diligence Studies, Programming, and Master Planning.*
- *Project Design Fees.* Regardless of project delivery method, fees associated with design of the project are a significant component of the project budget. Fees for architects, engineers, and their consultants are normally included.
- *Commissioning.* These include commissioning agent fees, other management fees depending on the type of project delivery selected, and testing and inspection service costs.

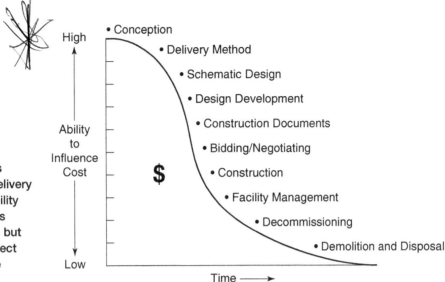

Figure 6.2
As a project proceeds through the project delivery process (time), the ability to influence the cost is high at the beginning, but decreases as the project advances through the various stages.

- *Jurisdictional Fees.* These are fees imposed by the AHJs over the project for zoning and variance applications.
- *Relocation.* These costs are the costs incurred by the owner for relocating to a new facility, and the cost of temporary facilities while existing facilities are being renovated or expanded.
- *Terminating Leases or Rental Agreements on Existing Facilities.* If they do not affect the decision to relocate, highly restrictive leases or rental agreements may affect the feasibility of the project. The cost of renewing a lease on a month-to-month basis may also influence the construction schedule, with penalties for the delayed project.

Project budget hard costs include the following:

- *Site-Related Costs:*
  - The direct costs associated with acquiring a site for the project, including the cost of the site and associated real estate fees, settlement costs, and taxes.
  - If a contaminated site, whether existing or newly acquired, requires rehabilitation.
  - For undeveloped sites, the costs for utilities will be significant. For existing facilities, upgrades may be required depending on the proposed uses, occupancy levels, or the cost of upgrading outdated or inadequate service.
  - Topographic surveys.
  - Geological surveys or soil analysis.
  - Environmental issues and cost of mitigating them, including wetlands, stormwater management, and other protective measures.
  - In some jurisdictions, a development permit application including an associated processing fee is required, depending on project type. Variances in existing zoning regulations may require specialized assistance and associated fees, particularly if a public review or appeal is involved in the process.
  - Site preparation, including decommissioning of existing improvements, abatement of hazardous materials or conditions, deconstruction, demolition, and site restoration. The required demolition may be minor, such as removing a small shed, or it may include the full removal of an existing building plus removal of underlying contaminated soil.

- *Construction.* This includes the estimates for the probable cost of constructing the project, including building permit fees, materials, labor, tools and equipment, bonds, insurance, and initial maintenance agreements associated with construction. During the project conception stage, this cost is estimated. As a result of the procurement process, the cost will be more clearly defined; however, the cost of construction will not be fully known until the project is completed.
- *Furniture, Furnishings, and Equipment (FF&E).* Movable items necessary to outfit the facility.

6.7.3 Construction Budget

The construction budget usually accounts for the biggest portion of the project budget. It includes the cost of bonds, insurance, products and systems, and labor both to construct the facility and to verify and administer the construction process (e.g., materials testing and inspection). Preparing a budget for the construction cost of a project is accomplished by several methods:

- *Cost per Measured Units.* The total number of measured units in a project is multiplied by a predetermined cost per measured unit; for example, $100 per square foot for a 50,000-square-foot project equals an estimated construction cost of $5 million. A steel structure may be estimated using tons of steel as a measured unit. Estimating guides (available from various industry sources) provide the average unit costs for various project types, such as art museums, retail facilities, or restaurants. This is used for very preliminary budgeting, as published guides are often not site specific and do not take into account local market conditions and labor rates.
- *Component Cost.* If the proposed facility is a multiple of components, such as a hotel or an individual storage facility, then a component cost can be derived. The costs for a hotel, for instance, may be arrived at by estimating a cost per room, then multiplying that by the number of rooms in the facility. The component cost would include a percentage of the support functions required by that type of facility. In this example, the component cost of the hotel rooms would include a percentage of the cost of the lobbies, corridors, elevators, and common areas. Depending on the complexity of the facility, additional costs for restaurants, convention facilities, and recreation areas may be determined separately and by other methods.
- *Systems.* The Construction Specifications Institute (CSI) *UniFormat*™ can be used as a cost guide format. *UniFormat*™ breaks down a facility into systems—such as substructure, shell, interiors, services, equipment and furnishings, special construction and demolition, sitework, and general. Each of these systems is priced so that a total for all systems pertaining to the facility can be determined.

Utility projects, highway development, and special projects such as waste processing may be estimated according to methods other than square foot or unit cost.

6.7.4 Contingencies

All estimating requires contingencies to account for the unquantifiable effects of unknowns, such as funding sources, weather, labor and material shortages, governmental and regulatory restrictions, and construction delays related to known and unknown geological conditions and the possible presence of hazardous materials. Budgets should include an escalation factor that relates to the time required to complete programming, design, procurement, and construction, as well as commissioning.

The accuracy of the project budget is affected by several important factors, some of which will be unknown during this project conception stage, when the initial budget is compiled. Therefore, the owner and A/E or adviser assisting with the budget should include contingencies to account for those unquantifiable factors. Some of the factors include:

- Economic climate at the time of bidding or negotiation. The number of other projects being bid in the local construction market will affect the availability of products, labor, and services required for the project.
- Environmental factors, including weather, transportation routes, and the condition of available infrastructures. Natural disasters can greatly affect both the labor market and availability of materials in specific areas of the country; these in turn can affect pricing throughout the adjoining geographic areas.
- Availability of and proximity to labor and services.
- Accuracy and completeness of information produced during preliminary studies and programming.
- Unknown and concealed project conditions, including unexpected subsurface conditions such as rock or unsuitable soils. This is especially important in remodeling/rehabilitation projects where the extent of concealed conditions is significant.

Contingencies are critical for schedule and budget preparation. They account for the possible influence of unknown factors to prevent disruption of subsequent budget or scheduling activities. The contingency factor can be as high as 20 percent during project conception, 15 percent during programming, and 3 to 10 percent during construction. The more thorough the preparation during project conception and the more that is known, the fewer the contingencies that will be required for the project's later stages. However, the experienced estimator never rules out the need for contingencies, regardless of the project stage.

6.8 | Setting the Scheduling

A well-prepared project schedule can make the difference between a project that progresses smoothly and one that is characterized by delays and other problems. It serves as a road map, plotting out a logical succession of steps, from which a series of smaller, more specific tasks emanates. It also serves as a script showing the interactions of key project participants.

Schedules must be reasonably accurate and contain a level of detail appropriate for each stage of the project life cycle. They must be easy to read and understood by all project participants. And they must reflect the owner's requirements by identifying project milestone dates, including the estimated time of preliminary studies, site acquisition, design, marketing the project, the selected commissioning process, procurement (bidding/negotiating/purchasing), construction, and occupancy.

A good schedule clearly identifies the owner's project delivery requirements and provides a tool for managing each stage. A/Es, design-builders, contractors, and construction managers can work with the owner in each stage of the project to refine the project schedule. The project schedule developed during project conception differs from the construction schedule. It is, first of all, substantially broader. The project schedule is first formulated during this conception stage and often contains tasks, such as programming, site studies and acquisition, design, and other activities that must be completed before the physical construction is begun. The schedule may then progress as much as a year beyond the project completion. The construction schedule is just one part of the overall project schedule, albeit an important part.

Precise milestone dates may not be possible to determine during project conception. When first developed, broad time blocks are represented. As project conception tasks are completed, dates may become clearer to the key participants and more detail may be added.

Other elements include milestones, which are important dates or accomplishments. The schedule is also separated into tasks, along with the duration of these tasks. The tasks may be divided into subtasks, or the series of steps required before a task may be completed. The timely preparation of contract documents, labor, relationships, and resources should also be included.

The overall project schedule must identify decisions to be made and milestones to be achieved at each project stage and the ramifications when the milestones are not met. Deliverables are tasked items or components, performed or provided, to complete project conception/design stages of the project. Deliverables allow milestones to be achieved, with timely decisions. The overall project schedule must identify the decisions to be reached and key deliverables at each critical project stage, and the potential effects when these milestones are not met. It should identify when the owner's decisions, actions, and approvals must be made and the time periods allotted for these. A/Es can assist the owner in producing a realistic project schedule, using experience and professional tools such as scheduling software that can add value and efficiency to the process. As with all other studies and tasks performed during project conception, the services of a specialist bring value to the project if the owner is not experienced with this type of activity.

Depending on project delivery method, milestones of a project schedule developed during project conception may include durations for:

- Predesign activities
- Site acquisition
- Project delivery and team selection processes, including requests for qualifications, interviews, and negotiation of agreements
- Design and construction documents, and deliverables required at completion of each phase and stage
- Approval processes such as plan review and permit, zoning approval, and approvals of other regulatory agencies
- Procurement (bidding/negotiating/purchasing) activities and construction contract award
- Construction-stage activities, including lead times for major activities components, systems, and subsystems
- Project commissioning activities
- Contract completion and occupancy activities

The following factors (among others) require the inclusion of scheduling contingencies to allow adjustments to the schedule without totally disrupting the concept or overall project duration:

- Discovery of new project information, including unexpected results of site investigations
- Changes in laws, regulations, and codes that affect design or construction

- Length of approval processes
- Social factors, such as labor strikes or political events
- Economic factors, such as the state of the economy, the prevailing lending rates, and availability of key products and components
- The effects of weather conditions

Schedules can be developed by a variety of approaches. One approach provides for the establishment of a required date of occupancy or use for the project, then identifying all preceding milestone dates by working backward from this date. This approach is utilized when the completion date is the most important scheduling criterion. Schools, universities, dormitories, retail complexes, and other time-critical or revenue-generating projects may be scheduled according to this method.

The alternative to the methods technique is the critical path method (CPM) approach to project scheduling. CPM determines activities that are dependent upon each other and the longest path for completion of those activities. In this approach, the schedule is dictated by the activities that are on the critical path to the completion date of the project. As the project progresses, those managing the schedule can compare actual versus predicted performance times for each step and adjust the rest of the schedule accordingly.

Chapter 7
Project Delivery

7.1 Influencing Factors

7.1.1 Introduction

All projects, from the simplest buildings to the most complex infrastructure work, require a number of specialized individuals, firms, and companies that participate in a vast array of complex activities to design and construct a project. The size of this group may be large or small, depending on the project type, size, and complexity.

7.1.2 The Nature of Project Delivery

Before discussing the nature of project delivery in detail, it is helpful to examine how project delivery is defined by other professional organizations.

7.1.2.1 American Institute of Architects (AIA)

The Architect's Handbook of Professional Practice, 14th edition, published by John Wiley & Sons in 2008, page 1000, defines project delivery as "… the method selected to allocate roles, responsibilities, risks, and rewards among the parties accomplishing the design, preparation of construction documents, construction, and management of a construction project."

7.1.2.2 The Associated General Contractors of America (AGC)

Project Delivery Systems for Construction, published by the Associated General Contractors of America in 2004, page 3, defines project delivery as "… the comprehensive process of assigning the contractual responsibilities for designing and constructing a project …" and "… is fundamentally a people method …" because the "… success or failure of any delivery method depends upon the performance, trust, and cooperation among the parties."

7.1.2.3 Integrated Project Delivery (IPD)

The AIA California Council has issued *Integrated Project Delivery—A Working Definition,* published by McGraw-Hill Construction, updated May 15, 2007, which defines project delivery as the "… approach that integrates people, systems, business structures and practices into a process that collaboratively harnesses the talents and insights of all participants to reduce waste and optimize efficiency through all phases of design, fabrication and construction."

7.1.2.4 Construction Specifications Institute (CSI)

Project delivery encompasses the contractual relationships necessary to establish a sequential process of design and construction activities that converts a conceptual idea into a completed and occupied facility. Project delivery can be accomplished by any of the following methods:

- Design-bid-build (D-B-B)
- Design-negotiate-build (D-N-B)
- Design-build (D-B)
- Construction management (CM)
- Owner-build (O-B)
- Integrated Project Delivery (IPD)

Competitive market forces frequently compel owners to select a project delivery method that will achieve a balance between the following factors to establish the quality of the project, as illustrated in Figure 7.1:

- Extent (scope)
- Cost (budget)
- Time (schedule)

These three factors comprise the essence of any contractual arrangement. How these are defined by the project priorities, as well as the owner's capacities are necessary for the owner to make an informed decision about which project delivery method to select. Selection of the project delivery method will also directly influence the nature and extent of the work required for the design and construction of the project, including the contracts among the participants.

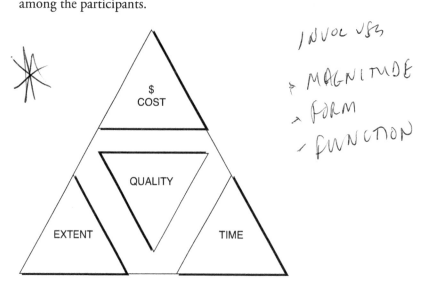

Figure 7.1

Cost, extent, and time factors affect the quality of a project, and influence which project delivery method is used.

7.1.3 Owner's Capability

There is a wide variety of experiences and qualifications that owners can have regarding the design and construction of a new project. The success of the delivery of a project depends heavily on the owner's having a good understanding of the many decisions required to direct and guide the design and construction process. Many factors determine if the owner has the experience, qualifications, and capability to handle the project, or whether the owner should take another course of action to ensure expectations are met. The owner's capabilities directly influence which project delivery method is selected.

The complexity of a project delivery method requires specialized knowledge. Having an intimate familiarity with the design and construction process is an important asset of an owner. Since the new facility will be for specific purposes of an owner, the owner is better than anyone for ensuring the project priorities are accomplished and their interests are protected, especially when the owner is assisted by design and construction professionals.

Owners experienced with one or more of the project delivery methods will be in a position to effectively direct, administer, and manage the complex delivery process. They will be aware of the importance of timely decisions and will be familiar with the implications and issues of the many process activities. A smooth process depends on managing those activities that are the responsibility of the owner and are important to the other participants in the process.

It is not unusual for owners that regularly build buildings to have entire departments devoted exclusively to the design and construction of new buildings and other facilities. It is common that the staffs of these departments are architects, engineers, or other design and construction professionals. In a few cases, the owners may be able to act as their own designer and contractor without requiring assistance.

For owners that build a project only occasionally, a lack of familiarity with the design and construction process will in all likelihood be a liability. Owners with little or no experience will either place their trust and protection of their interests in the design and construction professionals that participate in the delivery process, or will retain a construction management firm to assist with directing and administering the various stages, phases, and individual activities. Also, an owner with little or no experience may impede the process because of the decisions that are required or how to handle the issues that arise.

7.1.4 Extent of Work

The magnitude, form, function, and complexity of a project will have a direct bearing on the project delivery method and the number and role of the participants. Generally, the greater the magnitude of the project, the greater the number of participants, and the more the construction process is intensified. Small projects and projects of limited extent of work may involve only the owner, architect/engineer (A/E), and contractor. For example, for the construction of a small pedestrian bridge, the owner may rely solely on the services of an A/E and a contractor, or a design-builder, to complete the work. The A/E will probably not require the services of large numbers of consultants, perhaps only a landscape architect and a structural engineer. The contractor may do much of the skilled work using direct-hire employees rather than relying primarily on subcontractors to accomplish the work.

On large projects with a complex scope, large teams will be necessary to complete the design and construction. The A/E will have many consultants on the design team to complete the portion of the design within their area of expertise. The A/E will be required to carefully coordinate the work and the contributions from the different consultants. The contractor will require the services of many different subcontractors and suppliers. For example, a new performing arts facility will require a large, multidiscipline team for design and construction. Such a project will include not only the site and the structure, but also the interior spaces, performance facilities, sound systems, acoustics, lighting, seating, and public facilities. On projects with complex scopes of work or multiple-facility requirements, the services of multiple design and construction professionals may most likely be needed. Examples of such projects are a hospital, a multiple-structure manufacturing/process facility, or a campus-type facility for senior living, education, or business use.

7.1.5 Time

The commonly quoted and frequently used phrase "time is of the essence" expresses an important concept about establishing the time necessary for the design and construction of a project, and may be an overriding criterion for its completion. An equally quoted and used phrase that is often associated with it is "time is money." From the time an owner decides that a new facility is needed to the time occupants move in and start using the facility for its intended purpose, vast sums of money are expended with virtually no return on the investment because the facility is not available to the owner for use. In addition, many owners see the project delivery process as losing income for every day the new facility is not available for use. Consequently, time is of the essence for the owner because the time necessary for the design and construction of a project represents a significant cost to the owner.

The time necessary for a project is generally established by the owner in the project schedule developed during project conception. Construction contracts stipulate the amount of time for the completion of the construction between a notice to proceed to the date of substantial completion, which is usually expressed as a future date or a specific quantity of days. Days are usually defined in the conditions of the contract as calendar days. However, on certain projects, days might be defined as working days, which are weekdays, but excluding weekends, holidays, and special event days.

Completion of the construction is defined in the contract as beginning with "substantial completion" and ending with "final completion," which can create complications with multiple-prime or separate contracts. The need by owners to shorten the project duration for large or complex projects often results in the requirement for the construction work to begin prior to the completion of the design (see fast-track scheduling technique later in this chapter). The time required for project completion is dependent on the efficiencies utilized to sequence and schedule the work.

7.1.5.1 Sequencing

Not to be confused with scheduling, sequencing means performing one portion of the work prior to another portion in either a logical order or a predetermined order. For example, the design of a project is performed in a logical sequence, beginning with programming the project, conceptual design, schematic design, design development, procurement documents, construction documents, and ending with construction. The construction of a project also is conducted in a logical sequence, beginning with preparing the ground for construction, placing the foundation, erecting the structural frame, enclosing the structure with an exterior envelope, building out the interior spaces, and ending with taking occupancy.

In addition to sequencing normal construction activities, activities within and around existing facilities might require the portions of the work to be sequenced in a predetermined order. For example, in the case of improvements or additions to existing facilities, business operations and functions may need to be maintained while the new portion is under construction. This might require one portion of the work to be completed prior to another in order to relocate ongoing activities. Another example is for road widening or improvement projects where the entire road cannot be closed for an extended period. Work in and around existing facilities often requires relocation of existing functions to temporary locations and provisions for temporary utilities and support systems. Modifications of existing facilities often require protection of existing construction that will not be demolished, pedestrian protection, detours or other road traffic diversion, and other special sequence considerations. Most sequencing of projects will be accomplished during design, documentation, and construction stages; however, existing facilities might require careful consideration of project delivery methods to meet project requirements.

7.1.5.2 Scheduling

Not to be confused with sequencing, scheduling involves establishing time frames for activities by establishing starting and finishing dates for each activity. Significant dates are sometimes referred to as *milestones*. Determining the appropriate scheduling for a project may influence the decision for which method of project delivery should be selected.

If projects are not completed within the time frame designated for the work, the consequences can be onerous for all concerned.

- For the owner, it could mean decreased revenue from business lost because of a delay, additional rental expense to accommodate occupants longer than anticipated, or finding temporary space for occupants who cannot move into a new facility at the appropriate time.
- For the contractor, it may affect scheduled new work, the loss of early-completion incentive payments, paying liquidated damages to the owner, and damage to the contractor's business reputation for not completing the project on time.
- For the A/E, it may mean additional construction administration work, due to the extended period of time, until the work is completed, the cost of which may not be recovered.

In addition to a construction schedule, it is prudent to have a master project schedule that involves all stages of a project from conception through occupancy, and includes the variety of participants and their involvement in the project. This plan of activities illustrates the relationship of design and construction, as well as significant decisions that are involved with the project. The project schedule may include program development (owner's requirements), site acquisition, separate contracts for remedial measures such as hazardous materials removal, different design phases, and construction. Construction is usually separately scheduled, with its many activities, and should coordinate with the master project schedule to ensure completion within the time frame or by the dates established.

There are several types of schedules and usually they are presented graphically.

- The simplest form of a schedule is a Gantt Chart, which is a type of bar chart. A list of sequential activities is developed and listed vertically. Start dates, finish dates, and duration times are assigned to each activity and shown horizontally. The schedule is then articulated such that a continuous path can be traced through all activities and time frames. The simplicity or complexity of a Gantt Chart is determined by the number of activities that are developed and the level of detail in the time that is assigned to each.

- A more sophisticated scheduling technique is known as the critical path method (CPM). A computer-based schedule, CPM utilizes mathematically based algorithms to establish various types of relationships between activities and the dates when they start and stop. The goal is to establish the sequence of activities that constitutes the shortest path through all of the activities, which is identified as the critical path. If the work follows the critical path through the schedule, the work will be completed in the shortest amount of time.

7.1.5.3 Fast-Track Scheduling Technique

Fast-track is not a project delivery method by itself, but instead is a scheduling technique that, while it can be used with any project delivery method, is primarily used with the two construction management project delivery methods. Fast-track often utilizes the technique of separating work into multiple contracts based on project scheduling to ensure project completion in a condensed period of time. Fast-track is the process of overlapping activities to permit portions of construction to start prior to completion of the overall design. The project schedule may require that portions of the design and construction occur concurrently. For example, the lengthy process of site preparation, earthwork, and foundations may be under construction while the balance of the project design is being completed. With fast-track, the overall project cost may be difficult to determine, as certain portions may not be bid or contracted for until later in the project schedule. Adjustments to the contract amounts may be required as each portion of the design work is completed. The preparation of separate bid packages and contract documents for each additional portion of the work requires significant additional work and experience by the A/E.

The nature of fast-track is such that the A/E may be simultaneously involved in design, construction documents, development of contract packages, procurement (bidding/negotiating/purchasing), and contract administration. This multiplicity of activities and required staffing may add considerably to the cost of the A/E services. Figure 7.2 illustrates the overlapping activities of fast-track process.

In addition to preparing numerous contract packages, the A/E may also be required to review the detailed applications for payment from multiple contractors. Each contract package also requires coordination with adjacent or prior construction to ensure that nothing required for the complete installation of a product or system is omitted. This requirement of multiple contract packages adds to the responsibilities of the A/E, and a larger portion of construction document time is necessary than for an identical project for which the design is completed prior to obtaining construction contracts. In the D-B-B project delivery, the combined specification sections define the materials necessary for the entire project while the contractor determines the scope of subcontracts. In a fast-track project, the combined specification sections of each separate package describe the total project, and packages represent the individual extent of these intended contracts. The scope of work for each package needs to be determined. In order to monitor

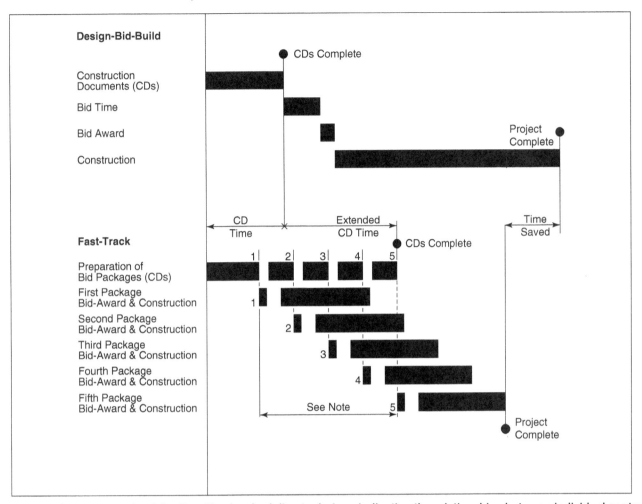

Figure 7.2 **An example of the Fast-Track scheduling technique indicating the relationships between individual contract document packages and individual construction activities.**

costs and keep the owner informed, the A/E, construction manager, or design-builder must periodically prepare and revise estimates of construction costs based on constantly changing design documentation.

When portions of the work are completed, subsequent changes to in-place construction may be unavoidable and, hence, more costly as modifications become necessary. For example, a fast-track project with a bid package for precast concrete must clearly indicate whether embedded items to attach to the adjacent construction are included in this or in another contract package. If embedded items are required, it may be necessary to include miscellaneous steel and other specification sections in addition to the precast concrete sections. The size and number of contract packages will vary depending on the size, scope, and type of project. There are several typical fast-track document packages:

- *Permit.* Documents required by the regulatory authorities to evaluate the project and issue permits
- *Demolition.* Removal of existing structures and materials that may interfere with the placement of new construction
- *Site Preparation.* Remedial work, site clearing, grading, excavation, sod and topsoil stockpiling, and other earthwork

- *Underground Utilities.* Water, sewerage, storm drainage, natural gas piping, as well as electrical and communications services on the site and below the facility
- *Civil.* Foundations such as piles or caissons, concrete forms, reinforcement, cast-in-place concrete, retaining walls, foundation drainage piping, and waterproofing.
- *Long Lead-Time Items.* Usually separate packages for elevators, escalators, chillers and boilers, transformers, switchgear and substations, or specialized equipment and systems.
- *Structural.* Structural steel, steel joists, load-bearing masonry, structural concrete, metal deck for concrete fill, concrete fill, and metal roof decks. Another package may include precast concrete columns, beams, and tees with concrete fill for decks and roofing
- *Exterior Envelope.* Curtain wall, storefront, window units, glazing, masonry, clapboarding, Portland cement plaster (stucco), exterior insulation finish system, precast architectural concrete, composite panels, skylights, roofing, joint treatments, flashings, weather barriers (air, water, and moisture), thermal insulation, and other related components
- *Mechanical.* Heating, ventilating, and air conditioning systems; fire protection systems; communications equipment; and controls
- *Plumbing and Fire Protection.* Hot and cold water piping and equipment, and sprinkler piping and equipment
- *Electrical.* Motors and generators, distribution systems, life safety systems, communications equipment, and controls
- *Communications.* Structured cabling and enclosure, and services for voice, data, audiovisual, fire safety, building controls, and nurse call
- *Interior Finishes.* Ornamental metal, carpentry, woodwork, cabinetry, partitions, floor tiles of various types, carpeting, ceilings, paint, wall covering, specialties, and other finish items
- *Landscaping.* Lawns and grasses, perennial plantings, trees, shrubs, irrigation systems, curbs, gutters, paving (walkway, parking, and drives), fountains, and site improvements such as benches and accessories
- *Security.* Control room furniture and equipment, access controls, sensors, and video surveillance
- *Furniture, Fixtures, and Fittings.* Desks, chairs, filing cabinets, beds, window treatments, wall decorations and sculpture, manufactured casework, rugs, and miscellaneous furnishings

The construction documents may have to be prepared in bursts of concentrated effort for each package instead of flowing from a natural design sequence. The time necessary to prepare contract packages for a project and to coordinate the interfaces of each is greater than typical preparation of all construction documents at one time. Additional time requirements are necessary for fast-track contracts. Allowances for these time increases should be made by including adequate professional service fees in the owner-A/E contract. Major items with large time impacts include the following:

- Extended contract document preparation due to fast-track multiple contract packages
- Reassembly of the separate packages into one coordinated set of contract documents
- Extensive preparation and coordination time for development of contracts, conditions of the contract, and Division 01—General Requirements for each separate contract
- Detailed review of multiple monthly applications for payments

The effort required of the A/E and owner for a fast-track project is greater with multiple contractors because it is administratively more complex, since simultaneous contract document production, procurement, and contract administration will occur during a large portion of the construction stage. Design development and changes during a fast-track project may affect long-lead-time items that have already been ordered or a part of the construction already in place. Design modifications may also affect multiple design phases. Due to the changing nature of design completion on fast-track projects, it is not unusual to have a greater number of requests for information and change orders than on a similar project where the design was completed prior to construction.

7.1.6 Cost of the Work

Contracts record the agreed-upon cost of the work and establish the basis of payment. A number of different methods are used for determining and stating amounts of cost or compensation within contracts. When a contract is bid or negotiated, the basis of payment that will be used in the contract is clearly stated in the procurement documents. When the contract is executed, the bid or negotiated basis of payment is included in the contract.

7.1.6.1 Stipulated/Lump Sum

A lump-sum price (sometimes called a *stipulated sum*) is an agreed amount for a described extent of work, based on complete or partially complete construction documents. This is the simplest method of stating the basis of payment wherein a single amount is agreed upon for completion of the entire contract. The principal advantage to the parties to the contract is that the amount is clearly established in advance.

7.1.6.2 Unit Price

Payment is made at a stipulated rate multiplied by the quantity completed. Unit prices are used in cases where the exact extent or quantity of work cannot be calculated accurately or otherwise determined in advance of actually performing the work. The unit price basis of payment is commonly used for civil engineering projects where the types of work, such as unsuitable soil or rock excavation, can be identified during the design of the project but the actual quantities of such work items can only be estimated. The types of work are divided into specific items with estimated quantities of each type. A cost per unit of work is established during the procurement (bid/negotiation) process for each identified type of work. The contract would then contain these established unit prices as the basis of payment. As the work is performed, the completed work is documented and verified with the contractor compensated only for actual quantities of completed work.

7.1.6.3 Cost Plus a Fee—Fixed Fee—Guaranteed Maximum Price

The cost-plus-a-fee basis of payment is usually used only with negotiated contracts. The contract calls for compensation for the actual cost of direct expenses, plus an additional fee for overhead and profit. The fee is usually a percentage of the direct expenses but also may be a fixed fee amount. In most cases, this type of contract also contains contract language that establishes a guaranteed maximum price (GMP). A GMP may be negotiated when the project design is in the early design phase, such as design development, and may be only sufficiently complete to allow adequate project definition. A contingency amount in the project budget should be included to allow for the inevitable changes and a resulting increase to the GMP. Schematic design or design development documents with "preliminary project descriptions" or "outline specifications" are not complete construction documents, and assumptions and omissions may occur during the negotiating (pricing) stage. The thoroughness of these suppositions is influenced by the contractor's prior experience and ability to forecast the undocumented items. The types of items that might lead to additional costs are usually details and specifics that are developed during the final completion of construction documents. Items that may be overlooked can include scheduled items such as finishes and details such as flashings and connections. These design refinements, if not considered initially by the contractor, may lead to claims of increased project costs along with an accompanying change to the GMP.

The cost-plus-fee arrangement provides significant control over such things as scheduling commitments and flexibility in such things as refinements, but also means that there is risk to the owner for the cost and final outcome of the project. The cost-plus-fee method also allows the entire team the opportunity to be involved in preconstruction budget and control of extent (scope). As the design of the project evolves to its final form, cost estimates can be refined and constructability reviewed. With contractor input, the design may be altered to maintain the project cost within the owner's budget.

The owner may try to control costs by negotiating the cost of the work plus a fee as a basis for payment. The fee may be a fixed fee or a percentage fee, and the project program may not yet be established. If the contractor has a percentage fee connected to the cost of construction, there may be little motivation to control construction costs since to do so will also reduce the fee. The owner may provide an incentive for cost control by including a shared savings clause in the owner-contractor contract. The owner is partially protected from excessive costs if the contract includes a shared savings clause. The contractor will usually establish a GMP that is somewhat higher than the estimated costs of construction in order to cover contingencies, since the estimated costs might be derived from incomplete construction documents. When the construction contract is based on a GMP with a fixed fee and a shared savings, the contractor will be encouraged to find ways to reduce construction costs. If the owner and contractor have a shared savings clause, the A/E can expect to review many product and system substitutions. The submittal review time for these shared savings may exceed the review time normally expected of a conventional construction project. A project with a shared savings clause obligates the A/E to spend more review time and possibly assume more liability, consequently reducing the A/E's own profit while helping the contractor make money and the owner save money. On most cost-plus contracts, the contractor is required to submit detailed supporting documentation with each application for payment. This may include receipts for materials, labor, equipment rental, and costs associated with administrative and procedural requirements.

7.1.6.4   Penalties, Bonuses, and Incentives

In addition to the basic elements of contracts, provisions are sometimes added to contracts to ensure completion in a timely manner. These provisions are important to emphasize that "time is of the essence" and to avoid compounding financial damage by the owner.

There are a number of different methods to encourage on-time completion. These contract clauses are employed in different ways and with varying results. They may be very effective if properly supported by all members of the project team.

A clause providing a penalty of a daily amount for not completing the work in the allotted time or by the agreed-upon date can be included in the contract. However, if there is a penalty clause in the contract, it is best accompanied by language that pays the contractor a bonus/incentive amount for early completion. Usually, the per-day amount for penalty and bonus/incentive are the same amount. The benefit of early completion may save financing charges and allow the owner earlier occupancy and leasing of retail or commercial space.

7.1.6.5 Shared Savings

A shared savings provision can be utilized to reduce initial costs and may be used with a GMP contract as an incentive for completing the project below the GMP contract price. With this form of "shared savings," the amount is made based on an agreed-upon portion, usually a percentage, of the difference between the original cost (stated or agreed) and the actual amount spent for the work. The savings are shared on a percentage basis between the parties to the contract. This incentive provision may require additional A/E fees to evaluate the proposed changes to the design and contract requirements.

7.1.6.6 Liquidated Damages

A delayed occupancy may extend interest financing charges, delay mortgage closing during a rising interest rate period, add rent to extend existing leased facilities, or delay income from leasing of project spaces.

Examples of situations resulting in liquidated damages include the following:

- A retail project that is not occupied for the holiday season, which is normally a very profitable time for retailers, may experience a substantial loss of income, or it may experience a delay in leasing by tenants, which is also a loss of income.
- Paving projects in the northern portions of the United States need to be completed early in November when the asphalt plants close due to cold weather conditions. Not completing the paving by this time may defer the work until the next paving season, with the added cost for contract administration work for both the owner and A/E.
- Not having classrooms ready for students at the beginning of the school year may mean relocation of students and teachers into temporary space, or delaying the opening of the school for a year, which could cause a significant loss of funds by a school district.

Liquidated damages are usually a fixed monetary amount per day, deducted from monies due the contractor for failure to substantially complete the work within a stipulated time or by a stated calendar date. Some form of documentation is desirable to substantiate the potential loss from delay of completion. If the amount for liquidated damages is not based on financial loss and is an excessive arbitrary amount, disproportionate to the value of the performance, it might be considered a penalty and become unenforceable. Penalties may be considered unreasonable if a dispute results from the claim of failure to complete. Other causes, such as unusual weather conditions, may create claims for change in the contract time. Projects constructed under multiple contracts do not lend themselves to the provisions of liquidated damages because of the difficulty in assessing the independent responsibility for time delays of several contracts. Liquidated damage clauses should not be confused with penalty clauses. The courts have stated that a penalty clause for delay is not enforceable unless there is also a bonus clause for early completion.

7.1.7 Methods of Delivering a Project

As indicated at the beginning of this chapter, there are six types of project delivery methods, each of which include a different mixture of contractual arrangements and processes that optimize the primary factors indicated previously. Understanding each delivery method requires an understanding of the roles of the stakeholders and participants, as well as their benefits and limitations. The decision to utilize a particular delivery method affects the participant relationships and how they will design and construct a project.

Project delivery requires significant decisions early in the facility life cycle. These decisions involve consideration of services, delivery methods, and participants to carry a project from conception to physical reality. Assembling the necessary participants and establishing the basis of contracts along with the elements of extent, time, and cost will determine the type of project delivery method to be utilized to accomplish the project. The project delivery method will define the relationships of the participants and their respective roles and responsibilities.

The owner's, A/E's, and contractor's capabilities and experience, along with the type of project, will affect the decision for the project delivery method. The selected project delivery method will determine how the project is designed, procured, and constructed. The subsequent stages of the project life cycle can be performed under individual contracts such as D-B-B or as a part of consolidated project delivery such as D-B. The requirements established during project conception can now be given to the project team to execute in a manner that will utilize the efficiencies of the selected project delivery method.

7.2 Design-Bid-Build

7.2.1 Introduction

As illustrated in Figure 7.3, the design-bid-build project delivery method, abbreviated as D-B-B, is the most traditional method of moving a project from its conception to its completion, and has the longest history of use. D-B-B is a linear sequence of activities generally occurring in the following order: project conception, design (including schematic design and design development), bidding and construction documents, competitive bidding, and then construction. The basis of D-B-B is twofold:

- The design and construction documents are completed prior to bidding and construction.
- The contractor is determined by selecting one of several bidders that have bid the work competitively.

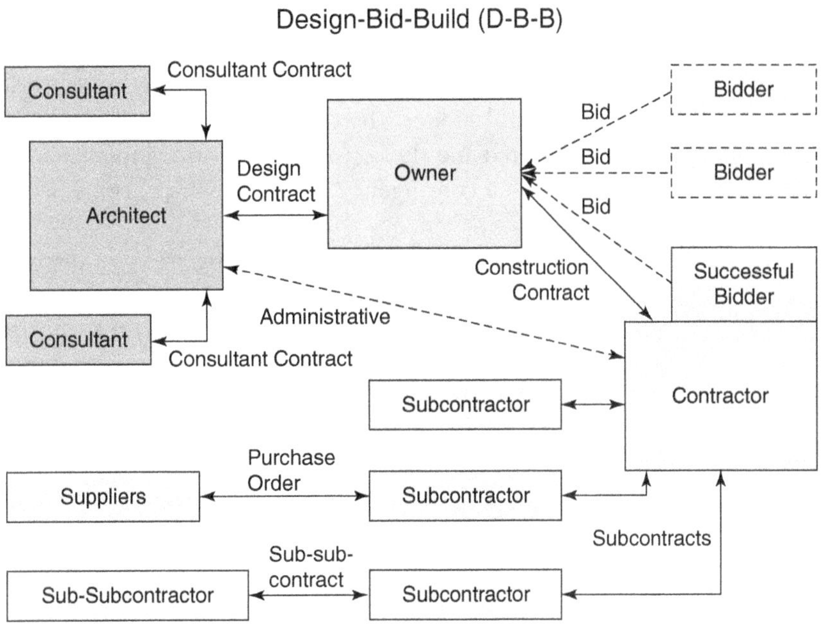

Design-Bid-Build (D-B-B)

Figure 7.3
The Design-Bid-Build (D-B-B) Project Delivery Method

7.2.2 The Nature of Competitive Bidding

Competitive bidding is the most effective method of determining the least cost for constructing the work that is described and defined by the bidding documents. Competitive bidding creates an environment where bidders at every level, contractor, subcontractor, and supplier, must carefully and seriously consider every aspect of their bid in the attempt to be awarded the work by providing a lower price than any of the other bidders. A bid states, or stipulates, the price the bidder will charge to perform the work (including overhead and profit) and may, if requested by the bidding documents, include the length of time required to complete the work.

The project design is developed and bidding documents prepared by the A/E for the owner that are then made available to bidders. There are two categories of bidders, and the owner generally determines which category should be used for a project:

- *Open Bidding.* Any interested bidder that has the experience and qualifications, if specified, may submit bids.
- *Closed Bidding.* Only those bidders that have been prequalified, preselected, or invited by the owner may submit bids.

In order for the bidding process to be equally fair and openly competitive among the various bidders, the process requires a specific set of rules for preparing and submitting a bid. Also, the process should include procedures for proposing substitutions and alternate product proposals.

Bids are confidentially prepared by each respective bidder and are submitted to the owner at a specified time, date, and place, after which the bids will be compared and evaluated. Unless there is a compelling reason to do otherwise, such as bid irregularities, the owner usually selects the most responsible bidder with the lowest price and whose bid is in conformance with the requirements of the bidding documents. Bids may be considered irregular for various reasons, including but not limited to bids containing incomplete information, bids improperly prepared, bids submitted after the required time and date, or bids with questionable information.

While the initial construction costs are established when the owner contracts with the successful bidder, the total costs cannot be known until all changes in the work are discovered and the contract is almost complete. To manage this risk, prudent owners establish a contingency amount to cover revisions, scope changes, or changed site conditions.

When the extent of work is contingent upon the funds available, certain provisions may be necessary to obtain costs for specific portions of the work. These portions of the work can be defined as alternates that will permit separate costs to be determined. After a project is bid, the extent of work can be adjusted based on the alternate bids and the owner's priorities. This process of alternate bids allows the owner to expand or contract the extent of work in order to align the cost with the funds available.

Finally, for projects that are time sensitive, bidders might also be required to compete and propose a construction schedule or a completion date.

7.2.3 Roles of the Stakeholders and Participants

The most basic relationship between the owner, the A/E, and the contractor is shown in Figure 5.1 and is known as the tripartite relationship. The tripartite relationship is first established by the owner-A/E contract and then, second, by the owner-contractor contract. While there is no contractual relationship between the A/E and the contractor, a third-party relationship is established between the two by the two contracts with the owner. For example, the owner-A/E usually specifies certain duties be performed by the A/E acting on behalf of the owner. The contractor has a right to rely on the proper performance of these duties. The A/E, similarly, relies on the contractor to perform certain duties identified in the owner-contractor contract.

7.2.3.1 Owner

As discussed in Chapter 2, the owner may be a private company, business, or individual, or it may be a public or governmental agency. The owner contracts first with an A/E to design the project and to prepare bidding documents. The owner then obtains bids through the competitive bidding process from bidding contractors. When one of the bidders is selected by the owner, the owner will either directly enter into the contract (such as for a project to be constructed with public funds), or negotiate the final cost and then enter into the contract (such as for a privately funded project).

7.2.3.2 A/E

Since D-B-B is the most traditional delivery method, the A/E usually provides full professional design services, the scope of which begins at project conception and includes schematic design, design development, construction documents, competitive bidding, and construction contract administration.

7.2.3.3 Contractor

The contractor is the bidder that has been selected and awarded the contract by the owner. The contractor provides construction project management to construct the project according to the contract documents and includes contracting with various specialty subcontractors and suppliers.

7.2.3.4 Subcontractors and Suppliers

To determine the price to bid, a bidder obtains subbids from specialty subcontractors and material suppliers that are based on respective portions of the bidding documents. When the owner enters into a contract with the selected bidder, that bidder becomes the contractor who then enters into individual subcontracts with specialty subcontractors and purchase orders with material suppliers. Subcontractors and suppliers then provide the required labor and materials to construct the project according to the contract documents. There being no contractual relationship between the A/E and the contractor, there is also no contractual relationship between the A/E and the subcontractors and suppliers.

7.2.3.5 Product Representatives

Product representatives can be a good resource to the owner, A/E, and contractor by providing accurate technical information about the products they represent. For those materials that benefit from or require the installers to be certified, approved, authorized, or otherwise acceptable, representatives can identify those that are so qualified. They can also assist those specialty subcontractors and material suppliers by ensuring their bids are properly based on their products that are specified.

7.2.4 Benefits of the Design-Bid-Build Method

The most significant advantage of D-B-B is that all participants in the design professions and construction industries are familiar with this method of delivering a project. Participant roles and responsibilities are well established, contract relationships are well understood, and conditions of the contract are similar from project to project. Familiarity with D-B-B promotes efficiencies in conceiving, designing, and constructing a project.

The owner is entitled to expect the contractor to construct the project for the cost that was bid and made the contract sum. Also, the contractor is entitled to expect the construction documents to be sufficient to accurately bid and construct the project. While this is true of every delivery method, it is especially true for D-B-B projects.

Project schedules are easier to establish because the various stages and phases of the project are easier to estimate since they do not overlap, as do other delivery methods.

An owner who does not have a staff with construction experience, qualifications, or the ability to bid and negotiate construction contracts might consider D-B-B as the most desirable delivery method. Boards of directors may require use of D-B-B to ensure that the lowest cost is obtained.

Competitive bidding is frequently required by public and governmental agencies to ensure that the taxpayer is paying a fair price for public facilities.

7.2.5 Limitations of the Design-Bid-Build Method

One of the primary disadvantages of D-B-B is "bid-day surprise" which occurs when all of the bids received exceed the owner's budget for the project. Should the owner decide to not immediately proceed with the project at a higher cost, significant time delays and additional costs will occur while the project is being redesigned and rebid. It is also possible that the project may be postponed or even canceled altogether.

The D-B-B is inherently adversarial by its very nature. Competitive bidding requires that a contractor bid as low as possible to obtain the work and still make a profit. Unfortunately, on occasions when market conditions are extremely competitive, bidders may be tempted to bid the project with little or no profit in order to survive as a business and maintain profitability by continuing to construct projects. In this scenario, the contractor may be motivated to extract as much profit from the project as possible by constantly seeking change orders.

Unlike the other delivery methods, contractors that bid and construct D-B-B projects cannot rely on the owner's carrying a contingency fund for scope of work inconsistencies that develop. Since it is not possible to prepare perfect construction documents or to perfectly bid the work, scope-of-work inconsistency problems develop when errors, discrepancies, omissions, and/or contradictory information are found in the construction documents or the contractors bids, which can lead to change orders, claims, and disputes. Just as competitive bidding provides the lowest cost, it also allows little margin for error. Every scope of work inconsistency can place an A/E firm or contractor in an unfortunate, difficult situation, where that firm will need to minimize any potential loss from that error.

Sometimes a bid for a D-B-B project may become a gamble when some unknowns are not considered. Some bidders may be tempted to bid a low price, knowing that there are unknowns, and then try to capitalize on the unknowns during construction for the purpose of making up the differences between the bid and the actual cost. D-B-B projects can result in a considerable number of requests for information and multiple changes. The shortness of the bid period forces everyone to respond quickly without proper consideration.

Just as the name implies, the competitive bidding process makes everyone an individual competitor and places participants on opposite sides of the playing field, which requires some form of refereeing. In the competitive bidding process, the A/E has a duty to administer the construction contract by contract.

Another limitation of D-B-B is that when the owner selects a bidder to be the contractor, the selection also includes accepting whichever subcontractors and suppliers the contractor intends to use. Also, the owner has no influence on how the contractor buys out the work or if the contractor engages in an unfair practice of "bid shopping" among the potential subcontractors and suppliers in the effort to improve the contractors profit. Unlike the other project delivery methods, the owner usually has no influence with how the contractor conducts construction project management.

7.2.6 Decision to Use the Design-Bid-Build Method

Public agencies are required by law (statutes at federal, state, and local levels of government) to be effective stewards of taxpayers' money and to obtain the best possible price for the project by utilizing the competitive bidding process. This process permits the cost of the project to be known before contracts are executed. To facilitate the bidding process, public agencies are obligated to establish an environment in which bidders can fairly and competitively compete for the work and protect the objectivity of the contract award process.

Historically, D-B-B has been the primary process of fulfilling these requirements and obligations on behalf of the taxpayers. Many projects have been successfully constructed for decades by this method. However, in some instances D-B-B is being replaced by one of the other project delivery methods that also utilize the competitive bidding process, such as the construction manager project delivery method.

When D-B-B is used, the A/E represents the owner, provides services throughout the project, and makes design decisions based on the project and the best interests of the owner. The contractor provides a completed project that complies with the contract documents for a stipulated price. The contractor cannot represent the owner because the contractor has interests that are different from owner.

A frequent reason for D-B-B is to obtain the contractor's bid for an early completion time. Bidding the time of completion or the construction schedule can be a consideration of the bid. The bid can also be conditional on time restrictions and a stipulated construction time period. This construction schedule may be subject to liquidated damages to ensure the project is completed on time.

7.3 Design-Negotiate-Build

7.3.1 Introduction

As illustrated in Figure 7.4, the design-negotiate-build project delivery method, abbreviated as D-N-B, is closely related to the design-bid-build project delivery method (D-B-B). They are similar in the following ways:

- The services provided by the A/E for the design and construction contract administration
- The construction project management services provided by the contractor

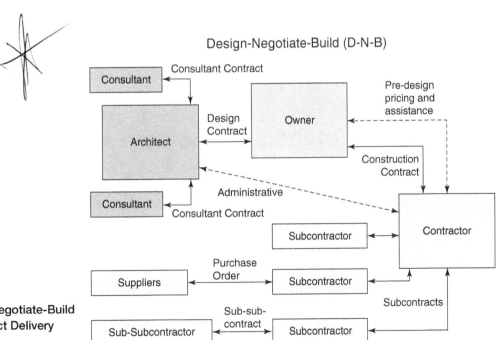

Figure 7.4
The Design-Negotiate-Build (D-N-B) Project Delivery Method

However, the following is more characteristic for D-N-B than D-B-B:

- The construction documents do not necessarily need to be completed before a cost is negotiated between the owner and the contractor.
- A specific set rules for preparing and submitting a bid is not necessary.
- Negotiating with a contractor is more informal than competitively bidding among several bidding contractors.
- Negotiating the work results in a less adversarial construction phase.
- How the contractor is selected.
- The manner in which the cost is determined.
- The owner is permitted to participate in the selection of the subcontractors and suppliers if desired.
- Negotiations are rarely used for public projects.

7.3.2 The Nature of Negotiations

When the owner and the contractor negotiate a construction contract, the goal is to achieve mutual benefits to each and to avoid the inherent risks of a competitive environment among contractors (however, competition still occurs between specialty subcontractors and material suppliers). The negotiated contract is based on a combination of factors, such as the following:

- Specific contractor expertise
- Project completion can be expedited
- How effectively construction costs can be controlled
- Project type
- Owner's capability or priorities
- Issues related to the construction process

It should be noted that an owner is not obligated to negotiate with only one contractor. An owner can actually negotiate a project with more than one contractor and then choose the one that is more responsive than the others.

7.3.3 Roles of the Stakeholders and Participants

For D-N-B, the roles of participants are slightly different from those for D-B-B. The various stakeholders and participants have more opportunity to discuss the project, or any aspect of the project, on a face-to-face basis and work toward informed, consensus decisions.

7.3.3.1 Owner

The owner will select a specific contractor and then negotiate the contract as the design and construction document process proceeds. Proper selection of the contractor is important for the optimum project results, and the owner must evaluate the risks pertaining to cost, extent, and time when negotiating.

7.3.3.2 A/E

The A/E usually provides full professional design services as for D-B-B project. Traditional bidding documents such as the invitation to bid, instructions to bidders, bid forms, and bid bonds are not usually necessary.

7.3.3.3 Contractor

The contractor is typically selected directly by the owner on the basis of the contractor's reputation, expertise, or a previously established working relationship. The selected contractor then can participate in the design process and can contribute to refinements of time schedules, cost estimates, and details.

The contractor can have influence over or even determine the scope of the bid/subcontract packages to expedite the construction process and to avoid disputes.

7.3.3.4 Subcontractors and Suppliers

Unlike D-B-B, the owner may choose to participate in the evaluation and selection of specialty subcontractors and material suppliers with the contractor. Like working with favored contractors, owners may want to work with favored subcontractors and suppliers as well.

7.3.3.5 Product Representatives

As with D-B-B, product representatives can be a good resource to the owner, A/E, and contractor.

7.3.4 Benefits of the Design-Negotiate-Build Method

There are numerous benefits of using a negotiated construction contract, because many aspects of the contract can be negotiated between the owner and the contractor.

The owner can select a contractor based on experience, expertise, and interest in the project, as well as reputation and financial capacity. Sometimes cost is not the primary consideration for selection. A contractor's history of successfully completing complex projects on time or early will usually mean an ultimate savings of time and money, along with the probability of better results.

In the process of negotiating with a contractor, the owner can work with the contractor to determine the scope of work that can be accomplished within the funds available. This refinement of the scope of work can frequently be determined with design development documents. Optional design schemes or documents can be prepared to establish alternate pricing. As the scope of work is finalized with preliminary estimates, construction documents can be prepared to determine the contract costs.

A construction contract can be negotiated at any time during the design process. Early participation by the contractor permits the A/E to benefit from the contractor's advice on constructability, emerging construction techniques, special materials and products, scheduling, and definition of bid/subcontract packages. The early addition of the contractor adds a dimension to the design process that provides a balance between cost, extent, and time. The contractor can periodically refine cost estimates to ensure that the project stays within budget. Value analysis may involve the use of negotiated substitute products or processes to reduce construction time or cost.

Early cooperation among A/E, contractor, and subcontractors may facilitate mutual product selections, choice of construction techniques, surveyed conditions, and mutual determinations of circumstances governing the work. This negotiation process allows concerned parties to have a better knowledge of the work necessary and clarifies ambiguities before preparing documents and contracts, thus resulting in more accurate costs.

7.3.5 Limitations of the Design-Negotiate-Build Method

One of the primary disadvantages of D-N-B is that the lowest cost may not be obtained due to the absence of competition because without bidding competition, the possibility exists for inflated prices.

Modifications to design documents may become change orders that affect time and cost. These modifications are sometimes referred to as *scope creep*. Change may lead to claims and disputes. The owner may not have expected cost increases even though the negotiated cost was established on partially completed construction documents.

D-N-B usually requires the use of contingency allowances for unforeseen circumstances due to the incomplete nature of the information available at the time of negotiations. If not spent, this contingency amount may be returned to the owner.

When a negotiated contract is based on partially complete construction documents, cost adjustments for unanticipated, unexpected, or newly completed aspects of the design may be requested by the contractor as the construction documents continue to be developed. Conflicts may ensue on apparent cost overruns because the negotiated price was established on incomplete information. What was included or excluded from the negotiated price is not always obvious. Scope of work that may have been typically detailed on the construction documents may not have been included in the negotiated price based on partially complete construction documents. The A/E might expect a contractor to intuitively anticipate and price the scope of work implied on partially complete construction documents but not actually shown. Without documentation, it may be unfair to assume the contractor would include the cost of this scope of work.

As cost oversights or assumptions become apparent, pressure may develop to reduce the construction cost by reducing aspects of the scope of work. What may be value analysis at another stage may be more like cost cutting at this stage.

Negotiated contracts may limit some responsibilities or may expand the effort required by others and may impact the cost required by others. Cost-saving incentives or value analysis may require considerably more review and research time by the A/E. Also, negotiated contracts that may limit A/E involvement in administration of the construction contract may be detrimental to the project. Multiple contracts can also require additional time for coordination, detailed progress payment reviews, and administration of these contracts.

Time constraints for contract package preparation are sometimes such that elements of surrounding construction can be easily overlooked. For example, a package for foundations might fail to include the requirements for installation of conduits, sleeves, and anchor bolts.

By negotiating contracts, the owner becomes financially committed to the project without knowing the final construction cost. Even with contingency allowances, there is a risk of financial loss if the owner becomes fiscally unable to complete the project.

When cost is given primary consideration, both extent and time may be compromised, which, in turn, will affect the cost. The owner accepts the risk of not knowing the final construction cost until the contract is almost complete. To manage this risk, some owners may elect to utilize the GMP approach. Negotiated contracts tend to encourage the owner to utilize "value analysis" and "constructability" reviews early in the design process.

7.3.6 Decision to Use the Design-Negotiate-Build Method

Privately funded projects for any type of new construction, renovation, alteration, or remodeling are candidates for negotiated contracts. Negotiated contracts are rarely used for publicly funded projects because laws requiring competitive bidding to protect the public interest prevent the start of construction before the final construction cost is known. An exception may be made, however, when project complexity limits the number of qualified bidders.

Negotiated contracts are intended to facilitate the construction of projects in the shortest possible time at the lowest cost. The stakeholders and participants would like to achieve all three of these objectives, but normally only two are possible. In negotiated contracts, construction quality and time are usually the primary considerations. Ultimate project costs may be reduced even though construction costs are typically increased. Negotiated contracts with a GMP can be beneficial if parties involved understand their roles and respect the roles of others. The key to successful negotiated contracts is finding the compromises needed to achieve balanced results and forging a cohesive relationship between the owner, the contractor, and the A/E.

Owners familiar with the construction process who desire to be active in the selection of materials and systems may want to consider negotiated contracts. Owners who have an understanding of the construction process may have the ability to negotiate with contractors to find alternatives that could result in cost savings.

In negotiating a contract, the owner may seek a contractor that is able to begin the project immediately and complete the project in the shortest time. In this situation, extent and time takes precedence over cost. Using a faster method of delivering the completed project may increase cost but will shorten the total time. The shortened time, in turn, may reduce the ultimate project cost because of savings of interim finance charges and increased income resulting from early use.

7.4 Construction Management

7.4.1 Introduction

Factors influencing the selection of a project delivery method include the experience and qualifications that the owner may or may not possess. It is prudent for an owner to be represented by knowledgeable professional expertise before proceeding with a project. This assistance can be provided by the construction management (CM) project delivery method.

7.4.2 The Nature of Construction Management

CM is the process of applying professional management expertise to a construction project for the purposes of managing the project extent, cost, and time. It is most often implemented on projects with complex schedules or budgets, those that require extensive coordination between disciplines, and those where the owner has limited expertise with regard to design and construction. Used appropriately, the additional fees paid by the owner to a construction manager are offset by removing the burden of oversight of complex projects from the owner or the owner's staff.

A construction manager is an individual frequently having a background as an architect, engineer, or contractor. Construction managers are granted differing degrees of authority by the owner, depending on how the project is organized and the contracts arranged.

CM can be used on private or public projects.

There are two variations of CM:

- Construction manager as agent or adviser (CMa)
- Construction manager as contractor (CMc)

7.4.3 The Nature of Construction Manager as Agent or Adviser

As illustrated in Figure 7.5, one variation of CM is when the construction manager serves as an agent or an adviser to the owner, and is characterized by the following:

- The role of the CMa is to advise the owner on the management of the design and construction of the project.
- Depending on the contractual arrangement, the CMa may or may not have the authority to represent and act on behalf of the owner.

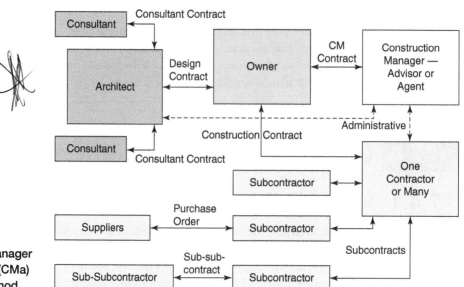

Figure 7.5

The Construction Manager as Agent or Advisor (CMa) Project Delivery Method

- The owner maintains direct contractual relationships with the A/E and either a single-prime contractor, or multiple-prime contractors (actually specialty subcontractors and material suppliers) depending on the project structure.
- The CMa does not bear financial risk for the design and construction.
- CMa may be used for any type of project but is most appropriate for owners who do not have the expertise or the time to manage a complex or difficult project.

7.4.4 The Nature of Construction Manager as Contractor

As illustrated in Figure 7.6, the other variation of CM is when the construction manager serves as, and bears the financial risk in the same manner as, a contractor.

The CMc consults with the A/E and owner, prepares a preliminary project schedule, makes recommendations for phased construction, prepares preliminary cost estimates, and, when documents are sufficiently complete, proposes a cost that is usually a GMP, and finally executes the construction as a contractor.

7.4.5 Roles of the Stakeholders and Participants

The construction manager's relationship with the owner is different from the relationship with either the A/E or the contractor and depends on whether the construction manager is performing the role of agent or adviser, or as a contractor at risk. The construction manager may provide professional management services throughout the project from the conception of design through postconstruction services, regardless of which type of CM the owner elects to utilize. As an advisor or agent, the construction manager is generally acting in that role earlier in the project than the construction manager would be in the

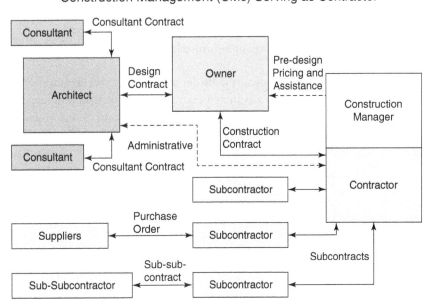

Figure 7.6

The Construction Manager as Contractor (CMc) Project Delivery Method

at-risk role. These services may include cost management, detailed estimating, constructability reviews, milestone and critical path scheduling, and value analysis.

7.4.5.1 Owner

Because the owner will contract with each prime contractor, the construction manager should review these contracts and make recommendations to the owner before the owner executes them.

The owner must establish budget and program requirements and convey this information to the construction manager.

7.4.5.2 A/E

The A/E is responsible for producing design and construction documents that comply with the owner's requirements and applicable codes and ordinances. The A/E services under CM are similar to those provided to an owner under D-B-B or D-N-B. These services include review of the owner's requirements, preparation of alternate designs, schematic design documents, design development documents, and construction documents. The A/E determines the design and selects materials consistent with the cost limitations set by the owner's requirements and budget. The construction manager may make recommendations during the design phases that influence the budget and ensure constructability. If the construction manager has budgetary oversight or control, these decisions may also influence the A/E's design.

CM may diminish the A/E's role, especially during construction. The following responsibilities may shift from the A/E to the CM:

- Prequalification of bidders
- Evaluating change orders
- Providing full-time on-site representation
- Processing applications for payment
- Providing interpretations of scope issues for each contract
- Preparing change documentation
- Resolving claims and avoiding disputes
- Communicating directly with the owner
- Processing submittals

Some owners consider shifting site representation from the A/E to the construction manager an advantage because of the construction manager's knowledge of construction. This also allows the A/E to concentrate on design issues, not construction issues.

The A/E should recognize and understand the additional time requirements necessary for CM projects and make allowance for these differences by including adequate professional service fees in the owner-A/E agreement. Major items with lengthy time requirements include the following:

- Extended contract document preparation time due to multiple bid packages
- Reassembly of these separate packages into one complete set of contract documents
- Preparation and coordination for the owner-A/E agreement, the owner-construction manager agreement, the conditions of the contract, and Division 01 sections of the specifications

- Extended substitution review time because of value analysis, which may include redesign to accommodate substituted items
- Detailed review of numerous monthly applications for payments on multiple-prime projects
- More complex submittal process

The administrative effort required of the A/E for a fast-track CM project is more complicated than for a conventional D-B-B or D-N-B projects because simultaneous contract document production, procurement, and contract administration will occur for a portion of the project life.

7.4.5.3 Construction Manager

The construction manager usually develops a CM plan, often consisting of the following items:

- Project description
- Milestone schedule
- Project schedule
- Project organization chart and staffing plan
- Explanation of roles, responsibilities, and authority of team members
- Reference to project procedures (i.e., documenting activities throughout the design and construction)
- Bid packaging, contract scoping, and contracting strategy
- Site mobilization and use plan

The construction manager manages quality assurance (QA) and quality control (QC) activities, including site observation and payment requests, and is responsible for ensuring that the completed project complies with the plan.

When the construction manager has responsibility for providing services that influence the design process, a conflict of interest may develop. For example, the construction manager may encourage use of an inexpensive product without the necessary performance characteristics. The relationship between the construction manager and the A/E is critical to a successful project. Mutual respect and open communication are necessary to allow each party to perform properly without duplicated effort.

7.4.5.4 Contractors

Companies that can be general contractors for D-B-B or D-N-B can be a single-prime contractor under CMc, but can also be one of multiple-prime contractors under CMa, depending on the contractual arrangements.

7.4.5.5 Subcontractors and Suppliers

Companies that can be specialty subcontractors and material suppliers for D-B-B or D-N-B can not only be a subcontractor for a single-prime contractor under CMc, but can also be one of multiple-prime contractors under CMa, depending on the contractual arrangements.

7.4.5.6 Product Representatives

Product representatives can be a good resource to the owner, A/E, and the construction manager by providing accurate technical information about the products they represent. For those materials that benefit from or require the installers to be certified, approved, authorized, or otherwise acceptable, representatives can identify those that are so qualified. And they can assist those specialty subcontractors and material suppliers by ensuring that their bids are properly based on their products that are specified.

7.4.6 Benefits of the Construction Management Method

CM projects are usually those involving multiple contracts, fast-tracking, or are of such a complex nature that intense professional management is necessary. Such projects usually require services beyond those the A/E generally provides through its basic services, and typically exceed the capability of the owner's staff. The use of CM and the respective contracts will most likely offset additional A/E fees and costs associated with developing bid packages.

The construction manager's knowledge of construction, systems cost, and scheduling is a good reason to involve the construction manager during the design phases. This allows the construction manager to influence product selections by providing information regarding costs, availability, and performance. The construction manager may also have helpful information regarding design and constructability of project elements, components, and details. Many CM entities are staffed with architects, engineers, contractors, estimators, value analysts, and other professionals knowledgeable about design and construction. Construction managers usually have particular expertise in the following areas:

- Coordination of construction
- Information management
- Cost management
- Time management
- Quality assurance
- Job-site safety

A construction manager can help reduce change orders and cost overruns by aiding communications among the parties, during the design and construction stages.

Assistance given to the A/E during design activities is another substantial benefit of CM. The A/E's design can benefit from information provided by those who will be responsible for construction. Because the construction manager usually monitors selection of products during the design, the construction manager may maintain budgetary control by initiating contracts for early purchase of materials and equipment.

When the construction manager has control of early purchase, construction progress schedules can be prepared with increased accuracy. The construction manager's expertise and participation can help achieve an effective design, by avoiding redesign, to meet budget requirements. Usually, the A/E is relieved of primary budgetary responsibility when the construction manager provides cost management. The construction manager's responsibility for complying with the budget should give the A/E some assurance that the A/E will not have to perform costly redesign.

CM by its very nature can be tailored to fit the needs of a particular project. CM's flexibility allows application of selected services required to supplement those already available to the owner through an in-house staff.

7.4.7 Limitations of the Construction Management Method

Projects that are small and simple in scope and contracted under a single stipulated sum are usually not suitable for CM. Also, projects that have little or no time constraints may not be appropriate. If an owner requires single-source responsibility or does not have time to devote to a construction project involving multiple phases or multiple contracts, then another type of project delivery method may be more appropriate.

The owner often pays a greater total amount for professional fees to the construction manager and A/E than would be paid on the same project where only an A/E and contractor are employed. Also, the selection and hiring process for a construction manager can increase the overall time frame for the project.

The additional level of authority resulting from the use of a construction manager requires communication, reporting, and other contract administration paperwork to be passed through the construction manager for processing and record keeping. An increase in these types of requirements can reduce overall contract administration efficiency and can be time consuming and expensive for the A/E and the contractor(s). These hidden cost increases are typically passed on to the owner through higher fees and prices.

The use of a construction manager may restrict direct communication between the owner and the A/E or contractor. This may result in the owner's having to compromise on some aspect of the design or constructed work. When using CM, the owner is relying heavily on the expertise and professional integrity of the construction manager, A/E, and contractor to deliver a project that will meet expectations.

When one party is advising the owner as well as constructing the project, the potential exists for conflicts of interest. The greater the financial stakes that one person has, the greater the potential for conflicts. When a CMc performs a portion of the work, the CMc assumes a direct financial interest in producing a profit on that portion of the work, which may not always be in the owner's best interest. The CMc may be reluctant to make changes that will directly influence its profitability.

7.4.8 Decision to Use the Construction Management Method

No specific rules determine when CM would be more beneficial than another delivery method. However, general factors to consider in the decision include the project's size and complexity, as well as economic considerations, including projected inflation and interest rates, short time schedules, and success of previous construction projects. When owners have critical needs to achieve project completion on time or have to achieve very ambitious project schedules, CM may be used beneficially. Conditions requiring project leadership not available from within the owner's staff are another reason for choosing CM.

The use of CM does not affect whether the contracts are bid or negotiated. Therefore, CM can be used in the private and public sectors. However, using CMa may be unacceptable for public work, as some governmental groups may not be allowed to delegate their fiscal duties to an agent. Also, some jurisdictions mandate that certain portions of a project, such as mechanical and electrical work, be bid separately. Such projects are likely work prospects for CM.

The following questions and issues should be considered before deciding to use CM:

- Does the project's complexity necessitate intense professional management?
- Does the owner have capable personnel to assign to the project?
- Are multiple contracts including several parties involved?
- Are long-lead items involved?
- Will using CM be cost effective, or will it add a layer of management that provides no significant value?
- Is there a need to reduce the risk of potential cost and schedule overruns?

Management of construction time is another reason for choosing CM. Events may be sequential; that is, contract documents are completed before construction begins. However, the fast-track method of scheduling is generally used. The fast-track scheduling encourages design decisions to be made and documented earlier in the process through the cooperative efforts of the project team, consisting of the owner, construction manager, A/E, and contractor. Fast-tracking creates an overlap in contract documentation and construction, with construction beginning before all contract documents are complete. Some projects may be divided into several contracts, each of which can be fast-tracked.

The decision to use CM should take into consideration the type of project, the owner's resources for preparing project requirements, the legal requirements in the area of the project, and the availability of construction managers. Construction managers provide benefits that some owners want, including specialized expertise during design, economy in cost and time, and maximized value of the finished project.

When the owner decides to use CM, the owner then must decide which form of CM meets its objectives: adviser or at-risk.

The roles of the parties involved in a CM contract should be carefully defined in their respective contracts. The capability of the owner's staff to respond to the issues involved should be closely evaluated. When an A/E or a contractor acts in a dual role, the potential for conflict exists and should be evaluated. CM firms are usually staffed with personnel from the design professions and the construction industry. This allows the construction managers to provide management services from project conception through construction stages of a project.

CM allows owners to control the project from beginning to end with a higher level of assurance that the project will be on time and within budget.

7.5 Design-Build

7.5.1 Introduction

Some owners, projects, and circumstances have unique requirements and need a more simplified contract arrangement. Selection of the design-build project delivery method, abbreviated as D-B, may be preferred because the owner can contract with a single entity to provide all the design and construction services necessary for a project as illustrated in Figure 7.7.

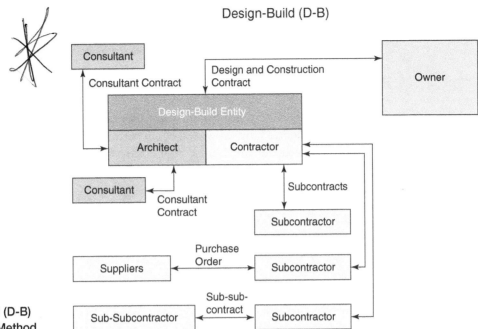

Design-Build (D-B)

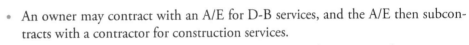

Figure 7.7
The Design-Build (D-B)
Project Delivery Method

7.5.2 The Nature of Design-Build

D-B entities exist in a variety of forms, depending on the type of firm that offers the primary services in the D-B entity. In each of the following D-B variations, the principles are similar:

- An owner may contract with an A/E for D-B services, and the A/E then subcontracts with a contractor for construction services.
- An A/E and a contractor may form a joint venture and contract with an owner to provide D-B services.
- An owner may contract with the contractor and then subcontract with an A/E for architectural and engineering services.
- A design-builder may be a single company capable of providing both design and construction services from the staff.

There are several ways an owner can utilize D-B; however, the process starts by the owner's preparing a project description of the performance-based requirements that establishes the required extent (scope), time (schedule), and cost (budget). How the project design is established is the principal difference in the several variations of D-B.

One way is when the owner contracts directly with a design-builder, who is then responsible for developing the design, providing the contract documents, and finally constructing the project.

A second way is when the owner wishes to have greater control over the design decisions of the project and engages a design A/E to create the project design and prepare schematic design documents, known as *bridging documents,* that become the basis of the contract with a D-B entity. The design A/E is not the "A/E of record" and is precluded from also being retained by the design-builder.

Third, some owners may be inclined to request competitive proposals for design and construction services from several D-B entities. To reduce the risks involved in competitive bidding, a modified selection process may be used that uses a combination of negotiations and competitive bidding. Initially, the owner prepares the project description, then requests proposals in two phases:

- *Phase I.* Usually requiring only minimal investment, a proposed project design and cost is submitted to the owner by each participating design-builder. The proposals are evaluated and either one design is selected or several designs are selected if the process is competitive. The preferred design, or designs, may not always provide the least initial cost, so value decisions may have to be made. The selection process may conclude in negotiations with each of the design-builders, or the process may continue to a second phase requiring more developed design and cost for each of the D-B proposals being considered.
- *Phase II.* The second phase can be time consuming and expensive for design-builders since only the selected design-builder will be fully compensated. To encourage participation, the owner may offer to pay a fee to cover all or part of the expenses involved in preparing second-phase proposals. Participating design-builders submit more developed versions of the design and cost selected in the first phase. Again, the proposals are evaluated and the owner makes a final selection and then negotiates the contract.

An additional feature of D-B is that other professional services can be offered that are in excess of the traditional design and construction services. Such services might include, but not be limited to, purchase and financing of the land, purchase and installation of specialized furnishings and equipment, building commissioning, and facility management. If these services are included in the D-B contract, then the contract could be considered a turnkey contract. Turnkey contracts mean that one entity provides all the services an owner needs to accomplish a new facility ready for occupancy and use.

While some public agencies continue to utilize D-B-B, many public and governmental agencies have turned to D-B as a more efficient way of obtaining new facilities. D-B fulfills the need for agencies to be stewards of taxpayers' money and obtain the best possible price for a project. Even when competitive bidding does not occur between design-builders, it occurs among specialty subcontractors and material suppliers for the purchase of materials and their installation in the project. Selection of firms providing D-B services for design and construction may not be subject to the same requirements as for competitively bid D-B-B contracts.

7.5.3 Role of the Stakeholders and Participants

D-B places the design-builder, including the A/E member, in a relationship with the owner that is similar to the relationship of a vendor with a purchaser: the design-builder agrees to provide a completed project that meets the owner's requirements for an agreed-upon price.

7.5.3.1 Owner

The owner is responsible for preparing a project description that establishes the required extent (scope), time (schedule), and cost (budget) upon which prospective design-builders can base their proposals or upon which a contract can be negotiated. For large projects, this can be a complex task, and the owner may elect to have the project description prepared by a separate entity, usually an architect or engineer. Many of the subjects that should be addressed in the project description reflect early design decisions made during the project conception and programming. At a minimum, the project description should include the following items:

- Project overview
- Project timing
- Performance program requirements
- Submittal, testing and inspection, substitution, and warranty requirements
- Environmental requirements and site information
- Proposal requirements
- Proposal evaluation criteria
- Contract type

After the D-B contract is awarded, the owner may be left out of many day-to-day decisions and will have less contact with project activities than in D-B-B. The owner should, however, be actively involved in the process unless an administrative professional, under a separate contract with the owner, provides these services for the owner. The design A/E may be retained by the owner to provide some of these services, such as oversight of QC/QA activities during design and construction and/or construction contract administration.

7.5.3.2 Design-Builder

The design-builder is responsible for providing a completed project that meets the owner's project description. QA and QC activities, including site observation, and payment requests are all managed by the design-builder with oversight by the owner or the owner's administrative professional. The combined activity of design and construction results in efficient project management since the process inherently ensures cooperation between the designer and the contractor.

7.5.3.3 Architect/Engineer

As previously mentioned, the A/E is not a representative of the owner because the A/E's services are performed in the interest of the design-builder and there is no contractual obligation or contractual relationship between the architect and the owner. The A/E services provided to the design-builder are similar to those provided to an owner using D-B-B. These services include review of the owner's project description, preparation of alternative designs, preparation of design documents, and preparation of construction documents. The A/E determines the design and selects materials consistent with the cost limitations set by the design-builder and the owner's project description and budget, and in compliance with applicable codes and ordinances. All communication with the owner is conducted through the design-builder.

The design-builder has final responsibility for the project design, not the A/E as under other project delivery methods.

7.5.3.4 Contractor

The contractor, as a member of the design-build entity, performs the construction work. The construction activities of the project include not only providing materials, labor, and equipment necessary to complete the work, but also control over the means, methods, and techniques necessary to complete the project. This means that the contractor lends the necessary skills to the D-B entity, including project management, subcontractor management, supervisory duties, and superintendence for the work.

Because the D-B entity provides a proposal to the owner for the project before the construction documents are complete, the contractor is heavily involved in the preconstruction activities. This input allows the contractor to provide construction experience, cost estimating, logistics, and other project management expertise to the design as it is developed. The contractor can also make suggestions during the design phases regarding materials and systems selections. Working together as part of the D-B entity, both the contractor and the A/E have an obligation to the owner to meet the project requirements.

The design-builder has final responsibility for the project construction, not the contractor as under other project delivery methods.

7.5.3.5 Subcontractors and Suppliers

Companies that can be specialty subcontractors and material suppliers for D-B-B or D-N-B can not only be a subcontractor for D-B, but can also be prime contractors depending on the contractual arrangements.

7.5.3.6 Product Representatives

The design-builder determines the most economical and efficient materials and methods to produce a project complying with established requirements. The product representative should work closely with the D-B and the A/E to offer products that fit the project description established by the owner.

7.5.4 Benefits of the Design-Build Method

The primary benefit to the owner is that a single entity is responsible for design and construction. The single-contract arrangement also offers more control over project timing and costs. Fast-track scheduling is an available option for minimizing construction time and the design-builder is able to maximize the value of the project by fulfilling the project description in the shortest time for the least cost.

Because of the close coordination between the A/E and contractor during the design phases, the contractor can influence product selections by providing information regarding cost, availability, and performance. The design-builder may also have specialized information regarding design and constructability of project elements, components, and details. Examples include:

- Structural systems (e.g., using a precast concrete system may avoid the cold-weather delays of cast-in-place concrete)
- Exterior wall component supports (e.g., panelized components may save expensive field labor)
- Details involving multiple trades

Design-builders usually specialize in particular types of projects, such as institutional facilities, manufacturing facilities, utilities, speculative offices, or warehouses, where their construction experience is a significant factor. Design-builders provide benefits that some owners desire, including specialized expertise during design, economy in cost and time, and maximized value of the finished project.

7.5.5 Limitations of the Design-Build Method

Preparation of the project description may be a difficult task for the owner. If the project requirements are complex and the owner does not have in-house staff familiar with construction projects, a third party may be needed to assist the owner.

Because the A/E is working for the design-builder, the owner should not expect the same level of professional service to protect the owner's interest as normally performed during a conventionally delivered project. Some owners engage the services of an administrative professional to act in the owner's interest.

Since the design-builder is creating the project design, the extent of documentation may not be the same (e.g., specifications may be replaced by manufacturer's data sheets). The design-builder usually will not perform any services not required by the owner's project description. Items normally taken for granted, such as shop drawings, product data, samples, testing and inspection, and extended warranties, may not be provided to the owner at all if not required by codes and regulations or by the owner's project description.

If not stated otherwise in the project description, material selections are usually left to the design-builder. If the owner wants to change a material or upgrade the design, a change order will likely be necessary. The owner's project description should clearly indicate necessary submittals, including the design documentation, as well as QA/QC submittals such as shop drawings, samples, testing and inspection, extended warranties, and product requirements.

D-B contract administration requires attentive management on the part of the owner. Although the design-builder is responsible for site administration and verification that the materials and products are included as specified, the owner may employ a separate administrative professional to monitor the project during the construction stage. The owner's administrative professional may perform such activities as submittal review, site observation, payment request assistance, and determination of compliance with the contract.

Dispute resolution may require more of the owner's time. In D-B-B, the A/E, as a representative of the owner, maintains records of project administration, which are valuable in helping to resolve disputes when they arise. The owner in a D-B situation should also maintain such records for use if disputes arise.

The design-builder may have increased risk due to expanded roles in design and construction. In a stipulated sum contract between the owner and design-builder, the design-builder bears the risk of design and construction cost increases. The design-builder has made assurances to the owner that the work will meet the owner's project description, which usually includes limitation on contract sum and time. Any errors, discrepancies, omissions, and/or contradictory information in the contract documents also become a liability of the design-builder.

7.5.6 Decision to Use the Design-Build Method

The most important benefit to the owner is the single point of accountability that a single contract offers. Having a single contract also improves coordination between design and construction. Any type of project may be a candidate for D-B; however, these projects are usually those with reasonably predictable project requirements that the owner is able to describe clearly and completely.

D-B is used primarily where contracts can be negotiated. Legal requirements influencing the decision to use D-B include the existence of state licensing laws permitting such entities to be formed. In most states, both the contractor and the A/E must be licensed to perform their respective services. The decision to use D-B should consider the availability of qualified design-builders for the project.

The roles of the parties involved in a D-B contract should be carefully defined in the contract. The owner's loss of a direct relationship with the A/E and reduced contact with construction activities should be evaluated and possibly offset by employing an administrative professional to act as the owner's representative.

7.6 Owner-Build

7.6.1 Introduction

Some large-scale real estate developers and private companies that have experienced and qualified on-staff professionals may construct projects without retaining an independent contractor or construction manager according to the owner-build project delivery method, abbreviated as O-B, as illustrated in Figure 7.8. Alternately, other owners may contract with independent A/E firms to provide a full range of design and contract administration services.

7.6.2 The Nature of Owner-Build

When constructing a project by the O-B project delivery method, the owner is involved in each and every aspect of construction contracting for each and every portion of the

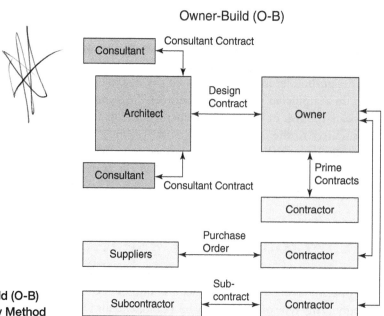

Figure 7.8

The Owner-Build (O-B) Project Delivery Method

project. Similar to CMc, the owner does not retain another entity to provide construction services. The construction contracts are executed directly between the owner and companies that are traditionally specialty subcontractors and material suppliers but become multiple-prime contractors under this delivery method.

O-B is not a viable option for public and governing agencies.

7.6.3 Roles of the Stakeholders and Participants

The owner exercises direct control of the project. Whether or not the owner hires an A/E to design the project and prepare the construction documents, there is no obligation for the O-B to adhere to the construction documents, except as required by authorities having jurisdiction.

Even though it is in the best interest of the owner to get the approval of the A/E for any changes or deviation from the design, there is no contractual requirement to do so. Not involving the A/E in changes or deviations can lead to liability and violation of professional licensing laws. Also, the owner may perform the duties that the contractor would otherwise perform. This means that the owner is also responsible for the means, methods, and techniques used to complete the work. The O-B project delivery provides the greatest possible control over the project by an owner. It also exposes the owner to the greatest risk.

7.6.3.1 Owner

The professional experience, qualifications, and expertise of the owner is the key to the successful use of O-B. Since the owner acts in the role of contractor, the owner must have the in-house capability to perform all of the duties that normally are the responsibility of the contractor. Broadly, these duties include project management, contract administration, and materials purchasing. O-B is normally used only by large developers and owners with large numbers of facilities and an ongoing capital construction program. Owners in these situations can benefit from having a staff of construction professionals in their direct employ, to take on the risk and responsibility required by O-B.

Some owners also have in-house capability for design services and may have architects, engineers, and drafters/technicians in their direct employ. In this case, the design of the project and the preparation of the construction documents are done by the owner's own design staff. However, many local regulatory jurisdictions may require that the construction documents be approved and stamped by an A/E licensed in the state before a permit can be issued. This is deemed necessary because A/E firms from outside the area may not be familiar with specific local conditions for certain critical elements such as foundation or roof design. In this case, the owner must hire a local A/E firm to assist with the design. Also, local A/E firms often provide the site adaptation to an existing design. For example, the owner of a group of chain stores may want to use the same design for all stores. The owner may hire a local A/E to adapt a previously completed project design for the specific site or local area where the new store will be constructed.

The owner, despite acting as a contractor, may not have all of the equipment, direct labor, or other essential elements that are usually associated with contractors. This means that the proper general support may not be able to be provided for the project. For example, minor work items that are not specifically made a part of a specialty contractor's work may be problematic for the owner to accomplish. This includes such work as periodic and final cleaning, trash removal, minor punch list work, expediting, and other miscellaneous work items that are inevitably a part of the project.

The owner must carefully determine how the tasks that are specified in Division 01—General Requirements of the project manual will be accomplished. Tasks such as traffic control, temporary utilities and other temporary facilities, employee parking, testing, and inspections are normally the responsibility of the contractor on a conventional project. The owner must require that these tasks become the responsibility of the individual specialty contractors or be accomplished by other means.

7.6.3.2 Architect/Engineer

When the owner hires an independent A/E, the A/E may provide the same services related to design of any other project. However, in most instances the owner will handle procurement and construction with little involvement of the A/E. Since the owner performs the role of the owner and the contractor, there may or may not be a need for A/E services during the procurement process and the construction stage. For example, the owner will determine the number of contractors (actually specialty subcontractors and material suppliers) and whether the contracts will be bid or negotiated. The A/E may or may not be involved in the preparation of the bid/subcontractor packages for the owner. Since the owner has control of the award of the construction contracts, the contract award may be based on low bid price or on the owner's own subjective internal criteria.

The A/E may have limited responsibilities under O-B and not include construction contract administration. Under these situations, consideration of the hold harmless clauses would be advised.

Whether or not the A/E is hired to provide construction administration services for the owner, the A/E will usually be required to serve as the interpreter of the design during the construction stage. Requests for information will be routed to the A/E, and the A/E will be required to provide the necessary responses throughout the construction stage. If the A/E firm is hired to provide construction administration services, these services would usually include construction evaluation, response to change order requests, decisions on claims, and conducting substantial and final inspections.

7.6.3.3 Contractors

The contractors who are awarded work under O-B are usually specialty subcontractors and material suppliers and are responsible for a specific portion of the project work that falls within their area of expertise. Since these contractors are in direct contract with the owner, they are technically not considered subcontractors but are actually prime contractors. Payment for work completed, including progress payments and final payment, is issued directly to the contractors from the owner.

Under O-B, the contractors assume a more expanded role in the project than they would in a typical role as a subcontractor to a prime contractor on a conventional project. For example, the contractors may be required to provide all of their own equipment, which is often provided by a prime contractor on a conventional project. This can include such items as forklifts for material staging and handling, man-lift equipment, scaffolding, trash containers, and other general use items.

7.6.3.4 Subcontractors

Companies that can be specialty subcontractors for D-B-B or D-N-B are prime contractors under O-B.

7.6.3.5 Product Representatives

An owner-build project is, by its very nature, a specialized facility and is directly related to the owner's operations. A product that provides unique long-term benefits or is particularly suited to the owner's operations could be an opportunity to establish an ongoing relationship resulting in future sales. A product representative can provide data on specific features, budgetary information, availability, and other data that can become a part of the owner's standards.

7.6.4 Benefits of the Owner-Build Method

One of the primary benefits of O-B is that the owner can achieve a cost savings by performing the duties that the contractor would for other delivery methods. The ability to actually realize these cost savings depends on a number of factors:

- The owner must have the experience and expertise in-house to successfully perform all of the duties of a contractor.
- The owner must have the financial backing to absorb the risk of problems or other losses that may develop during construction.
- Since the owner relies so heavily on the specialty contractors hired to work on the project, the owner must establish mutually beneficial business relationships with these contractors to effectively and efficiently complete projects.

Another benefit of O-B is control over the project, particularly during the construction stage. For example, under D-B-B, any changes to the work that affect the contract sum or time must be negotiated with the contractor to the satisfaction of the owner and the A/E. Under O-B, changes are negotiated directly with the multiple contractors and can be implemented at any time, since the owner functions as both the contractor and the owner. This provides the owner with significant flexibility and control over the project outcome.

7.6.5 Limitations of the Owner-Build Method

The primary limitation of O-B is the significant risk assumed by the owner. The control of the project afforded to the owner by functioning as the contractor also transfers much of the risk for project completion and quality to the owner. On D-B-B projects, in order to allay the primary risk of not being able to complete the project, the contractor is often required to provide performance and payment bonding. The owner may require any contractor to provide performance and payment bonds for its portion of the work; however, this does not mean that the entire project is bonded.

Another substantial limitation of O-B occurs when the owner also performs the design work in-house. Hence, there is no recourse for errors, discrepancies, or omissions from the construction documents. When the owner hires an independent A/E, there is the benefit to the project of having an experienced, licensed, and insured A/E completing the design and construction documents. The owner can select an A/E with a successful record of project design work for projects of the same type, complexity, and character as the owner's planned project.

Also, owners do not normally have employees who function to provide direct labor for the project, as contractors do. This means that each contractor must accomplish all of the work on the project, including mobilization/demobilization, provision of all of the tools and equipment necessary to complete the work, and other administrative and procedural requirements that are usually provided by a contractor.

7.6.6 Decision to Use the Owner-Build Method

As previously stated, most owners that participate in O-B are large corporate entities and contractor-developers who do large-scale development or housing projects. They may also be owners with a large numbers of built facilities and an ongoing capital construction program. This usually means that owners are engaged in constructing projects that are similar in nature. Examples include the following:

- An organization that builds and operates nationwide stores or franchised operations such as gas stations or fast-food outlets
- A large manufacturing company that builds a number of manufacturing plants in several locations
- A restaurant chain that builds the same or similar buildings over and over in many different locations

7.7 Integrated Project Delivery

7.7.1 Introduction

A study of the history of the design and construction of facilities in the United States reveal that the evolution of project delivery methods is a logical progression of sophistication that parallels the increase in complexity of facilities as can be seen by the arranged order of the project delivery methods in this chapter. In the past, designs were much simpler, there were far fewer individual building products and systems, and most of the construction work that was performed was based on verbal descriptions and handshake agreements with constructors that were masters of their craft. For many projects, there were very few graphic or written documents such as contracts, conditions, drawings, specifications, or submittals.

As design and construction began to become more involved, and activities and facilities increased in sophistication, the need for graphic and written documentation began to develop. The increase in complexity in relationships fostered the need for more formalized contracts and conditions. The D-B-B project delivery method became the first widely accepted and employed method of delivering a project. After a time, experienced owners started negotiating construction contracts with contractors to control costs and to have greater influence in the construction process. As contractual relationships, process management, and schedules continued to grow in complexity, professional management expertise became important. Thus was born the construction management project delivery method.

In the years when the D-B-B and D-N-B project delivery methods were dominant, the design and construction aspects were separate activities. As the construction management project delivery method evolved, the lines between design and construction began to blur. Construction professionals began to participate in the design process, and subcontractors began to produce more detailed shop drawings that supplemented the graphic and written documents produced by the design team. The assumption of design responsibility by the construction industry became the basis of the development of the D-B project delivery method and the similar O-B project delivery method.

At the beginning of the new millennium, the design and construction of facilities reached a more complex and sophisticated state that is characterized by many of the following aspects:

- Facility designs that involve a considerable number of functional relationships and a vast variety of building products, materials, and systems that require a larger number of specialty suppliers and installers
- An increased number of specialty design professionals to supplement architects and engineers
- Scheduling techniques and software that facilitated a reduction of the time between project conception and occupancy
- The need for professional management expertise to control, direct, and monitor the many diverse parts of the project delivery process
- Large projects involving hundreds of millions of dollars

Because of these and many other characteristics, the progression of project delivery methods has evolved into the Integrated Project Delivery (IPD) method. In its simplest form, a project delivery method is reducible to two groups of individuals and companies: those that decide, design, and determine, and those that supply, construct, and install. The operative component in IPD is the integration of these two broad activities to capitalize on the unique contributions each individual and company can make to the delivery process.

7.7.2 The Nature of Integrated Project Delivery

IPD is anticipated by many as the delivery method that will transform the way future projects are conceived, designed, documented, constructed, and operated. IPD is driven by a belief that effective solutions can be found for the following project delivery problems:

- Insufficient collaboration among stakeholders and participants
- Design, construction, and delivery of projects that is not fast enough
- Excessive cost overruns
- Facilities that are not sustainable
- Reduction of construction waste
- Design and construction errors
- Conflicting goals and interests among stakeholders and participants
- Construction schedules that take too long or are extended
- Project objectives, design, fabrication, construction, and operations information isolated among the stakeholders and participants and not mutually shared

One of the first working definitions of IPD was proposed by the AIA California Council and is included in a publication called *A Working Definition—Integrated Project Delivery*, Version 2, dated June 13, 2007:

> Integrated Project Delivery (IPD) is a project delivery approach that integrates people, systems, business structures and practices into a process that collaboratively harnesses the talents and insights of all participants to optimize project results, increase value to the owner, reduce waste, and maximize efficiency through all phases of design, fabrication, and construction. [Refer to Figure 7.9.]

The AIA California Council proposed that the flow of an IPD project from conceptualization through implementation to occupancy differs from other project delivery methods, as illustrated in Figure 7.10. That process is based on the premise of moving design decisions forward in time as much as possible that was proposed in 2004 by HOK CEO Patrick MacLeamy. This idea is graphically shown in the MacLeamy Curve, Figure 7.11, that was introduced in the Construction Users Roundtable's *Collaboration, Integrated Information, and the Project Lifecycle in Building Design, Construction and Operation* (CURT WP-1202, August, 2004).

IPD has energized the design and construction professions and industries in the common goal of developing the most optimized method of designing and constructing a project. The converging of technological advancements, risk management, leveraging of

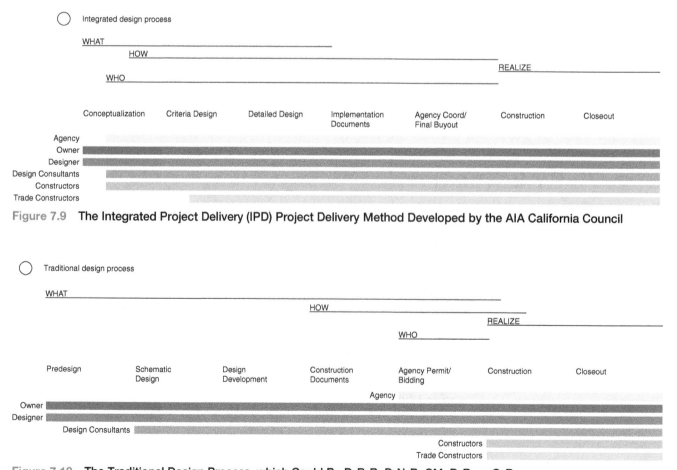

Figure 7.9   The Integrated Project Delivery (IPD) Project Delivery Method Developed by the AIA California Council

Figure 7.10   The Traditional Design Process, which Could Be D-B-B, D-N-B, CM, D-B, or O-B

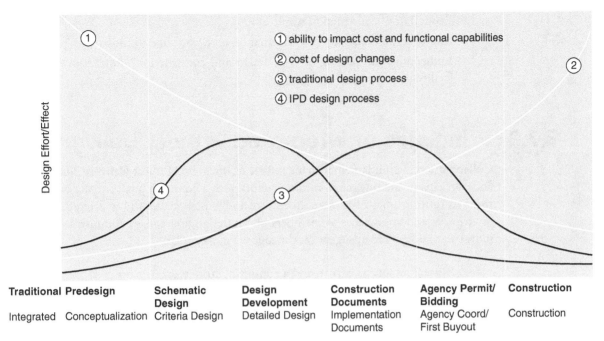

① ability to impact cost and functional capabilities
② cost of design changes
③ traditional design process
④ IPD design process

Design Effort/Effect

Traditional	Predesign	Schematic Design	Design Development	Construction Documents	Agency Permit/ Bidding	Construction
Integrated	Conceptualization	Criteria Design	Detailed Design	Implementation Documents	Agency Coord/ First Buyout	Construction

Figure 7.11
MacLeamy Curve

knowledge during the process, evolving business models, changes in the design professions, collaboration techniques, and owner demands are combining to force a more efficient method of delivering a project. The AIA has pioneered an entire family of contract forms specifically tailored for IPD.

One of the core elements around which IPD is structured is the technological development of Building Information Modeling (BIM), which is the basis of how design and construction documents should be prepared and used. BIM is also defined by *A Working Definition—Integrated Project Delivery* as the following:

> A Building Information Model, or BIM, utilizes cutting edge digital technology to establish a computable representation of all the physical and functional characteristics of a facility and its related project/life-cycle information, and is intended to be a repository of information for the facility owner/operator to use and maintain throughout the lifecycle of a facility.

In "Optimize BIM to Achieve the Promise of Integrated Project Delivery," a paper authored by Forrest R. Lott, AIA LEED AP, dated June 25, 2008, BIM is seen as a promise to fuel IPD for success by being "a digital representation of the building process," that "facilitates exchange and interoperability of information throughout the life cycle of a building" that benefits the design and construction process in the following ways:

- A better understanding of the design with a greater design option evaluation
- Improved visualization of the facility before it becomes a project
- Detection and resolution of conflicts between building components
- Increased coordination of construction documentation
- Greater prefabrication opportunities
- Optimized site utilization
- Efficiently scheduled delivery of product, materials, and equipment

- Reduction of construction waste
- Improved predictability of performance, cost, and time to construct
- Embedding and linking of vital design and construction information for use in facility management

7.7.3 Principles of Integrated Project Delivery

Collaboration is a fundamental characteristic of Integrated Project Delivery. Stakeholders and participants are integrated into one effort with a common goal, and are encouraged to focus on outcomes of projects instead of individual goals. IPD will require changes in attitudes and approaches of members of the design and construction professions and industries. Success is contingent on the following principles:

- Mutual respect and trust, and a commitment to work as a team
- Mutual benefit and reward, and because of early involvement, compensation based on the value added and what's best for the project
- The free exchange of ideas, decisions, and innovation, which are judged on their merits by the team
- Influx of knowledge and expertise in the early formative stages of projects to capitalize on informed decisions
- Project goals that are developed early and agreed upon by the team
- Recognition that intensified planning results in efficiency and savings during execution
- Open, direct, and honest communications among team members in a no-blame culture and the resolution of problems rather than determination of liability
- Reliance on cutting-edge technologies to maximize functionality and interoperability
- Team structure and leadership appropriate for the project that makes a commitment to the team's goals and values

Chapter 8
Design

Introduction

At the conclusion of the project conception stage, a project delivery method is determined, and a design team is selected by the owner. The owner provides the initial program and other relevant information to the design team, marking the beginning of the design stage of the project. From this point forward, a variety of stakeholders and participants will become part of the decision-making process, each providing services and information that will shape the character of the project.

Design is the arrangement of project elements and components, expressed in graphic and written documents, responding to:

- The owner's program, requirements, and budget
- Requirements of authorities having jurisdiction (AHJs)
- Climate and conditions at the site
- Suitability of available products
- The owner's functional, aesthetic, and sustainability requirements

The processes of design convert the owner's program into documents that allow stakeholders and participants to perform their roles, responsibilities, and activities related to the project.

During design, the design team, through interaction with other stakeholders and participants, will:

- Study the owner's program and related data produced during the project conception stage.
- Research the applicable requirements of AHJs.
- Propose solutions to satisfy the owner's and AHJs' requirements.
- Develop various forms of graphic documentation, artistic renderings, computer renderings, drawings, walk-through or fly-through computer videos, Building Information Modeling (BIM) models, and scale models to communicate the design that best satisfies the requirements and enhances understanding of the design intent by stakeholders and participants.
- Obtain product information.
- Incorporate project systems and assemblies into the design.
- Develop written documents to detail the technical aspects of the design, including preliminary project descriptions (PPDs) or outline specifications.

- Estimate project construction cost.
- Obtain the owner's approval at each phase of the design process.

The responsibilities of the participants in the design team are determined by the project delivery method used:

- In design-bid-build (D-B-B), design-negotiate-build (D-N-B), construction management (CM), and owner-build (O-B) forms of project delivery, the architect/engineer (A/E) executes the design phases and delivers the documents to the owner according to the owner-A/E agreement.
- Design-build (D-B) project delivery differs in that the A/E is retained by the design-builder, and the design-builder executes the design phases.
- The Integrated Project Delivery (IPD) method integrates the stakeholders and participants and, while the A/E may have the most control over the design, others will participate and make contributions to the evaluation and selection of products, systems, and assemblies.

At the conclusion of the design stage, stakeholders and participants should have a full understanding of the project's size, its functions, components, appearance, and probable cost so that construction documentation of the design for procurement (bidding/negotiating/purchasing) purposes can proceed.

8.2 Dual Nature of Design

Every project, facility, building, structure, or other embellishment to the built environment is birthed through a sophisticated process that is called design and construction. The process is essentially the same for every physical object in the built environment.

- Design is thoughtful, intellectual, analytical, functional, and many times original— an act of thinking. The tangible production of the design portion of the process is the documents required to give physical form to the creative ideas.
- Construction is a physical activity involving human labor, tools, equipment, manufacturing, and fabrication—an act of doing. The nonphysical and intangible production of the construction of the process are the efforts invested in planning, managing, and executing the manufacturing, fabrication, and installation of products necessary for physical form.

The quality of each physical object in the built environment in every respect is directly related to the time and effort invested by those charged with its design or, more aptly, its creative design. It is also influenced by the skill, talents, education, and experience of the designers. Creative design is the generation of ideas that give physical form to the needs, desires, and aspirations of an owner.

The quality of a creative design is based on the dual nature of the merging of aesthetic ideas and decisions and technical ideas and decisions. While the nature of design is being presented as two entities, they are in reality so intertwined as to be inseparable:

- Aesthetic design articulates products and materials into pleasing arrangements that form structures, forms, and spaces for specific purposes to house human activities.
- Technical design determines the requisite qualities and attributes of those products and materials for the purpose of successfully constructing the facility so that it will durably fulfill its intended function and perform properly throughout its life cycle.

These two portions are not equal in the amount of time and effort that are necessary. The technical portion consumes considerably more time and effort than the aesthetic portion. Also, the separation of creative design into two portions is not to say that one is more important than the other. While much emphasis is usually placed on the aesthetic design of a facility, it is the technical design that ensures the facility will exist for whatever time is allotted for its existence.

Before the aesthetic and technical ideas can be finalized, there are many other things that must be considered that will influence those decisions.

8.3 Design Considerations

Design considerations are requirements the A/E must take into account in designing the project. These requirements influence the size, arrangement, and extent of project elements, systems, subsystems, and components.

Essentially, the A/E must account for two types of requirements: regulatory requirements and owner requirements. Regulatory requirements include the state, federal, and local laws, as well as requirements for public input that affect the project. Owner requirements include functional, sustainability, aesthetic, and financial requirements of the project. Owner requirements are first expressed in the program developed during project conception and are further defined during the design stage.

8.4 Aesthetics

The owner's program, authorities having jurisdiction (AHJ) requirements, and cost information are some of the practical responsibilities of the A/E during design. But, for many projects, aesthetic requirements are also important considerations. In these cases, the A/E must address the practical and legal requirements while also satisfying the owner's personal tastes to establish a specific identity or image in the project.

Aesthetic design incorporates components that elicit sensory responses, primarily but not exclusively visual, in anyone who may have contact with the project, with the intention of communicating the owner's values and the facility's purpose. This is true of any project that affects the sensory perceptions of the user or the public at large, including buildings, landscapes, bridges, and towers—in short, all but the most rudimentary or utilitarian structures have aesthetic characteristics that result from the owner-A/E collaboration.

Many projects communicate abstract images representing important aspects of the owner's purpose, such as power, wealth, or security. The A/E must understand the owner's identity and make appropriate aesthetic decisions to ensure that the desired image is communicated effectively.

The owner and the A/E rely on each other to establish the aesthetic requirements. Some owners express them by identifying constructed projects they like. This method helps the A/E, but it may leave important requirements unexpressed until design is under development. Other owners may be able to identify only what they do not like, making interpretation difficult. The more precisely the owner expresses the aesthetic requirements, the more accurately the A/E can interpret them and the more completely the design will communicate the owner's identity and image.

A/Es invariably influence design with their own tastes. Therefore, aesthetic design is rarely a pure translation of the owner's aesthetic vision, and the A/E's influences may or may not meet the owner's expectations. The A/E designs at the risk of misinterpretation and the possibility of exceeding the owner's expectations.

To steer the aesthetic design process, an A/E may:

- Identify and discuss the effectiveness of aesthetic design components in the owner's existing facilities, when applicable.
- Discuss the message the owner wishes to convey in the design. The owner's program, mission statements, promotional literature, and public relations personnel may contain some of this information.
- Learn how the owner's clients respond to abstract images and messages.
- Through photos, renderings, and tours, show the owner examples of projects that successfully convey similar messages and images.
- Identify and discuss individual project components that might convey the owner's message visually. Building skin materials, signage, colors, and lighting are very effective.
- Engage the owner in a design charette to discover the fundamental forms, colors, and other subjective characteristics the owner favors.
- Develop digital (BIM) and physical models and renderings to establish and confirm the aesthetic design.
- Develop PPDs or outline specifications.

Some aesthetic requirements may be established during project conception, but the process begins in earnest when requirements are refined as the project moves from schematic design into design development, when the project's texture, color, and shape, and other aesthetic characteristics are more specifically defined.

Aesthetic requirements can be achieved in many ways, including:

- Complementing and contrasting textures
- Visual form, shape, and volume
- Color, light, and shadow
- Juxtaposition of elements according to size or shape
- Quantities and arrangements of elements
- The location or position of the project on the site
- Topography
- Harmony and dissonance of project components
- Context with surrounding facilities

Aesthetic effects are not limited to the visual. Acoustical, tactile, and other characteristics of project elements can also strongly influence the aesthetic effect of a design.

The A/E's interpretation will be judged as the owner responds to design development drawings, renderings, and models throughout this phase. Adjustments may be required once a starting point is established. The design becomes more refined as products are reselected. However, even as approvals are made, adjustments and reinterpretations may be required as the owner's budget and additional AHJ requirements force modifications. The process is the interplay of demands on the A/E's design capabilities.

Understanding the owner's aesthetic requirements and interpreting them accurately are some of the A/E's greatest challenges. The A/E designs functional environments and therefore has responsibilities to the owner, AHJs, and society at large. To fulfill these responsibilities, the A/E must continually adjust methods and suppress personal preferences to satisfy the owner's aesthetic requirements and design a functional project.

Context—the compatibility of the project with its surroundings—is an aspect of design related to aesthetic requirements. Some communities and municipalities control architectural style and other aesthetic characteristics of a project to ensure that they are consistent with the surroundings. Some contextual requirements are legislated and enforced by the AHJ, which can withhold approval of zoning or building permits if a design is not responsive to the values of the community in which the project will be located. This is primarily done to control the appearance of facilities. The owner or A/E must ensure conformance of the design to these values before the project can proceed to construction.

Contextual compatibility often has a financial basis. Some jurisdictions receive financial incentives from governmental authorities and private associations for preserving the historic character of communities.

Context applies to all structures and the effect they have on the environment, people, and community in which they are to be located.

8.5 Functional Requirements

The A/E must design the project elements and their relationships in a manner that ensures proper function of the project in accordance with the owner's program and related AHJ requirements. Considerations include:

- The size of project elements to ensure adequate space is provided
- The performance capacity of project elements to ensure that they serve the owner's requirements and AHJ requirements
- The arrangement of project elements so that they complement each other and provide efficient flow to the owner's operations, thus enhancing the project elements

Functional requirements will influence other decisions the owner and A/E must make to complete the design, including aesthetic requirements and product selection.

The systems should be selected based on how they fit the function, the intended design, and their suitability to the construction type selected. For example, an open-area glass and steel building would require a larger mechanical system than a heavily insulated masonry building with less glazing.

8.6 Constructability

Constructability is a review of the design to determine if it is practical to construct with the means, methods, and products available at the proposed time of construction, within the owner's budget, and within the proposed time requirements for the project. Although the means, methods, and techniques of construction are not documented, the A/E might have to modify a design to ensure that it can be constructed with the materials, labor skills, and funds available in the vicinity of the project.

A constructability review identifies areas of the design that may be difficult or impractical to execute and recommends options to the A/E or owner to make the design more practical. A constructability review is normally an evaluation of the overall design; however, major project elements, systems, and subsystems may be evaluated for their constructability. Although a constructability review is not a cost evaluation, the cost of executing the project is a consideration insofar as it relates to practicality. A constructability review is advised when:

- Innovative or unusual design techniques are proposed.
- Unfamiliar project components are considered for the project.
- The project will be constructed in an unfamiliar location.
- The site presents unusual challenges or constraints.
- There are specific budget constraints.
- There are specific time constraints.

A constructability review should be performed by a participant with experience in constructing similar projects. Design-builders may have personnel on staff to do this, because constructability is an important aspect of the design process under the D-B project delivery method. A/Es who do not have experienced construction participants on staff may have to contract with a qualified consultant for this service. Construction managers, contractors, and subcontractors may make constructability reviews a part of their available services. Product representatives may also participate in constructability reviews.

Constructability reviews are best performed when details have been sufficiently developed but before construction documents have been finalized, thus minimizing disruption to the design schedule. Evaluation includes the following:

- The design is compared with completed projects of similar function. Differences are identified.
- Elements, systems, and subsystems are reviewed to ensure they are properly coordinated.
- Estimated cost, schedule, and site conditions are considered.
- Areas of practical difficulty are identified. Options are considered.
- Recommendations are made to the A/E or owner.

The A/E should consider the recommendations of the constructability review and discuss them with the owner to determine if and how the design might be modified. Under D-B project delivery, the process may take place internally, and a conference with the owner might not be conducted. If changes are necessary, they should be prioritized. The following types of changes should be considered:

- Design changes that do not compromise the owner's program
- Design changes that do not compromise life cycle value
- Design changes that do not substantially modify the established aesthetic requirements
- Design changes that impact initial construction cost

8.7   Sustainability

Depletion of natural resources, deteriorating environmental conditions, rising human population, loss of animal and plant species to extinction, and economic competition from developing nations have raised public awareness of facility design. Environmental preservation has become an important issue in public policy as well as private enterprise, and several prominent national and international organizations provide resources to A/Es to ensure that design and construction industries respond appropriately.

According to the Environmental Protection Agency (EPA), green or sustainable building involves developing healthier methods of construction, operation, and demolition of buildings while at the same time using resources more efficiently. The need for green or sustainable design has been embraced by the design and construction communities and is being implemented in many facilities.

American Society for Testing and Materials (ASTM) E 2114, Standard Terminology for Sustainability Relative to the Performance of Buildings, defines a green building as one that meets performance requirements with minimal negative impact on and maximum improvement of the ecosystem during and after construction and expected service life.

8.7.1   Sustainable Design

The emphasis of sustainable design is the environmental performance of a facility and its components over the course of its life cycle, from planning through deconstruction. There are numerous organizations that have proposed approaches to applying sustainable design, and while there are variations among them, there are six fundamental sustainable design approaches that seem to be common to all:

- Site Optimization:
  - Selection of sites according to criteria, and utilizing it to its best advantage
  - Encouraging rehabilitation or reuse of existing buildings and contaminated sites
  - Evaluating the impact of improvements on ecosystems, transportation, energy and other utility use
  - Increasing rainwater percolation into the land by reducing or eliminating impermeable surfaces
  - Reducing site erosion by slowing and treating rainwater runoff
- Use of Energy:
  - Reducing energy usage and increasing its energy efficiency
  - Reducing or eliminating generation of greenhouse gases
  - Increasing the use of renewable energy resources such as solar, wind, hydroelectric, and geothermal

- Maximizing daylighting to reduce energy used for artificial lighting, and for passive solar heating
- Water Use:
  - Protecting existing fresh water resources
  - Conserving the use of water
  - Reducing, controlling, or treating water runoff
- Building Materials and Products:
  - Constructing with materials and products that minimize life cycle environmental impacts to resource depletion and human toxicity
  - Improving worker safety and health
- Indoor Environmental Quality:
  - Improving quality for occupant health, comfort, and enhancing worker productivity
  - Maximizing daylighting to enhance worker productivity
  - Improving ventilation and moisture control for good indoor air quality
  - Avoiding the use of materials and products with high volatile organic compound emissions
  - Mitigating exposure to toxic chemical, harmful biological, and radioactive materials
- Optimizing Operational and Maintenance Practices:
  - Using durable materials and products that reduce maintenance and life cycle costs
  - Cleaning materials and products that require less water and energy to use, and are non-toxic

Once voluntary, sustainable design approaches are being adopted as part of the building codes of local AHJs, and as regulations of federal and state AHJs. In addition to the various green building application programs like the U.S. Green Building Council's (USGBC) Leadership in Energy and Environmental Design (LEED ™) program which may be adopted as a part of a building code, the entrance of sustainable design approaches into building codes and regulations is also reflected in the International Green Construction Code (IGCC) developed and published by International Code Council (ICC).

Sustainable design can be defined by a code or regulation enforced by the AHJ, as rebate programs offered by local utilities, and as an owner initiative. For the requirements, each team member has responsibilities, as follows:

- The owner should understand sustainability design principles and approaches and how they might affect construction cost. The owner should prioritize sustainability as a goal early during project conception and maintain those goals throughout design, construction documentation, procurement (bidding/negotiating/purchasing), and construction.
- The A/E should be knowledgeable of sustainable design principles and approaches in order to assist in realizing the owner's sustainability goals. The A/E should understand how sustainability affects construction cost and other owner values, applying the concepts properly to fulfill the owner's requirements.
- The contractor should understand the project's sustainability goals, have experience in the type of construction required, and ensure that construction methods and techniques, purchasing of products, and management of construction waste are applied in a manner that fulfills the owner's sustainability requirements.
- Facility managers should implement maintenance procedures that support the sustainable design principles an approaches. Special training might be required to

ensure that facility systems, subsystems, and components perform their designed functions in order for sustainability to be properly realized.

8.7.2 Environmental Design Tools

In 1994, the National Institute of Standards Technology (NIST), a branch of the U.S. Department of Commerce, implemented its Building for Environmental and Economic Sustainability (BEES) program, a model for evaluating environmentally preferable building products. The BEES Technical Manual and User Guide explains the program's goals. The BEES project aims to create and implement a system for choosing building products that offers the best balance between environmental and economic considerations.

The EPA administers the Energy Star program in which individual building products are rated for compliance with sustainability criteria, based on standardized testing procedures of their energy consumption. The EPA also enforces many regulations regarding the environment, including air quality, water quality, emissions, and pollutants.

USGBC, a private corporation, developed the LEED™ program, which certifies the sustainability of new, remodeled, or existing facilities based on their compliance with USGBC criteria. According to its Product Development and Maintenance Manual, LEED™ works to promote sustainable green building and development practices by developing and applying universally accepted standards, tools, and performance criteria.

Sustainable design takes place at the product level and at the facility level. For example, the EPA's Energy Star program and NIST's BEES program evaluate design at the product level. Energy Star rates manufactured products, including appliances, equipment, building products, and manufactured structures, according to their energy efficiency. Manufacturers must obtain evaluation and certification of their manufacturing practices from the EPA so they can use Energy Star branding in their product marketing programs. NIST's BEES program differs in that it evaluates building products based on their environmental impact at each stage in the life cycle of the product. At the facility level, USGBC's LEED™ program evaluates whole facilities rather than individual products, including new construction, major renovations, and existing buildings, according to their theoretical environmental performance throughout their life cycle. Each organization has developed criteria and rating systems to aid the user in obtaining certification of their sustainability, or green, status.

Product manufacturers have responded to the demand for sustainable design by:

- Modifying their manufacturing and distribution processes to comply with sustainability concepts
- Researching and developing products that contribute to the sustainability of a project

Contractors have responded by adjusting their means, methods, and techniques of construction to comply with environmental requirements and sustainability concepts by:

- Minimizing and recycling construction waste
- Controlling pollution discharge
- Documenting environmental control procedures

A/Es have responded by:

- Implementing green design concepts
- Seeking a Green Building rating system certification
- Selecting products that comply with sustainability requirements

8.7.3 Assessing Product Sustainability

Determining whether a product or facility is sustainable requires a life cycle assessment by a qualified project participant. According to the BEES model, the life cycle of a product is a 50-year period, the stages of which are as follows:

- Raw materials acquisition
- Product manufacture
- Transportation
- Installation
- Operation and maintenance
- Recycling and waste management

These stages generally correspond with the construction (acquisition, manufacture, transportation, and installation) and facilities management (operation and maintenance, recycling, and waste management) stages of the project life cycle. Sustainability Life Cycle Analysis under the BEES model evaluates six impacts a product makes on the environment during each of the aforementioned stages. The six impacts are:

- Global warming potential
- Acidification
- Nitrification potential
- Natural resource depletion
- Solid waste produced
- Indoor air quality

ASTM E 2129, Standard Practice for Data Collection for Sustainability Assessment of Building Products, provides an alternative approach to the assessment of building products by providing a series of questions related to product sustainability under the following five headings:

- Materials
- Manufacturing
- Operational Performance of Installed Product
- Indoor Environmental Quality
- Corporate Environmental Policy

The standard is supported by ASTM E 2114, Standard Terminology for Sustainability Relative to the Performance of Buildings. Although the methods differ slightly in their organization and methodology, the goal of the cited organizations is rational assessment of the environmental impact of building products.

Although products may contribute to sustainability, the mere combination of products purported to be green does not constitute sustainable design. Product selection is an important step in fulfilling sustainability in a project design.

8.7.4 Assessing Facility Sustainability

A prominent method for assessing the environmental performance of new and existing facilities is the USGBC's LEED™ Green Building Rating System, which sets a standard for developing high-performance sustainable buildings, the core of which is its accreditation system. There are rating systems for the following:

- New Construction
- Core and Shell
- Schools
- Existing Buildings: Operation and Maintenance
- Commercial Interiors

There are other groups that provide design guidance, environmental objectives, and rating systems, such as the following:

- Advanced Buildings (www.advancedbuildings.net)
- Green Guidelines for Healthcare Construction (www.gghc.org)
- Green Globes (www.greenglobes.com)
- GreenGuard Environmental Institute (www.greenguard.org)
- STARS, a program for higher education institutions developed by the Association for the Advancement of Sustainability in Higher Education (www.aashe.org)

Sustainable design affects the activities of multiple participants in multiple project stages. Merely incorporating green products in a design does not constitute sustainable design. The considerations necessary for achieving sustainability require education, thorough planning, and commitment to the underlying principles. Continuing education, research, and proper application of sustainability principles is required for responsible sustainable design practice.

8.8 Design Phases

All projects proceed through multiple stages from conception to facility management, with variations depending on the nature of the work and the needs of the owner.

The American Institute of Architects (AIA) defines design as occurring in three distinct phases: schematic design, design development, and construction documents. The Engineers Joint Contract Documents Committee (EJCDC) defines design in two phases: preliminary design and final design phase, which includes construction documents. The Design-Build Institute of America (DBIA) defines design in two phases: schematic design and design development, which includes construction documents. For the purposes of this practice guide, design is defined as having two phases: schematic and design development. At the conclusion of each design phase, the A/E will deliver design documents that express the progress of the design and updated cost estimates to ensure that the design is consistent with the owner's program requirements and budget.

During design, the A/E and the owner use drawings and written descriptions, such as preliminary project descriptions, and outline specifications to communicate the design of a project. Drawings used during the design phases are primarily tools to convey ideas of the visual effect of a project. They show the nature of space in terms of surface texture, finishes, light, and color more fully than the drawings used for construction. Written documents, which should be developed concurrently, complement the drawings and aid participants in understanding the design as it develops.

8.8.1 Design Variations

Design is not always limited to a single project or a single location. In some cases, an owner's requirements may include multiple projects executed over an extended period of time in different locations to fulfill a comprehensive facility program. For these owners, master planning, prototype design, or a combination of the two may be required. Private and public owners alike may require these design variations in anticipation of growing demand for their respective businesses or services.

8.8.1.1 Master Planning

Master planning is the design of multiple projects with integrated and complementary functions on the same site or contiguous sites to fulfill the requirements of an extensive program. Master planning allows for future growth or alteration of an owner's facility with minimum obsolescence or loss of function. Master planning requirements should be defined in the owner's program during project conception.

The owner may require design of all or only a portion of a master plan at one time. Accordingly, the A/E may be engaged to design all or only a portion of the facilities required in a master plan.

Types of projects that normally require master planning include:

- Utilities and infrastructures
- Schools and universities
- Corporate campuses
- Manufacturers requiring warehousing, distribution, and point-of sale facilities in different locations
- Transportation projects, including ground, rail, and airport facilities

Master planning design requires thorough knowledge of the owner's present and future requirements and may require more time to complete than an equivalent number of individual project designs of similar extent.

8.8.1.2 Prototype Design

A prototype design is a single design developed for multiple projects on different sites. Minor modifications are made to the design to suit site conditions and the requirements of AHJs. Prototype design establishes a consistent project identity and purpose that are readily identifiable by facility users. Retail outlets, public buildings, multifamily housing, wastewater treatment plants, bridges, and entertainment facilities are examples of projects executed using prototype design. Prototype designs can enhance the efficiency of design, construction, and facility management stages of the project life cycle.

8.8.2 Conceptual Design

The creative design process is similar to the process of solving problems and starts with an original idea, also known as a concept. Concepts are mental representations of an abstract object that are creatively given shape, form, and meaning. Design is a journey of exploring and defining possibilities and constraints by using critical thinking skills.

As an A/E begins the process of designing a facility, it is not uncommon to start with a conceptual idea for the facility. One of the artistic values of some facilities is whether the built facility conveys its conceptual idea. A classical example of a facility that successfully conveys a concept is the TWA Terminal at John F. Kennedy International Airport in New York. Designed by Eero Saarinen, the design concept was to convey the sense of flight to air travelers.

8.8.3 Schematic Design

In the schematic design phase, the A/E reviews and evaluates the owner's program and budget requirements and discusses alternative approaches to the design and construction of the project based on those requirements. As mutually agreed upon, the A/E then prepares schematic design documents for the owner's approval. These may include preliminary sketches, small-scale schematic plans, elevations, sections, diagrams, renderings, digital (BIM) models, and other graphic and written documents that illustrate the general extent, scale, and relationship of project components and describe in general the type of construction and equipment proposed.

During schematic design, site plan and area relationships may be defined; the general size, shape, and massing of building elements determined; elevations and exterior finishes established; and conceptual design criteria for structural, mechanical, and electrical systems identified. Written documents usually consist of preliminary project descriptions and preliminary cost projections.

Schematic design phase drawings may include sketches, renderings, or conceptual diagrams. These drawings describe the size, shape, volume, spatial relationships, and functional characteristics of project components. They are usually general in nature, with few dimensions.

If the owner's program requirements are expressed in very general terms, the A/E may need to produce diagrams of major project elements in rudimentary geometric form to demonstrate their relationships and their relative sizes compared to the whole project. Once these diagrams are approved, the A/E produces sketches and schematic drawings to demonstrate the relationships of spaces and functions of the project in more tangible form. As schematic design proceeds, the A/E might further refine the schematic design by producing elevations, sections, diagrams, renderings, and written documents to illustrate and describe the form, configurations, and relationship of project components.

8.8.4 Design Development

The design development phase follows approval of the schematic design and any necessary program or budget adjustments. The emphasis shifts from overall relationships and functions to more technical issues of constructability and integration of systems and components. Aesthetic concerns move from massing and arrangement to materials, surfaces, and details. Design development phase documents fix and describe the size and character of the entire project, including architectural, structural, mechanical, and electrical systems. Drawings at this phase include plans, elevations, and sections that provide more detail of the various systems and components. The structural, mechanical, and electrical systems are usually developed by selecting the type of system and then determining preliminary sizes of equipment and routing of services. Site plans and floor plans are developed, elevations refined, typical construction details worked out, and many product and material selections made. Outline specifications are used to record such decisions and to describe to the owner the materials, products, and systems selected, as well as any special construction conditions or special contract requirements. The graphic and written documents serve as the basis for revised cost projections, and the outline specifications also serve as a checklist for the subsequent development of detailed documents.

During the design development phase, more detailed information is required. Drawings in this phase may show multiple views of the project in order to describe materials and basic systems and their interrelationships.

For infrastructure projects and large civil engineering projects, the A/E often incorporates standard designs and details provided by AHJs to satisfy the requirements of the jurisdiction. Constructability is an important design consideration. Constructability is evaluation of the practical and economic effects of design decisions manifested during the pricing and the construction stages. Constructability reviews, in which systems and components are reviewed and evaluated, should be performed by a project participant with construction and estimating experience. The simplicity or complexity of design can have a direct effect on construction costs and schedule. A constructability review should be conducted when details are developed to the point that project components can be identified but before the design is fully documented so that necessary changes can be implemented without disrupting the design schedule.

The criteria for the design decisions up to this point are revisited and reevaluated. The basic systems of the project are evaluated for suitability and cost versus the final use or design intent. Changes to the project or its major systems can be made at this time with relative ease compared to later in the design/construction process. Major changes made later during design or after construction has begun can have a significant impact on the total cost and schedule of the project.

8.9 | Quality Assurance/Quality Control Requirements

The quality of a project is the result of a process that is continuously defined throughout the life cycle of the project from conception through facility management. There are not levels of quality. There is not "low quality" or "high quality"; there are simply lesser or greater requirements. Since the requirements for the project start with the owner's program requirements, including AHJ requirements, schedule, and budget, they are the requirements for the design quality.

- *Quality.* Refers to the project requirements established in the contract documents. The contract documents will be prepared resulting from the design process.
- *Quality assurance (QA).* Refers to the procedures for guarding against defects and deficiencies before and during the execution of the work. During design, QA may include procedures such as obtaining data indicating performance, properties, and other attributes, which meet the requirements. This may include lists of certified products.
- *Quality control (QC).* Refers to the procedures for evaluating completed activities and elements of the design for conformance with the requirements. Procedures during design may include document reviews, simulations, and other forms of validation and review, such as meetings with AHJs.

- Quality assurance (QA) and quality control (QC) are not exclusive of each other. QC for one process may serve as QA for a subsequent process. For example, the QC testing by a manufacturer may be the basis for QA for its intended use. All participants perform various forms of QA/QC, whether or not this is specifically stated in the agreements. Refer to Table 8.1 for example phases of QA and QC.

Table 8.1   **Example Phases of Quality Assurance and Quality Control for Concrete Work**

Quality Assurance Activities	Quality Control Activities
Industry Associations	
Establishment of quality standards for reinforcement and concrete materials	
Material Manufacturer	
Review material requirements in contract documents	Testing of reinforcement and concrete materials by testing laboratory
Concrete Supplier	
Review performance requirements for cast-in-place concrete in contract documents	Analysis of previous mix designs for optimum performance match
Select concrete mix design and submit to A/E via contractor	Testing of mix design by testing laboratory
Review of mix design by A/E and consultants	
Concrete Subcontractor	
Prepare and submit product data and shop drawings, e.g., reinforcement and form materials, for A/E review	
Preconstruction conference with suppliers, subcontractors, contractor, testing laboratory, and A/E	
Construction of a cast-in-place concrete panel mock-up by subcontractor for review by contractor, A/E, and owner	
Formwork and Reinforcement Installer	
Tagging reinforcement and coordination with drawings and required locations	Inspection and observation of formwork and reinforcement by contractor and A/E, respectively
Concrete Placement Crew	
Observation of concrete placement by contractor and A/E	
Taking test cylinders and slump measurement by testing laboratory	Compressive strength testing of test cylinders by testing laboratory
	Tolerance measurements of placed concrete by contractor and A/E

Total project commissioning is a quality process utilizing an independent company providing services that may include monitoring the owner's project requirements and verifying that the requirements are incorporated into the basis of design. Commissioning continues through the construction stage of the project providing certain QA/QC services.

8.9.1   Establishing Quality

The owner establishes the basis for quality in the program, budget, and schedule. The AIA states that the A/E, during the design phases, reviews and provides a preliminary evaluation of the owner's program, schedule, and construction budget requirements. That evaluation should determine whether project requirements are feasible and realistic. It is prudent to inform the owner about what can be realistically achieved with these controlling factors. Owner expectations can vary, depending on their prior experiences and perception of what can be realistically achieved.

The A/E prepares design documents to convey a physical form and materials that should be consistent with the owner's quality requirements. The developing phases of design are forms of QA/QC. Obtaining approvals at each phase verifies the design as a QC. Procedures utilized by the A/E, such as uniform documentation systems, ensure a greater degree of QC.

8.9.2   Participants Affect Quality

The A/E performs QA/QC in the design of the project, preparation of contract documents, and administration of the construction contract. Selecting products and determining specific project requirements are part of the process of establishing the quality of the project. Documenting each decision, monitoring the costs, and verifying the constructability are other aspects that set the requirements to be included in the construction documents. It is the documented requirements that will establish the requirements for quality.

8.9.3   Concurrent Quality Assurance/Quality Control Processes

QC for one action may become QA for the next step in a process. Quality controls such as testing provide results that, if satisfactory, can provide QA that a product will be suitable for an intended use. In each step of the manufacturing process, the previous QC becomes part of QA for the next step. The International Organization of Standardization (ISO) developed ISO 9000. It is a series of related standards that have become an internationally accepted framework for developing internal improvement procedures based on quality management and QA. The standard is written in broad terms to cover various aspects of manufacturing and service industries. Compliance is established by third-party independent certification such as Underwriters Laboratories, Inc. This process is referred to as a quality loop or quality spiral by the American Society for Quality Control (ASQC).

8.10 | Budgets

Many projects require substantial financial investment, so the owner's budget requirements significantly influence design decisions on many projects. The A/E must understand and account for the owner's financial requirements and design the project accordingly. During each phase, the A/E may continuously evaluate design and budget to ensure they remain in agreement.

The owner must also be aware of the limitations that the project budget places on design. The A/E is responsible for informing the owner whether or not design and budget are in agreement. If the owner desires to increase the extent and value of the project, the A/E should evaluate how such design changes will affect the budget and advise the owner on their impact.

Design and budget are ultimately tested when the project is priced during procurement (bidding/negotiating/purchasing). Substantial differences between the owner's budget and the prices or bids received may indicate that design was not executed with a clear understanding of the budget requirements. Depending on the terms of the owner-A/E agreement, redesign may be necessary to reconcile the differences. Redesign is a common problem with design-bid/negotiate-build projects in which construction participants do not advise the A/E on budget and design during the design stage.

Because it contractually binds the contractor and the A/E, many owners view D-B project delivery as more reliable than design-bid/negotiate-build project delivery to ensure the project is designed according to the established budget. In O-B project delivery, the owner is directly involved in coordinating design and budget requirements for the project. Regardless of the project delivery method, the owner and A/E must have a common understanding of how budget will influence the design of the project.

8.11 | Cost Estimates

Traditionally, the A/E's scope of service for design normally requires cost estimates at the conclusion of each design phase. However, for all the project delivery methods except the D-B-B delivery method, the cost estimates are normally prepared by the contractor, construction manager, or design-builder.

An estimate is not a price. It is more like an opinion of the probable cost of construction based on:

- The cost of similar constructed projects
- Published cost data
- Input from construction participants
- Economic conditions prevailing at the proposed time of construction
- Contingency for inestimable factors, such as unknown details, unforeseen or hidden construction, soil conditions, changed market conditions, and weather delays

Estimating helps ensure that design is proceeding in accordance with the owner's budget. When estimates exceed the owner's budget, changes to the design may be required. The earlier changes are recommended and made, the less impact the changes will have on the design schedule.

8.11.1 Balancing Costs against Resources and Extent

It is important to maintain a balance between the proposed design and the project budget. A modification to either design extent or budget must result in a corresponding change in the other. For example, an increase in project size must result in either a corresponding increase in the project budget or a reduction in the cost of the components required in constructing the project. Conversely, an increase in the cost of the required components must result in a reduction in the project size or an increase in the project budget, and sometimes both. Without this understanding, design decisions by the A/E or owner can lead to misunderstandings as design progresses and the project is documented and subsequently priced.

A successful project is one in which the owner receives a project at a reasonable price, the A/E sees the project originally envisioned successfully completed without having to compromise design concepts or features, and the contractor has the work done on time and within budget so a reasonable profit can be realized. Project participants should be aware that a successful project can benefit all concerned parties and the project users, building occupants, and/or the public, too.

8.11.2 Estimating Techniques

Estimating techniques used during the design stage include any of the following:

- Order of magnitude
- Unit of measure
- Assemblies/systems
- Unit price

Each technique requires different information, will require different amounts of time to complete, and will produce a greater or lesser degree of accuracy.

Order of magnitude is the quickest estimate to complete and is also the least accurate. An order-of-magnitude estimate will provide a ballpark estimate for the project cost, typically with a degree of accuracy of 20 to 25 percent. The order-of-magnitude estimate uses per unit of occupancy costs such as a cost per bed price for a nursing home or hotel or cost per seat prices for a theater or a restaurant. Order-of-magnitude estimates are usually based on historical cost information available from proprietary cost databases, estimator's databases, or owner-supplied data. An order-of-magnitude estimate is used to provide cost information while the project concept or program is still at its earliest stages of development or during schematic design when project details are not yet determined.

A unit-of-measure estimate is a somewhat more accurate method of predicting constructed costs than the order-of-magnitude estimate. The construction must be defined and the approximate total facility size must be known. Usually, two unit costs per square foot/cubic foot are established for the gross area/volume and the net area/volume. The gross area/volume is determined for the entire facility. The net area/volume is the area/volume dedicated for the facility's intended primary use. The total project cost is then calculated in accordance with the facility's total size category. Necessarily, larger projects will realize an economy of scale, and the unit price will generally be somewhat lower. The gross area/volume unit cost and net area/volume costs are added together to achieve a total project cost. By using the square foot or volume method, a more accurate project cost, usually in the range of 15 to 20 percent, will be achieved. A square foot or volume estimate is often used during the schematic design phase.

An assemblies or systems cost estimate requires more detailed information about the project construction. A cost per unit of assembled construction is used to form the project estimate. For example, typical costs per square foot of area will be developed for the roofing assembly, the roof structural system, the floor structural assembly, and the exterior wall assembly, as well as all other units of construction throughout the project. Costs per unit will be applied for items such as windows, doors, and bathroom fixture groups. The costs for each assembly, item, or group will be totaled to achieve an estimate of total project costs. An assemblies or systems cost estimate requires the kind of project information that is determined during the design development phase. Assemblies or systems cost estimates will achieve an accuracy of 10 percent.

A unit price estimate utilizes a complete, detailed list of the project materials, components, and other cost items for the entire project. A unit cost estimate is the most accurate type of estimate and usually will result in a cost estimate that is accurate to 3 to 5 percent. The unit price estimate requires a significant amount of effort and time to complete and utilizes the completed construction documents. A complete quantity survey or takeoff is done to establish quantities of all work items in the project. Materials, labor, and equipment costs are assigned to each unit of work determined by the quantity survey. The unit price method is usually the method used to establish the final design estimate.

8.12 Life Cycle Costs

Life cycle costs are the estimated expenses for a project, or a specific material, equipment, or system, including:

- Design
- Construction
- Operation
- Maintenance
- Resale, demolition, or salvage

Life cycle costs are based on the total cost of ownership rather than just the initial cost.

Life cycle costs can be applied to the overall project or to individual components of the project such as materials, systems, or equipment. For example, the initial cost of a light wood frame structure might be lower than one constructed with cast-in-place concrete. The concrete structure, however, may have a substantially longer anticipated life. A life cycle study would demonstrate that a stone or ceramic tile floor would initially cost substantially more than carpet, but would have a much longer life with less maintenance, thereby making it economically more prudent for the long-term facility owner.

The A/E makes design recommendations based on life cycle cost when selecting products and materials as part of the design process. Using documented life cycle cost data, the A/E can determine overall value based on life cycle attributes. Some owners require documented life cycle cost information.

Life cycle costs require several considerations, including:

- Design costs affecting the initial construction cost as well renovation, remodeling, and improvements.
- Initial cost of construction including the cost of materials and the labor required for proper installation. The cost of labor may be higher than the material cost if it requires unusual skill or equipment to execute the work. If minimum initial cost is a priority, then design details must be kept simple and in accordance with common trade practices.
- Cost of operating the product or equipment. Chief among operating costs is the cost of energy consumed. Energy costs relate to numerous products from windows and insulation to water heaters and other equipment.
- Maintenance and replacement cost over the life of the product. The anticipated frequency of product replacement due to projected wear and deterioration due to use is a factor in determining life cycle costs. A comparison should be made between the product's predicted replacement cycles with the owner's projection of the life of the project. Inexpensive products sometimes become the most expensive when their maintenance and replacement costs over the life of the project are included. Obtain the owner's input regarding the quality and life expectancy of the facility.
- Alteration, renovation, and improvements.
- Salvage value or expense. This may be a value or an expense, depending on the nature of the product, material, or constructed project.

Once these expenses are estimated and the expected life is established, the anticipated life cycle costs can be forecasted.

The expected life of a project may be up to 100 years or more. The portion that the owner is concerned about often depends on the length of time the owner expects to use it. A public owner may derive value from a facility for 100 years or more, whereas a private owner may intend to use the facility for a far shorter period and sell it to a new owner. Each owner will place a different value on the expected life of the facility; therefore, the A/E must account for different life cycle value requirements in design. If the life cycle information is not reasonably documented, then the cost-per-year expenses cannot be determined.

Obsolescence, economic factors, and technological advances can also affect the life cycle value of a facility. An asset's value may be significantly diminished by changes such as purchasing policy, the color or texture no longer being in vogue, government legislation, competitive pressure, or a newer or more appealing design. These factors may be very difficult to predict.

Usually, in order to establish the expected physical life of an asset, projections are based on historic data gleaned from similar projects. If the expected economic life of a project is being determined, then statistical accounting data, compiled and reported on regularly, is the basis for forecasting future economic performance. The life of any asset can be terminated when it either is no longer profitable or has simply deteriorated to a point where the cost of maintenance exceeds the cost of replacement.

The salvage value or expense of a facility is difficult to accurately predict. The A/E may rely on the opinion of an experienced appraiser for estimating the future value of projects. However, at some point the facility might actually become a liability rather than an asset, as many building owners learned when the hazardous attributes of asbestos-containing materials, lead paint, and polychlorinated biphenyl (PCB)–filled transformers became understood.

Life cycle cost studies can be valuable information for the owner and the design team because they provide an important tool that benefits the design and there is no present consequence if the distant predictions do not actually come to pass.

8.13 Value Analysis

Value analysis, also called value enhanced design or value engineering, is the process of evaluating documented design to identify potential alternative methods, systems, or materials that will benefit the owner by enhancing the life cycle value of the project. To be effective, it requires a high level of cooperation among project participants, each of whom can contribute valuable perspective in achieving the most effective design for the owner's requirements.

Timing is also an important factor in value analysis processes. The earlier it is implemented in the design process, the more efficient and effective it can be. The later it occurs in the project, the more disruptive it can be to design and scheduling, resulting in less value retained in the project.

Value analysis can be used to enhance project value or to reduce initial or long-term costs. Ideally, value analysis is the process in which construction cost, maintenance costs, and replacement costs are evaluated and brought into balance to provide optimum net value over the life cycle of the facility.

One or a combination of the following project participants can provide value analysis services:

- The A/E and subconsultants
- Contractor
- Design-builder
- Construction manager
- Special consultant retained by owner

8.13.1 Value Analysis Processes

8.13.1.1 Data-Gathering Phase

Value analysis begins with compiling relevant project information, including:

- Project program to understand the owner's goals and requirements
- Code analysis
- Geotechnical information
- Energy analysis
- Design documents
- Construction documents, if completed

8.13.1.2 Investigation Phase

In this phase, the value analysis team considers potential alternatives and options applicable to the project. Those with the most potential for success are selected for further evaluation. The first step in this phase is to examine changes that have minimal impact on the project yet save the greatest amount of money, such as large components where a small change in one unit cost will have large savings impact. Issues include the perceivable impact on design, building function, and constructability.

8.13.1.3 Analytical/Development Phase

In this phase, the short-listed concepts are evaluated in detail, including:

- Cost analysis, including initial costs, maintenance costs, and replacement costs
- Impact on other work
- Schedule impacts
- System performance
- Plan of implementation
- Recommendations, including a ranking of the short-listed options in terms of their overall project impact

8.13.1.4 Report Phase

In this phase, the value analysis process is documented. Recommendations are presented for the owner's consideration and approval, and the A/E prepares to implement them accordingly.

8.13.1.5 Implementation Phase

In this phase, the implementation plan is executed.

8.13.1.6 Evaluation Phase

The evaluation phase is a combined assessment of the performance of the change and an extrapolation of how other alternatives might have performed differently.

8.13.2 Recommendations

Common recommendations resulting from value analysis include:

- Identification of new technologies. These tend to be higher-risk alternatives, but have greater return potential.
- Substituting desired products for less expensive products. When lower construction cost is the primary objective, life cycle value may be reduced.
- Constructability and simplification in detailing to reduce cost. This can affect the aesthetic value of the project.
- Changes in product types. These require the participation of the A/E, subconsultants, and owner to ascertain their practicability.
- Modifications to mechanical, electrical, and plumbing systems.
- Elimination of nonessential items.
- Reduction or elimination of nonessential details.
- Identification of items that can be eliminated from initial construction and added at a later time without disruption.

Value analysis used solely for reducing construction costs can be problematic. For example, size matters. Because size is directly related to functional attributes of the project, the owner is usually reluctant to reduce project size in order to reduce cost. Without size to consider, value analysis must focus on other project requirements, potentially reducing the project's life cycle value, eroding the project's net value, and violating an underlying principle of value analysis.

8.13.3   Documenting Decisions

When value analysis occurs during design, it impacts fewer related decisions. As projects progress to the pricing stage, relatively simple value analysis decisions can still be implemented without disrupting the project schedule, and the competitive influence is still prevalent. Complex changes may force redesign of portions of the project, thus extending the project schedule. Once a contract is awarded, the dynamics change significantly. The contractor has now joined the project team and can offer useful participation in the value analysis process. However, scheduling and project costs are at greater risk, and a concerted team effort is required to keep the project in balance.

8.14   Controlling Variables

There are occasions when it will be necessary for the A/E to consider special procedures for certain variables in a project, including:

- Indeterminate items, unknowns, and contingencies
- Postponement of decisions until adequate information is available
- Flexibility and adjustment for variables
- Identification and control of construction costs

8.14.1   Types of Variables

The procedures used for specifying these special applications are allowances, alternates, and unit prices.

8.14.1.1   Allowances

An allowance is a specified monetary sum or a specified quantity of work not otherwise defined by the specifications and drawings, but which the contractor is required to include in the bid or price. Two types of allowances are:

- *Cash allowance.* A monetary sum that the bidder includes as part of the contract sum to account for certain items to be determined at a later time.
- *Quantity allowance.* A specified quantity of a product or assembly that the bidder includes in the scope of the work even though the location of the product is not defined on the drawings or in the specifications.

8.14.1.2 Alternate

An alternate is a defined portion of the work that is priced separately and thus provides an option for the owner in determining the final scope of the project. The alternate provides the owner with a choice between different products or it can define the addition or deletion of a portion of the work.

8.14.1.3 Unit Prices

A price can be stipulated or quoted by a bidder or proposer for a single, specified unit of work. Unit prices are useful where the type of work is defined, but the extent of the work is not known or is likely to change. Unit prices are also utilized when quantity allowances are specified, providing a means of adjusting the contract sum once the full extent of the work becomes known. The contractor is asked to submit prices for work items that are undetermined at the time of procurement, but will be determined after the agreement has been executed.

8.14.2 Allowances

Allowances and unit prices provide a means for documenting certain information that cannot otherwise be specified or shown on the drawings. Alternates provide a method of pricing a portion of the work so that the owner can choose the actual scope of work after bids or prices have been received and evaluated. Ideally, the exact scope of a project should be understood before documents are released for procurement (bidding/negotiating/purchasing). However, variations in the scope often occur during construction, and special pricing procedures enable construction to proceed without rebidding or renegotiating the entire project. Once a project has been analyzed to determine where changes may occur, then an allowance, alternate, or unit price can be used to minimize the impact of such variables. Too many alternates, allowances, and unit prices complicate procurement and awarding activities. If undue burdens are placed on the prospective contractors, higher costs may result for the owner. Therefore, these special procedures should not become a substitute for accurate and complete documents. Refer to Figure 8.1.

8.14.2.1 Cash Allowances

The cash allowance is a monetary sum specified by the A/E and included in the price of the project to pay for products that are unspecified at the time of pricing. A cash allowance allows pricing to proceed before all products have been selected and documented in the design. For example, if brick has been determined as a building shell component but the size, type, and color have not been selected, the construction and supplier teams cannot accurately determine the material price. In the absence of complete information, the A/E can request that the prospective contractors include a predetermined sum in the construction price for the purchase of brick, thus postponing the selection but not delaying pricing procedures. When the actual selection is made, the contractor will be required to submit a price for the specified brick, and an adjustment will be made in the contract sum to account for the difference between the actual price and the allowance sum. Traditionally, cash allowances are intended to be used for purchasing the product, with labor costs, overhead, and profit included in the price over and above the cash allowance sum. The description of each allowance should state exactly the allowance sum and how it will be expended.

CONDITIONS OF THE CONTRACT
Supplementary Conditions

Delete Paragraph 11.8 – Case Allowances, and substitute the following:

11.8 – Allowances: Include in the Contract Sum all allowances stated in the Contract Documents. Allowances include specific monetary sums and quantities of work for certain scheduled items. Refer to Section 01 21 13 – Cash allowances and Section 01 21 19 – Quantity Allowances for allowance descriptions and requirements.

SPECIFICATIONS
Division 01 – General Requirements

SECTION 01 21 13
CASH ALLOWANCES

1.06 SCHEDULE OF CASH
ALLOWANCES

A. Section 04 20 00 – Unit Masonry: Include the unit price of $350.00 per thousand for purchase and delivery of facing brick. Stipulate the estimated quantity on the Bid Form. Include installation costs in Contract Sum.

Division 04 — Masonry

SECTION 04 20 00
UNIT MASONRY

1.05 ALLOWANCES

A. Provide selected facing brick under cash allowance specified in Section 01 21 13 – Cash Allowances

SECTION 01 21 19
QUANTITY ALLOWANCES

1.06 SCHEDULE OF QUANTITY
ALLOWANCES

A. Section 09 68 00 – Carpeting: Provide 200 SY, including purchase, delivery and installation of Type "A" Sheet Carpet.

B. Section 09 68 00 – Carpeting: Provide 400 SY, including purchase, delivery and installation of Type "B" Carpet Tile.

Division 09 — *Finishes

SECTION 09 68 00
CARPETING

1.05 ALLOWANCES

A. Provide carpet quantities specified under Section 01 21 19 – Quantity Allowances

Figure 8.1
Sample Use of Allowances

When using a cash allowance, the A/E must clearly specify which of the following costs are to be included:

- Product cost
- Taxes
- Delivery, storage, and handling costs
- Installation labor
- Overhead
- Profit
- Performance and payment bond cost

When to Use Cash Allowances. Cash allowances should be avoided if their use is the result of the failure of the owner or A/E to make necessary decisions before issuing procurement (bidding/negotiating/purchasing) documents. Cash allowances should not be used to postpone decisions. However, when necessary, cash allowances do offer unique advantages and may be best for the following:

- Items that cannot be designed or selected until the project is partially complete, including murals, sculptures, furnishings and accessories, and landscaping
- Items such as testing, the magnitude of which can be determined only during construction
- Acceleration of the design schedule when the benefit outweighs the potentially higher cost involved with items purchased with cash allowance funds.

Disadvantages of Cash Allowances. Cash allowances can be problematic. Although they establish the product price, the prospective contractors are, to some degree, blindly pricing installation. Some products satisfying the cash allowance description can be installed at less cost than others. This applies particularly to brick, hardware, and some kinds of equipment. Hardware selections, for instance, will affect hardware preparation cost for doors and frames.

Cash allowances have other disadvantages that almost always increase project costs. They effectively suspend competitive bidding on the specified product. When they are used in place of a detailed specification, they also deprive the bidders of essential information. For example, if the documents are not clear about the exact type, size, and quantity of products that will be purchased under the terms of an allowance, installation labor and the effect of the products on interfacing construction may be difficult for the contractor to price accurately. This can lead to disputes and cost-related claims. For example, labor costs to install jumbo brick and standard modular brick differ.

It is important to estimate cash allowance sums accurately. When the final cost differs considerably from the cash allowance, project participants can suffer financially. If a cash allowance is unrealistically high, the contractor's percentage of overhead and profit is proportionately high and becomes an unfair expense to the owner. If it is set too low, the overhead and profit percentage are low and become an unfair burden to the contractor.

8.14.2.2 Quantity Allowance

When the quantity of work is unknown during design, the A/E may establish quantity allowances and unit prices to allow pricing to proceed. In this procedure, the contractor bids or prices the work according to the specified quantity and provides a supplementary unit price related to the type of work specified under the quantity allowance. When the required quantity of work becomes known, work is completed, the actual quantity of work performed is measured, and the unit price is used to adjust the contract sum.

For example, in the construction of a multistory office building, the exact layout of the interior partitions often cannot be determined until the space is leased and each tenant's requirements determined. In order to allow for future work in the construction contract, the bidders will be asked to include quantity allowances for items such as specific unit measurements (e.g., square yard, square meter) of finished interior partitions, doors and frames, acoustical ceilings, and recessed lighting. In this way the cost of the anticipated work can be included in the contract sum even though the items are not shown on the drawings.

Quantity allowances may also be used in purchasing contracts for the purchase of fixtures, furniture, and equipment.

8.14.3 Alternates

Alternates are optional work items that may or may not be made part of the contracted work and are used when bids are solicited or invited. Alternates may be used for alternative design approaches or for pricing alternative materials. For example, an alternate may be prepared for adding an additional wing to a building or for using a brick exterior finish instead of wood siding. Alternates are priced during the procurement (bidding/negotiating/purchasing) stage of the project and may be additive or deductive work items. If bids are low enough for the owner to have additional funds available in the project budget, additive alternates may be awarded to the contractor. If the bids are higher than expected, deductive alternates maybe utilized to reduce the total contract amount.

Alternates should be carefully expressed in the pricing documents, including the criteria by which alternates will or will not be awarded. Alternates should be clearly delineated on the drawings as well as addressed appropriately in the specifications. If this is not done carefully, misunderstandings and misinterpretations can occur regarding the scope of an alternate.

The use of alternates is often encouraged or mandated by project owners to make use of the funds available for a project, particularly on public projects where the project funds must be expended or the project administrator will lose the funds. The design team must spend additional time and effort to prepare the construction documents containing numerous alternates. The bidders must also spend additional time and effort to prepare accurate bid prices for alternates. Bidders have to consider the impact to the project that an alternate may have—if it is accepted. This can be a difficult task for bidders depending on the complexity and the number of trades involved in the work of each alternate. Contractors must protect their profit margins to remain in business. If an alternate is not fully documented, the contractor must account for unknown factors by including additional funds in the alternate price to safeguard against financial loss. For this reason, the alternate prices may not be truly competitive market prices for the additional work.

Alternates often increase the complexity of procurement (bidding/negotiating/purchasing), evaluations, and contracting procedures. From the contractor's perspective, an extensive number of alternates can indicate that the design is not fully determined or the owner's budget may not support the desired design.

Some owners use alternates as advisory prices or breakout costs for their internal management and accounting purposes. Given the potential inaccuracy of alternate prices, this practice should be avoided.

Overreliance on alternates should be discouraged to avoid the complexity of determining the low bidder. If the design team has sufficient time to execute the design and prepare accurate and complete cost estimates, alternates are usually not necessary.

Chapter 9
Design Documents

9.1 | Introduction

As covered in Chapter 8, the design process documentation for the stages of design begins broad and proceeds to specific, or, from the general to the detailed. This is also generally true of design stage documentation, regardless of the project delivery method used.

Documentation is especially important in the design and construction process because without graphic representations of the project design, it would be difficult for anyone to understand the three-dimensional spatial and functional proposal to fulfill the owner's aspirations, requirements, and need for a facility. Graphic representations present and communicate the design intent in different ways for each of the following:

- The three design stages, as will be described later in this chapter
- The documents necessary to construct the project, as will be described in Chapter 11
- The documents required by the contractors, subcontractors, and suppliers for their respective purposes (i.e., shop drawings), as will be described in Chapter 13
- The documents necessary for facility management, as will be described in Chapter 14

9.2 | Design Concept Phase Documentation

Documentation necessary to communicate the design concept is usually the most generalized and abbreviated information that will be prepared for a project. The objective is for stakeholders and participants to get a general understanding of the project design and the various systems being contemplated.

9.2.1 | Drawings

Drawings are frequently free-hand sketches and illustrations because the objective is to communicate the overall organizing idea and basic appearance of the project design, and not detailed and technical information.

9.2.2 Narrative Description

Descriptions are presented in a narrative form and briefly list the major products, assemblies, and systems included in the project design. Detailed technical information and specifications are not necessary at this point. An example of a narrative description of the exterior of a building might be something like the following:

> The exterior appearance of the new facility, together with its parking garage and entry pavilion, will convey an impression of permanence, strong civic presence, and a timelessness. The materials employed on the building's facades will be durable and from local sources. The design precedents and elements of the existing 19th and early 20th century commercial buildings that still dominate the city will be included in this facility.

9.2.3 Design Team Coordination

The design portion of the project delivery method begins when a design professional formulates design ideas that give physical form to the design requirements. Before the design ideas can be finalized into the design concept for the facility, design professionals for the various other design and engineering disciplines formulate and coordinate their respective ideas into a finalized design concept.

9.2.4 Estimates

While any of the estimating techniques detailed in Chapter 8 could be used, the order of magnitude technique is the most appropriate because it is consistent with the other project concept documents because it provides a ballpark estimate.

Estimates typical for this stage are usually no more than a simple list of the cost for the major components and building systems of the project design.

9.3 Schematic Design Phase Documentation

During the schematic design phase, both the American Institute of Architects (AIA; Document B101) and Engineers Joint Contract Documents Committee (EJCDC; EJCDCE-520) standard forms of agreement between owner and architect/engineer (A/E) require the A/E to furnish the owner with a report. This report should include preliminary schematic drawings and a preliminary project description (PPD) that together clearly indicate the extent and relationship of the project components.

9.3.1 Drawings

The extent of schematic design drawings depends on the complexity of the project and the terms of the owner-A/E agreement. Schematic design drawings give a more organized form to the design concept and begin to describe the following about the project design:

- Aesthetics
- Size, shape, and volume
- Spatial relationships
- Functional characteristics
- Code and life-safety requirements
- Materials
- Major building systems

Drawings are not technical in nature and may include any of the following:

- Site plan
- Floor plans
- Elevations
- Building sections
- Perspective and renderings
- Digital modeling (Building Information Modeling)
- Scaled models

9.3.2 Preliminary Project Descriptions

A preliminary project description (PPD) is a method of describing aspects of the schematic design in a written form.

Preparing the PPD requires the design team to think through the project and document decisions and design criteria in broad terms. Changes can be made without disrupting the ongoing design process during document development throughout subsequent refinement and value analysis stages. The document should include information suitable for preliminary cost estimates, time schedules, and initial value analysis studies.

The emphasis of the PPD is on describing the physical requirements of the project. Identification of actual materials to be used is often tentative and may change during later stages of design.

A PPD may include both performance criteria and product descriptions, depending on the progress of the design and the decision-making process. The document should be organized to describe groups of construction systems, assemblies, and components in a logical sequence. Refer to Figure 9.1 for an example of a portion of a PPD.

9.3.2.1 Format

A PPD organizes and defines major project elements, systems, and subsystems in their basic construction sequence rather than the individual products that comprise them. *UniFormat™* provides an efficient organizational and numbering system for creating PPDs, especially for large projects with multiple elements. As a design tool, a PPD can be expanded with detail as design develops, using *UniFormat™* numbering with *MasterFormat®* suffix numbers to identify smaller components.

ELEMENT B SHELL		
B20	EXTERIOR ENCLOSURE	
B2010	EXTERIOR WALLS	Thermal Performance: Minimum assembly U-value of 0.06 per International Energy Conservation Code. Aesthetic Requirements: Match appearance of existing building
B2010.001	Masonry Veneer Exterior Walls	Brick: Match existing jumbo size brick. Precast Trim: Match existing. Portions will have decorative moldings with multicolor painted finish to match existing building.
B2010.002	Metal Panel Exterior Walls	Aluminum-faced composite metal panel cladding system with face sealed joint; 4 mm thickness, factory-applied fluorocarbon coating in metallic color. Sealant: Medium modulus silicone.
	Exterior Wall Construction	6-inch deep cold formed metal framing with 1/2-inch glass-mat faced gypsum sheathing.
	Exterior Wall Vapor Retarders, Air Barriers, and Insulation	Insulation: R-10 extruded polystyrene continuous insulation in drainage cavity, unfaced R-13 fiberglass batts in stud cavities. Weather Barrier: Liquid-applied vapor permeable air and water barrier membrane.
	Exterior Wall Interior Skin	Gypsum board, painted finish.
	Exterior Louvers	Aluminum louvers, drainable storm-proof blades, welded construction, factory-applied fluorocarbon finish that matches metal cladding panels.
	Exterior Soffits	Direct-applied exterior finish system (DEFS) on gypsum sheathing over CFMF framing with R-19 unfaced fiberglass batt insulation.
END OF ELEMENT		

Figure 9.1   A Portion of a PPD for the Exterior Enclosure of a Project

Although the headings relate primarily to buildings, non-building-type projects may be described using some of the categories mentioned. Following schematic design, a PPD may be maintained and updated for use as an instrument of communication between project participants and as a source of information when developing outline specifications during design development.

9.3.2.2   Design Decisions

The PPD follows the same logical sequence as the major elements of the design. The document should include proposed design solutions and decisions made, or to be made, and serve as a master guide for the project from which all subsequent project documentation will flow. Documents prepared by the A/E during schematic design serve to:

- State the A/E's understanding of the method of construction delivery (e.g., bid or negotiated, construction management, design-build, owner-build) intended by the owner, and the conditions of the contract proposed to support the method of delivery.
- Inform the owner of the proposed design elements, components, and systems to be used in the project.
- Describe systems meeting the design and budget constraints.
- Document the basis for time schedules and estimates of probable construction costs.
- Aid the design process by documenting decisions between the owner and the project team members.
- Provide the reference point on which subsequent decisions and stages of the project will be based.
- Provide the documented basis for the owner's approval of decisions made during the schematic design phase.

9.3.2.3 System Descriptions

There are two principal methods for defining building systems.

- The first is to describe and list products and systems, including restrictions and possible alternatives that meet the design criteria. Cost estimating, scheduling, and value analysis can then take place for each of the products and systems, including alternatives that may perform satisfactorily.
- The other method is to list performance criteria along with supplementary descriptions. PPD describes the project as a system of components rather than actual products. A level of general performance may be described instead of providing detailed information. When using the performance criteria method, include relevant information so that unsuitable systems can quickly be identified and eliminated from consideration.

The PPD is organized to describe the various groupings of facility construction systems and components in a logical sequence from the ground up and from the outside in. The facility systems and components may be defined in terms of performance criteria or generic or proprietary product listings. The information provided should be in sufficient detail to serve as the basis for a preliminary cost estimate.

9.3.3 Design Team Coordination

The other engineers and consultants usually have been developing their design concepts for the program and conceptual design provided by the A/E. These documents are included with the schematic design documents prepared by the A/E.

9.3.4 Estimates of Probable Construction Cost

While any of the estimating techniques detailed in Chapter 8 could be used, the unit of measure technique is the most appropriate because it is consistent with the other schematic design documents.

Schematic design estimates of probable construction cost may be formatted using *UniFormat*™ categories for identifying costs of major project elements. Because the design is broadly defined, the estimate will be similarly broad with a substantial contingency category to account for unknown factors.

9.4 Design Development Phase Documentation

AIA Document B101 requires the A/E to prepare drawings and other documents sufficient to describe the character of the project and its major elements, including architectural, structural, mechanical, and electrical systems, and materials as appropriate, along with adjustments to the preliminary cost estimate. EJCDC E-520 requires production of final design criteria, preliminary drawings, outline specifications, and written descriptions of the project along with a revised estimate of probable project cost.

9.4.1 Drawings

The drawings at this stage are more detailed than the schematic design drawings, but are not suitable as construction drawings. Artist's renderings are not typically used because at this point the stakeholders and participants are familiar with the aesthetic aspects of the project design. The emphasis during this time is shifting from aesthetics to the technical aspects of the project design in anticipation of producing construction drawings.

The objective of the drawings is to fix and describe the size and character of the project design and will typically include drawings for the following project aspects:

- Civil and site development
- Architectural
- Structural system
- Mechanical, electrical, plumbing, and fire protection systems
- Landscaping
- Other aspects necessary to communicate design development information, such as access security, food service equipment, or any of the many specialty consultants

The U.S. National CAD Standard for Architecture, Engineering, and Construction (NCS) provides the recognized standard format for organizing design information on design development drawings.

9.4.2 Outline Specifications

Outline specifications aid in the design process and are the basis for revising estimates of probable construction cost, schedules, and value analysis studies. They also serve as a checklist for the project team when selecting products and methods during development of the project manual.

They are a means of communication among members of the project team and between the team and the owner. Outline specifications help control the decision-making process and encourage clarity in the construction documents. The use of well-prepared outline specifications reduces the potential for design and drawing changes at later stages and the consequent inefficient use of design team time. Outline specifications can also be useful for the coordination of terminology between drawings and specifications. Outline specifications contain more detailed design decisions than system descriptions. System descriptions can usually be changed with less impact on the production of contract documents than changes in the outline specifications.

Outline specifications can help the owner become more familiar with and understand building elements, products, and standards. They also serve a variety of purposes for other entities, including lenders, estimators, construction managers, and code officials. Outline specifications are more than a table of contents for the final project manual. They are a record of decisions about specific materials, equipment, systems, methods, manufacturers, and special fabrication requirements.

Outline specifications are not construction documents nor do they become a part of, or a substitution for, the project manual. Effective outline specifications contribute to the successful accomplishment of the following tasks:

- Making product selection decisions early in the documentation process
- Recording product selection decisions and code requirements
- Making cost estimates for budget control
- Preparing time schedules
- Assisting the owner in understanding what materials and systems are proposed
- Coordinating construction documents
- Preparing the project manual

9.4.2.1 Format

Technical information documentation for the design development phase is frequently in the form of outline specifications, which are more technical than the general and narrative information of the schematic design phase. Outline specifications are typically in a format that can form the basis for the construction specifications and can be organized according to *MasterFormat*®.

MasterFormat® level-two numbers and titles are recommended for outline specifications. However, level-three and level-four numbers and titles may be used if suited to the materials selected.

An outline specification presents pertinent data in brief, concise statements, sometimes using the streamlining technique that is a method of reducing verbiage, as explained in Chapter 11. The three-part *SectionFormat*™ is not necessary, but listing the information in the same sequence will simplify production of the project specifications later during the construction documents stage of the project. Refer to *SectionFormat*™ for information about the three-part section format. Refer to Figure 9.2 for an example of an outline specification.

9.4.2.2 Content

Outline specifications typically include information about manufacturers, materials, manufactured units, equipment, components, and accessories. They also may describe

SECTION 08 44 13
GLAZED ALUMINUM CURTAIN WALLS

PART 1—GENERAL
1.1   SECTION INCLUDES
  A.   Conventionally Glazed Aluminum Curtain Walls Installed as Stick Assemblies.
1.2   PERFORMANCE REQUIREMENTS
  A.   Delegated Design: Provide structural design for glazed aluminum curtain walls.
  B.   Structural Performance:
    1.   Wind Loads: As indicated on drawings.
    2.   Live Load Vertical Deflection: 1/4 inch.
    3.   Maintenance Equipment Loads: As indicated on drawings.
  C.   Deflection of Framing Members:
    1.   Standard: AAMA TIR-A11.
    2.   Deflection Normal to Wall Plane: Limited to L/175.
    3.   Deflection Parallel to Glazing Plane: Limited to L/360 or 1/8 inch, whichever is smaller.
  D.   Windborne-Debris-Impact-Resistance Performance: Pass missile-impact and cyclic-pressure tests for Wind Zone 1.
  E.   Air Infiltration: 6.24 lbf/sq. ft.
  F.   Water Penetration: 15 lbf/sq. ft.
  G.   Condensation Resistance: Not less than 55.
1.3   QUALITY ASSURANCE
  A.   Manufacturer Qualifications: 10 years.
  B.   Fabricator Qualifications: 10 years.
  C.   Installer Qualifications: 10 years.
  D.   Mockups: 10 foot square.
  E.   Preinstallation Conference.
1.4   WARRANTY
  A.   Materials and Workmanship: 5 years.
  B.   Finish: 20 years.
PART 2—PRODUCTS
2.1   FRAMING
  A.   Framing Members: ASTM B 209 and ASTM B 221 extruded or formed aluminum.
    1.   Construction: Thermally broken.
    2.   Glazing System: Retained mechanically with gaskets on four sides.
    3.   Glazing Plane: Front.
  B.   Concealed Flashing: Dead-soft, 0.018-inch thick stainless steel.
  C.   Corrosion-resistant Fasteners and Anchors.
  D.   Framing Sealants.
2.2   ALUMINUM FINISHES
  A.   Aluminum Finishes: AAMA 2605, high-performance organic (three coat metallic).
2.3   FABRICATION
  A.   Shop Fabrication.
  B.   Provisions for Field Replacement of Glazing from Interior.
PART 3—EXECUTION
3.1   FIELD QUALITY CONTROL
  A.   Testing: By owner-engaged agency.
  B.   Testing Services:
    1.   Air Infiltration: ASTM E 783.
    2.   Water Penetration: ASTM E 1105.
    3.   Water Spray Test: AAMA 501.2.

END OF SECTION

Figure 9.2 An Example of an Outline Specification for a Glazed Aluminum Curtain Wall.

material mixes, fabrications, and finishes, along with installation, erection, and application procedures if the information is special or unique to the project. Only a few items from PART 1—GENERAL of *SectionFormat™* are necessary in outline specifications. Reference standards involving products and installation may be listed. Special submittal requirements beyond the norm, such as unusual samples, mock-ups, special testing requirements, and maintenance materials, should be listed. Special qualifications for manufacturers, fabricators, or installers may also be included, as well as a description of any extended or special warranty requirements. Include fabrication and workmanship requirements only when such information has an impact on product or installation grades, cost, or time scheduling.

Outline specifications aid in the design process and help form the basis for revised cost estimates and schedules. As the design process continues, they become the basis for preparation of the project specifications. Outline specifications serve as a checklist for the project team for choosing products and methods for later incorporation into the project specifications. Properly developed outline specifications establish criteria for the final contract documents. They also help to eliminate fragmented decision making, which can affect previous decisions and cause unnecessary changes and extra work.

9.4.3 Design Team Coordination

Prior to completing design development documents, the A/E must review the design and estimate of probable construction cost information provided by the owner and subconsultants to ensure that the documents are coordinated and within budget. The key to effective design team coordination is good communication. Time must be dedicated to performing coordination tasks. A well-planned, executed, and enforced coordination program can result in fewer addenda items, fewer change orders, fewer disputes, and reduced project costs. Ideally, the final documents will be as consistent as if they were prepared and produced by one source.

Complete coordination may be just as difficult when project design team members are on the A/E staff as when they are multiple outside consultants. There are three components to project design team coordination:

- *Organization.* Selecting team members and establishing management procedures
- *Execution.* Project design and production of construction documents
- *Quality Assurance.* Meetings, checklists, communication, and checking and cross-checking construction documents

Incomplete coordination among design team members can be a problem within the construction industry. Following are some of the issues that can result from incomplete coordination:

- *Duplications.* Duplications violate the Construction Specifications Institute (CSI) principle of "say it once and in the right place." Duplication is an opportunity for discrepancies that alter the uniform basis for procurement (bidding/negotiating/purchasing) and cause confusion. In turn, this can result in higher construction costs, faulty construction, disputes, decreased document credibility, and increased exposure to liability.
- *Omissions.* Omissions are defined as information concerning an element of work that is inadvertently excluded from the construction documents and are often

caused by a lack of understanding of the responsibilities of the various design disciplines and the absence of a joint checklist.

- *Errors or Discrepancies.* Conflicting information in the construction documents can be due to the lack of knowledge by the team leader or team members of the procurement (bidding/negotiating/purchasing) requirements, contract document requirements, agreements, insurance, bonds, or the conditions of the contract increases the possibility of discrepancies and conflicts.
- *Division 01 Responsibility.* Although Division 01—General Requirements is usually the responsibility of the design team leader, it affects all divisions and requires input from all disciplines.
- *Terminology Differences.* Differences in the technical and descriptive terms used on drawings and specifications of the various design disciplines can occur because the documents are not prepared by the same individual or in the same office.

9.4.4 Estimates of Probable Construction Cost

Design development activities include selecting products, systems, and equipment, which require more detailed cost information than for the previous stages. While any of the estimating techniques detailed in Chapter 8 could be used at this phase, the assemblies/systems or unit price methods may be used more frequently. Or one of the techniques used for developing a construction budget could also be used, as described in Chapter 6.

Estimates of probable construction cost should be prepared in a format and language that can be understood by all project participants and comply with the terms of the owner-A/E agreement. Sufficient detail should be provided to enable the owner and the A/E to recognize the major aspects of the design and how funds are allocated in each. A useful estimate should enable participants to identify problematic areas of the project and propose solutions. Design development estimates of probable construction cost may be formatted using *UniFormat*™ supplemented by *MasterFormat*® section numbering references. Because design and construction are assembly-based processes, *MasterFormat*® by itself may not be a satisfactory basis for estimates during the design phases.

Chapter 10
Product Selection and Evaluation

Introduction

In Chapter 8, the dual nature of design was introduced and it emphasized that the creative design of every facility of the built environment is accomplished by ideas and decisions of the merging of an aesthetic nature and a technical nature. The most significant place where these two natures are especially intertwined is in the realm of products, materials, assemblies, components, and equipment. While there are many materials that are exposed to view and are selected based on aesthetic decisions, there are many more that are concealed that are crucial to the performance of the facility over its life cycle. It is the technical portion of the dual nature that selects the materials that are concealed and evaluates the technical qualities of all materials and then makes decisions about their use in the aesthetic design.

By identifying, selecting, and evaluating individual products, the documents necessary for the manufacturing, fabrication, and installation can be produced. Who produces which documents depends on the project delivery method selected. For example, for the design-bid or negotiate-build project delivery methods, the architect/engineer (A/E) produces all of the documents that are necessary for procuring (bidding/negotiating/purchasing) and awarding a contract for construction.

Thorough product selection is required to:

- Establish performance requirements for the products, assemblies, equipment, as well as the facility itself.
- Identify types of products with attributes that comply with the performance requirements that are established for the project.
- Obtain product information from product representatives.
- Select specific products based on their history of performance in like applications, their compatibility with other selected products, and their life cycle value.
- Consider alternatives.
- Present product selections to the owner.
- Document selections.

This series of activities introduces the product representative as an important project participant. The A/E relies on trained manufacturer's representatives to identify products available in the marketplace and provide the technical support necessary to make informed product selections.

Product selection is the result of a process that involves every member of the designer, owner, constructor, and supplier teams at one time or the other depending on the product under consideration. The overall selection process includes establishing product requirements, and identifying and evaluating products for incorporation in the project. Products are evaluated during the preparation of construction documents and the bid process, and purchased and installed during construction. To complete the process, owners, facility managers, and A/Es often call on product representatives for advice on service and maintenance.

10.2 Types of Products

The term *product* is not only used in the traditional sense to identify manufactured units, but is also used generically to include materials, assemblies/fabrications, and equipment. Products can be categorized into the following types.

10.2.1 Materials

Materials tend to be naturally occurring substance, compound, liquid, or resource that is extracted, harvested, recycled, processed, or otherwise converted from a raw state into an asset with desirable physical properties useable for the construction of facilities. Materials are frequently intended for a single purpose or function, included in the manufacture of products, or can be directly installed or incorporated in the work. Examples include sand, Portland cement, stone, brick, lumber, various metals, and glass.

10.2.2 Commodities

A commodity can be defined as goods that can be uniformly and consistently produced by various manufacturers with the same predetermined quality. Materials become commodities when they are specified without a specific manufacturer being named, and material from any manufacturer will be acceptable.

10.2.3 Products

Configurations of various materials that are manufactured into a self-contained unit that has certain physical properties that is intended for a specific purpose or function that can be installed, applied, or incorporated into the work. Examples include paint, roofing membranes, sealants, windows, fasteners, plumbing fixtures, and glazed concrete masonry units.

10.2.3.1 Standard Products

Most manufacturers have a standard product line. The manufacturing equipment is set to fabricate the product in a certain way and can do so in the most expeditious time and efficient manner. Standard products are produced in quantity and stocked for shipment on receipt of a purchase order. Quite often, special design services are available to modify the product to fit a specific situation. This service is usually provided for an additional cost because the special design requires alteration of the standard equipment settings, resulting in increased production costs.

10.2.3.2 Custom Products

Products with nonstandard characteristics are considered custom products. Because of more sophisticated manufacturing processes and more efficient distribution capabilities, the distinction between standard and custom products is not as dramatic today as it was in the past. It is important for the A/E to understand the consequences of selecting and specifying custom products. When evaluating the use of custom products, the following situations may arise:

Prepayment   Manufacturers often require prepayment on orders for custom products to ensure that payment is made even if the product is not used, or the project is not constructed.

Submittals The request for a custom product often requires more extensive shop drawings, finish samples, and occasionally a mock-up prior to fabrication to assist the owner and A/E in communicating specific situations and desired results to the manufacturer.

Minimum Purchase Orders Custom products may have a minimum quantity or purchase order cost requirement for the product. This minimum order can increase the cost substantially if the minimum purchase order quantity is significantly more than the buyer actually needs.

Custom Colors Because custom colors are produced for a specific project, minimum orders are usually necessary. The buyer should also be informed that a custom color may be difficult to match when a future addition or renovation occurs.

Lead Time Because custom products are produced on demand, the manufacturer rarely stocks the product, and an extended lead time may be necessary.

Testing and Certification Custom products may alter the characteristics of standard products that have previously been tested and certified to meet industry standards. Often, additional testing is required before acceptance of the custom product to verify that it meets industry standards or code requirements. The testing process for required approvals or certifications may be costly and time consuming. The possibility also exists that the custom product may not pass the testing procedures and as a result be rejected.

Proprietary Products Proprietary products are often unique, high-performance materials without comparable competitively priced or functionally equivalent products. They may have limited distribution based on the geographic boundaries with distributors, installers, and manufacturers. Because of few approved installers or applicators in some areas, the product may not be available without paying a premium.

10.2.4 Assemblies/Fabrications

Assemblies/fabrications are configurations of materials and products that are assembled, fabricated, built, formulated, or mixed on-site or off-site prior to being installed or incorporated in the work. Examples include precast concrete panels, unitized curtain walls, drywall partitions, and wall louvers.

10.2.5 Equipment

Equipment are configurations of materials, products, and assemblies/fabrications in a self-contained form with an operational function either within a larger equipment unit or for a single purpose, that can be installed or incorporated in the work, and frequently connected to some form of building utility service. Examples include water heaters, pumps, elevators, control devices, fans, and packaged air conditioning units.

10.3 Importance of Product Selection and Evaluation

Every facility can be seen as a convergence of a vast number of diverse materials, products, components and equipment into a completed entity that encloses physical space for a specific purpose. Because of this, materials, products, components and equipment should be appropriate, suitable, functional, and compatible for the project and for the completed facility. Thus, it is important that designers and decision makers should be skilled in making selections and value judgments necessary to accomplish the project objectives.

The selection and evaluation process requires that numerous questions be answered before the necessary decisions can made. The following is a sampling of these questions:

- Do the various individual selections fit the project budget?
- Does each selection satisfy the project objectives?
- Of all the product attributes, which are important to what the product will be expected to do?
- Are the selected products available?
- Other than products that are periodically replaced due to wear and tear, will each product be durable for as long as it needs to be without being a burden on the owner?
- Will each product be satisfactory with the surrounding products?
- What are the advantages and limitations of each product?
- Does each product comply with an applicable standard?
- Will a product be a liability for the owner?
- What are the risks of selecting a particular product?
- Does each product have a record of success?

10.4 Obtaining Product Information

Just as the advent of the Internet has caused major paradigm shifts in the way society generates, absorbs, and disseminates information about anything, the product information world has also been permanently shifting in the way information is made available to the design professions and the construction industries. As the Internet has grown in popularity and usefulness in the first decade of the new century, what was once a large volume of library shelves packed with product information binders has been slowly giving way to product search engines and long lists of bookmarks and favorites on individual computers.

Because the Internet provides a relatively lower cost when compared to the cost of printed information, manufacturers are making much more information available than ever before. Also, most manufacturers are aware that current and accurate technical information is required for the design and construction of projects, so they have been more aggressive about providing customer service to those that make evaluations, selections, and decisions about products.

Sources of information about the aesthetic and technical attributes of products include the following:

- Product representatives, either manufacturer or independent
- Continuing education presentations and seminars
- Local suppliers, distributors, or providers
- Product shows
- Contractors and subcontractors
- Fabricators and installers
- Internet search engines
- Manufacturers' Internet web sites and proprietary specifications
- Trade-specific periodicals
- Trade associations, societies, councils, and institutes
- Technical manuals and books
- Owners and owner organizations
- Architects, engineers, and specialty consultants
- Master guide specifications writing companies
- Research agencies and testing laboratories
- Professional associations, societies, councils, and institutes

10.5 The Evaluation and Selection Process

Effective evaluation and selection of products for the design and construction of a project is an important responsibility of those that make design decisions. The process should be disciplined and thorough, and should conclude with products that are suitable for the project design and its location. While there are no perfect products, the products that are ultimately selected should be those that most favorably address the evaluation criteria—if grades were given for the evaluation process, the product receiving the highest grade should be the selection. Ferrous metals will always rust and wood will always rot, however, the question is not if they should be used on a project, but instead, if they are used, what are the criteria for them to remain serviceable and useful for the duration of the life cycle of the facility?

10.5.1 Initial Product Identification

As the design concept for a project is developed and the aesthetic design begins to give physical form to the desired project, products should be identified as generic products. Since the aesthetic design is still fluid at this point, it is too early to expend much time and effort evaluating and selecting the actual products that will be specified.

10.5.2 Establishing Product Criteria

As the design is developed further and in more detail, such as with design development or construction documents, the unique attribute of each product should be evaluated according to the product criteria that are established for the project.

10.5.2.1 The Nature of Attributes

The performance attributes of products should be evaluated to determine the suitability of any particular product for installation on any specific project. For example, when considering the suitability of a window, beyond its configuration and operational characteristics, the structural attributes, water resistance, air infiltration, and thermal performance are essential performance attributes. Many other specific attributes of the windows may be decided later, such as the window finish, window hardware, and mounting accessories. Attributes are the means by which performance characteristics are identified.

An attribute can be defined as a characteristic of performance. There are three essential considerations of an attribute:

- *Requirements.* Desired results, usually in qualitative terms. More than one requirement may be defined for a single attribute.
- *Criteria.* Performance criteria for a particular requirement, stated in quantitative or qualitative terms. Criteria must be either measurable or observable. Several criteria may be needed to completely and accurately define a requirement.
- *Tests.* Means of verifying conformance with performance criteria and a measure of actual or predicted performance level. A test will be associated with each criterion and may be based on a recognized industry test method, calculation or engineering analysis, observation, or professional judgment. Test results may be evaluated by conducting the specified test or simply by submitting certified results of previous testing.

For example, when considering a product for a ceiling, the following would be used for the evaluation:

- Attribute: Surface burning characteristics
  - Requirement: Flame spread
  - Criteria: A rating of less than 25 on a scale of 0 to 100
  - Test: ASTM E 84

Figure 10.1 is a reference guide that lists various attributes along with sample requirements, criteria, and tests.

Attribute	Requirement (R)/Criteria (C)	Test
HEADING I: SAFETY AND PROTECTION		
11 Fire Safety		
(01) Fire Areas	R: Control fire hazard neighboring structures.	
	C: Limit distance between structures: limit area within fire barriers; limit ceiling height.	
(02) Fire Barriers	R: Control the spread of fire.	1
	C: Require fire walls, fire stops, fire-resistance separation between egress openings; require that barrier penetrations maintain rated fire endurance; require fire dampers.	1
(03) Egress Means	R: Provide means for emergency evacuation.	
	C: State minimum number of exits, maximum travel distance to exits and other means of egress; require minimum width for public corridors and public stairways; limit obstruction by door swing or equipment installation; require exit signs.	1
(04) Protective Devices	R: Provide warning devices and automatic fire extinguishing equipment.	
	C: State conditions under which automatic fire detection systems, smoke detection systems, sprinkler systems, extinguishing systems, or other protection devices should be provided.	1.5
(05) Fire Resistance/Combustibility	R: Maintain integrity for sufficient time to permit evacuation or control of fire.	
	C: Require use of noncombustible materials, state minimum hours of fire resistance or classification.	1.3
(06) Fire Load/Fuel Contribution	R: Control fuel contribution of materials.	
	C: State maximum potential heat (contribution to fire load) in BTU per hour or BTU per square foot of material.	3
(07) Surface Spread of Flame	R: Control surface spread of flame.	
	C: State maximum flame spread or flammability of rating.	3
(08) Flame Propagation	R: Control propagation of flame through enclosed spaces.	
	C: State maximum flame propagation index.	1,3
(09) Smoke Generation	R: Control amount and toxic effect of smoke produced.	
	C: State maximum smoke development rating; state maximum optical density and maximum time to reach critical density; limit toxicity of smoke, require that smoke be non-noxious.	3
(10) Smoke Propagation	R: Control propagation of smoke through enclosed spaces.	
	C: Require smoke-tight joints, provide for venting of smoke areas.	1,3
(11) Accidental Ignition	R: Protect against accidental ignition of fire.	
	C: Design to prevent spark formation; limit equipment overheating; require equipment mounting to permit adequate ventilation.	1
12 Life Safety (other than fire)		
(01) Physical Safety	R: Protect against physical hazards.	
	C: Require guardrails, handrails, protective covers on moving parts; slip-resistant surfaces.	1
(02) Electrical Safety	R: Protect against electrical hazards.	
	C: Require protective cover, insulation, and grounding: require safety controls and interlocks.	1
(03) Toxicity	R: Control dangerous materials and substances.	
	C: Limit toxicity of materials; surfaces and finishes; limit toxic emissions below stated temperatures; limit toxic venting and leakage.	3
(04) Chemical Safety	R: Protect against hazard from chemical substances.	
	C: Identify chemicals and agents, including concentration and anticipated frequency of use, to which the system will be exposed; indicate the level of atmospheric pollution permitted.	1

Test Codes:

1. Design Drawings   2. Design Calculations   3. Laboratory Certification   4. Prototype Testing   5. Inspection

Figure 10.1   **Suggested Attributes/Requirements/Criteria/Tests**   *(continued)*

Attribute	Requirement (R)/Criteria (C)	Test
(05) Azoic Protection	R: Protect against infection from biological sources.	
	C: Identify insects, vermin, fungi, microorganisms and other biological contaminants likely to be encountered and state level of protection to be provided.	1
13 Property Protection		
(01) Theft Security	R: Protect equipment and eontents against theft.	
	C: Design to control unauthorized entry and access.	1
(02) Security against Vandalism	R: Protect against malicious damage.	
	C: Design to resist malicious damage.	1,5
(03) Resistance to Misuse	R: Protect against accidental or deliberate misuse.	
	C: Design to prevent improper usage. Design for failsafe operation. Perform factory adjustment. Provide instructions.	1,5
14 Accessibility Considerations		
(01) Physical Access	R: Provide for physical access by impaired individuals.	
	C: Design to provide at least one means of ingress and egress for individuals in wheelchairs.	1
(02) Mobility-Impaired Usage	R: Provide for building usage by mobility-impaired individuals, if appropriate.	
	C: Design to permit mobility-impaired individuals access to and use of facilities and equipment, such as restrooms, drinking fountains, vending machines, elevators.	1
(03) Vision-Impaired Usage	R: Provide for building usage by vision-impaird individuals, if appropriate.	
	C: Design to permit vision-impaired individuals access to and use of facilities and equipment, such as restrooms, drinking fountains, vending machines, elevators.	1
(04) Hearing-Impaired Usage	R: Provide for building usage by persons with hearing deficiencies, if appropriate.	
	C: Design to permit hearing-impaired full usage of building services, such as, fire alarm systems, door bells, audible signals system.	1
HEADING 2: FUNCTIONAL		
21 Strength		
(01) Static Loading	R: Sustain gravity loads and superimposed and specified vertical and lateral loads.	
	C: State dead loads to be supported, including forces transmitted from other systems. Specify how and were loads shall be transmitted from other systems.	2
(02) Live Loading	R: Sustain dynamic loads.	
	C: Describe live loads to be supported, including snow load. Identify concentrated loads and state design floor loads.	2
(03) Horizontal Loading	R: Sustain wind loads and other lateral loads.	
	C: For exterior walls, state design wind speeds and other live loads. State typhoon or hurricane conditions. For partitions state lateral design load per square foot of partition area.	2
(04) Deflection	R: Limit deflection.	
	C: State maximum acceptable deflections.	2
(05) Thermal Loading	R: Sustain loads due to temperature change.	
	C: State the temperature extremes to be used for design.	2
(06) Structural Serviceability	R: Retain serviceability under load and deflection.	
	C: Require structure to sustain design loads without causing local damage.	2
(07) Seismic Loading	R: Sustain earthquake loads.	
	C: State the seismic zone to be used for design.	2

Test Codes:
1. Design Drawings   2. Design Calculations   3. Laboratory Certification   4. Prototype Testing   5. Inspection

Figure 10.1 *(continued)*

Attribute	Requirement (R)/Criteria (C)	Test
(08) Impact Loading	R: Sustain impact loads and forces.	
	C: Describe the source and magnitude of any impact loads to be sustained.	2
(09) Penetration Resistance	R: Protect against damage from concentrated loads.	
	C: Describe magnitude and location of concentrated loads.	2
22 Durability		
(01) Impact Resistance	R: Resist surface degradation due to point impact.	
	C: Limit surface indentation due to specified impact load.	3
(02) Moisture Resistance	R: Resist degradation when exposed to water or water vapor.	
	C: Design for use in specified range of humidity. Limit permanent effect to exposure to water, water retention, and absorption.	3
(03) Thermal Resistance	R: Resist degradation when exposed to temperature ranges expected in normal use.	
	C: Limit physical change when exposed to specified temperature range.	3
(04) Corrosion Resistance	R: Resist degradation when exposed to corrosive agents.	
	C: Limit corrosive effect observed after specified exposure to salt spray or fog; require corrosive-resistant surface treatment: design to avoid contact of dissimilar metals.	3
(05) Chemical Resistance	R: Resist degradation when exposed to chemicals. Resist staining or damage from soluble and insoluble salts, alkali attack, and oxidation.	
	C: Limit changes in appearance or other specified property after exposure to specified chemicals.	3
(06) Weather Resistance	R: Resist degradation when exposure to specified period of simulated weathering.	
	C: Limit changes observed after exposure to specified period of simulated weathering.	3
(07) Ultraviolet Resistance	R: Resist degradation due to exposure to ultraviolet light.	
	C: Limit discoloration after ultraviolet exposure.	3
(08) Surface Serviceability	R: Resist cracking, spalling, crazing, blistering, delaminating, chalking, and fading.	
	C: Limit surface changes observed after exposure to simulated conditions of use.	3
(09) Stain Resistance	R: Resist permanent discoloration when exposed to staining agents and chemicals.	
	C: Limit visual evidence of permanent stains due to treatment with identified agents.	3
(10) Absorbency	R: Resist tendency to absorb and retain water.	
	C: Limit quantity of water retained after specified exposure.	3
(11) Cleanability	R: Resist damage from routine maintenance and cleaning; permit removal of identified stains.	
	C: Limit discoloration or surface change after simulated cleaning with specified cleaning agents.	3
(12) Color Resistance	R: Resist fading over time	
	C: Limit discoloration after stared period.	3
(13) Friability/Frangibility	R: Resist crumbling and brittle fracture.	
	C: Limit damage observed after specified loading.	3
(14) Abrasion Resistance	R: Resist degradation due to rubbing.	
	C: Limit weight loss after specified number of abrasion cycles.	3
(15) Scratch Resistance	R: Resist degradation due to scratching.	
	C: Limit rating on pencil hardness scratch scale.	3
(16) Dimensional Stability	R: Control dimensional changes resulting from changes in environment.	
	C: Limit volume change and movement under specified exposure to moisture and temperature variation.	3
(17) Cohesiveness/Adhesiveness	R: Resist peeling and delamination.	
	C: Limit peeling or delamination failures under specified simulated loading.	3

Test Codes:
1. Design Drawings   2. Design Calculations   3. Laboratory Certification   4. Prototype Testing   5. Inspection

Figure 10.1   (*continued*)

Attribute	*Requirement (R)/Criteria (C)*	*Test*
(18) System Life	R: Function properly for identified period.	
	C: Limit failure under accelerated life test. Design life of components consistent with specified life of system.	3,4
23 Transmission Characteristics		
(01) Heat	R: Control heat transmission.	
	C: Design for specified thermal transmittance ("U" value).	2
(02) Light	R: Control light transmission.	
	C: Design for specified percentage of light or radiation transmission.	2
(03) Air Infiltration	R: Resist leakage of air.	
	C: Limit infiltration under specified pressure or wind load. Design for specified maximum leakage.	2,3,4
(04) Vapor Penetration	R: Resist vapor penetration.	
	C: Design vapor barrier for minimum vapor permeability.	2,3,4
(05) Water Leakage	R: Resist water leakage.	
	C: Limit infiltration under specified pressure or wind load design for specified maximum leakage.	2,3,4
(06) Condensation	R: Control admission and condensation of moisture.	
	C: Design to provide moisture barriers and thermal breaks.	2,4
24 Waste Products and Discharge		
(01) Solid Waste	R: Control production of solid waste. Provide for elimination or emission and prevent undesired accumulation.	
HEADING 3: SENSIBLE	C: Design to accommodate waste produced or accumulated. Require identification of wastes produced.	1,2
(02) Liquid Waste	R: Control production of liquid waste. Provide for elimination or emission and prevent undesired accumulation.	
	C: Design to accommodate waste levels produced, accumulated or omitted. Require identification of waste produced.	2
(03) Gaseous Waste	R: Control production of gases. Provide for elimination and prevent undesired accumulation.	
	C: Design to accommodate levels of gas accumulated or emitted. Require identification of gaseous waste emitted.	1,2
(04) Odor	R: Control formation and persistence of odors.	
	C: Design to prevent odor formation.	1
(05) Particulate Discharge	R: Control production of particulate wastes. Provide for collection of waste and prevent undesired accumulation.	
	C: Design to accommodate amount of particulate waste produced. Limit particulate concentration.	1,2
(06) Thermal Discharge	R: Limit of thermal energy and vibration. Provide for control or reabsorption.	
	C: Design to control thermal discharge produced below specified levels.	2
(07) Radiation	R: Limit emission of radiation. Provide for control or reabsorption.	
	C: Design to control radiation discharge produced below specified levels.	2
25 Operational Characteristics		
(01) Method of Operation	R: Provide operating methods consistent with function.	
	C: List desired operating modes.	1,2,3,4
(02) Results of Operation	R: Provide output consistent with function.	
	C: List desired output quantities and rates.	1,2,5
(03) Cycle Time/Speed of Operation	R: Provide cycle times to accommodate functional requirements.	
	C: List desired repetition rates.	1,2,5

Test Codes:

1. Design Drawings   2. Design Calculations   3. Laboratory Certification   4. Prototype Testing   5. Inspection

Figure 10.1   (*continued*)

Attribute	Requirement (R)/Criteria (C)	Test
31 Aesthetic Properties		
(01) Arrangement	R: Provide order, organization or relationship appealing to visual perception.	
	C: Design for pleasing relationships between elements and components.	1
(02) Composition	R: Provide unified appearance appealing to visual perception.	
	C: Design for pleasing overall appearance.	1
(03) Texture	R: Provide surface finishes appealing to tactile perception.	
	C: Design surface finishes pleasant to touch and feel.	1,4,5
(04) Color/Gloss	R: Provide finishes with pattern or luster appealing to visual perception.	
	C: Design surface finishes for pleasing appearance.	1,4,5
(05) Uniformity/Variety	R: Provide appropriate consistency or variety of visual environment.	
	C: Design to provide pleasing variety of colors, textures, and glosses. Limit visual confusion.	1,4,5
(06) Compatibility/Contrast	R: Provide appropriate consistency or variety of visual environment.	
	C: Design appearance of elements in a pleasing and harmonious combination.	1,4,5
32 Acoustical Properties		
(01) Sound Generation	R: Control undesirable sound and vibration generation.	
	C: Limit sound generation. Provide specified decibel rating.	2,3,4,5
(02) Sound Transmission	R: Control transmission of sound.	
	C: Design for specified sound transmission classification. Provide STC or SPP rating.	1,2,3,4,5
(03) Reflectance	R: Control reflection, reverberation, and echo production.	
	C: Design for specified reverberation time, and sound path length.	1,2,3,4
33 Illumination		
(01) Level	R: Control quantity of illumination provided.	
	C: Design for specified illumination intensity level. Design to provide specified level of natural light.	2,5
(02) Color	R: Control color (wavelength) of illumination.	
	C: Require lamp color and specified range of correlated color temperature.	
(03) Shadow/Glare	R: Control illumination uniformity.	
	C: Design for specified variation in illumination level over room area.	2,3,4
(04) Reflection	R: Control undesirable reflection.	
	C: Limit reflected light.	2,5
34 Ventilation		
(01) Air Quality	R: Control air quality.	
	C: Design for specified natural ventilation. Design to control rate of air removal and supply design to control odors.	1,2
(02) Velocity	R: Control air movement.	
	C: Design to maintain air motion between specified limits.	1,2
(03) Distribution	R: Control temperature gradients.	
	C: Design to control temperature gradients within specified limits.	1,2
(04) Pressurization	R: Control pressure differential.	
	C: Design to limit air leakage.	2
(05) Temperature	R: Control air temperature content.	
	C: State exterior design conditions. Design to control rate of change of mean radiant temperature within specified range.	
(06) Moisture	R: Control air moisture content.	
	C: State exterior design conditions. Design to provide specified range of relative humidity.	2
35 Measurable Characteristics		
(01) Levelness	R: Control deviation from identified horizontal.	
	C: Require level installation. Design for case of level installation.	5
(02) Plumbness	R: Control deviation from identified vertical.	
	C: Require plumb installation within specified tolerance. Design for case of plumb installation.	5

Test Codes:

1. Design Drawings   2. Design Calculations   3. Laboratory Certification   4. Prototype Testing   5. Inspection

Figure 10.1 (*continued*)

Attribute	Requirement (R)/Criteria (C)	Test
(03) Dimension/Tolerance	R: Control spatial extent for installation or fit within available space.	
	C: Conform to specified spatial dimensions and tolerances.	5
(04) Volume	R: Control volumetric measure or capacity.	
	C: Conform to specified limits of volume or capacity.	5
(05) Flatness	R: Control planar surface characteristics.	
	C: Limit deviation from flat, smooth, or planar surface.	5
(06) Shape	R: Control surface configuration, contour, or form.	
	C: Conform to specified shape limitations.	5
(07) Weight/Density	R: Control weight or density.	
	C: Conform to specified weight or density limitations.	5
36 Material Properties		
(01) Hardness	R: Control resistance to penetration.	
	C: Limit penetration under specified load.	3
(02) Ductility/Brittleness	R: Control capability to shape by drawing. Control tendency to shatter.	
	C: Limit percentage elongation or percent change in cross section before rupture.	3
(03) Malleability	R: Control capability to shape by hammering.	
	C: Limit choice of materials.	
(04) Resilience	R: Control capability to store energy.	
	C: Limit residual deformation after impact load.	3
(05) Elasticity/Plasticity	R: Control capability to retain original shape when load is removed.	
	C: Limit residual deformation after removal of load.	3
(06) Toughness	R: Control capability to change shape without rupture.	
	C: Limit energy absorption before rupture.	3
(07) Viscosity	R: Control fluid resistance to flow.	
	C: Limit coefficient of viscosity.	3
(08) Creep	R: Control permanent change in shape after prolonged exposure to stress or elevated temperature.	
	C: Limit permanent deformation under specified load or temperature conditions.	3
(09) Friction	R: Control tendency of two bodies in contact to resist relative motion.	
	C: Limit coefficient of friction.	3
(10) Thermal Expansion	R: Control change in unit dimension resulting from change in temperature.	
	C: Limit coefficient of thermal expansion.	3
HEADING 4: PRACTICAL		
41 Interface Characteristics		
(01) Fit	R: Control size and shape of interface elements.	1,4,5
	C: Design for physical compatibility with specified elements.	
(02) Attachment	R: Control physical and electrical connection at interface.	1,4,5
	C: Design to use specified connections.	
(03) Tolerance	R: Control variation in interface dimension.	1,4,5
	C: Design to accommodate specified tolerance.	
(04) Modularity	R: Control standardized unit dimensions or repating dimension.	1,4,5
	C: Design for compatibility with the specified module.	
(05) Rotability	R: Control orientation at interface.	1,4,5
	C: Design to provide or permit specified orientations.	
(06) Relocatability	R: Control ability to disassemble move or relocate.	1,4,5
	C: Design to provide specified flexibility to dismount and re-erect.	
(07) Erection Sequence	R: Control order of erection or installation.	1,4,5
	C: Design to provide specified flexibility to dismount or re-erect.	
42 Service		
(01) Repairability	R: Provide for repair or replacement of damaged or inoperative elements.	
	C: Design for ease of repair. Limit use of special tools, limit amount of labor required.	1,4,5

Test Codes:

1. Design Drawings   2. Design Calculations   3. Laboratory Certification   4. Prototype Testing   5. Inspection

Figure 10.1 *(continued)*

Attribute	Requirement (R)/Criteria (C)	Test
(02) Interchangeability	R: Provide for interchangeability of elements.	
	C: Design for interchangeability.	1,4,5
(03) Accessibility	R: Provide access for service and maintenance.	
	C: Design with access panels. Avoid placing connections in inaccessible locations.	1,4,5
(04) Replaceability	R: Provide for substitution of equivalent elements.	
	C: Design to permit substitution.	1,4,5
(05) Inconvenience	R: Limit disturbance during maintenance and repair.	
	C: Design to minimize inconvenience. Provide backup or alternate elements.	1,4,5
(06) Extendibility	R: Provide for capability to increase capacity.	
	C: Design to permit or accommodate extension or expansion.	1,4,5
(07) Adaptability	R: Provide for alteration or modification.	
	C: Design to use industry standard connectors and interface elements.	1,4,5
(08) Replacement Sequence	R: Provide for identified order for removal and replacement.	
	C: Design for identified replacement sequence.	1,4,5
(09) Service Frequency	R: Control repair and maintenance frequency.	
	C: Design for identified failure rates and maintenance schedules.	1,4,5
43 Personnel Needs		
(01) Maintenance Personnel	R: Control skill levels required for maintenance.	
	C: Design for maintenance by personnel with identified skills.	2
(02) Training	R: Control availability of trained personnel.	
	C: Require provision for training operators and maintenance personnel.	2

Test Codes:
1. Design Drawings   2. Design Calculations   3. Laboratory Certification   4. Prototype Testing   5. Inspection

Figure 10.1 **(continued)**

10.5.2.2 Project Requirements

Early in the project delivery process, a project program sets the requirements for form and function, creating project requirements that will influence product selection decisions.

The project budget directly influences decisions by setting price parameters for products. As will be discussed later, an important aspect of the selection of products is aligning each product with criteria that will be established for making decisions.

The project schedule has two basic influences:

- One influence is the schedule for design delivery. Although the project delivery process accelerates projects through the design phases, it may not allow sufficient time for product evaluation. If the time allotted for product evaluation is limited, the documents may be limited to only those product options that are already known or the few that were evaluated within the limited time frame. This, in turn, increases the occurrences of substitution requests and often increases construction prices.
- Another schedule influence is product delivery. Product availability and delivery become crucial factors. These influences are normally secondary considerations to prices, but are sometimes important factors.

Regulatory requirements also exert influence product selections. Building codes and statutes have a direct influence on product selection. These are discussed in more detail in Chapter 4.

Finally, marketplace considerations introduce competitive influences on product selection. Some products may not be available within the project schedule. Fabricators and manufacturers cannot produce products until submittals are approved, and submittals cannot be produced until a contract is in place, and a contract cannot be in place until the construction documents have been produced. If it takes months or a year or two to produce the products, but only a few months are scheduled between submittal approval and the time the products are required on site, then that product is not a viable option for selection. This is one of the issues that the Integrated Project Delivery method takes into account by moving the decision to a point much earlier in the delivery process.

10.5.2.3 Project Delivery

Table 10.1 illustrates the stages of a project and the types of decisions made during each stage. Activities are performed during the design phases that create a setting for progressive decisions leading to a final product selection. These progressive decisions begin at an elemental level in the early phases and become more detailed as the design progresses.

During the schematic design phase, the project program requirements discussed earlier are developed. Basic decisions are made such as whether the structure should be steel or concrete and whether the exterior skin should be an aluminum curtain wall or brick veneer. These decisions are conceptual and require only basic information. This information focuses primarily on aesthetics, form, function, and budgets. Other product information needs at this phase are applicable code and regulatory requirements, site characteristics, and budget prices for comparison of various products and systems. These decisions are required so that informed decisions on basic functional requirements and basic building construction elements.

Table 10.1 **Project Stages, Decisions, and Information Needs**

	Project Conception	Design	Construction Documentation	Bidding/ Negotiating/ Purchasing	Construction	Facility Management
Activities	Programming, Concepts, and Budgeting Schedule	Product and Systems Decisions Value Analysis	Working Out Details for Incorporation of Products into Project Value Analysis	Quantity Takeoffs and Estimating	Sales and Delivery Installation and Startup Procedures	Operation and Maintenance Services
Documents	Preliminary Project Descriptions Sketches Renderings Models	Outline Specifications Preliminary Drawings Statement of Probable Costs/ Cost Estimate	Project Manuals Construction Drawings Statement of Probable Costs/ Cost Estimate	Bid Forms Contract Forms Addenda	Purchase Orders Submittals Delivery Slips Modifications	Operation and Maintenance Data Record Documents Warranties
Information Needs	Code and Regulatory Requirements Product Characteristics Budget Pricing Product Literature	Product Availability Code Approvals Installed Costs Warranty	Installation Details Compatibility Requirements Technical Data Comparable Manufacturers Quality Standards	Price Information Product Compliance Data Substitution Requests	Submittals Installation Requirements Qualified Installers Delivery Schedule Warranty Inspections	Operation and Maintenance Instructions Personnel Training Demonstrations

During the design development phase, decisions are more focused on determining the details of the project design so that the appropriate products can be evaluated and selected, and the appropriate drawings and specifications can be prepared.

10.5.3 Determining Applicable Criteria for Evaluation

At some point between the schematic design phase and the later stages of the construction document phase, but before the final decisions are made on the selection of products, criteria for product selection should be developed based on the project design, the project requirements, regulatory requirements, and the project location. Products do not need to be evaluated according to each and every product criterion known, but only those that apply to the specific project.

10.5.4 Attribute Categories for Evaluation

The attribute categories that follow, while an extensive list in itself, is probably only a small number of the possible categories and attributes that could be developed for a product. There are so many products that can be used in so many projects in so many locations that it is impossible to compile a single list that is useable for every project.

10.5.4.1 General Considerations

In addition to evaluating the qualities of a product, it should also be evaluated in the context of the entire project. Some products affect the performance, function, or appearance of other products and thereby affect subsequent product selections. To make the evaluation and selection process efficient, major systems and subsystems should be selected first, and then smaller components selected based on their performance attributes as well as their compatibility with prior product selections.

Compatibility is an important concern. Knowledge of material, assembly, and system characteristics and methods of alleviating or eliminating potential problems is an essential consideration. Two products may each be proper selections when evaluated separately, but when installed together, one or both may fail because of incompatibility (e.g., the galvanic corrosion that occurs when dissimilar metals are placed in contact in a damp or wet environment). Products must be evaluated together as parts of a system and require coordination among the design disciplines.

The performance, function, and appearance of a product, and its level of importance, is not the same for every project. The attributes of each product should be considered for each project—just because a product is suitable for one project, does not automatically mean that it is suitable for another project.

Product criteria should be established so that actual products can be selected from the available options. Care should be exercised to ensure that products are available for selection when evaluated according to the product criteria.

Since the owner establishes the quality of the facility based on the project requirements and budget, products should be evaluated to determine if they are appropriate for the owner's intentions.

Architectural and engineering licensing regulations, under state jurisdiction, require that those professionals who seal the drawings and specifications are responsible for the nature, quality, and execution of the products indicated, specified, or required for construction. Because of this liability, the A/E will normally make the final selection of products even if the decision is based on the result of a group discussion and consensus. The architect usually influences the choice of aesthetic products, the structural engineer for the structural aspects of the project design, and the mechanical and electrical engineers for their systems, and so forth for each professional providing services on the project. In almost every case, A/Es, because of their knowledge of products, will also be heavily involved in the process and are expected to exercise professional judgment. This is one of the most important responsibilities of an A/E.

If the construction documents are performance based or list optional products, final product selection might be performed by the contractor after the contract for construction is awarded. However, each of the products that are named should have been duly evaluated. In these cases, it may not be known which product will be selected until manufacturer's product data and other information is submitted during the construction phase.

In spite of their similarities, construction products will have different characteristics, making no two identical in every respect. A determination should be made of the degree of variance in product characteristics can be allowed and still be acceptable.

A determination should be made if the product is recommended by the manufacturer for the use intended for the project. The product's documented properties and limitations should be compared against the criteria established for the project. Evaluations should reveal whether the product is domestic or imported, whether delivery will be a problem, whether replacement parts will be excessively expensive, and whether any of these factors will affect the design.

The effects of varying climatic conditions on the product should be evaluated (e.g., temperature and humidity, effect of condensation, alternate wetting and drying conditions).

It is often difficult to verify information presented in promotional literature. Test reports can be helpful but are inconclusive unless conducted according to recognized standards by a reliable independent testing laboratory or agency. Testing laboratories and agencies must be acceptable to authorities having jurisdiction (AHJs) for the test data to be accepted. Standardized tests can be valuable for comparing the properties of one product to another, although the usefulness of this kind of information may be difficult to assess. Ideally, tests should duplicate site conditions as nearly as possible. Performance history as well as the following should be evaluated:

- Product history and development
- Length of time on the market
- Conditions and circumstances of other installations
- Optimum conditions of use
- Maintenance requirements

It may be helpful to obtain product performance information from others (such as building owners, A/Es, contractors, AHJs, and installers-applicators) who have had experience with the product under consideration. Inquiries should be made into recently completed projects and older installations, and not only the ones recommended by the product representative. It is a good policy to use only those products that have been adequately field-tested. Selection of new products should be undertaken only with the project owner's consent and understanding of potential risks. AHJs may be hesitant to accept a new product as complying with the requirements of code, and considerable effort may be necessary to gain approval for its use in some jurisdictions. Determine whether changes in the manufacture of a product have been made recently. The new product may not perform the same or as well as the old product. Product failure does not necessarily mean the product is not good, but that it may be misapplied. Much can be learned from the experiences of others.

Not all products require in-depth evaluation for each project. Products of a generic nature may be used so often that their attributes are known and, thus do not require an evaluation every time they are selected. Their attributes, cost, and life cycle value are well understood because of their widespread use. One of the hallmarks of empirical experience is that knowledge and experience is cumulative, and unless project criteria are different from previous projects and evaluations, a product may not necessarily need to be evaluated.

10.5.4.2 Physical Properties

A physical property of a product is any aspect that can be measured by repeatable testing.

As discussed above, the most frequently used method of determining if a product will comply with the criterion of an attribute requirement is to test its physical properties. While there is not a perfect way to be certain that a product will be suitable for project, laboratory testing and inspection is the most practical method. The following are only a few of the many physical properties for which resistance can be tested or inspected:

- Corrosion
- Ultraviolet light degradation
- Impact
- Chemical
- Abrasion
- Stain
- Conductance
- Wind loading
- Seismic

The following are a few of the physical properties for which performance can be measured:

- Density
- Dimensional stability
- Absorbency
- Thermal resistance
- Hardness
- Ductility
- Malleability
- Elasticity
- Viscosity
- Flow rate

10.5.4.3 Performance

In many instances it is necessary to determine if a product, or in some case an assembly of products, can perform in a certain way, such as the following:

- Moisture vapor transmission rate
- Air infiltration
- Water penetration
- Condensation
- Expansion and contraction
- Deflection
- Windborne impact resistance
- Energy

10.5.4.4 Sustainability

Because of the popularity of the green building movement and the subsequent development of many guides and rating systems, there are a considerable number of criteria that can be used to determine the sustainable attributes of a product, such as the following:

- Low embodied energy
- Recyclability, material reuse, or salvaged
- Natural or renewable resources
- Locally or regionally produced
- Energy efficiency
- Low environmental impact
- Durability
- Recycled content
- Waste minimization
- Promotes good indoor air quality
- Absence of unhealthful chemicals, toxic substances, or volatile organic compounds
- Biodegradable or bio-based composition
- Conservation of resources
- Responsible wood supplies

When products are evaluated according to sustainability criteria, the evaluation may require the selection of products that comply with the sustainability principles of a selected Green Building rating system. The Leadership in Energy and Environmental Design (LEED™) rating program is based on the following categories of environmental goals:

- Sustainable sites
- Water efficiency
- Energy and atmosphere
- Materials and resources
- Indoor environmental quality
- Innovations in design

Another important asset available for the evaluation of products are the various independent websites that provide product information arranged according to sustainability criteria such as the following:

- Building Green (www.buildinggreen.com)
- Cool Roof Rating Council (www.coolroofs.org)
- Ecolect (www.ecolect.net)
- Energy Star (www.energystar.gov)
- GreenFormat (www.greenformat.com)
- GreenSeal (www.greenseal.org)
- GreenSpec (www.greenspec.co.uk)
- Heartland Green Sheets (www.heartlandgreensheets.org)

10.5.4.5 Safety and Protection

There are several subcategories in which these attributes can be organized:

- Fire safety:
  - Fire resistance
  - Surface spread of flame
  - Fuel contribution
  - Flame propagation
  - Smoke propagation
- Life safety:
  - Electrical
  - Toxicity
  - Chemical
- Property protection:
  - Security against vandalism
  - Resistance to misuse

10.5.4.6 Manufacturers

There will be many instances when it will be preferable to identify the available manufacturers. For certain projects, it may be necessary to identify manufacturers' qualifications. The following information about the manufacturer is helpful when evaluating qualifications:

- Country of origin, which can affect delivery time, testing procedures, availability of parts, maintenance, warranty service, and so on, for the product
- Financial stability
- Distribution network
- Performance criteria and test results
- Extent of technical services and local representation network
- Warranty and service

10.5.4.7 Installers

Although the construction drawings and specifications describes work results rather than the means, methods, and techniques necessary to achieve them, which is the responsibility of the contractor, it is prudent to evaluate the manufacturer's instructions for installation or application to determine whether they are sufficiently specific to complement the specifications. Installation instructions may indicate:

- Required project conditions
- Alternative installation methods for different types of projects
- Manufacturer's field quality control requirements
- Maintenance requirements
- Installer qualifications
- Coordination requirements
- Delivery, storage, and handling requirements
- Site conditions at the time of installation or application

If the installation will be within an existing building, other special considerations are necessary. The effect the new work will have on existing areas that are not involved should be evaluated, including the following:

- Size of existing openings
- Presence of hazards, disturbances, or other hardships requiring precautionary measures
- Fumes and odors emitted during the installation of products in occupied buildings

It is important to be aware of preparation or finishing requirements not accomplished as part of the product installation that may have cost implications or affect sequencing of the work.

10.5.4.8   Cost

The installed cost of a product is a key concern. A product may have a low material cost but require expensive, labor-intensive installation. It is often possible to use a product in a number of different ways, some more expensive than others. If minimum initial cost is a prime requirement, then fabrication and erection details must be kept simple in accordance with common trade practices. Initial cost may not always be the dominant factor in selecting products. For many projects, life cycle cost may be a more appropriate measure of value. The anticipated frequency of product replacement due to the projected wear and deterioration is a factor in determining life cycle cost. The product's predicted replacement cycle with the owner's projection of the life of the project should be compared and evaluated.

10.5.4.9   Maintenance

Preventive maintenance requirements should be considered during product selection, because maintenance costs affect the life cycle cost of products and equipment. Maintenance considerations include the following:

- *Product Design.* Some products are designed in a manner that makes maintenance procedures easier to perform than with otherwise similar products. Products requiring complex multistep maintenance procedures may not be practical, a condition that may lead to poor product performance and reduced life cycle value.

- *Maintenance Cycles.* The frequency of maintenance and the effect of procedures on the operations of the facility should be considered.
- *Maintenance Training.* The cost of training in-house maintenance personnel should be compared to the cost of contracting maintenance to specialists.
- *Maintenance Supplies.* The availability and cost of maintenance supplies should be given consideration.
- *Manufacturer or Distributor Support Services.* Cost and availability of maintenance services offered by the manufacturer should also be considered.

For many projects, it is also prudent to discuss product selection with the management and maintenance personnel for the facility because they usually have valuable and useable insight into how certain products perform and their need for maintenance.

10.6 Services That Product Representatives Provide

To be effective in meeting the needs of the many that are involved in the design and construction of facilities, product representatives should strive to be in a position to provide accurate information with the necessary level of detail that is appropriate to the stage of the project to whomever needs the information.

A/Es need assistance in selecting the appropriate products for their projects. A product representative who exhibits detailed knowledge, competence, a willingness to consult, and has a history of honest and ethical dealings is an important resource for the design community. A/Es need product information, and access to current information is an important service.

In addition to supplying technical information used for product selection, the representative may provide assistance in preparing a specification and providing details for product installation for use on drawings. A/Es need to be aware of product costs, including installation costs, since they are responsible for designing projects to fit an owner's budget. They will often consult the product representative when preparing cost estimates and making comparisons and evaluations.

10.6.1 Technical Assistance

The A/E requires product information to create adequate drawings and specifications during design. Product representatives assist and advise the A/E in getting the product documented correctly.

Many products are incorporated into every project. Product costs may be affected dramatically by information such as lead times, custom orders, and special field testing, or inspections if not brought to the A/E's attention in a timely manner.

In addition to assisting the A/E with the product decisions, product representatives can add value to their service in other ways. These include providing product cost information, storage recommendations, and reference standards and making the A/E aware of related code requirements.

10.6.2 Assistance in Preparing Specifications

While many design and construction team members are involved in selecting and purchasing products and systems, the person actually developing the project specifications is the most likely to request comprehensive technical assistance. Product representatives should be able to perform the following tasks:

- Provide generic descriptions of products and systems.
- Understand the work of other trades that affects the proper installation and performance of the product.
- Point out the reference standards that relate to the product.
- Describe related work associated with the product.
- Assist in determining system or product options or accessories.
- Point out modifications necessary to integrate a system or product in a project.
- Clarify questions concerning delivery, storage, and handling of products.
- Explain installation procedures.
- Explain product and system limitations.
- State the required certifications.
- Discuss requirements for field quality control.
- Provide a guide specification.

10.6.3 Assistance in Preparing Drawings

Drawings also require technical assistance to verify proper use of the product, ensure accurate incorporation of the product in the project, and verify that special conditions are addressed correctly. Product representatives can provide technical assistance in drawing development in the following ways:

- Assist in establishing specific material locations and dimensions.
- Verify that products meet code requirements.
- Assist in the detailing of product interface with adjacent materials.
- Provide manufacturer's standard drawings for proper product application.

Although the product information may contain standard drawing details and specifications, the product representative may ask to review the drawings for a decision maker on a project in the construction documents stage. This may help the decision maker become more comfortable with the level of service that can be expected. This type of technical assistance builds the decision maker's confidence in the product representative and ensures that the product information is being provided.

10.6.4 Estimating Costs

Besides knowing the differences in product prices, product representatives should know the difference in total installed costs among the various grades, models, and finishes of the products they represent. Cost information that does not take project conditions into account is incomplete and may mislead participants who depend on that information. Product representatives should be able to make cost comparisons with competitive products and systems. Some information may be obtained from bids on public construction projects, but most product or system-installed costs are buried in the total figures. Generally, product representatives must collect installed cost information from recent projects or inquire about costs for competitive products from contractor contacts.

10.6.5   Representative Costs

When the owner or A/E needs to view a critical portion of the work before it is completely constructed to verify the work's aesthetic effect or the qualifications of the installer, representative construction, including mock-ups and field samples, may become a project requirement. Mock-ups are representative assemblies to demonstrate the coordination and interfacing of different products, such as a window assembly built into a masonry wall. Field samples are representative applications of finish materials.

Mock-ups and field samples add cost to the project because they require materials and labor and may be required to be performed out of the sequence of normal construction activities. When they are specified, they should be included in the project cost. The cost and time involved in providing them should be discussed with the A/E prior to procuring (bidding/negotiating/purchasing); it is possible an existing installation or display may serve as the project standard. Consideration should be given to whether the carefully constructed mock-up truly represents the results expected at the actual field installation. Samples should be oriented similarly to the intended installation. For example, a spray-applied finish may look quite different on a ceiling than on a wall, or in direct light rather than in shadow.

10.6.6   Project Conditions

Occasionally, product representatives may be asked to visit the project site and make recommendations. Site visits are good opportunities to confirm ideas, voice a new opinion, or suggest specific products or systems and a course of action. Well-respected product representatives have earned a great degree of trust from the A/E, and professional written reports are a contributing factor. These reports should be logically composed with the basis for assumptions, choice of products or systems, and recommended actions clearly expressed.

Products are affected to a varying extent by the conditions to which they are exposed during the construction and facility management stages of a project's life cycle. The A/E should research manufacturer's product information, test reports, and other available information for facts related to product exposure to conditions prevailing at the project site and should understand and consider their effects when making product selections. Products are designed and manufactured to withstand a limited set of prevailing conditions, including:

- Temperature
- Humidity
- Wind exposure
- Atmospheric pressure
- Exposure to chemicals and pollution

- Solar exposure
- Frequency of use
- Intentional abuse or theft
- Accidental damage
- Owner's maintenance procedures

Few products can reasonably withstand the conditions prevailing at all projects, but many products can perform satisfactorily within a reasonable set of limits. When conditions are unusual, a special product designed to perform accordingly should be selected. The A/E and the qualified product representative may collaborate to determine the appropriateness of a product for the prevailing project conditions.

Project specifications often require materials, products, systems, and equipment to be stored in a safe place. Improper storage areas—too hot, too cold, too dusty, too dirty, too wet, and too dry—may seriously affect the material, product, or system application and performance. The A/E and the contractor should be informed of possible ramifications if these requirements are not met. Product representatives should also guide the A/E in developing specifications that specify proper storage. Improperly stored materials usually result in damaged products and rejection by the A/E.

10.6.7 Manufacturers

Product representatives should be familiar with available products from various manufacturers other than those they represent.

Because relatively few projects name only one source, product representatives should be prepared to name other qualified competitive sources. Product representatives normally prefer to bid against qualified products rather than risk having to bid against potentially cheaper but inferior products.

The A/E and the owner are sometimes wary of such recommendations from product representatives. The integrity of product representatives and the A/E's knowledge and experience are tested when deciding to include or exclude a particular product or system. Product representatives often serve as qualified consultants to A/Es and owners. They get products specified by representing product lines skillfully, knowledgeably, and honestly. They assist in selecting products and systems based on merit, availability, and costs. When appropriate, product representatives should be familiar with and have honest opinions about competitive products. Product representatives should not hesitate to advise an A/E if their product is not the appropriate product for the application in question. This kind of honesty builds respect.

10.6.7.1 Fabrication—Shop Assembly, Shop Finishing, and Tolerances

To ensure controlled production or to comply with regulatory requirements, the owner, A/E, or AHJs may require that certain project components be fabricated or finished under the controlled conditions of a qualified shop, rather than fabricated and finished at the construction site. Such components may be fabricated, inspected by AHJs and other participants, partially disassembled into manageable parts, packaged and transported to the project site, and reassembled during installation. Components that are normally shop-fabricated include:

- Drainage structures
- Prestressed structural concrete members

- Precast concrete components
- Structural steel members
- Metal fabrications, such as stairs, railings, ladders, cages, ornamental metalwork, and column covers
- Cabinetry and casework
- Decorative panels
- Roof accessories, such as hatches, scuttles, and vents
- Fire-rated doors and frames
- Preglazed doors and windows
- Custom doors and frames
- Demountable partitions
- Special coatings and finishes
- Panelized acoustical components
- Furniture
- Equipment
- Prefabricated shelters and other special construction
- Vertical transportation equipment
- Plumbing equipment, such as packaged pump stations
- Heating, ventilating, and air conditioning (HVAC) equipment, such as unitized condensing units and heaters
- Electrical equipment, such as emergency power generation systems

The A/E and construction participants may need assistance in collecting information concerning shop-fabricated components in order to understand proper substrate conditions, framing and blocking requirements, structural requirements, and other conditions affecting installation.

10.6.7.2 Testing and Certification

Product testing and certification requirements may be required by:

- AHJs to verify requirements with regulatory requirements
- The owner or A/E for quality assurance or quality control purposes

National and international standards have been developed for evaluating the capabilities and competence of testing laboratories.

It is impractical to subject each manufactured product to testing. To ensure product quality control, representative samples of products are randomly selected from production runs and subjected to standardized testing procedures, and the results are reported to concerned participants, thus certifying that the manufacturing process complies with a specified standard. The A/E or owner may require a copy of a certification to ensure that the selected product will meet the project requirements.

To further verify compliance with the requirements, the product may be tested by a qualified testing and inspection agency after it is fabricated or installed, and the results are reported to the owner or A/E. This is known as quality control testing.

Several laboratories specialize in quality assurance and certification. A few of the more prominent are Underwriters Laboratories Inc. (UL), Factory Mutual Engineering and

Research Corporation, and Intertek Testing Services. It is important to know that the laboratory must be current in its certification for its tests to be valid. The certification process is complex and does not prohibit noncertified manufacturers from being bid or provided with a specific product.

10.6.7.3 Installer and Fabricator Qualifications

The A/E or owner may require qualifications of installers or fabricators of certain project components as a quality assurance provision. Installers and fabricators may be qualified by manufacturers, trade associations, or testing and inspection agencies. The A/E must be aware that qualification of installers and fabricators may limit the number of participants who can bid or negotiate for work on projects. Therefore, there must be clear reasons for requiring qualification statements. Requiring certified installers and products might increase project costs because of the limited availability of certified manufacturers and applicators in the project locale. If the contractor needs to obtain products from manufacturers that are not represented in the immediate area, additional shipping and handling costs may further increase construction costs.

10.6.7.4 Cost Considerations

Product representatives should be able to assist the A/E in estimating installed costs based on the following:

- *Size of Project.* On the basis of the product and installation or application requirements, a small amount of installed material may cost more than a large amount. If a long drying time is needed before another coat can be applied, the applicator must visit a small project more often than a large one. On a larger project, the required time lapse may be met once the first application is completed.
- *Choice of Contractor Installer/Subcontractor.* Product representatives should be able to provide information regarding which installers are qualified, available, and competitively priced.
- *Time of Year.* Weather affects the installed prices quoted for products and systems. Exterior painting and roofing are two examples of trades that may charge more in winter than summer because they must take into account the lost time due to inclement weather. Product representatives may be able to advise when work is generally slow for a particular trade and prices are lower.
- *Use of Standard Materials.* The A/E may not recognize when drawing details indicate nonstandard products or systems that are more costly. Small modifications in design may permit less expensive standard products or systems without materially changing the anticipated result.
- Other factors that affect estimated costs include actual site conditions, labor rates dictated by law (commonly referred to as prevailing wage rates), and the availability of authorized or experienced installers in the project area.

10.6.7.5 Code Considerations

It is important for product representatives to understand local codes and the effect on the products. Some codes create conflicts and require interpretation by the AHJs. Many manufacturers belong to code development agencies. Manufacturers can use their participation as an opportunity to influence the code development process.

Product representatives should be able to reference applicable codes and identify requirements that must be met for the project to comply. Some product representatives may meet with code officials personally. Such meetings may be necessary when the product meets the code but requires a local interpretation, or when variances from codes are being requested. Meetings may also be necessary when an interpretation is sought that is different from specified code requirements. This procedure may require drawings, references, literature, ratings of materials, and certifications. If product representatives anticipate a need for an interpretation, information should be forwarded to the A/E before submittal to the local building code authorities. This process may require coordination with the manufacturer's technical or research and development departments. The product representative may introduce a new product or process to the AHJ for placing on a list of approved products when required by the local jurisdiction. The product representative may provide technical assistance to the A/E who submits a product to an AHJ as an equivalent to the strict requirements of the code.

Codes vary from state to state and differ between local jurisdictions as well. A city may adopt codes different from those of the county in the same area. Product representatives should be aware of applicable codes and inform the A/E of any potential effects they may have on the product's use. The International Building Code establishes minimum regulations for building systems using prescriptive and performance-related provisions. The building code provides the model code with a development process that offers an international forum for design and construction participants to discuss performance and prescriptive code requirements.

Chapter 11
Construction Documents

Introduction to Construction Documents

11.1.1 Introduction

Successful, timely, and cost-effective construction relies on appropriate communication of a project design by the design team to the contractor and supplier team on behalf of the owner. From project conception through design and construction to facility management, effective communication of the project requirements depends largely on having construction documents that are sufficient for their intended purposes.

The responsibilities of the participants on the design team are determined by the project delivery method used. In the design-bid-build (D-B-B), design-negotiate-build (D-N-B), construction management (CM), and owner-build (OB) methods of project delivery, the architect/engineer (A/E) executes the design phases and delivers to the owner the documents according to the owner-A/E agreement. Design-build (D-B) project delivery differs in that the A/E is employed by the design-builder, and the design-builder executes both the design and construction. Integrated Project Delivery (IPD) differs from all the other delivery methods and restructures the process.

Many product decisions are made throughout the development of the contract documents. Product representatives can be a part of those decisions by providing technical assistance to the A/E, owner, or contractor in the early stages of a project and continuing the assistance through the development of the contract documents. Product representatives should be familiar with the overall concepts of drawings and specifications and understand the implications of contract modifications. Thorough knowledge of all aspects of the represented product is essential when assisting the A/E with the development of the documents used for construction.

Product representatives should be technical resources for the proper use and incorporation of reference standards, specifications, testing and certification, and applicable codes. The ability to review documents and advise on a cost-effective method of installation, or a new product that would contribute to the project's success, is a valuable service and can build credibility.

Construction documents define the rights of, responsibilities of, and relationships among the parties. As discussed in Chapter 5, standard documents have been published by the several professional organizations for the various project delivery methods and basis of payment customarily used for construction. The advantage of a standard document is that it provides familiarity through repeated use and also that this repeated use has resulted in clear and well-coordinated documents.

This standardization has been extended to the project specifications and drawings as well:

- *MasterFormat*® presents a master list of numbers and titles for divisions and sections, providing a uniform location for administrative, procedural, and product information for any type of construction project.
- *SectionFormat*™ and *PageFormat*™ set up standard formats for the presentation of requirements within a specification section and on each specification page.
- *UniFormat*™ provides a standard for organizing information on construction systems, assemblies, and elements.
- The U.S. National CAD Standard for Architecture, Engineering, and Construction (NCS), including the Uniform Drawing System (UDS), provides a standard for defining and locating information on the drawings, including the identification of standard symbols, abbreviations, and notations.

Through the use of such standardization, information can be placed properly in a predetermined location for each construction project, thereby making the task of using the documents much easier. Specifications can be more easily coordinated with the drawings, specifications sections can be coordinated with each other, and A/E consultants can correctly integrate their work with less effort and error.

It is not practical to include descriptive notes on construction drawings to describe in detail all of the product qualities and installation methods. Separate written descriptions, referred to as specifications, more effectively communicate this type of information. The drawings and specifications are complementary to one another.

Proper methods of writing specifications or developing master guide specifications should be employed. The information should be clear to the user and presented in a concise manner, and it should also be technically correct and complete. Specifying methods include descriptive, performance, reference standard, and proprietary. The preparation of conventional specifications, as well as particular procedures such as specifying for the purchase of goods or for public agencies or the preparation of shortform specifications, requires an understanding of construction documents.

11.1.2 Construction Documents

Construction documents are defined as the written and graphic documents prepared for communicating the project design for construction and administering the construction contract.

A standardized approach to the location of project subject matter for both written and graphic documents greatly simplifies the retrieval of information and reduces the possibility of conflicts, discrepancies, errors, and omissions. Written project requirements are organized in an orderly fashion, following the project manual concept. A properly assembled project manual with each document in its assigned location will facilitate checking and coordination. Likewise, a drawing set organized in a standard format with uniform location for information will be easier to coordinate with the project manual and itself.

Another important principle governing the production of construction documents is that each document, written or graphic, has a specific purpose and should be used for that purpose. Each requirement should be stated only once and in the correct location. Information in one document should not be repeated in other documents. Whether a project is simple or complex, the basic concepts for preparing, organizing, and coordinating construction documents are applicable.

As indicated in Figure 11.1, construction documents include two major groups of documents:

- *Procurement Documents.* Procurement involves bidding (public and private), negotiating, and purchasing that require documents to communicate project information to the bidders or proposers and to facilitate the project delivery and pricing process.
  - Before bids or proposals can be solicited, prospective bidders or proposers must be made aware of the project and sufficient data must be furnished for them to determine the requirements of the project. They need specific information that will enable them to:
    - Comply with required procurement procedures.
    - Understand procurement and awarding requirements.
    - Understand the intent of the construction documents.
    - Submit bids or proposals that will not be disqualified for technicalities.
    - Understand conditions that apply after bid or proposal submittal and prior to contract award.
  - The documents that furnish this information are the procurement documents, which include the following, that, with the exception of the resource drawings (if any), become contract documents when the owner-contractor agreement is executed:
    - Drawings
    - Specifications
    - Contracting requirements
    - Resource drawings (if any)
    - Precontract revisions (addenda)
- *Contract Documents:*
  - The contract documents describe the proposed construction (referred to as the work) that results from performing services, furnishing labor, and supplying and incorporating materials and equipment into the construction. Contract documents consist of both written and graphic elements and typically include the following:
    - Contracting requirements
    - Drawings
    - Specifications
  - *Contracting and Project Forms:*
    - *Notice of Award.* A written notice issued by the owner to inform bidders of the owner's intent to award a contract to a successful bidder. The notice of award establishes the beginning of any challenge periods.
    - *Agreement.* A legal instrument executed by the owner and the contractor binding the parties to the terms of the contract. The agreement defines the relationships and obligations between owner and contractor. It incorporates all other contract documents by reference.
    - *Bonds:*
      - A performance bond provides a guaranty that if the contractor defaults or fails to perform, the surety will either complete the contract in accordance with the terms or provide sufficient funds up to the penal amount for such completion.

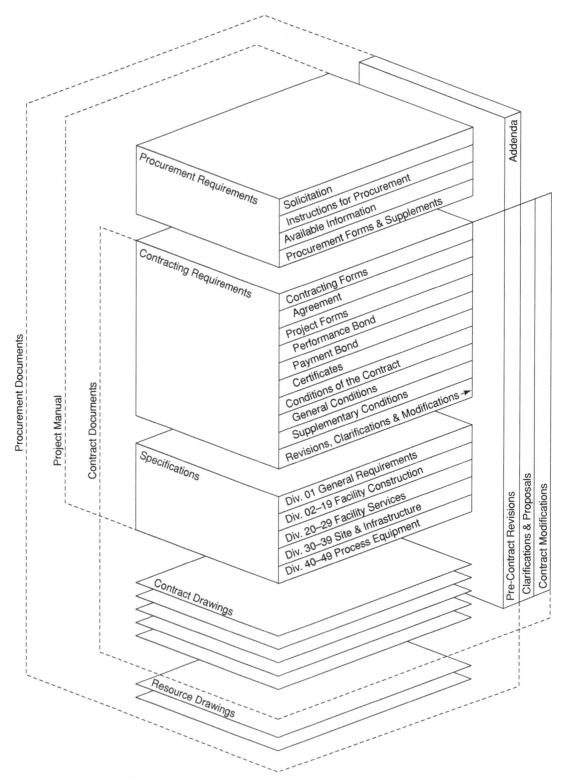

Figure 11.1 This graphic illustrates the distinction between procurement documents and contract documents.

- A payment bond provides a guaranty that subcontractor, material suppliers, and others providing labor, material, and services to the project will be paid.
- *Certificates.* Includes certificates of insurance and certificates of compliance with applicable laws and regulations. Although the procurement documents

may include blank samples of these forms, the executed copies become part of the contract.

- *Conditions of the Contract.* The conditions of the contract are written provisions that define the basic rights, responsibilities, and relationships of the parties associated in the construction of a project.
  - General conditions have wide applicability to almost all projects and are available as standardized documents that are prepared by various professional associations.
  - Supplementary conditions modify the requirements of the general conditions when necessary to fit the needs of a specific project.
- *Revisions, Clarifications, and Modifications:*
  - Precontract revisions include revisions made prior to signing the agreement. Addenda are written or graphic documents issued to clarify, revise, add to, or delete information in the original procurement documents or in previous addenda. Typically, an addendum is issued prior to the receipt of bids or proposals. Other revisions may include bid or proposal revisions when permitted.
  - Clarifications and proposals include documents initiating changes or clarifications that have not been incorporated into the contract by formal contract modifications. These documents include requests and proposals.
  - Contract modifications include modifications after the construction agreement has been signed and additions to, deletions from, or modifications of the work to be done are accomplished by change orders, construction change directives, work change directives, field orders, architect's supplemental instructions, orders for minor changes, and written amendments. These can be issued at any time during the contract period.

11.1.3 Drawings

Drawings are graphic representations of the work upon which the contract is based. As the graphic documents usually contain more than plan views, the preferred term is drawings rather than plans. They show the quantitative extent and relationships of elements to one another.

11.1.4 Specifications

Specifications define the requirements for products, materials, and workmanship upon which the contract is based and requirements for administration and performance of the project. They are generally written for each subject as sections and organized by divisions under *MasterFormat®* or by categories under *UniFormat™*.

11.1.5 Contracting Requirements

Contracting requirements, though not specifications, are legal documents that describe contractual requirements. Contracting requirements define the processes, rights, responsibilities, and relationships of the parties to the contract.

11.1.6 Procurement Requirements

Procurement requirements instruct the bidders or proposers about the established procedures for preparing and submitting their bids or proposals. Procurement requirements are addressed to prospective bidders or proposers interested in the project. Although not necessarily part of a contract, the procurement requirements are usually bound with other written construction documents into a project manual.

11.2 Drawings

11.2.1 Introduction

Drawings are the first of the two major categories of construction documents prepared by the design team. A variety of drawing types and views are used to convey comprehensive information about a project. A particular drawing may vary with the intended user, the project stage, and the information that must be communicated. Regardless of how drawings are prepared (manually or electronically), certain standards should be followed.

Preparation of drawings also requires technical assistance to verify proper use of the product, ensure accurate incorporation of the product in the project, and verify that special conditions are addressed correctly. Trained and knowledgeable product representatives can provide technical assistance in drawing development in the following ways:

- Assist in establishing specific material locations and dimensions.
- Verify that products meet code requirements.
- Assist in the detailing of product interface with adjacent materials.
- Provide manufacturer's standard drawings for proper product application.
- Verify that products are being used in the manner intended by the manufacturers.

The product representative may ask to review the drawing details and specifications for a project in the construction documents stage. This type of technical assistance ensures the product information is used correctly and is being provided to the appropriate people. In this way, the project participants become more comfortable with the level of service that can be expected and confident in the product representative's abilities.

A revolution is taking place in the design and construction universe. Building Information Modeling (BIM) is not only a new and sophisticated way of producing drawings to be used for construction, it is also providing a wide variety of capabilities that changes the way professional services are provided and how the technical information is made available.

11.2.2 The Nature of Drawings

Drawings are graphic and textual information organized on a two-dimensional surface for the purpose of conveying data about a specific portion of a project. Drawings convey design intent and may show multiple views, either of the whole project or of its parts. Drawings indicate relationships between elements and may show the following for each material, assembly, component, piece of equipment, and accessory:

- Location
- Identification
- Dimension and size
- Details and diagrams of connections
- Shape and form

11.2.3 Role and Function of Drawings in Project Stages

Construction drawings are not produced in full detail from the outset of the project but in steps at a level consistent with that of the specifications and the level of development of the design concept. All construction projects proceed through multiple stages, from conception to completion, with variations depending on the nature of the work and the needs of the owner. The schematic design drawings and preliminary project descriptions complement each other following project conception when the owner's initial needs are assessed and information is gathered and reviewed. At each phase, design decisions may require more fully developed drawings and specifications.

11.2.3.1 Drawing Users

A/Es, owners, contractors, subcontractors, product representatives, and material/equipment suppliers are the traditional users of drawings. Related professions using drawings include financial advisers and lenders and cost estimators. Authorities having jurisdiction (AHJs) review drawings for compliance with codes and regulations. Each group uses drawings for different purposes and to different degrees during each of the project stages. It is the A/E's responsibility to identify what is required and determine how it is to be presented in the construction documents.

11.2.3.2 Design Stage Drawings

During the design stage, the A/E and the owner use drawings to establish the extent and design of a project.

Schematic design phase drawings may include sketches, renderings, or conceptual diagrams. These drawings describe the size, shape, volume, spatial relationships, and functional characteristics of project components. They are usually general in nature, with few dimensions. Preliminary project descriptions are prepared to complement the schematic design drawings to describe the requirements at this phase.

During the design development phase, more detailed information is required. Drawings in this phase may show multiple views of the project in order to describe selected materials and basic systems and their interrelationships. Outline specifications are prepared to complement the design development drawings to describe the requirements at this phase.

Drawings used during the design phases are primarily tools to convey aesthetic aspects of a project. They show the qualities of space in terms of surface texture, finishes, lighting, and color more fully than do the drawings used for construction.

11.2.3.3 Construction Drawings

After the design stage, construction documents are prepared, which include detailed drawings and specifications that describe the work. The drawings and specifications are complementary to one another, and the information contained within one should not duplicate information in the other.

Construction drawings consist of contract drawings and resource drawings. Contract drawings are those that describe the work of the project. Resource drawings show existing conditions or new construction related to the work, but are not included in the contract.

Contract drawings are legally enforceable and, depending on the requirements of a project, may include drawings that show the following:

- Deconstruction/demolition of existing construction to be removed
- Alterations of existing construction to be modified
- New construction

Construction drawings are the basis of other drawings that are produced during construction:

- Drawings during construction
- Record drawings

11.2.3.4 Drawings during Construction

During the construction stage of a project, several types of supplemental drawings are prepared, which are necessary to further illustrate portions of the project. One such drawing is called a shop drawing. Shop drawings are not contract documents. Shop drawings may be prepared by the contractor, subcontractor, or material/equipment supplier and show how a particular aspect of the work is to be fabricated and installed in compliance with the information provided and design concept described in the contract documents. The A/E reviews shop drawings for conformance with the design concept only. This review does not extend to shop fabrication processes, field construction techniques, or coordination of trades.

Changes in the work or clarifications to the contract documents during construction may require the A/E to prepare drawings or sketches that supplement the contract documents. The changes shown on these supplemental drawings are often marked by placing a bubble or a cloud around the revised area. A unique identifier is usually associated with the revised area and is used as a reference for correspondence and change orders.

11.2.3.5 Record Drawings

During the project, the contractor is often required to maintain record drawings. Record drawings are marked-up or corrected contract drawings that identify changes incorporated into the work during construction as well as actual locations of items shown diagrammatically. These changes include field changes, modifications, and supplemental drawings.

The purpose of record drawings is to provide the owner with a set of documents that describe the actual construction of the project and that will serve to facilitate operation, maintenance, and future modifications of the facility throughout its useful life. Sometimes the owner will contract with the A/E to incorporate the changes shown on the contractor's record drawings into a copy of the original drawings produced by the A/E.

11.2.4 Categories of Drawings

Just as drawings can communicate some spatial relationships more clearly than can the written word, different types of drawings can more effectively describe specific conditions.

As indicated previously, drawings are used to communicate the design concept in a form that is useable for constructing a facility. Each type of facility has its own unique requirements for the types of drawings that are necessary. The drawings for a freeway are dramatically different than those for a high-rise building. However, most design and construction drawings consist of the following types:

- *Plans:* Refer to Figure 11.2 for a design floor plan and Figure 11.3 for construction drawing examples of a floor plan, a reflected ceiling plan, and a roof plan.
- *Elevations:* Refer to Figure 11.4 for construction drawing examples of an exterior elevation and an interior elevation.
- *Sections:* Refer to Figure 11.5 for construction drawing examples of building section and a wall section.
- *Details:* Refer to Figure 11.6 for a construction drawing example of a detail.
- *Schedules:* Refer to Figure 11.7 for a construction drawing example of a schedule.

Developing digital models of facility designs makes possible several additional types of drawings that, prior to BIM, usually required specialized skill and time to prepare. While the following drawing types might have been traditionally reserved for expressions of design concepts, they can easily be produced from the digital model and used for construction:

- *Perspectives:* Refer to Figure 11.8 for an example of a design rendering and an example of how a perspective is used as a construction drawing.
- *Isometrics:* Refer to Figure 11.9 for an example of an isometric drawing that can be used as a construction drawing.

11.2.4.1 Views

Each view is prepared for an ability to demonstrate unique information in the most logical and understandable way. Views can represent a whole project or only portions of it. All design and construction drawings, however, can be classified as one of two types of views: scaled or nonscaled. To draw a view to scale means to prepare the view to accurate dimensions at something other than actual size, using a known proportion.

11.2.4.2 Scaled Views

Scaled views are the most common form of drawings. Scaled views include orientations in the horizontal plane and in the vertical plane and vertical cuts through the project. These views can be drawn at any scale, depending on the information that needs to be shown. The scale of a view is usually indicated on the drawing, either by a numeric scale, 1:100 or 1/8 inches = 12 inches, or by a graphic scale.

Views of horizontal planes are known as plans. Refer to Figure 11.2 for an example of the floor plan for a fire station. Plans show project materials and components in their horizontal relationship. Typical types of plans include floor plans, roof plans, site plans,

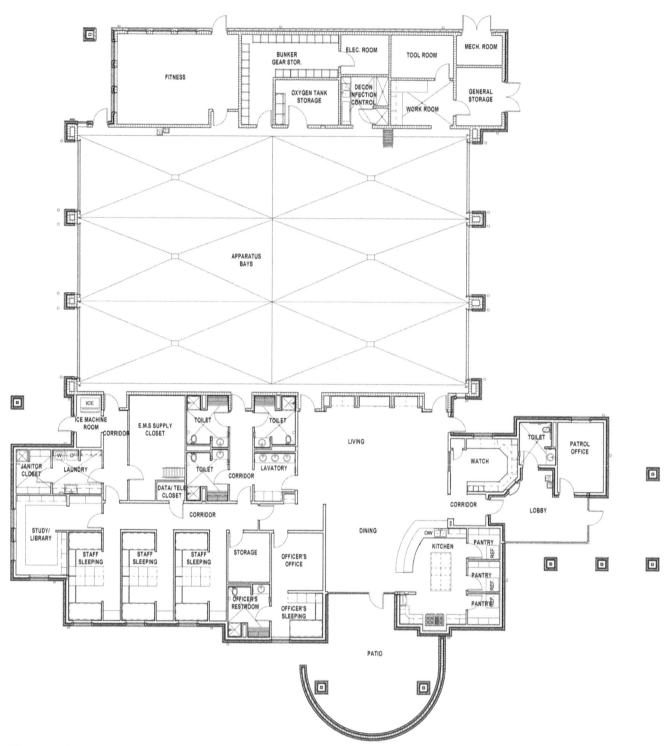

Figure 11.2 An example of a floor plan for a fire station used as a design drawing; reproduced with permission of Wiginton Hooker Jeffry, PC Architects. The lower right area of the fire station floor plan, around the building entrance and lobby, is used as the focus for many of the construction drawing examples included in Figures 11.3 through Figure 11.9.

framing plans, reflected ceiling plans, and plans for specialized engineering disciplines such as topographical surveys. Floor plans and reflected ceiling plans, are horizontal cross-section cuts taken at a selected vertical elevation that is perpendicular to project materials and components. Other types of plans, such as site plans and roof plans, are views

(a)

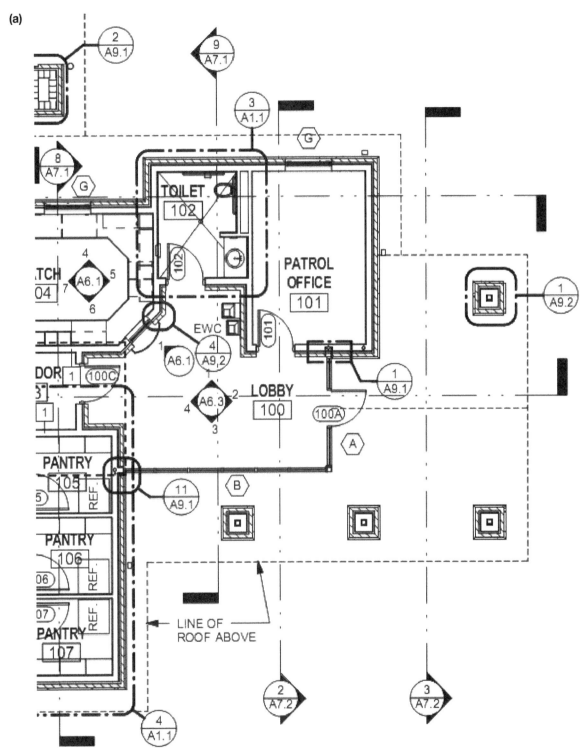

of a horizontal plane, viewed perpendicularly from a selected plane. Refer to Figure 11.3 for examples.

Views of vertical planes are known as elevations. Elevations show project materials and components in their vertical relationship, viewed perpendicularly from a selected

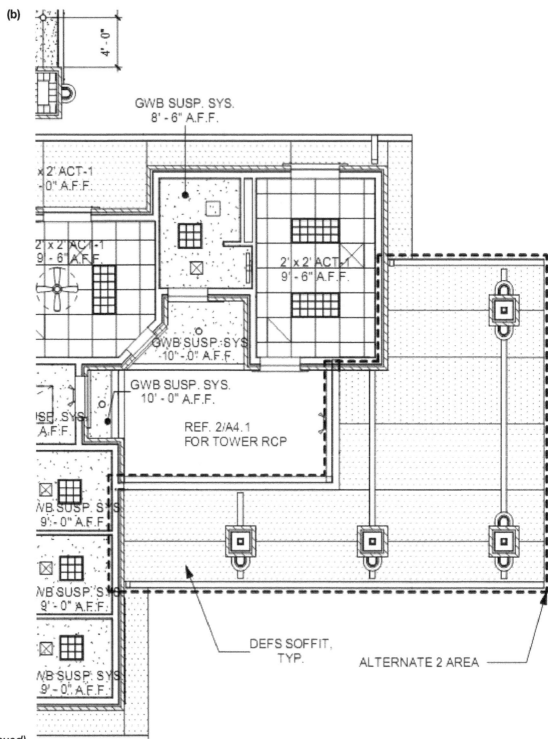

(b)

Figure 11.3 *(continued)*

vertical plane, generally retaining their true scale, shape, and proportion. When project components are not perpendicular to the selected vertical plane, such as sloped roofs and curved or oblique surfaces, they appear foreshortened and distorted from their true shape. Typical types of elevations include exterior building elevations, interior room elevations, and elevations of specialized components or engineering applications, such as an electrical panel board layout. Refer to Figure 11.4 for examples.

(c)

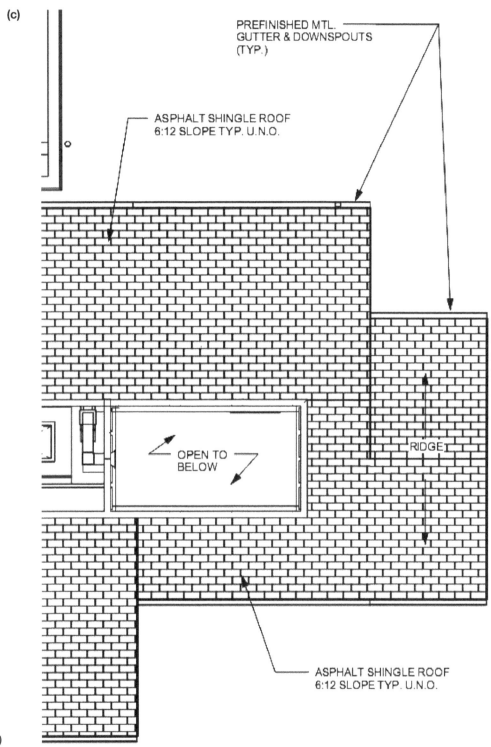

PREFINISHED MTL.
GUTTER & DOWNSPOUTS
(TYP.)

ASPHALT SHINGLE ROOF
6:12 SLOPE TYP. U.N.O.

OPEN TO
BELOW

RIDGE

ASPHALT SHINGLE ROOF
6:12 SLOPE TYP. U.N.O.

Figure 11.3 *(continued)*

Sections are cut vertically through and perpendicular to project materials and components and show their detailed arrangement. Typical types of sections include building sections, wall sections, site sections, and sections of specialized engineering applications. Refer to Figure 11.5 for examples.

(a)

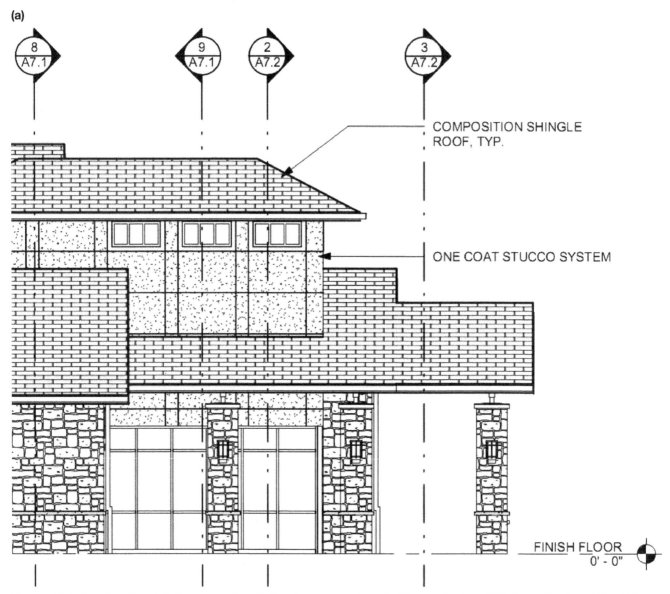

Figure 11.4 **Construction drawing examples of elevations; reproduced with permission of Wiginton Hooker Jeffry, PC Architects. (a) Exterior elevation. (b) Interior elevation.**

A detail may be shown as a plan, an elevation, or a section view. Details show more specific information about a portion of a project component or element than can be provided by smaller-scale drawings. Examples of detail drawings include joints and connections between materials and products. Refer to Figure 11.6 for an example.

11.2.4.3 Nonscaled Views

Nonscaled views do not necessarily relate to perpendicular plane orientations as do scaled views. Typical types of nonscaled views are diagrams, key plans, schedules, perspectives, isometrics, and title sheet drawings. These views are drawn in widely differing ways, depending on the information that needs to be shown, the needs of a project, and the intended user of the drawing.

Diagrams show arrangements of special system components and connections generally not possible to clearly show in scaled views. Engineering disciplines often use

(b)

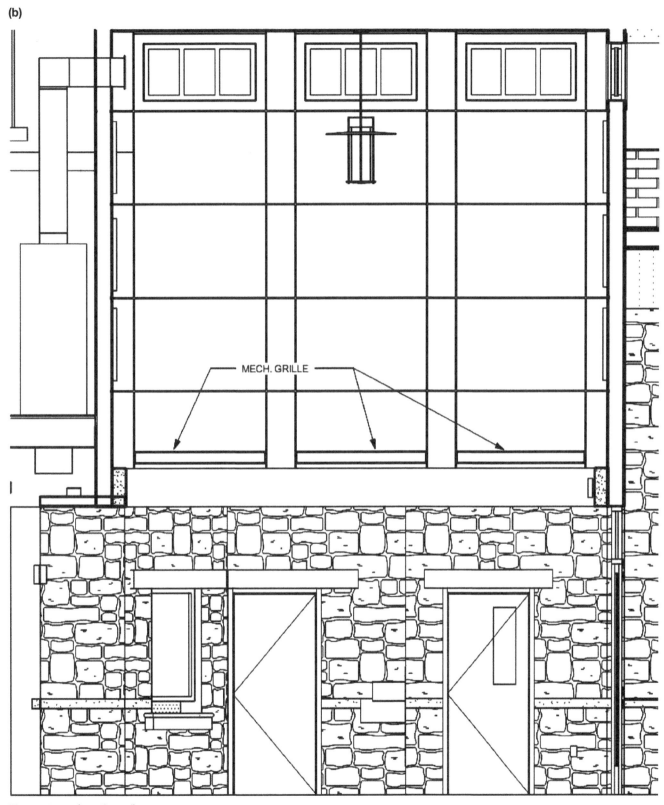

MECH. GRILLE

Figure 11.4 *(continued)*

(a)

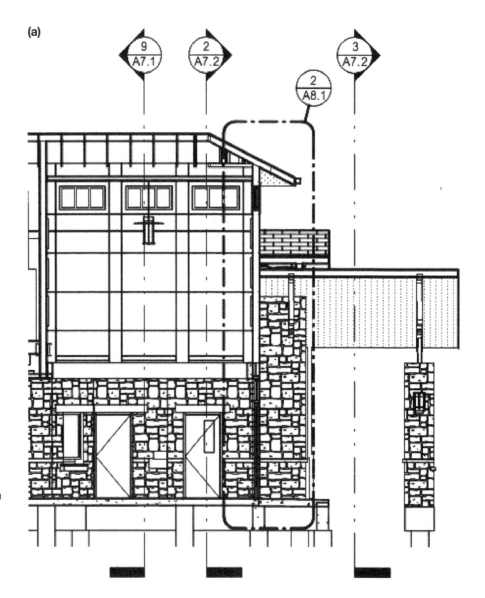

Figure 11.5 Construction drawing examples of sections; reproduced with permission of Wiginton Hooker Jeffry, PC Architects.
(a) Building section.
(b) Wall section.

diagrams to show entire project systems in a single drawing, in addition to showing portions of a system in scaled views. This allows all of the system components and their relationships to be seen at once and to be more easily understood. Typical types of diagrams include electrical single-line diagrams and plumbing riser diagrams.

A key plan is a small diagram that symbolically shows the relationship of a portion of the project to the whole. It is usually used in combination with a plan view when the larger-scale plan presents only a portion of the project. Schedules supplement the specifications. Schedule information may include data about materials, products, and equipment. Typical types of schedules include room finish schedules, door schedules, and equipment schedules. Refer to Figure 11.7 for an example.

A perspective is a type of drawing that illustrates objects as they appear to the eye, with reference to relative distance and depth. An isometric is a type of drawing that shows horizontal and vertical surfaces not in perspective, but equally foreshortened in all three dimensions. Both perspectives and isometrics provide easy and rapid visual means to grasp spatial and physical relationships. Refer to Figures 11.8 and 11.9 for examples.

(b)

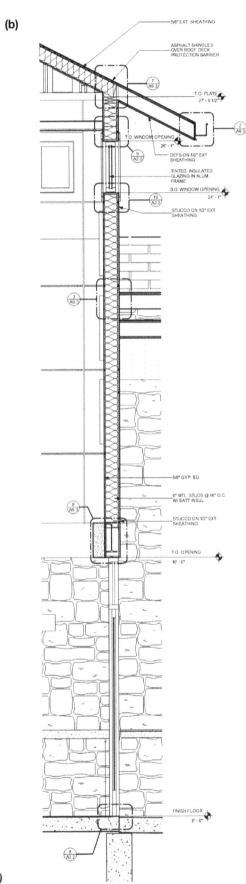

Figure 11.5 *(continued)*

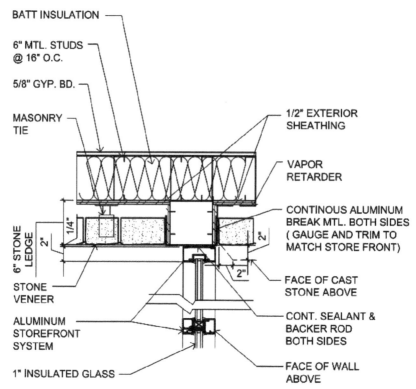

BATT INSULATION

6" MTL. STUDS
@ 16" O.C.

5/8" GYP. BD.

MASONRY
TIE

1/2" EXTERIOR
SHEATHING

VAPOR
RETARDER

CONTINOUS ALUMINUM
BREAK MTL. BOTH SIDES
(GAUGE AND TRIM TO
MATCH STORE FRONT)

6" STONE LEDGE
2"
1/4"
2"
2"

STONE
VENEER

FACE OF CAST
STONE ABOVE

ALUMINUM
STOREFRONT
SYSTEM

CONT. SEALANT &
BACKER ROD
BOTH SIDES

1" INSULATED GLASS

FACE OF WALL
ABOVE

Figure 11.6 **Construction drawing example of a detail; reproduced with permission of Wiginton Hooker Jeffry, PC Architects.**

11.2.5   Features of Drawings

11.2.5.1   Drawing Standards

In addition to the UDS, large organizations and many public agencies have created their own individual drawing standards for use by in-house A/Es and consultants. Some private-sector owners may require conformance with their own or another organization's specific drawing standard. Drawings used for construction, however, have common conventions that distinguish them from other types of drawings. These features include construction-related symbols and abbreviations, dimensions, drawing identification, notes or keynotes, and various types of graphic representations.

11.2.5.2   Drawing Identification

Individual drawings on a sheet, regardless of whether they are scaled or nonscaled, are uniquely identified to provide a logical method for easily locating individual elements. These identifiers may indicate the units of work or the A/E discipline responsible for producing the drawing.

11.2.5.3   Cover Sheet

Typically, the first sheet in the drawing set, the cover sheet often shows the name of the project, the name of the owner, the name of the A/E and consultants, and general project data such as location map, code information, and a list of included sheets. On small projects, title sheet information may be included on other drawing sheets.

UNIFORM DRAWING SYSTEM

SCHEDULES

DOOR AND FRAME SCHEDULE

MARK	DOOR								FRAME						FIRE RATING	HARDWARE		NOTES
	SIZE			MATL	TYPE	GLZ	LOUVER		MATL	TYPE	GLZ	DETAIL			LABEL	SET NO	KEYSIDE RM NO	
	W	HT	THK				W	HT				HEAD	JAMB	SILL				

© Copyright 2004, Construction Specification Institute, 99 Canal Center Plaza, Alexandria, VA 22314-1588

08 10 00–01 · DOOR AND FRAME SCHEDULE

UDS-03.53

Figure 11.7 Construction Drawing Example of a Schedule

(a)

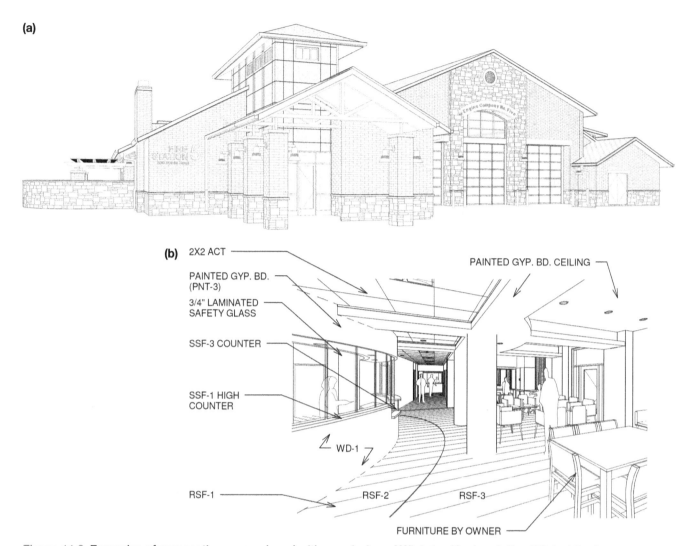

(b) 2X2 ACT

PAINTED GYP. BD. (PNT-3)

3/4" LAMINATED SAFETY GLASS

SSF-3 COUNTER

SSF-1 HIGH COUNTER

WD-1

RSF-1   RSF-2   RSF-3

PAINTED GYP. BD. CEILING

FURNITURE BY OWNER

Figure 11.8 Examples of perspectives; reproduced with permission of Wiginton Hooker Jeffry, PC Architects.
(a) Design drawing example of an exterior perspective.
(b) Example of interior perspectives, top as a design drawing and bottom as the same perspective used as a construction drawing.

11.2.5.4 Graphics

The graphical portions of drawings are called drawing blocks and are constructed of various types and shapes of lines (such as straight lines, arcs, and circles, some of which are combined to create shading or hatching). Lines may be solid, dashed, or a combination of both to create a special line type.

Solid lines are most often used to designate new construction or existing conditions that are to be modified. Dashed lines can represent construction to be demolished, elements in front of or behind the view plane, or items that are not included in the contract (e.g., furniture or equipment).

Special line types may be used for modular grid or reference lines, property lines, and match lines. Modular grid and reference lines provide a basis for describing the location of an item on a drawing. Property lines show the property boundary for a site. Match lines are used to indicate where a portion of a project continues onto another drawing, usually on another drawing sheet. Drawings requiring multiple match lines

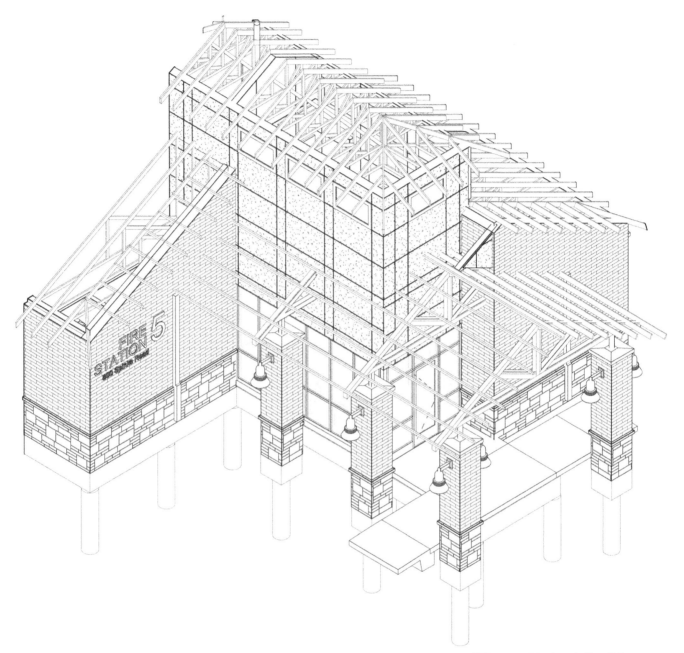

Figure 11.9 A digital example of an isometric drawing; reproduced with permission of Wiginton Hooker Jeffry, PC Architects. The roofing is not shown so the portion of the building below the roof can be seen. A digital drawing with this level of detail can be easily produced using building information modeling and can be used as a construction drawing.

are often necessary when the project size or orientation does not allow effective use of a drawing sheet.

Shading and hatching may be used to indicate special conditions or requirements in areas of a project. Examples of the use of shading or hatching on a drawing would be to indicate a fire-resistive wall or to distinguish between new and existing construction.

Color may be used to differentiate types of project components and materials.

Photographs may be incorporated into drawings. In a renovation project, for example, photographs may be used as a background to show the extent and condition of existing construction. Notes and graphics may then be added over the photograph to describe the project requirements.

11.2.5.5 Symbols

A symbol is a scaled or nonscaled graphic representation of a product or material. For clarity and efficiency of drafting, these representations are usually drawn with a minimum amount of detail or texture.

Symbols may also indicate abstract conditions such as north arrows or direction-of-view indicators. Refer to CSI UDS Chapter 6, Symbols, for standard symbols used in construction documents.

Symbols may also be used as reference identifiers for items such as doors, windows, or equipment.

11.2.5.6 Dimensions

Drawings may include dimensions to delineate the actual size of an object. They may also be used to demonstrate extent or required clearances. The referenced end points of dimension lines are usually shown with arrowheads or slash marks.

11.2.5.7 Notations

Textual information on drawings is usually in the form of notations or notes on the drawings. Because the drawings and specifications complement each other, the same terminology should be used on the drawings as in the specifications. Text should be kept to a minimum and should only identify an item and its extent or location. Specific product characteristics and installation requirements should be described in the specifications. Phrases such as "See specifications" or "Refer to specifications" are obvious and should be avoided.

General notes are text information that applies to an entire collection of drawing sheets in a drawing set and are usually found near the cover sheet. These notes should be used sparingly and only when the information cannot be covered effectively in the specifications. General discipline notes are specific to each sheet in a discipline.

Notes that apply only to a particular sheet or drawing are called sheet keynotes or reference keynotes. These are generally used where, for clarity and drafting efficiency, the note or text is replaced with an identifying symbol. The identifying symbol then refers back to the full text, which is reproduced elsewhere on the drawing sheet.

11.2.5.8 Abbreviations

Abbreviations of construction terms are used on drawings and in schedules where space for textual information may be limited. In general, construction documents should include an edited list of abbreviations that are tailored to the project and not the long, all-inclusive list of widely used standard abbreviations. It is recommended that abbreviations used on the drawings be listed on the drawings rather than in the specifications. It is generally recommended that you avoid the use of abbreviations, especially for words of five letters or less.

Abbreviations may vary with the A/E disciplines, but the terms abbreviated should be consistent with those used in the specifications. For example, do not use WDW for windows on the drawings when curtain wall is specified. Verify that abbreviations used on drawings are not shared by different items, such as PLAS for PLASTER in one place and for PLASTIC in another. Verify that abbreviations do not have a different meaning on drawings from a different discipline; for example, SD may be SMOKE DETECTOR on one set of drawings and SUPPLY DUCT on another. Refer to CSI UDS Chapter 5, Terms and Abbreviations, for a listing of common construction terms and their abbreviations.

11.2.6 Drawing Set Organization

A collection of sheets of drawings related to a project is known as a drawing set. The traditional method for organizing drawing sets is to group the A/E sheets by A/E discipline; within each discipline, the sheets are further grouped by drawing types (i.e., plans, elevations, sections).

Certain aspects of a project might influence the organization of a drawing set, including:

- Number of disciplines
- Number of project parts (e.g., individual buildings)
- Number of contracts
- Project phase
- Construction sequence
- Number and extent of systems
- Project delivery method

11.2.7 U.S. National CAD Standard

The United States National CAD Standard (NCS), administered by the buildingSMARTalliance (www.buildingsmartalliance.org), a council of the National Institute of Building Sciences, streamlines and simplifies the exchange of building design and construction data from project development throughout the life of a facility. It coordinates the efforts of the entire industry by classifying electronic building design data consistently allowing streamlined communication among owners and design and construction project teams.

The NCS is a consensus standard incorporating industry publications. It comprises of interrelated standards, guidelines, and tools for uniformly organizing and presenting facility planning, design, construction, and operation drawing information. NCS comprises the following:

- National Institute of Building Sciences' Forward and Administration
- AIA CAD Layer Guidelines
- CSI Uniform Drawing System
- Plotting Guidelines

11.2.7.1 National Institute Building Sciences' Foreward and Administration

The foreward and administration provides a brief history of the development of the NCS and the process for its future evolution and development.

11.2.7.2 AIA CAD Layer Guidelines

The CAD Layer Guidelines provide a hierarchical organization for describing drawing layers. The user can identify or name layers on the basis of the level of detail provided in each drawing layer. The guidelines define four data fields within layer names:

- *Discipline Designator* data field identifies the discipline and content of the specific layer. Examples of disciplines include Hazardous Materials, Structural, Architectural, Fire Protection, Mechanical, Electrical, and Telecommunications.
- *Major Group* data field defines a major building system (e.g., WALL).
- *Minor Groups* further describes the Major Group field preceding it. For example, WALL—FULL or WALL—FULL—TEXT.
- *Status* defines the data on the specific layer as to the status of the work or its construction phase. Examples of work status include New Work, Existing Work, Temporary Work, Not in Contract, and Phase Numbers.

These data field identifiers are alphanumeric characters and, when grouped in a string, describe a drawing sheet's contents as to its construction discipline, building system, and work status. In addition, the drawing layers can be given identifiers to organize the drawings by type, such as elevation, section, or detail. Additional data field identifiers can be used to create a layer for notations, dimensions, borders, title blocks, and similar text.

11.2.7.3 CSI Uniform Drawing System

The CSI UDS organizes and presents the drawings and project information in a standard format for use in planning, design, construction, and operation of facilities throughout its lifecycle. As the life cycle stage of a facility changes, graphical information used previously for this project can be retrieved and reused. UDS provides a standard drawing organization whereby only the desired or necessary information can be efficiently and accurately retrieved.

UDS consists of an open structure of a series of application chapters that are organized around the stages of a facility life cycle. Elements such as *MasterFormat*® and *UniFormat*™, keynotes, specifications, and other special applications can be inserted.

The hierarchical set of systems and subsystems of the UDS organization is flexible enough to meet the requirements of various users of the drawings at different stages of the project life cycle. It provides a method by which undesired information may be filtered out depending on the needs of the discipline or user. It can perform within different project delivery methods such as design-build, construction management, or the traditional design-bid-build method.

UDS also establishes a uniform set of standards for different types of drawings. This standardization contributes to a consistency of drawings among multiple design professionals and aids in clear communication. This uniformity allows for accurate integration of information and better coordination of documents. UDS formats provide standards for linking notes and terminology to specifications, facility management information, and other electronic applications tied to project information.

Currently, the UDS consists of eight interrelated chapters:

- *Chapter 1—Drawing Set Organization.* Establishes drawing set content and order, sheet identification format, file naming standards for a set of construction drawings, and standard designators for each discipline.
- *Chapter 2—Sheet Organization.* Provides a format for drawing sheets defining the drawing area, the title block, and production data areas of the sheet. The Sheet

Organization Chapter establishes a grid system for organizing drawing blocks on the sheet, and includes a system for identifying each drawing block and its location on the sheet based on this grid system.

- *Chapter 3—Schedules.* Provides a standard for schedules with a consistent format, terminology, and organization of content. It also includes requirements for schedules located on the drawings or in the specifications.
- *Chapter 4—Drafting Conventions.* Provides standard conventions used in drawings such as orientation, layout, symbols, material indications, line types, dimensions, drawing scale, diagrams, notations, and cross-referencing.
- *Chapter 5—Terms and Abbreviations.* Provides consistent spelling, terminology, and abbreviations.
- *Chapter 6—Symbols.* Provides standard symbols, classifications, graphic representation, and organization.
- *Chapter 7—Notations.* Provides notation classifications, use of notes, notation format, notation components, notation location, and linking of notations to specifications.
- *Chapter 8—Code Conventions.* Identifies types of general regulatory information that should appear on the drawings, locates code related information in a set of drawings, and provides standard graphic conventions.

11.2.7.4 Plotting Guidelines

The plotting guidelines provide details for plotting drawings in gray scale, color, and line width tables.

11.2.8 Building Information Modeling

With advances in information technology and widespread use of the Internet, the distinction between drawing and specification is blurring. For example, graphic information may be stored in an electronically generated drawing as a database with related nongraphic attributes. When a graphically represented object on a drawing—a door, for example—is selected, information for its size, material, fire rating, and finish may be retrieved and displayed. Quantities may be extracted by querying the database, and access to the specifications may be made possible by linking the object to the specification text. Similarly, objects on a graphic display can be linked to a manufacturer, supplier, or installer, and detailed drawings can be retrieved.

While the construction industry is adopting a holistic philosophy that guides facility design and construction from conception through construction to operation and maintenance, advances in information technology have led to a parallel evolution in construction drawing. Building Information Modeling (BIM) is rapidly shifting the emphasis from two-dimensional CAD drawing to three-dimensional thinking. Simple CAD is a relatively "dumb" method of drafting based on geometric attributes such as the size and location of points, lines, and planes and gives little information beyond the relationship of these attributes. BIM is a database of building information and uses an integrated object based model that describes the parameters or attributes of building objects and the relationships of those objects to each other. Geometric entities are just a subset of the building parameters and can be developed as 3D objects. Building data can be retrieved from the database and used during schematics, design development, and construction and facility management for visualization, analysis, and record keeping. The intent of BIM is to achieve interoperability among the various softwares used in the construction industry. One method of interoperability presents a process whereby multiple disciplines could store building information in a central location using prescribed standards to define the attributes. A connected discipline could then retrieve total building information stored by other users at one time, rather than piecemeal, in order to perform a fuller structural analysis, energy usage calculations, value analysis, and layout of mechanical, electrical, and plumbing systems, for example.

Another method by which interoperability can be achieved is by providing an open unifying framework or platform that can be used by a variety of coordinated applications that are spread across a number of disciplines. This open platform would be useful for distributed multidisciplines using their own systems and sharing information, or possibly for very large projects. As with the first method, the data would be managed to maintain correct relationships of attributes and to update changes across the system.

The advantages of BIM are much like those provided by the CSI formats and principles. The information is stored on standardized platforms for multidisciplinary retrieval and use, the building attributes are described only once in the data model, and changes can be tracked and managed with a greater degree of accuracy and consistency across the separate interfaced applications.

BIM applications include the use of building walk-through, verification of design intent, work sequencing for a multiphase project, simulation of emergency exiting patterns, development of fire-spread models, and time sequenced shadow casting including the usage of various other audiovisual files. These applications involve simulations of potential circumstances.

11.2.9 Coordinating Drawings with Specifications

The drawings and the specifications are complementary, and both are needed to fully describe a construction project. The drawings show size, form, quantity, relationship, generic type, and graphic representation of construction materials. The specifications define the qualitative requirements for products, materials, and workmanship on which the construction contract is based. The specifications also describe administrative procedures regarding both drawings and specifications. The drawings and specifications may separately describe limits of work or construction phases.

Aspects of the specifications and the drawings may be clear, concise, correct, and complete, as to the information they convey, but unless the parts are coordinated with each other, the construction project may experience many problems and discrepancies. Effective coordination and quality assurance programs must begin early in the design process and depend largely on continuous and effective communication among project team members. The level of detail in the drawings should be consistent with the level of requirements in the specifications.

Coordination must occur at all levels of the project team. Consultants must ensure that the drawings and specifications within their offices are fully coordinated. Various consultants must also coordinate their graphic and written materials among their respective offices. The responsible A/E must not only coordinate the drawings and specifications within the A/E's own office, but also be responsible for coordinating the entire construction document package and for maintaining the communication process that will facilitate this coordination.

11.2.9.1 Drawings

A particular material or component may appear many times throughout the drawings, but is specified in only one location. In order to simplify and coordinate the documentation process, only generic notes should be used on the drawings to identify, but not describe, a material or component. Overly detailed notes may obscure the drawings and increase the possibility of inconsistencies and duplications. Detailed written information should be reserved for the specifications so that minor changes during development of the documents can be accommodated by revising only the specifications. For example, if the drawings have been noted to include concrete pavers, a design decision changing to brick pavers would necessitate finding and changing several drawing notes as well as the specifications. However, if the drawings had indicated only unit pavers, those notes would be unaffected by the change, and only the specifications would have to be modified. Minimizing the number of required changes to written information on the drawings diminishes the opportunities for discrepancies among the various drawings and between the drawings and specifications.

Whenever a change of materials is made, the corresponding symbols must be changed throughout the drawings, so symbols referring to a generic class of material, such as concrete or wood, are preferable over symbols referring to specific materials, such as walnut and oak. Thus, a change in wood species, for example, would not affect the drawings. Also, when more than one type of a generic class of materials is used, then such differentiation can be shown in the drawings with short notation such as "Wood-A" and "Wood-B."

Items of equipment, such as pumps or valves, should be identified on the drawings by a short generic name or coded symbol. For example, power roof ventilators (PRVs) might be indicated by PRV-1 and PRV-2. The graphic representation on the drawings should be only a representative outline rather than a detailed drawing. Proprietary product information should not appear on drawings unless a closed proprietary specification limits options to a single product. Even when specifications refer to products by their proprietary names, the notes on drawings should remain generic. If proprietary names are used on drawings, acceptance of a substitution could require revision of each proprietary reference by addendum or contract modification.

Material systems should also be identified on the drawings with only generic notes. For example, either a four-ply built-up roof with gravel surfacing or a loose-laid and ballasted ethylene propylene diene monomer (EPDM) roof could be noted on the drawings simply as "roof membrane." If more than one type of membrane is used in a project, the drawings should identify roofing Type A, B, C, and so forth, where the letter symbolizes a specific system described in the specifications. Where different design strengths are specified for structural steel, reinforcement, concrete, or other structural elements, the drawings may be used to indicate the boundaries between the materials of different capacities, which also may be designated as Type A, Type B, and so on.

Do not cross-reference between drawing and specifications with notes such as "refer to specifications" or "manhole cover—see specifications." Drawings and specifications are complementary parts of the same set of contract documents, and including references from one to the other is not recommended. However, it is acceptable to refer to specific specification sections. For example, a note on a floor plan could state "provide firestopping at wall penetration—see specification Section 07 84 00." This concept is consistent with similar techniques on drawings, where one drawing references another specific drawing or detail in the drawing set.

The drawings should not attempt to define the work of specific subcontractors or trades. However, the drawings may be used to indicate the extent of alternates, areas of construction phasing, limits of work, and specific items of work by the owner or by separate contract. On multiple-prime contract projects, the drawings can be used to designate work of separate contracts. Although these items may be graphically delineated on the drawings, the written descriptions and scope of work requirements should be defined in Division 01—General Requirements and PART 1—GENERAL of the specification section.

11.2.9.2 Specifications

In contrast to the generic notes and symbols on the drawings, the specifications provide detailed requirements for the physical properties, chemical constituents, performance requirements, and standards of workmanship associated with the manufacture and installation of materials, equipment, and components. For example, whereas the drawings might simply refer to a vapor retarder, the specifications define minimum perm rating, physical properties, and required installation methods. The specifications usually do not, however, include information that belongs more appropriately on the drawings, such as quantity, capacity, and location.

11.2.9.3 Schedules

Schedules help simplify communication by presenting data in a tabular form or in a matrix. The location and content of schedules may vary widely among A/Es. When placed in a specification section, schedules are included at the end of PART 3—EXECUTION. Although not technically part of execution, the schedules are placed there for convenience in specification preparation, although they can be included in the specifications or on the drawings. Examples of schedules are hardware schedules and sealant schedule. Schedules that include materials from multiple specification sections should be included in the drawings.

11.2.9.4 Coordination

Specifications complement, but should not repeat, information shown on the drawings, nor should the drawings duplicate information contained in the specifications. If a requirement on the drawings or in the specifications is duplicated in the other, an opportunity arises for a discrepancy between the two. An addendum covering a design change may correct the item in one location but overlook it in the other. Last-minute changes are most likely to create discrepancies of this sort. Such discrepancies may cause bidders/proposers to make different interpretations of what is required, often resulting in change orders and extra costs. Properly prepared drawings and specifications should dovetail like a jigsaw puzzle, without overlaps or gaps. To facilitate coordination, especially on complex projects with many different materials, components, subcontractors, and trades, adhere to the CSI principles established or locating information properly within the contract documents.

Preliminary Coordination. Construction documents are generally reviewed at set milestones such as 50 percent completion and 90 percent completion. Drafts of interim specification sections and copies of interim drawings from consultants should be collected and reviewed for coordination of information:

- Within the project manual
- Within the drawings of each separate discipline

- Between the drawings of separate disciplines
- Within the specifications of each separate discipline
- Between the specifications of separate disciplines
- Between the project manual and drawings

Consultants should review the drawings and specifications of other disciplines and forward corrections and comments to the A/E for communication to the other project team members. In addition to obvious graphical, dimensional, and typographical errors, documents should be carefully checked and compared to eliminate:

- Omissions
- Overlaps and duplications between disciplines
- Noncompliance with laws and regulations
- Conflicts and discrepancies with locations of equipment and components
- Incompatible materials and components
- Difficult or impossible construction methods
- Inconsistent terminology and abbreviations
- Inconsistent units of measure
- Incorrect or unspecified materials, components, or equipment
- Errors in extent of alternates
- Errors in defining areas of construction phasing
- Errors in defining limits of work
- Errors in identifying work by the owner or work not in contract
- Errors in designating work of separate contracts
- Inaccurate or unnecessary cross-referencing

Checking construction documents is not the same as coordinating the separate portions. A drawing may be found correct unto itself but may be totally inconsistent with other parts of the construction documents. Particular attention should be given to coordinating Division 01 sections with the conditions of the contract. The level of specification detail should complement the level of drawing detail. Early coordination with sufficient time devoted to the task will help achieve design intent and promote elimination of problems during the construction stage.

Final Coordination. Final construction documents should receive final coordinating and checking prior to issuance:

- Verify that all previously noted inconsistencies, errors, and inaccuracies have been corrected.
- Verify that the construction documents are complete, with final check of project manual table of contents and drawing table of contents.
- Verify consistency of all schedules.

Terminology and Abbreviations. Use consistent terminology and abbreviations throughout the contract documents to avoid confusion among the various users. The "service sink" in the specifications should not become the "janitor's sink" on the drawing, nor should "bituminous surface course" become "asphalt topping." The use of inconsistent terminology and abbreviations may create confusion in preparing specifications. It wastes time and can easily raise construction costs and cause delays, and may even result in faulty construction. The A/E should take responsibility for enforcing consistent terminology and abbreviations. Inconsistent and inappropriate terminology is perpetuated by such poor practices as the indiscriminate reuse of detail drawings and poorly edited specifications from previous projects.

Order of Precedence. Questions of precedence often arise among large-scale drawings, small-scale drawings, and specifications. However, the use of statements in the project manual to establish the precedence of the various contract documents is not recommended because the documents are complementary. The general conditions of the contract should indicate only that in a case of conflict between drawings and specifications, the A/E will make a documented interpretation.

Responsibility for Coordination. One person should be the coordinator and should have the responsibility for reviewing consistency between the drawings and the specifications. Good coordination policies include establishing effective intraoffice and interteam communication procedures. In preparing drawings and specifications, the specifier and A/E should work together, keeping in mind the difficulties faced by estimators, bidders, contractors, inspectors, and product representatives. In many instances, the A/E is also the specifier. As the project design stage begins, a conference should be held that includes the A/E, the consultants, the drafters, and the specifier. A preliminary project description or outline specification should be developed as a checklist and additional conferences should be held as the design progresses. Specification preparation should proceed concurrently with design, and coordination should become a continuous process from the beginning of the project.

Using Checklists. The coordinator should use checklists to ensure that necessary items are included in the specifications, that specified items are consistent with the drawings, and that drawings do not duplicate the specifications.

The form of a checklist will vary depending on its purpose. Forms may be designed to address specific office problems such as omissions, discrepancies, or duplications. For example, rather than putting overly specific or detailed notes on a drawing, drafters and CAD operators might simply keep a list of catalog references used in preparing details of particular products and equipment. These lists may be maintained in specification outlines that the specifier can later consult when preparing each section. A coordination checklist designed to avoid omissions in the specification of essential items noted in the drawings might have lists of materials, systems, and products by specification system. Check marks can be used to indicate inclusion in the design, and space should be provided for notes regarding coordination with other work and other items requiring special attention. *MasterFormat*® is one basis for an effective coordination checklist. The designer or drafter should fill in appropriate information on the list as work progresses to inform the specifier of required items.

11.2.10 Considerations for Different Delivery Methods

The extent of drawing and degree of detail may vary with the project delivery method, depending on the needs of the construction document user. For instance, the level of detail may not need to be as great for an owner-build or for a design-negotiate-build project delivery method as for one that is constructed under a design-bid-build method. Similarly, a design-builder entity may not require, or even desire, a great deal of detail. Construction management delivery methods generally require much more product description and installation detail.

Similarly, projects with phased scheduling or multiple contracts may also have different construction drawing needs. For example, a fast-tracked project may have a fully coordinated set of drawings that is developed as discrete packages of information that are required at predetermined construction milestones. Multiple prime contract projects may require different sets of construction drawings containing information specific to each contract but that also include commonly shared drawings, such as site plans or limit-of-work diagrams.

Regardless of the level of drawing detail required, the A/E must develop drawings that are in conformance with the requirements of the agreement and conditions of the contract. The A/E must also be aware that the level of drawings needed by the owner or contractor often may not be sufficient for the AHJ to complete its code compliance review or to document code compliance.

11.3 Specifications

11.3.1 Introduction

This chapter presents an overview of specifications. For more detailed information, refer to *The Construction Specifications Practice Guide*.

Specifications are the second of the two major categories of construction documents prepared by the design team.

11.3.2 The Nature of Specifying

A simple definition of the word *specify* is to describe or define an object, idea, or concept in such detail that it is easily understood by most people. It is not practical for construction drawing notes to include sufficient information to properly specify products and their installation. While construction drawings show products, materials, and equipment quantitatively, specifications detail their qualitative requirements. A specification is a precise statement describing the characteristics of a particular item that complements the graphic representations on the drawings. Whether specifying curtain wall systems, buildings, civil structures, or bridges, specifications should describe each product, material, or piece of equipment in sufficient detail so each can be purchased, manufactured, or fabricated according to the contract requirements. It is not necessary for a specification to include every attribute, physical property, or characteristic of a product, only those that will facilitate its incorporation into the project.

11.3.3 Evolution of Specifications

A fundamental question in creating specifications is how to organize the multiple pieces of information necessary. Years ago specifications were as different as the projects and the architects/engineers (A/Es) who designed them. No two A/Es followed the same method of organizing information. There was no consistency or uniformity. Such diverse organization caused difficulty in preparing bids, and important and costly items were easily overlooked. Particular information was difficult to locate, and coordination was difficult and last-minute changes troublesome.

Originally, specifications were simply a compilation of notes determined to be too long to place on the drawings. Other information and contractual provisions were later added, and as construction methods and systems increased in complexity, lengthy specifications became commonplace.

It is very important to establish a standard location for specific information and to state that information only in that location. This provides an orderly and logical arrangement for both the writer and reader. It also provides a standard, fixed framework for organizing specifications; provides a standard sequence for arranging specification sections; and it enables easy retrieval of information.

As will be seen later in this chapter, *MasterFormat*® has advanced over the last half-century into a 50-division organization that still dominates the design professions and construction industries.

11.3.4 Practices

11.3.4.1 Project Manual Concept

The documents commonly referred to as the specifications normally contain much more than that name implies. The procurement requirements, contracting forms, and conditions of the contract are usually included, but they are not specifications. In most cases, these are prepared by, or in coordination with, the owner and the owner's legal counsel and insurance adviser. This information, along with the specifications, is, in fact, a collection of certain written construction documents and project requirements whose contents and functions are best implied by the title *Project Manual*. With different methods of construction procurement, some documents become unnecessary. For example, in the owner-build delivery method and with negotiated contracts, bidding requirements are not applicable.

11.3.4.2 Developing Specifications

The techniques used in the preparation of specifications usually involve development of sections from product reference material or editing sections from master guide specifications. Regardless of who writes the specification sections or how they are developed, products must be researched, selected, evaluated, coordinated with other products, specified in a consistent and clear manner and coordinated with the drawings.

Gathering Information. Before beginning to write a section of specifications, the A/E must have the necessary information pertaining to that product, equipment, system, or assembly. Two kinds of information are needed. The first is information regarding the specific project requirements. The second kind of information is reference material pertaining to products and construction methods applicable to the particular specification section.

Many manufacturers offer suggested proprietary or guide specifications to relieve the A/E from some of the tasks of researching and writing a particular specification section. These specifications must be reviewed carefully to determine whether they have biases and whether they accurately state the necessary information. Product representatives should be able to perform the following tasks:

- Provide generic descriptions of products and systems.
- Understand the work of other trades that affects the proper installation and performance of the product.
- Identify the reference standards that relate to the product.

- Describe related work associated with the product.
- Assist in determining system, assembly, or product options or accessories.
- Identify modifications necessary to integrate a system or product in a project.
- Answer questions concerning delivery, storage, and handling of products.
- Explain installation procedures.
- Explain product and system installations.
- Identify the required certifications.
- Discuss requirements for field quality control.
- Answer questions regarding composition and manufacturing processes to produce products.
- Provide a guide specification in a format compatible with the A/E's computer system.
- Provide information regarding codes and regulations related to the use of a product or process.
- Assist in obtaining AHJ approval for installation of a product or process.

Product Selection Decisions. This requires systematic and progressive compiling of information, beginning with the early design phases. Selecting products for construction is like selecting goods for any other purpose. As discussed in Chapter 10, selection is based on evaluation of the products against specific criteria derived from the owner's requirements. There are several factors to consider in evaluating a product:

- The product
- The manufacturer
- The installation
- The cost

11.3.4.3 Specifications Organization and Preparation

Several decisions are required at the outset of the development of a specification section. On small, limited-scope projects, remodeling work, and work under the control of an owner-builder, the decision may be made to use a shortform specification or to record only the basic product selections and requirements. Conversely, highly detailed language may be needed for certain sections where requirements are critical or have been the subject of extensive investigation. Specific project requirements of the owner should be reviewed at this time, along with any requirements imposed by outside sources, such as regulatory agencies.

Format. Information collected should be developed in the three-part *SectionFormat*™.

Method of Specifying. A decision must also be made as to the appropriate method of specifying:

- Descriptive
- Performance
- Reference standard
- Proprietary

At times more than one method may be necessary in the same specification or even within the same section. If a project is for a government agency, nonrestrictive methods will generally be required, and it is essential to be aware of this limitation before beginning to prepare specifications.

Specification Language. Competent specification writing requires the correct use of vocabulary and grammar along with correct construction of sentences and paragraphs. Always use the four principles of effective communication:

- Clear
- Concise
- Correct
- Complete

The imperative mood should generally be maintained throughout a specification. Consistent use of terminology and language contributes to better communication. Avoid duplicating or contradicting requirements contained elsewhere in the project manual. Because the contractor and owner are the only parties to the owner-contractor agreement, all instructions are addressed to the contractor. Consistency in the use of terms will help minimize confusion and ambiguity.

Preparing Specifications. Specification sections can be newly written, derived from a previous project specification, or edited from a master guide specification. With the use of commercial master guide specifications, editing rather than writing is usually the primary means for producing project manuals or specifications.

Division 01—General Requirements. Early distribution of the Division 01 draft to consultants and other contributors to the specifications will help eliminate overlapping requirements and omissions.

Section Title List. Once basic requirements for the project are known, a list of section titles is developed, along with the scope of work associated with each. This list should also indicate related work that is specified in other sections. The section title list serves as a device for coordination among the sections and helps prevent overlaps or omissions in the specifications.

Coordinating with Consultants. Major portions of the project specifications may be written by consultants. This is often the case for the mechanical, electrical, structural, and civil engineering sections. Some sections may also be written by specialists such as theater consultants, lighting designers, and landscape architects. Such situations require special coordination among entities involved to ensure that the specifications are complete, compatible, consistent, and without duplication or overlap.

11.3.4.4 Specifying Workmanship

Workmanship is often confused with the term *quality*. As quality is a mirror of the requirements, the requirements need to reflect what is intended. Workmanship generally refers to precision, and craftsmanship. These requirements have measurable properties and can be specified with a means to verify compliance. Workmanship can be controlled in several articles of a specification section. These articles specify qualifications, tolerances, and various other aspects of quality assurance and quality control. Workmanship can be divided into two main categories:

- Workmanship relating to the manufacturing and fabrication of products
- Workmanship relating to the application, installation, or erection of products

It is a combination of materials and workmanship that results in the final characteristics of the product. Workmanship requirements are specified to an appropriate level in accordance with the needs of the project. Project requirements should be specified without demanding conformance to unattainable standards or to standards exceeding those necessary for the requirements of the overall project. Workmanship requirements should be measurable. Avoid broad generalities such as "best possible workmanship."

Appropriate methods for achieving desired workmanship include:

- Referring to applicable standards and codes
- Establishing qualifications of manufacturer, fabricator, and installer
- Referring to workmanship requirements of trade associations
- Requiring samples to establish an acceptable level of workmanship and a basis for judging subsequent work
- Specifying tolerances and performance or physical requirements
- Establishing testing and inspection requirements

11.3.4.5 Considerations during Development of Specifications

Economic Implications of Each Choice. The A/E should be aware of the economic impact of the requirements stated in the specifications.

Work Results Structure. The A/E must understand that neither the section titles nor their arrangement defines how the work of the project is to be assigned to various construction trades and subcontractors.

Industry Conditions and Availability of Products. The A/E should consider the availability of products being specified. A product available today may not be available some months later when the project is under construction. Similarly, some products require long delivery times and may not be appropriate for projects with short construction periods or when early completion of the project is extremely important.

11.3.4.6 Specifying Quality Assurance and Quality Control

The agreed upon requirements, schedule, and budget establish the project quality. Specifications generally stipulate qualitative requirements and the drawings generally indicate quantitative requirements.

Quality Assurance in the Conditions of the Contract. The basis for quality assurance is included in the conditions of the contract. Some assurances are based in the legalities of the contract. Most standard general conditions include warranty provisions requiring the contractor's affirmation that materials and equipment will be new and of good quality, unless otherwise required or allowed; will be free from defects not inherent in the quality required or allowed; and will conform to the requirements of the contract documents.

Quality Control in the Conditions of the Contract. The quality control (QC) provisions in the conditions of the contract are to verify conformance with the contract requirements. Many standard general conditions require the contractor to supervise the work using expertise, skill, and attention. The contractor is solely responsible for controlling the means, methods, techniques, sequences, and procedures for construction and is therefore responsible for controlling the quality of the work. The A/E usually visits the site to become familiar with the progress and quality of the completed work. On the basis of field observations, the A/E reviews the contractor's applications for payment and certifies or recommends payment of amounts due. Standard general conditions typically give the A/E authority to reject work that is defective or does not conform to the contract documents. This authority does not constitute control of the work, nor does this authority establish a responsibility for means, methods, techniques, sequences, or procedures for construction. The A/E may require additional independent inspection and testing.

Division 01—General Requirements. The following are several Division 01 sections that often include provisions for quality assurance or establish quality controls over the work:

- Regulatory Requirements
- Project Management and Coordination
- Submittal Procedures
- Quality Assurance
- Quality Control
- Substitution Procedures
- Commissioning

Specifications. Divisions 02 through 49 are composed of individual sections, each addressing a distinct subject area. The issues and requirements concerning quality assurance and quality control specific to that section are addressed. The contract documents are so interrelated none of them can stand alone. An examination of *SectionFormat*™ in the appendix will help clarify the interrelationships between the requirements of articles within individual sections in Divisions 02 through 49 and Division 01 specification sections. The requirements in Division 01 are dependent upon provisions in the conditions of the contract.

- PART 1—GENERAL of a specification section includes articles on administrative matters. Three articles that deal specifically with quality are "Administrative Requirements," "Submittals," and "Quality Assurance."
- PART 2—PRODUCTS of a specification section includes articles related to the manufacture and fabrication of products. Following are several articles that specifically address quality control:
  - Assembly or Fabrication Tolerances
  - Source Quality Control
  - Tests
  - Inspections
  - Nonconforming Work
  - Manufacturer Services
- PART 3—EXECUTION of a specification section covers work performed at the project site. The following articles in PART 3 relate to quality control:
  - Tolerances
  - Field or Site Quality Control
  - Field or Site Tests
  - Field or Site Inspection
  - Nonconforming Work
  - Manufacturer's Services

11.3.4.7   Coordination of the Specifications

Continuous communication and coordination of information among the project team members is essential to reduce errors, omissions, duplications, and inconsistencies within the project manual and with the construction drawings. Sharing of design and product decisions with project team members must begin at the earliest phases of the project, and the A/E should assume the responsibility for coordinating the flow and documentation of project information.

Refer to Figure 11.10 for an example of a construction specification.

11.3.4.8 Variations Required by Project Delivery Methods

The preceding discussion is based on the traditional design-bid-build project delivery method. Other project delivery methods require some variation in the construction documents. Some other variations for project delivery may be simple and others may require multiple project manuals and separate packages of drawings.

Document Variations for Design-Negotiate-Build Project Delivery Method. The A/E will not necessarily be the sole decision maker on all the items that would normally be the A/E's responsibility. Decisions are often shared by other project team members.

- *Procurement Requirements.* The contractor might prepare the contractor's own procurement requirements for subcontract packages.
- *Contracting Forms.* If the contract is negotiated between the owner and contractor, the A/E may not be involved in preparing contracting forms, bonds, and certificates.
- *Conditions of the Contract.* The general conditions might be standard documents published by the AIA or the EJCDC or might be general conditions offered by the proposer. Some owners, especially large developers, prefer to use their own general conditions, which are usually based on AIA or EJCDC general conditions.
- *Division 01—General Requirements:* Division 01 requirements should be prepared in conjunction with the conditions of the contract. Special coordination might be necessary for certain procedures that are to be negotiated, such as payment procedures, construction progress schedules, submittals, substitutions, warranties, and contract closeout.
- *Divisions 02 through 49—Specifications:* Writing specifications for this delivery method would not be significantly different. The decisions to utilize specific products might be the result of prior negotiations or value analysis; however, the specification would be similar. If pricing and negotiations have determined specific products, then the specification might be written as proprietary, eliminating a level of detail.

Document Variations for Construction Management Project Delivery. The nature of construction management is to provide management services and generally divide the project into various "packages" representing discrete scopes of work that are released at different times.

The A/E will not necessarily be the sole decision maker on all the items that would normally be the A/E's responsibility. Decisions are often shared with other project team members.

- *Procurement Requirements.* The CM may prepare the procurement requirements for the bid packages. The process of obtaining separate bids is not significantly different from that of a traditional design-bid-build project delivery method.

SECTION 12 31 23
MANUFACTURED STAINLESS STEEL CASEWORK

PART 1—GENERAL
1.1   SUMMARY
   A.   Section Includes: Manufactured stainless steel casework and supplementary items necessary to complete their installation.
1.2   SUBMITTALS
   A.   Product Data: Manufacturer's technical literature for each product indicated, specified, or required; include installation details, material descriptions, dimensions of individual components and profiles, and finishes.
   B.   Shop Drawings: Submit including plans, elevations, sections, details, and attachments to other work.
      1.   Indicate locations of blocking and reinforcements required for installing casework.
      2.   Indicate locations of and clearances from adjacent walls, doors, windows, other building components, and other equipment.
      3.   Include coordinated dimensions for equipment specified in other Sections.
   C.   Samples for Verification Purposes: Submit 6 inch square sample for each type of finish.
1.3   QUALITY ASSURANCE
   A.   Product Quality Standard: SEFA 8.
1.4   DELIVERY, STORAGE, AND HANDLING
   A.   Handling: Protect finished surfaces during handling with protective covering.
PART 2—PRODUCTS
2.1   MANUFACTURERS
   A.   Available Manufacturers: Subject to compliance with requirements of Contract Documents, manufacturers offering products that may be incorporated into Work include, but are not limited to, those listed alphabetically below.
      1.
      2.
      3.
2.2   METAL
   A.   Stainless Steel Sheet: Mild, cold-rolled and leveled, ASTM A 666, Type 304; No. 4 satin finish; suitable for exposed applications, thicknesses indicated.
2.3   FABRICATION
   A.   General:
      1.   Assemble and finish units at point of manufacture.
      2.   Use precision dies for interchangeability of like-size drawers, doors, and similar parts. Perform assembly on precision jigs to provide units that are square.
      3.   Reinforce units with angles, gussets, and channels.
      4.   Integrally frame and weld to form a dirt and vermin-resistant enclosure.
      5.   Maintain uniform clearance around door and drawer fronts of 1/16 inch.
   B.   Flush Doors:
      1.   Outer pans, made of not less than 0.050 inch thick sheet, and inner pans, of not less than 0.038 inch thick sheet, that nest into box formation, with full-height channel reinforcements at center of door.
      2.   Fill doors with noncombustible, sound-deadening material.
      3.   Mortise for hinges and reinforce angles, of not less than 0.038 inch thick sheet, welded inside inner pans at hinge edge.
   C.   Drawers:
      1.   Fronts of outer and inner pans, of not less than 0.038 inch thick sheet, that nest into box formation, with no raw metal edges at top.
      2.   Sides, back, and bottom, of not less than 0.038 inch thick sheet, fabricated in one piece with rolled or formed top of sides for stiffening and comfortable grasp for drawer removal.
      3.   Weld drawer front to sides and bottom to form a single, integral unit.
      4.   Provide drawers with rubber bumpers, ball-bearing slides, and positive stops to prevent metal-to-metal contact or accidental removal.
   D.   Base Units:
      1.   Wrap-around side and back construction of not less than 0.050 inch thick sheet.

MANUFACTURED STAINLESS STEEL CASEWORK
12 31 23 - 1

Figure 11.10 **An example of a construction specification.**

2. Vertical uprights for shelving, with holes at 1/2 inch increments for clip attachment, made of not less than 0.050 inch thick sheet.
3. Shelves of not less than 0.038 inch thick sheet; front, back, and ends formed down, with edges returned horizontally at front and back to form reinforcing channels; with center-mounted hat channel reinforcing for shelves longer than 36 inches.
4. Front rail of not less than 0.078 inch thick sheet.
5. Intermediate front rail of not less than 0.063 inch thick sheet.
6. Bottom and toebase of not less than 0.050 inch thick sheet; fully enclosed, 4 inches high by 3 inches deep, with no open gaps or pockets.
7. Accessible hex-head leveling screws at each corner.
8. Holes for attaching countertops.

2.4 HARDWARE
A. General: Manufacturer's standard satin-finish, commercial-quality, heavy-duty hardware complying with requirements indicated for each type.
B. Hinges:
1. BHMA A156.9, Grade 1, 5-knuckle stainless steel hinges with antifriction bearings and rounded tips.
2. 2 for doors 48 inches or less in height and 3 for doors more than 48 inches in height.
C. Pulls: Stainless steel; fastened from back with two screws.
D. Door Catches:
1. Nylon-roller spring catch or dual, self-aligning, permanent magnet catch.
2. 2 catches on doors more than 48 inches in height.
E. Drawer Slides: BHMA A156.9, Type B05091, powder-coated, full-extension, self-closing, heavy-duty drawer slides; designed to prevent rebound when drawers are closed; with nylon-tired, ball-bearing rollers; rated for 150 pounds.

PART 3—EXECUTION
3.1 EXAMINATION
A. Acceptance of Surfaces and Conditions:
1. Examine substrates to which casework attaches for compliance with requirements for installation tolerances and other conditions affecting performance of assemblies specified in this Section.
2. Do not proceed with installation until unsatisfactory conditions have been corrected.
3. Starting work within a particular area will be construed as applicator's acceptance of surface conditions.
3.2 INSTALLATION
A. General: Install level, plumb, and true; shim as required, using concealed shims. Where casework abuts other finished work, apply filler strips and scribe for accurate fit, with fasteners concealed where practical.
B. Base Units: Fasten cabinets to reinforcements in partitions with fasteners spaced not more than 24 inches o.c. Bolt adjacent cabinets together with joints flush, tight, and uniform.
C. Hardware: Install uniformly and precisely. Set hinges snug and flat in mortises.
3.3 ADJUSTING
A. Final Adjustments: Adjust casework and hardware so doors and drawers align and operate smoothly without warp or bind and contact points meet accurately. Lubricate operating hardware as recommended by manufacturer.

END OF SECTION

MANUFACTURED STAINLESS STEEL CASEWORK
12 31 23 - 1

Figure 11.10 *(continued)*

- *Contracting Forms.* Agreement forms are usually prepared by the construction manager for each bid package.
- *Conditions of the Contract.* General conditions for construction management project delivery require unique provisions ensuring cooperation between and mutual responsibility among multi-prime contracts.
- *Division 01—General Requirements:* Division 01 requirements for multiple-prime contracts should be prepared with specific regard for the scope of each contract. Special coordination is necessary for certain procedures such as

payments, progress schedules, product submittals, QC, substitutions, warranties, and contract closeout.

- *Divisions 02 through 49—Specifications.* On multiple-prime contracts, the CM may request changes to ensure clear definition of the responsibilities of various contractors. It is possible that a particular product specification section will be tailored differently for each bid package.

Document Variations for Design-Build Delivery Method. The owner might issue a request for proposal (RFP), conditions of the contract between the owner-design-builder, technical specifications or performance specifications, and the design requirements. The design-builder will respond to the RFP and negotiate an agreement. The construction documents for a D-B project are prepared by an A/E for the design-builder. Though performed in the interest of the design-builder, the basic services provided by the A/E may be similar to those of a traditional contract.

- *Procurement Requirements.* The design-builder will prepare any necessary procurement for subcontracts, including instructions to bidders.
- *Contracting Requirements—Agreements and Conditions of the Contract.* The design-builder may also have the design-builder's own general conditions tailored for a specific project type. Most standard agreements are written for two phases: the preliminary design phase and the construction phase.
- *Division 01—General Requirements.* The design-builder should prepare the general requirements as part of the construction documents.
- *Divisions 02 through 49—Specifications:* The design-builder should prepare specifications to secure accurate subcontract bids and ensure clear definition of the responsibilities of various subcontractors. The design builder may desire brief specifications that allow wide latitude in product requirements and selections, or the owner may have stringent project requirements that dictate the level of specification detail required.

Document Variations for Owner-Build Project Delivery Method. Owners who are capable of preparing their own designs and documentation might have an in-house department with an A/E or facility manager. Documentation may be performed in-house or under agreement with an independent A/E.

- *Procurement Requirements.* The procurement requirements will be developed similar to other delivery methods and will depend on the nature of the project and whether it is to be bid, negotiated, purchased, or some form of services.
- *Contracting Forms.* The A/E might not always participate in this process. The A/E might simply include the owner's standard documents that have been prepared by the owner's attorney or in-house legal department.
- *Conditions of the Contract.* The conditions of the contract may also be standard documents that have been prepared by the owner's attorney or in-house legal department.
- *Division 01—General Requirements.* Division 01 requirements should be prepared in conjunction with the conditions of the contract.
- *Divisions 02 through 49—Specifications.* Writing specifications for this delivery method are not usually different; however, some firms will have specific requirements for products that have become standard in their identity or operations.

11.3.5   Specification Language

As legally enforceable contract documents, construction specifications should be prepared with concern and respect for their legal status. The four Cs for effective communication are:

- *Clear.* Use proper grammar and simple sentence construction to avoid ambiguity.
- *Concise.* Eliminate unnecessary words, but not at the expense of clarity, correctness, or completeness.
- *Correct.* Present information accurately and precisely. Carefully select words that convey exact meanings.
- *Complete.* Do not leave out important information.

Since specifications are a form of technical writing that are of a specialized nature, there are certain rules and characterizations that are appropriate.

11.3.5.1   Writing Style

Good writing style is characterized by accuracy, brevity, and clarity:

- Use simple sentences; long, complex sentences and stilted language do not contribute to effective communication. Avoid complicated sentences in which inadvertent omission or insertion of punctuation could change meaning or create ambiguity.
- Use words and terms that are simple and clearly understood.

11.3.5.2   Sentence Structure

Two basic grammatical sentence moods can be used to clearly convey specification requirements:

- *Imperative Mood.* The imperative mood is the recommended method for instructions covering the installation of products and equipment. The verb that clearly defines the action becomes the first word in the sentence, such as: spread adhesive with notched trowel. The imperative sentence is concise and readily understandable.
- *Indicative Mood.* The indicative mood, passive voice requires the use of shall in nearly every statement. This sentence structure can cause unnecessary wordiness and monotony, such as: adhesive shall be spread with notched trowel.

11.3.5.3   Abbreviations

While abbreviations are effective when used on drawings, they are not effective in specifications and should be generally avoided.

11.3.5.4   Symbols

Symbols as substitutes for words or terms should be avoided.

- Symbols may conflict with command characters in software programs.
- There are potential font translation problems when converting from one software to another.
- Small symbols may bleed together and become unreadable in a poorly printed text.

- Use of parentheses and quotation marks should be minimized or avoided.
- Underlines should not be used.

11.3.5.5   Numbers

Use numerals whenever possible because they are easy to identify. However, when numbers are used to define both size and quantity, the written word should be used for the quantity.

11.3.5.6   Capitalization

Capitalization should be consistent throughout the contract documents. Capitalization of the initial letter of certain specific nouns and of proper names defined in the conditions of the contract is appropriate.

11.3.5.7   Punctuation

Because specifications are legal documents, the formal rules of punctuation must be observed. Sentences should be constructed so that the misplacement or elimination of a punctuation mark will not change the meaning. Commas should be used after each item in a series, including the item preceding a conjunction, and in other locations where the clarity of the statement will be improved.

11.3.5.8   Grammar

Subject and Verb Agreement. Subject and the verb must always agree in number. Singular verbs should be used with singular subjects and plural verbs with plural subjects. An error in number is easy to make when a sentence is long and complicated. The singular subject of a sentence can be confused with a plural modifier.

- Incorrect: One of the elongated central fasteners are to be placed around the eye of the panel and bolted.
- Correct: One of the elongated central fasteners shall be placed around the eye of the panel and bolted.
- Preferred: Bolt one elongated central fastener to panel eye.

Parallel Construction. Good grammar also requires the use of identical style in both parts of a compound subject or predicate. The use of identical style in a series of nouns, adverbs, or prepositional phrases is also recommended.

- Incorrect: Tests shall be performed to determine strength and establish qualities.
- Correct: Tests shall be performed to determine strength and to establish quality.
- Preferred: Perform tests to determine strength and to establish quality.
- Incorrect: Heating, ventilation, and air-conditioning.
- Correct and preferred: Heating, ventilating, and air conditioning.

11.3.5.9   Inappropriate Terms

Avoid using words such as the following:

- as approved; as indicated; as required
- hereinafter; hereinbefore; herewith

* any, such
* etc.
* as per
* in a workmanlike manner
* to the satisfaction of the architect/engineer
* also

11.3.5.10 Pronoun Reference

The use of pronouns in specifications should be minimized or avoided. Personal pronouns should not be used.

* Repeating the noun is better than risking possible misunderstanding.
  * Poor: Apply coating with pneumatic equipment when it is above 40°F.
  * Better: Maintain pneumatic equipment above 5 degrees C (40 degrees F) or apply coating only when ambient temperature is above 5 degrees C (40 degrees F).
* *Which* and other relative pronouns should be used sparingly, if at all.
  * Poor: Contractor shall install bathroom accessories which are to be purchased under an allowance.
  * Better: Contractor shall install bathroom accessories to be purchased under an allowance.
  * Preferred: Install bathroom accessories purchased under allowances specified in Section 01 21 00.
* The word *same* should not be used as a pronoun.
  * Poor: If materials are rejected, the contractor shall replace same at no additional cost.
  * Better: Contractor shall replace rejected materials.
  * Preferred: Replace rejected materials.

11.3.5.11 Unnecessary Words

* Definite article the and indefinite articles a and an need not be used in most instances.
  * Poor: Apply an oil paint with a brush to the wall.
  * Better: Apply oil paint with brush to walls.
* Use of the word all is usually unnecessary.
  * Poor: Store all millwork under shelter.
  * Better: Store millwork under shelter.
* Avoid using contractor as the subject of the sentence.
  * Poor: Contractor shall lay brick in common bond.
  * Better: Brick shall be laid in common bond.
  * Preferred: Lay brick in common bond.

11.3.5.12 Prepositional Phrases

Sentences may be shortened in specification language by using modifiers in place of prepositional phrases.

* Correct: Top of platform.
* Preferred: Platform top.

11.3.5.13 Streamlining

Attempts to reduce verbiage in specifications are recommended if the meaning can still be clearly conveyed. Although difficult to adapt to descriptions or instruction, streamlining is used to list products, materials, reference standards, and other itemized specifications. This technique places the subject first and provides keywords for quick reference.

- Adhesive: Spread with notched trowel.
- Equipment: Install plumb and level.
- Portland cement: ASTM C 150, Type 1.

11.3.5.14 Specification Detail

Language style should not be confused with specification detail. Specification detail should be commensurate with the requirements of the project, and method of project delivery. Specifications for a large housing project may be more complex than those for a small vacation cottage, but the same general rules for clarity and conciseness apply to both projects. Degree of detail is a matter of judgment and is often tempered by economic considerations. A specification is complete when it covers important details without elaborate or unnecessary language.

11.3.6 Methods of Specifying

There are four methods that are used for writing specifications:

- *Descriptive.* A prescriptive method—products and processes are specified but not the results.
- *Performance.* A method of specifying results, but not the means to achieve them.
- *Reference standard.* A method that can be used for prescriptive or performance specifications.
- *Proprietary.* A prescriptive method—products and processes are specified but not the results.

Project specifications typically employ more than one specifying method. All four methods may be used in a single specification section. There is no clear rule for using either one method or a combination of methods.

11.3.6.1 Descriptive Specifications

A descriptive specification is a detailed, written description of the required properties of a product, material, or piece of equipment and the workmanship required for its installation. Proprietary names of manufacturers are not used. The burden of performance is assumed by the A/E when a descriptive specification is used. Once widely preferred, the descriptive method is being used less frequently as projects become more complex and as better reference standards become available. Writing a descriptive specification is a lengthy and tedious process.

11.3.6.2 Performance Specifications

A performance specification is defined as a statement of required results with criteria for verifying compliance, but without unnecessary limitations on the methods for achieving the required results.

- *A Statement of Required Results.* Desired end results must be specified; an incomplete performance specification results in a major loss of quality control over the materials, equipment, and workmanship going into a project.
- *With Criteria for Verifying Compliance.* Criteria for measuring, testing, evaluating, or other acceptable assurances are required before production, at the time of production, in place at the site, or after a period of service.
- *Without Unnecessary Limitations on the Methods for Achieving the Required Results.* Only essential restrictions are placed on the system; limitations on the means should be avoided.

Performance specifying will be discussed in more detail later in this chapter.

11.3.6.3 Reference Standard Specifications

As discussed in Chapter 4, a standard is a document established by consensus that provides rules, guidelines, or characteristics for activities or their results. Standards are incorporated by reference into the specifications and thus become commonly known as reference standards. They are published by trade associations, professional societies, standards-writing organizations, governments, and institutional organizations. Typical authors are architects, engineers, scientists, technologists, manufacturers, and product users who are extremely knowledgeable about the particular reference standard subject. Where applicable, use standards listed in the model or local codes to ensure acceptability with the AHJ.

Reference standards are incorporated into the specifications by referring to a number, title, or other designation. The provisions of standards so referenced become a part of the specifications just as though included in their entirety. Their incorporation into the specifications by reference saves the A/E the work of writing an elaborate and lengthy text. Accompanying these benefits are some liabilities:

- Inadequate reference standards coexist with stringent ones.
- Reference standards can create duplication and contradiction within the contract documents.
- Standards can contain embedded options.
- Standards generally refer to minimum requirements.
- Reference standards might contain undesired requirements.
- Various AHJs may enforce different editions of the same standard, which might have conflicting requirements.

11.3.6.4 Proprietary Specifications

Proprietary specifications identify the desired products by manufacturer's name, brand name, model number, type designation, or other unique characteristics. When a manufacturer's name is not stated, a specification is considered proprietary when the product specified is available from only one source.

- Advantages of proprietary specifications are as follows:
  - Product selection can be closely controlled.
  - More detailed and complete drawings can be prepared based on precise information obtained from selected manufacturer's data.
  - Reduced cost and time benefits may be obtained from use of shorter specifications and reduced drawing production effort.
  - Bidding may be simplified by narrowing competition and removing product pricing as a major variable.

- Disadvantages of proprietary specifications include the following:
  - Competition for products is reduced or eliminated.
  - Products may be specified with which the contractor may have had little or an unfavorable experience.
  - Certain products and manufacturers may be favored over others.
  - An error might occur when specifying model or product designations.

Closed and Open Proprietary Specifications. Proprietary specifications can be either closed or open, and there are fundamental differences between them.

- *Closed Proprietary Specification.* The closed proprietary specification permits the design to be completed to a high level of detail. This reduces variables and promotes accurate pricing; however, it does not offer protection against possible higher costs. The supplier of a specified proprietary product could take unfair advantage of being the sole source and increase the price of the product. A closed proprietary specification can list one product or name several products as options. In either case, substitutions are not allowed.
- *Open Proprietary Specification.* Open proprietary specifications may alleviate the problem of overpriced sole-source items.
  - *Requested Alternates.* There are several ways that proprietary specifications can be opened to allow alternate products. One method is to request proposals for alternate products. This form of proprietary specification defines the materials in the same way as a closed specification (i.e., only one brand is named for each material or item of equipment specified). Alternates to the specified products are named in the specification. The terms *alternate* and *substitute* are often misused. An alternate is something that is named for which alternative pricing is requested; a substitute is something that is requested to replace an item as specified.
  - *Proposed Substitutions.* This form of open proprietary specification is prepared in much the same way as a specification requesting alternates. However, no alternates are named in the specifications. The bid/proposal must be based on the specified materials, but the bidder/proposer is permitted to submit requests for substitutions, provided the bidder indicates the difference in cost that will result if the substitutions are accepted.
  - *Controlled Substitutions.* In this type of open proprietary specification, specific products are named but substitutions are allowed under specified procedures. A requirement may be met with the specified item or by a similar product that is not necessarily identical but that is alike with respect to performance. This method saves time during the development of a specification because only one product needs to be investigated and specified for each requirement. The principal problem associated with this type of proprietary specification is that attempts are often made to substitute materials of different characteristics or requirements than those specified.

Selection of Proprietary Methods. There are many useful proprietary techniques that consider the bidder's/proposer's right to select products. Closed methods generally give the bidder/proposer little or no choice. Open methods give the bidders/proposers a wide choice.

The acceptance of substitutions opens the project to the possibility of accepting unknown and perhaps inferior products. If the specified item is part of a vital system, the situation may call for a proprietary specification prohibiting substitutions entirely. However, if keen competition and low construction cost are more important than completely assured performance, then substitutions should be permitted.

Open specifications generally place a greater workload on the A/E, increasing in direct proportion to the degree of choice available to the bidders/proposers. From the standpoint of reducing the design and specifying effort, the closed proprietary method is best. Because only one product is named for each application, the drawings and specifications can be completed quickly and precisely. There is no need to accommodate several combinations or construction options.

When substitutions are allowed, competition is keenest. Material costs are nearly certain to be less, but this method is conducive to permitting products of lesser requirements. The apparent savings can easily be lost through subsequent high maintenance and replacement costs. A proprietary designation establishes a basis for determining quality, including performance, appearance, and cost. A proprietary name also establishes that the designer has considered the characteristics of the specified product, has decided upon its incorporation into the project, and has used its dimensions in the drawings. Any coordination effort resulting from the use of a contractor proposed substitution should be the responsibility of the contractor.

Nonrestrictive Specifications. Nonrestrictive specifications may be developed from descriptive, performance, reference standard, or proprietary specifications or from a combination of these four methods.

Descriptive and performance specifications can easily be used for nonrestrictive specifications. However, care must be taken to ensure that descriptive and performance requirements can be met by several manufacturers or suppliers. Failure to do so will make the specifications restrictive, even though a proprietary name has not been used.

A proprietary specification masquerading as a performance specification is not nonrestrictive. The A/E may delete the identifying name of the product and then list the salient qualities verbatim from the manufacturer's literature as product requirements. Without any ranges of characteristics and performance being given, this method results in a fully proprietary, closed specification and is not a suitable solution for a nonrestrictive project.

11.3.7 Formats

A number of organizational standards, loosely referred to as *formats,* have been developed to organize all of the information that needs to be addressed from the inception of a project throughout its life cycle. These formats can each be employed for a variety of applications; the chief advantage they carry is a standardized means of organizing, storing, retrieving, and communicating this enormous body of data.

Figure 11.11 illustrates the hierarchies and relationships among the several formats that will be discussed in the following sections.

11.3.7.1 OmniClass™

OmniClass™ is a multi-table framework for organizing information used by the architectural, engineering, and construction industry (www.omniclass.org). Ultimately serving all participants who work to sustain the built environment throughout the entire life cycle of a facility, *OmniClass*™ is useful for many applications, from organizing library

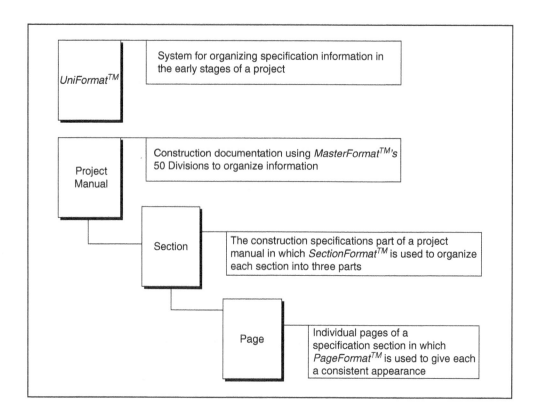

Figure 11.11
Hierarchy of the Formats

materials, product literature, and project information, to providing a classification structure for electronic databases. It is based on the other following systems:

- *MasterFormat*® for work results
- *UniFormat*™ for elements

The 15 *OmniClass*™ classification tables are organized by segregating types of information about the built environment into a set of discrete, coordinated tables. The information contained in each table exists and is organized based on a specific facet, or view, of the information for the subject matter addressed by that table.

- Table 11: Construction Entities by Function
- Table 12: Construction Entities by Form
- Table 13: Spaces by Function
- Table 14: Spaces by Form
- Table 21: Elements-UniFormat™
- Table 22: Work Results-MasterFormat®
- Table 23: Products
- Table 31: Phases
- Table 32: Services
- Table 33: Disciplines
- Table 34: Organizational Roles
- Table 35: Process Aids
- Table 41: Information

- Table 42: Materials
- Table 49: Properties

OmniClass™ classification tables can be used together or individually to manage information about all aspects of the facilities that compose the built environment over their entire life cycle. *OmniClass*™ concepts are derived from internationally accepted standards developed by the International Organization for Standards (ISO) and supported by the International Construction Information Society and the International Alliance for Interoperability.

11.3.7.2 *UniFormat*™

UniFormat™ is a uniform classification system for organizing preliminary construction information into a standard order or sequence on the basis of systems and assemblies. By establishing a uniform list of identifiers and titles, *UniFormat*™ promotes standardization and facilitates the retrieval of information. *UniFormat*™ can be used to organize preliminary project descriptions, preliminary cost estimates, and drawing detail filing in the early stages of a facility's life cycle. *UniFormat*™ organizes construction information based on physical parts of a facility called systems and assemblies. These systems and assemblies are characterized by their function without identifying the products that compose them. Systems and assemblies present a view of a proposed facility separate from the view presented by a breakdown of building materials, products, and activities.

UniFormat™ classifies information into the following categories that constitutes a Project Description:

Introduction
- A: Substructure
- B: Shell
- C: Interiors
- D: Services
- E: Equipment and Furnishings
- F: Special Construction and Demolition
- G: Building Sitework
- Z: General

These nine categories can each be used to arrange preliminary project descriptions and preliminary cost information, such as the following example:

Level 1   A   SUBSTRUCTURE
Level 2   A10   Foundations
Level 3   A1010   Standard Foundations
Level 4   A1010.10   Wall Foundations
Level 5   A1010.10.CF   Continuous Foundations

Titles in Levels 1 through 3 can be applied to most preliminary project descriptions and preliminary cost estimates. Levels 4 and 5 are available for use on detailed, complex projects. Levels 4 and 5 titles and detailed listings provide a checklist to ensure comprehensive and complete application of *UniFormat*™. Figure 11.12 is a list of Level 1 through 2 alphanumeric *UniFormat*™ designations and titles.

```
A  SUBSTRUCTURE
   A10   Foundations
   A20   Basement Construction

B  SHELL
   B10   Superstructure
   B20   Exterior Closure
   B30   Roofing

C  INTERIORS
   C10   Interior Construction
   C20   Stairways
   C30   Interior Finishes

D  SERVICES
   D10   Conveying Systems
   D20   Plumbing Systems
   D30   Heating, Ventilating, and Air-Conditioning (HVAC)
         Systems
   D40   Fire Protection Systems
   D50   Electrical Systems

E  EQUIPMENT AND FURNISHINGS
   E10   Equipment
   E20   Furnishings

F  OTHER BUILDING CONSTRUCTION
   F10   Special Construction
   F20   Selective Demolition

G  BUILDING SITEWORK
   G10   Site Preparation
   G20   Site Improvements
   G30   Site Plumbing Utilities
   G40   Site Heating, Ventilating, and Air-Conditioning
         (HVAC) Utilities
   G50   Site Electrical Utilities
   G60   Other Site Construction

Z  GENERAL
   Z10   General Requirements
   Z20   Bidding Requirements, Contract Forms, and Conditions
   Z90   Project Cost Estimate
```

Figure 11.12
Levels 1-2 of Uniformat™

Preliminary project descriptions (PPDs), based on *UniFormat™*, provides a system to describe a project by its basic systems and assemblies before the particular materials and methods have been chosen. A/Es use PPDs to organize project descriptions and help estimators formulate early cost estimates. PPDs can also be used for the following:

- Preliminary cost estimates
- Drawing detail filing

11.3.7.3 *MasterFormat*®

MasterFormat® is an organizational structure providing numbers and titles for the variety of subject matter necessary for the construction, operation, and maintenance of a facility. *MasterFormat*® provides a system of six-digit and eight-digit numbers and titles for organizing construction information into a standard order or sequence. By establishing a master list of numbers and titles, *MasterFormat*® promotes standardization, facilitates the placement and retrieval of information, and improves construction communication.

Divisions. *MasterFormat*® arranges related construction practices, or work results, into a series of level 1 titles called Divisions (www.masterformat.com). The 50-division format does not follow the sequence of construction nor is it organized around traditional subcontracts or construction trades. However, it does follow an organization that is logical and the groupings lend themselves to convenient subdivision. If there is no work within a division, then that division is simply not used in the project specification. However, the remaining divisions are not renumbered.

In addition to listing the work results within each division, *MasterFormat*® also organizes the section locations so sections related to operations and maintenance, common work results, schedules, or commissioning will always be located in the same area of each division.

Central to the arrangement and use of contents of the divisions in the groupings in *MasterFormat*®, and the sections that make them up, is the notion that all of the different types of construction are addressed equally. The basic organizational structure of the *MasterFormat*® groups and subgroups is as follows:

- *Procurement and Contracting.* Introductory information and procurement information as well as the location for information defining the relationships, responsibilities, and processes for construction
  - *Requirements Group:*
    - *Division 00—Procurement and Contracting Requirements.* Solicitation, instructions for procurement, procurement forms and supplements, contracting forms and supplements, project forms, conditions of the contract, and revisions, clarifications, and modifications
- *Specifications Group.* Administrative requirements and the physical aspects of construction
  - *General Requirements Subgroup:*
    - *Division 01—General Requirements.* General and administrative requirements, procedural matters, and temporary facilities and controls that apply to all the other sections contained in Divisions 02 through 49
  - *Facility Construction Subgroup:*
    - *Division 02—Existing Conditions.* Existing conditions assessment, investigation, demolition and structure moving, remediation, contaminated site material removal, water and facility remediation
    - *Division 03—Concrete.* Concrete, including forms and accessories, reinforcement, and cast-in-place and precast items
    - *Division 04—Masonry.* Brick, block, stone, simulated masonry, other masonry units and assemblies, and associated mortars and accessories
    - *Division 05—Metals.* Structural metal framing, metal joists, metal deck, metal fabrications, and ornamental metal
    - *Division 06—Wood, Plastics, and Composites.* Rough carpentry, finish carpentry, architectural woodwork, structural plastics, and plastic fabrications
    - *Division 07—Thermal and Moisture Protection.* Thermal and moisture protection including damp-proofing and waterproofing, insulation, siding, roofing, flashing, sheet metal, roof accessories, and joint sealers
    - *Division 08—Openings.* Most types of doors, frames, storefronts, curtain wall, windows, skylights, hardware, and glazing

- *Division 09—Finishes.* Finishing work and materials, such as plaster, gypsum board, tile, acoustical treatments, carpet, paints and coatings, and wall coverings.
- *Division 10—Specialties.* Miscellaneous manufactured items, such as visual display boards, toilet compartments and accessories, louvers and vents, fireplaces, signs, lockers, and operable partitions
- *Division 11—Equipment.* Specialized building equipment, such as security, library, theater and stage, audiovisual, parking control, loading dock, water and treatment, food service, laboratory, and medical
- *Division 12—Furnishings.* Art, window treatment, manufactured and specialty casework, furniture and accessories, multiple seating, and interior planters and site furnishings
- *Division 13—Special Construction.* Building components serving specialized purposes, including air-supported structures, radiation protection, lightning protection, preengineered structures, swimming pools, storage tanks, utility control systems, solar and wind energy equipment, and building automation systems
- *Division 14—Conveying Equipment.* Elevators, escalators, wheelchair lifts, material handling systems, cranes, and other powered transportation systems
- *Division 15.* Reserved for future expansion
- *Division 16.* Reserved for future expansion
- *Division 17.* Reserved for future expansion
- *Division 18.* Reserved for future expansion
- *Division 19.* Reserved for future expansion
- *Facility Services Subgroup:*
- *Division 20.* Reserved for future expansion
- *Division 21—Fire Suppression.* Equipment and systems involved in fire protection and controls
- *Division 22—Plumbing.* Equipment and systems involved in process piping, plumbing, drainage, and controls
- *Division 23—Heating, Ventilating, and Air Conditioning.* Equipment and systems involved in process piping, heating, ventilating, air conditioning, and controls
- *Division 24.* Reserved for future expansion
- *Division 25—Integrated Automation.* Hardware and software for integrated automation network (building automation)
- *Division 26—Electrical.* Electrical work, including power distribution, lighting, and instrumentation and controls
- *Division 27—Communications.* Structured cabling, data, voice, and audiovisual communications, and distribution and monitoring systems
- *Division 28—Electronic Safety and Security.* Electronic access control and intrusion detection, electronic surveillance, monitoring, detection and alarm systems and controls
- *Division 29.* Reserved for future expansion
- *Site and Infrastructure Subgroup:*
- *Division 30.* Reserved for future expansion
- *Division 31—Earthwork.* Site clearing, earth moving, earthwork methods, shoring and underpinning, excavation support and protection, special foundations and load bearing elements, and tunneling and mining
- *Division 32—Exterior Improvements.* Bases, ballasts, and paving, site improvements, wetlands, irrigation, and planting

- *Division 33—Utilities.* Water utilities, wells, sanitary sewerage and storm drainage, fuel distribution, hydronic and steam energy, electrical and communication utilities
- *Division 34—Transportation.* Guideways/railways, traction power, signaling and control equipment, fare collection equipment, transportation construction and equipment, and bridges
- *Division 35—Waterway and Marine Construction.* Signaling and control equipment, waterway and marine construction and equipment, coastal construction, and dam construction
- *Division 36.* Reserved for future expansion
- *Division 37.* Reserved for future expansion
- *Division 38.* Reserved for future expansion
- *Division 39.* Reserved for future expansion
- *Process Equipment Subgroup:*
  - *Division 40—Process Integration.* Piping for gas, vapor, liquids, solids and mixed materials, process piping protection, and process equipment commissioning and controls
  - *Division 41—Material Processing and Handling Equipment.* Bulk material, piece material handling, manufacturing, container processing and packaging equipment, material storage, and mobile plant equipment.
  - *Division 42—Process Heating, Cooling, and Drying Equipment.* Process heating, cooling, and drying equipment
  - *Division 43—Process Gas and Liquid Handling, Purification and Storage Equipment.* Process gas and liquid handling, purification, and storage equipment
  - *Division 44—Pollution and Waste Control Equipment.* Air, noise, water treatment, solid waste control equipment
  - *Division 45—Industry-Specific Manufacturing Equipment.* Specific manufacturing equipment including: oil and gas extraction, mining, food production, textiles and apparel, paper manufacturing, printing equipment, assorted material, electronic, and other product manufacturing equipment.
  - *Division 46—Water and Wastewater Equipment.* Equipment and work results for water treatment, wastewater treatment, and water reuse systems and processes, and related systems and equipment
  - *Division 47.* Reserved for future expansion
  - *Division 48—Electrical Power Generation.* Instrumentation and control of electrical power generation equipment and testing
  - *Division 49.* Reserved for future expansion

Standardized Numbers and Titles. *MasterFormat*® provides six-digit numbers only for the broad and medium scope level two and level three titles. The first two digits refer to one of the 50 divisions. Intervals have been left between level 2 and level 3 numbers so that numbers, in sequence, are available for use with the level 4 titles. Unused numbers are available between level 3 numbers to permit assignment of numbers to the selected level 4 titles needed to accommodate individual project requirements.

MasterFormat® identifies five levels of detail:

- Level 1: The 50 divisions
- Level 2: Sections of broad scope that provide the widest latitude in describing units of work
- Level 3: Sections of medium scope that cover units of work of more limited scope

- Level 4: Sections of narrow scope that cover extremely limited and very specific elements of work
- Level 5: User defined

MasterFormat® is used in a variety of ways in the design and construction of facilities:

- *Specifications. MasterFormat*® is most widely used for the purpose that drove its initial development: organizing specifications. Titles are provided in a logical sequence for the most common specification sections required for a construction project. Use of the numbers and titles shown in *MasterFormat*® will allow easy cross-referencing within the project manual because a section will always have the same number and title. *MasterFormat*® has been developed to provide the A/E with a standard yet flexible system for organizing specifications and construction information. However, *MasterFormat*® sections are not intended to correspond to the work assigned by the contractor to a single trade or subcontractor.
- *Data Organization.* The system of numbers and titles organizes technical data and product literature by work results. *MasterFormat*® is used by most construction product manufacturers for their product literature, allowing their products to be related to the work result sections in which they are used.
- *Cost Classification.* The number and title system serves as the basis for the organization of construction costs and parallels the organization of specifications.

Sections. A section is a part of the project specifications covering one portion of the project requirements. It describes particular materials or products and their installation, or particular administrative or procedural requirements. Individual sections dealing with related items are grouped together under the appropriate divisions. Specific sections are included in a project manual only as needed to meet project requirements. A section does not necessarily relate to the work accomplished by a single subcontractor. It is not the intent of the specifications to define the work of individual trades.

Specifications should always address the contractor rather than subcontractors. The contractor executes an agreement with the owner to construct the project and is therefore the only entity responsible to the owner. Responsibility for construction of the total project remains with the contractor no matter how the work is divided among subcontractors and suppliers.

In order to assist in preparing text for any section, the following fundamental questions and characteristics should be addressed:

- What products or systems are required?
- What shop or factory actions are required and how are the products or systems to be prepared for delivery?
- What on-site actions are required and how are the products or systems to be incorporated into the work?
- What are the specific administrative requirements for accomplishing this portion of the work?
- What are the specific procedures required for accomplishing this portion of the work?
- What special relationship exists with associated work to be described in other sections?

Collectively, the answers to these questions make up the essential portions of text of a specification section. When considered with the organization of text suggested by *SectionFormat*™, the answers can be easily placed in the appropriate parts and articles.

11.3.7.4 *SectionFormat™*

SectionFormat™ provides a uniform approach to organizing specification information by establishing a structure consisting of three primary parts. These parts organize specific information consistently within each section. Refer to Figure 11.13. A section is intended to cover one portion of the project requirements. It describes particular materials, products, systems, or assemblies and their installation and particular administrative or procedural requirements. Sections are included in a project manual specification only as needed to meet the project requirements. Specifications address the contractor. A section does not necessarily relate to the work accomplished by a single subcontractor. It is not the intent of the specifications to define the work of individual trades. Each contractor will divide the work differently among subcontractors. Responsibility for construction remains with the contractor regardless of how the work is divided among subcontractors and suppliers.

The specification information within sections is arranged in a three-part format:

- *PART 1—GENERAL.* Describes administrative, procedural, and temporary requirements unique to the section. PART 1 is an extension of subjects covered in Division 01 and amplifies information unique to the section.
- *PART 2—PRODUCTS.* Describes products, materials, equipment, fabrications, mixes, systems, and assemblies, and their quality requirements, that are required for incorporation into the project.
- *PART 3—EXECUTION.* Describes installation or application, including preparatory actions and postinstallation cleaning and protection. Site-built assemblies and site-manufactured products and system are included.

11.3.7.5 *PageFormat™*

There are advantages to standardizing the way information is presented on a page. A standard page format provides an orderly and uniform arrangement of text for each page of a specification section. The standard page format has three objectives:

- To present text clearly and at a density best suited for easy reading and rapid reference
- To provide an acceptable standard suitable for use in specifications throughout the construction industry
- To provide a flexible format compatible with most current production techniques and electronic software

Uniformity of presentation eases the tasks of preparation, review, and publication and saves the specification user time and effort.

11.3.8 Agreements

Discussed in more detail in Chapter 5.

11.3.9 Conditions of the Contract

Discussed in more detail in Section 11.5.4.

SectionFormat™ Outline

Standard Article titles in a section. **BOLD UPPERCASE:** Primary titles. Title Case: Subordinate titles that may be elevated to primary Article titles.

PART 1— GENERAL

SUMMARY

Section includes
Products Furnished Supplied But Not Installed
    Under This Section
Products Installed But Not Furnished Supplied
    Under This Section
Related Requirements

PRICE AND PAYMENT PROCEDURES

Allowances
Unit Prices
Alternates Alternatives
Measurement and Payment

REFERENCES

Abbreviations and Acronyms
Definitions
Reference Standards

ADMINISTRATIVE REQUIREMENTS

Coordination
Preinstallation Meetings
Sequencing
Scheduling

SUBMITTALS
ACTION SUBMITTALS/INFORMATIONAL
    SUBMITTALS

Product Data
Shop Drawings
Samples
Certificates
Delegated Design Submittals
Test and Evaluation Reports
Manufactures Instructions
Source Quality Control Submittals
Field Site Quality Control Submittals
Manufacturer Reports
Sustainable Design Submittals
Special Procedure Submittals
Qualification Statements

PART 2—PRODUCTS
OWNER-FURNISHED OWNER-SUPPLIED
PRODUCTS

New Products
Existing Products

**[SYSTEMS]/[ASSEMBLIES]/[MANUFACTURED UNITS]/
[EQUIPMENT]/[COMPONENTS]/[PRODUCT TYPES]/
[MATERIALS]/[USER-DEFINED HEADING]**

CLOSEOUT SUBMITTALS

Maintenance Contracts
Operation and Maintenance Data
Bonds
Warranty Documentation
Record Documentation
Sustainable Design Closeout Documentation
Software

MAINTENANCE MATERIAL SUBMITTALS

Spare Parts
Extra Stock Materials
Tools

QUALITY ASSURANCE

Regulatory Agency Sustainability Approvals
Qualifications
    Manufacturers
    Suppliers
    Fabricators
    Installers/Applicators/Erectors
    Testing Agencies
    Licensed Professionals
Certifications
Sustainability Standards Certifications
Preconstruction Testing
Field Site Samples
Mock-ups

DELIVERY, STORAGE, AND HANDLING

Delivery and Acceptance Requirements
Storage and Handling Requirements
Packaging Waste Management

FIELD SITE CONDITIONS

Ambient Conditions
Existing Conditions

WARRANTY BOND

Manufacturer Warranty
Special Warranty
Extended Correction Period

PART 3—EXECUTION
INSTALLERS

Installer List
Substitution Limitations

EXAMINATION

Verification of Conditions
Preinstallation Testing
Evaluation and Assessment

Figure 11.13 SectionFormat™ outline.

Manufacturers
    Manufacturer List
    Substitution Limitations
    Product Options

Description
    Regulatory Requirements
    Sustainability Characteristics

Performance/Design Criteria
    Capacities

Operation
    Operators
    Controls
    Operation Sequences

Materials

Assembly Fabrication
    Factory Assembly
    Shop Fabrication
    Assembly Fabrication Tolerances

Mixes

Finishes
    Primer Materials
    Finish Materials
    Shop Finishing Methods

ACCESSORIES

SOURCE QUALITY CONTROL
    Tests and Inspections
    Nonconforming Work
    Manufacturer Services
    Coordination of Other Tests and
        Inspections

PREPARATION
    Protection of In-Place Conditions
    Surface Preparation
    Demolition/Removal

**ERECTION/INSTALLATION/APPLICATION/
[USER-DEFINED PROCESS]**
    Special Techniques
    Interface with Other Work
    Systems Integration
    Tolerances

**[REPAIR]/[RESTORATION]
REINSTALLATION**

FIELD SITE QUALITY CONTROL
    Field Site Tests and Inspections
    Nonconforming Work
    Manufacturer Services

SYSTEM START-UP

ADJUSTING

CLEANING
    Waste Management

CLOSEOUT ACTIVITIES
    Demonstration
    Training

PROTECTION

MAINTENANCE

ATTACHMENTS
                    END OF SECTION
    Schedules
    Tables
    Illustrations
    Forms

Figure 11.13 *(continued)*

11.3.10 Division 01—General Requirements

The sections in Division 01, which are collectively referred to as the General Requirements, specify the following:

- *Administrative and Procedural Requirements.* Relates to the process of contract administration, the assignment of contractual responsibilities, and the methods of communicating, controlling, and assuring quality
- *Temporary Facilities and Controls.* Work put into place for use only during the period of construction and that will be removed when no longer required for construction operations
- *Performance Requirements.* Facility and system performance
- *Life Cycle Activities.* Commissioning, facility operation, facility maintenance, and facility decommissioning

Division 01 sections expand on certain of the administrative and procedural provisions in the conditions of the contract and apply broadly to the execution of the work of all the other sections of the specifications. Division 01 sections cover general requirements for execution of the work and should be written in language broad enough to apply to sections in Divisions 02 through 49. Without Division 01, these requirements would otherwise be repeated throughout the specifications, and the possibility of conflicts and omissions would be increased. This Division 01 concept adheres to the principle of stating information only once and in the right place. Figure 11.14 illustrates the relationships between Division 01 and each of the other construction documents.

Proper use of Division 01 avoids mixing conditions of the contract with the administrative and procedural details of the specifications. A comparison of conditions of the

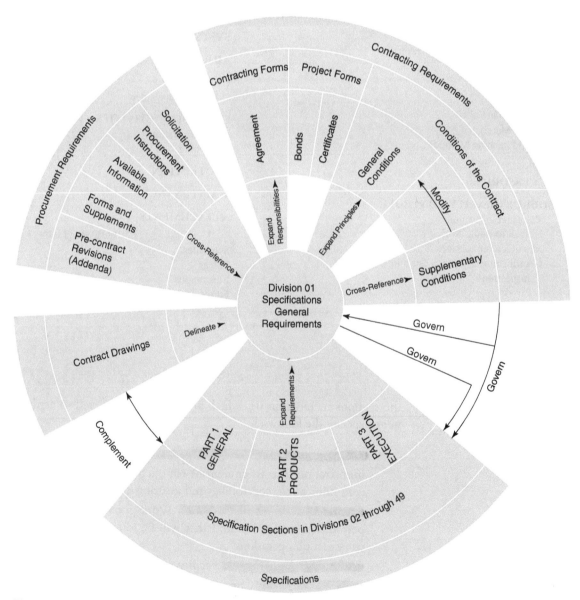

Figure 11.14 Division 01 Relationship to Other Documents

CONDITIONS OF THE CONTRACT	DIVISION 01—GENERAL REQUIREMENTS
Are inherent part of the Agreement	An inherent part of the Specifications
With the Agreement govern the content of the entire contract	Administratively governs the Specification sections
Contain contractual principles applicable to most projects with supplements for a particular project	Contains specifics directly applicable to a particular project

GENERAL CONDITIONS	SUPPLEMENTARY CONDITIONS	SECTIONS OF DIVISION 01
Are broad contractual conditions	Modify the contractual conditions	Contain specific administrative and procedural requirements
Contain the constants	Modify the constants for a specific region or project	Contain variables directly applicable for specific project
Relatively static content, thus allowing the use of published standard documents	Take precedence over general conditions	Must be written separately for each project
	Must be written separately for each project	

ARE NOT SPECIFICATIONS   **ARE SPECIFICATIONS**

Figure 11.15 **Conditions of the Contract versus Division 01—General Requirements**

contract and Division 01—General Requirements is shown in Figure 11.15. Coordination is necessary between each section of Division 01 and the respective specification sections of Divisions 02 through 49, and among the sections of Division 01 that cover interrelated administrative and procedural requirements.

11.3.10.1 Division 01 and *SectionFormat™*

Division 01 specifies procedural requirements common to many specification sections and to the project as a whole. Most of these requirements are related to the administrative activities of the project, and others govern products and execution requirements. Accordingly, the numbers and titles of Division 01 in *MasterFormat®* have been arranged to parallel the sequence of information in *SectionFormat™*. Figure 11.16 shows the parallel organization of Division 01 titles to *SectionFormat™*.

11.3.10.2 Division 01 Relationship to Other Documents

Each of the contract documents complements one another and should not duplicate specific information. The provisions of the conditions of the contract and the agreement apply broadly to the work of the project, and Division 01 expands on these provisions, giving just enough detail to apply broadly to the other specification sections. The

DIVISION 01
GENERAL REQUIREMENTS

SectionFormat^{TM}

01 00 00   GENERAL REQUIREMENTS

01 10 00   SUMMARY
Summary of Work
Multiple Contract Summary
Work Restrictions
Project Utility Sources

01 20 00   PRICE AND PAYMENT
PROCEDURES
Allowances
Unit Prices
Alternates
Value Analysis
Substitution Procedures
Contract Modification Procedures
Payment Procedures

01 30 00   ADMINISTRATIVE
REQUIREMENTS
Project Management and Coordination
Construction Progress
 Documentation
Submittal Procedures
Special Procedures

01 40 00   QUALITY REQUIREMENTS
Regulatory Requirements
References
Quality Assurance
Quality Control

01 50 00   TEMPORARY FACILITIES
AND CONTROLS
Temporary Utilities
Construction Facilities
Temporary Construction
Construction Aids
Vehicular Access and Parking
Temporary Barriers and Enclosures
Temporary Controls
Project Identification

01 60 00   PRODUCT REQUIREMENTS
Common Product Requirements
Product Options
Owner Furnished Products
Product Delivery Requirements
Product Storage and Handling
 Requirements

PART 1—GENERAL
SUMMARY
Section Includes
Products Supplied but Not Installed Under
 This Section
Products Installed but Not Supplied Under
 This Section
Related Sections

Allowances
Unit Prices
Alternates
Measurement Procedures
Payment Procedures
Alternates

REFERENCES

DEFINITIONS

SYSTEM DESCRIPTION
Design Requirements,
 Performance Requirements

SUBMITTALS
Product Data
Shop Drawings
Samples
Quality Assurance/Control Submittals
Closeout Submittals

QUALITY ASSURANCE
Qualifications
Regulatory Requirements
Certifications
Field Samples
Mock-ups
Preinstallation Meetings

DELIVERY, STORAGE, AND
HANDLING
Packing, Shipping, Handling,
 and Unloading
Acceptance at Site
Storage and Protection
Waste Management and Disposal

Figure 11.16
Division 01 Relationship to
SectionFormat™

DIVISION 01
GENERAL REQUIREMENTS

SectionFormat^{TM}

01 70 00   EXECUTION AND CLOSEOUT
REQUIREMENTS
Examination and Preparation
Execution
Cleaning and Waste Management
Starting and Adjusting
Protecting Installed Construction
Closeout Procedures
Closeout Submittals
Demonstration and Training

PROJECT/SITE CONDITIONS
Project/Site Environmental
Requirements
Existing Conditions

SEQUENCING

SCHEDULING

WARRANTY
Special Warranty

01 80 00   PERFORMANCE REQUIREMENTS
Facility Performance Requirements
Facility Substructure Performance
Requirements
Facility Shell Performance
Requirements
Interior Performance Requirements
Conveying Equipment Performance
Requirements
Facility Services Performance
Requirements
Equipment and Furnishings
Performance Requirements
Other Facility Construction
Performance Requirements
Site Construction Performance
Requirements

SYSTEM START-UP

OWNER'S INSTRUCTIONS

01 90 00   LIFE CYCLE ACTIVITIES
Commissioning
Facility Operation
Facility Maintenance
Facility Decommissioning

COMMISSIONING

MAINTENANCE
Extra Materials
Maintenance Service

PART 2—PRODUCTS
Not Used

PART 3—EXECUTION
Not Used

Figure 11.16 *(continued)*

specifications and drawings further expand on Division 01 and provide detailed requirements for specific portions of the work.

- *Procurement Requirements.* Procurement requirements are not usually part of the contract documents. Provisions that are stated only in procurement requirements are not enforceable during administration of the construction contract. The procurement requirements should not repeat Division 01 provisions but should instead refer to the appropriate Division 01 sections, by number and title, to direct the bidder to relevant information. Provisions applicable only during the bidding stage, such as document acquisition and cost, bid security requirements, and bid opening dates, should be stated in the procurement requirements rather than in Division 01.

- *Owner-Contractor Agreement.* The owner-contractor agreement includes by reference all other contract documents. Certain provisions of the owner-contractor agreement are supplemented by the provisions of Division 01 sections that define in greater detail the responsibilities of the parties to the contract.

- *General Conditions.* The conditions of the contract govern the execution of the work and apply broadly to sections of the specifications, including those in Division 01. Among the topics usually covered are property surveys, temporary utilities and services, warranties, progress schedules, record documents, submittals, cutting and patching, cleaning, schedule of values, applications for payment, and closeout procedures. As these topics are covered only in very broad terms, they must be specified in further detail in Division 01 to tailor requirements to a specific project.

- *Supplementary Conditions.* Supplementary conditions should not repeat information contained in the general conditions or encroach upon topics that belong more appropriately in Division 01. Proper coordination between Division 01 and supplementary conditions will avoid conflicts, omissions, and duplications. Other than a statement establishing the authority of Division 01, the supplementary conditions should not contain general references to Division 01.

- *Other Specification Sections.* Specification sections are subject to the administrative and procedural requirements of the conditions of the contract and of Division 01. As suggested in Figure 11.17, project requirements become more specific for each successive level of a three-tier hierarchy:

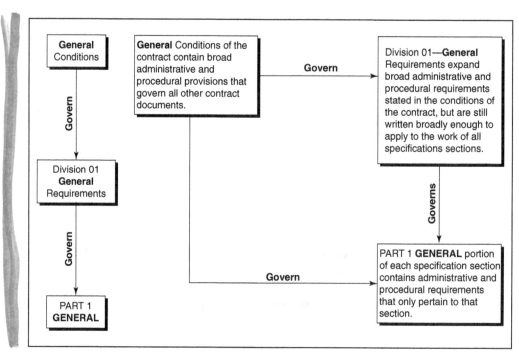

Figure 11.17
Hierarchy of General Administrative and Procedural Requirements

- The general conditions state provisions in broad terms.
  - Division 01—General Requirements elaborate on the broad provisions of the conditions of the contract, but are still written broadly enough to apply to the work of all specification sections.
  - PART 1—GENERAL in a specification section becomes very specific in project requirements for that section only.
- *Drawings.* Drawings graphically define certain Division 01 subject matter, such as the extent of work, and may define related work that may or may not be part of the contract. Purely procedural sections of Division 01, such as submittals, quality requirements, and closeout procedures, need no coordination with the drawings. Other sections, such as those covering use of the site, phased construction, and multiple-prime contracts, usually require extensive delineation on the drawings and close coordination between the drawings and Division 01.

11.3.10.3 Commonly Used Division 01 Sections

The more commonly used Division 01 specification sections are listed in the following paragraphs with some guidelines for the general types of information that might be included in each.

- Section 01 10 00—Summary
  - Section 01 11 00—Summary of Work
  - Section 01 12 00—Multiple Contracts Summary
  - Section 01 14 00—Work Restrictions
- Section 01 20 00—Price and Payment Procedures
  - Section 01 21 00—Allowances
  - Section 01 22 00—Unit Prices
  - Section 01 23 00—Alternates
  - Section 01 24 00—Value Analysis
  - Section 01 25 00—Substitution Procedures
  - Section 01 26 00—Contract Modification
  - Section 01 29 00—Payment Procedures
- Section 01 30 00—Administrative Requirements
  - Section 01 31 00—Project Management and Coordination
  - Section 01 32 00—Construction Progress Documentation
  - Section 01 33 00—Submittal Procedure
  - Section 01 35 00—Special Procedure
- Section 01 40 00—Quality Requirements
- Section 01 50 00—Temporary Facilities and Controls
  - Section 01 51 00—Temporary Utilities
  - Section 01 52 00—Construction Facilities
  - Section 01 53 00—Temporary Construction
  - Section 01 54 00—Construction Aids
  - Section 01 55 00—Vehicular Access and Parking
  - Section 01 56 00—Temporary Barriers and Enclosures
  - Section 01 57 00—Temporary Controls
  - Section 01 58 00—Project Identification

- Section 01 60 00—Product Requirements
  - Section 01 62 00—Product Options
  - Section 01 64 00—Owner-Furnished Products
  - Section 01 65 00—Product Delivery Requirements
  - Section 01 66 00—Product Storage and Handling Requirements
- Section 01 70 00—Execution and Closeout Requirements
  - Section 01 71 00—Examination and Preparation
  - Section 01 73 00—Execution
  - Section 01 74 00—Cleaning and Waste Management
  - Section 01 75 00—Starting and Adjusting
  - Section 01 76 00—Protecting Installed Construction
  - Section 01 77 00—Closeout Procedures
  - Section 01 78 00—Closeout Submittals
  - Section 01 79 00—Demonstration and Training
- Section 01 80 00—Performance Requirements
  - Section 01 81 00—Facility Performance Requirements
  - Sections 01 82 00 through 01 89 00
- Section 01 90 00—Life Cycle Activities
  - Section 01 91 00—Commissioning
  - Section 01 92 00—Facility Operation
  - Section 01 93 00—Facility Maintenance
  - Section 01 94 00—Facility Decommissioning

11.3.10.4 Specifying Allowances

The use of allowances requires written provisions in several of the procurement documents that must be carefully coordinated. Typically, allowance requirements will appear in the procurement requirements, conditions of the contract, Division 01—General Requirements, and the individual specification sections for the items covered by the allowances Figure 11.18. The documents must state exactly what is included under the allowance, who is to authorize items covered by allowances, and how costs will be adjusted if the actual price, quantity, or time varies from the amount stated.

Specification Section 01 21 00—Allowances should specify the dollar amount or quantities as well as administrative and procedural matters relating to handling allowances. The specific items of work covered by each allowance should be identified and referenced to the respective specification sections.

11.3.10.5 Specifying Alternates

Most master guide specifications and standard documents do not contain extensive provisions for alternates, as they are generally unique to each project. If alternates are to be used, special provisions must be incorporated in the documents to make them effective. Figure 11.19 illustrates how the requirements for an alternate for adding television sets to a hospital project might be stated in the various procurement documents.

Specification Section 01 23 00—Alternates should identify each alternate and describe the changes of work included in each and reference the respective specification sections affected by the alternates. If not shown on the drawings, certain areas or portions of the work may be described to clarify the locations of changes necessitated by the incorporation of alternates. The specification sections in Divisions 02 through 49 affected by the alternates should contain a coordinating or clarifying statement calling attention to the provisions for alternates.

BID FORM

If quantities for the following allowance items vary from the amounts specified in Section 01 21 29 – Quantity Allowances, the Contract Sum will be adjusted in accordance with the following unit prices:

ITEM DESIGNATION	UNIT OF MEASURE	UNIT PRICE
1. Tenant Corridor Entrance	Each	$ _____
2. Corridor Partition	LF	$ _____

SECTION 01 21 29—QUANTITY ALLOWANCES

1.06   SCHEDULE OF QUANTITY ALLOWANCES

A. Item No. 1 – Tenant Corridor Entrance: Allow a quantity of 55 installed entrances, each to include:
1. Fire-rated hollow-metal frames, Section 08 11 00 – Metal Doors and Frames:
2. 1-½ hour fire-rated wood doors, 3′-0″ by 7′-0″, Section 08 14 00 – Wood Doors, and Section 08 15 00 – Plastic Doors;
3. Hardware Set No. 3, Section 08 70 00 – Hardware;
4. Door sign, Section 10 14 00 – Identification Specialities.
B. Item No. 2 – Corridor Partition: Allow a quantity of 250 linear feet of installed 8′-0″ high partition including:
1. 3-5/8-inch, 25-gage steel studs spaced 24 inches on center, with two layers of 5/8-inch Type X gypsum board screw attached to each side, Section 09 21 16 – Gypsum Board Assemblies;
2. Tenant side finish: One coat of primer and two coats eggshell latex paint, Section 09 90 00 – Painting and Coating;
3. Corridor side finish: Type A vinyl wall covering, Section 09 72 00 – Wall Coverings.

Figure 11.18

Partial Bid Form and Corresponding Division 01 Schedule of Quantity Allowances

11.3.10.6 Specifying Unit Prices

Whether a project is based on a stipulated sum contract with a few unit prices listed for minor variables or is based entirely on unit prices, the requirements and procedures for handling unit prices must be defined in the procurement documents. These requirements will involve the bid or proposal form along with carefully written Division 01 sections, both of which must be coordinated with the respective specification sections in Divisions 02 through 49.

Specification Section 01 22 00—Unit Prices is generally the specification section for establishing procedural requirements for unit prices and should:

- Cover methods of determining actual quantities for both progress and final payments.
- Be coordinated with the general conditions to avoid conflicts, duplication of information, or omission of essential requirements.
- Define who is responsible for actual measurement of unit price quantities.

Figure 11.20 is a sample partial bid form and the corresponding Division 01 schedule of unit price allowances for tenant corridor entrances and corridor partitions.

PROCUREMENT REQUIREMENTS

Invitation to Bid

Type of Bids: Bids shall be on a stipulated-sum basis of the base contract, and include a separate price for each alternate.

Instructions to Bidders

Each alternate is described in the Specifications and is provided for in the Bid Form.

The price of the Bid for each alternate will be the amount to be added to or deducted from the price of the Base Bid if the Owner selects the alternate.

The Owner may accept alternates in any order; regardless of how they are listed, and determine the lowest responsible bidder on the basis of the sum of the base bid plus any selected alternates.

Bid Form

Alternate No. 1—Patient Room Televisions:
Add _____ Dollars ($_____)
(In Words)   (In Numerals)

CONTRACTING REQUIREMENTS

Agreement

The Contractor shall perform all work required by the Contract Documents for TLC Nursing Home at 123 Primrose Lane, Anywhere, USA, including Alternates No. 1, 2, 3 as described in Section 01 23 00—Alternates, of the Specifications.

SPECIFICATIONS
SECTION 01 23 00

1.06   ALTERNATE NO. 1—PATIENT ROOM TELEVISIONS
A.   Provide 72 bedside bracket-mounted television sets on the first floor of "A-Wing" as specified in Section 27 41 19—Portable and Spare Audio Video Equipment.

SECTION 26 61 50

1.04   ALTERNATES
A.   Refer to Section 01 23 00—Alternates, for description of work under this Section affected by alternates.

Figure 11.19
Samples Use of Alternates

11.3.11 Coordinating Drawings and Specifications

Discussed in more detail in Section 11.2.

11.3.12 Procurement and Contract Document Modifications

There is no effective substitute for clear, concise, correct, complete, and carefully coordinated construction documents. Despite best efforts and planning, situations requiring changes do develop. The A/E, owner, and contractor must have adequate means for dealing with such changes. Addenda and change orders may be employed to modify

BID FORM

SCHEDULE OF PRICES

ITEM NO.	DESIGNATION	UNIT OF MEASURE	UNIT OF PRICE	ESTIMATED QUANTITY	TOTAL PRICE
	Refer to Section 01 22 00 — Unit Prices		Dollars/Cts		Dollars/Cts
1	Earthwork for Utilities	CY	$_____	563	$_____
2	10-inch Ductile Iron Pipe	LF	$_____	62	$_____
3	30-inch Steel Pipe	LF	$_____	234	$_____
4	30-inch Prestressed Concrete Cylinder Pipe	LF	$_____	115	$_____
5	30-inch Valve and Vault	EA	$_____	2	$_____

TOTAL PRICE:_____   ($_____)

(In Words)   (In Numerals)

SECTION 01 22 00—UNIT PRICES

1.04 SCHEDULE OF UNIT PRICE ITEMS

A. Item No. 1 Earthwork for Utilities
 1. Trench Excavation, select granular backfill, and compaction in accordance with Section 31 23 00—Excavation and Fill.
 2. Unit of Measure: Cubic yards of backfill compacted in place.

B. Item No. 2 10-inch Ductile Iron Pipe
 1. Pipe and fittings including pressure-testing in accordance with Section 33 10 00—Water Utilities.
 2. Unit of Measure: Linear feet of pipe installed.

C. Item No. 3 30-inch Steel Pipe
 1. Pipe and fittings including pressure-testing in accordance with Section 33 10 00—Water Utilities.
 2. Unit of Measure: Linear feet of pipe installed.

D. Item No. 4 30-inch Prestressed Concrete Cylinder Pipe
 1. Pipe and fittings including pressure-testing in accordance with Section 33 10 00—Water Utilities.
 2. Unit of Measure: Linear feet of pipe installed.

E. Item No. 5 30-inch Valve and Vault
 1. Valve, vault, roadway box, frames, and covers in accordance with DPW Standard No. 890.01 and Section 33 10 00—Water Utilities.
 2. Unit of Measure: Each valve with vault installed.

Figure 11.20 **Sample Schedule of Prices on the Bid Form and Sample Schedule of Unit Price Items in Division 01**

procurement and construction documents, but reliance on them to correct poorly prepared drawings and project manuals should be avoided. Addenda are modifications issued either prior to receipt of bids and proposals or in some cases prior to the time the agreement is executed.

11.3.12.1 General Criteria

Written construction document modifications are the means for communicating changes to the bidders or proposers during procurement and to the contractor during construction. Most changes are best expressed in words and augmented by drawings where necessary. Oral instructions or changes should be avoided, even where it is intended that an addendum or change order will be prepared later to cover the change. Instead of giving an oral interpretation, an A/E should state that an addendum or change order will be issued promptly to clarify the items in question. Most instructions to bidders or proposers state that oral interpretations are not binding, and the general conditions usually require all contract modifications to be in writing. There are two basic methods for preparing written changes to procurement and construction documents:

- *Narrative Method.* This method is characterized by clearly providing only enough information to make the change clear, without oversimplification, and making references to other construction documents.
- *Revised Page Method.* This method of preparing changes to written and graphic documents is a reissuance of affected pages or sheets with appropriate markings to identify the changed portions.

11.3.12.2 Procurement Documents Modification—Addenda

Addenda are written or graphic instruments issued to clarify, revise, add to, or delete information in the procurement documents or in previous addenda. Typically, addenda are issued before the opening of bids/proposals. An example is shown in Figure 11.21.

The primary purpose of addenda is to clarify questions raised by bidders or proposers; to issue new requirements, including changes to the extent of work; and to correct errors or omissions in procurement documents. When issued, addenda become part of the procurement documents, and those portions of addenda that affect the contract documents become part of the contract documents after the agreement is executed.

11.3.12.3 Contract Documents Modifications

The conditions of the contract establish procedures for the A/E to issue interpretations of contract documents and to order minor modifications of the work consistent with these interpretations. Provisions and procedures are also included for the contractor and owner to claim changes in contract sum or contract time if the contractor or owner believes such changes are justifiable based on the A/E's written interpretation. Types of modifications include the following, which are also discussed in more detail in Chapter 13:

- *Change Orders.* A written instruction that authorizes an addition, deletion, or revision in the work or an adjustment in the contract sum or the contract time that is signed by the A/E recommending the change, the owner authorizing the change, and the contractor accepting the change.
- *Construction Change Directive.* A written order directing a change in the work prior to agreement on adjustment and stating a proposed basis for adjustment, if any, in the contract sum or contract time, or both. With a construction change directive, the owner may, without invalidating the contract, order changes in the work within the general scope of the contract consisting of additions, deletions, or other revisions, the contract sum or contract time being adjusted accordingly. A construction change directive is used in the absence of total agreement on the terms of a change order. Upon receipt of a construction change directive, the contractor is required to perform the changes and advise the owner and architect of agreement or disagreement with the proposed method for adjusting contract sum or time. If the contractor agrees with the proposed method for adjusting

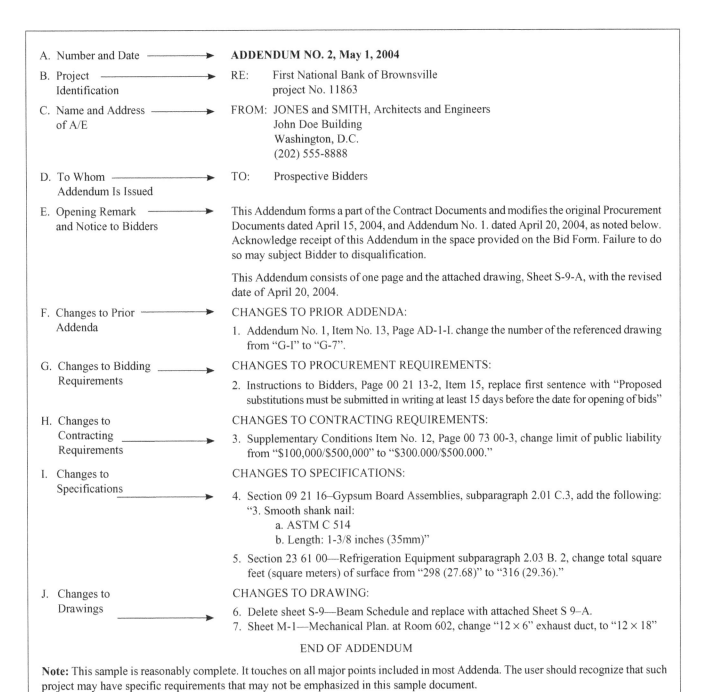

A. Number and Date ────────▶	**ADDENDUM NO. 2, May 1, 2004**
B. Project ────────▶ Identification	RE: First National Bank of Brownsville project No. 11863
C. Name and Address ────────▶ of A/E	FROM: JONES and SMITH, Architects and Engineers John Doe Building Washington, D.C. (202) 555-8888
D. To Whom ────────▶ Addendum Is Issued	TO: Prospective Bidders
E. Opening Remark ────────▶ and Notice to Bidders	This Addendum forms a part of the Contract Documents and modifies the original Procurement Documents dated April 15, 2004, and Addendum No. 1. dated April 20, 2004, as noted below. Acknowledge receipt of this Addendum in the space provided on the Bid Form. Failure to do so may subject Bidder to disqualification.
	This Addendum consists of one page and the attached drawing, Sheet S-9-A, with the revised date of April 20, 2004.
F. Changes to Prior ────────▶ Addenda	CHANGES TO PRIOR ADDENDA:
	1. Addendum No. 1, Item No. 13, Page AD-1-I. change the number of the referenced drawing from "G-I" to "G-7".
G. Changes to Bidding ────────▶ Requirements	CHANGES TO PROCUREMENT REQUIREMENTS:
	2. Instructions to Bidders, Page 00 21 13-2, Item 15, replace first sentence with "Proposed substitutions must be submitted in writing at least 15 days before the date for opening of bids"
H. Changes to Contracting ────────▶ Requirements	CHANGES TO CONTRACTING REQUIREMENTS:
	3. Supplementary Conditions Item No. 12, Page 00 73 00-3, change limit of public liability from "$100,000/$500,000" to "$300.000/$500.000."
I. Changes to Specifications	CHANGES TO SPECIFICATIONS:
────────▶	4. Section 09 21 16–Gypsum Board Assemblies, subparagraph 2.01 C.3, add the following: "3. Smooth shank nail: a. ASTM C 514 b. Length: 1-3/8 inches (35mm)"
	5. Section 23 61 00—Refrigeration Equipment subparagraph 2.03 B. 2, change total square feet (square meters) of surface from "298 (27.68)" to "316 (29.36)."
J. Changes to Drawings	CHANGES TO DRAWING:
────────▶	6. Delete sheet S-9—Beam Schedule and replace with attached Sheet S 9–A.
	7. Sheet M-1—Mechanical Plan. at Room 602, change "12 × 6" exhaust duct, to "12 × 18"
	END OF ADDENDUM

Note: This sample is reasonably complete. It touches on all major points included in most Addenda. The user should recognize that such project may have specific requirements that may not be emphasized in this sample document.

Figure 11.21 **Sample Addendum**

contract sum or time by signing the construction change directive, the agreement should be recorded as a change order. If the contractor disagrees with the proposed method for adjusting the contract sum or time, the work must still be performed and the architect is usually required to determine the method and amount of adjustment on the basis of reasonable expenditures and allowance for overhead and profit.

- *Minor Changes in the Work.* A written instruction or interpretation not involving adjustment to the contract sum or contract time. Such changes are made by the architect's supplemental instructions directing the contractor to make stated modifications. The architect's supplemental instruction does not require the owner's signature.

11.3.13 Master Guide Specifications

Most A/E firms, government agencies, and large corporations use master guide specifications as a basis for their individual construction documents. Developing and using master guide specifications is an efficient way of producing project specifications.

For any given specification section, there are two basic methods of preparation of text:

- Write the text from scratch.
- Edit prewritten text.

When using prewritten text, A/Es have a number of sources to draw from, including commercial master guide specification services, office master text, specifications furnished by product manufacturers, and previous project specifications. The most effective and efficient source is a set of text that is preedited to the A/E's principal project types and specification requirements.

The term *master specification* refers to the documents used as guides for preparing project specifications. Master specifications facilitate the preparation of project specifications by standardizing products, materials, and processes and their order of presentation. These specifications allow editing to adapt the guide specification to specific project requirements. These two terms are combined to become the term *master guide specification* used in this practice guide for prepared specification sections intended to be edited and used as project specifications. The term *office master specification* is also used, principally to distinguish an A/E's master specification from commercial master guide specifications. The office master specification may be derivative of commercial master guide specifications that were used as its basis.

A master guide specification ideally would include the types of items typically utilized for most projects. Each master guide specification section should include text written in a consistent style covering typical requirements and should also list possible options and choices. Instructional notes may be included and should provide direction, guidance, and notice of required decisions. The A/E edits selected master guide specification sections to suit the particular project. Paragraphs and articles that do not apply are deleted.

Master guide specifications have evolved from the need to compile a concise, centralized, and quick-to-edit source of information from the overwhelming amount of data and options available to the A/E. When new project experience is systematically incorporated into the master for future use, the master guide specification becomes a significant repository of knowledge for the firm (i.e., a part of the "corporate memory"). A master guide specification prepared and maintained with an emphasis on consistency of text and speed of editing makes project specifications more accurate and quicker to prepare. Investments in the firm's master guide specification will be returned through lower project specification preparation costs.

Using a master guide specification does not eliminate the need to understand the principles of specification writing. Master guide specifications are only tools. They require competence, skill, and construction experience for their proper use. Although master guide specifications are extensive, they might not cover every need of a specific project. These additional needs will require custom specifications to be written consistent with the master guide specifications. The use of a master guide specification requires an understanding of the basis of the conditions of the contract and general requirements for which they were prepared.

11.3.14 Shortform Specifications

Some projects of limited scope and extent may need less detailed descriptions than those provided by a typical or normal specification. Similarly, for projects with a negotiated contract or D-B delivery method, a specification with reduced detail may be appropriate. In these cases, an A/E may choose, or an owner may request, to use a shortform specification. Although the name might imply that documents are less than complete, the specification must provide sufficient detail to describe the requirements of the project.

11.3.14.1 Concept of Shortform Specifications

The purpose of shortform specifications is to provide a concise set of construction specifications commensurate with the size and extent of a project and to reduce the level of detail where it is appropriate. Project specifications can be as brief as a collection of detailed notes on the drawings or as lengthy as a traditional full-length specification.

11.3.14.2 Characteristics of Shortform Specifications

Shortform specifications are a part of the written portion of the contract documents and share the same characteristics as full-length specifications. These shortform specifications should:

- Express the design intent and a consistent level of project detail despite their short length.
- Include information necessary to achieve the design intent and the required level of detail. Not all requirements, however, can be described briefly and text should not be condensed solely for the sake of brevity. The level of project requirements expressed by the shortform specifications must be consistent with the level of detail necessary to meet the owner's project requirements.
- Be capable of being priced. Like typical specifications, they should be clear, concise, correct, and complete.
- Be made specific to a project. They should be coordinated with local codes and construction practices.
- Be fully enforceable.
- Parallel the level of drawing detail.

Shortform specifications are made cost effective by communicating the project requirements in the shortest possible form. They are compact and easy to read, and the language is concise and direct. Because there is less written material to review, coordination and document review are simplified. Less time and cost are usually required to assemble and edit shortform master guide sections.

Shortform specifications might impose limitations. The level of construction detail may be more difficult to maintain because there is less descriptive content. The A/E should carefully determine the amount of detail necessary for each individual specification section. The A/E must be skilled, knowledgeable, and experienced as a specifier to ensure that important items are not omitted and unnecessary detail is not retained. The risk of error might increase as the detail decreases and the A/E, not the owner, assumes this risk. The A/E and the owner should agree on an acceptable level of requirements for the project and determine the degree of specification detail required accordingly.

11.3.14.3 When to Use Shortform Specifications

Shortform specifications might be used for any project, though some types of projects lend themselves more readily than others:

- *Small Projects.* Projects of limited extent and cost. The use of a full-length specification may not be consistent with the scope of the project drawings. In such cases, the use of a shortform specification would be justified as long as the desired level of detail is maintained throughout. Similarly, shortform specifications can be used effectively on projects that use standard materials and traditional construction details, as they generally require less descriptive detail in the specifications.
- *Design-Negotiate-Build Project Delivery.* Where a contractor has had previous experience with the owner or A/E on a similar project type, there is usually better communication, so the chance of misunderstanding is lessened. The shortform specification can be effective because the contractor is familiar with the level of detail required by the owner, and less descriptive detail may be acceptable in the specifications.
- *Construction Management Project Delivery.* Multiple-prime contracts may present coordination complications, and unless the shortform specification is written to cover such situations, full-length specifications are usually more suitable.
- *Design-Build Project Delivery.* The level of detail provided by the shortform specifications will depend in large part on the completeness of the owner's project requirements. Shortform specifications can be used effectively in D-B projects because the single contract and single focus of accountability provide many of the same features of the negotiated contract. Because the A/E and the contractor are associated, coordination and communication are improved, which reduces the chance of misunderstanding, and less administrative detail is usually required. The level of detail is purposely reduced to decrease cost and to increase flexibility in product selection, subcontract negotiation, and installation. Items such as shop drawings, samples, testing, inspection, and extended warranties may not be included in the specifications unless required by the owner or by code. The owner will have limited influence and much of the decision making will be done by the D-B entity.
- *Owner-Build Project Delivery.* Because the administrative and installation details are reduced to the minimum, the A/E will have less influence, and more of the decision making will be done by the owner.
- *Interior Design and Tenant Improvement Projects.* These projects may involve the installation of standard finishes, furnishings, and equipment. Unless the materials or systems used are unusual, there is usually no need for detailed product descriptions or execution requirements. An acceptable level of detail may be specified by use of reference standards.
- *Single-Prime Contract.* Simple projects can work better with shortform specifications because there are generally fewer complex administrative issues.
- *Projects where a Shortform Specification Is Specifically Requested.* The owner should be informed of the reduced detail of the specifications and its limitations.

11.3.15 Performance Specifying

Performance specifying is a method of indicating characteristics and requirements with measurable properties. Performance specifying can be extended from a single attribute to an entire project, with numerous variations in between. By specifying the end result, performance specifying provides flexibility in optional solutions that all meet the same requirements.

11.3.15.1 Construction Systems and Assemblies

Performance specifying can be used to specify complete systems and assemblies as well as components and construction products. The primary advantage of performance specifying lies in the applicability of available products and systems to most traditional project requirements. Utilizing existing technology, performance specifying is practical even for smaller projects and can apply to a complete project or portions of a project. Entire systems and assemblies may require specialized engineering and performance-based criteria. This level of performance specifying may be subject to licensure and regulation by AHJs.

11.3.15.2 Utilizing Nonstandard Technologies

Many products and systems emerge from research and development before they evolve into standard configurations or solutions. Although they may not be entirely new technologies, their development and use may be at a stage where no alternatives are similar enough to specify descriptively without excluding other variations of that system. Some examples include alternative energy systems, environmental control systems, building monitoring systems, and data and communication systems.

11.3.15.3 Developing New Technology

Shortcomings in available technology may relate to technical capabilities, construction cost, or expediency. Performance specifying in this context gives the owner the advantage of attracting research and development expertise and resources from many elements of the construction industry. New technologies and products are being developed to meet the performance requirements of sustainable and green projects. New technologies include materials consisting of recycled postindustrial and postconsumer waste. These new materials can be utilized by providing performance requirements describing the salient characteristics.

There are also disadvantages for the owner involving the time and expense of developing requirements, solicitation, research, design and development, and prototype tests. The requirements must also be able to gain economies of scale of the newly developed technology because considerable expense might be incurred in producing a unique product, system, or assembly. The feasibility of using performance specifications to develop new technology will generally be limited to larger, corporate owners or public agencies with a large volume of construction.

11.3.15.4 Delegating Responsibilities

In many instances an owner may not wish to assume full involvement in the design and construction of a facility. Many owners with large, ongoing construction programs maintain architectural or engineering departments but do not assume full design or construction responsibilities. Performance specifying can be utilized by an owner to establish an owner's requirements for a project delivery method such as D-B. Using performance criteria, the owner delegates the tasks of definitive design and construction yet ensure that needs are met through well-developed performance specifications.

11.3.15.5   Roles of Participants

Performance-oriented design, construction documentation, procurement, and contracting alter some of the traditional roles and responsibilities normally assumed by participants in the construction project process.

Owner. Performance criteria might be utilized to prepare a request for proposals using a D-B delivery method. Under other delivery methods, performance specifying may be used to provide flexibility and alternative solutions through traditional construction documents. Using performance criteria, the owner will relinquish some control over the solution. Under this process, the owner must be willing to accept the results of performance criteria. Therefore, to ensure satisfaction with results, the owner must be able to communicate the criteria thoroughly. This feature of performance specifying may encourage the owner to perform a more comprehensive analysis of needs than might be done in a traditional relationship.

Architect/Engineer. Depending on the project delivery method, the A/E might be a part of a D-B entity providing design in response to performance-based owner's project requirements. In the traditional design role, the A/E might be a performance specifier, which is a significant departure from traditional design solutions, given that requirements, criteria, and test results, rather than actual products, must be described.

Construction Manager as Adviser. The CMa might assume a role of coordinating the work of multiple-prime contracts. The CMa might deal with both performance items and the interface of descriptive items with those performance elements. Details of some items may not be known prior to releasing the documents for procurement. Thus, the CMa will be involved in administering procurement of performance items, interfacing these with traditionally designed items, and coordinating with the A/E on matters affecting design.

Contractor. Contractors will have different responsibilities when responding to performance criteria. The contractor might be a part of a D-B entity where an A/E is also part of that entity and involved in providing solutions in response to the owner's performance criteria. The contractor or design-builder must be able to generate solutions within the bounds of performance criteria. This will require design and engineering capabilities and may also require closer liaison with suppliers and manufacturers to acquire supplementary engineering support for particular solutions.

Manufacturer. Performance specifications affect manufacturers by placing competing products on the common ground of performance. Manufacturers will be responsible, through contractual lines, for submitting proof of the product's compliance with specified performance criteria. A product's use will be based on performance rather than on a convincing advertising campaign. Manufacturers might be placed in a situation in which they provide additional assistance such as design services.

Authorities Having Jurisdiction. In performance-based procurement, AHJs generally will not have complete construction documents for review at the time of permit application or code reviews. Final documentation is often not completed until sometime after the contract is awarded and construction has begun. In such cases, AHJs review the available definitive material as well as the performance specifications for code conformance and, if no conflicts are in evidence, maybe asked to issue permits, contingent upon inspection and approval of final documentation.

11.3.15.6 Determining the Extent

Determining the extent of a performance specification involves two interdependent decisions:

- The elements (pieces, parts, components, assemblies, and systems) to be performance specified.
- The extent to which those elements will be performance specified. Although entire structures can be performance specified, it is rarely practical to do so.

11.3.15.7 Performance Specifying of Project Elements

The first determination is which elements of a project, if any, ought to be specified in performance terms. Which elements provide a range of available options where competition among those options will provide optimum solutions? The question applies to any scale of project element (i.e., part, component, assembly, or system). Where a range of options is available, the following conditions favor the use of performance specifications:

- No single, distinct solution is recognized as an exclusive choice in terms of material, configuration, or technique.
- Costs of options are reasonably competitive.
- A system or assembly is a substantial portion of the entire project and does not necessitate a configuration or require such specificity as to preclude options.

Performance specifications may also offer advantages under the following conditions:

- A project element embodies a technology where the state of the art has not yet evolved a standard solution for a given situation.
- Development beyond state of the art is required of an existing product or construction item.
- Nothing exists on the market that will satisfy the owner's design or construction needs.

11.3.15.8 Levels of Performance Specifying

Table 11.1 shows a range of specifying modes from full descriptive to full performance specifications. The broadest levels of performance specifying (H and J) are generally used only in design-build contracts. The middle levels (D–G) are usually the broadest practical levels that are typically used in traditional construction documents. Functional elements of the project are identified as systems, subsystems, assemblies, or components. Statements of functional requirements are attached to these elements and qualified with technical criteria. The narrowest levels of performance specifying (B and C) are practical for use in most construction, but, in some cases, may be too restrictive to allow the manufacturers to be innovative. Specific components or products are identified and statements of technical criteria are tailored to that type of component.

11.3.15.9 Drawings and Specifications Coordination

Most performance specifications will be accompanied by drawings that supplement written performance criteria. The drawings may include schematic diagrams, layouts, plans, maximum and minimum dimensions, nominal dimensions, critical dimensions, modular

Table 11.1 **Levels of Performance Specifying**

			Performance/Descriptive Mixture	Sample Text	
Typical Specification Using *MasterFormat*™	Conventional Specifying Degree to which sample support requirements can be performance specified	**A**	Total project specified in descriptive terms.	10-gage galvanized annealed steel wire hangers spaced 4 ft. o.c. both ways.	**FULL DESCRIPTIVE**
		B	Descriptive with performance criteria.	Galvanized annealed steel wire hangers of size and attachment sufficient to support 60 lb. each and spaced 4 ft. 0 in. o.c. both ways.	
		C	Descriptive with overall performance criteria.	Galvanized annealed steel wire hangers of size spacing and attachment sufficient to support a uniform ceiling load of 7.5 lbs/s.f.	
		D	A major assembly specified in *MasterFormat*™ as a self-contained component.	Integrated ceiling... capable of supporting based load + 6 lbs/s.f. live load.	
		E	Several major assemblies specified in *MasterFormat*™ with interface required.[2]	Integrated ceiling... capable of supporting dead load + 6 lbs/s.f. live load...with key slots along building module lines in order to receive top rail of partitions.	
Design-Build statement of system based upon *UniFormat*™	Degree to which systems projects can be performance specified using *PerSpective*®	**F**	Most major components specified as *UniFormat*™ systems with interface required.	Ceiling/illumination/HVAC component... capable of supporting dead load + 6 lbs/s.f. live load... capable of supporting partitions at any building module line capable of...etc.	
		G	Major components specified as *UniFormat*™ systems to be developed solely according to performance requirements.	Ceiling/illumination/HVAC component... capable of supporting dead load + 6 lbs/s.f. live load... capable of supporting partitions at any building module line capable of...etc.	
	Specifying by Determinates	**H**	Total project(s) specified to be developed as systems solely according to general statements of performance.	Ceiling/illumination/HVAC component... capable of supporting all dead and live loads necessary to structural integrity and the safety of the occupants... capable of receiving partitions universally along a building module grid...capable of...etc.	
		J	Total project(s) specified according to human requirements alone, requiring translation into suitable design, systems, and technical performance requirements.	...Building occupants shall be provided with adequate light for common office tasks, without harshness or deadening uniformity; attractive ceilings that absorb undesirable noise levels without denying sharpness of voice communication; constructed in such a way that partition may be attached and relocation can be accomplished with disturbance limited to the immediate area and of not more than a day's duration.	**FULL PERFORMANCE**

Table 11.1 *(continued)*

Technical Input	Source of Components	Testing/Inspection		
No design input required.	Off-the-shelf products.[1]	Check sample. Observe executed work.	**A**	*Typical Specification Using MasterFormat*™
Propose size.		Check sample and proposed size. Observe executed work.	**B**	
Propose, size, spacing, attachment.		Check sample and proposed size, spacing. Observe executed work.	**C**	
Propose many particulars of assembly and interface, depending on degree of performance specifying.	Assembled largely from available products.	Check mock-up, standard test data. Observe executed work.	**D**	
	Assembled largely from rationalized available products.		**E**	
Contractor must have design capability and ability to modify or produce components.	Assembled from rationalized available components or from project-designed components.	Design needed tests, test mock-ups, and prototypes for performance.[3] Check executed work for performacne.	**F**	*Design-Build statement of system based upon UniFormat*™
Contractor must have highly developed design and manufacturing capability.	Assembled largely from project-designed subsystems.[4]		**G**	
None, until architect/engineer has translated general statements down to the degree of Line G.			**H**	
			J	

[1] Off-the-shelf includes products traditionally fabricated for each project using existing technology.
[2] At about this degree consider switch to *UniFormat*™.
[3] Move testing as much as possible to the factory for intermittent production-line sampling or prototype destructive testing, conducted by national certifying organizations to replace on-site testing and review by local authorities and project architect/engineer. On-site testing will still be needed but at reduced levels.
[4] As first-generation systems develop into second-generation systems over a number of years, more and more project-designed products become off-the-shelf items.

increments, and component arrangements. A broad extent of performance specifying will dictate that these drawings be diagrammatic in composition and content. Conversely, a narrower extent of performance specifying requires more definitive drawings. Any drawings that represent only a suggested definition and do not require strict adherence to a particular configuration should be so noted.

11.3.16 Specifying for the Purchase of Goods

Purchasing is the direct acquisition of materials and equipment by an owner for the owner's use or for installation in the owner's project. The term *goods* is used in purchasing specifications to designate the materials or equipment to be purchased. This term is also used in the Uniform Commercial Code (UCC), which governs most purchasing contracts.

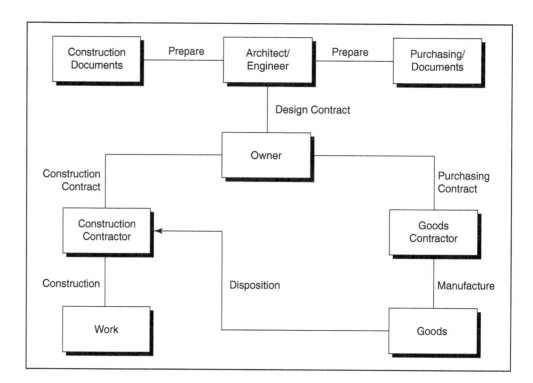

Figure 11.22
Purchasing Contract

The purchasing of goods necessitates a contract or agreement, so the vendor is called the *goods contractor*. Unlike the construction contractor, the goods contractor is involved in little or no on-site activity such as construction, installation, or erection. This is one of the distinguishing factors of a purchasing contract. The owner may purchase goods under a purchasing contract for installation by the construction contractor. But if the goods contractor is required to participate in the actual construction, the goods would be furnished and installed under a subcontract agreement between the goods contractor and the construction contractor, rather than under a purchasing contract.

The purchased goods may be for the owner's use, such as for maintenance or a manufacturing process. The goods may also be incorporated into the owner's construction project by another contractor. Figure 11.22 illustrates the case in which delivery and disposition of the goods is made to the construction contractor for installation in the work.

11.3.16.1 Use of Purchasing

Purchasing documents may be prepared to cover any of a number of activities by the goods contractor:

- To manufacture, fabricate, or supply and transfer to the owner at the goods contractor's plant
- To manufacture, fabricate, or supply and deliver to a designated location
- To perform additional services, which may include the preparation of shop drawings, the compilation of operation and maintenance data, technical assistance or guidance during on-site construction or installation of the goods by others, field checking or testing of the goods after installation or erection by others, start-up procedures, and training of the owner's personnel

Each of these activities has particular requirements that must be carefully considered and coordinated throughout the project manual. Note that these activities all stop short of actual on-site construction or installation by the goods contractor.

11.3.16.2 Differences between Purchasing Contracts and Construction Contracts

One of the principles of purchase specifying is that on-site activities by the goods contractor are limited, and no construction or installation is usually involved. The solicitation, procurement instructions, bid or proposal forms, agreement, conditions of the contract, and Division 01—General Requirements used in purchasing contracts will differ from those used in nonpurchasing construction documents. Most of these differences are readily apparent. The more subtle differences occur in the conditions of the contract. Several subjects should be carefully considered:

- Definitions
- Bonds
- Insurance
- Goods contractor's responsibilities
- A/E responsibilities
- Shop drawings, product data, and samples
- Operation and maintenance manuals
- Payment, completion, and acceptance

11.3.16.3 Uniform Commercial Code

The UCC governs contracts dealing with the sale of goods and, with minor variations, is the law in every state except Louisiana. The purpose of the UCC is to facilitate commerce by providing certainty and consistency in commercial transactions. Inapplicable provisions may be waived by mutual agreement of the parties to the contract; otherwise, the UCC applies to every situation falling within its terms. The provisions of the UCC become effective in the absence of, or may sometimes actually override, written contract provisions. The UCC is published by each of the using states as a part of its state statutes.

The UCC is composed of articles that govern a wide variety of frequently recurring business transactions, including the sale of goods, negotiable instruments, and financial transactions involving security interests. Article 2, dealing with sales, has the greatest effect on purchasing contracts. Its coverage is limited to sales of movable goods, so contracts that are primarily for services are excluded. The term *services* includes activities by the goods contractor such as technical assistance or an installation check.

The following four basic areas of contract law are covered by Article 2 of the UCC.

Contract Enforceability and Formation. Contracts for the sale of goods costing more than $500 must be in writing to be enforceable. Generally, a written contract without ambiguities will be construed as the total agreement between the parties and may not be contradicted by a prior agreement or a concurrent oral agreement. The strict common-law contract rules relating to offer and acceptance and to the formation of a contract are somewhat relaxed under the UCC. The thrust of Article 2 is to establish a contract if at all possible, even though there was never a true meeting of the minds, in the contract-law sense, as to all of the various terms and conditions. The legal test is whether the parties intended to make a contract. Terms, including price, may be left open, to be determined at a later date.

Warranties. The UCC attaches certain warranties, expressed and implied, to sales transactions and governs warranties provided by the seller. Generally, a seller warrants the transfer of clear title, free of any security interest of which the buyer is unaware. Express warranties may consist of:

- An affirmation or promise, such as a claim of performance
- A description of the goods such as photos, drawings, or specifications
- A sample or model that becomes a basis of the agreement

There are also two implied warranties under the UCC:

- *Merchantability.* If the seller is a merchant who deals with goods of the kind being conveyed, a warranty is implied that the goods are fit for the ordinary purposes for which such goods are used.
- *Fitness for a Particular Purpose.* If the seller has reason to know of any particular purpose for which the goods are required and that the buyer is relying on the seller's skill or judgment to furnish suitable goods for that purpose, an implied warranty of fitness for that particular purpose arises.

Contract Interpretation. The UCC acknowledges the common commercial practice by which the contracting parties leave certain terms to be agreed upon at a later date, or to be based upon reasonable commercial practices. Quantity must generally be agreed upon; however, details of payment, delivery, and even price may be supplied by the UCC if they are not covered by the written contract. Unless otherwise agreed, the UCC allocates risk of loss or damage to the goods between the buyer and the seller, depending on the extent to which the agreement has been performed. FOB (free on board), CIF (costs, insurance, and freight), and similar shorthand mercantile terms that place responsibility for transportation costs, insurance, and risk of loss are defined in the UCC.

The parties to an agreement governed by the UCC are bound by a requirement that they act in good faith, and unfair or unconscionable contracts are not enforceable.

Remedies. The UCC provides remedies for the seller in the event that the buyer becomes insolvent or breaches the contract by wrongfully rejecting the goods, refusing to pay, or revoking acceptance.

11.3.16.4 Format

The organization, concepts, locations of subject matter, and language established for construction specifications can also be adapted to purchasing documents. Use of documents similar to those already accepted and familiar to goods contractors and suppliers in the construction industry helps avoid confusion. Usually, a purchasing contract for goods and a construction contract that includes installation of those goods will be in force at the same time, in which case the two project manuals should be similar and must be coordinated.

Procurement and Contracting Requirements. A purchasing project manual customarily contains procurement requirements, contracting forms, conditions of the contract, and specifications. These documents are similar to those used for construction projects, but reflect the differences previously discussed.

The procurement requirements might include prebid information, instructions to bidders, information available to bidders, bid forms, and bid security forms. An agreement form, performance bond, general conditions, and supplementary conditions should also be elements of the purchasing project manual.

Division 01—General Requirements. Division 01 specifications are as important for purchase projects as they are for construction projects. The level 2 and level 3 sections listed in *MasterFormat*® fall into three categories with respect to purchasing contracts.

- The first category includes those sections that are generally applicable to all purchasing contracts:
  - Section 01 10 00—Summary
  - Section 01 30 00—Administrative Requirements
  - Section 01 40 00—Quality Requirements
  - Section 01 60 00—Product Requirements
- The second category includes those sections that are sometimes applicable to purchasing contracts, the determining factors being the level of activity required of the goods contractor and the particular aspects of the project:
  - Section 01 20 00—Price and Payment Procedures
  - Section 01 70 00—Execution and Closeout Requirements
  - Section 01 80 00—Performance Requirements
- The third category includes those sections that are generally not applicable to purchasing contracts because they relate to on-site activities:
  - Section 01 50 00—Temporary Facilities and Controls
  - Section 01 92 00—Facility Operation
  - Section 01 94 00—Facility Decommissioning

Divisions 02 through 49 Specifications. Depending on the goods to be purchased, the project manual may contain one or more specification sections. Many of the *MasterFormat*® titles deal exclusively with construction and would not be appropriate for purchasing, but others pertaining essentially to furnishings, furniture, equipment, or materials may be used.

Disposition of Goods. Preparation of purchasing documents must include consideration of the eventual disposition of the purchased goods, as each of the methods of disposition will have its own effect on various document sections. Three basic methods should be considered:

1. Retention by owner for own use and installation
2. Furnished by owner for installation by others
3. Assignment of purchasing contract to construction contractor

In any case, the method of disposition must be clearly stipulated in the purchasing documents. If a construction contract is also involved, the method of disposition must be stipulated in the construction contract as well, and the procedures definitively established with both the goods contractor and the construction contractor. The documents must state which items, appurtenances, accessories, or other parts are to be furnished under each contract and must establish responsibilities for the remainder. These procedures require particularly close study and coordination by the A/E.

11.3.17 Specifying for Federal Agencies

Many federal agencies administer construction programs, and each has different construction document preparation requirements. This section identifies some of the unique requirements involved in preparing contract documents for federal agency projects.

Many of the principles discussed here will also apply when the client is a city, county, or state government agency, or a school district with specific requirements for the form and content of its construction documents. *MasterFormat®* is often the common link between federal government and private-sector specifications. Most government agencies use *MasterFormat®* to organize their guide specifications.

11.3.17.1 Procurement and Contracting Requirements

Federal agencies usually do not require the A/E to prepare all the components of a document package that will be used for solicitation of bids on a construction contract. In some cases the A/E will prepare the general requirements and technical specifications, and the agency will prepare the procurement and contracting requirements. When agency-prepared documents are used, the content of Division 01 will vary greatly from a Division 01 prepared for use in the private sector.

The first difference regarding the conditions of the contract for a federal project is the name of the document. Unlike the standard forms published by AIA, EJCDC, DBIA, and AGC, the federal documents might be titled "General Provisions," "General Standards," "Special Provisions," or "Contract Clauses." They are all based on the Federal Acquisition Regulations (FAR) that can be found at www.acquisition.gov/far/.

There are other significant ways in which federal general conditions differ from their private-sector counterparts:

- A contracting officer, rather than the A/E, is responsible for administering the procurement and construction phases of the contract. The contracting officer is either a military officer or a civilian employee of the government. Consequently, the A/E does not exercise the same authority on federal projects that it ordinarily would on projects in the private sector.
- The federal government is both the owner and the primary regulating authority.
- Local building code authorities do not have jurisdiction on federal property, although other federal agencies may have authority. Local AHJs do, however, have jurisdiction on private property leased by federal agencies. Federal guide specifications may include requirements that take exception to or exceed local building codes.
- The federal government is self-insuring and does not procure commercial insurance for its buildings or their contents. Federal guide specifications may contain more stringent requirements for fire protection, safety, security, and component and construction durability than those in the private sector.
- The means of settling contract disputes are different from the means encountered in the private sector.
- Although this normally does not directly affect the preparation of specifications, it does have a significant impact on administration of the contract.

11.3.17.2 Social Value Regulations

Federal government contracts may include certain "social value" regulations designed to assist particular industries and other special interest groups. Some examples are wage rates, environmental regulations, preference for American shipping, affirmative action, utilization of small businesses, utilization of businesses owned by women and minorities, labor standards, environmental issues, and accessibility standards.

11.3.17.3 Use of Manufacturers' Names

In almost all situations, federal agencies prohibit the use of brand names, manufacturers' names, or other proprietary or restrictive requirements for products. The intention is to encourage unlimited competition consistent with the type and requirements of the work and to maximize the use of standard products and current models meeting the functional requirements of the project. Specifications for acquisitions should state only the government's actual minimum requirements and describe the supplies or services in a manner that will encourage maximum practicable competition. Brand names may be used in federal government specifications only under the following exceptional conditions:

- When there is no other feasible way of describing the essential functional or physical characteristics (such as to describe the color of a paint, appearance of stone, or the performance of a high-technology product).
- When an agency is extending or connecting to an existing system and the new portion or components must match the existing system. In this situation, the agency would prepare a justification and approval document for procurement of only one brand. Where a specific brand name is required, the A/E may be required to provide technical input for preparation of justification and approval as part of the specification preparation effort.
- When specifications include a statement explaining that the brand names are included only to describe stated salient characteristics such as color, pattern, and operational characteristics, and that other products having the same characteristics will not be excluded.
- When specifications list a minimum of three products and state specifically that acceptable products are not limited to the manufacturers of those products.

When brand-name descriptions are necessary, the specifications must clearly identify and describe the particular physical, functional, or other characteristics of the brand-name items that are considered essential to satisfying the requirement.

11.3.17.4 Reference Standards

There are four classifications of reference standards used for specifying government construction. Listed in the order of preferred usage:

- Private-sector standards
- Commercial item descriptions (CIDs)
- Federal specifications
- Military specifications

Federal specifications are documents issued by the General Services Administration (GSA) Federal Supply Service and cover a wide variety of items used by the federal government, including some construction products. They were originally established to meet a vital need, and many of them also have set standards for industry. However, current government policy encourages development and use of nongovernment standards to replace military specifications and federal specifications. Private-sector organizations such as the American Society for Testing and Materials (ASTM), National Fire Protection Association (NFPA), and American National Standards Institute (ANSI) are now more active in developing standards for construction products, and federal specifications are being replaced by these standards, or by CID, which include references to ASTM, ANSI, and other industry standards. Government policy currently favors the use of such private-sector standards when they exist and when they meet the needs of the agency concerned.

Military specifications are similar, except that they are issued by the Department of Defense (DOD) and include only a few construction products. Military specifications are organized with various classifications of type and quality.

11.3.17.5 Federal Government Agencies' Construction Documents Policies

Each agency involved in construction has its own policies and procedures for administering construction programs. Each agency also publishes its own construction documents and forms or has combined with other federal agencies to publish common documents. In Divisions 01 through 49, federal guide specifications are tailored to the specific project by the A/E. Procurement requirements and contracting requirements are later incorporated into the contract documents by the agency before issuance of the project for procurement.

Construction Criteria Base (CCB). Administered by the National Institute of Building Science (NIBS), and found on the Whole Building Design Guide web site (www.wbdg.org/references/docs_refs.php), the CCB was developed for electronic dissemination of specifications, technical manuals, standards, electronic details, and other documents. Use of the CCB is intended to improve the quality of construction, decrease overlap and conflicts that exist among criteria, speed introduction of new technology into the construction process, and improve dissemination of design and construction information.

11.3.18 Warranties

There are two basic types of warranties used in construction projects:

- *Extended Warranties.* Construction warranties or guaranties, which cover products and workmanship, are usually extended warranties specified in various specification sections.
- *Purchase Warranties.* Warranties that cover products only.

11.3.18.1 Definition of Terms

The following definitions are taken from *Black's Law Dictionary* and apply to construction and purchasing warranties and guaranties:

- *Guarantor.* One who makes a guaranty; one who becomes secondarily liable for another's debt or performance in contrast with a strict surety who is primarily liable with the principal debtor.
- *Guaranty.* To undertake collaterally to answer for the payment of another's debt or the performance of another's duty, liability, or obligation; to assume the responsibility of a guarantor; to warrant.
- *Warrantor.* One who makes a warranty; any supplier or other person who gives or offers to give a written warranty or who is or may be obligated under an implied warranty.

- *Warranty.* A promise that a proposition of fact is true or that certain facts are truly as they are represented to be and that they will remain so, subject to any specified limitations. In certain circumstances, a warranty will be presumed; this is known as an implied warranty.
- *Express Warranty:*
  - Express warranties are created by any of the following:
    - Any affirmation of fact or promise made that relates to the goods or installation and becomes a part of the basis of the bargain creates an express warranty that the goods or installation shall conform to the affirmation or promise.
    - Any description of the goods or installation that is made a part of the basis of the bargain creates an express warranty that the goods or installation shall conform to the description.
    - Any sample or model that is made a part of the basis of the bargain creates an express warranty that the whole of the goods or installation shall conform to the sample or model.
  - It is not necessary to the creation of an express warranty to use formal words such as *warrant* or *guarantee* or that the seller have a specific intention to make a warranty. An affirmation of the value of the goods or installation or a statement purporting to be merely an opinion or commendation of the goods or installation does not create a warranty.
- *Full Warranty.* A warranty as to full performance covering generally both labor and materials. Under a full warranty, the warrantor must remedy the consumer product within a reasonable time and without charge after notice of a defect or malfunction.
- *Implied Warranty.* A promise arising by operation of law that something that is sold shall be merchantable and fit for the purpose for which the seller has reason to know that it is required.
  - Unless excluded or modified, a warranty that the goods or installation shall be merchantable is implied in a contract for their sale if the seller is a merchant with respect to goods or installation of that kind. The serving for value of food or drink to be consumed either on the premises or elsewhere is a sale for this purpose.
  - Where the seller, at the time of contracting, has reason to know any particular purpose for which the goods or installation are required, and that the buyer is relying on the seller's skill or judgment to select or furnish suitable goods or installation, there is, unless excluded or modified, an implied warranty that the goods or installation shall be fit for such purpose.
- *Limited Warranty.* A written warranty that fails to meet one or more of the minimum standards for a full warranty. An example is a warranty limited to labor or to materials for a specified time. The UCC does not have a time limitation; thus manufacturers limit the time period.
- *Warranty of Title.* An implied promise that the seller owns the item offered for sale; the title conveyed shall be good, its transfer rightful, and the goods shall be delivered free from any security interest or other lien or encumbrance of which the buyer at the time of contracting has no knowledge.

11.3.18.2 Guaranties and Warranties

The terms *guaranty* and *warranty* are commonly used interchangeably to describe the responsibility of a manufacturer after delivery of a product and to describe the responsibility of a contractor after completion of construction. These same terms are also used for similar meanings in other contexts. According to *Black's Law Dictionary,* guaranty and warranty are derived from the same root, and are in fact etymologically the same word, the "g" of Norman French being interchangeable with the English "w." Though the two terms are frequently misapplied in business, the law has assigned slightly different meanings to them:

- Legally, a guaranty is a separate contract by a third party (analogous to a surety bond) who assumes responsibility in case the principal fails to perform.
- Conversely, a warranty is assurance by the principal that it will assume stipulated responsibilities for completed portions of the project.

Thus, a manufacturer warrants its material, whereas the construction contractor provides a third-party guaranty for those same materials and a warranty for the construction contractor's own workmanship in installing them.

11.3.18.3 Extended Warranties

It is common practice for warranties, usually for extended time periods, to be included in the specifications and are as important as specifying the physical properties of the products, materials, and equipment.

Terms and Conditions. Generally, the contractor warrants that products, materials, and equipment will be new, of good quality, free from defects, and will conform to the requirements of the contract documents. These warranty provisions go on to indicate defects and damage caused by insufficient or improper operation and maintenance, abuse, modifications, and normal wear and tear are excluded from the warranty. It should be noted that none of these warranties include a time limitation. The time limitation will vary, depending on the location of the project and the laws governing the contract. For the warranty to be effective, a condition stated in the warranty must be satisfied, such as periodically maintaining the thing warranted, otherwise the manufacturer can disclaim liability.

There is a widely held misconception that a contractor's responsibility for defective work lasts only until the end of the one-year correction period. However, the courts have consistently held that expiration of the guaranty period does not terminate the contractor's responsibility for defective work (*John W. Cowper Co. v. Buffalo Hotel Dev.,* 115 A.D. 2d 346, 496 N.Y.S. 2d 127 1985; *Omaha Home for Boys v. Stitt Construction Co., Inc.,* 238 NW 2d 470, 1976; *Baker-Crow Construction Co. v. Hames Electric,* 566 P2d 153, 1977; *City of Kennewick v. Hanford Piping,* 588 P2d, 1977) except for statute of limitations. In an attempt to clarify this misconception, standard forms usually have terminology in their standard general conditions that refers to correction period and do not use the term *warranty period.* This correction period is not a limitation of the warranty provisions of the general conditions.

The one-year correction period is simply a specific contractual obligation for the contractor and a remedy for the owner under the general contract. It is not intended to limit the effect of warranties provided in or required by the contract. The distinction between the obligations of the contractor under the general warranty and its one-year specific correction obligations is not always made. Some contracts, most notably federal construction contracts that use warranty language provided in FAR, actually limit the contractor's warranty obligations to a one-year period.

Purpose. Construction warranties are usually required for several reasons:

- To protect the owner against faults, defects, or failures, in spite of technical compliance with the terms of the contract

- To provide a remedy to the owner for nonconformance with the contract after completion and acceptance of construction
- To give the owner recourse against additional parties (manufacturers, subcontractors, and suppliers) who are not in a direct contractual relationship with the owner
- To extend the manufacturer's responsibility beyond the end of the correction period
- To allow a remedy beyond the normal statute of limitations

Benefits. The unpredictability of performance and replacement cost of some products, such as roofing, waterproofing, insulating glass units, compressors, and other equipment, causes many owners to insist on extended warranties. Extended warranties are not provided for in standard general conditions and should be specified in PART 1—GENERAL of the respective specification section.

To benefit from extended warranties, the manufacturer must be financially secure enough to cover its liabilities. Immediate benefits can be gained from an equitable extended warranty that could make it worth the cost to the owner. These benefits include the qualification of the installer by the manufacturer, the manufacturer's involvement in the construction process, and insurance against failure.

Limitations and Exclusions. Product warranties are frequently perceived as providing increased legal and financial protection to owners against product defects. This is usually an inaccurate perception. Most product warranties provide a limited warranty, which actually reduces the rights an owner may have by statute under a full warranty. Now that strict product liability has become a major concern for manufacturers, the terms of warranties have become a principal mechanism for limiting manufacturers' liability for products that are defective or fail to perform as expected.

When an owner decides to insure a facility, the insurer can evaluate its risk in terms of geography, facility type, facility contents, quality of construction, and so on. This can be done because a structure exists to evaluate. However, when a manufacturer sells a product, little is known of the exact circumstances under which its product will be required to perform. Therefore, a manufacturer can either limit its potential liability or choose not to and accept the risks associated with its decision. Generally, manufacturers choose to limit their exposure and price their products accordingly.

Common limitations in a warranty can exclude labor and consequential and incidental damages. Other limitations include the following:

- Conditions establish criteria that must be met by the buyer before the warranty will be honored.
- An extra fee may be required to register the warranty.
- There may be restrictions of use for the product.
- Specially qualified installers may be required.
- The warranty may be limited to the original purchaser.

Though a full warranty (materials and labor) is specified, there may be limitations that affect the warranty. Other limitations include the following:

- The cost of removal and replacement of other materials that covers a warranted product is generally not included in the manufacturer's warranty.
- It may be valid only if the sales receipt and original containers are returned.

- Some warranties may cover replacing the initially installed product but not cover the replacement product itself.
- Some products cannot be field modified without voiding their warranty, and others have strict limitations on how they may be modified.

As extended warranties are usually written from the manufacturer's perspective, even those issued in good faith invariably contain language that limits the scope of their coverage. Warranties usually exclude consequential damage to any facility component other than the warranted product itself. In many cases, coverage of a product or system is prorated; for each year of service the product or system has already provided, many warranties pay a smaller percentage of the repair or replacement costs.

When manufacturers delete exclusions from their warranties, they usually add other costs or terms and conditions to protect their interests. Prorated coverage, for example, is eliminated in no-dollar-limit roof warranties. In exchange for paying full replacement costs for a defective system, the manufacturer requires the use of all or almost all of the manufacturer's products within a warranted system.

Many manufacturers' warranties take away consumer protection normally included in the UCC, including the implied warranty of merchantability and fitness. A manufacturer's warranty may restrict repairs of failures only up to the cost of the original installation, not replacement costs. An extended warranty is of little benefit if nothing is covered. For example, an implied warranty becomes worthless if the written warranty states that a roofing material may be unsuitable for roofing.

An important factor is the financial backing of the warranty under consideration. Some manufacturers do not have or have not committed sufficient assets to satisfy all claims against their warranties. In either case, an owner may be left with a faulty product and no immediate remedy. It is also important to determine which companies have been in business long enough to have long-term experience with their products. A 20-year warranty issued by a company that has been in business for 5 years is questionable, just as a 20-year warranty on a new product is also questionable.

A repair or alteration to an item by a party other than the manufacturer or original installer will invalidate the remainder of the warranty period.

The following exclusions and limitations should be of particular concern:

- Language making the warranty the exclusive remedy
- Clauses limiting the scope of coverage to materials only
- Clauses limiting the assignability of the warranty
- A requirement stating that the owner must sign the warranty document
- Warranties containing a deductible
- Clauses limiting the time that the owner has to take legal action for breach of a warranty
- A requirement allowing the warrantor to recover legal costs in a proceeding involving the owner or contractor
- Unfair dispute resolution procedures when a difference in opinion occurs regarding the manufacturer's warranty
- Clauses that exclude installation of the replacement product

Remedies. The UCC permits the manufacturer to disclaim implied warranties of merchantability and fitness in writing, and also permits vendors to limit the duration of their responsibility as well as the remedies that are available to the buyer. The nature of those remedies and their limitations are the most important features of warranties.

In some instances, specifying a manufacturer's standard warranty could be giving the manufacturer the opportunity to limit its responsibility to a level that is unreasonable from the owner's standpoint. The owner may be better off having no warranty at all.

The time it takes to settle a claim can also cause problems. Most manufacturers have a procedure that contractors must follow to collect for repairs made under warranty. If the contractor proceeds immediately to make repairs without waiting for the manufacturer's approval, the repairs may not be compensated by the manufacturer. This can place contractors in a difficult situation. Contractors may jeopardize long-standing business relationships if they do not respond quickly to an owner's request to repair a defective product. When the owner is a large company with many facilities that require some sort of repair work, contractors should not jeopardize future work by being unresponsive in emergency situations.

Duration. The most commonly specified factor for warranties and the most common basis for comparison of warranties is their duration. Express time limits are generally stipulated in product warranties. The time limits often bear no direct correlation with the expected service life of the product, and in some cases it is unrealistic to expect a product to serve satisfactorily for the duration of its warranty. Rather than relying on a warranty, the performance history of a particular product should be known before specifying it for an application where duration of performance is critical. Another area worth analysis involves the extent of testing or other studies conducted by the manufacturer to verify that the system can reasonably be expected to function for the stated period.

11.3.18.4 Purchasing Warranties

Warranties effected by a sales transaction and governed by the UCC and other applicable state laws are referred to as *purchasing warranties*. Although purchasing warranties are seldom directly applicable to a construction contract, the UCC governs most transactions involving the sale of goods. The UCC attaches certain express and implied warranties to sales transactions and governs warranties provided by the seller. Any written warranty is called an *express warranty*. An *implied warranty* is derived from the nature of a transaction, applicable state law, and the position of the parties.

Express warranties may consist of:

- An affirmation of fact or promise related to goods, such as claim of performance
- A description of the goods, such as photos, drawings, or specifications
- A sample or model that becomes a basis of the agreement

Under the UCC, there are two implied warranties:

- Implied warranty of merchantability or "implied warranty that goods are merchantable," which means that the consumer goods are fair, average, medium quality (Richard A. Mann, Barry S. Roberts, and Len Young, *Smith and Roberson's Business Law,* 12th ed., Southwestern, 2002) and:
  - Pass without objection in the trade under the contract description
  - Are fit for the ordinary purposes for which such goods are used
  - Are adequately contained, packaged, and labeled
  - Conform to the promises or affirmations of fact made on the container or label
- The second is the implied warranty of fitness. A warranty of fitness means that when the retailer, distributor, or manufacturer has reason to know any particular purpose for which the goods are required, and further, that the buyer is relying on the skill

and judgment of the seller to select and furnish suitable goods, then there is an implied warranty that the goods shall be fit for the intended purpose. *Smith and Roberson's Business Law* states, "Any seller ... impliedly warrants that the goods (he sells) are reasonably fit for the particular purpose of the buyer for which the goods are required, if at the time of contracting the seller has reason to know such particular purpose and that the buyer is relying on the seller's skill and judgment."

The UCC also governs the manner in which warranties may be disclaimed. Exclusion of the warranty of title must be by specific language, or the circumstances of the sale must be such that the buyer should not expect a warranty of title. Express warranties can be disclaimed in the same manner in which they are created, but warranty language will take precedence over disclaimer language in the event of a conflict. Implied warranties may generally be disclaimed by the use of a conspicuous written disclaimer or by the use of the words "as is, with all faults" or similar language. Federal law requires that written warranties covering consumer products (often inapplicable to construction projects) fully and conspicuously disclose, in simple and easily understood language, the terms and conditions of such warranty, including whether the warranty is a full or limited warranty.

To obtain maximum advantage of the implied warranty of fitness, sellers should be informed of the specific uses to be made of their goods and that their recommendations are being relied upon. If the buyer requests or demands a particular brand, there is no implied warranty of fitness because the buyer is relying on the buyer's own skill or judgment (Mann, Roberts, and Young, *Smith and Roberson's Law*).

When specifying warranties, avoid:

- Relying on a warranty as a substitute for thorough investigation of a product and its manufacturer
- Requiring warranty coverage that is not available for a particular product
- Requiring or permitting a warranty that weakens, rather than strengthens, the owner's rights

11.3.19 Construction Bonds

There are three basic types of bonds used in construction projects:

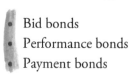

- Bid bonds
- Performance bonds
- Payment bonds

The decision whether to require bid, performance, or payment bonds should be made by the owner.

11.3.19.1 Definitions of Terms

A *surety bond* is a three-party contract under which one party promises to answer for the debt or default of another. The critical terms used in bonding include the following:

- *Principal.* The party who has the primary obligation to perform the undertaking that is being bonded. For example, the contractor on a bonded construction project is the principal.

- *Surety.* Also referred to as the bonding company, the surety is the party that guarantees the principal's performance. In essence, the surety agrees to be bound to the obligations of the principal should the principal fail to perform them.
- *Obligee.* The obligee is the person for whose benefit the bond is written. With respect to a performance bond, the obligee is usually the owner. Some performance bonds are written in favor of more than one obligee (e.g., a subcontractor's bond may be written for the benefit of both owner and contractor, or a contractor's bond for the benefit of the owner and the project lender). Such bonds are called dual obligee bonds.
- *Surety Bond.* The surety bond is the written document given by the surety and principal to the obligee to guarantee a specific obligation.
- *Indemnity Agreement.* An agreement between the principal and the surety whereby the principal guarantees the surety that the surety will incur no loss by reason of its providing the bond.
- *Penal Amount.* Bonds are written with a limit on the amount of the guarantee. This limiting amount, frequently 100 percent of the contract amount, is called the penal sum or penal amount of the bond.
- *Claimant.* Commonly used to refer to a party who files a claim against the bond. This could be the owner or a subcontractor or supplier seeking recovery under the payment bond.
- *Lien.* The legal right of a party, such as a subcontractor, to claim a security interest in the project or have it sold for payment of a claim.

11.3.19.2 Purpose of Bonds

Bonds generally provide the owner, subcontractors, and suppliers with assurance that should the contractor fail to make payments or complete the contract, there will be a financially solvent party, the surety, to perform these obligations. A surety bond is not an insurance policy; rather, bonding involves a three-way contractual relationship among the principal, surety, and obligee. A surety's obligation is analogous to the obligation of a cosigner on a note. The principal remains primarily liable to perform the bonded contract and is obligated to indemnify the surety against any loss.

11.3.19.3 Advantages and Costs of Bonding

There are numerous advantages of providing a fully bonded project:

- The bid bond protects the owner against the withdrawal of a favorable bid.
- The suppliers and subcontractors are protected against nonpayment of amounts due them. The owner is protected against mechanic's liens on the project.
- The owner is protected against default, breach of contract, and nonperformance by the contractor.
- The owner receives additional assurance of the stability of the contractor. Most bonded contractors are financially stable, and the bond guarantees that the surety will pay if the contractor fails.
- The indemnity agreement generally provides added incentive for the principals of the contractor to properly perform, as they may be personally liable to the bonding company for amounts paid on a bonded project.
- Bonding satisfies statutory requirements for publicly funded projects.

There is a cost for this protection. The bond premium will be included in the contractor's bid, and one of the functions of a bond requirement is to exclude contractors who cannot qualify for bonding.

11.3.19.4   Bid Bond

The purpose of the bid bond is to protect the owner from losing the benefit of an accepted bid. Issuance of a bid bond commits the bidder to enter into a contract and, if required, provide performance and payment bonds. The bid bond is provided by the bidder at the time of bid and is submitted with the bid. The bid bond generally provides for a penal amount expressed either in dollars or as a percentage of the total amount of the bid. In the event that the selected bidder fails or refuses to enter into a contract for the price that was bid, the surety is obligated to pay the owner's damages, up to the penal amount of the bid bond.

11.3.19.5   Performance Bond

The *performance bond* provides the most important protection for the owner by guaranteeing that if the contractor defaults, the surety will either complete the contract in accordance with its terms or provide sufficient funds, up to the penal amount of the bond, to fund such completion.

If there is a default and the owner makes a demand upon a surety to perform under the terms of the performance bond, the surety will investigate the owner's claim against the contractor. This investigation will include examining both the owner's and the contractor's positions and making an independent analysis of the situation. Once the validity of the claim has been established, the surety has a number of options as to how it will fulfill the bond obligation that includes the following:

- If the contractor's work is satisfactory and the problems are only financial, the surety may choose to finance the contractor to complete the project. Under this option, the surety provides funds to the contractor so that the contractor can pay subcontractors and suppliers, buy materials, make payroll, and take other steps necessary to complete the project.
- If the owner terminates the contract, the surety can complete the project by taking over the work itself and hiring another contractor, or by arranging for a completion contractor to work directly for the owner.
- The surety may also leave it up to the owner to finish the project and pay the difference between the balance left in the original contract and the actual cost of completion.

11.3.19.6   Payment Bond

The *payment bond,* sometimes referred to as the *labor and materials payment bond,* guarantees subcontractors, material suppliers, and others providing labor, material, and equipment to the project will be paid. This promise benefits the owner because it protects against mechanic's liens and delays caused by unpaid subcontractors and suppliers. The payment bond generally provides for payment not only to parties employed by or in direct contractual relationship with the contractor but also to sub-subcontractors and suppliers to subcontractors.

11.3.20 Construction Insurance

The owner of a construction project risks substantial assets and is exposed to significant legal liability throughout the life of a project. The owner also has a significant amount of money invested. The contractor performing the work also incurs risks that require insurance protection for itself, the owner, and third parties. The owner's interest is protected in part by requiring the contractor to carry specific types of insurance coverage, within limits determined to be adequate for the circumstances.

11.3.20.1 Definitions of Terms

The following definitions related to construction insurance are taken from the *Glossary of Insurance and Risk Management Terms* published by the International Risk Management Institute (IRMI).

- *All-Risk Insurance.* Protection from loss arising out of any fortuitous cause other than those perils or causes specifically excluded by name. This is in contrast to other policies that name the peril or perils insured against; refer to named peril.
- *Builder's Risk.* Indemnifies for loss of or damage to a building under construction from specified perils. Insurance is normally written for a specified amount on the building and applies only in the course of construction. Coverage usually includes fire and extended coverage and vandalism and malicious mischief coverage. Builder's risk coverage can be extended to an all-risk form as well. The builder's risk policy also may include coverage for items in transit to the construction site (up to a certain percentage of value) as well as items stored at the site.
- *Claim.* Used in reference to insurance, a claim may be a demand by an individual or corporation to recover, under a policy of insurance, for loss that may come within that policy.
- *Claims-Made Policy.* Policies written under a claims-made basis will cover claims made (reported or filed) during the year the policy is in force for any incidents that may occur that year or during any previous period the policyholder was insured under the claims-made contract. This form of coverage is in contrast to the occurrence policy that covers today's incident regardless of when a claim is filed, even one or more years later.
- *Completed Operations.* A form of liability insurance that provides coverage for bodily injury and property damage arising out of the operations that have been completed or abandoned, provided the accident occurs away from the premises owned or rented by the insured. Operations shall be deemed completed at the earliest of the following times:
  - When all operations to be performed by or on behalf of the insured under the contract have been completed
  - When all operations to be performed by or on behalf of the insured at the site of the operations have been completed
  - When the portion of the work from which the injury or damage arises has been put to its intended use by other than the contractor or subcontractor
- *Comprehensive General Liability (CGL) Policy.* A broad form of liability insurance usually covering business organizations to protect them against liability claims for bodily injury and property damage arising from operations, products and

completed operations, and independent contractors, but excluding coverage for liability arising from the use of automobiles.

- *Comprehensive Policy.* This term applies to a variety of policies that provide broad protection.
- *Contractual Liability.* Liability assumed under any contract or agreement over and above that liability that may be imposed by law.
- *Coverage.* In insurance practice, the word *coverage* is used synonymously with insurance or protection.
- *Employer's Liability Insurance.* This coverage is provided by Part 2 of the basic workers' compensation policy and pays on behalf of the insured (employer) all sums that the insured shall become legally obligated to pay as damages because of bodily injury by accident or disease sustained by any employee of the insured arising out of and in the course of employment by the insured.
- *Endorsement.* A form bearing the language necessary to record a change in an insurance policy.
- *Exclusion.* A provision of an insurance policy or bond referring to hazards, circumstances, or property not covered by the policy.
- *General Aggregate Limit.* The maximum limit of liability payable during any given annual policy period by an insurer under the CGL policy on behalf of an insured for all losses other than those arising from the products and completed operations hazards.
- *Hold-Harmless Agreement.* A contract under which legal liability of one party for damages is assumed by the other party to the contract. The basic types of such agreements are as follows:
  - Limited form, where Party A reaffirms responsibility for Party A's own negligent acts; Party B is thus protected when Party B is held vicariously responsible.
  - Intermediate form, where Party A reaffirms responsibility for Party A's own acts and agrees to share responsibility for joint and concurrent negligence of both parties.
  - Broad form, where Party A reaffirms responsibility for all liability, including that arising out of the sole negligence of Party B.
- *Indemnify.* To restore in whole or in part the victim of a loss by payment, repair, or replacement.
- *Indemnity.* Restoration to the victim of a loss up to the amount of the loss.
- *Insurable Interest.* An interest by the insured person in the value of the subject of insurance, including any legal or financial relationship. Insurable interest usually results from property rights, contract rights, and potential legal liability.
- *Insurance.* A contractual relationship that exists when one party (the insurer), for a consideration (the premium), agrees to reimburse another party (the insured) for loss to a specified subject (the risk) caused by designated contingencies (hazards or perils). The term *assurance* is ordinarily considered identical to, and synonymous with, insurance.
- *Insured.* The person(s) protected under an insurance contract.
- *Liability Insurance.* Insurance paying or rendering service on behalf of an insured for loss arising out of legal liability to others.
- *Limit of Liability.* The maximum amount that an insurance company agrees to pay in the case of loss.

- *Loss:*
  - The basis of a claim for damages under the terms of a policy.
  - Loss of assets resulting from a pure risk. Broadly categorized, the types of losses of concern to risk managers include personnel loss, property loss, time element, and legal liability.
- *Loss of Use Insurance.* Coverage to compensate the policyholder for loss suffered because the policyholder cannot use the property destroyed or damaged by an insured peril.
- *Named Insured.* Any person, company, or corporation or any of its members specifically designated by name as insured(s) in the policy as distinguished from others who, although unnamed, are protected by the policy definition. A named insured under the policy has rights and responsibilities not attributed to additional insureds, such as premium payment, premium return, notice of cancellation, and dividend participation.
- *Named Perils.* Named peril policies specify the perils that are insured against, as distinguished from the all-risk and broad-form policies.
- *Occurrence.* An event that causes injury to people or damage to property.
- *Occurrence (CGL).* This term means an accident, including continuous or repeated exposure to conditions, that results in bodily injury or property damage neither expected nor intended from the standpoint of the insured. Occurrence policies cover claims made that arise from injury or damage that occurs during the policy period, irrespective of when the claim is made against the insured. See claims-made policy.
- *Owner's and Contractor's Protective Liability (OCP).* Coverage for bodily injury or property damage liability caused by an occurrence and arising from the operations performed for the named insured by the contractor designated, or acts or omissions of the named insured in connection with the named insured's general supervision of such an operation. Coverage can be obtained by separate policy. The CGL policy provides the insured with automatic coverage for liability arising from independent contractors.
- *Peril.* The cause of a loss insured against in the policy (e.g., fire, windstorm, explosion).
- *Policy.* The insurance policy is a contract or agreement between the insurer and the insured.
- *Policy term.* The period for which the mode premium has been paid.
- *Property Damage.* As defined in the general liability policy, property damage means (1) physical injury to or destruction of tangible property that occurs during the policy period, including the loss of use thereof at any time therefrom, or (2) loss of use of tangible property that has not been physically injured or destroyed, provided such loss of use is caused by an occurrence during the policy period.
- *Property Insurance.* Insurance that indemnifies the person with an interest in the physical property for its loss or the loss of its income-producing ability. This is first-party insurance, which provides coverage for the insured's property damaged or destroyed by an insured peril, as contrasted with liability insurance, which covers the insured's legal liability to others. Examples of property insurance include builder's risk and fire insurance.
- *Replacement Cost.* The replacement value of the damaged property without deduction for depreciation.
- *Reporting Form.* A policy designed for use when values of the insured property fluctuate during the policy term. Usually, an adequate limit of liability is set, and

then the insured reports the values actually on hand on a given day of each month. At the end of the year or policy term, these reported values are averaged and the premium adjusted accordingly.

- *Subrogation.* The assignment to an insurer by terms of the policy or by law, after payment of a loss, of the rights of the insured to recover the amount of the loss from one legally liable for it.
- *Waiver of Subrogation.* The relinquishment by an insurance carrier of the right to collect for damages paid on behalf of the policyholder.
- *Workers' Compensation.* All states have laws that provide compensation to a worker if the worker is injured while at work for an employer, whether or not the employer has been negligent. The workers' compensation laws apply to all individuals, except those specifically excluded.
- *XCU Exclusion* (not defined by International Risk Management Institute [IRMI]): A common exclusion from liability coverage for damages to others caused by blasting and explosion, collapse of structures, and underground excavation damage to property.

11.3.20.2 Liability Insurance

Liability policies protect the named insured from losses arising out of legal liability to others caused by the insured's activities. Liability policies do not cover damage or loss of the insured's products, machinery, or equipment. Coverage is effective only at the project site. General conditions usually require the contractor provide liability insurance because it is the contractor who is responsible for activities at the project site.

Workers' Compensation Insurance. Workers' compensation insurance provides protection to an employee by an employer in accordance with a statutory no-fault/limited liability agreement. Under workers' compensation laws, some form of which exists in all states, employers must compensate their employees for employment related injuries, regardless of fault. The employee, in return, cannot bring legal action against the employer for compensation in excess of the statutory amount. Compensation includes reimbursements for medical costs and for lost wages, as well as a specific amount for certain permanent injuries. Without workers' compensation insurance, the employer does not have the protection of the state law and may be sued by the employee for unlimited damages.

General Liability. Under a general liability policy, often called public liability insurance or commercial general liability insurance, the insurance company agrees to pay all sums for which the insured becomes legally obligated to pay as damages. The insurance company also agrees to provide legal defense in any related suits brought against the contractor.

The terms *comprehensive general liability* and *commercial general liability* are both used to describe broad-based liability insurance, and there are two types of coverage:

- *Occurrence-Type Coverage.* Protection under the policy is fixed when the occurrence causing the damage is known. The policy must have been in force at the time of the occurrence, but need not have been in effect at the time the claim was made. Coverage remains effective after construction for claims resulting from the construction process. This type is easier to monitor and enforce, and provides better protection for the owner.
- *Claims-Made Type.* Protection under the policy is provided when the insurance is continuously in force from the time of the occurrence to the time

of the claim. Claims-made coverage is seldom used for construction projects because of problems with keeping the policy in force long after the project is completed.

When required by particular construction risks, certain important additions to the general liability coverage are advisable. In its basic form, the comprehensive general liability policy has an exclusion usually called the XCU exclusion, which is an abbreviation for explosion, collapse, and underground damage. Removal of this exclusion is required to provide coverage for claims arising from blasting, collapse of structures due to excavation or removal of shoring or support, and underground damage caused by mechanical excavation. It is also in the owner's best interest to require the contractor to provide personal injury coverage.

The commercial general liability policy is one that combines several coverage aggregates into a single general aggregate, which is the maximum amount that will be paid under the policy. The general aggregate may be modified to apply to each individual project, and the requirement for this modification should be identified in the supplementary conditions.

Six separate limits of liability are covered in commercial general liability policies. Following is the explanation of each of the six limits as contained in the *Guide to Construction Insurance* published by IRMI:

- *General Aggregate Limit.* Places an aggregate limitation on what the policy will pay for all medical expenses, personal/advertising injury, bodily injury, and property damage claims within the policy period.
- *Products/Completed Operations Aggregate.* Places an aggregate limitation on the amount of insurance available to cover any products/completed operations claims.
- *Personal and Advertising Injury Limit.* Constitutes the maximum insurance available to pay a claim for personal injury or advertising injury. The insurance available is further limited by the general aggregate limit.
- *Each Occurrence Limit.* Places a limitation on the amount of insurance available to pay bodily injury, property damage, and medical expense claims arising out of any one occurrence, subject to the general policy aggregate.
- *Fire Damage Limit.* Limits the amount of insurance available to pay for property damage (to premises rented to the insured) caused by any fire, subject to each occurrence limit as well as the general aggregate limit.
- *Medical Expense Limit.* Represents the amount of insurance available to pay for all medical expenses arising from bodily injury sustained by any one person.

Automobile Insurance. Ownership and operation of motor vehicles is one of the more risky business operations. From a contractor's standpoint, the liability for operation of owned or nonowned automobiles, including rented or hired vehicles, is generally secured through a business automobile coverage form. Where use of aircraft or water vessels is contemplated, the owner should require appropriate liability coverage for both the owned and nonowned vehicles.

Owner's Protective Liability. The general liability insurance policy regularly carried by the owner for normal operations may not include construction risks. Additional coverage, called owner's protective insurance, may be appropriate to cover the same hazards as those covered by the contractor's general liability insurance. It should include coverage for liability from claims arising from the contractor's operations and the owner's duties with respect to the construction project.

The contractor can be required to obtain the owner's protective insurance. The owner's interests are better served, and obtaining coverage from the contractor's carrier rather than the owner's carrier minimizes conflicts between insurance policies.

11.3.20.3 Property Insurance

Property insurance compensates the insureds for damages to covered property caused by insured perils. Builder's risk insurance is the cornerstone of the project's property insurance. Builder's risk insurance covers losses during the construction stage arising from the insured risks of fire, windstorm, collapse, and theft. The policy is designed to cover all property that has been or will be incorporated into the project. Builder's risk insurance is available in a named peril or an all-risk type policy. All-risk type policies are preferred by owners because coverage is for all perils except those specifically excluded in the policy. Typical exclusions include earthquakes, floods, loss of use or occupancy, penalties for noncompliance or noncompletion of the contract, normal wear and tear, latent defects, and loss caused by faulty workmanship or design.

The owner often obtains builder's risk insurance, because the owner has an insurable interest in the project. As materials are installed or stored on-site and title passes to the owner, the insured interest increases to the contract sum, to the insured limit, or until the owner occupies the project.

Builder's risk insurance is available in two forms:

- *Completed Value Form.* Written for the anticipated completed value of the project.
- *Reporting Form.* Written on the actual value of the project at the time the policy is written.

The owner should arrange for coverage of owner-furnished materials or equipment not included in the construction contract price. The owner should also determine whose insurance will cover the value of material or equipment in transit or stored by the contractor off-site during the course of the project.

Property of the contractor stored on the owner's premises but off the construction site should be addressed in either the owner's property insurance or the contractor's property insurance.

In the event the owner intends to furnish material or equipment to be incorporated into the project, care must be taken to secure coverage from the time the owner assumes title. The owner's property insurance may require adjustment for the storage of these materials, while the owner has the risk of loss.

Subrogation. The objective of comprehensive insurance planning is to create a network of policies to protect the collective and separate interests of parties engaged in the construction project. Subrogation allows the insurer to assume the insured party's rights against others in exchange for payment of the loss or damage.

Through subrogation, one party's settlement can become another party's lawsuit. Because of the threat of litigation, this situation may adversely affect the owner's relationship with the contractor and the A/E for the balance of the project. To prevent this situation, current contract practice suggests that all parties involved in the project waive all claims against one another to the extent covered by insurance. Because of this waiver, the right of subrogation does not arise. All parties involved in the construction contract should check whether such a waiver violates any term or condition of their individual insurance policies.

Boiler and Machinery Insurance. Insurance companies have traditionally separated certain risks from others. One example of such separation is boiler and machinery insurance. Typically, it is a policy separate from the builder's risk policy. The boiler and machinery policy insures against loss resulting from accidents to boilers and pressure vessels identified in the policy, including damage to the property of others.

Contractor's General Property and Equipment Insurance. The builder's risk policy covers the value of the construction, but it does not cover the value of the tools and equipment used to build the project. Loss of tools and equipment can affect the progress and, perhaps, the quality of the work, so either insurance covering construction equipment and tools used on the project, or the financial ability to replace them may be necessary.

Business Interruption. An accident during the course of construction, such as a fire, may prevent the owner from obtaining use of the project by the planned completion date. An owner may obtain loss-of-use insurance that protects against loss caused by the inability to occupy and use the project because of damage resulting from a covered peril. This coverage is available for a variety of risks, including fire, and can include compensation for additional business expense and for the rental of substitute facilities.

Umbrella Excess Liability. The umbrella excess liability policy provides a layer of insurance above the limits carried in the contractor's other liability coverage. Two purposes are served by specifying a relatively high limit umbrella excess liability policy. First, this is the most economical way to secure limits in excess of those normally offered by general liability and automobile policies. Second, the umbrella can broaden the coverage provided by those policies.

11.4 Procurement Requirements

11.4.1 Introduction

Procurement requirements are the procedures for soliciting pricing for the work of a project. Whether the work of a project is bid or negotiated is determined by the project delivery method selected by the owner. However, both methods of pricing need rules and procedures to manage the pricing process. Although the following text is applicable to bidding, the information needed for effective negotiating and purchasing is similar.

An effective manner of discussing contracting requirements is to organize this section according to a portion of Division 00 of *MasterFormat®*, and to list standard forms and documents that are available from AIA, EJCDC, DBIA, and AGC.

11.4.2 The Nature of Bid and Proposal

The terms *bid* and *proposal* as used in the construction industry are almost synonymous as an offer to perform work.

- *Bid.* An offer to perform a contract for work or to supply materials or goods at a specific price. A bid is a response to a solicitation such as an invitation to bid or an advertisement for bid.
- *Proposal.* An offer from one entity to another, of terms and conditions with reference to some work, which if accepted can form a contract. A proposal implies an opportunity for more consideration by the recipient and is sometimes utilized when project cost or other conditions will be determined by negotiation. A proposal is usually in response to a request for proposal.

Because they are owner-specific documents, procurement requirements should be provided by the owner or prepared by the owner with the A/E's assistance. An inexperienced owner may request that the A/E prepare procurement documents; however, the documents should receive the owner's final approval before being implemented. Procurement requirements should not become contract documents except in special circumstances, such as a detailed bid form for a complex unit price contractor when a combination bid guaranty and contract bond is used in public works agreements. In such cases, procurement requirements that will be incorporated into the contract should be clearly identified in the owner-contractor agreement.

The basic principle of saying something only once in construction documents does not preclude references to other documents. For example, in a typical procurement (bidding/negotiating/purchasing) process, the subject of bid security is referred to in the bid solicitation, but the detailed requirements of the bid security form and amount are included in the instructions to bidders and supplementary instructions to bidders. Similar situations occur throughout a project manual. Even though some items may be referenced in more than one location, it is best not to duplicate operative figures (dollar amounts, time, dates, etc.). In these instances insert the location of the primary reference in the phrase "as indicated in the [ ]" should replace the operative figures in all secondary locations. The following are particularly useful in determining the primary location of subject matter in procurement and contracting requirements:

- AIA Document A521, Uniform Location of Subject Matter
- EJCDC Document N-122, Uniform Location of Subject Matter

There are several guides published by professional associations for the owner to provide instructions regarding the desired contracting requirements:

- AIA Document G612, Owner's Instructions to the Architect Regarding the Construction Contract, Insurance and Bonds, and Bidding Procedures
- EJCDC Document C-050, Owner's Instructions Regarding Bidding Procedures and Construction Contract Documents
- EJCDC Document C-200, Guide to the Preparation of Instructions to Bidders
- EJCDC Document C-410, Suggested Bid Form for Construction Contracts
- EJCDC Document P-001, Commentary on Procurement Documents

11.4.3 00 10 00 Solicitation

11.4.3.1 00 11 00 Advertisements and Invitations

Bid solicitations fall into two categories: invitations to bid and advertisements to bid.

The invitation to bid is intended to attract qualified bidders and to help prospective bidders decide whether to obtain the procurement documents. It should be limited to pertinent data that will permit prospective bidders to judge whether the work is within their capability, whether they have the necessary qualifications, required licenses, and whether they will have time to prepare a bid.

The invitation to bid should be brief, simple, and free from irrelevant information. It is not intended to contain detailed requirements or instructions that belong elsewhere in the procurement documents. It should not contain information necessary for actual preparation of a bid, because that information belongs in the instructions to bidders. The invitation to bid should always be in writing to facilitate adequate distribution. A separate mailing to each prospective bidder is desirable. A sample invitation to bid is shown in Figure 11.23.

In public work, regulations or policy usually requires that an advertisement be published as a legal notice in designated publications or newspapers. In this case, the invitation takes the form of an advertisement for bids and is so identified. An invitation to bid implies that the owner will be selective by inviting only certain bidders to submit bids. An advertisement for bids, however, is notice to all qualified bidders, not just a select few. In order to save costs, the wording used in the advertisement is usually shortened from that in the invitation. In private work, the legal notice is usually omitted and the invitation to bid is issued to selected contractors only. A sample of an advertisement for bids is shown in Figure 11.24.

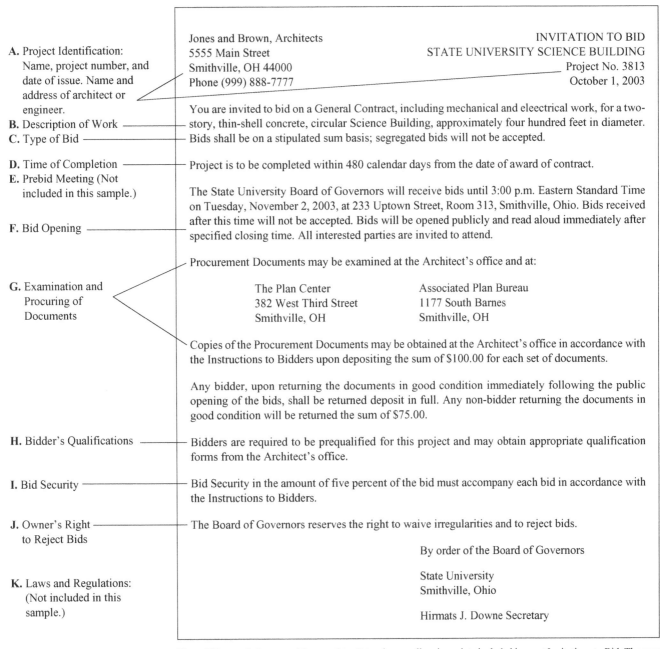

A. Project Identification: Name, project number, and date of issue. Name and address of architect or engineer.

B. Description of Work
C. Type of Bid

D. Time of Completion
E. Prebid Meeting (Not included in this sample.)

F. Bid Opening

G. Examination and Procuring of Documents

H. Bidder's Qualifications

I. Bid Security

J. Owner's Right to Reject Bids

K. Laws and Regulations: (Not included in this sample.)

Jones and Brown, Architects
5555 Main Street
Smithville, OH 44000
Phone (999) 888-7777

INVITATION TO BID
STATE UNIVERSITY SCIENCE BUILDING
Project No. 3813
October 1, 2003

You are invited to bid on a General Contract, including mechanical and eleectrical work, for a two-story, thin-shell concrete, circular Science Building, approximately four hundred feet in diameter. Bids shall be on a stipulated sum basis; segregated bids will not be accepted.

Project is to be completed within 480 calendar days from the date of award of contract.

The State University Board of Governors will receive bids until 3:00 p.m. Eastern Standard Time on Tuesday, November 2, 2003, at 233 Uptown Street, Room 313, Smithville, Ohio. Bids received after this time will not be accepted. Bids will be opened publicly and read aloud immediately after specified closing time. All interested parties are invited to attend.

Procurement Documents may be examined at the Architect's office and at:

The Plan Center
382 West Third Street
Smithville, OH

Associated Plan Bureau
1177 South Barnes
Smithville, OH

Copies of the Procurement Documents may be obtained at the Architect's office in accordance with the Instructions to Bidders upon depositing the sum of $100.00 for each set of documents.

Any bidder, upon returning the documents in good condition immediately following the public opening of the bids, shall be returned deposit in full. Any non-bidder returning the documents in good condition will be returned the sum of $75.00.

Bidders are required to be prequalified for this project and may obtain appropriate qualification forms from the Architect's office.

Bid Security in the amount of five percent of the bid must accompany each bid in accordance with the Instructions to Bidders.

The Board of Governors reserves the right to waive irregularities and to reject bids.

By order of the Board of Governors

State University
Smithville, Ohio

Hirmats J. Downe Secretary

Note: This sample is reasonably complete. It touches on all major points included in most Invitations to Bid. The user should recognize that each project may have specific requirement that may not be emphasized in this sample document.

Figure 11.23 **Sample Invitation to Bid**

ADVERTISEMENT FOR BIDS

A. Project Identification: Name, project number, and date of issue. Name and address of architect or engineer.

Bids: November 2, 2003
STATE UNIVERSITY
SCIENCE BUILDING
SMITHVILLE, OH
Project No. 3813

October 1, 2003

Jones and Brown, Architects
5555 Main Street
Smithville, OH 44000
Phone: (999) 888-777

B. Description of Work

The Board of Governors, State University, Smithville, Ohio, will receive sealed bids in a General Contract, including mechnical and electrical work, for a two-story, thin-shell concrete, circular Science Building, approximately four hundred feet in diameter.

C. Type of Bid

Bids shall be on a stipulated sum basis; segregated bids will not accepted.

D. Time of Completion (Not included in this sample)

E. Prebid Meeting (Not included in this sample.)

The State University Board of Governors will receive bids until 3:00 p.m. Eastern Standard Time on Tuesday, November 2, 2003, at 233 Uptown Street, Room 313, Smithville, Ohio. Bids received after this time will not be accepted. Bids will be opened and publicly read aloud immediately after specified closing time. All interested parties are invited to attend.

F. Bid Opening

Procurement Documents may be examined at the Architect's office and at:

G. Examination and Procuring of Documents

The Plan Center
382 West Third Street
Smithville, OH

Associated Plan Bureau
1177 South Barnes
Smithville, OH

H. Bidder's Qualification (Not included in this sample)

Copies of the Procurement Documents may be obtained at the Architect's office in accordance with the Instructions to Bidders upon depositing the sum of $100.00 for each set of documents.

I. Bid Security

Bid Security in the amount of five percent of the bid must accompany each bid in accordance with the Instructions to Bidders.

Any bidder upon returning the documents in good condition immediately following the public opening of the bids, shall be returned the deposit in full. Any non-bidder returning the documents in good condition will be returned the sum of $75.00.

J. Owner's Right to Reject Bids

Contracts for work under this bid will obligate the Contractor and subcontractors not to discriminate in employment practices. Bidders shall submit a compliance report in conformity with Executive Order No. 11246.

K. Laws and Regulations: Usually required for legal advertisements

This contract is Federally assisted. The Contractor must comply with the Davis-Bacon Act, The Anti-Kickback Act, and the Contract Work Hours Standard.

The Board of Governors reserves the right to waive irregularties and to a reject bids.

By order of the Board of Governors

STATE UNIVERSITY
SMITHVILLE, OHIO

Note: This sample is reasonably complete. It touches on all major points included in most advertisement for bids. The user should recognize that each project may have specific requirement that may not be emphasized in this sample document.

Figure 11.24 **Sample Advertisement for Bids**

Basic information incorporated into the solicitation should include the following items:

- *Project Identification.* Clearly identify the owner and the A/E issuing the documents, including full name, address, and telephone number. Show the name or title of project in a conspicuous manner and the project number, where applicable. Include the date of issue of the procurement documents.
- *Description of Work.* Briefly describe the project type and size and major characteristics of construction to give an idea whether the project is within the bidder's work capacity and financial capacity. This description should not be elaborate or detailed. It is intended only to help the bidder determine whether it is worthwhile to obtain documents. Estimated costs of the project should not be mentioned unless it is a legal requirement. Costs are a matter for the bidder to determine.
- *Type of Bid.* Indicate briefly the type of bid required, that is, whether stipulated sum, cost-plus fee, or unit price bids are required, and whether there are alternates or bidder proposed substitutions. If separate bids are allowed, indicate acceptable combinations. Give details on type of bid in the instructions to bidders.
- *Time of Completion.* If established, state the number of days allowed for constructing the project or the date by which substantial completion or final completion is desired. State whether the time of completion is stipulated or to be filled in by the bidder.
- *Prebid Meeting.* State date, time, and location. Advise bidders if this meeting is mandatory.
- *Bid Opening.* State who will receive bids, when and where bids will be opened, and whether the opening will be public or private. For private bid openings, state who can attend. Sometimes bidders are permitted to attend private openings that are closed to subbidders and trade publication representatives.
- *Document Availability.* List the locations and addresses where procurement documents may be examined. State where documents can be obtained and give information regarding charges, deposits, and refunds. Coordination between the solicitation and the instructions to bidders is necessary to prevent repetition or discrepancies.
- *Bidder Qualifications.* If required, the type of qualification should be mentioned.
- *Bid Security.* State whether bid security is required and whether it is a percentage of the bid or a fixed amount. Give details concerning the security in the instructions to bidders.
- *Owner Right to Reject Bids.* State that the owner reserves the right to waive irregularities and to reject bids.
- *Laws and Regulations.* Include specific laws and regulations, such as those covering nondiscrimination in employment and wage rates.

00 11 13 Advertisement for Bids
00 11 16 Invitation to Bid

Obtaining pricing and soliciting for proposals for work or a project may be accomplished using a less formal process. This proposal process also requires documents that provide information and procedures to ensure a proper understanding of the offer. Whether this pricing is obtained through bidding or through negotiation, certain rules and procedures are required to ensure communication of project intent. These rules and procedures deal with issues such as obtaining interpretations of documents, addenda, available information, contractor's qualifications, and the type of pricing or proposal form requested.

Soliciting a proposal requires a different type of solicitation process. This process is intended to seek out unique solutions using delivery methods other than the traditional bidding process. These documents have similarities but also differences. The terminology is different but the sequence of events is similar.

A request for proposal (RFP) is usually prepared by the owner to indicate what is desired. This RFP may be in letter form or may result from a face-to-face meeting with a company under consideration for negotiation. An RFP may follow a preliminary search to determine who is qualified. The preliminary search may involve a request for qualifications to narrow a field to a short list or single company.

An RFP is a solicitation and can be similar to a bid solicitation such as an invitation to bid. It should include pertinent data as outlined for the invitation to bid. The negotiation process may be less formal and not have an exact time when the proposal is required to be submitted. As this type of procurement does not involve numerous participants, document availability can be handled without a documented statement.

Depending on the project delivery method, an RFP may contain a significant description of the type of work or services required for the project. For example, documents prepared for a design-build project might include reference to an extensive project description. D-B procurement documents may be formatted differently, including performance specifications and other requirements based on *MasterFormat®* or *UniFormat™*.

00 11 19 Request for Proposal

Some owners may require bidders to provide information regarding their capability to do the work from both a physical and a financial standpoint. A form for this information can be provided in the project manual for submission along with the bid. AIA Document A305, Contractor's Qualification Statement, can be used for this purpose. The AIA form includes requests for information such as bank references and a financial statement; therefore, the information obtained in the qualifications should be kept confidential. If more detailed information is needed, it may be obtained after the bid opening. EJCDC does not publish its own form but endorses the use of a similar form published by the Associated General Contractors of America (AGC).

00 11 53 Request for Qualifications

- AGC Document 221, Standard Questionnaires and Financial Statement for Bidders (for Engineering Construction)

11.4.4 00 20 00 Instructions for Procurement

Standard printed instructions to bidders are published by professional associations and local, state, and federal agencies as companion pieces to standard printed general conditions such as the following:

- AIA Document A701, Instructions to Bidders
- AIA Document A751, Invitation and Instructions for Quotation for Furniture, Furnishings, and Equipment
- EJCDC Document C-200, Guide to the Preparation of Instructions to Bidders
- EJCDC Document P-200, Suggested Instructions to Bidders, Procurement Contracts

11.4.4.1 00 21 00 Instructions

The instructions to bidders are the requirements with which bidders must comply before and during submission of bids. The instructions to bidders will not be as brief as the solicitation because they contain specific information not included in the other procurement requirements; the instructions are the information a bidder needs to properly prepare and submit a bid. The instructions also describe conditions affecting the award of contract.

When standard printed instructions to bidders are used, it is often necessary to modify and sometimes expand on them in order to suit a specific project. This is done by use of supplementary instructions to bidders.

When EJCDC C-700, Standard General Conditions of the Construction Contract, and the corresponding EJCDC agreement forms are used, then EJCDC C-200, Guide to the Preparation of Instructions to Bidders for Construction Contracts, which is not intended to be inserted in the project manual, should be used as a guide for writing instructions to bidders in a manner similar to the way master guide specifications are used for writing specification sections.

Basic information incorporated into the instructions to bidders should include the following items:

- *Documents.* State whether documents will be issued to other than prime bidders. Include information about availability of documents to supplement information in the bid solicitation. Issuance of partial sets of documents should be avoided. Explain conditions and requirements governing return of documents by bidders, including time for their return and refund of deposits. Some A/Es prefer to include this information in the invitation to bid, rather than in the instructions, to eliminate repetition; however, the invitation is often limited in size through circumstances beyond the preparer's control. Minimum information should still appear in the invitation, but complete details should be given in the instructions.
- *Examination of Documents, Site, and Local Conditions.* Explain that the bidder is responsible for examining the documents and the site. Give limitations on time of examination and describe arrangements necessary for the examination, and, when applicable, give a name and telephone number of the person to contact.
- *Interpretations during Bidding.* Describe how discrepancies and ambiguities in the documents will be resolved during the bidding period and give instructions for obtaining the information.
  - Name and address of the entity to which inquiries and requests for clarification should be directed.
  - Manner in which such requests are to be made, including time limits.
  - How replies will be made. Replies should be issued as addenda. State how and when addenda will be issued and to whom they will be sent. Include time limits.
- *Substitution of Products.* The practice of listing more than one product or manufacturer for a given material description is preferred (and may also be required in some public work) by many A/Es in order to stimulate competition among suppliers. Some circumstances allow for substitution of products other than those specified. The A/E should state the requirements and procedures under which proposed substitutions of materials and methods will be considered. If such consideration is during the bidding period, include a date prior to bid opening after which requests for substitutions will no longer be considered. Refer the bidders to Division 01, Section 01 25 10 Substitution Procedures, for specific requirements and procedures for requesting substitutions.

- *Type of Bid.* Describe the type of bid required. There are several possibilities, and the instructions to bidders should clearly state the requirements and conditions for the bid type. The instructions to bidders should also include guidance for preparing items on the bid form, such as combined bids, allowances, alternates, and unit prices.
- *Preparation of Bid.* Inform bidders how bids are to be prepared, including instructions for forms to be used and the number of copies required. Give explicit instructions regarding the signatures required. Describe any additional information to be submitted with the bid.
- *Bid Security Information.* Inform bidders if and what amount and form of bid security will be required.
- *Performance Bond and Payment Bond.* Indicate if bonds will be required. Performance and payment bonds, each equal to 100 percent of the contract sum, are usually required for public work and are recommended for private work. If bonds are required, stipulate the period of time in which they must be furnished. Coordinate this requirement with conditions of the contract.
- *Subcontractor Listing.* Where applicable, explain conditions and requirements relating to listing and acceptance of proposed subcontractors. Instruct the bidders to submit the information as a listing on the bid form or as a supplement to the bid form, or to note that it will be furnished within a specified time after the bid opening. Where appropriate, give information about the significance of such a list in evaluating the bids and how binding the list may be. It should be noted that EJCDC C-200 states that the contractor should be able to employ subcontractors of their own choosing and provides recommended wording if the owner chooses to use this approach.
- *Identification and Submittal of Bid.* Indicate how to identify the bid, the project name, number, contract number, owner, bid date and time, and name of bidder. Give instructions regarding submittal of the completed bid and whether a sealed envelope is required.
- *Modification or Withdrawal of Bid.* Indicate whether bids may be modified between submittal and opening. Explain circumstances under which a bidder may not withdraw the bid. Include a list of conditions under which bids may be withdrawn without forfeiture of bid security and describe procedures to be followed when so doing. State the length of time the owner may hold bids before any withdrawal is permitted.
- *Disqualification of Bidders.* List conditions or irregularities under which a bidder may be disqualified.
- *Special Applicable Laws.* List applicable federal, state, and local laws and regulations. Avoid an exhaustive list and avoid implying that the list is complete. The listed items may include:
  - Licensing of contractors for special requirements
  - Requirements for special construction permits
  - Exemption from sales tax, if applicable
  - Wage rates and employment requirements when required by law or by the owner
  - Local labor agreements
  - Nondiscriminatory hiring practices
- *Prebid Meeting.* Refer the bidder to the solicitation and provide any supplemental information not included in the solicitation.
- *Liquidated Damages.* Provide information about provisions relating to liquidated damages.

- *Opening of Bids.* Refer the bidder to the solicitation for information about date, time, and place for opening of bids.
- *Evaluation and Consideration of Bids.* Describe the basis under which the owner will award the contract, including considerations of alternates and unit prices. If applicable, the order in which alternates are to be accepted should be stated, if there is one. Reserve for the owner the right to waive irregularities in a bid or to reject all bids.
- *Execution of Contract.* List requirements and conditions for execution of the agreement, including the preparation and examination.

The bid form is prepared to ensure a uniform arrangement that facilitates comparison and equal consideration for awarding the contract. Although the bid form is usually not one of the contract documents, some of the information contained on the successful bidder's bid form, such as contract prices, unit prices, prices of alternates, and time of completion, will be incorporated into the owner-contractor agreement. Many civil engineering projects are bid on a unit price basis, and the bid form and unit price schedule may be attached to the agreement to avoid lengthy transcription and potential errors.

00 21 13 Instructions to Bidders

Unlike the bidding process, the proposal and negotiation process has not generated standard printed documents. Even without preprinted documents, there is a need to establish some ground rules to prevent misunderstandings and incomplete proposals. Instructions serve the purpose of establishing proper methods of obtaining clarifications or interpretations and define documents such as addenda.

The arrangement of typical instructions to bidders can be used to develop these instructions to proposers. Because the process is less formal, many of the details and formalities on preparing bids might not be applicable. In the proposal process, other elements, such as qualifications of team participants and a completion schedule, could be primary considerations of the proposal.

00 21 16 Instructions to Proposers

11.4.4.2   00 22 00 Supplementary Instructions

When standard printed instructions to bidders or proposers are used, a common method of modifying the information in those documents is to include project specific information as an additional document.

00 22 13 Supplementary Instructions to Bidders
00 22 16 Supplementary Instructions to Proposers

11.4.4.3   00 23 00 Procurement Definitions

Sometimes there is a need to provide project specific definitions of terms that are used in the procurement documents.

11.4.4.4   00 24 00 Procurement Scopes

There are occasions when additional information is necessary to describe how various scopes of work will be arranged contractually, such as if there will be multiple contracts or there will be multiple-prime contracts.

00 24 13 Scopes of Bids
00 24 16 Scopes of Proposals

11.4.4.5 00 25 00 Procurement Meetings

Generally, the date, times, and location of prebid or preproposal meetings are provided in the advertisement or instructions to bidders or proposers; however, additional information is sometimes necessary.

> **00 25 13 Pre-Bid Meetings**
> **00 25 16 Pre-Proposal Meetings**

11.4.4.6 00 26 00 Procurement Substitution Procedures

When substitutions are permitted during procurement, the procedures should be provided. The procedures in this location are in addition to those that are located in Division 01, Section 01 25 00 Substitution Procedures, which are generally for substitutions during construction. The procedures in this location may or may not be the same procedures in the Division 01 Section.

11.4.5 00 30 00 Available Information

There are various types of information that should be made available to bidders, proposers, and contractors during procurement and execution of the work however, they are not contract documents.

To prevent the owner and the A/E from being held responsible for conclusions drawn from this information, a disclaimer may be advised; however, relevant and accurate information should be provided. Withholding relevant information could be construed as misrepresentation. Care should be used in preparing and issuing this information. The procurement (bidding/negotiating/purchasing) requirements should contain provisions that the bidder may conduct additional investigations to verify the thoroughness of information made available to bidders.

This information, when provided, is for the bidders' use in preparing bids, but is not part of the contract documents and does not relieve the bidders from doing their own investigation to determine the accuracy of the information. However, owners and A/Es should not knowingly include inaccurate or misleading information. Recommendations included in this information may be contradictory with the contract documents. For example, geotechnical evaluations and recommendations may recommend a compaction test that differs from that specified.

The AIA and EJCDC documents approach this subject differently. AIA Document A201, General Conditions of the Contract for Construction, requires that if physical conditions are encountered at the site that are subsurface, concealed, or of unusual nature and that differ materially from those shown in the contract documents, then the observing party will notify the other party within 21 days of observing the condition. The A/E will investigate and recommend an equitable adjustment to the contract sum or contract time, or both, if the conditions differ materially from the contract documents.

EJCDC C-700, Standard General Conditions of the Construction Contract, requires that if subsurface or physical conditions at the site are revealed and believed to be a material inaccuracy in the technical data on which the contractor is entitled to rely, or may require a change in the contract drawings, or differ materially from the contract documents, or are of an unusual nature, then the contractor will notify the owner and A/E before the conditions are disturbed. The A/E will review the conditions and advise the owner of the need for further tests or exploration and, if necessary, an equitable adjustment to the contract price or the contract time. Similar procedures are described for those instances when underground facilities and hazardous materials are encountered. In addition, the subject is addressed in EJCDC C-800, Guide to the Preparation of Supplementary Conditions, and EJCDC C-200, Guide to the Preparation of Instructions to Bidders. EJCDC places the reference to the information and where it may be obtained in the supplementary conditions. A cross-reference is made in the instructions to bidders, but they also state that the information is not part of the contract documents.

Information included at this location is not considered a part of the contract documents, unless specifically included in the agreement.

11.4.5.1 00 31 00 Available Project Information

Preliminary schedule information, when provided, is normally included as advisory data to be used by the bidders in preparing their bids. This information is not part of the contract documents unless specifically incorporated in the agreement. This schedule information does not replace requirements for submission of a progress schedule as indicated in the conditions of the contract or Division 01. Dates (including milestones) or time for completion might also be included in the bid form, agreement, or Division 01.

00 31 13 Preliminary Schedules

There are occasions when it is necessary for the owner to make bidders, proposers, and contractors aware of the owner's budget.

00 31 16 Project Budget Information

For projects that involve renovations or additions to existing facilities, it is common to provide bidders, proposers, and contractors with information about the existing conditions that might even include construction documents.

00 31 19 Existing Condition Information

Virtually every project requires the owner to disclose essential information about the project site, such as the location of property lines and boundaries, descriptions of site conditions and existing facilities, topography, and underground utility locations that are known.

00 31 21 Survey Information

- AIA Document G601, Request for Proposal—Land Survey

Environmental assessments studies are sometimes required to be disclosed. Examples include soil contamination reports, environmental impact study report, or environmental impact mitigation report.

00 31 24 Environmental Assessment Information

For projects involving renovations or additions, there may be existing materials that should be disclosed, such as for concrete, masonry, metals, wood, plastics, or thermal and moisture protection.

00 31 25 Existing Material Information

It is good professional practice to make bidders, proposers, and contractors aware of hazardous materials that might be present in existing facilities that are to undergo renovations or additions, such as the presence of asbestos, lead, polychlorinated biphenyl, mold, or hazardous waste drums.

00 31 26 Existing Hazardous Material Information

Some building sites may require more sophisticated investigations to discover and document seismic, magnetic, electromagnetic, electrical resistivity phenomenon, and like geotechnical data needs to be disclosed to the bidders, proposers, and contractors.

00 31 31 Geophysical Data

It is common to make bidders, proposers, and contractors aware of the findings discovered by a geotechnical investigation prior to solicitation, such as soil boring data, subsurface drilling and sampling information, soil and rock strata formations present.

00 31 32 Geotechnical Data

- AIA Document G602, Request for Proposal—Geotechnical Services.

Bidders or proposers may need to be made aware of a building code or regulatory requirement that would not ordinarily discovered during the procurement process that may affect the bid, proposal, or execution of the work. An example might be a permit that is required for a project in close proximity to an airport, a major highway, a facility being built over a railway, or within a particular governmental jurisdiction.

00 31 43 Permit Application

11.4.6 00 40 00 Procurement Forms and Supplements

The form of bid or proposal is based on the project delivery method and the intended basis of payment for the agreement. An owner may request several types of bids or proposals:

- *Stipulated Sum.* A stipulated amount for a described scope of work based on complete construction documents. A stipulated sum is usually requested for architectural-type projects. Stipulated sum bids may be included within bids that are basically unit price. For example, a stipulated sum bid may be asked for a pump station that is part of a pipeline projector a toll station in conjunction with a highway project. The pipeline or the highway work itself is generally awarded under a unit price bid to provide for adjustment of actual measurements and other field variations. In some cases, stipulated sum bids are adjusted by using allowances, alternates, or unit prices.

- *Cost-Plus Fee.* Cost of the actual direct expense of construction work plus a fee for overhead and profit usually based on partially completed construction documents for a defined scope of work. The fee can be fixed, a percentage of the actual direct cost or some other arrangement. A cost-plus basis of payment is not usually bid; however, to establish an agreement, proposals may be requested or offered for the amount or percentage of fee. These cost-plus proposals might also include a guaranteed maximum price (GMP).

- *Unit Price.* Estimated quantities are provided for various items and the bidders or proposers quote a price for each, resulting in a total bid for the project. This basis for payment is most often used where the extent of the work cannot be fully determined or where quantities cannot be accurately calculated until the actual work is performed. Unit prices are more prevalent in civil engineering–type projects such as utilities, highways, and dams. Unit prices are frequently used in building construction for items that are indefinite at the time of procurement (bidding/ negotiating/purchasing) (e.g., partitions, doors, hardware, painting, and flooring in an office building where rental space is not yet leased). They are also used for items that may be modified in quantity by conditions at the site (e.g., length of piles, excavation, reinforcement, and concrete in conjunction with foundations).

- *Combined Bid.* Bidders might be allowed to bid on an individual part, or a combination of parts, when the work may be subdivided into two or more separate parts or phases. When a combination bid is permitted, the bidder may quote an amount to be subtracted from the total of the separate bid parts. This separation of bids may be utilized for multiple-prime contracts.

11.4.6.1 00 41 00 Bid Forms

The bid process requires a bid form that is prepared as a document that the bidder will submit to the owner. It contains blank spaces completed by the bidder and a place for the bidder's signature (and for the seal of corporate entities) to indicate that the bidder agrees to all provisions. The bid form should be prepared to ensure a uniform arrangement that facilitates comparison and equal consideration for awarding the contract.

The bid form is not considered a part of the instructions to bidders; the two are separate, but related, documents. The bid form is bound into the project manual. For the bidder's convenience, an additional unbound copy of the bid form may be provided with the project manual or separately with a bid packet consisting of all forms required to be submitted and a bid envelope.

The following information, an example of which is shown in Figure 11.25, should be included in the bid form (note that not all conditions are addressed in the sample):

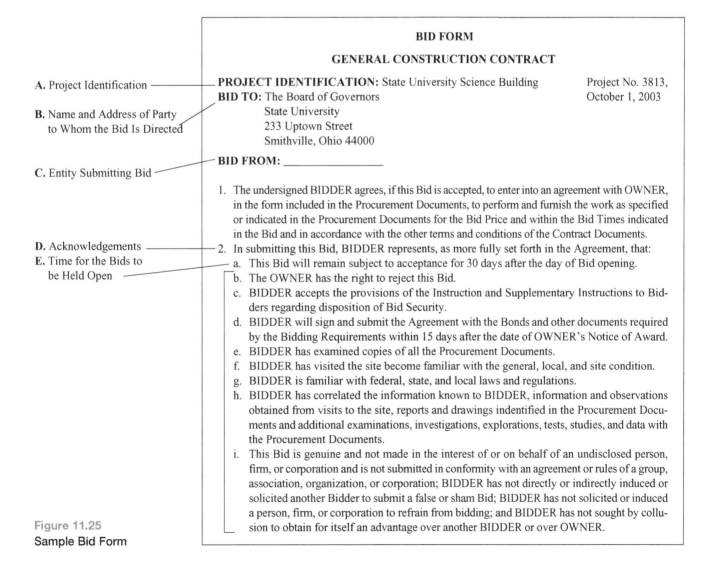

A. Project Identification

B. Name and Address of Party to Whom the Bid Is Directed

C. Entity Submitting Bid

D. Acknowledgements
E. Time for the Bids to be Held Open

BID FORM

GENERAL CONSTRUCTION CONTRACT

PROJECT IDENTIFICATION: State University Science Building   Project No. 3813,
BID TO: The Board of Governors   October 1, 2003
        State University
        233 Uptown Street
        Smithville, Ohio 44000

BID FROM: _____

1. The undersigned BIDDER agrees, if this Bid is accepted, to enter into an agreement with OWNER, in the form included in the Procurement Documents, to perform and furnish the work as specified or indicated in the Procurement Documents for the Bid Price and within the Bid Times indicated in the Bid and in accordance with the other terms and conditions of the Contract Documents.
2. In submitting this Bid, BIDDER represents, as more fully set forth in the Agreement, that:
   a. This Bid will remain subject to acceptance for 30 days after the day of Bid opening.
   b. The OWNER has the right to reject this Bid.
   c. BIDDER accepts the provisions of the Instruction and Supplementary Instructions to Bidders regarding disposition of Bid Security.
   d. BIDDER will sign and submit the Agreement with the Bonds and other documents required by the Bidding Requirements within 15 days after the date of OWNER's Notice of Award.
   e. BIDDER has examined copies of all the Procurement Documents.
   f. BIDDER has visited the site become familiar with the general, local, and site condition.
   g. BIDDER is familiar with federal, state, and local laws and regulations.
   h. BIDDER has correlated the information known to BIDDER, information and observations obtained from visits to the site, reports and drawings indentified in the Procurement Documents and additional examinations, investigations, explorations, tests, studies, and data with the Procurement Documents.
   i. This Bid is genuine and not made in the interest of or on behalf of an undisclosed person, firm, or corporation and is not submitted in conformity with an agreement or rules of a group, association, organization, or corporation; BIDDER has not directly or indirectly induced or solicited another Bidder to submit a false or sham Bid; BIDDER has not solicited or induced a person, firm, or corporation to refrain from bidding; and BIDDER has not sought by collusion to obtain for itself an advantage over another BIDDER or over OWNER.

Figure 11.25
Sample Bid Form

F. Identification of Addenda ——

G. Prices ——
H. Combined Bids:
   (Not included in this
   sample.)

I. Alternates ——
J. Allowances: (Not included in
   this sample.)

K. Unit Price ——

L. Completion Time

M. Liquidated Damages:
   (Not included in this
   sample.)
N. Supplements
O. Closing ——

---

j. BIDDER has received the following Addenda receipt of which is hereby acknowledged:

   Date   Number
   _____   _____
   _____   _____
   _____   _____

3. BIDDER will complete the Work in accordance with the Contract Documents for the
    following price(s):
    STIPULATED-SUM BID PRICE _____ ($_____)
                                        (use word)   (figure)
ALTERNATES
Alternate No. 1 (use of brick in place of granite)   ($_____) (add)
                                                         ($_____) (deduct)
Alternate No. 2 (chiller as manufactured by XYZ, Co.)   ($_____) (add)
                                                         ($_____) (deduct)

UNIT PRICES
If the required quantities of the items listed below are increased or decreased by Change Order,
the adjustment unit prices set forth below shall apply to such increased or decreased quantities:
Rock excavation_____($_____CY)

4. BIDDER agrees that the Works will be substantially complete and ready for final payment
    in accordance with the General Conditions on or before the dates or within the number of
    calendar days indicated in the Agreement.

5. The following documents are attached to and made a condition of this Bid:
    (a) Required Bid Security in the form of _____.
    (b) Required BIDDER's Qualification Statement with supporting data.

SUBMITTED on _____, 20_____.

By _____(SEAL)
              (Firm Name)

_____
        (Name of Person Authorized to Sign)
Business Address: _____

_____
Phone No.: _____

Figure 11.25 *(continued)*

Note: This sample is reasonably complete. It touches on major points included in most Bid Forms. The user should recognize that each project may have specific requirements that may not be emphasized in this sample document.

- *Project Identification.* The bid must identify the project and work (including the designated portion of the project for which the bid is submitted) by referring to the title, project number, contract number, and date that appear on the drawings and the project manual.
- *Name and Address of Party to Whom the Bid Is Directed.* This is usually the owner or public agency soliciting the bids. The name may appear on one line, following the words "BID TO" or "THIS BID IS SUBMITTED TO."
- *Entity Submitting Bid.* The name and address of the company submitting the bid, preferably following the words "BID FROM."
- *Acknowledgments.* The bidder is asked to provide statements regarding the following basic information:
  - The owner has the right to waive irregularities and to reject this bid.
  - The bidder agrees to abide by instructions to bidders for disposition of bid security. This places the bidder in the position of agreeing to forfeit bid security

if the bidder refuses to execute the agreement. This provision is included by reference to avoid lengthy repetition.

- The bidder agrees, if the bid is accepted, to enter into an agreement with the owner and to use the required agreement form.
- The bidder acknowledges receipt of the procurement documents. The bidder's signature will testify to the bidder's receipt.
- The bidder has examined and is familiar with the site conditions.
- The bidder has examined and is familiar with local conditions, laws, and regulations.
- The bidder accepts the determinations regarding information upon which the bidder can rely, as well as the bidder's responsibility to obtain additional data.
- The bidder acknowledges that the bid is genuine.

- *Amount of Time for the Bids to Be Held Open.* A statement that the bidder agrees to hold the bid open (continue to honor the bid price) for a stated period of time. This period is usually a minimum of 30 days after bid opening for private work and 60 to 90 days after bid opening for public work. If the low bidder defaults for any reason, this provision allows the owner to award the contract to another bidder, without repeating the entire bidding process. The number of days the bid is to be held open must be coordinated with the general conditions and instructions to bidders. Any change to this length of time on the bid form might require a change to the other related documents.

- *Identification of Addenda.* A place for the bidder to fill in the identifying number of all addenda received during the bidding period. The bid form should include a statement that addenda were received and that their costs have been included in the bid.

- *Prices.* Blank spaces for the bidder to fill in all prices. Usually, the stipulated sum or total base bid price is quoted in both words and figures. Separate items according to the breakdown needed for each particular project. The language concerning the bid amounts should be identical to the applicable portion of the agreement. When there are numerous unit price items or quantity allowance items, a separate bid schedule should be made a part of the bid form. When allowances are part of the bid, include a statement on the bid form that the amounts and the quantities of the allowances are included in the bidder's stated price.

- *Combined Bids.* If multiple or separate bids are solicited or permitted, the bid form should indicate acceptable methods for combining separately listed bids (e.g., a stipulated sum or percentage deduction from the total of separate bids).

- *Alternates.* Alternates should be requested only when they are believed to be of special importance to the owner, either as a means of ensuring bids within available funding or to provide an opportunity to make an important determination in the selection of materials or processes.
  - Alternates may be either additive or deductive to the base bid, the stipulated sum bid, or the total unit-price bid. Appropriate blanks should be provided on the bid form. They must be clearly described in Division 01, Section 01 23 00—Alternates. The instructions to bidders should contain guidance for preparing alternate bids.
  - Alternates may be used in conjunction with unit price bids or stipulated sum bids. They should be used with discretion and carefully prepared to eliminate doubt and confusion. Avoid alternates, if possible, because they may complicate the procurement (bidding/negotiating/purchasing) process and may result in higher prices.

- *Allowances.* An amount (cash allowance) or quantity (quantity allowance) that each bidder is required to include in the bid to cover specific work that has not been specifically defined.

- *Cash Allowances.* The dollar amount for a specific item or items is specified.
- *Quantity Allowances.* A quantity of each item may be specified. Request a price on each item, and provide a blank if the total amount bid for each bid item is to be based on the specified quantities. When there are numerous quantity allowance items, a separate bid schedule may be made a part of the bid form.
- *Unit Prices.* Where the extent of work cannot be determined or accurately calculated until the work is performed, quantities are estimated and a unit price quoted for each item.
- *Completion Time.* A statement concerning the completion date of the work or project either by designating a specific date or by designating a number of days (usually calendar days). The language in this paragraph should be identical to the language in the agreement.
- *Liquidated Damages.* If applicable, include acknowledgment of provisions for liquidated damages. Because the bid form is not usually a contract document, care should be taken to ensure the amount of liquidated damages is included in the agreement or conditions of the contract. This amount should not be repeated in several locations, as it could result in a conflict.
- *Supplements.* Statement that the required supplements are enclosed, such as:
  - The bid security
  - A proposed subcontractor listing
  - Statements of evidence of bidder's qualifications
  - Bidder's financial statement
  - Noncollusion affidavit
- *Closing.* The closing of the bid includes the signature of the appropriate party or parties, the date, and, where appropriate, the corporate seal of the bidder.

00 41 13 Bid Form—Stipulated Sum (Single-Prime Contract)
00 41 16 Bid Form—Stipulated Sum (Multiple-Prime Contract)
00 41 23 Bid Form—Construction Management (Single-Prime Contract)
00 41 26 Bid Form—Construction Management (Multiple-Prime Contract)
00 41 33 Bid Form—Cost-Plus-Fee (Single-Prime Contract)
00 41 36 Bid Form—Cost-Plus-Fee (Multiple-Prime Contract)
00 41 43 Bid Form—Unit Price (Single-Prime Contract)
00 41 46 Bid Form—Unit Price (Multiple-Prime Contract)
00 41 53 Bid Form—Design/Build (Single-Prime Contract)
00 41 56 Bid Form—Design/Build (Multiple-Prime Contract)
00 41 63 Bid Form—Purchase Contract

Currently, AIA documents do not include a suggested bid form. The EJCDC documents include the following, which includes suggested language and choices specific to the EJCDC documents:

- EJCDC Document C-410, Suggested Bid Form for Construction Contracts
- EJCDC Document P-400, Suggested Bid Form for Procurement Contracts

11.4.6.2   00 42 00 Proposal Forms

The proposal process can utilize a form offered by the proposer or can be a form required in a procurement process. Whether the process is formal or informal, the proposal forms could be similar to a bid form.

A formal proposal form provides assurances that the requested information is included. The proposal form can be as outlined for a bid form and would provide spaces for the desired considerations. If alternates, allowances, or unit prices are desired, they can be included. The benefit of a stipulated proposal form is that it can include acknowledgments, similar to a bid form, for such items as having visited the site and considered existing conditions. This proposal form, when reviewed by the owner's legal counsel, can ensure that the proper elements are included to permit it to be accepted as an agreement or incorporated into a formal agreement form.

00 42 13 Proposal Form—Stipulated Sum (Single-Prime Contract)
00 42 16 Proposal Form—Stipulated Sum (Multiple-Prime Contract)
00 42 23 Proposal Form—Construction Management (Single-Prime Contract)
00 42 26 Proposal Form—Construction Management (Multiple-Prime Contract)
00 42 33 Proposal Form—Cost-Plus-Fee (Single-Prime Contract)
00 42 36 Proposal Form—Cost-Plus-Fee (Multiple-Prime Contract)
00 42 43 Proposal Form—Unit Price (Single-Prime Contract)
00 42 46 Proposal Form—Unit Price (Multiple-Prime Contract)
00 42 53 Proposal Form—Design/Build (Single-Prime Contract)
00 42 56 Proposal Form—Design/Build (Multiple-Prime Contract)
00 42 63 Proposal Form—Purchase Contract

11.4.6.3 00 43 00 Procurement Form Supplements

Various forms and attachments might be required to supplement the procurement form or accompany a proposal. These forms may be required by public agencies or to provide additional information. This information is best placed on separate forms to prevent the procurement form from becoming unmanageable and important data from being lost. These forms may be documentary information or can be considerations for award.

Bid security guarantees that if a bid is accepted within the specified time, the bidder will enter into a formal agreement with the owner (usually 30 to 90 days from the opening of the bids) and will furnish the required construction performance and construction payment bonds. The purpose of the bid security is to compensate the owner for damages incurred if the selected bidder does not accept the contract award.

If the selected bidder does enter into an agreement with the owner, the bid security should be returned to unsuccessful bidders. After the performance and payment bonds are provided and the agreement executed, bid security should also be returned to the successful bidder, who is now the contractor.

The details of the bid security requirements are addressed in the instructions to bidders and should cover the following:

- Required amount of the bid security (normally a percentage of the bid price or a stipulated sum)
- Form of the bid security (cash, certified check, bank draft, cashier's check, money order, or bid bond)
- To whom the security is to be payable
- Required licensing or rating of the surety
- Length of time that bid securities will be retained
- Description of the conditions under which the bid security will be returned to unsuccessful bidders
- Description of the bid security forfeiture conditions

The bid security is acknowledged on the bid form and submitted with the bid. Usually it should be included in the same envelope as the bid form. If a specific form is required to be used, it should be included in the project manual and a statement provided that only this form is acceptable. A separate unbound form may be provided for the bidders' convenience.

00 43 13 Bid Security Form

- EJCDC Document C-430, Bid Bond, Penal Sum Form
- EJCDC Document C-435, Bid Bond, Damages Form

On some occasions allowances, unit prices, and alternates are itemized on forms (rather than included in the bid or proposal form) that become attachments to the bid or proposal.

00 43 21 Allowance Form

- CSI, Allowance Authorization

00 43 22 Unit Prices Form
00 43 23 Alternates Form

If substitutions are permitted during procurement, it is helpful to the bidders and proposers to include a particular form that is required to be submitted before or with the bid or proposal.

00 43 25 Substitution Request Form (During Procurement)

- CSI, Substitution Request (During the Bidding/Negotiating Stage)
- CSI, Product Substitution Checklist

Some projects may require estimated quantities of some or all of the products that will be procured; if so, a particular form may be provided that is to be submitted with the bid or proposal.

00 43 26 Estimated Quantities Form

Some projects may require disclosure of some or all of the products that will be procured; if so, a particular form may be provided that is to be submitted with the bid or proposal.

00 43 33 Proposed Products Form

Some projects may require disclosure of some or all of the subcontractors that will be employed; if so, a particular form may be provided that is to be submitted with the bid or proposal.

00 43 36 Proposed Subcontractors Form

- CSI, Subcontractors and Major Material Suppliers List
- AIA Document G705, List of Subcontractors

Projects constructed with public funds frequently require bidders and proposers to provide a statement of intent to utilize minority businesses; if so, a particular form may be provided that is to be submitted with the bid or proposal.

00 43 39 Minority Business Enterprise Statement of Intent Form

Also for projects constructed with public funds, disclosure of the wage rates that will be paid for particular categories of work may be a condition of the work; if so, a particular form may be provided that is to be submitted with the bid or proposal.

00 43 43 Wage Rates Form

Some projects may require a schedule of values to be submitted with the bid or proposal; if so, a particular form may be provided.

00 43 73 Proposed Schedule of Values Form

Since contractors usually determine the time required for construction, bidders and proposers may be required to submit a proposed construction schedule; if so, a particular form may be provided that is to be submitted with the bid or proposal.

00 43 83 Proposed Construction Schedule Form

Some projects may have multiple scopes of work, or components, that require bidders and proposers to provide a work plan detailing the sequence of construction activities; if so, a particular form may be provided that is to be submitted with the bid or proposal.

00 43 86 Proposed Work Plan Schedule Form

When the bidding or proposal process require numerous forms to be submitted, it is helpful to the bidders and proposers to include a checklist that identifies the various documents that are to be included in the bid or proposal.

00 43 93 Bid Submittal Checklist

- CSI, Bid Checklist

11.4.6.4   00 45 00 Representations and Certifications

It is not unusual for an owner to require more information from bidders or proposers than can be typically provided in a bid or proposal. To obtain this information, there may be a procurement requirement for the execution of single purpose forms, usually provided by the owner, as a means of substantiating that a bidder or proposer has a particular qualification or capability that is important to the project. Executing representation forms or providing certifications are more frequently required for public projects than for private projects. If bidders or proposers are not prequalified prior to solicitation, representations and certifications is an effective manner of obtaining information to be evaluated.

00 45 13 Bidder's Qualifications

- AIA Document A305, Contractor's Qualification Statement

00 45 16 Proposer's Qualifications
00 45 19 Noncollusion Affidavit
00 45 23 Statement of Disposal Facility
00 45 26 Workers' Compensation Certification Schedule
00 45 33 Nonsegregated Facilities Affidavit
00 45 36 Equal Employment Opportunity Affidavit
00 45 39 Minority Business Enterprise Affidavit
00 45 43 Corporate Resolutions
00 45 46 Governmental Certifications

11.5   Contracting Requirements

11.5.1   Introduction

As discussed and emphasized throughout this practice guide, contracts are a crucial part of the design and construction industry. Depending on the project delivery method chosen for a project, the number of forms and documents necessary to establish contractual relationships can vary from one to many.

An effective manner of discussing contracting requirements is to organize this chapter according to a portion of Division 00 of *MasterFormat*®, and to list standard forms and documents that are available from AIA, EJCDC, DBIA, and AGC.

11.5.2 00 50 00 Contracting Forms and Supplements

There are several standard forms and documents published by professional associations for the owner to provide instructions regarding the desired contracting requirements:

- AIA Document G612, Owner's Instructions to the Architect Regarding the Construction Contract, Insurance and Bonds, and Bidding Procedures
- EJCDC Document C-050, Owner's Instructions Regarding Bidding Procedures and Construction Contract Documents
- EJCDC Document C-051, Engineer's Request for Instructions on Bonds and Insurance
- EJCDC Document C-052, Owner's Instructions Concerning Bonds and Insurance for Construction

11.5.2.1   00 51 00 Notice of Award

After bids have been evaluated to the satisfaction of the owner, it is customary for the owner to notify the company with the winning bid or proposal that they will be awarded the contract for the work. In its simplest form, a notice of award may be as short as a one-sentence statement in a personal letter.

For some projects involving the use of public funds, and in the interests of fairness, there may be a need to notify all bidders or proposers of the intent to award the contract. Also, there may be some projects, requiring qualified bidders, proposers, contractors, vendors, or subcontractors, that are required to provide a specific period of time after notification of intent to award the contract during which a challenge may be made. For example, a bidder that was not selected may believe they were unfairly treated or were not given sufficient consideration, and who wants to challenge the selection appealing to the authority having jurisdiction over the project. A form that includes a description of the rights of those bidders or proposers that were not selected is the best way of fulfilling this requirement. And if the form is included in the project manual, then each bidder or proposer would have the opportunity to become familiar with the contents of the notice.

- EJCDC Document C-510, Notice of Award

11.5.2.2   00 52 00 Agreement Forms

The nature of a contract, or an agreement, in general has been previously discussed in Chapter 5. The essence of an agreement is the meeting of the minds of two parties about a specific scope of work in exchange for an amount of compensation, which is then put in written form. While an owner has a right to use whatever form of contract desired, it is prudent to use preprinted standard forms by one of the several national professional associations.

00 52 13 Agreement Form—Stipulated Sum (Single-Prime Contract)
00 52 16 Agreement Form—Stipulated Sum (Multiple-Prime Contract)

- AIA Document A101, Standard Form of Agreement Between Owner and Contractor Where the Basis of Payment Is a Stipulated Sum
- AIA Document A105, Standard Form of Agreement Between Owner and Contractor for a Residential or Small Commercial Project
- AIA Document A107, Standard Form of Agreement Between Owner and Contractor for a Project of Limited Scope
- AIA Document A151, Standard Form of Agreement Between Owner and Vendor for Furniture, Furnishings, and Equipment Where the Basis of Payment Is a Stipulated Sum
- EJCDC Document C-520, Suggested Form of Agreement Between Owner and Contractor for Construction Contract (Stipulated Price)

00 52 23 Agreement Form—Construction Management (Single-Prime Contract)
00 52 26 Agreement Form—Construction Management (Multiple-Prime Contract)

- AIA Document A101, CMa, Standard Form of Agreement Between Owner and Contractor Where the Basis of Payment Is a Stipulated Sum, Construction Manager-Advisor Edition
- AIA Document A121, Standard Form of Agreement Between Owner and Construction Manager Where the Construction Manager Is also the Constructor (AGC Document 565)
- AIA Document A131, Standard Form of Agreement Between Owner and Construction Manager Where the Construction Manager Is also the Constructor and Where the Basis of Payment Is the Cost of the Work Plus a Fee and There Is No Guarantee of Cost (AGC Document 566)
- AIA Document B801, Standard Form of Agreement Between Owner and Construction Manager

00 52 33 Agreement Form—Cost-Plus-Fee (Single-Prime Contract)
00 52 36 Agreement Form—Cost-Plus-Fee (Multiple-Prime Contract)

- AIA Document A102, Standard Form of Agreement Between Owner and Contractor Where the Basis of Payment Is the Cost of the Work Plus a Fee with a Negotiated Guaranteed Maximum Price
- AIA Document A103, Standard Form of Agreement Between Owner and Contractor Where the Basis of Payment Is the Cost of the Work Plus a Fee without a Guaranteed Maximum Price
- EJCDC Document C-525, Suggested Form of Agreement Between Owner and Contractor for Construction Contract (Cost-Plus)

00 52 43 Agreement Form—Unit Price (Single-Prime Contract)
00 52 46 Agreement Form—Unit Price (Multiple-Prime Contract)
00 52 53 Agreement Form—Design/Build (Single-Prime Contract)
00 52 56 Agreement Form—Design/Build (Multiple-Prime Contract)

- AIA Document A141, Agreement Between Owner and Design-Builder
- AIA Document A142, Agreement Between Design-Builder and Contractor

- EJCDC Document D-520, Standard Form of Agreement Between Owner and Design/Builder on the Basis of a Stipulated Price
- EJCDC Document D-525, Standard Form of Agreement Between Owner and Design/Builder on the Basis of Cost-Plus

00 52 63 Agreement Form – Purchase Contract

- EJCDC Document P-520, Suggested Form of Agreement Between Buyer and Seller for Procurement Contracts

11.5.2.3 00 54 00 Agreement Form Supplements

00 54 13 Supplementary Scope Statement
00 54 21 Allowances Schedule
00 54 22 Unit Prices Schedule

11.5.2.4 00 55 00 Notice to Proceed

The notice to proceed directs the contractor to begin the project on a specific date. Establishing this date is important because the time designated in the agreement to construct the project officially begins on the date designated in the notice to proceed.

- CSI, Notice to Proceed
- EJCDC Document C-550, Notice to Proceed

11.5.3 00 60 00 Project Forms

11.5.3.1 00 61 00 Bond Forms

When bonds are required by the owner, it is customary to provide the particular form that will be required.
00 61 13 Performance and Payment Bond Form

- EJCDC Document C-610, Construction Performance Bond
- EJCDC Document C-615, Construction Payment Bond
- EJCDC Document D-610, Design/Build Contract Performance Bond
- EJCDC Document D-615, Design/Build Contract Payment Bond
- EJCDC Document P-610, Suggested Performance Bond for Procurement Contracts
- EJCDC Document P-615, Payment Bond for Procurement Contracts

00 61 16 Lien Bond Form
00 61 19 Maintenance Bond Form
00 61 23 Retainage Bond Form
00 61 26 Special Bond Form

11.5.3.2 00 62 00 Certificates and Other Forms

00 62 11 Submittal Transmittal Form

- CSI, Submittal Transmittal

00 62 16 Certificate of Insurance Form

- AIA Document G715, Supplemental Attachment for ACORD Certificate of Insurance 25-S

00 62 19 Infection Control Form
00 62 23 Construction Waste Diversion Form
00 62 33 Products Form
00 62 34 Recycled Content of Materials Form
00 62 39 Minority Business Enterprise Certification Form
00 62 73 Schedule of Values Form
00 62 76 Application for Payment Form

- AIA Document G702, Application and Certificate for Payment, and, G703, Continuation Sheet
- AIA Document G702 CMa, Application and Certificate for Payment, Construction Manager-Advisor Edition
- AIA Document G722 CMa, Project Application and Project Certificate for Payment, Construction Manager-Advisor Edition, and, G723 CMa, Project Application Summary, Construction Manager-Advisor Edition
- EJCDC Document C-620, Contractor's Application for Payment
- DBIA Document 500-D1, Project Schedule of Values and Design-Builder's Application for Payment

00 62 79 Stored Material Form

- CSI, Stored Material Summary

00 62 83 Construction Schedule Form
00 62 86 Work Plan Schedule Form
00 62 89 Construction Equipment Form

11.5.3.3 00 63 00 Clarification and Modification Forms

00 63 13 Request for Interpretation Form

- CSI, Request for Interpretation
- CSI, Request for Interpretation Log
- AIA Document G716, Request for Information

00 63 19 Clarification Form

- CSI, Clarification Notice
- CSI, Clarification Notice Log

If substitutions are permitted during construction, it is helpful to include the form that is required to be used.

00 63 25 Substitution Request Form (During Construction)

- CSI, Substitution Request (After the Bidding/Negotiating Stage)
- CSI, Substitution Request Log
- CSI, Product Substitution Checklist

AIA Document A201 defines minor changes to the project or clarifications of the contract documents as instructions or clarifications not involving adjustment of the contract sum or time.

00 63 33 Supplemental Instruction Form

- AIA Document G710, Architect's Supplemental Instructions

Some A/Es use a field order to make minor changes to the project. EJCDC C-700 allows the engineer to authorize or order minor variations to the project by use of a field order.

00 63 36 Field Order Form

- CSI, Field Order
- CSI, Minor Change/Field Order Log
- EJCDC Document C-942, Field Order

00 63 43 Written Amendment Form

Sometimes a construction change directive is necessary to direct the contractor to make a change to the project before the owner and contractor have agreed upon the proposed changes in the contract sum or time.

00 63 46 Construction Change Directive Form

- AIA Document G714, Construction Change Directive
- AIA Document G714 CMa, Construction Change Directive, Construction Management-Advisor Edition

00 63 49 Work Change Directive Form

- EJCDC Document C-940, Work Change Directive
- DBIA Document 500-D5, Design-Build Work Change Directive Form

00 63 53 Request for Proposal Form

- CSI, Request for Proposal Log
- AIA Document G709, Work Change Proposal Request

00 63 54 Proposal Worksheet Summary Form

- CSI, Proposal Worksheet Summary

00 63 55 Proposal Worksheet Detail Form

- CSI, Proposal Worksheet Detail

00 63 57 Change Order Request Form

- CSI, Change Order Request (Proposal)
- CSI, Change Order Request Log

A change order is a written instruction to the contractor issued after execution of the agreement that authorizes an addition, deletion, or revision to the project in consideration of an adjustment in the contract sum, contract time, or both.

00 63 63 Change Order Form

- CSI, Change Order Log
- AIA Document G701, Change Order
- AIA Document G701 CMa, Change Order
- EJCDC Document C-941, Change Order
- DBIA Document 500-D2, Design-Build Change Order Form

11.5.3.4 00 65 00 Closeout Forms

00 65 13 Certificate of Compliance Form
00 65 16 Certificate of Substantial Completion Form

- AIA Document G704, Certificate of Substantial Completion
- AIA Document G704 CMa, Certificate of Substantial Completion, Construction Manager-Advisor Edition
- AIA Document G704/DB, Acknowledgment of Substantial Completion of a Design-Build Project
- EJCDC Document C-625, Certificate of Substantial Completion
- DBIA Document 500-D4, Certificate of Substantial Completion Form

00 65 19 Certificate of Completion Form
00 65 36 Warranty Form
00 65 73 Statutory Declaration Form

11.5.4 00 70 00 Conditions of the Contract

Conditions of the contract define basic rights, responsibilities, and relationships of the parties involved in the performance of the contract. These conditions are an inherent part of the owner-contractor agreement and are considered to be the general conditions of the agreement. Limited services or abbreviated agreements normally contain the general conditions within the agreement. However, the involvement of other participants (e.g., A/E or construction manager) and the delegation of responsibilities to subcontractors lead to the relatively public nature of the conditions of the contract. The need for review by those not signatory to the agreement has led to the use of conditions of the contract separate from the agreement.

Though not a signatory to the owner-contractor agreement, the A/E commonly has duties and responsibilities described in the conditions of the contract and may assist in their preparation. A/E duties and responsibilities under conditions of the contract generally include construction administration:

- Acting as an owner's representative for matters concerning the work
- Visiting the construction site to become familiar with the work, confirming the work is in conformance with the contract documents, and evaluate progress
- Validating the progress of the work for the purpose of authorizing progress payments
- Preparing the following:
  - Architect's Supplemental Instructions (ASI) or field orders
  - Construction change directives or work change directives
  - Change orders

- Clarifying and interpreting the contract documents
- Reviewing, approving, or taking other appropriate action on submittals such as shop drawings, mock-ups, and samples
- Rejecting defective work
- Determining dates of substantial completion and final completion

Conditions of the contract need to be closely coordinated with related documents such as the design and construction agreements and Division 01—General Requirements. Changes in one document may necessitate changes in the other documents.

General and supplementary conditions are conditions of the contract and have legal consequences. The A/E should not prepare general or supplementary conditions without explicit approval and guidance from the owner, the owner's legal counsel, and the owner's insurance adviser.

11.5.4.1   00 71 00 Contracting Definitions

Sometimes there is a need to provide project specific definitions of terms that are used in the contracting documents.

11.5.4.2   00 72 00 General Conditions

General conditions for a project can be any of a number of standard documents published that are applicable to the project delivery method. Provisions of general conditions have broad application and include practices common in the United States. Standard general conditions for construction are prepared and published by professional associations such as the AIA, EJCDC, and DBIA.

Standard general conditions benefit the construction industry by providing documents with a history of many years of use and refinement. The language and provisions of these standard documents have been tested and interpreted by the courts and are well understood and familiar to those concerned. The use of standard general conditions also establishes a baseline from which exceptions, modifications, and additions of the supplementary conditions are clearly identified and evaluated. Writing new general conditions for a project will conceal the unique requirements rather than make them clearly understood.

Standard general conditions are normally based on the concept of a single-prime contract for the work. When a project will be constructed under multiple-prime contracts, each contract should use the same general conditions with emphasis on mutual responsibilities. The general conditions should always be bound into the project manual, not simply included by reference, so that they are easily available during progress of the work.

Federal, state, and local government agencies usually produce standard general conditions specifically for use on their projects. Some large corporations have also developed their own general conditions for their projects. When working with unfamiliar general conditions, the A/E must use particular care to adapt the wording of contract documents to the differing provisions to avoid conflicts or omissions. Changes may be required in provisions that the A/E would otherwise treat as standard or routine. Provisions that might be affected include substitutions, submittal procedures, naming of manufacturers, and temporary facilities.

AIA Document A201, EJCDC Document C-700 and DBIA Document 535, Standard Form of General Conditions of the Contract Between Owner and Design-Builder address common project concerns. Each document deals with these concerns in a similar manner but with language determined to be in accord with the needs of each organization. In general, the DBIA general conditions provide fewer details and requirements than do the EJCDC and AIA documents because the designer and the builder are acting as a single entity. Some of these common articles deal with:

- *Work.* Each of the three documents describes work under the basic definitions in the respective first articles. Whereas all three define work as the construction and other services required by the contract documents, including labor, material, equipment, and services, AIA Document A201 additionally refers to the contractor's obligation to perform. EJCDC C-700 includes a reference to the documentation required to produce the construction, and DBIA 535 requires the procuring and furnishing of all materials, equipment, services, and labor that are reasonably inferable from the contract documents. Although both the AIA and the EJCDC general conditions go on to describe the project as the total construction, of which the work under the contract documents may be the whole or part, the DBIA general conditions do not make this additional distinction.

- *Contract Documents.* AIA Document A201 lists the documents that make up the contract documents as the agreement, conditions of the contract, drawings, specifications, addenda issued prior to execution of the contract, other documents listed in the agreement, and modifications issued after execution of the contract and excludes certain procurement documents. EJCDC C-700 simply states that the contract documents are those printed or hard-copy documents listed in the agreement, excluding shop drawings, other contractors' submittals, and reports and drawings of subsurface and physical conditions. DBIA Document 535 refers to contract documents throughout, but does not define what they are composed of within these general conditions.

- *Payments.* The articles dealing with payment procedures are fairly detailed in each of the three general conditions. Each sets out requirements for a schedule of values and a method of request for payment and review of application, withholding payment, substantial completion, and final payment. Both AIA Document A201 and EJCDC C-700 define a contract sum, whereas DBIA Document 535 does not.

- *Termination.* Each of the three general conditions provides detailed procedures for both the owner and the contractor or design-builder to suspend the work without cause or to terminate the contract for cause. In general, the reasons for suspension or termination are similar for each of the general conditions and include failure to make payments, failure to provide adequate work force or materials, flagrant disregard for laws and regulations, or a breach of the contract documents. The time periods allowed under each general condition vary. In addition, AIA Document A201 allows the contractor to terminate the contract if the work has stopped for 30 consecutive days as a result of a declaration of a national emergency. DBIA 535 also provides for the possibility of bankruptcy by either the owner or the design-builder.

- *Claims and Dispute Resolution.* Both the AIA and EJCDC general conditions refer most claims or disputes to the initial decision maker first, who is most likely the A/E, and a decision is made at this level if possible. AIA Document A201 exempts any claims dealing with hazardous materials, but EJCDC C-700 has no similar exception. For both AIA and EJCDC, the next step after failing resolution with the A/E is to take the dispute to mediation and, failing that, next to arbitration for resolution (that is unless the parties have agreed to other stipulations). DBIA

Document 535 addresses this concern by first emphasizing dispute avoidance and a commitment to working with each other at all times to minimize disputes and losses. In this case, the design-builder's representative and the owner's representative first attempt to resolve the dispute together. Failing that, the dispute is taken to senior representatives of both parties, then failing that to a nonbinding mediation, and failing that, to binding arbitration.

Each of the three standard general conditions, though similar in many respects, has developed over time and has evolved into a document that serves the basic requirements of its sponsoring organization.

00 72 13 General Conditions—Stipulated Sum (Single-Prime Contract)
00 72 16 General Conditions—Stipulated Sum (Multiple-Prime Contract)

- AIA Document A201, General Conditions of the Contract for Construction
- AIA Document A201 SC, Federal Supplementary Conditions of the Contract for Construction
- EJCDC Document C-700, Standard General Conditions of the Construction Contract
- AGC ConsensusDOCS Document 200, Agreement and General Conditions Between Owner and Contractor (Lump Sum)

00 72 23 General Conditions—Construction Management (Single-Prime Contract)
00 72 26 General Conditions—Construction Management (Multiple-Prime Contract)

- AIA Document A201 CMa, General Conditions of the Contract for Construction, Construction Manager-Adviser Edition

00 72 33 General Conditions—Cost-Plus-Fee (Single-Prime Contract)
00 72 36 General Conditions—Cost-Plus-Fee (Multiple-Prime Contract)

- AGC ConsensusDOCS Document 235, Short Form Agreement Between Owner and Contractor (Cost of Work)

00 72 43 General Conditions—Unit Price (Single-Prime Contract)
00 72 46 General Conditions—Unit Price (Multiple-Prime Contract)
00 72 53 General Conditions—Design/Build (Single-Prime Contract)
00 72 56 General Conditions—Design/Build (Multiple-Prime Contract)

- EJCDC Document D-700, Standard General Conditions of the Contract Between Owner and Design/Builder
- DBIA Document 535, Standard Form of General Conditions of the Contract Between Owner and Design-Builder
- AGC ConsensusDOCS Document 410, Agreement and General Conditions Between Owner and Design-Builder (Cost of Work Plus Fee with Guaranteed Maximum Price)
- AGC ConsensusDOCS Document 415, Agreement and General Conditions Between Owner and Design-Builder (Lump Sum Based on the Owner's Program Including Schematic Design Documents)

- AGC ConsensusDOCS Document 500, Agreement and General Conditions Between Design-Builder and Construction Manager (Guaranteed Maximum Price with Option for Preconstruction Services)
- AGC ConsensusDOCS Document 510, Agreement and General Conditions Between Design-Builder and Construction Manager (Cost of Work with Option for Preconstruction Services)

00 72 63 General Conditions—Purchase Contract

- EJCDC Document P-700, Standard General Conditions for Procurement Contracts
- AIA Document A251, General Conditions of the Contract for Furniture, Furnishings, and Equipment
- AGC ConsensusDOCS Document 300, Tri-Party Agreement for Collaborative Project Delivery

11.5.4.3 00 73 00 Supplementary Conditions

The requirements of the general conditions can be modified or expanded in the supplementary conditions to accommodate specific project conditions, owner's requirements, or unusual aspects relating to the roles, rights, duties, and responsibilities of the parties to the contract for construction. Supplementary conditions are not standard for every project and must be prepared based on requirements of the specific project.

Some modification of standard general conditions is almost always necessary. Regardless of the efforts to develop standardized documents, modifications are necessary to customize the requirements to the project. Published guides for preparing supplementary conditions give examples of wording for modifications that occur frequently, with a recommended procedure for the preparation of the supplementary conditions.

Deletion or rewording of provisions in standard general conditions should be avoided. The provisions and terminology have been carefully coordinated with companion documents and the deletion or change of requirements of a provision may affect other documents. When rewording of the general conditions is necessary to adjust for local conditions, owner's requirements, or other legitimate reasons, advice of legal counsel is necessary to avoid conflicts with, or weakening of, unmodified statements elsewhere in the contract documents.

Modifications, deletions, and expansions of articles in the general conditions are written in the supplementary conditions in the same order as the related articles occur in the general conditions, and are referenced specifically to the article, paragraph, subparagraph, or clause in the general conditions. Additional articles, paragraphs, subparagraphs, or clauses of supplementary conditions are added by using the next consecutive article, paragraph, subparagraph, or clause number consistent with the provisions of the general conditions.

Properly prepared contract documents agree with one another as integral parts of a whole. The documents should agree with one another in terminology and nomenclature. Modifications made to one of the documents should not contradict provisions contained in the other documents. The supplementary conditions must, therefore, be carefully coordinated not only with the general conditions, but also with the other documents, including procurement requirements and the various agreements.

AIA Document A503 contains supplementary conditions for the standard AIA Document A201 general conditions; these supplementary conditions are applicable for certain federal government requirements. Additional conditions that may also be required to adapt the documents to project requirements should be provided in addition to AIA Document A201/SC for a specific project.

The practice of printing standard supplementary conditions is not recommended. Supplementary conditions are based on the unique requirements of each specific project. Recommended additions or modifications to the standard general conditions commonly illustrated in published guides are not applicable for every project, and other changes are frequently required. In addition, the supplementary conditions are prepared in conjunction with the procurement requirements because of their interrelationship.

The published guides for preparing supplementary conditions give examples of wording for modifications that occur frequently, with a recommended procedure for the preparation of the supplementary conditions.

The AIA and EJCDC electronic versions allow for direct modification of standard general conditions. The resulting project-specific general conditions contain both the original text and the supplementary modifications. In this case, there might not be separate supplementary conditions. There are several guides that are published by the professional associations that can be used for the preparation of supplementary conditions:

- AIA Document A503, Guide for Supplementary Conditions
- AIA Document A511, Guide for Supplementary Conditions, Construction Manager-Advisor Edition
- EJCDC Document C-800, Guide to the Preparation of Supplementary Conditions
- EJCDC Document P-800, Guide to the Preparation of Procurement Supplementary Conditions for Procurement Contracts

00 73 16 Insurance Requirements
00 73 19 Health and Safety Requirements
00 73 23 Purchase Contracts
00 73 26 Assigned Contracts
00 73 33 Non-Segregated Facilities Requirements
00 73 36 Equal Employment Opportunity Requirements
00 73 43 Wage Rate Requirements
00 73 46 Wage Determination Schedule
00 73 49 Labor Stabilization Agreement
00 73 53 Anti-Pollution Measures
00 73 63 Security Requirements
00 73 73 Statutory Requirements

Chapter 12
Procurement

The transition from the design stage to the construction stage of a project is the bidding/negotiating/purchasing stage collectively known as procurement. During this stage, owners make the proposed construction documents available to prospective contractors, through either direct selection or open solicitation. The prospective contractors assemble, calculate, and formally present to the owner their prices to complete the project described in the procurement documents. Construction prices become the financial basis of the contract for construction.

The documents used to obtain pricing from prospective contractors are referred to as the procurement documents and are based on the project delivery method selected. In a competitive bidding process, the documents are used for bidding. In a negotiating process, the documents are used for developing proposals. Pricing activities include:

- Examining the procurement (bidding/negotiating/purchasing) documents
- Investigating the site and conditions affecting the work to acquire additional information about the project
- Requesting clarifications, interpretations, and additional information if procurement documents and physical conditions are not in agreement
- Proposing substitutions for specified products, when permitted, according to documented requirements
- Soliciting prices from prospective subcontractors and suppliers
- Providing a bid/proposal security when required by the owner
- Compiling prices and calculating overhead and profit
- Submitting prices and supplemental information in accordance with the owner's requirements

A price is presented in one of two ways:

- A bid that will be compared with other bids submitted by other prospective bidders in a competitive bidding process
- An offer in the form of a proposal in a negotiating process

12.2   Pricing Methods

A price can be presented as:

- *Stipulated Sum (also known as a Lump Sum) including Cost of the Work, and Contractor's Overhead and Profit.* By this method, the design is completed before pricing and the price is known by the participants before construction begins. This pricing method is used for public and private projects that will be competitively bid.

- *Cost of the Work Plus a Fee, sometimes, with a Guaranteed Maximum Price (GMP).* The prospective contractor's price includes the cost of the work as defined in the procurement documents and the prospective contractor's fee for administering construction, including overhead and profit. The contractor's fee can be stated as a stipulated sum (fixed fee) or as a percentage of the cost of the work. The cost of the work combined with the contractor's fee can be established as the GMP. If the design is fully documented at the time pricing is requested, the GMP is essentially an estimate.

The GMP is a guarantee not to exceed the amount for completion of the work. It may be based on construction documents ranging between 30 percent and 70 percent complete. The contractor and subcontractors guarantee their price will not exceed a sum for the work indicated, including a reasonable amount of anticipated work for the items not shown on the provided documents.

Obtaining a GMP requires an experienced participant to review partially complete documents and to understand the scope of work necessary to achieve the final project. Often, if the final cost after completion is below the GMP, the difference between the actual cost and the guaranteed cost may be shared between the owner and the contractor in an agreed-upon ratio of the savings.

This pricing method is most effective for negotiated contracts. The contractor may decide to negotiate subcontracts for materials, equipment, and systems or seek competitive bids for these items to determine the actual costs. Bid packages or subcontract packages for subcontractors may be negotiated or combined with procurement requirements assembled by the contractor for bidding subcontracts. Accordingly, many portions of a project may be competitively bid at the subcontractor/supplier level even when the prime contract for the project is to be negotiated.

- *Time and Material with an Estimate of Probable Cost.* As an alternative to a cost-plus with a GMP, the contractor and the owner might agree to proceed on a time and material basis. In the owner-contractor agreement, the contractor states the percentages of overhead and profit that will be added to documented labor and material costs incurred while constructing the project and an overall estimate of probable cost. This pricing method is also effective for negotiated contracts.

- *Unit Price.* The type of work is known at the time of pricing, but the limits (extent) of the work will not be known until the project is constructed. The prospective contractor presents the owner with a price per unit of measure for designated items (e.g., price per square foot or price per item), including labor, material, equipment, overhead, profit, applicable taxes, and other pricing considerations. When the project is completed, the amount of work is measured or counted, usually by a designated entity, and the contract price is calculated based on the unit prices. This is a popular method of pricing for public or private projects that are not possible to accurately define prior to construction, such as utility work, highway construction, extensive excavation work, and maintenance projects. Unit prices are also used to price certain aspects of otherwise definable projects.

Once formalized in the owner-contractor agreement, a price can be modified only when mutually agreed upon by the owner and contractor. Whether a project is competitively bid or negotiated, a price or method of determining a price is the financial basis of an enforceable contract and requires documents defining the extent of work and sets of rules for the processes to be fair and complete and to proceed in an efficient manner.

12.3 | Purchasing

Purchasing is the direct acquisition of materials and equipment, and in some cases special services, by the owner (referred to as the buyer) for installation in the project or use in the constructed facility. Materials and equipment acquired under a purchasing contract may include supplies, furniture, furnishings, or equipment necessary for the facility to function during the facility management stage. The supplier is not normally engaged in project-site installation, except when special services are provided.

As with bidding and negotiating, purchasing requires documents that define the extent of goods and related services to be purchased and rules defining the manner in which the supplying contractor's price is to be presented. The documents and rules of purchasing are usually governed by the Uniform Commercial Code (UCC), which covers commercial transactions in most of the United States. Prices can be presented as stipulated sums for defined quantities of goods or as unit prices. Buyers may also request that suppliers define price breaks or discounts for larger quantities of goods. Discounts may also be offered when payment is made within a defined period following receipt and acceptance of goods.

To procure goods at the most competitive prices, private buyers may request bids or proposals from more than one prospective seller at the same time so that price comparisons can be made. Depending on the material cost, public buyers might be required to solicit purchasing prices through public advertisement similar to public bidding processes, because the funds used to purchase the goods are derived from public sources.

12.4 | Pricing Considerations

Pricing is a complex evaluation process for determining cost and profit. Pricing involves a comprehensive cost analysis of the project requirements, based on the information contained in the procurement documents and other information obtained during the period preceding bidding or negotiating.

Pricing requires a network of resources the contractor has developed. Such a network derives from

- Experience on completed projects
- Published cost guides
- Participation in construction-related associations structured to promote contractor business interests

12.4.1 Pricing Categories

In preparing a price, the following categories are considered:

- *Construction Costs.* The calculable costs the contractor will be required to pay.
- *Contingency.* An estimated monetary amount to account for the risk to the prospective contractor for performing the work, including unknown physical conditions that might arise.
- *Contractor's Overhead.* The contractor's business costs unrelated to an individual project.
- *Profit.* The financial benefit realized by the contractor after all costs have been paid and all related claims settled.

Because contingency, profit, and, to a degree, overhead, are essentially incalculable, they must be estimated. Successful pricing involves calculating known costs accurately and estimating incalculable factors prudently so that the contractor may realize a reasonable profit for performing the work.

12.4.1.1 Construction Costs

Costs include:

- Labor and personnel costs. Wages or salaries and associated benefits for:
  - Workers employed by the contractor to execute the work
  - On-site supervisory or administrative personnel
  - Travel expenses
- Subcontractor costs
- Products, including:
  - Costs of products incorporated into the work
  - Excess products allowed for unsalvageable waste
  - Maintenance materials for the owner's use in maintaining the project during the facility management stage
  - Costs of transportation, storage, handling, and special insurance or bonds associated with products
- Allowances identified in the procurement documents
- Mock-ups and sample panels not incorporated in the work
- Tools and equipment specially required for and consumed or depreciated in executing the work
- Rental charges for tools and equipment required for executing the work
- Fuel for operations

- Safety and security procedures and personnel
- Special training required for the work
- Temporary facilities and controls, including field offices, temporary heat and light, signage, safety provisions, environmental protection, and other items consumed but not incorporated into the work
- Waste removal and disposal costs
- Administrative costs attributable to the work:
  - Document reproduction and distribution
  - Payroll services
  - Data processing
  - Telephone and Internet charges, facsimile charges, postal and delivery service charges, and other site-related office expenditures
  - Shop drawings, samples, quality assurance (QA) and quality control (QC) submittals
  - Contract closeout costs, operations and maintenance manuals, record documents, demonstration and training, maintenance agreements, warranties and bonds, final cleaning.
- Fees for permits, inspections, and approvals by authorities having jurisdiction (AHJs)
- Field engineering and testing procedures
- Project coordination with prime contractors working concurrently:
  - Coordination of separate contractors
  - Coordination drawings
  - Owner-furnished products and services
  - Scheduling services
  - Progress documentation, such as photography
- Mobilization and start-up costs, including transportation, installation, maintenance, and removal of temporary facilities, protections, and controls between stages of extended projects
- Costs related to site restrictions, including off-site storage and parking expenses
- Royalties, licenses, and fees for use of patented designs or products
- Delegated design costs for engineering of products based on performance criteria
- Insurance and bonds
- Applicable taxes
- Deductions for:
  - Cash discounts and rebates from manufacturers and suppliers
  - Salvage value of waste, existing components not retained by the owner, extra products not retained by the owner
  - Shared savings with the owner resulting from value analysis

12.4.1.2 Contingency

Contingency is the summary risk factor the contractor perceives in the project arising from:

- Incomplete documents
- Estimated sums for unverified cost factors
- Errors made in pricing
- Costs related to dispute resolution, legal fees, and claims against the contractor

- Costs and penalties related to scheduling delays due to weather and other circumstances beyond the contractor's control, such as strikes and civil disturbance
- Default by a subcontractor or supplier, resulting in delays and monetary losses

Unspent contingency funds result in additional profit when all costs and claims are settled.

12.4.1.3 Contractor's Overhead

Overhead is the cost incurred for maintaining a viable business but not directly attributable to an individual project, including:

- Licensing required for conducting business in a jurisdiction
- Salaries, wages, and benefits for office personnel, general management, warehouse personnel, maintenance workers, and other employees engaged in daily operations at the place of business
- General office expenses not related to an individual project, including rent, leases, mortgages, utilities, and related services
- Leased or rented equipment and furniture not used on the project site
- Office supplies

Overhead is usually calculated as a percentage against the cost of a project.

12.4.1.4 Profit

Profit is the financial benefit that the contractor will realize after all costs and claims for the project are paid. It is often expressed as a percentage of the total costs.

12.5 Competitive Pricing

Competitive pricing depends on:

- Seeking the lowest prices available from subcontractors and suppliers for known cost factors
- Accurately estimating contingency factors without overestimating or underestimating their economic effects
- Determining reasonable sums for overhead and profit

The speed and accuracy with which the contractor compiles prices can also affect the outcome. Because important project information often is not known until the pricing period has commenced, the contractor must develop ways to process new project information in compressed time periods, often when prices for other projects are also being estimated. This requires an office of sufficient size, experienced staff, good organizational skills, and modern estimating and communication tools for efficient collaboration with other project participants.

Ideally, project information is received in a timely manner; however, this is not always possible. A contractor's office is extremely busy as subbids and quotes from suppliers are received with little time to spare before prices are due. Whether or not the contractor is successful in securing a contract, prices require considerable financial resources and time for preparation.

A competitive price (i.e., a low, yet fully considered price) represents an accurate analysis of the project, without underestimating or overestimating any applicable factor. However, prices vary significantly from contractor to contractor for one or a combination of the following reasons:

- Product costs vary among different suppliers because of quantity discounts, payment history, and the credit rating of the purchaser.
- Labor costs and time estimates will vary among contractors and subcontractors.
- Labor rates vary with skill and experience.
- Costs vary with composition of the workforce.
- Costs vary with the contractor's perception of difficulty in executing the project.
- Profit margins vary with other work available.
- Competition for the project is a factor, involving the number and skill level of other prospective contractors pricing the project.

Human error can also influence pricing, thus straining the contractor's resources at some point in a project. Project participants might be adversely affected when this occurs. A careful review of a price prior to award of a contract can reveal problematic areas, which in some project scenarios can be remedied before commencement of work. Hence, open dialog between the prospective contractor and the owner might be necessary for clarifications before a contract can be awarded.

12.5.1 Value Analysis of Proposed Substitutions

When substitutions are permitted and proposed during procurement (bidding/negotiating/purchasing), value analysis procedures determine their acceptability. Prospective contractors should also employ sound value analysis principles when considering possible substitutions.

12.5.2 Pricing under Design-Bid-Build Project Delivery

In design-bid-build (D-B-B) project delivery, most pricing activities take place between participants (bidders, subbidders, and separate contractors) during a defined bidding period (refer to Figure 12.1). A bid represents the prospective contractor's best compilation of the pricing factors applicable to the project. However, it is not always possible to obtain all of the pricing information necessary for a complete price within the time allowed for bidding. In some cases, a prospective contractor must estimate the cost of portions of the work for which accurate pricing information is not available, causing pricing activities to continue after the contract has been awarded.

Project participants might be exposed to potential financial risk when a construction price contains significant unverified pricing factors at the time of bidding under the D-B-B delivery method. If the estimated amounts are lower than the market value

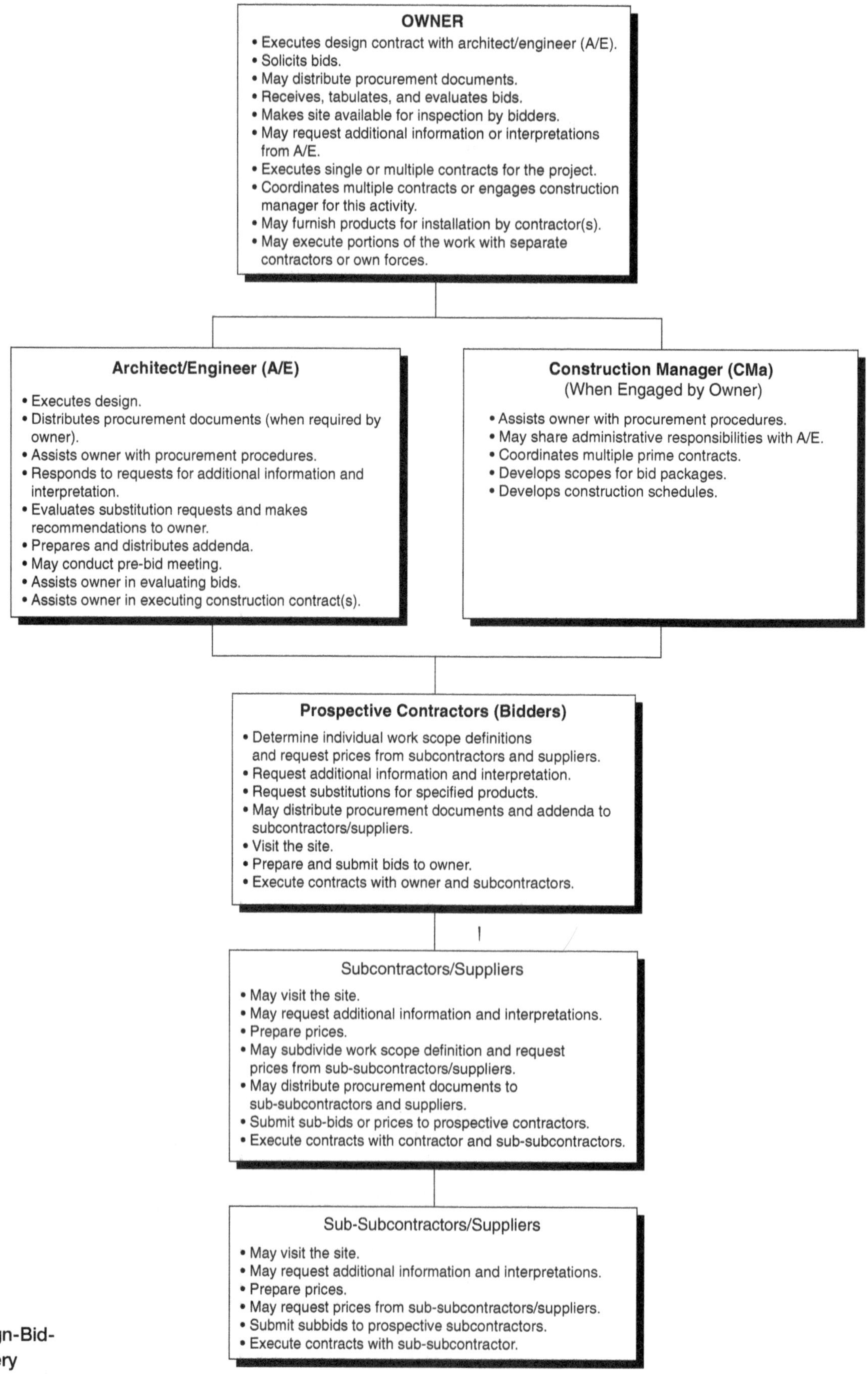

OWNER
- Executes design contract with architect/engineer (A/E).
- Solicits bids.
- May distribute procurement documents.
- Receives, tabulates, and evaluates bids.
- Makes site available for inspection by bidders.
- May request additional information or interpretations from A/E.
- Executes single or multiple contracts for the project.
- Coordinates multiple contracts or engages construction manager for this activity.
- May furnish products for installation by contractor(s).
- May execute portions of the work with separate contractors or own forces.

Architect/Engineer (A/E)
- Executes design.
- Distributes procurement documents (when required by owner).
- Assists owner with procurement procedures.
- Responds to requests for additional information and interpretation.
- Evaluates substitution requests and makes recommendations to owner.
- Prepares and distributes addenda.
- May conduct pre-bid meeting.
- Assists owner in evaluating bids.
- Assists owner in executing construction contract(s).

Construction Manager (CMa)
(When Engaged by Owner)
- Assists owner with procurement procedures.
- May share administrative responsibilities with A/E.
- Coordinates multiple prime contracts.
- Develops scopes for bid packages.
- Develops construction schedules.

Prospective Contractors (Bidders)
- Determine individual work scope definitions and request prices from subcontractors and suppliers.
- Request additional information and interpretation.
- Request substitutions for specified products.
- May distribute procurement documents and addenda to subcontractors/suppliers.
- Visit the site.
- Prepare and submit bids to owner.
- Execute contracts with owner and subcontractors.

Subcontractors/Suppliers
- May visit the site.
- May request additional information and interpretations.
- Prepare prices.
- May subdivide work scope definition and request prices from sub-subcontractors/suppliers.
- May distribute procurement documents to sub-subcontractors and suppliers.
- Submit sub-bids or prices to prospective contractors.
- Execute contracts with contractor and sub-subcontractors.

Sub-Subcontractors/Suppliers
- May visit the site.
- May request additional information and interpretations.
- Prepare prices.
- May request prices from sub-subcontractors/suppliers.
- Submit subbids to prospective subcontractors.
- Execute contracts with sub-subcontractor.

Figure 12.1
Pricing under Design-Bid-Build Project Delivery

at the time services or components are required, the contractor's financial condition will be strained, or the documented requirements for construction components or services might be compromised, affecting the value received by the owner. Conversely, if estimated amounts exceed the market value, the prospective contractor's price might not be competitive or the owner might overpay for components. Requiring lists of subcontractors as a bid form supplement can reduce this risk by ensuring a bid is complete.

12.5.3   Pricing under Design-Negotiate-Build Project Delivery

The pricing process under design-negotiate-build (D-N-B) delivery is similar to the process under the D-B-B method, but might be protracted if counteroffers by the owner or negotiator are considered, prompting repricing of certain project elements and components (refer to Figure 12.2). Because negotiation requires dialog between the owner and the prospective contractor, the process is more conducive to value analysis and repricing as negotiations proceed.

12.5.4   Pricing under Construction Management Project Delivery

Under construction management (CM) project delivery, the pricing process is similar to that used in D-B-B or D-N-B. CM usually involves multiple-prime contracts, each bid separately. The construction manager may act as an adviser or agent (CMa), to the owner or may act in the capacity of the contractor (CMc).

12.5.5   Pricing under Design-Build Project Delivery

Unlike D-B-B and D-N-B project delivery methods, pricing under design-build (D-B) project delivery takes place early in the design stage of the project, because pricing and design are performed by the same coordinate identity. Estimates may be the basis of pricing in the early stages of design-build. Pricing is confirmed by the D-B company through either competitive bidding or negotiation with subcontractors and suppliers as design and construction documents are developed (refer to Figure 12.3).

12.5.6   Pricing under Owner-Build Project Delivery

Under the owner-build (O-B) delivery method, contractors negotiate or bid directly with the owner, who defines the scope of the project and engages separate contractors for their portions of the work. Pricing may be phased or take place at a fixed point in time similar to D-N-B or D-B-B as applicable (refer to Figure 12.4).

12.5.7   Pricing under Integrated Project Delivery

One of the principal assets of Integrated Project Delivery (IPD) is that because of the early involvement of material and product suppliers and trade contractors during the

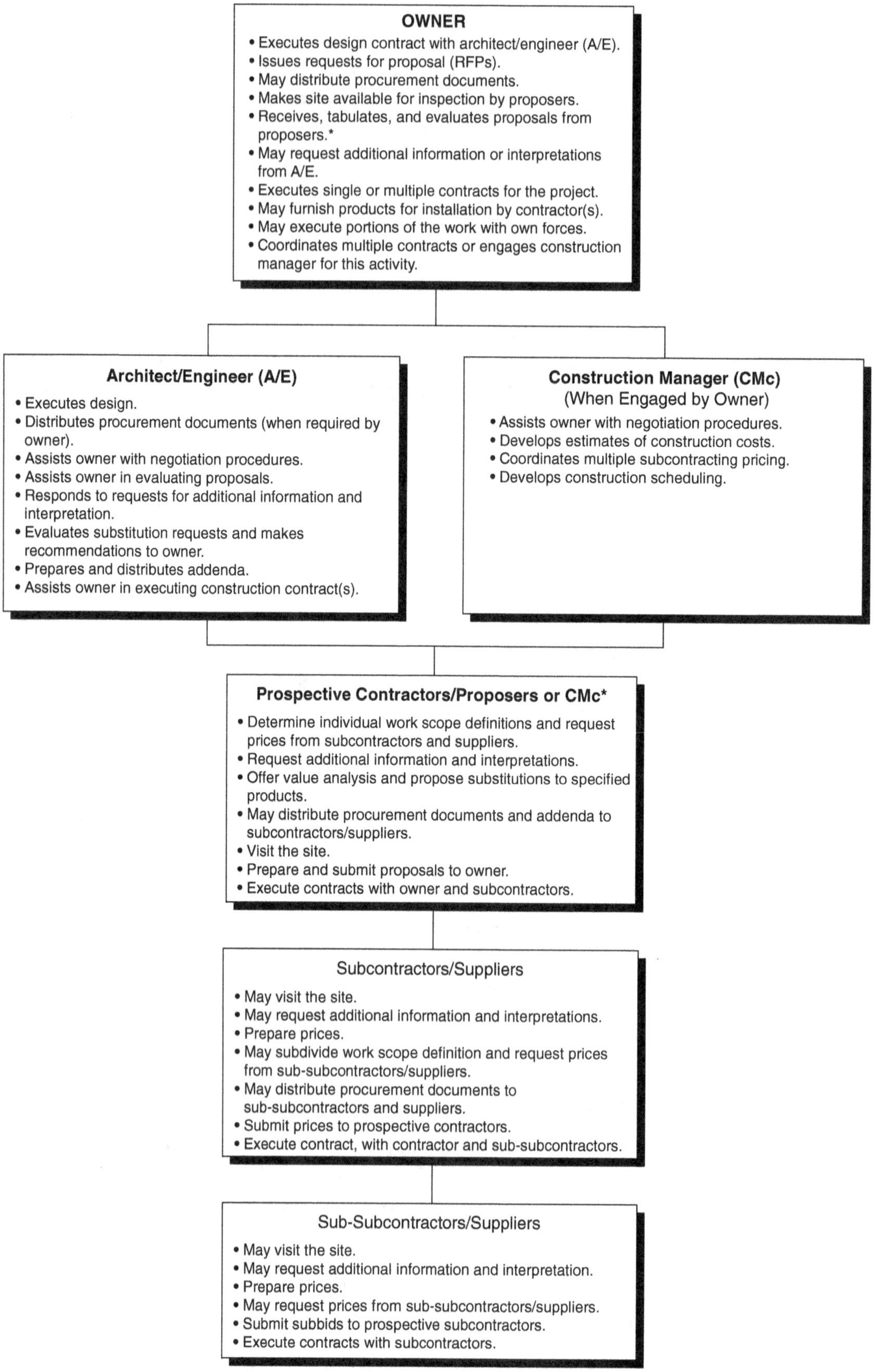

OWNER
- Executes design contract with architect/engineer (A/E).
- Issues requests for proposal (RFPs).
- May distribute procurement documents.
- Makes site available for inspection by proposers.
- Receives, tabulates, and evaluates proposals from proposers.*
- May request additional information or interpretations from A/E.
- Executes single or multiple contracts for the project.
- May furnish products for installation by contractor(s).
- May execute portions of the work with own forces.
- Coordinates multiple contracts or engages construction manager for this activity.

Architect/Engineer (A/E)
- Executes design.
- Distributes procurement documents (when required by owner).
- Assists owner with negotiation procedures.
- Assists owner in evaluating proposals.
- Responds to requests for additional information and interpretation.
- Evaluates substitution requests and makes recommendations to owner.
- Prepares and distributes addenda.
- Assists owner in executing construction contract(s).

Construction Manager (CMc)
(When Engaged by Owner)
- Assists owner with negotiation procedures.
- Develops estimates of construction costs.
- Coordinates multiple subcontracting pricing.
- Develops construction scheduling.

Prospective Contractors/Proposers or CMc*
- Determine individual work scope definitions and request prices from subcontractors and suppliers.
- Request additional information and interpretations.
- Offer value analysis and propose substitutions to specified products.
- May distribute procurement documents and addenda to subcontractors/suppliers.
- Visit the site.
- Prepare and submit proposals to owner.
- Execute contracts with owner and subcontractors.

Subcontractors/Suppliers
- May visit the site.
- May request additional information and interpretations.
- Prepare prices.
- May subdivide work scope definition and request prices from sub-subcontractors/suppliers.
- May distribute procurement documents to sub-subcontractors and suppliers.
- Submit prices to prospective contractors.
- Execute contract, with contractor and sub-subcontractors.

Sub-Subcontractors/Suppliers
- May visit the site.
- May request additional information and interpretation.
- Prepare prices.
- May request prices from sub-subcontractors/suppliers.
- Submit subbids to prospective subcontractors.
- Execute contracts with subcontractors.

Figure 12.2
Pricing under Design-Negotiate-Build Project Delivery

*Note: The owner may negotiate with more than one prospective contractor simultaneously.

```
┌─────────────────────────────────────────────┐
│                   OWNER                       │
│ • Issues request for proposal (RFP) to        │
│   design-builder.                             │
│ • Executes design-build agreement with        │
│   design-builder.                             │
│ • Makes site available for inspection by      │
│   participants.                               │
│ • Receives, tabulates, and evaluates proposal │
│   from design-builder.                        │
│ • May request additional information or       │
│   interpretations from design-builder.        │
└─────────────────────────────────────────────┘
                      │
┌─────────────────────────────────────────────┐
│               DESIGN-BUILDER                  │
│ • Responds to owner's RFP.                     │
│ • Prepares design based on owner's program     │
│   and budget requirements.                     │
│ • Visits the site.                             │
│ • Conducts pre-proposal meeting with           │
│   prospective subcontractors and suppliers.    │
│ • Determine individual work scope definitions  │
│   and distributes pricing documents to         │
│   subcontractors and suppliers.                │
│ • Responds to requests for interpretation from │
│   owner, subcontractors, and suppliers.        │
│ • Prepares and distributes modifications to    │
│   owner, subcontractors and suppliers.         │
│ • Requests prices from subcontractors and      │
│   suppliers.                                   │
│ • Executes contracts with subcontractors and   │
│   suppliers.                                   │
│ • Proposes pricing changes to owner.           │
│ • Modifies design to comply with the owner's   │
│   budget.                                      │
└─────────────────────────────────────────────┘
                      │
┌─────────────────────────────────────────────┐
│           Subcontractors/Suppliers            │
│ • May visit the site.                          │
│ • May request additional information and       │
│   interpretations.                             │
│ • Attend pre-proposal meeting convened by      │
│   design-builder.                              │
│ • Prepare prices.                              │
│ • May sub-divide work scope definition and     │
│   request prices from sub-subcontractors/      │
│   suppliers.                                   │
│ • May distribute pricing documents to          │
│   sub-subcontractors and suppliers.            │
│ • Submit prices to design-builder.             │
│ • Execute contract with design-builder and     │
│   sub-subcontractors.                          │
└─────────────────────────────────────────────┘
                      │
┌─────────────────────────────────────────────┐
│         Sub-Subcontractors/Suppliers          │
│ • May visit the site.                          │
│ • May request additional information and       │
│   interpretation.                              │
│ • May attend pre-proposal meeting convened by  │
│   design-builder.                              │
│ • Prepare prices.                              │
│ • May request prices from sub-subcontractors/  │
│   suppliers.                                   │
│ • Submit prices to prospective subcontractors. │
│ • Execute contract with sub-contractor.        │
└─────────────────────────────────────────────┘
```

Figure 12.3
Pricing under Design-Build Project Delivery

design phases, the cost of the work develops and evolves along with the project design. Identified as the buyout phase, advantages include the following:

- The owner, design, contractor, and supplier teams can interact before the construction documents are completed to make decisions and commitments about the design that have cost implications.

- Decisions can be made and orders placed for materials, products, and equipment that require long lead times.

- The buyout phase can be managed better because of the team interactions and extended time for making effective decisions.

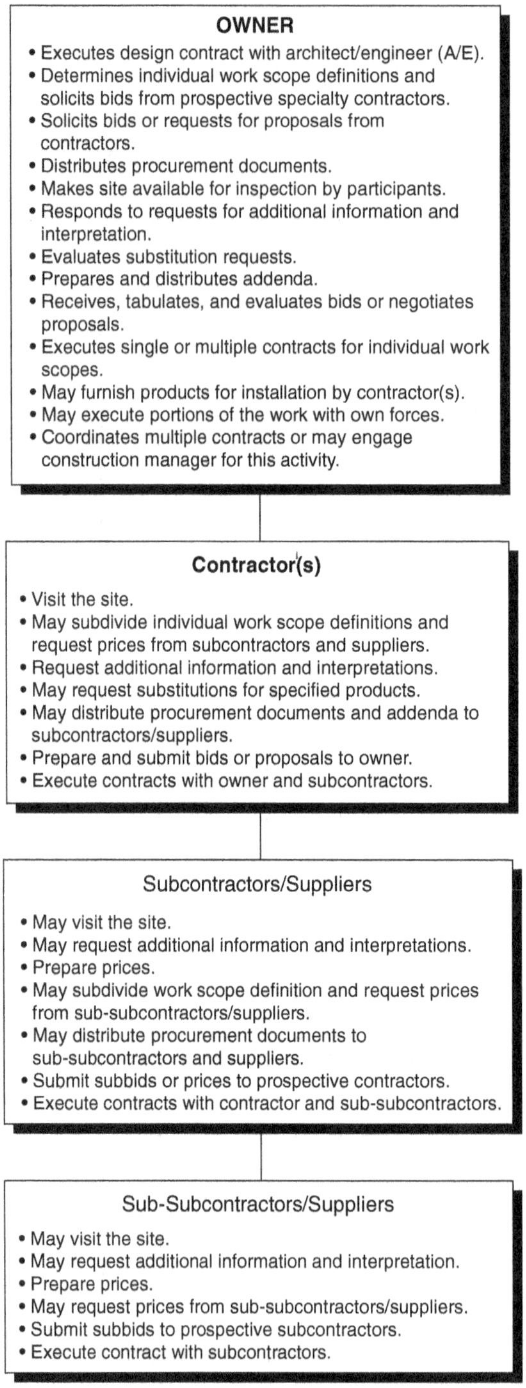

OWNER
- Executes design contract with architect/engineer (A/E).
- Determines individual work scope definitions and solicits bids from prospective specialty contractors.
- Solicits bids or requests for proposals from contractors.
- Distributes procurement documents.
- Makes site available for inspection by participants.
- Responds to requests for additional information and interpretation.
- Evaluates substitution requests.
- Prepares and distributes addenda.
- Receives, tabulates, and evaluates bids or negotiates proposals.
- Executes single or multiple contracts for individual work scopes.
- May furnish products for installation by contractor(s).
- May execute portions of the work with own forces.
- Coordinates multiple contracts or may engage construction manager for this activity.

Contractor(s)
- Visit the site.
- May subdivide individual work scope definitions and request prices from subcontractors and suppliers.
- Request additional information and interpretations.
- May request substitutions for specified products.
- May distribute procurement documents and addenda to subcontractors/suppliers.
- Prepare and submit bids or proposals to owner.
- Execute contracts with owner and subcontractors.

Subcontractors/Suppliers
- May visit the site.
- May request additional information and interpretations.
- Prepare prices.
- May subdivide work scope definition and request prices from sub-subcontractors/suppliers.
- May distribute procurement documents to sub-subcontractors and suppliers.
- Submit subbids or prices to prospective contractors.
- Execute contracts with contractor and sub-subcontractors.

Sub-Subcontractors/Suppliers
- May visit the site.
- May request additional information and interpretation.
- Prepare prices.
- May request prices from sub-subcontractors/suppliers.
- Submit subbids to prospective subcontractors.
- Execute contract with subcontractors.

Figure 12.4
Pricing under Owner-Build Project Delivery

12.6 Project Information

An important pricing activity is exchanging complete project information. Each participant requires graphic and written documents upon which the price, and ultimately the contract for construction, will be based. The information must be complete and timely so participants can fulfill their pricing activities efficiently. Project information must be available to prospective contractors, subcontractors, suppliers, and other participants who contribute to the pricing process.

12.6.1 Distribution of Information

Methods of distributing project information include:

- Distributing to prospective contractors from the owner's or architect/engineer's (A/E's) offices
- Distributing to prospective subcontractors and suppliers from the prospective contractor's offices
- Distributing through construction trade associations
- Distributing through plan rooms
- Distributing through construction reporting services
- Distributing through subscription information services
- Use of project web sites and extranets
- Purchasing documents from document reproduction services

Depending upon the owner's and A/E's policies, documents may be distributed in printed form, reproducible media form, or electronic form. Normally, the owner assumes the cost of document reproduction and distribution. Refundable deposits may be charged to prospective participants who obtain document sets. Nonrefundable fees may be charged to prospective participants to offset the owner's reproduction costs; however, this might discourage participation.

For projects with a large number of potential participants, deposits are normally required to ensure that (1) only participants who intend to complete pricing activities request the documents and (2) documents are returned after pricing activities are complete, ensuring that the owner will have a sufficient supply of document sets to distribute to the contractor who will execute the work.

Attempting to defray or transfer document reproduction or costs to another participant can have an adverse effect on pricing because it increases the possibility that complete sets of documents are not being reproduced for all participants.

The speed and efficiency of information exchange have been enhanced by electronic tools. Although they might not fully supplant printed documents, electronic documents are rapidly becoming the primary means of information exchange in the design and construction industry. In the context of pricing, the major advantages of electronic transfer of project information are:

- Cost savings compared to traditional forms of exchange, including document reproduction and distribution (mailing) cost
- Time savings in transfer
- Enhanced ability to transfer complete sets of documents, reducing the possibility of incomplete pricing

12.6.2 Control of Information

For procurement (bidding/negotiating/purchasing) procedures to be fair and effective, project information is carefully managed to ensure that all participants receive project information complete and in time to perform their pricing procedures efficiently and accurately.

To overcome the potential misuse or loss of project information, the A/E and owner should have an information control plan in effect at the beginning of the procurement (bidding/negotiating/purchasing) stage. Such a plan should:

- Support the owner's disclosure and privacy policies related to the project
- Establish which reporting and document distribution services will be used
- Provide a system of quality controls on project information before it is issued to the participants
- Provide supplemental project information in a timely manner to participants
- Ensure the integrity of project information by exchanging it in secure forms, such as paper documents or read-only electronic formats
- Ensure that oral inquiries and information are documented

12.7 Bidding

12.7.1 General Considerations

In competitive bidding, prospective contractors are invited to prepare and submit bids stating, in a specified format, the sum of money and sometimes the length of time required to execute the project. It is a method of determining the lowest cost for accomplishing work defined by the procurement documents. The objective of competitive bidding is to ensure that the cost of the project is reasonable and consistent with prevailing conditions in the construction industry.

Competitive bidding occurs at multiple levels. In response to a bid solicitation from an owner, a prospective contractor solicits bids for portions of the project from a group of subcontractors and suppliers, either preselected or at large. In competitively bidding a complex project, the subcontractors and suppliers in turn may solicit bids from sub-subcontractors and suppliers. Theoretically, the tiers of competitive bidding are limited only by the project requirements. A bid states the price that the bidder will charge to perform the work and possibly the length of time to complete the work. Competitive bids from the prospective contractors are prepared confidentially by each bidder, sealed, and submitted to the owner to be examined and compared.

In publicly funded projects, the owner is normally required to award a contract to the lowest responsible and responsive bidder (i.e., the prospective contractor with the lowest price whose bid is also in complete conformance with the procurement documents). In private projects, however, the owner may rank any criteria including qualifications, experience, financial condition, and performance history in determining the most qualified bid.

A fundamental principle of the competitive bidding process is that bidders receive fair consideration by bidding on an identical basis. By soliciting bids, the owner states the procurement requirements and implies a question: "Who will do this work for the least cost?" This is a reasonable question and should receive a straightforward answer: the bidder implies, "I will do the work for $X million." Both question and answer are impersonal and unconditional.

12.7.1.1 Competitive Bidding Participants

The participants common to public and private competitive bidding include:

- Owner
- A/E
- Prospective contractors
- Prospective subcontractors and suppliers

Additional participants might be involved depending on the project delivery method, the project complexity, and the owner's administrative requirements.

12.7.1.2 Qualifications of Prospective Contractors

Some owners might request information regarding the skills and financial stability of prospective contractors. This is known as a request for qualifications (RFQ). AIA Document A305, Contractor's Qualification Statement, published by the American Institute of Architects (AIA) can be used to respond to this request. The Engineers Joint Contract Documents Committee (EJCDC) does not publish a contractor qualification form but endorses the use of Associated General Contractors of America (AGC) Document 221, Standard Questionnaires and Financial Statement for Bidders (for Engineering Construction).

Important qualification criteria for prospective contractors include:

- *Experience.* All projects require that the work be executed efficiently, by personnel trained in the type of work required. Experience is ascertained by evaluating the contractor's performance record on similar projects, which can be substantiated by references.
- *Special Training and Certification or Licensing.* Contractors might be required to have special training and licensing to perform certain work procedures. Examples include hazardous material abatement, life safety systems, elevators, electrical, and mechanical work, as well as work underwater or in confined spaces.
- *Personnel.* Project supervision and coordination, submittal procedures, payment procedures, contract modifications, and contract closeout procedures are contractors' qualifications required to execute administrative procedures for the project. The contractor's staff should be of sufficient size to administer and perform the work of the project efficiently and in accordance with the owner's schedule requirements.
- *Specialized Equipment.* Some projects might require special equipment for proper execution of the work.
- *Financial Stability.* Financial statements reveal the likelihood of the contractor to remain financially solvent for the duration of the project and avoid liens, bankruptcy, and other disruptive financial occurrences that affect the project schedule. This may include the bond limits and business rating.
- *History of Claims and Disputes.* Claims and disputes records provide the owner with important information about the way that a contractor conducts business.

Instructions to bidders define the general qualification criteria for prospective contractors. Special qualifications and supporting documentation for manufacturers, fabricators, and installers are specified in quality assurance articles of applicable specification sections. Prospective contractors may also develop similar qualification requirements for prospective subcontractors and suppliers.

12.7.1.3   Competitive Bidding Activities

Activities performed by participants during competitive bidding include:

- Bid solicitation to inform the prospective bidders about the project
- Distribution of procurement documents
- Prebid meetings to inform bidders and subbidders about the procurement and contracting requirements and project conditions
- Requests for interpretation from the owner or bidders
- Substitution requests
- Responses to requests for interpretations
- Addenda
- Pricing procedures
- Preparation of bids and supplements
- Submittal of bids
- Bid opening
- Evaluation of bids for compliance with requirements
- Bid tabulation
- Value analysis if bids exceed the established project budget
- Notification
- Award of contracts

12.7.1.4   Procurement Documents

Procurement activities require documents to communicate project information to the bidder and move the process to award of a contract. Before bids can be submitted, prospective contractors must be made aware of the project and sufficient information must be provided. They need specific information to enable them to:

- Understand procurement and contracting requirements.
- Comply with formal competitive bidding procedures.
- Understand conditions that apply after bid submittal and prior to contract award.

The procurement documents that provide this information include:

- Procurement requirements such as:
  - Bid solicitation
  - Instructions to bidders
  - Available information: subsurface investigations, surveys, records, and resource drawings
  - Bid forms and supplements
  - Addenda
- Contracting requirements such as:
  - Contracting forms
  - Conditions of the contract
- Specifications
- Drawings

Of these documents, the contracting requirements, specifications, drawings, and addenda become contract documents when the owner-contractor agreement is executed.

12.7.1.5 Establishing a Competitive Bidding Period

The extent of the project influences the length of time that is allowed for the preparation of bids. Although the length of the bidding period varies from project to project, all projects should allow sufficient time for participants to:

- Study the procurement documents including available information
- Attend a prebid meeting to obtain an introduction to the project and existing project conditions
- Visit the site to verify existing conditions and correlate the information in the documents with firsthand observations
- Make inquiries regarding existing conditions and the procurement documents
- Propose substitutions when permitted by the procurement documents
- Receive addenda resulting from bidder inquiries and substitution proposals
- Solicit, evaluate, and compile prices from subcontractors and suppliers
- Obtain bid security when required by the procurement requirements
- Prepare qualification statements when required by the procurement requirements
- Tabulate and submit bids within the designated time

The competitive bidding stage should allow a reasonable amount of time to perform these procedures and activities. Bidding periods for public projects must be structured according to prescribed time periods to ensure the activities are performed according to prevailing laws. Although private projects are not subject to the same restrictions as public projects, the length of the competitive bidding stage might affect the accuracy and number of bids submitted. The A/E should advise the owner about the activities of a well-structured bidding period.

12.7.1.6 Prebid Meeting

The prebid meeting, normally convened at the site, allows the owner, A/E, and consultants to orient the prospective contractors to conditions affecting the project. The owner may make attendance a mandatory condition of competitive bidding. The A/E normally prepares an agenda for this meeting, which includes the following points:

- A summary description of the project
- Availability of the site for examination
- Project time and phasing requirements
- Goals based on Minority Business Enterprise (MBE) participation and the Green Building rating system being applied
- Special pricing requirements, including allowances, alternates, and unit prices
- Distribution of contract documents (verify that all entities have complete and current sets)
- Work restrictions
- Communication protocol

- Use of the site during construction: storage facilities, parking, offices, temporary facilities and controls, staging, daily cleaning, waste management, security, working hours
- Owner's concurrent operations at the site (if applicable)

The date, time, and location of the prebid meeting is documented in the bid solicitation. The A/E should record and distribute the proceedings of the prebid meeting. Because meeting proceedings are not procurement or contract documents, oral interpretations and new information exchanged at this meeting should be documented in an addendum.

12.7.1.7 Substitution Requests

To preserve fair and open competition in the construction marketplace, substitution requirements for public projects are generally less restrictive than in privately funded projects. Therefore, with few exceptions, bidders and subbidders may propose substitutions for most components, subsystems, and systems during the competitive bidding stage in accordance with the instructions to bidders. The A/E needs a reasonable period of time to evaluate substitutions. If a substitution is adjudged acceptable, the A/E will issue an addendum to incorporate the substitution into the procurement documents so that it can be bid as an acceptable equivalent to comparable specified products.

12.7.1.8 Addenda

Addenda are issued prior to receipt of bids unless permitted to be issued prior to the time the agreement is executed by the procurement requirements for the project. Addenda clarify, revise, add to, or delete information in the procurement documents or in previous addenda. They are used to answer questions proposed by bidders; document new requirements, including changes to the work; and correct errors or omissions in procurement documents. Examples of addenda modifications include:

- Changing the date, time, or location of receipt of bids
- Adding to, deleting from, or revising procurement documents
- Including additional qualified products or approved substitutions

Administrative requirements for addenda, the method of issue, and other pertinent facts concerning addenda are included in the instructions to bidders and acknowledged on the bid form.

Addenda requirements applicable to the contract documents will be incorporated into the contract between the owner and contractor. Addenda must be issued to bidders in sufficient time for use in preparing bids.

12.7.1.9 Subcontractor and Supplier Bids

Unless a project is small or limited, it will require the participation of subcontractors and suppliers. Because most work is performed by subcontractors, most pricing for individual work components is prepared at the subcontractor level. Subcontractors are affected financially by the same pricing considerations as contractors. Their prices are based on the materials and labor required for their individual portions of work, as well as bonding requirements, contingencies for unknown risk factors, and other applicable factors previously described. In addition, subcontractors may solicit bids for portions of their work from sub-subcontractors and suppliers. Subcontractor prices may have stipulations on how long they will be honored without modification or withdrawal.

Contractors and subcontractors share responsibilities for basing prices on complete project information. Each subcontractor should understand its responsibilities regarding the procurement documents, not merely those applicable to its trade. The requirements of a specification section or division can be impacted significantly by requirements in other portions of the procurement documents, including the following:

- The conditions of the contract define insurance requirements, permits, taxes, and other contractual responsibilities.
- Division 01 requirements describe the work covered by the contract documents, alternates, allowances, unit prices, project administration and coordination, submittals, temporary facilities and controls, and contract closeout. Requirements, such as hoisting, can have an impact on costs. Other requirements affect overhead and profit and might necessitate the need for some form of price breakdown or unit costs.
- Work described in other specification sections and on drawings affects the work of the subcontractor's trade.

Subcontractors and suppliers prepare their prices based on their

- Project-specific requirements
- Special knowledge of individual products, subsystems, and systems
- Present contracted workload
- Experience on projects involving the prime contractors to whom they are bidding
- Experience on projects involving the owner of the project
- Experience on projects designed by the A/E

Whereas bids to the owner are submitted formally, subcontractor prices are sometimes submitted to prospective contractors informally (e.g., orally) to save time and are later formalized with written quotations. Figure 12.5 is an example of a subcontractor/supplier bid form that can be used to formalize a subcontractor's bid.

12.7.1.10 Preparing Competitive Bids

In the hours immediately preceding competitive bidding deadlines, numerous subbids, both solicited and unsolicited, are transmitted to the prospective contractors offices. The prospective contractor must quickly evaluate each subbid for its completeness and consider the qualifications of subcontractors and suppliers. The scope might vary between subbidders and might be based on a specific trade, a designated portion of the project, or certain documents. The contractor must ensure that the subbidders account for their responsibilities under the procurement documents. Subbidders might not have complete project information. Successful contractors maintain checklists to verify the completeness and accuracy of the subbids they receive. Items requiring verification include products, accessories, connections, hoisting, taxes, freight, required alternates, and the number of addenda received.

Some subbidders will withhold their prices until the final moments before the deadline to ensure that their price is not used to obtain a lower price from another subbidder.

Knowledge for Creating
and Sustaining
the Built Environment

SUBCONTRACTOR
SUPPLIER BID FORM

Project Location: _____

Bidder's Name/Address: _____
_____

Bid Due Date/Time: _____

Contractor's License #: _____
Tel: _____

Fax: _____

Bid Submitted To: _____

Mobile: _____

Pager: _____

E-Mail: _____

Acknowledgments:

Per Procurement Document: ☐ Yes   ☐ No — Identify Exceptions in Special Notes below

Addenda Received: ☐ #1   ☐ #2   ☐ #3   ☐ #4   ☐ #5   ☐ _____

Complete: ☐ Yes   ☐ No

Furnish Only: ☐ Yes   ☐ No   ☐ Some — List Specifics in Special Notes below.

Install Only: ☐ Yes   ☐ No   ☐ Some — List Specifics in Special Notes below.

Permits & Fees Included: ☐ Yes   ☐ No   ☐ Some — List Specifics in Special Notes below.

Certifications: ☐ WBE   ☐ DBE   ☐ MBE   ☐ ESB   ☐ _____

Bondable: ☐ Yes   ☐ No   ☐ N/A   Cost _____

Bid Valid For: _____ Days

Scope:

Bid Amounts:

Section	Base Bid (+/–)	Alt #	Alt #	Alt #	Alt #	Alt #

Unit Prices:

Description	Quantity	Unit Price	Extension

**Exclusions/
Clarifications:**

**Special Notes/
Conditions/
Allowances:**

Signed by: _____   Date: _____

Title: _____

Page _____ of _____

Form Version: June 2004
CSI Form 1.5B

Figure 12.5   CSI Form 1.5B, Subcontractor-Supplier Bid Form

Knowledge for Creating
and Sustaining
the Built Environment

SUBCONTRACTOR
SUPPLIER BID FORM

(Instructions)

1	**Project/Location:**		Identify the project name and location (exactly as listed in the bidding documents).
2	**Bid Due Date/Time:**		Insert the bid due date and time (exactly as Inserted in the bidding documents), including all addenda.
3	**Bidder's Name/Address:**		Insert the complete legal company name, street address or PO box, city, state & zip code of the firm submitting the bid.
4	**Contractor's License #:**		Insert current contractor's license number. If more than one contractor's license, insert the one that will be pertinent for the project being bid on.
5	**Tel:**		Insert the primary office phone number for the firm quoting.
6	**Fax:**		Insert the primary fax phone number for the firm quoting.
7	**Mobile:**		Insert the mobile number for the primary contact person submitting the bid or N/A (Not Applicable).
8	**Pager:**		Insert the pager number for the primary contact person submitting this bid or N/A (Not Applicable).
9	**E-mail:**		Insert the company's e-mail here, if any.
10	**Bid Submitted To:**		Insert the name of the company you are submitting your bid to, including person's name or dept.
11	**Acknowledgments:**	Per Procurement Documents:	Indicate Yes or No. If No, list exceptions in "Special Notes."
		Addenda Received:	Check all addenda received by the subcontractor firm.
		Complete:	Indicate Yes or No. If No, go to "Install Only" or "Furnish Only."
		Install Only:	Indicate Yes, No, or Some. If Some, list specifics in "Special Notes."
		Furnish Only:	Indicate Yes, No, or Some. If Some, list specifics in "Special Notes."
		Permits & Fees Included:	Indicate Yes, No, or Some. If Some, list specifics in "Special Notes."
		Certifications:	List any special certifications the quoting firm has.
		WBE:	Woman-Owned Business Enterprise
		DBE:	Disadvantaged Business Enterprise
		MBE:	Minority-Owned Business Enterprise
		ESB:	Emerging Small Business
		OTHER:	List any other certification(s) that may be pertinent but are not listed above. This would also be the area to identify whether your firm is union, non-union, or has any special qualifications pertinent to performing the work that has been quoted.
		Bondable:	This refers to payment and performance bond. Indicate N/A, Yes, or No. If Yes, indicate the cost, either as a $ figure or percentage of the total amount quoted. If nothing is marked, it will be presumed your firm can provide a payment and performance bond, if requested to do so.
		Bid Valid For ____ Days:	If the quoted bid is only valid for a specific period of time, enter the number of days the bid will be valid.
12	**Scope:**		Specifically identify the exact scope of work that is being quoted.
13	**Bid Amounts:**		Indicate the section number (as identified in the bidding documents), the base bid ($), and the alternate amount ($) for each alternate, if applicable. Clearly indicate whether alternate is additive or deductive.
14	**Unit Prices:**		Indicate the description of the item(s), quantity, if applicable, unit price and extension for any items that have been identified as unit price items.
15	**Exclusions/Clarifications:**		Specifically list any items excluded from your quote and/or clarify any items you feel are not clearly stated in all of the aforementioned steps. This is a very important step — if exclusions are NOT noted, your bid will be construed to include everything necessary to do the work complete, as identified in #12 above.
16	**Special Notes/ Conditions/ Allowances:**		List any special notes, conditions that your quote is based upon or expand on any information that may have been listed in #11 above requiring further information. If the bid requires any allowances, this is the area to list them.
17	**By:**		The person who has binding authority for the firm submitting the bid must sign here.
18	**Title:**		Insert the title of the person whose signature appears on this form.
19	**Date:**		Insert the date the bid is submitted here.

Page _____ of _____

Form Version: June 2004
CSI Form 1.5B

Figure 12.5 *(continued)*

This type of negotiating is the unethical practice referred to as bid shopping. In bid shopping the contractor asks subbidders to reevaluate their prices and find ways to lower them. This reduces the incentive for the product suppliers and installer to furnish materials and workmanship of the documented quality.

Once all of the subbids and supplier bids have been received and included with other pricing, such as work performed directly with the contractor's own forces, they are tabulated and filled in on the bid form.

12.7.1.11 Submitting Bids

The submission of the bid is one of the most important steps in the competitive bidding procedure. Given the time constraints related to construction pricing, many bidders are forced to finalize their bids with little time to spare before the deadline. Therefore, the final bid information may be communicated to an individual waiting near the location designated for receipt of bids. This individual receives the final numbers and information and completes the bid form. The bid is then sealed and deposited at the required location prior to the bid due date and time for receipt.

If a bid is submitted to the owner after the established deadline, it is sufficient cause for complete rejection of the bid, especially in public projects. A late bid is one that is submitted at any time following the official bid due date or time stated in the procurement documents. Bids that are received late should be marked accordingly and not opened. They may be returned to the bidder. Therefore, prospective contractors must follow procedures and ensure their bids are submitted on time.

A prospective contractor may be allowed to withdraw a bid before the established time for receipt of bids, but not after it has been received, unless the owner consents to the withdrawal. The instructions to bidders should state the time period in which the bid shall be held open by the prospective contractors for acceptance, and this period of time may be irrevocable. Once this period has elapsed, a prospective contractor may withdraw a bid without penalty. In two commonly used sets of documents published by the AIA and EJCDC, this time period is handled differently. AIA Document A701, Instructions to Bidders, does not state the time period; therefore, it should be identified in the supplementary instructions to bidders written to modify AIA Document A701. EJCDC uses the time period of 35 days in EJCDC C-200, Guide to the Preparation of Instructions to Bidders. Therefore, if this time period is to be changed, coordination is required among the other EJCDC documents since it is mentioned in various documents of the series.

Normally, once a prospective contractor has withdrawn a bid, that contractor is not permitted to submit another bid for the same project. Bid irregularities may be cause for a bid to be rejected and not considered for award.

12.7.1.12 Bid Depository

Bid depositories have been established in several states for use on publicly funded projects and, depending on location, may be either a voluntary or a mandatory procedure. The bid depository system was developed to improve the reliability of bids and to reduce potential unethical bidding practices. A bid depository system receives subcontractor bids for identified units of work. The units of work are usually significant parts of the total project. These subbids, depending on location, are then either analyzed by the client agency with the selected subbids assigned to the general contractor, or the subbids may simply be deposited for delivery to the prime bidders.

The bid depository system was also developed to ensure fairness and impartiality in subcontract bidding and to prevent a subbidder from being forced to reduce a bid quotation after it has been submitted. Bid depository systems are usually managed by local construction associations and usually include all of the major subcontract trades. Practice varies with the locality, so inquiries should be made to local construction associations for information.

The bid depositories usually receive subbids several days before the project bid date. For states that allow the prime bidder to select the subbids, this procedure allows the prime bidder sufficient time to review the subbids and to be sure that all required items are covered. This procedure also allows the prime bidder time to investigate the capabilities of the subbidders that the prime contractor has not employed on previous projects.

12.7.1.13 Evaluating Bids

Because it is more than a statement of price, a bid should be carefully reviewed, compared with other bids, and evaluated by experienced participants to determine compliance with the owner's requirements. Prior to reviewing and evaluating bids, the participants (normally the owner and the A/E) should review the instructions to bidders to ensure that the evaluation is a fair and equitable process. Points of bid review include:

- *Timeliness.* The bids should be submitted to the owner (or other designated participant) on or before the date and time established in the procurement requirements. The participant responsible for receiving bids should have a method of indicating the date and time that bids are received and keep them in a secure location until the designated time of bid opening. Bids received after the deadline, or in a manner not conforming to the procurement requirements, should not be opened or considered and should be clearly identified as not conforming.
- *Completeness.* All blank spaces on the bid form should be filled in according to the instructions to bidders, and the bid form should be duly signed by an individual who is authorized to conduct major business transactions for the prospective contractor. A bid form that describes multiple scopes of work should allow the bidder to bid only the scopes of work within its expertise, with all remaining scope provisions clearly marked as not applicable. Blanks not filled in or not otherwise acknowledged indicate that a bidder has not been responsive to all of the procurement requirements. In addition, all required bid form supplements, which can be extensive for some projects, should be attached to the bid in the sequence requested, with all requested information, authorizations, and signatures provided. When bid security is required, the security should be provided in the manner described in the instructions to bidders. Failure of the bidder to provide all required bid form supplements and security indicates that the bidder is not responsible and responsive. Responsive and responsible are important concepts and are the basis of acceptance or rejection of bids.
  - The bidder is responsive, meaning that the bidder has filled in all of the blanks on the bid form, has complied with the instructions to bidders, and has submitted all required bid supplements.
  - The bidder is responsible, meaning that there are no legal judgments against the bidder that would preclude competitively bidding the project and the bidder is financially solvent.

- *Variance from the Construction Budget.* Except in unusual economic circumstances, bids should be close to the established construction budget. Often, however, one or more bids might be significantly higher or lower than estimates, indicating possible errors. An inordinately low bid is especially problematic for the owner because the bidding contractor might experience financial problems and possibly default if the bid contains a substantial error and is accepted. And, although a private owner may reject a bid for any reason without legal consequences, a public owner must have a clear justification for such a rejection or the owner might face a legal challenge by the bidding contractor.
- *Competitive Bidding Irregularities.* Instructions to bidders should state the manner in which bidding irregularities will affect the acceptability of competitive bids. Material irregularities are normally a cause for rejection of a bid, whereas irregularities of an insignificant nature may not be cause for rejection. Competitive bidding irregularities include:
  - *Material Irregularities.* These are significant irregularities that result in sufficient cause for rejection of a bid. A material irregularity may include one or a combination of the following:
    - Submission of an incomplete, altered, obsolete, or unauthorized bid form
    - Absence of required bid form supplements
    - Absence of required bid security, or incorrect form or amount of bid security
    - Exclusion of work or limitations of bids
  - *Bid discrepancies*, as when statements filled in by the prospective contractor are at variance with other statements, such as a difference between the bid stated in numbers and the bid stated in words
  - *Nonrequired attachments*, such as information that was not required, which is attached to the bid. These might or might not affect the acceptability of a bid, depending upon the nature of the attachment. Bid limitations (e.g., statements of what a bid does not include) might disqualify a bid, whereas an unsolicited statement of a bidder's skills and experience might not.

The instructions to bidders should define the manner in which bids will be opened and evaluated and to whom the results will be reported. Private bid openings may be conducted at the owner's discretion, and bidding irregularities may be considered or waived according to the owner's judgment. Most public bids are required to be opened publicly, the rules regarding irregularities strictly followed, and the results reported to all bidders and the general public.

The time required for thorough review of bids and supplements varies according to the following factors:

- Bid form's complexity
- Number of required supplements
- Number of bids received

Therefore, the time between review of bids and determining the actual results varies from project to project.

Collusion in competitive bidding occurs when multiple participants attempt to unlawfully control the results of bidding by agreeing to fix construction prices at a level above fair market values to establish high profit margins or to ensure that a predetermined prospective contractor is awarded a contract. To discourage collusion, many public owners and some private owners require noncollusion affidavits to be submitted with bids.

12.7.2 Public Competitive Bidding Process

The traditional project delivery method in public projects is D-B-B with or without the involvement of construction managers, although D-B methods are growing to answer rising public demand to ensure cost within established budget and to prevent cost overruns.

12.7.2.1 Competitive Bidding Participants

The primary participants in D-B-B public projects include the following:

- Owner/public entity
- Construction managers
- A/E and consultants
- Contractors and subcontractors
- Supplier team participants
- Secondary participants, including sureties and insurers

12.7.2.2 General Characteristics of Public Projects

Most public funds are raised from taxes and public bond issues; however, private donations and grants might also be sources of public project funding. To preserve the public's rights, laws have significant restrictions on who may bid a public project and, except when a bid is obviously in error or the bidder cannot meet the specified qualifications, the lowest bid must be accepted. The public mandate requires contracting the project for the lowest available price. However, significant administrative resources may be expended by the owner and A/E in enforcing the project requirements when construction is procured in this manner. Nevertheless, the risk is open and obvious and should be anticipated by expressing appropriate contractor qualification requirements in the procurement documents.

Procurement and contracting requirements for public projects are more formal and subject to public scrutiny than privately funded projects. Public bidding is governed by the laws of the public authority controlling the project. The restrictions cannot be waived or modified for a participant's convenience. Changes in the restrictions must be made through formal legislative-administrative procedures.

Public projects can be initiated by the owner at the local, county, state, and federal levels:

- Local includes legally incorporated villages, parishes, townships, cities, and counties.
- State includes departments of education, transportation, utilities, and administrative services controlled by the state executive and legislative branches. State universities controlled by state boards of regents are also included in this category.
- Federal includes departments controlled by the federal government including the Departments of Defense (DOD); Housing and Urban Development (HUD); Transportation; the Interior; Health, Education and Welfare; Veterans Affairs (VA); and Homeland Security.

The source of public funds can be one or a combination of these levels of public authority. The laws of each level may govern a project, whether or not funding is provided by each level. The laws governing the public bidding processes normally become successively more restrictive when state or federal funds are wholly or partly involved.

12.7.2.3   Contractor Qualifications for Public Projects

Except in cases of highly specialized projects, the public owner cannot exercise control over who is eligible to bid public projects to the extent that the private-sector owner can. The basic eligibility requirements for bidding public projects include:

- Financial responsibility
- Ability to provide the required bid security
- Ability to provide the required performance and payment bonds if awarded a contract
- Nondelinquency in matters of taxes and other obligations to the controlling public authority
- Insurability
- Work capacity and previous experience with the public authority

12.7.2.4   Multiple-Prime Contracts in Public Projects

When the estimated cost of a major portion of the work (civil work, general trades, plumbing, fire protection, and electrical) exceeds a codified amount, the owner might be obligated to solicit separate bids for that portion, to run concurrently with the work of other contracts. In such cases, one prime contractor is assigned responsibility for project management and coordination and afforded the necessary authority to carry out that responsibility with efficiency.

Requirements for public projects with multiple-prime contractors often include provisions for combined bidding to reduce project management and coordination cost. The bid form is structured to allow bidders to submit bids for more than one major category of work with the potential for cost savings and reduced administrative burdens on the participants. If a combined bid is lower than the aggregate of individual bids, a combined contract can be awarded. For example:

- Individual plumbing bid: $45,000
- Individual heating, ventilating, and air conditioning (HVAC) bid: $37,250
- Individual aggregate total: $82,250
- Combined plumbing/HVAC bid: $81,425

Multiple-prime contracting generates a greater administrative burden during procurement (bidding/negotiating/purchasing) and construction. Combined bidding preserves the multiple-prime bidding concepts while providing an opportunity for simplified bidding and contracting administration. Multiple-prime contracts are inherent in construction management project delivery including fast-track scheduling.

12.7.2.5   Procurement Documents

Because the public bidding process is open to a greater number of bidding participants than private bidding, the owner requires information to be submitted with the bids to ensure the public's interests are not compromised. Thus, the bid form for many public projects requires all or a combination of the following supplements:

- Statement of qualifications
- Tax liability status
- Proof of insurance
- Bid security
- Noncollusion affidavit
- Minority and disadvantaged business participation
- Acknowledgments (the bid form usually contains statements that the bidder must acknowledge in writing).

12.7.2.6 Bid Solicitation

Laws require that information about public projects must be made available to the public through published advertisement. A bid solicitation containing essential information about the project must appear in periodicals of general circulation at predetermined intervals prior to the bid due date so that bidders and other project participants can respond.

Bid solicitations advertisements are normally published in newspapers and by notices posted in public locations. State and federal projects are advertised in state and federal registries, also available to the public.

12.7.2.7 Receipt, Tabulation, and Review of Bids

Public bids are required to be:

- Complete, including all required bid form supplements
- Signed by an authorized signatory of the company or individual responsible for the bid
- Sealed in an opaque envelope and identified as required in the instructions to bidders
- Submitted prior to the time established for bid opening

At the established time, the bids are opened by the owner in the presence of the public, and the bid sums are read aloud. Because of this open procedure, the apparent low bidder is immediately known. However, because the owner and the A/E must carefully review and evaluate the bids and supplements to verify strict compliance with the procurement requirements, the bidder to whom a contract will ultimately be awarded might not be known for days or weeks following the bid opening.

For convenience, bids are tabulated on a prepared form for easy comparison. A bid tabulation form should identify the following:

- Bidder's name, address, and telephone
- Contract being bid
- Form of bid security provided
- Base bid
- Unit prices
- Alternates

Public bid evaluation involves review of the bid form, bid security, and supplements to ensure that all procurement requirements have been satisfied. Informalities or omissions are strictly scrutinized and can be cause for rejection of a bid. The owner and the A/E may be involved in the bid evaluation process.

Under some circumstances, the owner may wish to interview bidders to verify certain information provided with their bids, or the owner may request additional documentation if a bid form supplement is unclear on a point of information or contains a minor irregularity. For complex projects, bid evaluations might become prolonged as information is compiled and verified. Above all, bid evaluation must be objective—a fundamental principle of competitive bidding.

After the evaluation process is complete, the owner may request the A/E's recommendation and board or committee approval before determining the successful bidder—the contractor who has submitted the lowest bid and complies with all of the procurement requirements. Once the successful bidder has been determined, the results are announced to all of the bidders and the public.

12.7.2.8 Award of Public Contracts

The prospective contractor with the lowest bid is usually awarded a contract if:

- The procurement requirements have been satisfied.
- The bid does not contain technical errors.
- The bidder is responsive and responsible.
- The bid is within the funds available.

In some jurisdictions, the lowest bid must not exceed the established project budget. If all bids for a contract exceed the budget, the bids for that contract are rejected, and bid security and deposits for documents are returned to the bidders. The project may be rebid following an evaluation and remedy of the cause. Generally, three things can be done:

- Increase the budget.
- Redesign the project in a value analysis process to be within the budget.
- Abandon the project.

Many owner-A/E agreements contain provisions that require the A/E to redesign the project to comply with the established budget when required by the owner. Most owners reserve the right to reject any individual bid or all bids when it is in their best interests to do so.

12.7.2.9 Additional Considerations

Additional issues affecting competitive bidding procedures for public projects include:

- *Wage Requirements.* When the estimated cost of a public construction contract exceeds a codified minimum, contractors are required to pay wages and benefits complying with state-established requirements. Federally funded projects must comply with requirements of the U.S. Department of Labor under the mandate of the Davis-Bacon Act, 40 U.S.C. 276a Rates of Wages for Laborers and Mechanics. The wage determinations under this act closely reflect the work classifications and wage/benefit scales of the labor unions in each project jurisdiction. Wage rates are required to be updated quarterly.

- *Percentage of the Bidder's Own Labor Forces Provided.* A degree of credibility is ensured when the prospective contractor intends to provide the contractor's own labor forces to perform a percentage of the work. The instructions to bidders of many public authorities identify a minimum percentage of work the prime contractor is required to perform.
- *Minority Business Enterprise (MBE)/Disadvantaged Business Enterprise (DBE).* Public authorities might be required to set aside a percentage of a project for minority or disadvantaged business participation to ensure the goals of affirmative action are achieved. These requirements are provided by the owner and included in instructions to bidders and the conditions of the contract. Sometimes the names of eligible MBE/DBE business are provided by public agencies and included in the procurement documents as additional information.
- *Environmental Requirements.* Special environmental restrictions might apply to projects in certain areas of the United States. Applicable information should be provided by the owner.
- *Liquidated Damages.* Public procurement documents may contain provisions for liquidated damages for failure of contractor performance.
- *Incentives.* In special circumstances, public procurement documents may provide monetary incentives for early completion of a project.

12.7.3 Private Competitive Bidding Process

The private owner is not subject to the same laws and restrictions that public owners are required to follow. Therefore, the competitive bidding procedures for private projects may be as formal or informal as the owner prefers within the framework of laws governing private enterprise. However, the owner should practice fair and reasonable competitive bidding procedures to ensure that reputable contractors will participate.

In the private sector, an owner may solicit competitive bids from a limited field of prequalified bidders, which will provide assurance that the project requirements will be achieved at a reasonable, but not necessarily the lowest, cost. The risk to the private owner is that the bids might not be as competitively priced as they would be if opened to all available bidders. The more complex or greater level of skill required to complete the project, the stricter the qualifications become, thus reducing the number of qualified bidders.

The owner's contractor qualification criteria can be as objective or subjective as the owner prefers.

The number of prospective contractors competitively bidding a private project is normally fewer than for a public project of equivalent scope, so communication with the owner and A/E might also be less restrictive.

Bid openings for private projects are not required to be open to the public. Therefore, the owner's actions are not under public scrutiny. Accordingly,

- A date and time for receiving bids may not be enforced.
- When evaluating bids, the owner may waive irregularities in competitive bidding in order to award a contract to a preferred contractor.
- The owner may award a contract to a bidder other than the lowest.
- The owner may or may not publish the results of competitive bidding.
- The owner may reject any or all bids for any reason, whether or not the bids satisfy the owner's financial requirements.

However, because the invited contractors are normally selected based on their qualifications, it is unusual to award a contract to a bidder other than the lowest responsible and responsive bidder.

12.7.3.1 Competitive Bidding Participants

The participants and their specific roles in private projects are determined by the project delivery method selected by the owner. The basic set of participants includes the owner, A/E, the contractor, subcontractors, and suppliers.

12.7.3.2 Design-Build Participants

The design-builder takes the place of the A/E and contractor, who are combined in the single D-B entity. The design-builder:

- Develops the contract documents and works with the owner to establish and maintain a project budget
- Coordinates and constructs the project with subcontractors and its own forces
- Provides construction administration services

12.7.3.3 Construction Management Participants

The construction manager advises the owner, may act as agent, and may become the contractor. The construction manager:

- Develops bid packages
- Assists in obtaining bids
- Coordinates agreements for the work with separate contractors
- Coordinates phased construction or fast-track scheduling
- Participates in value analysis with the A/E and owner in design, procurement (bidding/negotiating/purchasing), and construction stages
- Shares construction administration responsibilities with the A/E

12.7.3.4 Owner-Build Participants

The owner manages the entire project by engaging design services from an A/E, obtaining a site, soliciting bids, and contracting directly with multiple trade contractors, product manufacturers, and suppliers to execute the project.

12.7.3.5 Procurement Documents

The procurement documents for private projects are similar to those applicable to public projects. Exceptions include the following:

- The bid solicitation for private projects is usually an invitation to prequalified bidders. However, the owner may wish to solicit bids from the general bidding public, in which case an advertisement is used.
- The instructions to bidders are usually brief, as the private bidding process involves fewer formal procedures than public bidding.

- The bid form and supplements may be briefer and less standardized than for public projects.

12.8 Negotiating Process

Negotiating is a process of dialog, offer, compromise, and resolution between two parties, precedent to an agreement, or contract modification. Negotiating takes the place of bidding when:

- A contract can be awarded without a formal bidding process, as in private sector construction.
- The owner and contractor have established a level of trust that makes competitive bidding unnecessary.
- The contractor meets the owner's requirements for skill, timing, and cost in constructing the project.

12.8.1 Participants

The key participants in negotiation procedures can include the:

- Owner
- A/E
- Prospective contractor or contractors

Owners may also engage in negotiation for construction with design-builders and CMcs. Contractors may negotiate subcontract agreements with subcontractors and suppliers.

12.8.2 Procurement Documents

The documents for negotiating are similar to those required for competitive bidding. They include:

- *Request for Proposal (RFP).* Like an invitation to bid, this document invites a prospective contractor to submit an offer to perform the work of a project. The RFP may contain instructions and describe the offer format and time limit in which the offer is to be submitted. The RFP may also state the types of bonds and supplemental information required of the prospective contractors at the time a formal offer is made.
- *Drawings and Specifications.* In the case of D-B project delivery, a project description and criteria requirements may be accompanied by possible schematic design prepared by the owner.
- *Offer Forms and Supplements.* Similar to a bid form, the offer form reflects the way the owner wants to receive and evaluate what prospective contractors offer.

12.8.3 Negotiation Procedures

Negotiation procedures include the following steps:

- *An RFP by One Participant to Another to Engage in a Negotiation Process.* The RFP can be written or orally communicated. The owner invites a prospective contractor to negotiate a contract for a scope of work. A contractor can also invite subcontractors to negotiate subcontracts for limited scopes of work.
- *Discovery.* Exchange of documents that will become the basis of the negotiation, including drawings, specifications, and other negotiation documents. Review of project conditions, such as the site, resource drawings, test reports, and public records.
- *Pricing Procedures.* A construction price is prepared.
- *Offer.* A prospective contractor proposes to the owner a sum of money, and in some cases a length of time, to perform the work described in the procurement documents.
- *Counteroffer.* Unlike formal competitive bidding procedures, the owner may propose counteroffers to the prospective contractor's offer in negotiation. The prospective contractor may perform value analysis and repricing procedures to determine the acceptability of the owner's counteroffer. This process can be repeated several times if the participants believe the process is progressing.
- *Resolution.* Acceptance or rejection of the offer and counteroffers. If accepted, the final terms of the contract by one or a combination of the key participants are formalized.
- *Award of Contract.* The formal acceptance of the terms of negotiation by the participants.
- *Execution.* The work executed according to the terms of the contract.

Negotiation occurs at every level in the construction process when participants attempt to refine the terms of a contract or subcontract.

12.8.4 Value Analysis of Construction Prices

Following receipt and evaluation of prices, the owner might discover that the cost of the project will exceed the established budget unless significant design changes are made. Value analysis can determine how the project can be reduced in extent and still serve the owner's program requirements.

12.9 Purchasing of Goods

Although not identified as a project delivery method, purchasing can be used to obtain goods for a project or completed facility.

12.9.1 General Considerations

Purchasing is the direct acquisition by the owner of supplies, materials, furniture, furnishings, equipment, or special services necessary for one or more of the following:

 Installation by a contractor for the project, referred to as owner furnished and contractor installed

Installation by the owner's personnel or a separate contractor engaged by the owner, referred to as owner furnished and owner installed

 Use in the operation of the completed project during the facility management stage

Goods are products and equipment. Special services include testing procedures, start-up, demonstration, training, and similar services provided by the seller for the buyer's benefit.

The procedures for purchasing are similar to those for competitive bidding and negotiating. Public owners are required to obtain goods at the most competitive price available at the time the purchase is made. Therefore, public owners (referred to as buyers) solicit purchasing proposals by legal advertisement and distribute documents to prospective goods contractors (referred to as sellers).

Private buyers also need to purchase goods and special services at competitive prices. As with private construction procurement, however, a seller might be selected based on factors other than the price of the seller's goods or special services, such as the buyer's previous experience with a seller, exceptional service from the seller, reliability of the seller, and other qualifications.

12.9.1.1 National Accounts

As with construction, prices may be negotiated. A less commonly used form of negotiated purchasing is the use of national accounts. This pricing method is used when the contractor or owner has special or "fixed" pricing direct from the manufacturer, distributor, or supplier. The national account is guaranteed a price regardless of project location, which helps to keep costs known. This method might bypass the supplier in the sale. Many product representatives maintain the libraries for national accounts. In an effort to improve communication and make them uniform, some manufacturers have account executives dedicated solely to these accounts. All information is disseminated through them to the field.

12.9.1.2 Cooperative Purchasing

To obtain goods and special services at the lowest available prices, many government agencies, not-for-profit organizations, and small private businesses organize or join purchasing cooperatives. A purchasing cooperative is an organization of two or more buyers who solicit bids for goods and services from two or more sellers. Purchasing cooperatives can be formed at the local, state, regional, or national levels. By collecting buyers to purchase goods of common need, the cooperative enhances the purchasing power of the participants.

Types of organizations that participate in cooperatives include:

- Local, state, and federal government agencies
- Not-for-profit organizations
- Hospitals
- Schools
- Small businesses

Goods and services purchased by cooperatives include:

- Books, furniture, and supplies
- Maintenance supplies, such as lamps, belts, and filters

- Office furniture
- Janitorial supplies
- Bulk materials for road and highway maintenance
- Utility supplies, such as piping, wire, and cable
- Office supplies
- Health care supplies
- Materials-handling equipment
- Utility services, such as water, electricity, heating oil, and natural gas
- Telecommunications services
- Maintenance services
- Insurance

Public purchasing cooperatives may be administered by an independent agency of the government or a private administrator. Private purchasing cooperatives may be administered by the participants or by an independent purchasing management company. Participation fees for participating in cooperatives can be lump sum or percentage based.

The benefits of cooperative purchasing to participants are several:

- Sellers can price, contract, and deliver goods and services more competitively to cooperatives than to their individual members.
- Buyers receive better discounts in cooperation with others than they can when purchasing as individual participants.
- Public buyers may use cooperatives to avoid the cost of bidding and still comply with laws restricting use of public funds.
- Cooperatives are managed by review boards and experienced management personnel, reducing the administrative burden on the buyer.
- The cooperative can often control the value of goods and services through its enhanced purchasing power.

State and federal laws control the amount and type of goods and services that can be purchased by purchasing cooperatives serving public owners.

12.9.2 Participants

The participants in purchasing include the buyer (acting individually or as a member of a purchasing cooperative) and the seller (the goods contractor who bids and supplies the goods required by the owner).

12.9.3 Documents

As with other forms of procurement, purchasing requires procurement documents to communicate the buyer's purchasing requirements to the seller, including, as applicable:

- An RFP, like an invitation to bid, invites a prospective seller to submit a proposal to furnish a defined quantity or quantities of specified goods or special services within a specified time. The RFP may contain instructions to proposers and describe the format and time limit in which the bid is to be submitted. The RFP may also state the types of bonds and supplemental information required of the prospective sellers at the time a formal proposal to supply goods or special services is made.

- Procurement documents, including drawings, specifications, and procurement requirements describing the quantity and extent of goods required.
- Procurement forms and supplements.
- A contract or purchase order is issued by the buyer, in lieu of a construction contract, to secure the purchased goods or special services from the prospective seller. A purchase order is a form of purchasing contract. Figure 12.6 is an example of a purchase order form.

12.9.4 Processes

The steps required in securing a purchasing agreement include:

- Issuing an RFP to one or more prospective goods contractors to furnish the specified goods or special services. This is similar to an invitation to bid and may include many of the same provisions, except that the terms work, project, and site are not used.
- Visiting the point of destination (of goods) or the point of performance of special services. In some procurement instructions for purchasing, prospective sellers are encouraged and sometimes required to visit the point of destination or point of performance to review the existing conditions under which the goods will be delivered or special services will be performed.
- Performing Pricing Procedures: These are similar to the pricing considerations identified previously under "Pricing Considerations." The purchasing price includes:
  - The costs of goods, bonds, insurance, transportation, handling, applicable taxes, and performance of special services
  - Contingency
  - Overhead
  - Profit
- Submitting a bid in the specified format to furnish the specified goods or special services and in the detail required for evaluation and comparison with other bids to furnish goods or special services. Depending on the rules for purchasing established in the RFP, the buyer may elect to purchase all or only a portion of the goods specified. The buyer may therefore require unit prices or alternates related to the specified goods or special services, and the purchasing documents will be structured accordingly.
- Evaluation of Prices: The process is similar to evaluation of bids for construction. The completeness of the bid or proposal and the required supplements will determine whether or not the prospective seller is responsible and responsive. Several factors might influence the decision to purchase a product, such as:
  - Cost evaluation
  - Service
  - Delivery schedules
  - Acceptability to other participants
  - Product compatibility
  - Ease of installation
  - Performance and reliability

PURCHASE ORDER

Date: _____   **Purchase Order No.** _____

COMPANY NAME
Address
City/State/Zip Code
Telephone:
Fax:

Vendor:

Vendor Name
Address
City/State/Zip Code
Telephone No.
Authorized Agent

Ship To:

Reference	Payment Terms	Payment Method	Shipping Terms	Delivery Date

We submit the following:

Item No.	Description	Quantity	Unit	Unit Cost	Extended Cost

Subtotal	
Less Discount	
Tax	
Shipping Charges	
TOTAL	

TERMS & CONDITIONS: All work shall be performed in accordance with the contract documents dated XX/XX/XX Modification of the terms of the contract documents requires approval of all parties and a signed Change Order.

_____   _____   _____   _____
Buyer's Authorized Agent   Date   Seller's Authorized Agent   Date

Figure 12.6 Sample Purchase Order

Product prices vary based on delivery schedule, terms of pricing, and contract requirements and modifications. If the product cannot meet the standard delivery schedule because of extended lead times, unusual shipping requirements, or difficult destinations, the price might be affected. Product representatives are a good source of information to make the goods contractors aware of requirements that need to be met to avoid price increases.

Quantity discounts and minimum orders need to be taken into account in determining price. Some manufacturers offer discounts if a certain quantity is purchased; however, an additional fee might exist if less than the minimum quantity is ordered. Quantities are especially important when dealing with unit pricing. If the quantity is unknown but needs to be ordered, the price quote might include a cost differential for over or underestimating the quantity.

- *Executing a Contract.* Preparation and signing of the formal agreement by the buyer to purchase the specified goods or special services from the seller. The purchasing contract is similar to a construction contract, and each party has rights and responsibilities as defined. The conditions of the purchasing contract, similar to the conditions of the construction contract, might be a separate document or incorporated into the contract. Many buyers issue standardized purchase orders in lieu of purchasing contracts when it is in their best interest to do so. A purchase order is a document authorizing a supplier to furnish goods of a specific quantity and quality. A purchase order constitutes an offer that is accepted when the specified goods are delivered.
- *Purchasing Agreement Modifications.* A change in the terms of a purchasing contract is referred to as a change order.
- *Delivery to the Point of Destination.* Upon execution of the purchasing contract, the seller delivers the goods or special services to the point of destination specified in the documents. Failure to perform the terms of the contract may result in liquidated damages being assessed in the same manner as they may be assessed in performing a construction contract.
- *Performance of Special Services at the Point of Performance.* When the terms of the purchasing contract include special services, the seller performs the special services at the point of performance specified in the documents.

12.9.5   Purchasing—Cost Impacts and Concerns

The purchasing process is affected by a combination of events and factors in the supply chain, including delivery and distribution, lead-time requirements, special shipping and handling requirements, import and export restrictions, and payment terms. Product representatives can advise the A/E and owner about the actual effects of these factors on project cost and the project schedule.

12.9.5.1   Delivery and Distribution

Many factors can affect a product's delivery and distribution, and some of these factors might, in turn, affect payment.

Delivery influences the time required to manufacture and transport a product. Distribution is the method by which products are delivered to the purchasers. Delivery time has a direct correlation with the shipping method to be used.

A term commonly associated with delivery and distribution is free on board (FOB). "FOB—factory, freight, prepaid to the job site" means without charge to the buyer for delivering and placing a shipment on board a carrier at a specified location. Once on board the carrier, it belongs to the buyer.

Several concerns normally affect the anticipated schedule for product delivery. They include:

- Lead times
- Supply and demand
- Labor disputes and strikes
- Weather
- Special handling considerations
- Geographic influences
- Coordination with adjacent materials
- Shipping and packaging requirements and damage claims

Additional delivery issues include the origin of the purchase. Distributors might be stocking or nonstocking. If the product is purchased from a stocking distributor, it is more readily available than if the distributor places an order.

12.9.5.2 Lead Time

Lead time is the amount of time required from receipt of a purchase order by a seller to the time the product is delivered. Many of the issues related to delivery of construction products should also be considered by owners who procure goods for installation by their own employees or who furnish goods to a contractor for installation on a project.

12.9.5.3 Special Shipping and Handling Considerations

Shipping and handling affect the cost of procuring goods as well as their conditions when they are delivered to the buyer.

12.9.5.4 Import and Export

International distribution of products also affects the delivery and payment from the time of manufacture. Language might be a barrier to communicating product requirements and maintaining quality control. Some countries require labels and instructions in the native language and English prior to distribution and use of products not manufactured in the country.

Trade agreements affect distribution of products. The North American Free Trade Agreement (NAFTA) allows goods manufactured or grown in North America to cross borders between countries, either north or south, without incurring taxes. The General Agreement on Tariffs and Trade (GATT) is widely used throughout the world. This agreement sets a single standard tax amount based on the item being imported or exported.

The NAFTA and GATT agreements affect the manufactured prices as well as delivery costs. NAFTA enables manufacturers to produce a material in Canada or Mexico at a lower cost and to distribute it in the United States without incurring additional costs. GATT has the same effect on manufacturing. If the delivery stays in the country in which the product was manufactured, additional taxes are not incurred. Delivery costs when importing goods and applying the GATT are high.

Quality control of the manufacturing process such as the International Organization for Standardization's (ISO) ISO 9000 provides quality assurance to the end user. Products are usually manufactured from locally available resources. If they perform well in another part of the world, this does not necessarily mean they will perform well in a project location in the United States.

A concern with measurement and payment for products is the unit of measure and currency exchange. All countries today, other than the United States, use the International System of Units (SI) as their standard of weights and measurements. Soft conversion to SI units is required on projects for the U.S. government, but SI units are not widely used in other domestic construction projects. Soft conversion means using an exact conversion of measurement from one system to the other, but no actual dimensional change is required for the product. A hard conversion requires a physical change in product dimensions. The use of SI units affects measurement and payment in that the cost per square meter is significantly different from the cost per square foot. Terms of payment in the purchase order should specify the currency used for payment. If it is not expressed as U.S. dollars, provisions should be made to stipulate the exchange rates on a particular date or event in the purchase order, whether delivery, receipt of product, or date of manufacture.

12.9.5.5 Terms of Payment

The terms of payment affect pricing of materials when dealing with potential financial loss. Occasionally, a manufacturer asks for a down payment in advance of fabrication or even prior to releasing shop drawings. Sometimes, because of scheduling, the submittals need to be approved prior to product representatives receiving commitments from buyers. This might necessitate an increase in price or require a down payment to cover the necessary work effort prior to receiving the order.

In addition, it is standard practice for the owner to withhold a Retainage amount that is released on final acceptance of the project. Though this amount is usually nominal, it can be a burden on some product representatives, especially those who provide products in the early stages of a project. If product representatives are aware of this requirement, the price might include an additional cost to cover incidentals.

12.9.5.6 Role of Product Representatives

Product representatives are often aware of conditions affecting product delivery and distribution and might be able to advise the A/E of potential delays or complications during the product selection process. Once a purchase order for the product has been received, product representatives can also assist the contractor by facilitating timely delivery. If a product cannot be delivered by the desired date after placement of an order, the contractor should be informed immediately.

Product representatives should become aware of the construction progress schedule and the projected product delivery date to encourage the buyer to place an order in a timely manner.

Product representatives consider phasing of construction and sequencing of product installation when estimating a requested delivery date. A product delivered early might need storage or if delivered late might cause a construction delay. Product representatives review the purchase order prior to ordering the product to verify where it will be delivered. For example, if the final destination is the ninth floor of an office building, product representatives need to allow time to unload the product and transport it to the ninth floor, which might require additional labor and equipment.

After receipt of the purchase order, product representatives may assist the contractor in preparing submittals. The contract may require some manufacturers to submit shop drawings as a preconstruction submittal. If shop drawings are required, additional charges may be included in the purchase order because manufacturers sometimes charge for these shop drawings.

Product representatives should allow sufficient time for processing of required submittals to maintain the schedule. Submittal processing might take longer than expected if a change to the drawings has occurred or the submittal is rejected and needs to be revised and resubmitted. When a change order occurs after approval of shop drawings, revised shop drawings might be necessary to incorporate changes. Manufacturing of the product cannot begin until the A/E has approved the final submittal.

Product representatives should be aware of conditions affecting lead time and know the anticipated delivery schedule to receive approvals of submittals, order the product, and have it shipped in a timely manner. A tracking method should be developed that documents action taken on submittals, purchase orders, and delivery. Figure 12.7 is a suggested checklist of items to be included in this type of tracking form. Essential to the success is communication with the contractor to be aware of schedule changes and change orders that might affect the quantity of product ordered.

Product representatives might be able to assist the A/E, contractor, and owner to understand products manufactured overseas and how they perform in locales similar to the project location, and can be a valuable source of information on international shipping and payment policies.

12.10 Subcontracting

Subcontractors are the principal providers of labor, materials, and services in the commercial construction process. The term subcontractor defines a contractual relationship between a specialist trade contractor and a prime contractor on a construction project. As specialists, subcontractors can provide other project participants with important information useful for all project stages, including:

- Technical information about systems, subsystems, and products for design development and construction documentation
- Financial information for estimating the project
- Installation information for project coordination
- Manufacturing and delivery information for project scheduling purposes
- Information and services necessary for facility maintenance programs

These attributes make the subcontractor a valuable resource for the design and construction team, regardless of design or project delivery method.

12.10.1 Subcontractor Prices

Most construction contracts can be subdivided into smaller units of specialized work. Demolition, excavation, concrete, masonry, and roofing are a few examples. Within each area of specialization, separate competitive bidding occurs, with subcontractors

INFORMATION TRACKING CHECKLIST

Date: _____   Re: _____

A/E Number: _____   Manufacturer's Project No.: _____

Filing No.: _____   Contract For: _____

Customer Information:

☐ Architect Address/Contact Person (with phone and fax nos.)
☐ Bid Amount
☐ Bid Date
☐ Product(s)
☐ Project Name

☐ Customer Name/Address/Contact Person (with phone and fax nos.):
☐ Contractor
☐ Owner
☐ Subcontractor
☐ Other

☐ Project Number
☐ Sale Amount
☐ Status of Bid
☐ Requested Delivery Date

Sale Information:

☐ Amount Due
☐ Anticipated Due Date
☐ Estimated Date for Receipt of Commission

☐ Commission Paid/Date/Amount
☐ Invoice Date

☐ Invoice Number
☐ Manufacturer

☐ Order Date
☐ Paid Amount

Delivery:

☐ Estimated Date of Shipment from Manufacturer
☐ Estimated Arrival Date
☐ Actual Delivery Date

Purchase Order:

☐ Submitted
☐ Received

☐ Terms of Payment
☐ Remarks

☐ Changes/Exceptions
☐ Return Executed Purchase Order

Submittals:

☐ Date Ordered/Received Status:
  ☐ Shop Drawings
  ☐ Samples

☐ Date Submitted to Contractor
☐ Date Returned
☐ Action Taken

Contract/Subcontract:

☐ Terms Being Negotiated
☐ Change Order

Figure 12.7 CSI Form 20.5, Information Tracking Checklist

competing on a price basis within their specialty. The price submitted by a contractor often will be made up of prices from as many subcontractors as is appropriate for the project scope.

12.10.2 Subcontractor Issues and Concerns

Because of their unique role in the construction process, subcontractors have concerns that affect their relationships with A/Es, prime contractors, and owners. They include:

- Bid shopping
- Payment and Retainage provisions
- Labor availability and competency
- Liability risk management
- Legislative initiatives affecting labor

12.10.3 Bid Shopping

Bid shopping is the practice of revealing the subbid of one subcontractor to obtain a lower price from another subcontractor. It occurs during the procurement (bidding/negotiating/purchasing) process, and following award of a prime contract, or both.

Bid shopping has the potential for adversely altering project performance or imposing unanticipated risks on other project participants, because it encourages cost-cutting measures that might compromise project requirements and the owner does not always receive the financial benefit of the cost savings. It can lead to unauthorized substitutions and generally degrade the competitive bidding environment.

The organized efforts of all project participants can reduce the harmful effects of bid shopping in commercial and public work. Bid depositories, whereby prequalified sub-bidders submit their prices to the owner independently of the prime contractor, have been used with some success in public works projects. They strike a satisfactory medium between lowest price and reasonable requirements. Requiring bidders to list the subbidders they intend to use in their bids has also had some effect in controlling bid shopping. However, this method can restrict the contractor's ability to complete subcontract agreements if listed subcontractors fail to execute a contract or otherwise default. Provisions requiring the contractor to submit lists of subbidders and suppliers within a specified period prior to award of a contract can be effective in limiting bid shopping. The A/E and owner may include these provisions in the contract documents.

12.10.4 Subcontractor Bidding Environment

Although the A/E and owner should not intrude on the contractor's basic right to control the means, methods, techniques, and sequences of the work, they can substantially improve the competitive bidding environment, thereby improving project quality assurance, by implementing a few measures:

- Consult qualified subcontractors during design.
- Consider bid listing and bid depository provisions to preclude bid shopping.

- Control substitutions through clear bidding and contracting requirements and by evaluating proposed substitutions carefully.
- Produce accurate, concise contract documents.
- Document clear, adequate quality assurance/quality control provisions and submittals.
- Enforce contract documents.
- Promptly review submittals and payment requests.
- Encourage implementing reasonable retainage provisions.
- Administer contract closeout procedures effectively.

By such means, the chances for project success are greatly improved.

Chapter 13
Construction

Introduction

This chapter presents an overview of construction. For more detailed information, refer to *The CSI Construction Contract Administration Practice Guide.*

Construction is the execution of the work required by the contract documents. Construction is the coordinated effort of all those involved in providing the owner with a successful project. Construction activities can be divided into two broad categories:

Construction Contract Administration (CCA)   Activities related to administering the contract for construction, typically performed by the A/E.

Contractor Project Management (CPM)   Activities related to managing the construction process, typically performed by the contractor. Contractor project management should not be confused with construction management. Construction management is a delivery method. Contractor project management is managing the construction process, whether by a contractor, a construction manager, a design builder, or other entity responsible for constructing a project.

13.2 Construction as a Team Activity

The construction of a facility is the culmination of the collective ideas, talents, and services of a large and diverse group. The main participants are the owner team, the design team, the contractor team, and the supplier team.

The team member with the greatest number of project management responsibilities is the contractor who has the responsibility for maintaining project coordination, control of the project schedule; subcontractor and supplier performance; payment procedures; safety, insurance, and bonding requirements; quality assurance and quality control tasks; submittals; and a multitude of other business management functions.

The responsibility for CCA oversight typically rests with the architect/engineer (A/E). The A/E provides services to the owner through the design stage and usually continues to represent the owner during the construction stage, thereby allowing the A/E to maintain continuous involvement in both the design and construction processes.

13.2.1 Team Approach

The cumulative and coordinated efforts of the owner, the A/E, and the contractor, during design and construction, are the means that produce the end: the completed project. The success of the project is dependent on how well the participants understand their roles and responsibilities and those of the others, how well they carry out those roles, and how well they meet the expectations of the other participants.

13.2.1.1 Benefits to Working as a Team

There are many benefits to the project team working together in harmony. These benefits may include:

- Better communication and coordination
- Increased productivity
- Reduced project costs
- Earlier project completion
- Improved project team morale
- Fewer claims and delays

When project participants work together as a team, the participants usually benefit from increased productivity. Increased productivity results from reductions in downtime while waiting for response to questions, resolution of disagreements, reductions in work that needs to be redone, and reductions in paperwork associated with claims and disputes.

13.2.1.2 Obstacles to Working as a Team

There are obstacles inherent to every project. How the project team members manage these obstacles may affect how successful the project will be. These obstacles may include:

- Adversarial relationships/personalities
- Incomplete or inaccurate contract documents
- Unreasonable schedule requirements
- Unplanned or inordinate number of changes to the project scope
- Labor issues
- Delays in product fabrication or delivery
- Poor communications
- Delays caused by ineffective management

13.2.1.3 Team Building and Collaborative Effort

All projects benefit when the owner, A/E, and contractor work together in a collaborative effort. A collaborative effort includes an expressed commitment to proactive cooperation during the execution of the project. Each of the parties actively works to:

- Understand the extent of their contractual rights and responsibilities and effectively carry them out
- Work fairly, efficiently, and swiftly to solve problems through communication
- Act in an ethical manner

13.2.2 Understanding the Documents

Construction documents are defined as the written and graphic documents prepared or assembled by the A/E for communicating the project design for construction and administering the construction contract. Various documents constitute the contract documents that are the basis of the contract. Other documents are for reference, such as geotechnical data and surveys, and others are generated to carry out the requirements, such as shop drawings and test reports. Certain requirements used in the procurement of the construction contract may no longer apply once the agreement is signed and the contract is formed. These documents include procurement solicitations, instructions for procurement, bid security, and procurement forms.

13.2.2.1 Contract Documents

These documents are listed and enumerated in the agreement and referred to in the conditions of the contract for the work to be performed. They are the documents that are a legal part of the contract and describe the work. The contract documents describe the proposed construction (referred to as the work) that results from performing services, furnishing labor, and supplying and incorporating materials and equipment into the construction. Contract documents consist of both written and graphic elements and typically include the following:

- Agreement
- Conditions of the contract
- Addenda affecting contract documents
- Contract modifications such as change orders and change directives
- Drawings
- Specifications

The contractor signing the agreement with the owner has the responsibility of accomplishing the work in accordance with the contract documents. Therefore, the contract documents are addressed only to the contractor; however, owner responsibilities are also included within these "contract documents."

13.2.2.2 Drawings

Various drawings represent information about the work to be performed. The drawings illustrate relationships between elements as well as quantities, locations, dimensions, sizes, shapes, and forms of the elements and assemblies in the project.

Contract document drawings typically include plans, elevations, sections, details, and often diagrams and schedules. The drawings typically identify materials and assemblies in generic terms.

13.2.2.3 Specifications

Specifications are prepared by the A/E to describe a portion of the work to be supplied and installed by the contractor. The specifications define the quality of material and workmanship. The specifications are typically organized in accordance with the Construction Specifications Institute (CSI) *MasterFormat*® and the three-part *SectionFormat*™.

13.2.3 Administering Construction Based on Delivery Methods

Although there are many similarities, the CCA and contractor project management processes vary with the project delivery method selected for the project. A comparison of CCA and contractor project management requirements based on project delivery method is addressed in detail in *The CSI Construction Contract Administration Practice Guide.*

13.2.3.1 Design-Bid-Build and Design-Negotiate-Build Project Delivery

The most common form of construction contracting is the single prime contract. It involves negotiation or competitive bidding for a single construction contract, incorporating all work required to complete the project. Many people consider design-bid-build (D-B-B) to be the traditional method of construction contracting.

The A/E is typically responsible for:

- Representing the owner during the construction stage
- Observing the work for conformance with contract requirements
- Observing project progress for review of contractor applications for payment
- Preparing and recommending contract modifications
- Attending project meetings
- Inspecting the project to determine substantial and final completion

The contractor typically has a project manager on staff to handle contractor project management responsibilities. These responsibilities may include:

- Preparing applications for payment
- Administering subcontracts
- Purchasing
- Preparing, monitoring, updating, and revising project schedules
- Attending project meetings
- Communicating with the A/E and subcontractors
- Preparing proposal requests and responding to A/E issued contract modification proposals
- Preparing and implementing safety programs
- Requesting clarifications and interpretations of the contract documents
- Administering the submittal process

13.2.3.2 Construction Management Project Delivery

Construction management services are often provided in one of two basic forms: construction manager as constructor (CMc) and construction manager as adviser (CMa). The CMc is effectively the contractor and provides contractor project management services, while most or all of the construction work is subcontracted. The CMa usually divides the project into multiple contracts for procurement and award of contracts. The CMa provides management services to the owner and usually includes consolidating applications for payment and coordination among contracts. A construction manager may also provide construction expertise, cost estimating experience, and scheduling services to the A/E during the design stage of a project.

13.2.3.3 Design-Build Project Delivery

As project cost control and speed of delivery have become more important, the design-build (D-B) method of project delivery has become more popular. In the D-B project delivery method, the owner contracts with a single entity, the design-builder, to design and subsequently to construct the project. The design-builder may have a contract with an independent A/E for design services, or may provide A/E services as part of a D-B company. The significant difference is that the A/E services are provided for the design-builder, rather than the owner. The A/E does not represent the owner under a D-B delivery method. Standard AIA, DBIA, ConsensusDOCS, and EJCDC contract document forms are frequently used for the D-B project delivery method.

13.2.3.4 Owner-Build Project Delivery

When the owner-build (O-B) project delivery method is utilized, the owner provides many of the contractor's project management services and a layer of management is eliminated. Depending on the extent of the project, the owner may retain an A/E for design services and for obtaining required permits for the project. The A/E's construction contract administration services during the construction stage are at the direction of the owner. Depending on the level of participation desired by the owner and included in the owner-A/E agreement, the A/E might be very involved in the construction stage, even assuming responsibility for conducting the owner's communications with contractors and suppliers. At the opposite extreme, there may be no formal construction contract administration at all, other than that required by A/E licensing laws. Typical documents for the O-B delivery method are owner specific and may not be based on standard documents such as those from AIA or EJCDC. These documents may be prepared directly by the owner or the facility manager.

13.2.3.5 Integrated Project Delivery

Integrated Project Delivery (IPD) requires early collaborative contributions during the design phases of what are traditionally late applications of expertise. Contractors, facility managers, subcontractors, manufacturers, and suppliers become involved in the design process. Decisions are usually made based on the appropriate solutions for the project and the owner's needs rather than solely on first cost. The early involvement of more "team members" creates synergy and allows the project to yield the highest potential of good design and construction solutions meeting the owner's requirements. Since much of the work that has been traditionally performed during construction has moved forward into the design phases, construction contract administration should be simplified. For example, a particular manufacturer or supplier may have had input during design and their product information may have been incorporated into the contract documents. Therefore, review of submittals may be eliminated except to verify that the material that was documented is in fact being supplied and constructed into the project.

13.3 | Roles and Responsibilities

The contract documents establish the roles and responsibilities for construction contract administration. Construction contract administration and contractor project management processes require participants to:

- Know the documents used in construction
- Understand the role of each construction participant
- Be sensitive to the expectations each participant has of the others
- Communicate with each other
- Understand the effect various project delivery methods have on construction contract administration and contractor project management

The procedures utilized by the project participants during the construction stage vary depending on the project delivery method being utilized.

13.3.1 Owner

Whereas the owner typically places much of the construction contract administration responsibility on the A/E, the owner also has several important rights and responsibilities during the construction phase. Some of these rights and responsibilities include:

- Furnishing information to the contractor
- Payment of fees and charges associated with the work
- Making payment to the contractor
- Right to stop the work
- Right to carry out the work
- Right to perform construction
- Right to award separate contracts
- Right to clean
- Right to partial occupancy
- Termination for convenience
- Termination for cause

The owner may be the facility manager or may employ a separate facility manager. For the purposes of this Practice Guide, the owner is the entity who "pays" for the project while the facility manager is the entity who "manages the operation of the facility."

Ideally, the facility manager is involved in the construction stage as part of the owner's team. Involvement in the construction stage of the project allows the facility manager to:

- Observe construction of the facility for which it will be responsible
- Become familiar with the means and methods employed by the contractor
- Become familiar with the location of concealed items, such as piping, conduit, cabling, and structural connections
- Participate in decision making regarding contract modifications

13.3.2 Architect/Engineer

Most standard owner-A/E agreements require the A/E to administer the construction contract. Typical A/E responsibilities are to:

- Represent the owner
- Certify/recommend payments
- Interpret contract documents
- Resolve disputes
- Modify the contract documents
- Review submittals
- Observe the work
- Perform inspections

Dictionaries define observe as to perceive, notice, see, whereas inspect means to examine carefully and critically, especially for defects. In construction, the distinction between these two words has significance, and the individuals responsible for construction contract administration and contractor project management need to be familiar with the two terms.

13.3.3 Contractor

The contractor is responsible for accomplishing the work and for the contractor project management process. The conditions of the contract list the basic responsibilities of the contractor. Standard owner-contractor agreements typically require the contractor to conform to the construction contract, including the following tasks:

- Review contract documents
- Follow procedures for substitution of products
- Furnish competent supervision
- Maintain accessible up to date construction documents
- Schedule and coordinate material deliveries and subcontractor's work
- Furnish payment and performance bonds
- Furnish contractor's liability insurance and workers' compensation insurance
- Implement and enforce project safety rules and regulations
- Schedule and facilitate testing
- Implement and monitor quality control (QC) and quality assurance (QA)
- Promptly pay subcontractors and suppliers
- Furnish submittals and samples as required by the contract documents
- Schedule and obtain required inspections by authorities having jurisdiction (AHJs)
- Submit record drawings, operation and maintenance (O&M) manuals, and other project data

13.3.4 Subcontractors and Suppliers

Contractors typically employ subcontractors and suppliers to assist in accomplishing the work required by the contract. Because the terms of the contract cover all work related to performance of the contract, agreements and conditions of the contract require that work performed by subcontractors and suppliers is bound by the same terms of the contract that bind the contractor.

13.3.4.1 Subcontractors

Subcontractors may or may not furnish materials but almost always furnish labor on the project as part of their subcontract work. A contractor often subcontracts segments of work that the contractor does not want to "self-perform."

13.3.4.2 Suppliers

Suppliers typically do not furnish on-site labor. They furnish materials or supplies for installation by the contractor or subcontractors. There are, however, exceptions. A supplier may provide for a manufacturer's representative or product representative to visit the site and train, oversee, or assist in the installation of the supplier's product.

13.3.5 Consultants

A variety of consultants may be involved in the design, construction contract administration, and contractor project management processes. Consultants frequently engaged by the A/E include:

- Mechanical engineers
- Electrical engineers
- Structural engineers
- Plumbing engineers
- Civil engineers
- Fire protection engineers
- Interior designers
- Landscape architects
- Sustainability professionals
- Vertical transportation specialists
- Life-safety specialists
- Estimating professionals

Consultants frequently engaged by the owner include:

- Geotechnical engineers
- Surveyors
- Traffic engineers
- Hazardous material abatement consultants
- Commissioning authority
- Sustainability professionals

Consultants frequently engaged by the contractor include:

- Erosion and sedimentation control engineers
- Surveyors

- Structural engineers
- Fire protection engineers
- Project schedulers
- Safety consultants
- Waste management consultants (for demolition and recycling)
- Sustainability professionals

Consultants are bound by the terms of their contracts with the A/E, owner, or contractor. Contracts for consultants engaged by the contractor should include flow-down language. This language ensures that the duties, rights, and responsibilities are properly delegated and the terms are consistent with the provisions of the agreement between the owner and the contractor.

13.3.6 Authorities Having Jurisdiction

The project type and location often determine which authorities have jurisdiction over a project. Often multiple agencies have jurisdiction over a project. For instance, a project located within the city limits may be governed by the city building department, but the county health department, state fire marshal, and state elevator inspectors may also have jurisdiction. The AHJs do not have contractual relationships with the project participants but have regulatory authority granted by the permit process and local, state, and federal regulations and laws.

13.3.7 Testing Agency Inspectors

The types and quantity of tests and inspections that may be required on a project are typically determined by the facility type and extent and materials and methods being utilized. Independent testing and inspections are often required by code, the owner, A/E, or contractor as part of QA and QC processes. Common testing requirements include soil and asphalt compaction, concrete strength, structural steel bolted and welded connections, critical structure inspections, fireproofing, and paint/coating thickness.

13.3.8 Commissioning Authority

The commissioning authority may be hired by the owner to help ensure that the completed facility, or portions thereof, meet the owner's requirements. The commissioning authority may be involved in total project commissioning or may be limited to building systems commissioning. With total project commissioning, the commissioning authority is already part of the project team when construction begins and is typically involved throughout the construction stage. With building systems commissioning, the commissioning authority typically becomes involved in the project near the end of the construction stage and is responsible for ensuring that systems are properly tested and will perform in accordance with the design. The commissioning authority's duties may include obtaining, reviewing, and approving O&M manuals. The commissioning authority uses measurement and verification equipment and procedures for monitoring optimum system performance.

13.3.9 Product Representatives

Individuals, either independent or within companies involved in the promotion and sale of construction products and systems, are product representatives. Product representatives are a critical component to the success of a company. Product representatives need to be aware of project requirements, including specified functional and performance criteria, submittal requirements, delivery dates, and procedures for requesting substitutions. The most effective assistance occurs when product representatives interact with members of the project team and review the construction documents to determine the requirements. Product representatives advise A/Es, owners, contractors, and subcontractors on products and systems to be incorporated into a project.

13.3.10 Communication

Construction contract administration, contractor project management, and communication during the construction stage are integral activities. The contract documents establish the lines of communication and might describe how the communication process is to work. The basic lines of communication as identified in the AIA and EJCDC general conditions include the following:

- Between owner and contractor, through the A/E
- To design consultants, through the A/E
- To subcontractors and suppliers, through the contractor
- To separate contractors, through the owner, construction manager, or coordinating contractor

In traditional agreements, the A/E and contractor have no contract with each other; however, their individual agreements with the owner and the conditions of the contract make it their duty to have certain communications. Although the owner and the contractor have a direct contract, the contract documents stipulate that communication between them flows through the A/E. Although the construction process encourages communication among the participants, it is important that participants follow the contractual lines of communication to ensure proper documentation and coordination. The communication roles may be different on D-B and IPD methods.

13.3.10.1 Oral and Written Communication

Communications may be oral, such as telephone calls or field resolution of design or construction issues, but oral communications should be followed with written documentation confirming decisions or interpretations. After a meeting with several participants present, a copy of the minutes of the meeting should be sent to the attendees. An opportunity should be offered to each party to review and correct the documented information within a specified period of time.

13.3.10.2 Electronic Communication

The use of electronic communication has become prevalent in construction. It includes faxes, electronic mail, digital photos, project web sites, text messaging, and voicemail.

When electronic communications are integrated into a project, it is important to establish the following:

- Rules that clearly identify an official communication
- Types of communication that will be legally binding
- How distribution to other parties will be handled
- Record-keeping procedures

The procedures for utilizing electronic communications are established by the construction documents or agreed to at the beginning of the project. The participants need to understand the forms of communication that will be considered legally binding, how they will be recorded, and how and to whom they will be distributed.

13.4 Preconstruction

13.4.1 Contractor's Organization

The contract documents require many preconstruction activities. Other preconstruction activities are determined by good business practices, the contractor's organization, duration of the project, interaction with outside agencies, and interface with the project team. Preconstruction activities begin when the contractor has received an executed agreement or a notice to proceed. Occasionally, a "Letter of Intent to Award" may initiate this phase as well. Prior to starting preconstruction activities, the contractor should review the conditions of the contract and Division 01 for requirements that will impact the contractor's project management procedures including communications, submittals, meetings, sustainability requirements, contract modifications and interpretations, payment processes, and project closeout.

13.4.1.1 Award of Subcontracts

Subcontracts are contracts between the contractor and subcontractors. Each subcontract identifies the work required and is subject to compliance with the contract documents. Similarly, subcontractors can establish contracts with sub-subcontractors. Subcontract issues may include the number of mobilizations and demobilizations, required inclusions and exclusions, project schedule, special requirements for subcontracted work, testing requirements, submittals, and samples.

13.4.1.2 Purchase Orders

Purchase orders are contracts for materials being purchased, reference the project specifications, and include pertinent terms such as discounts, cost escalations, submittals, certifications required, samples required, freight, taxes, delivery schedule, and quantities. The fewer ambiguities in the purchase order, the fewer the problems that may be encountered later in the project. Purchase orders reflect the terms of the supplier's quote: the quote was the offer; the purchase order is the acceptance in the contract process.

13.4.2 Notice to Proceed

The project time limit provisions are normally established by the date of commencement stated in the agreement. The date of commencement may be established by a notice to proceed. The agreement for a design-build project or a negotiated contract that has the contractor performing value analysis and constructability reviews during the design stage may not establish the construction start time or duration. In this case, the notice to proceed issued by the owner to the contractor establishes the construction start date and the construction duration.

13.4.3 Contract Documents

The CCA and contractor project management procedures established by documents published by AIA and EJCDC have become standards of the industry in defining the rights, duties, and responsibilities of the various parties to a construction contract. Although ConsensusDOCS promulgated by several construction related associations, and some private companies and governmental agencies use other documents, the following information focuses on those published by the AIA and EJCDC.

The documents typically used in the administration of a construction contract include:

- Owner-A/E agreement
- Owner-contractor agreement(s)
- Conditions of the contract
- Specifications
- Drawings
- Bid form or proposal, when attached as an exhibit to the agreement (EJCDC)
- Precontract revisions, including addenda with items relating to contract documents
- Notice to proceed (as required by most EJCDC contracts, and as required by some public- and private-sector projects utilizing standard or modified AIA contracts)
- Contract modifications, including change orders

These documents are related, and it is necessary that those responsible for CCA and contractor project management have a working knowledge of each of the documents that are included in the project's contracts. While the agreements are not usually shared among the project participants, the rights, roles, and responsibilities of the participants are covered in the conditions of the contract. The tendency to skim over apparent boilerplate provisions must be avoided, lest a seemingly insignificant detail escape the reader's attention, only to prove very important later.

13.4.4 Preconstruction Submittals

Generally, no work begins until required preconstruction submittals have been submitted by the contractor and reviewed by the A/E and owner. When the contractor receives the notice to proceed, preparation and delivery of the preconstruction submittals should begin as soon as possible. These submittals may include:

- Certificates of insurance and worker's compensation coverage
- Payment and performance bonds

- Proposed subcontractor and product lists
- Preliminary construction and submittal schedules
- Proposed use of the site and site logistics, including signage
- Erosion control plan
- Pollution control plan
- Traffic control plan

13.4.5 Permits and Regulatory Issues

Nearly every project requires that appropriate permits be obtained before construction can begin. The permit process begins when an owner or A/E submits a set of construction documents to the AHJ for review. For any given project, an AHJ may be a city, county, state, or federal agency. There might be more than one AHJ, which might involve several agencies. An AHJ reviews the documents and requests additional information or clarification if necessary, then issues the appropriate permits for construction. These permits usually include an overall building permit, supplemented by specialty permits for specific portions of the project such as temporary erosion control, surface water management, environmental mitigation work, traffic control, mechanical work, plumbing work, fire sprinkler system, electrical work, and fire alarm system.

13.4.6 Preconstruction Meetings

Preconstruction meetings are important for establishing the ground rules for communication and for explaining the administrative process. In many cases, a single meeting is all that is required; however, large or complex projects may require more than one meeting.

13.4.7 Verification of Site Conditions

It is important to establish the site conditions prior to starting any construction activities, including mobilization. The documented conditions establish the existing circumstances in case damage occurs to existing facilities or adjacent properties, or if unknown or concealed conditions are encountered later in the project. When foundation work is required in a project, often geotechnical data such as boring logs will be part of the construction documents to help indicate the subsurface conditions. Boring logs represent the various materials, such as soils, clay, cemented gravels, sand, rock, and water that are likely to be encountered in the boring location during excavation or deep foundation work. These subsurface reports are typically furnished for "Informational Purposes Only." The geotechnical data and subsurface condition reports are not usually a part of the contract documents and should not be used as a basis for bid preparation concerning the site. Existing conditions may also include an existing facility and drawings previously prepared for the existing facility's construction. This information might be included in the procurement documents as "Available Information". When the information is made available, it can reduce the likelihood of unknown or concealed conditions claims during the project.

13.4.8   Mobilization

The contractor's first activity on the project site is typically mobilization. Mobilization entails setting up the temporary facilities that the contractor will need to perform the work required by the project. Mobilization typically occurs after receipt of a notice to proceed and following a preconstruction meeting and a site mobilization meeting. The mobilization process has several elements that need to be carefully planned and followed. These include:

- Use of the Project Site
- Project Site Security
- Temporary Facilities
- Temporary Utilities
- Temporary Controls
- Equipment
- Environmental Protection Requirements
- Project Site Safety
- Utility Locations
- Survey/Layout/Datum

13.5   Meetings

Effective meetings are an important part of CCA and contractor project management. They give the participants an opportunity to share information, exchange ideas, and make decisions. Meetings facilitate coordination of the work and resolution of issues and help to prevent or resolve problems. Effectively administered meetings have a PAL—a purpose, an agenda, and a time limit. Meetings with published agenda and on-topic discussions that convene and adjourn on schedule will contribute to a team approach in construction.

13.5.1   Procedures and Administration

The specification sections in Division 01 typically identify the types of meetings to be held during the construction stage. The Division 01 specifications may also establish the administrative and procedural requirements for the meetings, including the frequency of meetings, the participants, meeting administration, topics for discussion, and the meeting facilities required. In addition, sections in Divisions 02–49 may also contain requirements for meetings, such as meetings required prior to installation of certain products and coordination meetings.

13.5.2   Types of Meetings

Many types of meetings are convened during the course of a project.

13.5.2.1   Preconstruction Meetings

Preconstruction meetings are important for introducing the project team, establishing the ground rules for communication, and explaining the administrative process. On some projects, a site mobilization meeting may be held separately from the preconstruction meeting. Typically held at the project site, a site mobilization meeting addresses issues about site use.

13.5.2.2 Progress Meetings

Progress meetings concern the progress of the work. They provide a forum in which matters pertinent to the timely completion of the work can be discussed. The frequency and length of progress meetings depend on the extent of the project and the project delivery method. For complex projects or projects of short duration, daily or weekly meetings might be necessary. Regular progress meetings facilitate coordination and administration of a project.

13.5.2.3 Contractor/Subcontractor Meetings

Contractor/subcontractor meetings address the progress and scheduling of the work, coordination between the contractor and subcontractors, and coordination between two or more subcontractors. These meetings frequently address contract issues such as applications for payment, project site safety, requests for interpretations (RFIs), and contract modifications.

13.5.2.4 Preinstallation Meetings

Preinstallation meetings help to clarify installation procedures, phasing, and coordination of the participants and processes involved in the installation of a specific product or system. These meetings are usually specified to focus on specific concerns and do not relieve the contractor of the responsibility to coordinate the work.

13.5.2.5 Closeout Meetings

The closeout meeting is used to review requirements for the completion of the contract and to obtain submittal of the necessary final documents. Separate meetings may be required for substantial completion, final completion, and warranty reviews. Review of closeout procedures at the initial progress meeting or preconstruction meeting is recommended. Many of the closeout documents are prepared during construction, even though their submission is not required until the project is nearing completion. These documents might include record documents, operations and maintenance (O&M) data, manufacturer certification of installations, and interim inspections and testing. As a project nears completion, a review of the requirements for substantial completion helps to facilitate a smooth conclusion.

13.5.2.6 Other Meetings

Other meetings may be scheduled by the contractor, owner, A/E, construction manager (CM), or design-builder on an as-needed basis. The contractor may schedule meetings to address internal management, organization, operation, coordination, and safety issues. The owner may schedule meetings to address coordination with separate contractors, select colors, or coordinate move-in plans. Special meetings may also be scheduled to coordinate sustainability issues. A design-builder may schedule meetings to address coordination between the contractor and the A/E. Special meetings scheduled for a specific purpose usually do not involve or require attendance of the entire project team.

13.6 | Submittals

During the construction of a traditional D-B-B delivery method for a project, the contractor is usually required by the contract documents to submit product data, shop drawings, samples, informational submittals, closeout submittals, and maintenance material submittals to the A/E for review. These submittals are not contract documents, unless specifically identified as such in the contract documents, and are not to be used by the contractor or the A/E to modify the contract. Submittals convey information about systems, equipment, materials, products, and administrative matters. They provide important information to the A/E and, through the A/E, to the owner. Submittals are also an important part of the quality assurance for a project. They indicate how the contractor, subcontractors, fabricators, and suppliers intend to fulfill portions of the contract document requirements. They also provide the owner with information on products and equipment incorporated into the facility. This information, in combination with O&M data, is useful for facility management activities and when future facility modifications or replacement are being considered.

13.6.1 Contract Documents

Administrative and procedural requirements governing submittals during the construction stage are contained in the conditions of the contract and Division 01—General Requirements. Standard general conditions, such as AIA Document A201, General Conditions of the Contract for Construction, and the EJCDC C-700, Standard General Conditions of the Construction Contract, require the contractor to prepare, review, and forward various submittals to the A/E. The conditions of the contract also clarify the A/E's role in using professional judgment to review, approve, or take other appropriate action on the submittals.

Both AIA Document A201 and EJCDC C-700 require the contractor to submit a schedule of submittals coordinated with the construction progress schedule to allow for timely submission and adequate review time of construction submittals.

The Division 01 submittal section will usually stipulate the amount of review time needed by the A/E to render professional judgment on submittals. The Submittal section also often states that the contractor should allow sufficient time in the submittal schedule for a review, rejection, resubmittal, and re-review of a submittal without causing delay to the project.

13.6.2 Preconstruction Submittals

Generally, no work should begin until required preconstruction submittals have been submitted by the contractor and reviewed by the A/E and owner. When the contractor receives the notice to proceed, preparation and delivery of the preconstruction submittals should begin as soon as possible.

13.6.3 Construction Submittals

Specified submittals relating to a portion of the work must be acted upon by the A/E before work on that portion begins. AIA Document A201 indicates that the contractor shall perform no portion of the work requiring submittal and review of shop drawings, product data, samples, or similar submittals until the respective submittal has been approved by the architect and that such work shall be in accordance with approved submittals.

In the traditional D-B-B project delivery method, submittals are processed during the construction stage of a project.

13.6.3.1 Action Submittals

Action submittals are submittals requiring responsive action by the A/E, normally review and approval. These include the following.

Product Data. Product data include illustrations, standard schedules, diagrams, performance charts, instructions, and brochures that illustrate physical appearance, size, and other characteristics of materials and equipment for some portion of the work. This information is helpful to both the contractor and the A/E. It is used by the A/E to determine whether the contract requirements are being met.

Shop Drawings. Shop drawings are drawings, diagrams, illustrations, and schedules specifically prepared by the contractor to illustrate and depict more clearly some portion of the work. Shop drawings assist the contractor and the A/E in determining how a certain portion of the project will be constructed and how this portion interfaces with adjacent construction.

Samples. Office samples show color, texture, and other appearance items. Samples and color selection items are physical examples of materials, equipment, or workmanship that illustrate functional and aesthetic characteristics of a material or product and establish standards by which the work will be judged. Inclusion of a detailed color schedule with the construction documents helps to avoid delays, changes, and additional costs.

13.6.3.2 Informational Submittals

Informational submittals are submittals not requiring responsive action by the A/E. AIA Document A201 states that informational submittals upon which the architect is not expected to take responsive action may be so identified in the contract documents. This information deals for the most part with the verification and certification that the installed work or portion of the work meets the specified quality requirements. This information is used by the A/E to evaluate the performance and quality of project components. These may include design and delegated data, test and evaluation reports, manufacturer's instructions, manufacturer's reports, certificates, and qualification statements. Many of these submittals are processed as a record of the construction and do not require approval by the A/E or the owner. These informational submittals may include:

- Coordination drawings
- Certificates
- Design and delegated design data
- Test and evaluation reports
- Manufacturer's instructions

- Manufacturer's reports
- Sustainable design reports
- Qualification statements
- Construction photographs

13.6.3.3 Closeout and Maintenance Submittals

At or near completion of a project, a number of submittals are processed, including:

- O&M data
- Bonds
- Special warranties
- Record documents (shop drawings, record drawings and specifications, addenda, change orders, field orders, photographs)
- Spare parts and maintenance materials (sometimes called attic stock)
- Keying

13.6.4 Submittal Preparation

Submittals are normally prepared and assembled by suppliers, fabricators, and subcontractors for the contractor's submittal to the A/E. Division 01—General Requirements typically includes a section on submittal procedures containing information applicable to all submittals required for the project. In addition, specific requirements are included in the sections in Divisions 02–49. By referring to Division 01 and the specification requirements, the preparer can determine the extent of the submittal, the suggested format, how the submittal must be prepared, how it is to be identified, drawing size, the required number of copies, and distribution requirements. The total number of copies of each submitted item usually includes the copies retained by the A/E, the owner, and consultants, plus those required by the contractor, subcontractors, and suppliers. If the contract documents do not refer to a specific submittal form, product representatives should coordinate required information with the contractor prior to submittal. If the specified requirements are followed, the submittal can be processed easily.

13.6.5 Submittal Review

Submittals are reviewed and approved by the contractor to ensure that contract document requirements have been met, to check dimensions, and to coordinate with subcontractors. In order to maintain proper lines of communication, the A/E receives submittals only from the contractor. Once approved by the contractor, they are submitted to the A/E for review and processing. The A/E's review is limited to determining whether the submittal is consistent with the design intent indicated in the contract documents. The A/E's review is not to determine accuracy and completeness of dimensions or quantities; these are the contractor's responsibility. The submittal review process may include the A/E's consultants. In some cases, submittals are also reviewed by the owner after they have been reviewed by the A/E. In those cases, the owner transmits the reviewed submittals back to the contractor through the A/E.

If the A/E determines that the contractor has not properly reviewed and approved an item before submitting the item for review, the A/E returns the item to the contractor with a request that the item be properly reviewed and resubmitted. The rejection of a submittal for good cause is not a cause for a delay claim on the part of the contractor. The contractor should anticipate the potential need to resubmit incomplete or rejected submittals in the submittal schedule.

AIA Document A201 states that the contractor shall review, approve, and submit to the architect, shop drawings, product data, samples, and similar submittals required by the contract documents. It also states that the architect will review and approve or take other appropriate action upon the contractor's submittals.

Though many standard general conditions documents do not require the contractor and A/E to specifically stamp the submittal, Division 01 sections that address submittals usually require the use of a submittal stamp to verify that the contractor and A/E have completed their obligations to review and approve the submittals. Submittal stamps with specific language are used by the contractor and by the A/E to identify the status of a reviewed submittal. In many cases, the language on the stamp is suggested by a legal counsel or liability insurance company. The critical issue is that the contractor and A/E need to be responsible for processing submittals in accordance with the requirements stated in the contract documents.

13.6.6 Participant Responsibilities

Each member of the construction team has responsibilities in the processing of submittals. Subcontractors and suppliers are responsible for:

- Reading and understanding the contract documents
- Knowing the construction progress schedule and allowing adequate time for contractor and A/E review
- Properly preparing submittals
- Submitting in a timely manner
- Using a transmittal form
- Reviewing other submittals and coordinating with them
- Maintaining records and current status

The contractor is responsible for:

- Reading and understanding the contract documents
- Establishing a realistic submittal schedule that allows for resubmittal
- Coordinating submittals including by owner's separate contractors
- Reviewing submittals for compliance with contract documents, site conditions, dimensions, and construction means and methods
- Approving submittals before transmitting them to the A/E
- Using a transmittal form
- Distributing approved submittals to subcontractors and others
- Maintaining copies of all approved submittals at the site for reference
- Maintaining logs and tracking progress

The A/E is responsible for:

- Specifying reasonable requirements
- Reading and understanding the contract documents

- Verifying that the contractor has reviewed, stamped, and approved submittals
- Reviewing and approving submittals in a timely manner or taking other appropriate action
- Reviewing submittals for conformance with design intent
- Using a transmittal form
- Forwarding submittals to consultants and the owner
- Maintaining a copy of approved submittals
- Maintaining a submittal log and tracking progress

Consultants are responsible for:

- Specifying reasonable requirements
- Reading and understanding the contract documents
- Reviewing and approving submittals in a timely manner or taking other appropriate action
- Reviewing submittals for conformance with design intent
- Using a transmittal form
- Returning submittals to the A/E

The owner is responsible for:

- Reading and understanding the contract documents
- Reviewing and approving submittals, when appropriate, in a timely manner
- Coordinating owner-furnished items that are to be installed by the contractor, including obtaining, reviewing, submitting, and processing of required submittals for coordinating this work
- Coordinating contractor-furnished items that may be installed by the owner or under a separate contract
- Coordinating work to be completed under a separate contract
- Using a transmittal form
- Allowing the A/E to comply with contractual obligations and responsibilities
- Following project requirements

13.6.7 Record Keeping

Record keeping is a vital part of any project. A record of submittals is necessary for checking on the status of specific items and ensuring their timely review. The submittal process should be given high priority by each participant, whether it is preparation of submittals, assembly of information, or review. A submittal log should be maintained by both the A/E and the contractor.

13.6.8 Processing Procedures

Although there are numerous kinds of submittals common to projects, some standard processing guidelines can be followed. Submittals should be complete and accurate, in conformance with specified requirements, and consistent with project conditions. Only specified submittals should be processed. Submittals should be prepared, submitted, and reviewed in a timely manner according to the approved submittal schedule and the current construction progress schedule. Each submittal must clearly indicate project name, A/E's project number, date, specification section reference, drawing reference, and a sequential submittal number. Sequential numbering allows easy tracking. The preparer should specifically indicate any part of the submittal that does not conform to the contract requirements. Preparers should avoid submitting information that is not applicable to the project or not required by the contract documents.

13.7 Site Visits, Observations, and Inspections

All participants in the construction process have certain responsibilities for making observations and inspections. This process of monitoring the work is basic to quality control.

Dictionaries define *observe* as to perceive, notice, see, whereas *inspect* means to examine carefully and critically, especially for defects. In construction, the distinction between these two words has significance, and the individuals responsible for CCA and contractor project management need to be familiar with the two terms.

Most standard owner-A/E agreements and conditions of the contract indicate the A/E will perform construction contract administration and will periodically visit the construction site to (1) ascertain progress and quality of the work, (2) inform the owner of known deviations from the contract documents and defects and deficiencies observed in the work, (3) keep the owner informed of the progress of the work, and (4) conduct inspections to determine the dates for substantial and final completion. The responsibility for observations and inspections by the A/E varies, depending on the owner-A/E agreement and project delivery method utilized.

The standard agreements between owner and contractor require the contractor to visit the site prior to bidding or commencing work to correlate conditions and coordinate observations with the contract documents and report any discrepancies to the A/E. The contractor is responsible for directing and supervising the work and has control over means, methods, and techniques. The contractor is also responsible for continual inspection of the work to ensure that each portion is ready to receive subsequent portions and to arrange for inspections required by AHJs. To achieve substantial completion of the work, the contractor is required to inspect the work and prepare a list (i.e., the punch list) of items required to be completed or corrected prior to final payment.

13.7.1 Contract Requirements

AIA agreements between owner and architect, and EJCDC agreements between owner and engineer are coordinated with respective versions of general conditions of the contract for construction. In the same manner, agreements between owner and contractor are coordinated with the same respective general conditions, such as AIA Document A201, General Conditions of the Contract for Construction, and EJCDC C-700, Standard General Conditions of the Construction Contract. These agreements and conditions of the contract are similar for construction management but can be significantly different under design-build project delivery. It is important that the individuals involved in a project understand the responsibilities and limitations contained in the agreements and the general and supplementary conditions of the contract.

13.7.2 A/E's Responsibilities

Typical and traditional agreements require the A/E to consult with and advise the owner and act as an owner's representative during construction, as provided in the general conditions. The standard agreements also require the A/E to make site visits at intervals appropriate to the stage of construction and to become generally familiar with the progress and quality of the contractor's work. In addition to these requirements, the standard agreements and general conditions state that the A/E:

- Is the communicator between owner and contractor
- Has the right to reject defective work
- Conducts inspections to determine the date of substantial completion and to verify final completion

Standard AIA and EJCDC general conditions state that the A/E is empowered to act on the owner's behalf only to the extent provided in the contract documents. Therefore, it is important that the A/E advise the owner and keep the owner informed of activities at the site.

The A/E's consultants are normally required to be involved in CCA to the extent necessary for the specific discipline. For example, consultants are required to make periodic site visits to observe the progress of work related to their discipline.

The standard AIA and EJCDC documents limit the number of inspections required of the A/E to two. These inspections are to determine the dates of substantial and final completion, which are part of project closeout. A/E inspections help to determine:

- When the project, or a portion of the project, is sufficiently complete to allow the owner beneficial use
- Which items are incomplete or not in compliance with the contract documents
- When the project is complete, and when the contractor is entitled to final payment

Substantial completion is the date established by the A/E when the project, or a portion of the project, is so nearly complete that the owner may use the project for its intended purpose. Final completion occurs when the contractor has completed the contract requirements, the A/E has inspected to determine completion, the owner has made final payment to the contractor, and the contractor has accepted final payment.

13.7.3 Contractor's Responsibilities

The contractor is required to supervise and direct the work. The contractor has complete responsibility for and control of means, methods, techniques, sequences, and procedures for all portions of the work under the contract. The contractor is required to ensure that the work is done according to the contract documents. The typical provisions of the conditions of the contract require the contractor to:

- Observe conditions at the site affecting the work and correlate them with a review of the contract documents and report any errors, omissions, and inconsistencies to the A/E.
- Inspect each portion of the work prior to performing subsequent work.
- Inspect work performed by the owner or separate contractor if the contractor's work depends on that work.
- Prepare and submit a comprehensive list (initial punch list) of items to be completed or corrected prior to final payment.

13.7.4 Owner's Responsibilities

The owner is obligated to provide information about the physical characteristics, legal limitations, and utility locations upon which the contractor can rely, subject to proper precautions taken by the contractor to ensure safe performance. The owner also is obligated to furnish other information or services under the owner's control, upon request of the contractor. The owner is also responsible for work performed by the owner or separate contractors that will affect the work of the contractor performing subsequent dependent work and may be required to correct deficiencies reported by the contractor affected.

Depending on the knowledge, experience, and capability of the owner and the complexity and extent of the project, the owner may have full-time, periodic, or no on-site personnel. Many public-sector projects have full-time owner representatives.

Neither the AIA nor EJCDC standard documents require the owner to perform site observations. In most instances, the owner relies on the A/E for these services. Some owners have experienced staff to perform site-related activities. Usually these activities are not intended to replace the A/E site observations, but only to supplement them. When the owner performs site activities, clear lines of responsibility and communication need to be established to prevent erroneous presumptions by any entity performing construction-related activities. These responsibilities are usually incorporated into the conditions of the contract, but it is helpful to reiterate the responsibilities at the preconstruction meeting.

13.7.5 Authorities Having Jurisdiction

Federal, state, county, and city authorities oversee the safety and welfare of the public they serve. In doing so, they verify that code and ordinance requirements have been met. The AHJs usually perform reviews of the contract documents before issuing permits. They verify that the regulatory requirements are being met by performing building, mechanical, electrical, elevator, fire, life safety, health, zoning, accessibility, and critical structural inspections at the project site.

If the authorities discover work not in compliance with code requirements during a site inspection, they will not approve the work. The noncomplying work must be corrected by the contractor and approved by the AHJs. The contractor is not required to ascertain that the contract documents comply with applicable regulations and code. If the rejected work conforms to the contract documents, the contractor may be entitled to a change order to correct the defective work. However, the contractor may be responsible for correcting, at no additional cost, work the contractor knew to be contrary to applicable regulations and codes.

13.7.6 Working Relationships

A good working relationship among the owner, the A/E, and the contractor, with the primary focus on the quality of the construction, helps to resolve problems and conflicts quickly. The owner, the A/E, and the contractor must work together to construct a facility that complies with the requirements of the contract documents. The A/E should insist that the requirements be met, but allow the contractor some latitude in the methods of obtaining that quality. The A/E's obligations during administration of the contract should be met within the time limits stipulated in the contract documents and as agreed to in the construction and submittal schedules.

Contract document interpretations by the A/E must be impartial. Quick judgments and decisions by the A/E should be avoided unless it is certain that the decision is correct. Only the contractor has a construction contract with the owner. The contractor is responsible to the owner for performance of that contract.

13.7.7 Conduct at the Project Site

All participants should exhibit proper conduct at the project site. Proper conduct includes:

- Maintaining professional demeanor
- Being polite and courteous
- Showing respect
- Following proper lines of communication
- Adhering to the contractor's procedures for visitors

13.7.8 Project Site Safety

The standard general conditions clearly establish the contractor as being responsible for planning, maintaining, and supervising construction safety measures and programs.

The issue of construction safety cannot be ignored by the owner and the A/E. The owner and the A/E are responsible for the safety of their employees at the project site. Therefore, it is important that the owner and the A/E educate the personnel who will be visiting the project site about procedures that are to be followed. Although the owner and the A/E do not participate in the planning of the contractor's safety program, they are to follow the safety procedures established by the contractor.

13.7.9 Defective and Nonconforming Work

Every project has the potential for including work that may not conform to contract document requirements. The AIA and EJCDC general conditions have provisions that require the contractor to allow the A/E to have access to the project. The standard general conditions also state that if work is concealed contrary to the written request of the A/E, the A/E has the right to request that the work be uncovered. Reinstallation may be at the contractor's expense.

The A/E has the authority to reject work that does not conform to the requirements of the contract documents. However, the authority for rejecting work is not a required duty or responsibility of the A/E for the benefit of the contractor. AIA Document A201 states that work not conforming to the requirements of the contract documents may be considered defective. Only the owner can accept nonconforming work; the A/E is not authorized to do so. The A/E, upon discovery of nonconforming work, should document the deficiencies in a field observation report and present copies to the contractor and the owner. The contractor has the obligation to promptly correct nonconforming or defective work. The contractor is responsible for the cost of corrective work, including the costs for additional testing and inspection. The contractor is also responsible for removing the defective or nonconforming work from the project site. The A/E should follow up on deficient work to verify that the deficiency is corrected and that work is proceeding according to the contract documents.

13.7.9.1 Stopping the Work

Forcing a contractor to stop work on a project is a severe action that can have ramifications on both cost and time. The standard general conditions do not give authority to the A/E to order the contractor to stop work. The standard general conditions stipulate that if a contractor fails to correct work that is not in compliance with the contract documents, the owner may order the contractor to stop work until the reason for the stoppage has been eliminated.

The contractor has the right to stop work if the owner has failed to pay the contractor within the time stipulated in the contract documents. AIA and EJCDC documents allow the contractor the right to terminate the contract if work has stopped, through no fault of the contractor, for a stipulated period of time. The conditions of the contract describe the conditions under which the contractor can stop work or terminate the contract and the procedures the contractor must follow when doing so.

13.7.10 Delivery, Storage, and Protection of Products

13.7.10.1 Delivery

The contractor is responsible for receiving, unloading, and handling products delivered to the project site. An exception may be for delivery of owner-furnished products the owner may be required to accept at the site. The contractor schedules deliveries and arranges for the delivered products to be suitably stored at the time of delivery. Products should be inspected for damage upon delivery. Damage discovered during unloading should be noted on the delivery ticket and reported to the carrier immediately.

13.7.10.2 Storage

Products are often stored at on-site and off-site locations before being incorporated into the project. The contractor's use of the site for storage and construction operations may be confined to certain areas identified in the contract documents. The standard general conditions prohibit the contractor from unreasonably encumbering the site with products and equipment.

13.7.10.3 Protection

The contractor is responsible for adequately protecting stored products. Requirements may vary depending on the manufacturer's requirements, industry standards, and common sense. The A/E normally reviews stored products to verify that they are adequately protected. The manufacturer should submit material safety data sheets (MSDS) to the contractor for those products deemed by the manufacturer to contain hazardous substances. Manufacturer's requirements for protection are normally followed to ensure that products are not damaged and that warranty provisions will not be voided.

13.7.11 Progress Schedule Review

The contractor is required to submit construction progress and submittal schedules. The A/E reviews these schedules before making site visits. Review of the construction progress schedule assists the A/E in determining the percentage of project completion. An accurate construction progress schedule is essential when payment requests on lump-sum projects are evaluated.

Review of the construction progress and the submittal schedules helps the A/E to recall the status of submittals and to anticipate when products will be arriving at the site. The schedules are effective as a point of reference during site visits to help the A/E observe areas that will soon be concealed. The submittal schedule should be coordinated with the construction progress schedule.

13.7.12 Record Keeping and Reporting

Documentation created by CCA is effective for communication as well as for a historical record of the construction stage activity. These records serve as an aid in future recollection of construction activity. Construction documentation should be well prepared and include important transactions arising from the construction process. The documentation should be maintained in a format that can be easily retrieved.

Use of both hard copy and electronic media is helpful for documenting construction activities. Printed copies of reports and correspondence are necessary for distribution to others and for record-keeping purposes. Electronic media ease the task of searching for specific activities, thanks to the ability to electronically search for and retrieve documents.

The A/E maintains records of many items during the construction of a project. These include:

- Field observation reports
- Correspondence
- Meeting minutes
- Communication reports (telephone and meeting)
- Submittals
- Test reports
- Payment requests and certifications
- Schedules
- Requests for interpretation, clarification, or information
- Proposal requests and change order requests
- Contract document modifications

13.7.13 Establishing a Field Office

The specifications may include requirements for a structurally sound, weather-tight structure equipped with heating, air-conditioning, electrical and data communication outlets, and lighting for the A/E's and contractor's field offices. This is normally accomplished through the use of portable facilities. When an existing facility is being renovated or the project is on a restricted site such as a downtown location, it may be possible to establish field offices using designated space within an existing facility or to lease space within an adjacent facility. The specifications may require that the field office be equipped with a telephone, a computer with Internet connection, and a fax machine to expedite communications.

13.7.14 Record Documents

Record documents are kept in the field office and are used to record actual construction. The contractor is required by both AIA and EJCDC standard general conditions to maintain record documents. Division 01 specification sections specify the procedural requirements for record documents. The contractor usually obtains one set of drawings for recording changes and modifications. These documents are stored in the field office apart from the documents used for construction. The record documents should be labeled and filed according to the specification section number. Each item should be labeled "RECORD DOCUMENT" with a stamp or in printed letters. The documents should be maintained in a clean, dry, and legible condition and should not be used for construction purposes. Information should be placed on the record documents concurrently as construction progresses. The record documents should be available for review by the A/E and the owner during the entire construction stage.

13.7.15 Review, Analysis, and Evaluation

Regular feedback based on actual project experience is valuable for the improvement of future documentation and project procedures. Feedback should occur during each stage of a project, especially during the construction stage. It is during the construction stage that lessons learned should be documented, in writing, in order to improve the project team's corporate memory and quality management programs. During large or complex projects, feedback to the project team should be continuous rather than periodic.

It is usually helpful to briefly record the history of the construction stage as a prelude to a thorough review of the project upon its completion. This history includes:

- Successful product uses and techniques, as well as those that need improvement
- Successful coordination and communication situations, in addition to those requiring refinement
- Successful techniques in handling difficult situations
- Details of construction
- Interface of products and systems
- Identification of problems, delays, conflicts
- Identification of construction-related factors that could be useful on future projects
- Subcontractor and vendor performances
- Review of approved change orders to analyze the reasons for these changes
- Review of denied or rejected change proposals to determine potential document clarification needed

13.8 Quality Assurance and Quality Control

The construction stage of a project is the process of executing the requirements of contract documents and thus providing the required quality. Contractor project management and CCA involve QA and QC processes. Quality refers to the project requirements established by the contract documents.

- *Quality Assurance (QA):* Refers to the procedures for discovering defects and deficiencies or deviations to the contract documents before and during the execution of the work. It includes submittals, certifications, and other actions to ensure that the proposed products and services meet the contract requirements.
- *Quality Control (QC):* Refers to the procedures for evaluating completed activities and elements of the work for conformance with contract requirements. Procedures include testing and inspection. Contractual agreements may include the responsibility and authority to find and correct causes of unsatisfactory performance.

13.8.1 Participants Affect Quality

Each of the participants in the construction process has a role in achieving quality in a project. The rights and responsibilities of the owner, contractor, and A/E are addressed in the conditions of the contract. Procedures are addressed in Division 01—General Requirements within 01 40 00, Quality Requirements of the specifications.

In the course of administering a construction contract, the A/E endeavors to verify that the required quality of work is being provided and to inform the owner of known deviations from the contract documents and defects and deficiencies observed in the work. Acting as interpreter of the contract documents, the A/E provides the continuity in the understanding of the intent of the contract documents.

The contractor's QA process begins when the contractor visits the site to become familiar with conditions under which work will be performed. The process continues with field measurements, coordination, scheduling, and the preparation and review of submittals.

The contractor's QC process originates when the contractor assumes responsibility to supervise and direct the work using the contractor's expertise, skill, and attention. The contractor also assumes control over the means, methods, techniques, sequences, and procedures for construction.

13.8.2 Examples of Quality Assurance

Before actual execution of the work, QA activities help to ensure a common understanding of the contract documents and prevent future problems. These QA activities are in the best interest of all participants. Examples of early QA activities are:

- Verifying site conditions, taking field measurements, correlating the information with the contract documents, and reporting any errors, inconsistencies, or omissions
- Reviewing drawings and specifications to uncover any coordination items, errors, omissions, or inconsistencies prior to construction
- Correlating proposed solutions with the contract requirements
- Scheduling and sequencing of the work

- Meeting with others to resolve unclear or conflicting matters
- Submitting satisfactory evidence of the kind and quality of products
- Obtaining manufacturer's certifications

13.8.3 Examples of Quality Control

QC consists of procedures used to determine whether completed items meet the required quality. Features, characteristics, and functional performance are measured and compared with contract requirements. These procedures may be based on objective, scientific evidence or on a more subjective, aesthetic judgment. Testing may be destructive or nondestructive and may be performed in place or on representative samples. Some of the more common forms of QC include:

- Comparing items to an acceptable standard
- Determining whether items are within an acceptable range of deviation of tolerance
- Checking against a list of contract requirements
- Monitoring, verifying, and substantiating requirements
- Testing and inspection

13.8.4 Concurrent Quality Assurance/Quality Control Processes

QC for one action may become QA for the next step in a process. Raw material suppliers implement QC procedures before shipping to manufacturers. Manufacturers incorporate QC procedures in their manufacturing processes. Following these procedures, manufactured components may be fabricated into more complex units. In each step of the process, the previous QC becomes part of the QA for the next step. This process is referred to as a quality loop or quality spiral by the American Society for Quality Control.

13.8.5 Quality Established by the Contract

The contract documents establish requirements for the work and procedures for administering the contract. Specifications generally stipulate qualitative requirements and the drawings generally indicate quantitative requirements. Therefore, the major criteria for quality are described in the specifications. Every specification requirement influences the quality of work, which is not always limited to articles that use the word quality. Requirements range from procedural issues to performance criteria and workmanship.

13.8.6 Team Approach

The responsibilities and performance of each participant affect overall project quality. The success of a project depends upon all participants being committed to a team approach for meeting the requirements. A team approach is a cooperative effort in which each participant is involved in accomplishing the overall goals. The team approach involves procedures that make the achievement of quality a manageable task:

- The owner must have realistic goals and a reasonable program, budget, and construction schedule. The owner's selection of an A/E and the extent of basic services are necessary to the realization of these goals.
- The A/E's ability to develop the owner's requirements into a documented design is critical to defining the quality and the basis for evaluation (such as tolerances and standards).
- The contractor's performance and the completed project will be evaluated based on conformance to the contract documents.

13.9   Interpretations and Modifications

There is no substitute for clear, concise, correct, and complete contract documents. However, the extent of the design and construction process is such that contract document modifications and changes to a project are sometimes made. The contract documents are not perfect and the A/E is normally called upon for interpretations, clarifications, and modifications. Some changes, such as those resulting from concealed and unknown conditions, cannot be avoided. Part of the A/E's construction contract administration responsibility is having orderly procedures for managing these situations, whenever they occur.

There are two types of modifications: those that require a change to the contract sum or time, and those that do not. Changes to the contract sum or time require a change order. Changes that do not affect cost or time are minor changes in the work and may take the form of substitutions, supplemental instructions, or field orders.

13.9.1   Interpreting Contract Documents

Well-coordinated contract documents minimize the potential for conflicts and the need for contract interpretations and modifications. Information should be stated clearly, but only once. Information in the drawings and specifications should complement each other, but should not be repetitive. If similar information appears in both the drawings and specifications but is in conflict, document interpretation or modification will be needed. Standard contract documents prepared by the AIA and the EJCDC prescribe the role of the A/E to act as the impartial interpreter of the documents and render decisions regarding the documents' intent. A change directive, minor change, change order, notice of claim, or claim may result from a contract interpretation, depending on whether the contractor and owner agree with the interpretation.

13.9.1.1   Contract Document Relationships

AIA Document A201, General Conditions of the Contract for Construction, and EJCDC C-700, Standard General Conditions of the Construction Contract, describe the contract documents as complementary, and state that what is required by one is as binding as if required by all. When the contract documents are being interpreted, the contents of the drawings and the specifications must be considered together.

13.9.1.2 Requests for Interpretations

The acronym RFI is sometimes used to mean Request for Information. AIA Document A201 states that the architect will review and respond to requests for information about the contract documents. As stated and with respect to the A/E as the interpreter of the documents, RFIs should be limited to requesting an interpretation of the documents or may be a request for information that may be missing.

RFIs may occasionally be an attempt to make a product, material, or system substitution after expiration of the time limit for submitting requests for substitutions. The contractor should not attempt to transfer the contractor's responsibility for a timely and thorough review of the contract documents to the A/E through the issuance of RFIs. The contractor should be limited to the submission of valid RFIs, and the A/E should render interpretations in a timely manner. RFIs and the responses to them should be referenced to the contract documents if possible.

13.9.2 Contract Modifications

Contract modifications are required whenever a change will modify the contract documents, whether or not the change will affect the time or cost. Change orders are used to modify the contract documents when cost, time, or both are affected. Minor changes in the work are issued when neither time nor cost are affected. Prior to preparation of a change order, the contractor is usually asked to respond to a proposal request or submit a request for proposal, in which the cost of the change and schedule impact is identified. If the A/E is in agreement with the proposed change, cost, and time revisions submitted by the contractor, a change order will be issued. If the A/E is not in agreement with the contractor's proposal, a change directive may be issued. A change directive directs the contractor to proceed with the work. A change directive may result in a claim later when the contractor is not in agreement with all of the change directive terms. Contract modifications are not required when an RFI does not affect cost or time.

Properly prepared contract documents include provisions for modifications along with commensurate adjustments in the contract sum and time without invalidating the contract; however, the modification must be within the general scope of the contract. The A/E should avoid relying on modifications to correct inadequately prepared drawings or specifications.

Well-prepared and coordinated conditions of the contract and Division 01 describe the conditions under which modifications to the contract documents will be allowed.

13.9.2.1 Construction Change Process and Documentation

A request for a contract modification can be initiated by the owner, the contractor, or the A/E. It is important that the parties identify those individuals who are authorized to act on proposed changes.

Several methods are available to request and to make contract document modifications to the project:

- Written requests for change (not a directive to make a change):
  - Proposal request
  - Change order request
  - Request for substitutions

- Minor changes (that do not affect contract sum or time):
  - Architect's supplemental instructions (AIA)
  - Field order (EJCDC)
  - Written interpretation or clarification (EJCDC)
- Change directives (directs change to be made; contract sum or time adjusted at a later date in the form of a change order):
  - Construction change directive (AIA)
  - Work change directive (EJCDC)
- Change orders (directs change to be made with contract sum or time adjustments stipulated).

13.9.2.2 Minor Changes

Minor changes to the project or clarifications of the contract documents are defined as instructions or clarifications not involving adjustment of the contract sum or time. AIA Document A201 does not identify a specific document for minor changes, but AIA Document G710, Architect's Supplemental Instruction, is commonly used. EJCDC C-700 allows the engineer to authorize or order minor variations to the project by use of a field order. Minor changes may be initiated by the architect's supplemental instructions or the engineer's field orders, or another document identified in the contract documents that direct the contractor to make stated modifications. The architect's supplemental instruction does not require the owner's or the contractor's signature.

13.9.2.3 Change Directives

AIA Document G714, Construction Change Directive, and EJCDC C-940, Work Change Directive, direct the contractor to make a change to the project before the owner and contractor have agreed upon the proposed changes in contract sum or time. Change directives are used in the absence of an agreement between the owner and the contractor on the terms of a change order or when the value of a change cannot be determined until after the work is performed. The change directive may or may not affect the contract sum or time; however, the change directive serves as notice that the change will be incorporated in a change order once the value of the work is established. This is in contrast to a change order in which the parties have agreed on the adjustment in contract sum or time before the work is accomplished. The change directive is prepared by the A/E and signed by both the A/E and the owner. The contractor is directed to proceed with the change even if the proposed adjustment in the contract sum or time is subject to later acceptance or rejection. Once the cost or time is agreed upon, the change directive is incorporated into a change order.

13.9.2.4 Change Orders

A change order is a written instruction to the contractor issued after execution of the agreement. It authorizes an addition, deletion, or revision to the project in consideration of an adjustment in the contract sum, contract time, or both. A change order is used for changes to the contract documents that affect contract sum or time. A principle of most standard general conditions is that only the owner has authority to execute a change order. The term execute, as used here, means an owner authorization for the change order. The A/E usually prepares and signs the change order, and then the contractor signs the change order indicating acceptance of the change. The owner then signs the change order to formally authorize the change. Change orders may originate by issuance of a change directive, change order request, or proposal request.

The AIA standard general conditions state that time limits in the contract documents are of the essence. The time limit usually is the period of time allotted in the contract documents to achieve substantial completion of the project. By signing the agreement, the contractor agrees that the time limit stated is a reasonable period of time to construct the project. Careful monitoring of the contract time provisions is necessary during construction.

13.9.3 Substitutions

AIA Document A701, Instructions to Bidders, states that substitutions will not be considered after the contract award unless specifically provided for in the contract documents. EJCDC documents allow for material substitutions after bidding and negotiating.

Product, material, or system substitutions may be handled in many ways. Procedures applicable to substitutions proposed after execution of the agreement are described in Division 01. If Division 01 allows for substitutions after the procurement, acceptance of the substitution may be accomplished by use of a substitution request form. EJCDC C-700 has a provision that requires the contractor to reimburse the owner for the engineer's time in reviewing and evaluating a substitution, whether or not the proposed substitution is approved. Charges for A/E services to evaluate substitutions initiated by the contractor, to make subsequent revisions to drawings and specifications, and to prepare other documentation resulting from a proposed substitution should be addressed in the owner-A/E agreement and added to supplementary conditions or Division 01—General Requirements.

Substitutions should not be considered when:

- The substitution request is made as an RFI.
- The substitution is indicated or implied on shop drawings, in product data submittals, or as samples without a prior formal request being submitted and approved according to Division 01.
- The submitted substitution request has not been reviewed and approved by the contractor.
- Acceptance will require substantial revision of contract documents or other items of the project, unless the participants involved agree to reimburse costs for changes to the contract documents.
- The substitution request does not include an itemized comparison of the proposed substitution with the specified product.

13.9.3.1 Substitutions after Award of Contract

There are occasions when substitutions after award of the contract may be allowed. Under certain project delivery methods the owner may encourage the contractor to propose alternatives during the course of construction. This is often allowed to reduce costs and evaluate alternative products and systems.

13.9.3.2 Substitutions during Construction

Most contracts have very specific procedures for requesting a substitution. Substitutions during construction can be disruptive and should be avoided as much as possible. There are, however, several legitimate scenarios when substitutions during construction may be required or allowable.

- *Owner-Initiated Substitutions.* After contract award, the owner may decide to change a certain product, system, or other element of the project.
- *Contractor-Initiated Substitutions.* After contract award, many developer type owners may encourage the contractor to propose changes of products, systems, or other elements of the project in order to save money.
- *Integrated Project Delivery (IPD) Substitutions.* By the nature of the IPD process, there may be multiple modifications to products, systems, or elements of the facility. These modifications typically occur during the design process and involve the entire team.
- *Unavailability of Product.* On occasion, a product or system that has been specified cannot be obtained. There can be several reasons: it is no longer manufactured or there has been a labor strike, as examples.

13.9.3.3 Evaluation of Substitution Requests

A number of items are considered when evaluating substitutions. The first and foremost of these is whether or not the proposed substitution meets the requirements of the contract documents. These include the product, the manufacturer, the product representative, the installation, operating costs, maintenance costs, and warranty concerns. Equipment operating costs such as energy demands, replacement part life cycles, and routine maintenance costs are all factored into the evaluation process.

There is no substitute for a complete review of the proposed deviation from original contract requirements. The amount of time devoted to a request should be in proportion to the item's importance to the project. A request for approval of a curtain wall system requires considerably more attention and time than a request for approval of a towel dispenser. If a request is submitted with inadequate documentation, the request should be rejected and returned for resubmittal. It is the responsibility of the entity requesting the substitution to research and document the substitution to prove equivalency.

The A/E determines the acceptability of proposed substitutions and should review valid requests with reasonable promptness. The decision to approve or reject a requested substitution should be indicated on a substitution request form. Rejection of the proposed substitution usually requires use of the specified product. Most owners and most courts will hold the A/E, not the proposer of the substituted product, to be responsible as the ultimate judge. A simple principle applies: the same liability exists whether a product is specified or is accepted as a substitution.

13.9.4 Feedback

Once interpretations or modifications have been accepted, a determination should be made on whether the interpretation or modification was specific to a project or more general in nature, requiring a revision to the A/E's standards or system. If a standard detail or specification item requires an interpretation or clarification, the A/E should review the appropriate drawing or specification system to prevent future need for interpretations and clarifications. Failure to improve the system will only perpetuate the problem and generate more requests for information or requests for clarification on future projects. The time required to make interpretations becomes costly if the same item needs repeated clarification.

To be effective, feedback should occur on a continual basis. The purpose of evaluation and feedback is to provide information to the project team so that they may learn from actual experience. The benefits of feedback include:

- Enhanced experience in various project types, materials, systems, and processes
- Input of valuable information for use on future projects
- Better quality assurance and control methods
- The refinement of innovative designs, materials, and construction techniques
- Identification of correctable situations for the benefit of future projects

13.10 Executing the Work

13.10.1 Field Engineering

Field engineering consists of taking the measurements, facility placement, and layout from the contract drawings and laying them out on the project site. Field engineering includes site surveying and layout. It is important that this work be performed by properly trained and experienced personnel, which may include a licensed land surveyor, the contractor's superintendent, or project engineer. Mistakes made in field engineering can result in significant construction and legal problems. Errors made in field engineering become compounded as the project is constructed.

13.10.2 Supervision of Construction

Qualified and competent supervision of construction is often the difference between a successful project and one that is not. The contractor's project manager and superintendent(s) are responsible not only for getting the project constructed correctly, but also for safety, coordination, scheduling, dealing with media inquiries, dealing with project visitors, and a large variety of other tasks.

13.10.2.1 Contractor Responsibilities for Supervision of the Work

The agreements and conditions of the contract state that the contractor is responsible for supervision of the project work. Several forms of agreements have language that is specific as to the experience requirements for the contractor's project manager and superintendent, how much time the individuals must physically be on the project site, and define their responsibilities.

13.10.2.2 Complying with Contract Documents

The contract documents represent what is to be constructed. The agreement obligates the contractor to comply with the contract documents. Standards and other reference documents are included by reference in the contract documents. The participants need to be familiar with the referenced documents and comply with requirements. This includes obtaining the proper inspections, tests, transmittal of requested and required information, and routing of correspondence, and not deviating from the contract documents. The contractor is not required to confirm completeness and accuracy of the contract documents, nor is the contractor required to ascertain that the contract documents are in accordance with applicable codes and regulations. However, if the contractor discovers errors, omissions, or inconsistencies in the contract documents, or discovers nonconformity with applicable codes and regulations, the contractor is obligated to notify the A/E as soon as the issue is discovered as a request for interpretation.

13.10.2.3 Quality Assurance and Quality Control Procedures

The contractor must verify that the work being performed complies with the contract documents. This verification is a primary aspect of QC. This QC provides QA for subsequent operations. Each participant should verify that existing or preceding work is proper and does not contain obvious defects that will affect subsequent work. Verification of work varies, depending on who is verifying, on which portion, and at what time during the process. This verification may include inspecting, testing, and reporting the results. Other verification may be a simple review of work for accuracy and workmanship. The contractor needs to continuously verify that the work performed is according to the planned schedule and sequence. The contractor also prepares progress billings on the basis of verification of the quantity of work performed. Similarly, the A/E verifies the quality and quantity of work that has been completed, so the A/E can recommend to the owner whether the requested payment should be made.

13.10.3 Coordinating Construction Activities

Coordinating construction effectively is the most important activity contributing to a smoothly running project. The contractor must coordinate all of the subcontractors, suppliers, inspections, testing agencies, consultants, and other project participants at the correct times in order to ensure success. Preparation of an accurate, concise, properly sequenced, and thorough construction progress schedule is paramount to being able to coordinate all the various elements of a project.

13.10.4 Sequencing the Work

Effective sequencing of the work requires an understanding of the construction processes required for the project. The list of tasks that are dependent on each other in a project is extensive. For example, concrete forms are built first, then reinforcing steel is placed, and then the concrete can be placed. Walls are framed, then electrical, plumbing, and mechanical rough-in are completed before the wall framing is covered. Although common sense will dictate a lot of the sequencing, there is no substitute for adequate experience. Someone who does not have the appropriate experience may make some sequencing decisions that are not correct and that may cost the contractor money and time if work has to be rescheduled or corrected later. Contract documents may specify certain sequences required for the project. As an example, a specification may require resilient flooring to be installed prior to cabinetwork being installed.

13.10.5 Scheduling the Work

Regardless of the project delivery method, the contractor is responsible for scheduling and timing the work. Given this authority, the contractor has an obligation to keep all members of the project team informed of progress, expected delivery dates, start dates for tasks, and other issues that may affect milestone dates or the completion date. This is easily performed when a good updated construction progress schedule is shared with the participants on a regular basis. Weekly scheduling meetings are an excellent way to accomplish this. The owner, A/E, contractor, subcontractors, sub-subcontractors, suppliers, consultants, and any appropriate agencies, such as testing laboratories or inspection agencies, are invited to attend these meetings as deemed appropriate. By maintaining the schedule and communicating with all members of the construction team, there are fewer surprises and the participants know what is expected of them and when it is expected to occur.

13.10.6 Construction Means and Methods

Construction means and methods are the techniques and procedures that will be used to construct the project, the "how to" aspects of performing the work. Means and methods involve the planning and sequencing of activities, assignment of labor, use of the site, logistics of materials, coordinating with other activities, and executing the work. Means and methods involve how the work is carried out. A product or system may be assembled on- or off-site, in a single process or a series of processes, or it may be delivered to the site in components to be assembled in its final location. Means and methods involve the specific selection of equipment and personnel to perform the work, expeditiously and cost effectively. Power equipment, such as nail guns, backhoes, cranes, and lifts, may be used in lieu of hand tools to expedite the work and improve efficiency.

Construction means and methods are the sole responsibility of the contractor, unless specified otherwise in the contract. Whereas the contract documents specify what is being constructed and where it will be located, means and methods deal with how it will be constructed. Both the owner and the A/E must be very careful not to direct the means and methods. The A/E's responsibility is to ensure that the project is constructed as indicated in the contract documents.

13.10.7 Examination and Verification

Each installer should inspect previously completed work prior to starting the installer's own work. This is especially true for specialized subcontractors, such as cabinet installers, floor covering installers, glazers, and finish carpenters. This may include verifying actual field dimensions with dimensions on shop drawings; ensuring that openings, built-in anchorage, and reinforcing are in place and correctly sized; and ensuring that all work required prior to the start of the installer's work has been completed. This examination is intended to identify defects in previously completed construction. It is advisable to not begin work until defects and deficiencies have been noted and brought to the attention of the contractor. This procedure is a QA action that will help prevent compounding defects.

13.10.8 Preparation

After examination and verification of previously completed work, each installer needs to make necessary preparations for installation of the installer's work. These preparations may include verifying that the materials to be installed are at the project site, obtaining the tools and equipment required for the work, confirming that environmental requirements in the contract documents or of the manufacturer have been met, and coordinating the construction progress schedule with the contractor and other installers performing related work or work in the affected area of the project. Once the installation work begins, it is presumed that the substrate upon which that work is installed is acceptable and meets applicable standards for the new material being installed.

13.10.9 Erection, Installation, and Application

The contractor determines the means and methods of how to construct a project. The contractor's means and methods include erection, installation, and application of products and materials. This includes verifying that required materials are available, access to perform the task is adequate, and sufficient labor and equipment are on-site. A preinstallation meeting at the site often precedes these activities. The attendees at preinstallation meetings may include the contractor or a subcontractor, the manufacturer's representative when applicable, and the A/E.

13.10.9.1 Tolerances and Clearances

The quality of workmanship required for each project is established by the contract documents. Construction specifications identify the qualitative requirements for products, materials, and workmanship upon which the construction contract is based. Tolerances are QC requirements for construction items in the specifications, or by references to various industry or trade association standards related to product or equipment. Tolerances vary depending on the material and its use. Tolerances may be industry standards or they may be special project requirements. For example, the tolerance for concrete floors will be different for superflat warehouse floors than for concrete floors that will receive carpet in an office building. The specifications normally recognize the difference in requirements between these areas. The concrete floor standards for flatness in carpeted areas may not need to be verified if spot checks prove acceptable. However, because of the precise project requirements for a superflat floor, testing methods are normally required to verify compliance with the contract documents.

13.10.9.2 Contractor's Inspections

The contractor should perform regular inspections throughout the project, to ensure that the project is being constructed per the contract documents. This means that, in addition to supervising and inspecting the contractor's own work, it is also the contractor's responsibility to inspect the work of those under the contractor's control. The fact that the contractor did not perform an element of work with the contractor's own forces, does not excuse the contractor from compliance with the contract documents.

13.10.10 Cleaning and Construction Waste Management

Cleaning and removal of construction waste are a necessary aspect of construction. A poorly maintained site can be a safety hazard as well as being unsightly. Even though each individual may be responsible for their own debris, there needs to be central control of construction waste and debris. This overall control of cleaning and construction waste management may vary depending upon the project delivery method. Division 01—General Requirements may specify the procedures and responsibilities for cleaning and construction waste management.

Many projects, whether sustainable or not, have requirements maximizing the amount of construction waste being sent to recycling facilities. Many contractors have discovered that in certain urban project locations, it makes very good business sense to recycle as much construction waste as possible because the costs are far less than the cost of using landfills. Many projects have recycled more than 75 percent of construction waste, including material packaging.

13.10.10.1   Progress Cleaning

Regular cleaning is important during construction for several reasons. It presents a better project image to the public and visitors to the site. Having a clean work site reduces accidents such as tripping and stepping on nails, as well as making access easier for all workers. Often the requirements of regular project cleaning may be spelled out in the contract.

13.10.10.2   Construction Waste Management

Part of an efficient project-cleaning program includes construction waste management. Having adequate construction waste receptacles to isolate recyclable materials from trash going to a landfill is important.

In order to comply with sustainable requirements, the contractor may be required or simply desire to provide for salvage and reuse of existing materials and minimization of construction waste through recycling. As sustainability and reuse of construction materials become a higher priority, recycling and reuse opportunities are increasing. Often a recycling company provides receptacles on-site for collecting construction materials, which are then picked up and hauled away at no cost to contractor or owner. In several instances, the contractor or owner can make nominal revenue from the recycling efforts. Scrap steel and reuse of existing wood beams are good examples of constructive reuse of materials.

13.10.10.3   Final Cleaning

Final project cleaning is performed just before turning the project over to the owner. Timing is important so that the cleaning is performed only once. Usually, professional cleaning services are enlisted for this important cleaning. It is common to have a line item in the schedule of values for final cleaning. The requirements of final cleaning may be spelled out in the contract or at the preconstruction or site mobilization meetings. On sustainable projects, compliance with industry recognized referenced standards for stewardship of cleaning commercial and institutional facilities is often required.

13.10.11   Protecting Installed Construction

Protection of installed construction, while the contractor's responsibility, becomes everyone's job as the project progresses. Subcontractors are also responsible for protection when they perform their work. Even the owner and the A/E need to exercise care when at the project site to ensure that they do not inadvertently soil or damage completed work. This becomes more critical toward completion of the project, especially when finishes have been completed.

13.10.12 Testing and Inspection

There are numerous requirements for testing and inspection from a variety of AHJs and testing agencies throughout a project. Total facility commissioning may be a significant component of the testing and inspection required for a project. Commissioning is a critical component in the QC processes for a project. Whereas testing and inspection typically focus on specific items of work or systems, total facility commissioning checks the entire project to verify that it will meet the needs identified by the owner in the design stage.

The type of project determines which of the numerous tests will be required throughout a project. These may include pile-driving bearing tests, rebar and concrete QC inspections and tests, rock and asphalt compaction tests, structural steel-welding tests, and fireproofing tests. The contract documents specify who is responsible for testing. The party responsible for payment of the testing agency may vary from project to project, but the contractor is always responsible for scheduling the testing. The results of the test or inspection should be clearly documented, including whether the time tested passed or failed to meet the requirements, and issued in a report within a day or two after the test or inspection. Test reports are submitted to the contractor and the A/E to document required testing. The contract documents may also require the testing agency to submit copies of test reports to the owner, the A/E, the applicable subcontractor, and AHJs. Codes and applicable regulations often require the owner to provide special inspections and testing for portions of the project. The owner may rely upon the A/E for assistance in securing names and proposals for these services from independent testing laboratories and inspection agencies. The A/E may also be required to monitor these testing and inspection services to verify that required tests and inspections are taking place in a timely manner.

13.10.13 Project Site Safety

Project site safety is important to all of the construction team participants. Whereas the contractor is responsible for the overall project safety, the owner and A/E are obligated to abide by the contractor's safety rules when at the project site.

As construction has become more complicated, so have the health and safety issues facing the contractor. The contractor must be cognizant of a myriad of agencies and regulations. The Occupational Safety and Health Administration (OSHA) dictates many of the safety requirements that must be adhered to in construction. Furthermore, many states and local jurisdictions have safety requirements in addition to those mandated by OSHA. The owner and A/E should not direct the contractor in matters of safety, or they may be liable for the consequences that arise from their direction. In addition to OSHA, most companies have their own safety rules. These may include issues such as personal protective equipment, safety meetings, safety committees, new employee orientation, and accident/incident reporting. Personal protective equipment includes a variety of devices designed to protect the employee from the hazards found on a construction site. Some common types of personal protective equipment and related hazards are as follows:

- Hard hats—falling objects
- Ear protection—high-decibel noise
- Dust masks and respirators—sweeping, grinding, and spray applications
- Safety glasses, goggles, and face shields—airborne particles that may enter the eyes, such as sawdust, grindings, chemicals, and dust
- Safety vests—increased visibility to the traveling public and construction traffic

- Safety harnesses, lanyards, and lifelines—fall protection for overhead and elevated work
- Gloves—hand protection from abrasive and sharp objects
- Boots—foot protection from dropped material, sharp penetration, or other hazards

13.11 Claims and Disputes

The successful project is one completed on time, within budget, and with all claims resolved. Contract document modifications are a natural part of the construction process. When either an interpretation or a modification affects contract sum or time for completion of construction, a claim may be submitted. An unresolved claim may lead to a dispute. Whatever the sources of construction claims may be, the success of the project depends, to a large extent, on how well the owner, A/E, and contractor manage these claims.

Project participants need to understand the contract provisions governing claims and disputes and the way claims may be managed in order to avoid disputes. Claims are initial requests for adjustment in contract sum or time. For example, change order requests and proposal requests are claims. They are open to challenge but are not necessarily a matter in dispute. Disputes are claims that cannot be resolved by the parties to the construction contract without the intervention of an independent third party.

13.11.1 Claims

Generally, three sources of claims may occur on a project. Two sources of claims include claims by the contractor (often on behalf of their subcontractors and suppliers) against the owner, and claims by the owner against the contractor or the A/E. The third source is a claim initiated by someone other than a party to the construction contract.

13.11.1.1 Contractor Claims

A contractor prepares pricing based on the procurement documents and other factors that are reasonably foreseeable at the time. If, during the course of the project, the contractor encounters conditions contrary to those stipulated or inferred in the contract documents, a claim may be initiated. Changed conditions include:

- Active interference by the owner or A/E
- Conditions beyond the control of either the contractor or the owner
- Unknown or concealed conditions that affect the extent of the work
- Modifications made to the contract documents
- Errors and omissions in the contract documents

The contractor is required to provide clear documentation that a changed condition actually was not foreseeable at the time of pricing and resulted in demonstrable damages. Claims resulting from changed conditions may also be submitted by the contractor on behalf of the contractor's subcontractors and suppliers.

13.11.1.2 Owner Claims

In most cases, except in the case of cost-plus fee contracts, the owner has received a firm price from the contractor to perform the work of the project. When the owner believes the value of the work received is not commensurate with the contract price, or the owner's costs are increased because of actions or inactions by the contractor, the owner may initiate a claim. Claims initiated by the owner may include:

- Correction of nonconforming or defective work
- Contractor's failure to clean up
- Repair of damages to existing property
- Liquidated or compensatory damages for late performance
- Ineffective management and/or control of the work by the contractor resulting in added costs for:
  - Inordinate re-reviews of shop drawings
  - Reviews of substitution requests
  - Interferences with the owner's operations
  - Additional site visits, inspections, and related administrative time

These types of claims are also grounds for withholding payment. It is important that the owner understand that the general conditions require the party initiating the claim to provide documentation establishing the claim. Therefore, the owner should carefully document such claims, attempt to settle the claim, and unilaterally withhold payment only as a last resort to satisfying the claim.

13.11.1.3 Third-Party Claims

The various types of third-party claims are too numerous to name. Injury or death to persons and property damage claims are high on the list in terms of frequency and severity. The methods of claim prevention and resolution for these types of claims are very different and are not addressed in this chapter.

13.11.2 Entitlement

Entitlement is defined as the right to benefits specified by law or contract.

13.11.2.1 Contractor Entitlement

The contractor's entitlement to a claim involves two separate determinations. First, the claim is evaluated to determine whether the contract documents adequately identify the claim as being within the contractor's contractual obligations. If the work in question is found not to be reasonably inferred, the contractor is entitled to a contract modification. If the work in question is found to be reasonably inferred, the entitlement to the claim is denied.

The second determination of contractor entitlement is the timing of the claim. The general conditions require the contractor to notify either the A/E or the owner before performing extra work. In special instances, the contractor must notify the A/E and the owner within a specified period of time after performing the extra work. Receipt of proper notification by the contractor is a right reserved by the owner. This allows the owner to evaluate extra work situations with the A/E and attempt to identify the most cost-effective action. It also is intended to avoid situations where the passage of time has prejudiced the owner's ability to challenge the claim. Failure to properly notify the A/E and the owner can result in a forfeiture of entitlement to the claim.

13.11.2.2 Owner Entitlement

The determination of owner entitlement similarly involves determining whether the work in question required of the contractor by the owner may be reasonably inferred from the contract documents. If the work in question may be reasonably inferred, the owner's claim may be upheld without a modification of the contract. If the work in question cannot be reasonably inferred, the owner's claim is denied and the work in question either dismissed or provided for as a contract modification.

13.11.3 Resolving Claims

Upon receipt of a claim, the A/E or initial decision maker may request additional information to support the claim. Once the claim is clearly documented and understood, it may be appropriate to generate a written preliminary response summarizing the essence of the claim, identifying any concerns requiring reconciliation, and establishing a proposed schedule for resolving the claim.

The justification for many claims is often apparent at the outset, and such claims can be handled with much less effort by promptly addressing the issues and negotiating a settlement, if at all possible.

Claims involving adjustments in contract sum or time require supporting documentation. It is the responsibility of the party making the claim to prove the claim and it is the responsibility of the A/E or initial decision maker to evaluate the supporting documentation. On stipulated sum contracts, claims for additional cost are reviewed against the A/E's independent estimate of cost, based upon the contractor's schedule of values and published estimating guides. On unit price contracts, estimating guides are used if none of the unit price items apply to the extra work. The A/E should also attempt to verify with the contractor that the costs claimed are representative of the total impact of the conditions giving rise to the claim. The A/E evaluates the submitted documentation to determine the validity of the claim and presents the findings to both parties.

13.11.3.1 Dispute Avoidance

Because unresolved claims, or disputes, have become so commonplace in the construction industry, claims avoidance has become a common term applied to the management of claims and disputes. Because a claim is defined as a request for adjustment to the contract, it is more appropriate to think in terms of dispute avoidance.

Each party understanding the interests and limitations of the other is a first step to avoiding disputes. The owner holds the contractor accountable for only those cost elements of the project that are reasonably documented or foreseeable at the time of pricing. The contractor should understand the owner's need for thorough documentation justifying a claim. The contractor should reference the specific parts of the contract documents that support the contractor's claim and also provide sufficient cost breakdowns to permit a complete analysis of the costs. The contractor must accept that the owner also has the right to claim compensation for nonperformance, poor performance, or negligence resulting in damages to the owner.

When any of the participants refuses to accept its contractual responsibilities, disputes occur. Therefore, the process of submitting, processing, and successfully settling claims relies on individual integrity and cooperation among the participants.

13.11.4 Disputes

Disputes often occur when the A/E's or the initial decision maker's decision on a claim is not accepted by one or both parties and the claim cannot be resolved through negotiation. A claim may become a dispute no matter how responsibly the parties attempt to resolve it. Each party may be convinced its position is correct and that there is no further room for compromise. In most cases, the failure to negotiate effectively is due to one or more of the participants failing to understand and accept the rights, responsibilities, and requirements established by the contract documents.

When attempts at reaching a mutually acceptable settlement have been unsuccessful, the parties are obligated under the conditions of the contract to use the specified method of dispute resolution indicated in the contract documents. Both AIA Document A201 states that if no resolution is reached after the Initial Decision Maker's decision, then either party can demand the other party file for mediation. If the other party does not file for mediation, then both parties waive mediation and any other dispute resolution method with respect to the initial decision. EJCDC C-700 also identifies mediation as the first attempt to resolve a claim. If mediation is unsuccessful, the parties may choose to invoke any dispute resolution process provided for in the conditions of the contract.

13.12 | Measurement and Payment

Measurement means quantifying the amount of work eligible for payment, and payment is the disbursement of money proportionate to that quantity of work. Under some contracts, measurement may involve only identifying the attainment of specified milestones for which predetermined amounts of payment are to be paid. Under other contracts, particularly unit price contracts, measurement means verifying the quantities of work submitted for payment based on unit prices.

13.12.1 Applications for Payment

Most contracts specifically stipulate the requirements for preparation and delivery of the application for payment. The contractor needs to clearly understand the requirements for submitting an application for payment and follow procedures correctly, so that payment is not delayed. Most contracts require that a schedule of values be submitted to the A/E for approval prior to the first application for payment. It is not uncommon for the contractor to be required to submit an updated construction progress schedule, test reports, material certifications, and other accompanying information as a prerequisite for payment.

13.12.2 Payment Intervals

The interval between payments is normally identified in the contract documents. The payment interval specified should reflect the nature of the work of the project. Common payment intervals are as follows:

- *Periodic Progress Payments.* Monthly progress payments are appropriate for most projects, including those of long duration and high cost, where the rate of progress will vary from month to month. Twice monthly or even weekly progress payments may be appropriate for small projects performed by small contractors or large fast-track projects where large amounts of money are expended over brief periods on a regular basis.

- *Provisional Payments.* Provisional payments are predetermined partial amounts of the total contract sum tied to the attainment of identifiable milestones. The milestones may be percentages of the total quantities in the project, or they may be certain portions of the entire project that have been assigned a predetermined value.
- *Single Payment.* When projects are of a size that enables the work to be completed in a short period, the contract sum is small, or the vast majority of the contract sum is earned in the latter stages of the project, a single payment of the entire contract amount may be appropriate.

13.12.3 Basis of Payment

The contract sum may be established by a combination of base bid items, including unit prices, allowances, and alternates.

The payment administration process depends on the basis of payment identified in the contract documents for the various contract items. There are generally three bases of payment, and each places different demands on the project team. The three bases of payment are as follows:

- *Stipulated Sum.* On stipulated sum or lump sum contracts, a single price becomes the amount agreed upon for completion of the entire contract.
- *Unit Price.* Common to civil engineering projects where final quantities can be measured only upon completion but cannot be determined at time of pricing. Under unit price contracts, the actual quantity of work is measured and verified as it is completed and payments are made at the agreed-upon unit price rates.
- *Cost-Plus Fee.* Utilized where both the quantity and the cost per unit of work are uncertain or when the contract sum is a cost of the work plus fee not to exceed a guaranteed maximum price contract. As the term cost-plus implies, the contractor is reimbursed the contractor's actual cost of labor, equipment, and material, plus a predetermined fixed fee, or percentage of costs, for overhead and profit.

13.12.4 Contractual Responsibilities

The owner-A/E agreement establishes that the A/E will certify the amounts due the contractor based on the A/E's observations of the work in progress and evaluation of the contractor's application and certification for payment. The A/E's certification is a representation that the contractor is entitled to payment of the amount certified. The A/E's certification is based only on the A/E's knowledge, information, and belief that the work has progressed to the point indicated and the quality of work conforms to the requirements of the contract documents.

The contract documents contain terms, conditions, and procedures for payment application and certification by the contractor; review and certification by the A/E; and payment by the owner. Contract documents addressing payment usually include the following:

- Agreement
- General Conditions

- Supplementary Conditions
- Division 01—General Requirements, Section 01 20 00—Price and Payment Procedures

13.12.5 Measurement

There are three methods of measuring or quantifying the amount of work eligible for payment:

- *Stipulated Sum Contracts.* For stipulated sum or lump-sum contracts, progress payments are related to a schedule of values. The schedule of values serves as a basis for estimating percentage payments for partially completed work.
- *Unit Price Contracts or Items.* Unit price contracts generally consist of items that are measurable units suited to progress payments, such as lineal feet of storm sewer pipe or cubic yards of topsoil.
- *Cost-Plus Fee Contracts.* Cost-plus fee contracts are administered on the basis of receipts for materials and equipment and on payroll records to establish values for progress payments.

13.12.6 Schedule of Values

The schedule of values is prepared by the contractor according to the contract documents. It is an itemization of the costs of various portions of the work, which together comprise the total contract sum. Each line has a value that is a proportionate fraction of the total value of the whole project.

The first step to orderly payment administration on stipulated sum contracts is to secure a properly proportioned schedule of values. This is normally done after award of the contract and before processing of the first progress payment. The contractor submits the schedule of values to the A/E for review. The level of detail required by the contract documents should be sufficient to establish the proportionate cost of each of the various items of work in the project.

13.12.7 Application for Payment

Both AIA and EJCDC application for payment forms require significant representations of both the contractor and the A/E to the owner. Therefore, it is important to recognize that the application forms, schedule of values, contractor's preparation, and A/E's review and certification/recommendation are significant parts of the payment process.

13.12.7.1 Application Forms

AIA Document G702, Application and Certification for Payment, and EJCDC C-620, Application for Payment, are two commonly used application forms for payment prepared by the contractor and reviewed by the A/E. Some public owners may have their own forms. The forms contain representations made by both the contractor and the A/E to the owner.

The contractor prepares the application and certifies that the work covered by the application conforms with the requirements of the contract documents and that all the previous amounts paid to the contractor have been properly applied to discharge the contractor's obligations to others furnishing materials and labor on the project.

The A/E's representation is that to the best of the A/E's knowledge the work covered by the application has progressed as indicated and is in general conformance with the requirements of the contract documents.

13.12.8 Progress Payments

Upon receiving the contractor's application and certificate for payment with the A/E's certification, the owner is obligated to make payment on or before the time established in the contract documents. When the progress payment has been made to the contractor, the owner has discharged the owner's payment obligation for work completed to date. The contractor then becomes responsible for making payments to the various subcontractors, suppliers, and others with a vested interest in the work.

The conditions of the contract usually stipulate that progress payments do not constitute acceptance. Progress payments are made in response to representations and certifications by the contractor that the work conforms to the requirements of the contract documents. The A/E represents that the A/E's certification is not based on exhaustive inspections. Therefore, the conditions of the contract make provision for the owner to reject work and adjust payment accordingly any time up to final acceptance.

13.12.9 Retainage

Progress payments are usually subject to the Retainage of a prescribed percentage of the amount due for payment. This retainage is not to force the contractor to perform. It protects the owner against errors in estimating the value of work completed or defective work and is used to settle other participant (third-party) claims against the contractor before the release of final payment. If portions of the work paid for have latent defects, or if simple errors in estimating quantities have been made, the Retainage is available to the owner to correct the situation. Retainage reduction may be specified to occur at the attainment of some milestone such as 50 percent completion or substantial completion of the project.

13.12.10 Withholding Payment

The A/E has the right, and the responsibility, to withhold certification of the whole or any part of the payment application in order to protect the owner. AIA and EJCDC standard general conditions contain provisions for the owner to withhold payment to the contractor in whole or in part under certain conditions. Among the more common conditions for the A/E to recommend the withholding of payments to protect the interest of the owner are:

- Damaged or nonconforming work requiring repair or correction
- Damaged property adjacent to the project, caused by the contractor and requiring repair or replacement

- Failure by the contractor to meet specified schedule milestones or the contractor's own approved schedule to the extent that liquidated or compensatory damages may reasonably be anticipated
- Claims made against the owner on account of the contractor's failure to perform or furnish work without interference and damage to others
- Liens filed in connection with nonpayment of subcontractors, suppliers, laborers, and mechanics furnishing material and labor for the work of the project
- Failure to keep record documents up to date if required by the contract documents
- The cost of doing cleanup work, by the owner or others, resulting from the contractor's failure to perform cleanup work as specified in the contract

13.12.11 Failure to Make Payments

The A/E will have a prescribed time after receipt of the contractor's application for payment to make certification of payment, and the owner will also have a prescribed time after receipt of the A/E's certification to make payment to the contractor. These requirements are identified in the owner-contractor agreement and the conditions of the contract. If there is a failure to make payment within the prescribed times, without cause under the contract conditions, the owner may be in material breach of contract. In this situation, the contractor is protected under the conditions of the contract and may, upon prior written notice, stop work if payment is not made within the notice period. The owner's exposure to liability in such an occurrence may include the contractor's cost of demobilization and the cost of delay and remobilization after the breach is rectified by the owner. If the breach is not rectified by the owner and the contract is terminated, the owner may also be liable for damages resulting from the contractor's loss of profit.

13.12.12 Liens

A lien is the legal right of a party or claimant, such as a subcontractor, to control the improved property of another or have it sold for payment of a claim. Virtually every state has established laws that permit contractors performing work on real property to file a mechanic's lien against the property.

Typically, if a contractor, subcontractor, sub-subcontractor, or material supplier is not paid, they have a right to file a lien against the property where the project was performed. Such liens are similar to placing a mortgage on the property except that often mechanic's liens will have a higher priority than most mortgages —in other words, if the property is sold, payment of the mechanic's lien is a higher priority than payment of the mortgage.

13.12.13 Liquidated Damages and Penalty/ Bonus Clauses

Liquidated damages stated in the agreement are usually invoked when substantial completion is not achieved by the indicated date or within the indicated time. Liquidated damages or penalties are normally deducted from the final payment, and bonuses are added to the final payment. Both actions require a change order to modify the final contract amount.

Just because liquidated damages are not specified in a contract does not mean that the contractor is immune from claim for damages from the owner for late delivery of the project. Absent a specific amount for liquidated damages, the owner can document and make a claim for actual damages, which in some cases will far exceed the amount that could have been applied if a liquidated damages clause had been included in the contract.

13.12.14 Substantial Completion, Partial Occupancy, Final Acceptance, and Payments

The date of substantial completion is when the project, or a portion of the project identified by the construction contract, is determined by the A/E to be sufficiently complete so that the owner can use it for its intended purpose. If progress payments have been properly administered and if provided for by the contract, the Retainage may be reduced to an amount sufficient to complete the project.

Neither progress payments nor acknowledgment of substantial completion or partial occupancy constitute acceptance of work not completed according to the contract documents. The punch list, or list of items to be completed or corrected, must be completed prior to final payment. Some agreements for A/E services end within a certain period of time after substantial completion. Considering the time required for correcting or completing work, the contractor could be responsible for the cost of additional or extended services required by the A/E.

13.12.15 Final Payment

Final payment often requires the processing of a final change order to balance previous payments against the final payment and final contract amount. Typical final change order items may include:

- Adjustments to unit price item quantities
- Adjustments to stipulated allowances
- Adjustments for liquidated damages or penalty/bonus clauses
- Adjustments for testing reimbursement when the owner employs the testing services and pays for only passing tests
- Adjustments for reimbursement of utilities
- Adjustments for reimbursement of the owner's expense for additional A/E services

13.13 Project Closeout

13.13.1 Participant Roles

Construction contract administration culminates in project closeout and includes activities involved with the orderly transfer of the completed project from the contractor to the owner. The closeout process begins with starting and adjusting systems, and ends with the contractor accepting final payment from the owner. Following is a list of the participants and some of their major closeout responsibilities:

- *Manufacturer.* Inspects installed work and provides special warranties.
- *Supplier.* Assembles O&M data.
- *Subcontractor.* Starts systems and equipment, prepares record documents, prepares O&M data, completes the punch list, demonstrates systems, and provides training.
- *Contractor.* Makes inspections, coordinates completion of the punch list, assembles record documents, assembles O&M data, prepares and coordinates starting of systems and equipment and operational tests, provides demonstration and training, and performs final cleaning.
- *Consultant.* Assists with inspection of the project, reviews record documents, adds items to punch lists, certifies compliance of installed work with the contract documents, and reviews O&M data.
- *A/E.* Inspects the project, compiles supplementary punch lists, reviews record documents, reviews O&M data, prepares final change order, certifies substantial and final completion and the final application for payment.
- *Commissioning Authority.* Completes project commissioning.
- *Sustainability Consultant.* Receives sustainable submittals, prepares necessary paperwork, and submits evidence of sustainable accomplishments to certifying authority.
- *Owner.* Accepts the project, makes final payment and releases any retained funds, attends commissioning, attends demonstration and training programs, and arranges for transfer of the facility from the contractor to the owner.
- *Facility Manager.* Assists in the successful transfer of the completed facility for the owner's use. Major responsibilities may include:
  - Identifying maintenance-staffing requirements; assigning and training staff
  - Accepting delivery of extra stock and maintenance equipment and supplies included in the construction contract
  - Coordinating installation of owner furnished furniture, furnishings, and equipment
  - Participating in systems start-up and testing
  - Participating in systems demonstration
  - Participating in systems O&M training
  - Accepting and managing the record documents

Typical closeout process includes the following:

- The contractor inspects the project and prepares a comprehensive list of items to be completed or corrected (initial punch list).
- The contractor submits notice of substantial completion.
- The A/E inspects the project to verify substantial completion and prepares a supplement to the contractor's list (final punch list).
- The A/E prepares the certificate of substantial completion.
- The contractor completes the items on the punch list.
- The contractor submits notice of final completion and final application for payment.
- The A/E inspects the project to verify final completion.
- The A/E processes the final application for payment and closeout submittals.
- The owner makes final payment.

13.13.2 Closeout Meeting

A closeout meeting may be arranged by the A/E to review closeout procedures, or they can be discussed at a regular project meeting. Closeout procedures and submittal requirements may have been discussed during the preconstruction meeting, but several months or years may have passed since that meeting and the participants may need to review the process.

13.13.3 Closeout

Adhering to a comprehensive set of closeout procedures allows the project to be completed in an orderly and timely manner. Following are basic steps to project closeout:

- Start-up, testing, adjusting, and balancing of systems and equipment
- Project record documents
- Demonstration of systems and equipment and training
- Completion of the commissioning activities
- Substantial completion
- Final completion

13.13.3.1 Starting of Systems and Equipment

There is a particular time in every project when the facility must become functional. This initial functioning of permanent systems and equipment, such as the mechanical, electrical, and elevator systems, is known as start-up. Proper systems operation is a prerequisite for the project to be accepted by the owner.

The scheduling and coordination of starting of systems is specified in Division 01. These requirements establish the contractor's responsibility for coordinating start-up procedures as follows:

- The subcontractor completes a system
- The subcontractor notifies the contractor that the system is ready for start-up
- The contractor field-verifies compliance with the contract documents
- The contractor coordinates related work necessary for start-up
- The contractor arranges a time and date with the A/E and the owner to observe starting procedures
- The subcontractor starts systems and equipment according to the manufacturer's instructions, often in the presence of the manufacturer's representative
- Testing is completed according to the contract documents and manufacturer's recommendations
- Reports are submitted to the A/E for review

13.13.3.2 Project Record Documents

Project record documents include the construction submittals, record drawings, record specifications, addenda, contract modifications, photographs, start-up logs, test reports, certifications, and other documents, which are assembled by the contractor. They are used by the owner and facility manager as a resource in facility O&M. The number of copies required and the submittal format (electronic, hard copy, or both) are specified in Division 01.

13.13.3.3   Demonstration of Systems and Equipment and Training

Because a substantially complete project is one that the owner may occupy and use, it is important that the owner understand its operation. A project may not be certified as substantially complete by the A/E until the contractor has demonstrated the various systems and equipment and trained the owner's and facility manager's personnel, and the O&M data has been submitted by the contractor, approved by the A/E, and sent to the owner.

13.13.3.4   Commissioning

There are two basic types of commissioning: total project commissioning and systems and equipment commissioning. Total project commissioning, also referred to as total facility commissioning, begins during project conception and continues through facility management and use. Total project commissioning documents the owner's facility criteria and verifies that the criteria are achieved and that the facility is placed into proper operation. System and equipment commissioning includes detailed operational testing, adjusting, and training of specific systems or equipment to ensure their readiness for use in the facility.

13.13.3.5   Time of Completion

There are two significant dates in project closeout: substantial completion and final completion. Substantial completion occurs when the project, or a portion of the project, is sufficiently complete according to the contract documents to allow the owner to use it for its intended purpose. Final completion is when the project is complete according to the contract documents and the contractor is no longer involved on the project. Both dates are established by the A/E after conducting inspections of the project. Final completion of the project is evidenced by the contractor's acceptance of final payment from the owner. In the event of an outstanding claim, the contractor may refuse to accept final payment.

13.13.3.6   Substantial Completion

Most standard general conditions state that the date of substantial completion is the date established by the A/E when the project is sufficiently complete to permit the owner to use it for its intended purpose. The date of substantial completion is established by the A/E and documented by the issuance of a certificate of substantial completion. At substantial completion, the owner (or the facility manager on behalf of the owner) typically assumes responsibility for routine maintenance, utilities, security, property insurance, and liability for the facility and its adjacent grounds. At substantial completion, the correction period begins, and specified product warranties typically begin. If the contractor has been responsible for property insurance during the construction stage, this responsibility typically shifts to the owner at substantial completion. For these reasons, the date is important to the owner, the contractor, and the A/E.

13.13.3.7   Final Completion

Final completion occurs when the contractor has completed the contract requirements, the A/E has inspected to determine completion, the owner has made final payment to the contractor, and the contractor has accepted final payment. The final completion procedure begins when the contractor completes work on the punch list. The contractor removes any remaining trash, tools, construction equipment, temporary facilities, and surplus materials from the site. When this is accomplished, the contractor notifies the A/E in writing that the work is completed and submits required closeout documents.

13.13.4 Postconstruction Services

Sometimes the services provided by the A/E and the contractor continue beyond final completion. These services may include assistance with occupancy of the facility, more extensive training of owner's O&M personnel, and helping the owner with postoccupancy evaluations and inspections. A/E involvement in the project beyond occupancy can help the owner better understand the operation and performance of the project.

13.13.5 Facility Evaluation

The facility manager should develop and maintain an ongoing evaluation program. This process begins at occupancy with a postoccupancy evaluation and continues through the life of the facility. The format and content of the evaluations vary greatly depending on the facility type, and might include the following:

- *Building.* Structure, envelope, space allocation, interior and exterior finishes, mechanical and electrical systems, site development, and energy efficiency.
- *Tenant/User.* Efficient layout, signage, accessibility, interior finishes, mechanical and electrical systems, and leased area.
- *Highway.* Paving, striping, signage, lane width, on-ramps and off-ramps, lighting, shoulders, and landscaping.

Facility evaluations address facility use, effectiveness, efficiency, operational cost, maintenance, and environment. In preparing the evaluation format, the facility manager should try to envision the company's future. The forms need to incorporate relevant information for future decisions.

Facility evaluations assemble information that will assist in planning and scheduling routine and preventative maintenance, capital improvements, facility upgrades, and system and equipment replacement. Standard forms may be used to address component evaluations such as roofing, exterior wall finishes, landscaping, flooring, equipment and systems, and production processes. These forms facilitate quick field review and updating of facility records.

Facility evaluations should be made on a regular basis and records updated at regular intervals. An evaluation cycle should be set up for each facility component. The length of time between evaluations will also be affected by the age of the facility and the frequency of operational changes by facility users.

13.13.6 Project Feedback

It is common for the A/E and contractor to perform postoccupancy facility evaluations of completed projects. These evaluations may be performed in conjunction with the owner and the facility manager, or they may be performed to help the A/E or contractor in preparing for future projects. They also communicate to the owner that the A/E and contractor are genuinely concerned about the quality of the project. Lessons learned from a past project can prevent costly mistakes in future projects. These evaluations can also be used to address owner concerns, identify problems, and suggest solutions.

Chapter 14
Facility Management

Transition

14.1.1 Introduction

As will be discussed in greater detail in the following sections, management of the new facility becomes an important function after construction is completed, construction activities cease, and the facility is occupied and used for its intended function. It is not uncommon for facilities to be managed and maintained by a staff of skilled and training individuals. However, as the project transitions into a facility and goes through its various closeout activities, the facility manager can participate in the process in order to be ready for occupancy.

14.1.2 Role and Responsibilities of Facility Manager during Project Closeout

The facility manager is involved in project closeout to assist in the successful transfer of the completed facility for the owner's use. During project closeout, it is important for facility managers to:

- Understand their roles in and the construction contract requirements affecting commissioning, equipment and systems start-up, and project closeout.
- Identify maintenance-staffing requirements; assign and train staff.
- Take delivery of extra stock and maintenance equipment and supplies included in the construction contract.
- Coordinate installation of owner provided furniture, furnishings, and equipment.
- Participate in systems start-up and testing.
- Participate in systems demonstration.
- Participate in systems operations and maintenance (O&M) training.
- Understand the project correction period and warranties.
- Accept and manage the record documents.
- Accept and manage building information models.

It is necessary to pay close attention to project closeout issues and maintain contact with the contractor and A/E so that the facility manager becomes familiar with the facility and that O&M programs are established. It is important for the long-term success of the facility's O&M that project closeout activities include start-up and load testing of new and modified equipment and systems, demonstration of equipment and systems for new operators, operational training if necessary, and commissioning of systems and equipment. For example, the potential for outgassing of materials must be included in the time allocated for project closeout and start-up of heating, ventilating, and air conditioning (HVAC) systems. Multiple filter changes might be required in the first several weeks to ensure removal of fibers, dust, and potential allergens from indoor air.

The contract documents used for construction might require the contractor to provide several types of documents and materials to assist the facility manager in facility O&M. These documents are called record documents and include O&M data, materials and finishes data, record submittals and shop drawings, record drawings, and record specifications. The contractor might also furnish spare parts, extra materials, and specialized operating tools to the owner or facility manager as required by the construction contract. To ensure that the contractor submits this information during project closeout, it is essential that the requirements for these project closeout documents and materials be included in the contract documents for construction.

14.1.2.1 Operations and Maintenance Data

Prior to scheduling equipment and systems start-up and training sessions, the facility manager should receive O&M data for the facility. Submission of O&M data is typically a condition of substantial completion of the contract. This information is submitted by the contractor prior to start-up and training sessions to allow:

- Review by the architect/engineer (A/E)
- Revision by the contractor if required
- The facility manager to become familiar with the information

Prior to training sessions, the contractor should submit maintenance materials or specialty tools for O&M. The facility manager should have the O&M data available for review during the equipment and systems training sessions.

If the contract documents for construction did not require the contractor to provide the O&M data needed, the facility manager must obtain this information from other sources. A similar condition might occur when a facility manager assumes responsibility for operating an existing facility for which this information is not available. Potential sources for this information include the A/E, contractors and subcontractors who have worked on the facility, and manufacturers and suppliers of materials, systems, and equipment incorporated into the facility. For an existing facility, prior owners and tenants might be able to furnish useful information.

14.1.2.2 Demonstrations and Training

Equipment and systems operation and training sessions provide an opportunity for the facility manager to review and ask the trainers questions about the data, equipment, and systems. This review and training occurs prior to substantial completion, or when the construction contract stipulates that the facility manager accepts responsibility for O&M of the facility. The facility manager should ensure that the personnel responsible for the facility are present at the appropriate demonstrations and training sessions provided by the contractor. Prior to the sessions, the owner should receive, from the contractor, documentation indicating that the trainers are knowledgeable in the O&M of the systems and equipment.

After project closeout, additional training and operating information may be needed from the system or equipment installer or product representative. The facility manager should maintain a current contact list for product representatives and service organizations that may be needed to provide assistance in maintaining and operating facility systems and equipment.

14.1.2.3 Punch Lists

Prior to substantial completion of construction, most construction contracts require that the contractor prepare a punch list for the project. The punch list identifies incomplete work and items requiring correction. The owner and facility manager might not be contractually involved in the punch list process. However, if the owner or facility manager opts to be involved in this process, the owner or facility manager should limit personal involvement to avoid interfering with the contractor's and A/E's contractual obligations.

14.1.2.4 Authorities Having Jurisdiction

The owner is obligated to comply with regulatory requirements not included in the construction contract in order to meet requirements for use and occupancy. Requirements include installation of signage, safety devices, and other owner-furnished items. The owner needs to provide documents to various authorities having jurisdiction (AHJs). The facility manager is responsible for collecting and distributing these documents, including the following:

- *Bonds.* The owner might be required to provide bonds to ensure future performance, such as the establishment of landscaping, reforestation, or wetlands plantings, especially those done in compliance with mitigation negotiations.
- *Easements.* The owner might be required to dedicate easements to local utility providers for current utility service or future utility extensions.
- *Emergency Plans.* The owner might be required to submit and post written emergency plans for new or renovated facilities regarding fire equipment and exiting, emergency evacuation, and lockdowns.
- *Certificates of Occupancy and Inspection.* The owner is typically required to post certificates issued by the AHJ, such as the Certificate of Occupancy, elevator certificates, and boiler certificates.
- *Signed-off Permits.* The owner should obtain from the contractor the originals of permits for the project after final approval or sign-off by the AHJ. Approved permits for projects should be permanently retained and accessible. Some public agencies do not archive permit records; therefore, it is recommended that the owner retain copies in the event of any difficulty with permit processes.
- *Permit Review Documents.* The owner should obtain from the contractor the originals of permit review documents showing evidence of review, stamped by the AHJ for the project. These documents should be permanently retained.

14.1.2.5 Substantial Completion

Substantial completion of construction is the point at which the project is sufficiently complete for the owner to occupy or utilize the facility for its intended use. The date of substantial completion is established by the A/E and documented by the issuance of a certificate of substantial completion. On complex or phased projects, there might be more than one certificate and date of substantial completion. At substantial completion, the owner (or the facility manager on behalf of the owner) typically assumes responsibility for routine maintenance, utilities, security, property insurance, and liability for the facility and its adjacent grounds. It is important that trained staff is available and prepared to manage the facility starting on the day it is accepted as substantially complete.

14.1.2.6 Commissioning

There are two basic types of commissioning:

1. *Total Project Commissioning.* Also referred to as total facility commissioning, this type begins during project conception and continues through facility management and facility use. Total project commissioning documents the owner's facility criteria and verifies that the criteria are achieved and that the facility is placed into proper operation.
2. *System and Equipment Commissioning.* This type includes detailed operational testing, adjusting, and training of specific systems or equipment to ensure their readiness for use in the facility.

If a project includes total project commissioning, the facility manager should have been one of the key participants in developing the program facility criteria and making design decisions during project conception. This participation continues through the design, procurement, and construction stages. The facility manager works closely with the commissioning agent during project closeout and facility start-up. The facility manager's input and participation during this process may improve the effectiveness of the commissioning agent's work and will provide useful information for the facility manager's O&M procedures. The facility manager needs to be aware of the criteria upon which design was based and should be capable of the following:

- Identifying the systems and equipment to be included in the commissioning process
- Observing and participating in the commissioning process
- Confirming completion of items identified for correction
- Reviewing reports prepared by the commissioning agent
- Considering commissioning agent recommendations
- Ensuring that copies of the commissioning report are available for use in the facility and are archived for future use

If total project commissioning is not included in the project, the facility manager might consider obtaining the services of an independent commissioning agent who provides specialized expertise in system and equipment operation and performance that other project team members do not have. The commissioning agent helps ensure that the facility performs in accordance with the contract documents. This limited version of commissioning does not include the evaluation of original program or design and therefore cannot account for initial decisions.

14.1.2.7 Project Record Documents

During project closeout, the facility manager receives and reviews project record documents. Project record documents include contract drawings, the project manual, addenda, contract modifications, submittals, product data, shop drawings, samples, start-up logs, test reports, certifications, and other documents from the contractor. The requirements for these record documents are described in the contract documents to ensure that they will be submitted during project closeout. An owner might want to retain the A/E to incorporate the contractor's record information into the final record documents. Timely receipt of record documents prepared by the A/E is just as important as receipt of documents prepared by the contractor. Record documents should be permanently retained and accessible. The owner should make copies of these documents on which to record subsequent modifications.

As society continues to absorb technological advances and electronic "wizardry" becomes increasingly common, most, if not all, of the construction documents for facilities will be produced by building information model software. This is highly significant because the electronic model, originally created for the aesthetic and technical design and then used for construction, becomes the information-intensive foundation on which electronic record documents are produced for the owner to use for facility management purposes. If taken to its logical conclusion, the electronic model has the potential of becoming a virtual representation of the physical facility. The possibility exists that one day the design and construction electronic model could be integrated with the many other building monitoring systems, such as the fire alarm, system, the security and access control systems, the building mechanical and electrical systems, vertical transportation, and inventory control to form a single model of the facility.

14.1.2.8 Correction Period and Warranties

Contractors are typically required to provide a one-year correction period for the facility. This requirement might vary depending on the type of facility and construction contract. In addition to the correction period, the contractor is required to warrant the facility for a period of time established by law. Separate warranties and guaranties for specific products, equipment, and systems might be required by the contract documents. These warranties and guaranties might be furnished by the contractor, the installer, or the manufacturer and can have a longer or shorter duration than the contractor's one-year correction period. Most warranties and guaranties exclude misuse, abuse, and failure to maintain.

The facility manager carefully reviews warranties and guaranties to confirm:

- Products and materials included in or excluded by the warranty
- The warrantor or guarantor
- The duration of the warranty
- Conditions and restrictions included in the warranty. Most warranties include provisions that will void the warranty, depending on actions taken or not taken by the owner
- Authorization and activation of the warranty by the warrantor
- Whether owner acceptance of the warranty is required
- Coverage limitations that might result from acceptance
- Requirements for service contracts or approved service providers in order to maintain warranty

The provisions, restrictions, and limitations of warranties and guaranties should be clearly explained to maintenance and janitorial staff and service organizations to minimize potential for voiding warranty provisions. The original warranty documents should be maintained in a safe and secure location for easy access.

The contractor should be notified of warranty and correction items as they occur. Figure 14.1 illustrates a sample warranty action request. This allows the contractor to take corrective action, thereby reducing the potential for voiding warranties, further

WARRANTY NOTICE NO.: 1

PROJECT:	Administration Building 200 Main Street Anywhere, USA 00000	DATE:	June 20, 2005
		CONTRACT DATED:	May 17, 2003
TO CONTRACTOR:	ABC Construction Company Attention: T. Wilson Fax: (123) 555-7890 E-mail: twilson@abc.co	SUBSTANTIAL COMPLETION: A/E PROJECT NO.:	August 22, 2004 02-125
ISSUED BY OWNER :	123 Corporation Contact: B. Kent Fax: (123) 555-4567 E-mail: bkent@123corp.co	COPY TO A/E:	XYZ Architects Attention: B. Dawson Fax: (123) 555-7899 E-mail: bdawson@xyz.co

Purstrant to the Conditions of the Contract and Division 01 requirements of the Contract, notice is hereby given of an observed defect or deficiency in the Work as outlined below. Commence correction of the said defect or deficiency within ten days, and notify the Owner and A/E upon completion.

Subject:	Inoperative Override Button
Location:	Conference 207
Description:	The black override push button on the thermostat on the east wall of Conference 207 does not appear to operate correctly. We were unable to restart FC-207 after hours worked on Wednesday. We used the rotary override timer for zone #1, located in Custodial 127, to restart FC-207. Please repair override push button.

CONTRACTOR RESPONSE:

TO OWNER:	123 Corporation Contact : B. Kent Fax: (123) 555-4567 E-mail: bkent@123corp.co	COPY TO A/E:	XYZ Architects Attention: B. Dawson Fax: (123) 555-7899 E-mail: bdawson@xyz.co

Action Taken: _____

_____

_____

_____

Addressed By : _____ Date Addressed: _____

Contractor's Signature: _____ Date: _____

Figure 14.1 Sample Warranty Action Request

damage to the facility, and loss of productivity. With different project delivery methods, the facility manager contacts different team members. In a design-bid-build contract, the facility manager advises the contractor and the A/E of warranty items. In a design-build contract, the facility manager advises the design-builder of warranty items.

14.1.2.9 Warranty and Correction Period Inspections

The contractor's correction period and some manufacturer warranties might expire one year after substantial completion. Prior to expiration, the facility manager should review:

- Status of the facility with users
- Status of warranty notices
- Correction issues with the A/E
- The facility's condition

The inspection should be scheduled to allow corrections to take place prior to expiration of the correction period.

14.2 Occupancy

14.2.1 Introduction

As this practice guide has demonstrated, a sizeable number of professionals and significant monetary expenditures are necessary for the design and construction of facilities, both private and public. These facilities are properties owned by individuals or businesses and thus represent major assets. Effective management of these assets has grown increasingly important to owners and has given rise to the development of facility management as a formal profession and facility managers as a professional with its own course of study as can be seen by the website of the International Facility Management Association, IFMA (www.ifma.org).

14.2.2 The Nature of Facility Management

Facility management is defined by the International Facility Management Association (IFMA; www.ifma.org, accessed on February 13, 2010) as "a profession that encompasses multiple disciplines to ensure functionality of the built environment by integrating people, place, process and technology." For purposes of this practice guide, facility management is the process of allocating resources for the operation and maintenance of a facility to allow continued performance of the facility's intended function.

According to the *Facility Management Handbook* (David G. Cotts, New York: Amacon, 1988, p. 3), a facility manager integrates the people of an organization with its purpose (function) and place (facility). Other titles frequently used include facility director, property manager, support services director, or physical plant director.

The owner might perform the facility management function or it might be partially or totally outsourced to an outside company, with the facility manager serving under a separate agreement with the owner. Either way, the functions and roles played by the facility manager will be similar, as they are acting on the owner's behalf.

During the design and construction process, the facility manager can be an active participant and may be designated as the owner's representative during the project or act as a consultant to the owner. When doing so, a skilled facility manager should possess the following professional attributes:

- Effectively represent the interests of the owner.
- Have good oral and written communications skills.
- Understand the facility life cycle, especially the design decisions that are important to the use of the facility during its life cycle.
- Understand the design and construction process.
- Know and understand construction documents, especially those that are important to the management of the facility during its life cycle.
- Be familiar with construction, materials, equipment, and systems.
- Understand the codes and regulations that govern the facility and what is necessary for compliance.
- Understand budgeting.
- Understand planning.
- Know sources of products and services for the maintenance of the facility.
- Know and understand building information models and their inherent information assets.

14.2.3 Role and Responsibilities

A facility manager typically operates the facility and manages the support services of a facility in related areas such as maintenance, security, mail service, telecommunications and information technology, parking, fleet management, and transportation. The decision to develop in-house departments or groups to manage these tasks or to outsource them is typically based on:

- Costs of training, hiring, and paying benefits to full-time employees versus fee-for-services contracts in each type of business
- Flexibility associated with the use of outside vendors such as how they respond in the middle of the night and special service charges
- Relationship between employees and outside service providers, including how effectively employees work with outside service providers
- Benefits of outsourcing a piece of the task, as opposed to the entire function; for example, outsourcing cleaning rather than all maintenance functions
- Cost and effectiveness of the maintenance work
- Impact on employee morale when work previously performed by employees is outsourced

The facility manager's role and responsibilities are closely tied to planning for future facility needs. As a key member of the owner's strategic planning team, the facility manager is usually charged with long-term facility needs forecasting. Facility managers are typically involved in the development of master plans for facilities and properties, as well as budget projections for proposed projects. They frequently serve as lease managers for the owner's rental properties and are charged with tenant relations. The facility manager's responsibilities might include space planning, utilization studies, and space inventory and allocations. The facility manager might also be the owner's designated representative in work with independent developers, development consultants, or real estate agents to meet the owner's facility needs. In addition, the facility manager might be in charge of minor capital projects in the same location as contracted work and services.

It is not unusual to find architects, engineers, interior designers, construction managers, and related professionals on the facility manager's staff. This presents a unique opportunity and challenge, as in-house expertise might be closely involved in the evaluation of project progress. The size of the facility manager's staff depends on the size and complexity of the facility owner's company or organization and its operations. Very large companies might create a subsidiary to handle facility and property management. Other large companies could use independent companies to handle their property management, facilities, and development needs.

14.2.4 Operations and Maintenance

Operation activities include the management of the day-to-day functions of a facility and its systems such as utilities, production equipment, building and property infrastructure, mechanical and electrical, custodial and cleaning, and vertical and horizontal transportation.

The importance of facility standards cannot be overemphasized. When faced with the inevitable dilemma of where to allocate funds, the facility standards are a guide for determining appropriate budget preparation and adjustments. *Facilities Management* (Edmond P. Rondeau, Robert Kevin Brown, and Paul D. Lapides, Indianapolis: Wiley Press, 1995, p. 306) speaks of the basic components of standards:

The Design Standards for a particular facilities plan reflect:

1. Minimum requirements from architectural/engineering's standards, local and state codes, and any relevant federal requirements (e.g., Occupational Health and Safety Administration [OSHA] requirements, handicapped design requirements)
2. Special corporate requirements imposed on the particular activity or facility, or all facilities of the company
3. Requirements derived from user/occupant input
4. Budget constraints

The facility manager uses these standards to guide day-to-day operating procedures and as the basis for facility expansion, modification, and new construction.

14.2.4.1 Maintenance

Maintenance issues must be considered and addressed by the project team in the design of facilities, facility improvements, and selection of materials and finishes. Among the objectives of a good maintenance program are the following:

- Minimize interruptions that affect the facility's function and use.
- Minimize failures of equipment and facility structures that affect productivity.
- Select cost-effective repair and replacement methods and materials.
- Prevent hazards affecting health, safety, and welfare.

- Implement effective cost control systems that provide accurate data for review and methods for analysis.
- Implement effective energy conservation practices that support regulatory compliance and provide for a safe and healthy work environment.
- Maintain a clean and hazard-free environment that addresses appropriate disposal of waste, hazardous, and surplus materials.

14.2.4.2 Types of Maintenance

A variety of work processes are included in the realm of maintenance. Project team members should understand these common terms used by the facility management staff as they discuss issues in meetings during design and construction:

- *Maintenance.* Work needed to preserve or restore roads, buildings, landscaping, site improvements, utilities, equipment, and other facilities to original condition or such condition that they can be used for their intended purpose.
- *Emergency Maintenance.* Unscheduled work demanding immediate action to restore services or remove problems that could interrupt activities.
- *General Maintenance.* Unplanned maintenance of a "nuisance nature," requiring low skill levels for correction. Such problems are usually identified and reported by facility users.
- *Preventive Maintenance.* A planned and controlled program of periodic inspection, adjustment, lubrication, and replacement of components, as well as performance testing and analysis.
- *Routine Maintenance.* Repair or replacement of obsolete, worn, broken, or inoperative components or systems. This type of work might be scheduled, repetitive work, or might be a request of a nonemergency nature initiated by a facility user.
- *Renovation/Modification.* Basic changes to a facility or component to accommodate a new function. This work may be initiated either by the facility manager as part of ongoing upgrades to existing systems or at the request of a facility user.
- *Deferred Maintenance.* Work delayed on a planned or unplanned basis, often due to a lack of funds. This practice can be hazardous to maintaining warranties and a proper work environment for the long term.

14.2.4.3 Maintenance Records

To effectively manage these varied maintenance needs, the facility manager must keep accurate schedules, logs, and records to identify:

- Costs for budget purposes, especially life cycle costs
- Locations and systems with unusually frequent maintenance, repair, or replacement activity
- Schedules for equipment and property routine repair and replacement activity
- Evidence of compliance with regulation required inspections
- Compliance with emergency plans to ensure that emergency equipment is in working order
- Processes that can be provided more cost-effectively by outside companies (outsourced)

- Locations where an increase in personnel might be needed (either in-house or outsourced)
- Information that can be used to support increases in budget and labor allocations

Various computer software packages, varying in cost and complexity, can provide the structure for maintenance management (including elements from the preceding list). This software typically includes databases for recording maintenance activity. At a minimum, these records document:

- Identification
- Location
- Date of installation
- Component source
- Who maintains it
- Parts and service source
- Routine maintenance and monitoring requirements
- Regulatory tests and inspections
- Maintenance history

Maintenance history includes maintenance dates, personnel involved, costs, description of work performed, and recommendations for future maintenance work.

Software packages are also available to assist facility managers in tracking maintenance requests. Web-based maintenance software allows the facility manager, maintenance personnel, and building users to enter maintenance requests at a website. When accepted by the facility manager, work orders are generated and sent electronically to the appropriate maintenance personnel. Labor and materials required to complete requested work are posted to each work order account in the database. This information provides an ongoing record of maintenance expenses and activities. This type of system also facilitates monitoring of maintenance requests by the facility manager and the individual submitting the maintenance request. Figure 14.2 illustrates a sample maintenance and work order request.

14.2.4.4 Environmental Issues

A key element in facility O&M is compliance with environmental regulations. Facility managers must be knowledgeable about ordinances, regulatory requirements, and laws applicable to the facility and should determine O&M activities in consideration of their environmental impacts. Ignorance of environmental regulations can be costly and dangerous. Facility management staff must have appropriate training to handle these sensitive responsibilities. Key areas for which facility managers may be responsible include the following:

- *Recycling.* Recycling programs engage employees in responsible citizenship, generate good public relations about the organization, and help promote practices that benefit the community as a whole. Local regulations might require recycling programs to divert a portion of the refuse generated by a facility from landfill to recycling centers. Recycling centers, holding stations, and recycling equipment should be identified in the design stage.
- *Hazardous Wastes.* Regulations and laws require that hazardous materials and production waste materials such as asbestos, lead-based paint, and mercury are disposed of by trained personnel at specific disposal locations. This might require

Maintenance Request Number: 33230   **Status:** Accpted
Work Order Number: 1-51749   **Status:** Completed

Important:	Work order information is provided in real-time and is subject to change.

Building:	Building 15	**Subject:**	Infill floor in mechanical closets.
Location ID:	B-15		
Request Date:	08/10/05		
Accept Date:	08/14/05	**Reject Reason:**	N.A.
Reject Date:	N.A.		

Requestd Action:	In mechanical closets 202B and 220A, remove existing 2 × 4 mechanical curbs in floor and infill 3/4 inch thick wild flooring. Rough opening of framed hole in floor is approximately 19" × 30". Area of flooring to be filled is approximately 27" × 51".

Priority:	Normal	**Charge Account:**	GM05
Est. Completion:	09/24/05	**Task Code:**	GMMISC
Date Closed:	09/15/05	**Maintenance Trade:**	Carpenter Shop
		Contractor Name:	N.A.

Cost Summary:

Total Labor:	$311.74	Total Labor:	11.00 hours
Total Parts:	$0.00	Total Part Quantity:	0
Total Other:	$45.00	Total Cost:	$356.74

Labor Charge Detail:

Date	Name	Technician ID	Hours	Cost
09/13/05	T Wilson	236	4.50	$127.53
09/14/05	T Wilson	236	6.50	$184.21
		Total Labor:	**11.00**	**$311.74**

Parts Charge Detail:

			Total Parts:	$0.00

Other Charge Detail:

		Cost
Plywood		$30.00
Farming Lumber		$15.00
	Total Other:	**$45.00**

Page 1 of 1

Figure 14.2 Maintenance Request and Work Order

contracts with licensed hazardous waste haulers and disposers as well as personnel to manage this function. Hazardous materials removal costs should be included in a maintenance budget, especially for older facilities and sites previously used for industrial purposes. Attention should also be given to the smaller quantities of hazardous materials and waste generated by normal office operations, including toner, cleansers, solvents, light bulbs, photochemicals, paints, and similar substances.

- *Indoor Air Quality (IAQ).* The IAQ is monitored to mitigate airborne allergens and particulates, organic and chemical biohazards, and machine generated irritants in the workplace. Maintenance staff performing routine work on building air-handlings systems has an important role in maintaining good IAQ. The facility is checked on a regular basis for the presence of mold, mildew, and sources of bacteria that might be transported through space by the occupants, transfer of materials, and the heating, ventilating, and air conditioning (HVAC) system. The owner, facility manager, and A/E ideally discuss and include in the contract documents requirements to minimize IAQ concerns. Utilization of "green" materials in construction and operation may reduce long-term IAQ concerns. The project schedule must include time for off-gassing of chemicals from new materials. This can be accomplished in a variety of ways prior to facility occupancy. For example, taking early delivery of carpet and laying it out in a warehouse to air out prior to installing it in the facility will reduce the chemicals that the carpet might off-gas into the facility's air circulation system. While taking steps to minimize potential IAQ problems may impact the project schedule and costs, these impacts will likely be offset by earlier facility occupancy and the reduction or elimination of postoccupancy IAQ issues.

- *Energy Conservation.* The facility manager evaluates and monitors equipment, systems, and energy costs to identify potential savings. There are numerous public and private organizations and programs to assist facility managers in energy conservation efforts during facility design and operation. Public utilities and facility management professional organizations can provide information on this type of assistance.

ASTM International has developed standards for O&M work including cleaning, waste management, IAQ, and water management. Waste management programs should maximize use of source reduction and recycling procedures as outlined in ASTM D 5834, Standard Guide for Source Reduction, Reuse, Recycling, and Disposal of Solid and Corrugated Fiberboard (Cardboard). IAQ management programs should provide for evaluation of indoor carbon dioxide concentrations in accordance with ASTM D 6245, Standard Guide for Using Indoor Carbon Dioxide Concentration to Evaluate Indoor Air Quality and Ventilation, and evaluation of volatile organic compounds (VOCs) in indoor air in accordance with ASTM D 6345, Standard Guide for Selection of Methods for Active, Integrative Sampling of Volatile Organic Compounds in Air.

14.2.4.5 Regulatory Processes

Regulatory processes significantly affect facility management. The cost of complying with such regulations needs to be included in the annual budget. These costs range from construction permits to inspection contracts for life safety protection systems. Fees are assessed by local agencies for compliance monitoring, construction permits, life safety system inspections, and equipment inspections. Inspections by local, state, or federal inspectors are made regularly to ensure that equipment and facilities are properly maintained. Such inspections may be required by fire departments, health departments, and other agencies. These are referred to as AHJs. Qualified facility management personnel should assist inspectors.

Inspections for compliance with Occupational Safety and Health Administration (OSHA) regulations in the workplace result from accidents and the filing of health or safety complaints. The facility manager is responsible for accident prevention, including OSHA compliance and inspections. Material Safety Data Sheets (MSDSs), information about emergency exiting, procedures during disasters, and fire response procedures are required to be posted.

Regulatory requirements related to facility operation, processes, and material usage may change frequently. Previously approved conditions that may not meet current requirements are often considered to be acceptable as long as they are not modified or replaced. Accessibility is a notable exception. Accessibility requirements, also called barrier-free design, are enforced through implementation of the Americans with Disabilities Act (ADA) and local codes and ordinances. Not only are new facilities and facility improvements required to meet accessibility requirements, modifications are often required to bring nonconforming existing facilities into compliance with current accessibility requirements. Accessibility requirements may also regulate how a facility is used, including placement of furniture, workstations, equipment, materials, storage, and paths of travel. The regulatory impact of accessibility requirements may vary considerably based on the needs to employees with disabilities. The ADA requires that accommodations be made for individuals with disabilities. These accommodations may include specialized furniture or equipment, training, or specialized assistance for an individual. Facility managers need to understand regulations applicable to the facilities that they manage and need to consider the impact of these requirements when planning facility operations and facility modifications.

New laws and regulations affecting maintenance are instituted each year, and existing regulations are frequently amended. It is important for facility managers to keep abreast of pending legislation that might affect planning and budgeting and might have long-term implications for the costs of operating facilities and properties. Professional associations can be a primary source of information about state and national legislation, and local business organizations, such as chambers of commerce, are usually helpful on a local and regional level.

Facility managers must also comply with specific requirements mandated by agencies that enforce standards, laws, and regulations for certain types of facilities, such as medical, food processing, and manufacturing facilities.

14.2.4.6 Financial Issues

Developing a budget for the O&M of a facility requires that the facility manager anticipate maintenance needs, document the operations, and forecast future spending based on facility records and O&M data. The facility manager should develop a foundation for budget decisions based on actual costs. Such information would include cost areas such as personnel, materials and supplies, overhead charge rates, outside contract services, and utility rates. The facility manager should anticipate increases due to labor costs for cleaning during renovation projects. Annual energy cost increases can affect a budget by thousands of dollars.

Budgeting and Cost Control. Cost control and budgeting rely on accurate accounting. Effective cost control systems provide detailed comparisons between budgeted and actual expenditures. The facility manager reviews and analyzes results, anticipates and follows trends, and reacts to new challenges. Facility cost control requires the facility manager to emphasize the importance of accurate record keeping throughout the company for cost comparisons. A good database will supply the profiles and statistics needed to identify trends and support planning efforts. In addition, maintenance records and reports might be required by regulatory agencies for activities such as hazardous waste management and testing of life safety systems and equipment. In these instances, detailed records can provide information for cost control and regulatory compliance.

Budgeting for facility management depends on the development of this database, since O&M accounts for a significant percentage of a company's expenditures. The goal of O&M budgeting is to ensure the most effective and efficient use of resources toward meeting the company's stated facility objectives. The performance of a maintenance program, for example, can be evaluated by observing the degree to which a program operates within its budget and maintains the facility budget. A budget based on inaccurate data is ineffective.

In the facility budgeting process, two activities play important roles in describing facility needs: cost accounting and life cycle costing.

Cost Accounting. Cost accounting assigns costs to every activity, thereby creating data that can be used as part of a productivity measure. This is difficult to achieve without detailed record keeping and employee cooperation. Larger and more complex organizations now use handheld computers and bar code readers to record costs. Cost accounting is used to define and determine opportunity costs (those areas where the infusion of financial resources can affect long-term expenditures).

Life Cycle Costing. Life cycle costing analysis examines the relationship between present and future value of facilities and the equipment. This process is frequently used as the basis for making capital investments. The total sum of the initial investment, the cost of maintaining that asset over the expected life of the investment, operating costs, and costs of repair and replacement components are added together to obtain the total life cycle cost of the equipment or the facility under consideration. Life cycle costing can help the facility manager make informed decisions and recommendations about capital investments that consider the long-term implications of the use of resources. For example, the purchase of rooftop air-conditioning units for a climate-controlled laboratory benefits greatly from life cycle costing analysis, since it might clearly demonstrate the need for a more energy-efficient unit. This unit might cost more initially but generate substantial savings in utility costs over its 20-year life cycle.

Planning, Design, and Construction. Many owners rely on their facility managers for guidance and counsel on planning, design, and construction of facilities. Facility managers are often on the owner's selection team for A/Es and contractors. They may act as the owner's representative and prime contact for the project team, providing project team leadership in negotiating contracts and establishing project schedules. Because design has a substantial impact on the O&M of facilities, the facility manager is ideally involved in the project decision-making process. Space planning, changes in use, and tenant improvements should include consideration of the project's effects on the entire facility. Renovations and additions to facilities and other large-scale capital improvements should reflect the long-term goals and objectives of the company.

Cost estimates and analyses should include the following in any investment consideration:

- Initial capital investment
- Financing costs
- Design and engineering costs
- Costs of alternatives, including comparison of options
- Regulatory and permitting costs
- O&M costs

- Repair and replacement costs
- Salvage and disposal costs at the end of the life cycle

Value analysis can identify areas of potential cost savings and creatively propose options for the consideration of the project team.

14.2.5 Information Resources

The facility manager requires a variety of resource materials to ensure efficient and effective O&M. In order to receive these materials from the contractor and A/E during project closeout, the submission of these materials must be included in the requirements of the construction contract. The facility manager should request that the A/E include these requirements in the construction documents. These resource materials are used in a variety of ways by the following parties:

- The facility manager, in O&M planning and budgeting for the facility
- The facility manager, in planning for modifications, renovations, or additions in the future
- The custodial and maintenance staff
- Outsourced service providers working on-site

The storage and archiving of these materials is best organized into four categories:

- *Permanent Record Set.* One complete set of record documents, O&M information, warranties, and commissioning logs must be stored in a secure location where they are protected from damage or loss. The permanent record set should be removed from secure storage only to be copied and then returned.
- *Regular Use Set(s).* One or more complete sets of record documents, O&M information, warranties, and commissioning logs should be stored in an accessible location for regular use by maintenance personnel. Storage might be in the facility or at a central maintenance or operations site. These documents can be utilized in analysis of the existing facility and preparation of documents for new construction and renovation projects. Local fire and emergency response agencies might require sets of certain documents to be maintained at predetermined locations for emergency use.
- *Equipment and Systems Information.* Consideration should be given to storing a copy of record document information (such as schematic drawings, riser diagrams, and system design information), O&M information, and warranty information immediately adjacent to equipment or systems to which it pertains for use by maintenance personnel. Large-format documents can be reduced to 8½ by 11 or 11 by 17-inch format for ease of use. Documents receiving frequent use or being used outdoors or in areas with limited climate control can be laminated to extend their useful life and make them easier to handle.
- *Cleaning and Regular Maintenance Information.* Copies of cleaning and maintenance information should be furnished to custodial personnel.

14.2.5.1 Project Record Documents

Record documents are construction documents that are subsequently modified to show actual construction. Besides facility O&M, record documents are used in project conception, planning, design, and construction document preparation for modifications to and replacement of existing facilities. In addition to the modified contract documents, record documents might also include reviewed shop drawings, product data, samples, field test reports, inspection certificates, manufacturers' certificates, inspection reports from AHJs, documentation of special foundation depths, measurements or adjustments, surveys, design mixes, and project photographs and videos. Record drawings alone do not provide adequate record documentation without other record documents. Contract documents are not adequate record documents unless they have been accurately and completely modified to show actual construction. To facilitate accuracy and completeness, information is best noted on the documents during the construction stage as work progresses, rather than being prepared at the end of the project.

Record Drawings. Record drawings are frequently used by the owner, facility manager, and maintenance personnel to obtain information about concealed items. Record drawings are used by facility managers and A/Es in project conception, planning, design, and construction document preparation for modifications to and replacement of existing facilities and development of new facilities. Record drawings can include:

- Modifications made to the drawings by addenda, change orders, supplemental instructions, and field orders
- Revisions to materials, detailing, and dimensions incorporated into the project
- Revised locations of structural elements, mechanical equipment, controls cabling and equipment, piping, valves, filters, cleanouts, access panels, electrical raceway, cabling, and junction boxes
- Locations of underground utilities with horizontal and vertical dimensions

Record Project Manual. Record project manuals can include:

- Modifications made to the project manual by addenda, change orders, supplemental instructions, and field orders
- Identification of materials and systems incorporated in construction, rather than all manufacturers, materials, and systems identified in the contract documents

Record project manuals are used by the owner, facility manager, and maintenance personnel to obtain information about materials, systems, and equipment incorporated into the facility. They are helpful in identifying manufacturers, product names, and model numbers for maintaining, repairing, and replacing materials, system components, and equipment. Information included in the record project manuals can be supplemented by information included in the record submittals.

Record Submittals. Record submittals can include a complete set of shop drawings, product data, test reports, and other information on materials, equipment, and systems incorporated into the project. Record submittals are typically assembled and submitted by the contractor and organized according to project manual organization. Record submittals provide information on products, finishes, and equipment actually utilized in construction of the facility that is typically not included in other record documents.

Start-up Logs. Start-up logs record system information at the time of system and equipment start-up. This information assists the A/E in determining compliance with contract documents. Information included in the start-up logs assists maintenance personnel in servicing and adjusting equipment.

14.2.5.2 Operations and Maintenance Data

O&M data, incorporated in the O&M manuals, can include:

- Lists of products, materials, equipment, and systems incorporated into the facility, including manufacturer and supplier contact information
- Information on service contracts and warranty service, including contact information
- A complete list of colors, finishes, and textures for materials, with locations clearly identified. Information on paint and coatings include the manufacturer, product name or number, and the color name and mix formula
- Component diagrams for equipment and systems, including part names and numbers
- Installation, operation, and maintenance instructions
- Recommended cleaning, maintenance, and component or system replacement schedule
- Information to prevent voiding manufacturer or installer warranties

O&M data should be specific to the facility for which it is provided rather than generic product or system information. This data can be used by the owner, facility manager, maintenance staff, and outside service organizations in scheduling and performing routine cleaning and maintenance, and is also helpful in making emergency repairs.

14.2.5.3 Spare Parts and Extra Stock Materials

Spare parts and maintenance materials are provided by product, equipment, and system manufacturers and installers. This information can assist the facility manager in maintaining and operating the facility during the first year(s) of operation. These materials are important in assisting the facility manager to:

- Maintain equipment and systems
- Provide an initial supply of materials needed for routine maintenance
- Meet conditions of warranties
- Maintain the appearance of the facility

Typical spare parts and materials include:

- Keys, handles, fasteners, and specialized tools needed to access and work on equipment and systems
- Materials required for regular maintenance of equipment and systems, such as filters, lamps, lubricants, and batteries
- Specialized cleaning and patching materials required for cleaning and maintaining surfaces and product finishes
- Replacement parts for products susceptible to breakage or easily lost, such as keys and adjustable shelf clips
- Materials required for replacement and patching of finished materials that are subject to color, texture, and pattern variations, such as flooring materials, ceiling panels, drapery, plastic laminates, and coatings

Spare parts and maintenance materials are inventoried upon receipt by the facility manager and a schedule prepared for purchasing replacement materials required for routine maintenance. Spare parts and materials should be stored in a secure location near where they are likely to be used, or in a central location. Spare parts and materials not likely to be used in the immediate future should be clearly identified with product manufacturer name and model number, installed location(s), and the original date of installation.

14.2.5.4 Protecting Resource Documents

For fire and security reasons, copies of the most critical information should be maintained at a location away from the subject facility. Facilities located in a region subject to high security or natural disasters require copies of important documents to be stored in a location not likely to be affected by the same event. Electronic record copies can be more easily transferred to sites not subject to the hazards of the primary location and can be stored in a safe-deposit box.

14.2.6 Facility Evaluations

The facility manager develops and maintains an ongoing evaluation program. This process begins at occupancy with a postoccupancy evaluation and continues through the life of the facility. The format and content of the evaluations vary greatly, depending on the facility type, and might include the following:

- *Building.* Structure, envelope, space allocation, interior and exterior finishes, mechanical and electrical systems, site development, and energy efficiency
- *Tenant/User.* Efficient layout, signage, accessibility, interior finishes, mechanical and electrical systems, and leased area
- *Highway.* Paving, striping, signage, lane width, on-ramps and off-ramps, lighting, shoulders, and landscaping

Facility evaluations address facility use, effectiveness, efficiency, operational cost, maintenance, and environment. In preparing the evaluation format, the facility manager should try to envision the company's future. The forms need to incorporate relevant information for future decisions. Figure 14.3 shows an evaluation of an existing roof.

Facility evaluations assemble information that will assist in planning and scheduling routine and preventative maintenance, capital improvements, facility upgrades, and system and equipment replacement. Standard forms may be used to address component evaluations such as roofing, exterior wall finishes, landscaping, flooring, equipment and systems, and production processes. These forms facilitate quick field review and updating of facility records.

Facility evaluations should be made on a regular basis and records updated at regular intervals. An evaluation cycle should be set up for each facility component. The length of time between evaluations will also be affected by the age of the facility and the frequency of operational changes by facility users.

14.2.6.1 Postoccupancy Evaluation

Facility managers should perform a postoccupancy evaluation three to six months after initial occupancy. The postoccupancy evaluation becomes the baseline for the ongoing

---

ROOF EVALUATION   **Date:** June 6, 2002

Building:	Northwest High School
Address:	800 Fourth Street N. E. Cascadia. WA
Roof Location:	East Side of Center Roof at Music Building

Year Roof Installed:	1996	Roof Area:	1,804 s.f.
Year Bldg. Constructed:	1957	Overall Roof Condition:	Very Good

---

Roof Description

System:	Built-up Modified Bitumen Roofing
Surfacing:	Mineral Cap Sheet
Underlayment:	Modified Bitumen Felt - 2 Plys
Insulation:	Batt Insulation
Decking:	3/8" Plywood on 1×8 Shiplap
Base Flashing:	Mineral Cap Sheet and 2 Plys
Valley Flashing:	N.A.
Edge Flashing:	Painted Galv. Metal
Gutters:	N.A.
Downspouts:	N.A.
Slope/Drainage System:	1/2" per foot Slope Drains to Internal Pipes
	8:12 Pitch at Crickets
Venting System:	None
Penetrations:	4 Drains, 2 Mech., 4 Scuppers
Roof-Mounted Equipment:	None

Roof Condition

Surfacing:	Excellent	Gutters:	N.A.
Base Flashing:	Good	Downspouts:	N.A.
Valley Flashing:	N.A.	Drainage:	Very Good
Edge Flashing:	Very Good	Penetrations:	Very Good
Watertightness:	No Leaks Reported		
Ponding:	At Base of Crickets and Around Drains		
Mechanical Damage:	None		

Additional Comments:

1. Surface cracking present in base flashing at top of N.W. Cricket.
2. No blisters noted.

Prepared By:

Page 1 of 1

Figure 14.3 Evaluation of an Existing Roof

facility evaluation program. The postoccupancy evaluation and subsequent facility evaluations are performed to:

- Assist the facility manager in identifying nonconforming work and warranty items that were not identified prior to occupancy.
- Assist the facility manager in preparing for future projects. Lessons learned from existing facilities and past projects can prevent costly mistakes on future projects.
- Obtain information from facility users that can be used to determine the need for modifications to the facility to improve its usefulness.
- Assist the facility manager in anticipating future maintenance needs.

Effective postoccupancy evaluations record information from users, maintenance personnel, and other employees who use the facility on a regular basis. A separate postoccupancy evaluation is performed for each facility. Postoccupancy evaluations record:

- How the facility functions for the users
- Aesthetic issues that need to be addressed
- Perceived public or customer response to the facility
- Recommended changes to the facility
- Corrections or repairs that require immediate attention

14.2.6.2 Product, System, and Equipment Evaluations

A facility manager is in a position to evaluate the installation and long-term performance of products. Products and systems with acceptable performance are identified for use on future projects. If a product or system fails, it is identified as not being a recommended standard for the facility. Where products and systems have failed or performed unsatisfactorily, the facility manager should advise the owner and may request that the A/E or contractor investigate the problem, prepare a written report, and make remedial recommendations. Depending on the circumstances and applicable warranties, this work may be considered to be included in the contract or an additional service. Product representatives may be asked to provide information on adjusting equipment and systems, their operation and maintenance, and warranties. Product representatives may also be requested to provide additional operation and maintenance training for the facility manager.

14.2.7 Documents for Life Cycle Activities

Throughout the life of a facility, maintenance is a major factor, and contracts for maintenance may require various contractual documents. The cost of O&M will eventually exceed the original cost of the facility or a specific portion. Even though many decisions made about the facility and its products were based on life cycle cost, these decisions do not preclude maintenance or eventual replacement. The warranty for the original project and most manufacturers' warranties for products contain exclusions for failure to maintain. Failure to provide routine maintenance may even completely void a warranty.

The need to obtain O&M services begins a new project and the project lifecycle begins again. The project life cycle is the process of obtaining services and completion of work to provide or maintain a facility or portion of it for its useful purpose.

As indicated previously, O&M can involve everything from cleaning to parts replacement. The list of issues related to O&M can be long and seem never ending. A long-term plan requires outsourcing certain services. These services are documented in an agreement forming a contract. Most facility owners are familiar with purchase orders, but purchase orders are for purchase of goods and are not usually intended for on-site labor. An appropriate contract requires a description of time factors or frequency of service and may include specifications indicating the type of work to be performed along with some drawings indicating the extent of work. The principles and types of documents can be very similar to those used for construction. If the documents are prepared in this similar manner, the uniformity, consistency, clarity, and filing system will be the same as for the project record documents of the facility.

Similar to project delivery, the owner of the facility or the facility manager evaluates the needs, determines whether professional consultants are required, and determines how services are going to be provided. Services can range from forensic engineering to simple purchase of products. Each type of service requires appropriate documents. If the expected dollar value of services or work is minimal, short-form documents may suffice, whereas more detailed documents may be appropriate for extensive overhaul, alterations, or remodeling.

14.2.7.1 Procurement

As a part of the process of obtaining services, the owner determines the type of services and whether the services or items will be bid or negotiated and whether the contract will involve on-site labor or simply purchase of goods. This decision will affect how the procurement documents are prepared. Procurement documents include the proposed contract documents. Standard procurement documents can be developed providing procurement instructions, available information, and appropriate bid or proposal forms.

Solicitation. Similar to the procurement documents previously discussed, the procurement process may involve an invitation to bid for a few suppliers or an advertisement to the public for obtaining services required at a major institution. The invitation or advertisement includes the information about obtaining documents and types of bids or proposals, as well as the time and place to deliver them. This initial contact provides information on whom to contact and whether there will be a conference or access to the existing facility for review of conditions.

Instructions for Procurement. Procurement instructions may be preprinted forms explaining the procurement process and the intended method of award. As with construction documents, the procurement instructions explain the process for requesting document interpretations and how the answers will be distributed. Typically, precontract modifications are issued as addenda.

Available Information. Available information is an important aspect of dealing with existing conditions. Available documents may include review of record documents used to construct the existing facility. These may or may not represent as-built or exact circumstances, and some form of disclaimer may be necessary. Available information is important to ensure that compatible products, equipment, and materials are utilized for the proposed service, work, or goods. This information is for reference and is not the same information indicating the extent or requirements for the work being procured.

Procurement Forms and Supplements. Pricing, whether obtained by bid or proposal, should be uniform and easy to compare. To ensure uniformity, an owner-prepared form should be utilized that includes affirmations that the parties offering services are aware of project conditions such as delivery and access. If alternates or substitutions to the original specifications are permitted, the process and specifics should be stated. Unit prices, quantities, and tabulations may also require an appropriate form (possibly including a software-based spreadsheet).

Contracting. Contracting is the process of accepting an offer of a bid or proposal and developing it into a contract with contract documents.

Contracting Forms. The type of contacting forms should be reviewed by the owner's legal counsel for sufficiency and appropriateness to the purpose, such as service, labor and material, or purchase. The form of agreement includes the basic elements of time, cost, and extent. The agreement incorporates other contract documents by reference such as listing drawings, specifications, and other exhibits such as a list of unit cost or schedule of work.

Project Forms. Project forms may be included and can cover subjects from bonds and certificates to various owner requirements of documentation and reporting.

Conditions of the Contract. Conditions of the contract are usually standard documents that stipulate terms and conditions as well as duties, rights, and responsibilities of the parties to the contract. These types of terms are sometimes included on the back of standard purchase orders but do not include issues related to on-site labor. Of particular concern in general and supplementary conditions is the subject of insurance. The owner consults with the owner's insurance agent and explains the circumstances of any on-site work. These conditions of the contract also cover issues such as contract modifications, payment, and acceptance of work.

Revisions, Clarifications, and Modifications. Change is an inevitable part of any process. Precontract revisions such as addenda are issued during the procurement process. Other forms of clarifications and modifications might be required after the agreement is signed. The process of incorporating these clarifications and modifications is usually stated in the conditions of the contract.

14.2.7.2 Contract and Resource Drawings

Drawings are graphic illustrations of various portions of a facility. Simple single-line drawings may be developed to indicate the extent and quantity of work required for O&M. Drawings can also include a map of the vicinity, the site, and access to existing facilities. Drawings might be copied from existing record drawings and adapted to show work or maintenance required. Use of record documents should be limited to the existing facility for which they were prepared and not be used for another project that could violate copyrights. Record drawings should be reviewed against existing conditions, prior to distribution or release, to determine whether they are representative of the current conditions. Drawings may be derived from previous submittals that were made by contractors involved in the original constructions. These drawings may include manufacturers' shop drawings, catalog cuts, or other diagrams or schematics. Any drawings utilized should clearly distinguish between existing conditions and new work. Various techniques can be used to achieve the contrasting difference between new and existing features. Software vendors and reprographics/reproduction firms can suggest available techniques. In many cases it may be advisable to provide existing documents as "available information," for reference only, and indicate that the potential contractors or suppliers determine the existing conditions for themselves. For projects of limited scope, small drawings or reduced drawings may be combined with the procurement and contracting documents and specifications to be a part of the project manual.

14.2.7.3 Specifications

Specifications cover written specifics about the service, work, or product required. For small projects such as maintenance services, entire specification divisions may be specified in a single section. Refer to *MasterFormat* ® for appropriate numbers and titles.

Division 01—General Requirements. Division 01—General Requirements include specifications dealing with many administrative and procedural matters specific to the project. Sections at the beginning of Division 01 specify the nature of the work along with limitations on hours of operation, access, and use of the facility/site. Other sections can place restrictions on noise, dust, odors, and other environmental concerns including recycling of waste. This division also contains three sections of particular interest to facility management. One is Section 01 92 00 Facility Operation, another is Section 01 93 00 Facility Maintenance, and the other is Section 01 94 00 Facility Decommissioning. These sections can be utilized to explain existing O&M or to specify services needed. Other sections are listed under the broad heading of 01 90 00 Life Cycle Activities. Also included are headings that address Commissioning. Division 02 Existing Conditions includes headings adapted to other aspects such as specifying needed assessments, evaluation, and status report on existing systems.

Facilities Life Cycle Specifications. Throughout *MasterFormat*®are subtitles dealing with life cycle activities and O&M for various work results. These titles can be utilized to specify maintenance, repair, restoration, or alterations to existing products, equipment, or systems. Specifying life cycle activities is similar to specifying new work. Depending upon the nature of the service, work, or products needed, some of the three parts of the specification section may or may not be required. As an example, the purchase of goods may not require PART 3—EXECUTION, or the mowing of grass may not require PART 2—PRODUCTS. Specifying certain aspects of O&M work may require specifics that are concerned with means, methods, and techniques. Unlike construction where means, methods, and techniques are the sole purview of the contractor, these subjects may be required to ensure that O&M will not void manufacturers' warranties. An example might be carpet cleaning in which a wet process could damage backing and adhesion to the substrate. Specifying O&M requires significant understanding of the construction of the existing facility and the products, equipment, and systems utilized. Properly maintained record documents and maintenance history can be invaluable in developing the requirements for O&M work. For example, roofing work may require approval by the manufacturer providing a long-term warranty and may require written notice and limitations on installers utilized for the work.

14.2.7.4 Obtaining Services, Work, or Goods

Obtaining supplies for a facility is similar to obtaining other goods such as furniture, furnishings, and equipment. Proper preparation of documents used for procurement is important because the documents carry significant legal and financial implications. If the owner's staff is not familiar with these methods of preparing documents, the staff might be well advised to obtain the services of an A/E or specification consultant. These firms can assist in the procurement process and contract administration. During each stage of the project process, modifications and processing of information are required. Proper communications, formats, and procedures help ensure the contracts are executed in an efficient manner.

Facility management of existing facilities and infrastructure require significant commitment of resources, including time, money, and personnel. Numerous aspects require attention and continued O&M, and may require outsourcing of services, work, and goods. Each event requiring outsourcing requires proper documentation and processing to maintain continued operations. Each outsourcing creates another project and an individual project lifecycle. Each project begins with a conception stage and progresses through its documentation, procurement, and execution, returning to the facility management stage. Each project starts a new project life cycle. Several projects may coexist in various stages. Existing facilities, in whole or in part, require constant evaluation to determine whether they have become obsolete and need to be decommissioned, deconstructed or demolished, and recycled. Each time the life cycle begins again.

Index

About the Companion Web Site

Additional CSI publications that complement *The CSI Project Delivery Practice Guide* are available for download. The following documents can be obtained at www.wiley.com/go/csipracticeguides:

- MasterFormat® numbers and titles
- UniFormat™
- SectionFormat™/PageFormat™
- Sample CSI Forms
- GreenFormat™ questionnaire
- Practice Guide Glossary

To access the content on this site, you will need the unique Access Code printed on the card included with this book and follow these steps:

1. Navigate your web browser to:
   www.wiley.com/go/csipracticeguides
2. Click on the Download Access link for *The CSI Project Delivery Practice Guide* and follow the instructions on the page.
3. Enter your access code once to set up your account and access the material.

If you have purchased an ebook version of this title or if your access code is not working, please contact Customer Care at 877-762-2974 or at http://support.wiley.com for a unique Access Code in order to take advantage of the web site.